AF247603

Modern
Theories
of Language

MODERN THEORIES OF LANGUAGE

Philip W. Davis

Rice University, Houston, Texas

PRENTICE-HALL, INC., ENGLEWOOD CLIFFS, NEW JERSEY

Library of Congress Cataloging in Publication Data

Davis, Philip W   1939–
    Modern theories of language.

    Bibliography: p.
    1. Linguistics–History. 2. Grammar,
Comparative and general. I. Title.
P77.D3   410   73-1691
ISBN 0-13-598987-6

10 9 8 7 6 5 4 3 2 1

PRENTICE-HALL INTERNATIONAL, INC., London
PRENTICE-HALL OF AUSTRALIA, PTY. LTD., Sydney
PRENTICE-HALL OF CANADA, LTD., Toronto
PRENTICE-HALL OF INDIA PRIVATE LIMITED, New Delhi
PRENTICE-HALL OF JAPAN, INC., Tokyo

To My Parents

Carl and Sybil Davis

Contents

7 Prague School Theory

Preface

I should immediately qualify the title by which I mean simply the
nine theories of language proposed within the twentieth century which are
discussed here. Those nine are chosen primarily on the basis of influence or
number of adherents, but the selection remains arbitrary. Nothing is said,
for example, of Boas, Sapir, nor of any of those theories proposed by
Russian linguists.

Each theory is actually a cluster of closely related ones. Any theoretician
will change his mind on some points as his work progresses; and any time
more than one person works in the development of a theory, we are apt to
find differences of opinion. In choosing a theoretical variant for discussion,
I have tried to select that one which seems more closely representative of
work within a given approach or that one usually associated with the name
of the theory. Occasionally this forces concentrating on a single work or
two, e.g., Saussure's *Course in General Linguistics*, Hjelmslev's *Prolegomena
to a Theory of Language*, Bloomfield's *Language* and "A set of postulates
for the science of language," etc. Where such restriction is made, the first
paragraph or so of each chapter makes clear the basis of exposition. In
these and other instances the omission of variants (and of whole theories)
is not to be interpreted as adverse judgment of them but simply as a reflection of the tremendous amount of work done on the nature of language in
the past sixty years and the recognition of a limited amount of space.

The aim of this investigation is not proselytization but the objective
presentation of the essential characteristics of each theory within the meth-

odology of science so that the reader—whom I assume to have some knowledge of what linguistics is about—may make his own evaluation. It is assumed that the often repeated claim that linguistics is a science is to be taken seriously. In the Introduction, general principles of scientific methodology are presented and the discussion of theories is ordered to that framework. In some cases this involves an "interpretation" of the theory, but I have tried not to be arbitrary in this and to justify my opinion of how a theory may fit into the methodology of science (where this is not obvious) without making a Procrustean bed of the latter. The result is a view of a limited portion of linguistic theorizing divorced from development in time. Although such comments may form the basis of a historical treatment, the comparison of theories here (I assume such is possible in principle) is made without regard to historical influence.

I would like to acknowledge permission to reprint portions of Saussure's *Course in General Linguistics* granted by the Philosophical Library; portions of Louis Hjelmslev, *Prolegomena to a Theory of Language* (revised English edition), trans. Francis J. Whitfield (Madison: The University of Wisconsin Press; © 1961 by the Regents of the University of Wisconsin), pp. 11, 16–18, 39, 41, 60–61, 63–64, 66, 76–77, 83, 88, 96, 99, 118–19, 131–36; portions from *Language* by Leonard Bloomfield. Copyright, 1933 by Holt, Rinehart and Winston, Inc. Copyright renewed © 1961 by Leonard Bloomfield. Reprinted by permission of Holt, Rinehart and Winston, Inc.; portions of Kenneth L. Pike's *Language in Relation to a Unified Theory of the Structure of Human Behavior* and of Robert E. Longacre's *Grammar Discovery Procedures* granted by Mouton & Co.; portions of Trubetzkoy's *Principles of Phonology* originally published by the University of California Press and reprinted with the permission of the Regents of the University of California, and an illustration from Sydney M. Lamb, "The sememic approach to structural semantics," reproduced by permission of the author and the American Anthropological Association from American Anthropologist, Volume 66, No. 3 (2): 62, 1964.

I wish also to acknowledge the beneficial criticism of portions of the manuscript given by R. Saunders and E. W. Roberts, and especially the latter for the pleasure of extended conversation and argument. Finally, I wish to record here a very fundamental debt to the late Professor Richard Slade Harrell from whom I first heard of linguistics.

Philip W. Davis

CHAPTER 1

Introduction

We will assume that linguistics is a science. As a science it is subject to conditions and judgments that affect all fields that constitute the sciences. It is necessary, then, that we investigate these conditions and criteria for making judgments before we examine linguistics itself.

Three terms that appear in all scientific fields are *data*, *theory*, and an *accounting* of the data. The data of any science are initially defined by interest. Whatever seems to present a puzzle or to conflict with the prejudices of common sense may form the body of data. For example, a person may be puzzled by the movements of what seem to be twinkling lights in the night sky. He is moved to *say* something about them. Another person may be struck by things that "live" and want to discover the variety of life that exists. Or someone may be curious about sounds that people make and wonder how they can "have meaning." Any thing that a person can be curious about and wonder about may constitute data for a science. Initially, these data will usually form a superficially coherent set. No one would see any surface resemblance between the lights in the night sky and things that live, and think it possible to make meaningful statements in the same terms about both sets of phenomena. The first thing a curious person might do is to collect data. A person may satisfy his desire to know by writing down as accurately as possible the number of lights and their movements relative to one another, by listing as many living things as he can find or by recording sequences of sounds that humans make and associating these sequences with meanings.

That is, a person may account for sets of data by listing them. After this first accounting, he may discover something else. Some lights in the sky seem to move more than others. A given group of living things are more like some than others. Some sequences of sound that seem to be the same recur with what seem to be the same meanings. Patterns may be found, and names may be given to those things that seem to exhibit the same pattern. Those lights that move more than others may be called planets; the most stable lights may be called stars. Living things that seem more alike than others may be assigned to sets or classes called phyla. Recurring sequences of sounds that apparently mean the same things may be assigned to sets. The recorded data are searched until no more patterns are evident. In this way a second kind of accounting may be made that differs from the first in that it is more general; it is made not in terms of individual bits of data (lights, living things, sequences of sounds with their associated meanings) or of lists, but in terms of sets (planets/stars, phyla, sets of sound/meaning correspondences). These statements cover whole ranges of things, whereas in the first approach the statements relate to each individual piece of data.

This distinction between two kinds of accounting enables us to make judgments about them. The criterion is generality. The more general accounting is the better. We have also found one function for experimentation/observation: the collection of data to talk about. We see also why the ranges of data may be limited, at least initially. It is difficult to find patterns that are common to stars/planets and to living things or common to stars/planets and to sets of associations of sound sequences and meanings. In this way sciences may be roughly delimited. Patterns that are found to hold for one range of data become one science (astronomy for stars/planets, biology for living things, and linguistics for sound/meaning associations). If it should turn out that two patterns of what has previously been considered to be two sciences are somehow related, the boundaries between the sciences may be altered. For example, if the patterns that account for the movements of celestial objects turn out to account for the movement of objects on earth as well, one may say that there is now one science that has as its data the movement of objects relative to one another. This reduction in the number of sciences is justified again by the criterion of generality: one accounting covering a large range of data is better than two accountings for smaller ranges of data. If the patterns of some science also account for the data of what had been previously considered a separate science, but the reverse did not hold (if the patterns of the second did not account for the subject matter of the first), then again the number of distinct sciences may be decreased. In instances of this kind, the second science is said to be *reduced* to the first. For example, *if* living things can be accounted for in terms of patterns intended for celestial and nonliving earthbound physical bodies but the patterns of living things cannot be made to apply to nonliving things, then the science of biology may be reduced to the status of a branch, a special instance, of mechanics/physics called biophysics.

To this point we have said nothing explicitly about how the term "theory" fits into this scheme. One way of introducing it (because it is needed and not simply possible) is the following. Suppose we decide to concern ourselves with what seems to be a coherent range of data, say the lights again. This time let us also suppose that on examination, our recorded observations produce no obvious (or satisfactory) pattern. What then? We could possibly forget it. But patterns may be observable in other ranges of data. Why not here? The puzzle for the curious remains. One recourse is to make guesses. Suppose we *assume* that some pattern is valid for the movements of celestial lights. Then we could examine the results of our experiments to see if the assumed pattern is actually present. The pattern *predicts* that we will find observations that follow from it. Two things may result. We either find the observations predicted or we do not. If we do, we made a lucky guess. If we do not, either our guess was wrong or we made a mistake in our initial data-collecting experiments. Let us further assume that our guess was borne out, and add for some reason the additional ranges of data including movements of earthbound objects. Again if no pattern common to both is readily discoverable, we may guess. Obviously we cannot make guesses in terms of lights; projectiles and pendulums are not lights. We may choose to talk about X's and patterns that are assumed to be valid for X's. Once the guessing is finished, we may see whether it predicts what is found in the ranges of data when the X's are replaced by stars/planets or projectiles/pendulums. If our talk of X's and the patterns holding for them is verified by our observations, we have again been lucky.

But what of these X's? They form the *primitive terms* of our theory. The possible ways of relating them, the way the primitives enter into patterns and exhibit relationships, constitute the *axioms* or *postulates* of the theory. Given these two classes of elements, it is further possible to add a kind of secondary element to the theory: *definitions*, in terms of axioms and primitive terms. These three, primitives, axioms, and definitions, constitute a theory. With them it may be possible to construct a number of statements (possibly without limit) by adding further definitions, interrelating these with the primitives of theory, and so forth. The set of distinct possible statements consistent with the primitives, axioms, and definitions determines the set of possible accountings implied by the theory. An accounting is any member of this set of implied statement-sets.

Among our X's we might find the following: mass (m), acceleration (a) and force (F). The assumed patterns that hold among these factors may be formalized as Newton's three laws of motion, plus an additional force defined by each distinct pair of masses. But just as pendulums and projectiles were not lights, so these primitives are not any of the objects that are observed. Our primitives and axioms account for the data when these are applied to the data or when they are *interpreted*, when some substance or meaning is given them. To interpret an accounting one substitutes values known from the data for elements (X's) of the theory. For example, values for m may be replaced by the masses of the sun and some planet to obtain the value of a force acting on the planet. The movement of the planet that seems to contradict the axiom that masses move in a straight line unless some force acts upon them follows from the value F defined for pairs of masses. And the apparent erratic behavior in the movement of the planet is not erratic after all. It exhibits a pattern, although one not immediately apparent.

It is not necessary that the primitives and axioms of a theory have an interpretation to be a theory. It is possible that a set of primitives, axioms, and a set of definitions in terms of them imply an unlimited range of possible statements, but there are no known ranges of data for which the statements account. In this case the theory is nonetheless a theory; an interpretation is not a necessary condition for constructing a theory. It is also possible that the elements characterizing some theory also have an interpretation with reference to some range of data, but the predictions of an accounting in terms of the theory be contradicted by the data. The primitives, axioms, and definitions still constitute a theory: in this case an incorrect theory with reference to this range of data. It is not necessary that a theory have some *confirmed* interpretation to be a theory.

It is possible that two theories, when their accountings are interpreted, predict equally well the same range of data. The question arises: which is correct? Or are they both correct? To decide, one might have recourse to data collected by additional experimentation. That is, given the set of interpreted accountings of two competing theories, will the accountings of only one theory predict data that have not yet been observed? One can make this a criterion and discriminate between theories relative to predictability. Predictability is, however, a necessary condition of theories themselves. Thus no set of assumptions will be considered a theory if it is limited in time or space; the axioms and primitives are *universals;* a theory will necessarily account for future data. If this is the case, no theory can ever be fully confirmed, because it will never be possible to examine the theory in terms of data obtained at all times and all places. It will be possible, though, to invalidate theory at any time or place relative to a range of data. This possibility reveals a second function of experimentation: determining the fit between a theory and the data. Now in addition to performing experiments to find whether the interpreted accountings of some theory fit existing data, it will be necessary to perform experiments to find whether predictions of future data can be confirmed. This step in turn can lead to the discovery of new kinds of data (patterns) within the range of data that would have been ignored unless the predictions based on the theory had indicated their existence.

Let us assume that our two competing theories meet this condition of predictiveness, the additional requirement that assumptions must satisfy to be a theory. We have not yet found a way of distinguishing between them. It may be that the interpreted accountings of one bring about predictions that are a closer approximation to the data collected up to that time. For example, two competing theories of the movements of the planets will make predictions about their locations relative to one another and to the sun at given times. One of the theories may yield predictions that are closer to the actually observed positions than the predictions of the second. We may establish *relative* exactness of prediction as a criterion. If so, confirmation is not simply a yes or no matter but one of *degree* of fit. And the theory whose accountings produce predictions that are more closely confirmed by the data is the better one. Of the two, it may be that neither makes all the correct predictions. The one that comes the closer is the better. This situation provides one of the activities of science. The scientist may try to resolve the problem by determining whether the lack of fit lies in the data (it may be the fault of the experiment) or in the accounting (which may be incorrect, but for the present we ignore this possibility) or by trying to alter the theory in such a way that it will yield more accurate accountings. If an impasse is reached, we may accept the better of the two theories as the best one can do or, more likely, we will explore some third possible theory.

Let us assume again that our two competing theories are not differentiated with respect to exactness of prediction. We are again faced with the problem of evaluating them. It may be that of the two, one accounts as accurately as the other for the range of data that we were originally concerned with but also accounts for what had originally seemed to be a separate range of data, when an appropriate accounting and interpretation are established. The two theories will then differ with respect to *generality*. The less general theory will be incapable in principle of providing accountings for this additional range of data. We may then add a second criterion for evaluating theories: the more general theory (in the sense indicated above) is the better.

It is still possible that two competing theories will be undifferentiated, given the two criteria of relative exactness and generality. Let us assume again that our two theories are equally exact and equally general. It is possible that they differ internally, i.e., not with respect to data in terms of exactness or generality. One theory may rely on fewer assumptions; it may do the work of the second with fewer primitives or with fewer axioms or both. In this instance the two theories differ in *simplicity*. We may again make this a criterion in our evaluation of theories: all things being equal (exactness and generality), the simpler theory is the better.

The history of astronomy in outline over the past two thousand years mirrors concern with these three criteria. For approximately twelve hundred years after the work of Ptolemy, a theory of the planets was accepted in which it was assumed (1) that all planets moved about the earth as center and (2) their movement was circular. This theory required a rather complex accounting for the movements of planets in terms of epicycles—movement on the circumference of a circle, the circle itself describing a circle. Epicycles were added until the predicted positions of planets at given times approximated the observed locations. Copernicus proposed (1) that the planets, including

Earth, revolve about the sun and (2) that their movement is circular. This theory still requires epicycles, but a slightly *simpler* set. Kepler proposed changing the second assumption to one that claims an elliptical movement about the sun. The result is a *more accurate* and *simpler* prediction of the locations of planets at given times. Newton, by assuming his "laws," was able to show that the elliptical movement of planets about the sun followed as a special interpretation of statements following from his assumptions. And, in addition, by appropriate interpretation he was able to account for the data of terrestrial mechanics. Newton's proposal was *more general* than any of the preceding ones. The acceptance of each innovation was a function of accepting the criteria for evaluating theories that we have already outlined: simplicity, accuracy, and generality. (For a discussion of these developments in the history of astronomy, see Koestler 1959.)

There is still a fourth way in which theories may differ. Two theories may be equally exact in their predictions and equally general with respect to the ranges of data they account for, and perhaps equally simple or elegant, but still may differ in the following way. One theory, although accounting for a range of data, may include within its assumptions certain mechanisms that imply possible accountings for a kind of data that have not in fact been observed, but the second theory does not. We may assume two attitudes in this situation. One attitude is that the first theory is the more general; it just so happens we have not yet discovered the data that the accountings of the theory predict. This theory will then be the preferred one, according to our criterion of generality. There is, however, a factor that limits the generality of a theory, and that factor is contradiction. The assumptions of a theory cannot be contradictory. Were this the case, the theory could logically claim X and not-X, thus accounting potentially for a wider range of data than one limited to claiming either X or not-X. But such a theory of unrestricted generality is unacceptable, for it could not be invalidated. Neither data contradicting claim X nor not-X could possibly invalidate the theory, for the theory claims both. Hence, theories must be noncontradictory or *self-consistent*.

The second attitude is that the extra, predicted observations of the theory will not in fact occur; that the theory is too loose and is in fact inexact in a sense different from the sense introduced above. That is, the theory permits accountings that have no interpretation, that account for no observed data. In this instance the theory that predicted the more restricted range of data would be the preferred. This evaluation is the opposite of that based on generality and follows from the claim that the range of data excluded now in principle will never occur. It is not the nature of the possible data that such additional ranges exist. This claim (explicit in the form of a more restricted theory) is subject to invalidation (as are all theories). If one accepts the second theory as being the better one it is always possible to find at some point the exact range of data that was excluded by it. Should this happen, the criterion of generality would dictate that the first would be the preferred one.

This second attitude may be viewed as the other side of the criterion of generality. We want a theory that is general with reference to *possible* ranges of data and will evaluate it more highly than one that is less general; but we also want a theory that does not predict kinds of data that do not (or cannot) exist. It should be general but not too general. By successive approximations, through successive alterations of a theory, we approach this general, but not too general, point. In a sense then, the theory defines the possible range of the data; it defines the subject matter. At this stage the data do not define the theory; this follows from the universal character of theories. All the data cannot have been observed and hence could not have been determined the theory.

We may then assume that there are three criteria for evaluating theories and choosing the better one: exactness, generality in the revised sense, and simplicity. In this instance, wherein each of the three criteria has been derived independently of the others, any two may contradict each other. That is, given two competing theories, the first may provide more exact accountings for restricted ranges of data whereas the second will provide less exact accountings of more extended ranges of data. Or, of two theories, the first may provide accountings covering some range of data but be less simple than a theory that accounts for data whose range is more restricted. The problem is now one of establishing an evaluation if the chosen criteria conflict. One solution is to establish a hierarchy of criteria. One such is the following, in decreasing order of importance: exactness, generality, simplicity. Within this framework one would sacrifice simplicity for generality, and generality for exactness. Any such hierarchy, however, is unsatisfactory. In the first instance cited above, wherein exactness and generality conflicted, one would more likely choose the more general theory and try to refine it in such a way that its accountings fit the data more precisely. The same is true of the conflict between generality and simplicity. Intuitively, generality is perhaps the most attractive, most highly valued goal. Exactness, after all, can be met by simply listing the data.

We assumed in the instances of contradictory criteria that the evaluation based on a third criterion was in each case a constant. This is not necessarily what we would find. For instance, it may be that exactness will favor one theory but generality and simplicity favor the second. As before, the hierarchy is not absolute. The hierarchy may indicate which theory *seems* the better, which theory is more *likely* to succeed relative to all three criteria. In short, a conflict among these criteria identifies a point of flux in a science and a point for further research.

All sciences will at some time deal with theories and accountings of data. The picture of science and its methodology can be and is complicated by restrictions adopted in relation to what constitutes a possible theory and thus the set of possible accountings. Here we outline some of those attitudes that appear in the various sciences, including linguistics. A major distinction to be made is between an approach to science that limits the possible theories to asserting patterns that are *taxonomies* and the attitude that permits theories to assert a nontaxonomic pattern.

A taxonomic theory implies a set of accountings in which the data are fully dealt with when they are distributed among a set of classes defined by the theory. Let us take biology as an example. A taxonomic theory of biology may include a set of levels of classes related in a pattern of inclusion and defined by their place in the hierarchy of inclusion. The levels may be given names from lowest to highest in the hierarchy: specimen or population, species, genus, type, order, class, phylum, and kingdom. The population or specimens constitute the data to be accounted for. Each level consists of a number of distinct classes: $species_1$, $species_2$ . . . $species_n$ constitute the level of species. $Genus_1$ is defined by the species, say $species_7$ through $species_{12}$, included within it and by its inclusion within a type. $Genus_1$ . . . $genus_n$ constitute the level of genera, and so on to the level of kingdom. The patterns exhibited by the data of living organisms are exhaustively accounted for when the data are assigned their place in the taxonomy.

A nontaxonomic theory is one that relates terms in ways other than by class membership. A hypothetical science of chemistry that deals with protons, neutrons, and electrons and considers them and their patterns fully accounted for by their distribution into classes of atoms, on the order of Mendeleev's table of elements, would be a purely taxonomic science. The taxonomy may be expanded to include the pattern exhibited by grouping atoms into classes higher than elements themselves, or as compounds. If, however, we include chemical reactions, then these patterns require a way of relating classes and members (protons, neutrons, electrons, elements, and compounds) that is not taxonomic. The arrow symbol in a reaction indicates a relationship between terms to the left and right that cannot be stated in terms of class membership. What is required is a nontaxonomic relationship like "becomes," "yields," or "is replaced by."

All the theories of language that we will study are taxonomic, at least in part. All will contain statements equivalent to "X is a Y" wherein X is included in the class Y; but not all theories will limit relationships to this class-member one. The difference is not determined by the nature of theories themselves but by what kinds of patterns the theoretician conceives as attributable to language data.

The second major parameter along which theories may differ is derived from the distinction between *operational* and *explanatory* theories. We may restrict admissible definitions of theories to those that correspond to patterns derived from handling techniques or operations and observations that may be performed on a range of data. In this way the range of possible definition is restricted by the art of experimentation. Whatever operation or observation the laboratory provides may form the basis of an operational theory. No definitions beyond this basis may be part of such a theory. Taking again our example of biology, we may assume as primitives (1) a framework that permits us to record morphological properties of living organisms and (2) a relationship of conjunction. Conjunction of certain of these morphological properties defines a species. Having defined the level of species, we may define genus as the conjunction of certain properties present in a number of species; and as a species meets this criterion it is related to a genus, as member is to class. This process continues until we have decided that the theory is complete. To account for some organism is to assign it a place in the hierarchy of classes. To determine this, we first record its morphological traits in terms of our framework of morphological primitives; then by examining this first set of observations we determine its species, genus, and the like, as it matches the definitions of a particular species and genus. All organisms accounted for in the same way are identical with respect to the theory, although they may differ in size or some property irrelevant to the definitions of the theory. Whether or not we assign organisms their place in the hierarchy of classes by following the operations of the definitions step by step (we are not so obliged), it will always be possible to do so. This approach depends crucially on the applicability of a test: examining a population to discover characteristics such that the criteria for class membership are satisfied. And each class is directly or indirectly defined by these test criteria. This method of determining the classification (the operational theory and its accountings) is contingent on the success of the tests. Given the specimens and the criteria, a single accounting results if the criteria (1) can be applied, (2) are exhaustive, and (3) are noncontradictory. If the procedures indicated by the criteria are either not exhaustive or are contradictory, the accounting will be uncertain. We will return later to the problem of two or more possible accountings for the same data in a single theoretical framework. If one accepts this condition as a restriction on the class of possible theories then " . . .the meaning [interpretation] of every term must be specifiable by indicating a definite testing operation that provides a criterion for its application. Such criteria are often referred to as 'operational definitions' " (Hempel 1966:88–89).

An alternative to an operational attitude toward theories is one which requires that they be *explanatory*. An explanatory theory lacks the operational restriction. Without this condition we may construct theories such that it is not possible to apply to the collected data some test(s) and mechanically arrive at an accounting of the data. There is no mechanical procedure that leads to an accounting (unique or not) of the data. Within this approach, an accounting of a set of data is produced in the following way. One examines the data for possible obvious patterns and in a hit-or-miss way picks one of the possible accountings implied by the set of primitives and axioms as appropriate. One's choice of a particular configuration of statements is guided by past experience, intuition, luck, or chance. The derivation of an accounting is guided by the same factors that guided the choice of primitives, axioms, and definitions that make up the theory. By substituting particular values for the theoretical terms of the particular statements that render an accounting of the data, the description is interpreted. Here again there is no procedure to be mechanically followed.

Within the operational framework, the accounting that resulted from the operational tests was *by definition* an accounting of the data. Here, a particular description is the result of educated guesswork, and there is no assurance that the resulting account *is in fact* one of the data. There must be, then, a way of evaluating possible *accountings* relative to the data, just as there was a way of evaluating *theories*. Let us assume now that we have produced by this method two accountings (both consistent with some theory lacking the operational restriction) and want to determine which is the better. The criteria for this evaluation are similar to those for evaluating theories. The first criterion is *accuracy*; the more valuable accounting is the one that more closely approximates the data under consideration. Generality, in the sense introduced for evaluating theories, is not applicable in distinguishing better accountings from worse accountings. The data that are subjected to an accounting are fixed, well-defined; though the data may be infinite, they can be characterized. An accounting of the movements of the planets (their locations at fixed points in time) involves making an unlimited number of predictions from the accounting, but the data are nevertheless limited. An accounting of planetary movements is not expected to account for the movements of objects on earth. Hence, the question of generality as it was characterized in the discussion of theory evaluation does not arise with reference to accountings; it is not a possible variable. Within an accounting it is by definition a fixed quantity. Accountings may, however, be equally accurate in accounting for the same data but may differ in *simplicity*. The first of the two accountings may have involved more statements than the second accounting. If fewer statements in the second accounting predict with equal accuracy all the data of the first accounting, then *relative to these data*, the second is the simpler (or more general, in the sense that fewer statements account for equivalent data. This is "general" as distinct from its use in evaluating theories in which kinds or ranges of data were variable.)

Let us return to the problem of operational definitions that do not produce unique accountings as a result of lack of exhaustiveness or contradiction. In such cases two or more accountings of the data are possible. The problem in that instance may be resolved by imposing a hierarchy on the operational tests. If the tests are not well-enough defined to enable us to determine if the criteria have been met, then the theory is ill-defined either by accident or because the criteria (and theory) are indefinable. In this case, the solution to finding an accounting approaches in method the solution used in the explanatory theories; and the operational theory in part loses its operational character and approaches an explanatory one.

Given our distinction taxonomic-nontaxonomic and operational-explanatory, we may expect to discover theories that are taxonomic-operational, taxonomic-explanatory, nontaxonomic-operational, and nontaxonomic-explanatory. In the following chapters we will examine theories that exemplify all except the nontaxonomic-operational.

It is perhaps not apparent why the term "explanatory" should be applied to the second alternative attitude toward theories. An explanation is generally regarded as an appropriate response to the question "Why?" We can approach this problem by investigating some possible types of answers to this question. Nagel (1961: 15–26) presents four of these:

1. *Teleological*   Such a response is delivered in terms of intent, will, purpose, desire. For example, "Why did X rob the store?" X robbed the store with-the-intent/for-the-purpose-of/from-the-desire-to obtain the money to pay his rent.

2. *Statistical*   The statistical answer to the above question might be given in this way. It has been observed that 75 per cent of the people of a certain sex and age and education under certain social and economic conditions will resort to robbery. X exemplifies these stipulations; therefore it was more probable than not that X would rob a store in his circumstance.

3. *Genetic*   The genetic answer would follow in this way. People who have been taught that robbery is an acceptable method of obtaining money will rob stores. X was so instructed.

4. *Deductive*   A deductive answer to our question would involve an interpreted accounting consistent with some theory such that X's behavior followed from it *necessarily*. An answer in these terms differs clearly from the teleological, statistical, and genetic answers with regard to the stipulation "necessarily." Given X's desire, condition/environment, and his history, it does not necessarily follow that he would rob the store.

This fourth type of explanation is the one intended here when we say that some accounting out of those possible within a theory explains the data; the data follow (as predicted) from the accounting, hence necessarily. Instances to the contrary count as possible evidence for invalidating the accounting or the theory or both. And it is in this sense that the second alternative attitude toward theories is explanatory. An explanatory theory provides *explanations* of data; an operational theory provides *descriptions* of data. The neutral term "accounting" has been used to designate the set of possible statements within a theory without regard to whether these are explanations or descriptions of data.

There is a third class of attitudes one may adopt toward theories. These attitudes involve claims about the relation of theoretical terms (occurring in the accountings and theory) to the data without regard to their taxonomic/nontaxonomic or operational/explanatory character. One may claim that the theoretical terms are not "real." It may be claimed that the planets do not *in fact* circle the sun in elliptical orbits. An assumption to the contrary simply ensures a more accurate accounting of the data, the positions of the planets at given times. Such theoretical assumptions make no claims about the *actual* form of the movement of planets. The assumptions provide a tool that is used in accounting for observations. Given this attitude it is meaningless to claim that a theory is validated or invalidated; one merely notes that one theory is more or less *useful* than another in formulating accountings. Such an attitude is called *instrumentalism*.

The opposite attitude would claim that the theoretical terms are in fact "real" in some sense. One interpretation of "real" might be the following. Given some interpretation of a theory in which the theoretical term X occurs, there is an observation, experimentally accessible to all observers, that can be made and that corresponds to X under this interpretation. The theoretical term X is then "real" in that it is perceptible to all observers under the appropriate circumstances. A second sense of "real" is this. A theoretical term X, representing gravity defined in terms of masses and distance, is real if it appears in many confirmed accountings of data (positions of planets, movements of falling bodies, arcs of pendulums, etc.). In this sense of "real" the term X need not be physically perceptible to be counted "real." This attitude toward theoretical entities is called *realism*.

A third attitude is one somewhere between instrumentalism and realism, a kind of "temporary" instrumentalism. This attitude holds that theoretical entities should be real in one of the senses indicated above (or perhaps some other), but that before that stage can be reached there may be a stage in which theoretical entities are not real as indicated. The theoretical entities are justified instrumentally but not yet really. This attitude implies that the instrumentally justified terms should be translated or reduced into really justified terms. This last attitude has been named *descriptivism*.

Given this outline of scientific methodology, it is not surprising that there are a number of theories within any scientific field. There are a variety of ways theories can differ. First, it is possible that different thoreticians will regard as interesting different kinds or ranges of data and choose to develop theories differing in what they are theories of. Second, data may be freely chosen or their choice may be restricted in part by one of the attitudes, such as realism.

Assuming that the same range of data is regarded as interesting, the resulting theories may be distinct because of a choice between a taxonomic/nontaxonomic or an operational/explanatory theory, because of a choice among instrumental, realist, or descriptivist attitudes, or because the theories differ in their degrees of accuracy, generality, and simplicity. It is not surprising, then, that there are nearly as many distinct theories of language as there are theorists of language. This sketch of scientific methodology will serve as a framework for discussing a variety of theories of language proposed in the twentieth century.

ADDITIONAL READING

HEMPEL, CARL. G. 1966. *Philosophy of Natural Science*. Englewood Cliffs, N.J.: Prentice-Hall, Inc.

NAGEL, ERNEST. 1961. *The Structure of Science*. New York: Harcourt, Brace and World, Inc. Esp. pp. 1–152.

POPPER, KARL R. 1959. *The Logic of Scientific Discovery*. New York: Basic Books, Inc. Esp. pp. 59–145.

CHAPTER 2

Ferdinand de Saussure

As we pointed out in the preceding chapter, the range of subject matter one may be interested in is varied with respect to its attribution to language. The term "language" itself is necessarily defined differently from theory to theory. In beginning the study of a theory of language, the first order of business is to determine the nature of the data the theoretician takes as his subject matter.

Saussure's *Course in General Linguistics* was first published in 1916, three years after his death. The book is a compilation based on students' notes from the courses in linguistics taught by Saussure from 1906 to 1911 at the University of Geneva. This source makes it difficult to form definitive statements on several important points of Saussure's theory of language; such points will be noted in the course of the exposition. For philological studies of the *Course*, see Godel 1957 and Saussure 1967.

In the *Course in General Linguistics*, we find a discussion of a "speech act," a chain of communication between at least two people in which parts are identified and given names. Schematically, the speech act may be presented as follows (Saussure 1959: 11) on page 15. One part of this chain is bounded by the mouth and ear. This segment is termed the exterior or physical part. A second part, the psychological segment or "associative center," exists in the brain. The next division of this chain requires that a distinction be made between speaker A and listener B without implying that either is restricted to speaking or listening. The part of the act that is bounded by and includes the associative center of the speaker and the ear of the listener is active; the part bounded by

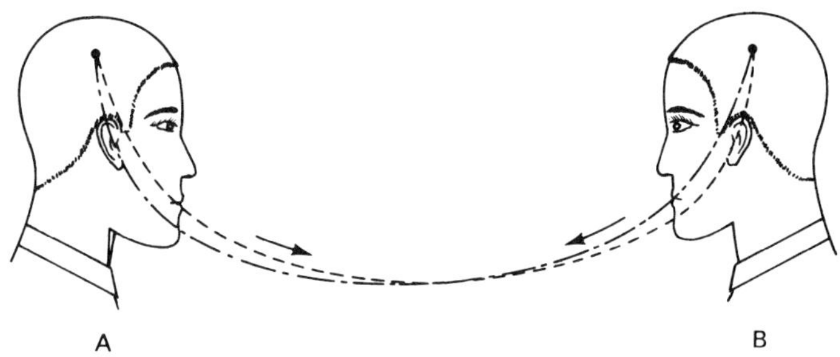

and including the ear of the listener and his associative center is passive. Notice that the three distinctions overlap in part. Some of these overlapping portions are of interest, in particular, the two defined by the overlap (1) of the psychological and the active and (2) of the psychological and the passive. These are termed (1) the executive and (2) the receptive.

At this point, we introduce three additional terms: *speaking* (*parole*), *language* (*langue*), and *speech* (*langage*), and examine the relationship of these terms to those derived from observations of the speech act. Speaking is defined as the "executive side" (Saussure 1959: 13), but we will see that this is not the same "executive" mentioned in the preceding paragraph. Language, according to Saussure, ". . . can be localized in the limited segment of the speaking-circuit where an auditory image becomes associated with a concept" (Saussure 1959:14). This localization does not imply the identification of language with that unidirectional association of auditory image and concept, but only that both are psychological phenomena located in the associative center. Language requires further characterization. Speaking and language together constitute speech.

The subject matter of linguistics proper is language. This does not mean that speaking cannot be studied, but simply that for Saussure speaking is not of primary interest. Saussure's theory of language excludes speaking. To see why language should be of primary interest, we must examine some of the characteristics attributed to it.

First, language is "social," whereas speaking is "individual." When speaking, one person talks or executes sound when he chooses. Neither what he says (the particular utterance) nor when he says it (the active) is socially determined. "Social" and "individual" are opposed. Similarly, the passive, which together with the active exhausts the speech chain A ⟶ B, is individually determined in that its functioning is occasioned by A's individual production of sound. Thus the term "individual," in characterizing the active and passive portions of the speech act, characterizes the entire speech act. If language is social, then it cannot be identified with the passive and unidirectional association of auditory image and concept, the receptive portion of the speech act, which is individual. The speech act, being wholly individual, may be assigned to speaking. And if speaking is individual, then the term "executive" asserted of speaking must not be identified with "executive" as label of the psychologically active; to interpret it otherwise would exclude the receptive portion of the speech act from speaking (and language) and eliminate it from any study. Language, existing in the brain, is social in an ontogenetic sense; it is social in terms of its acquisition. The particular associations of auditory image and concept are acquired by an individual as a function of those around the learner. All who learn a language acquire it in this way. Thus the nondirectional associations of sound image and concept are social in origin and are not the idiosyncracies of the individual learner. Because many people acquire language by exposure to the same milieu, it is shared by them and is social in a synchronic sense. Speaking, however, in its occurrences, does not have this character. Instances of speaking are idiosyncratically, individually determined, and hence, not social.

A second dichotomy paralleling the first involves willful and nonwillful. Language is nonwillful; speaking is willful. "Language is not a function of the speaker; it is a product that is passively assimilated by the individual. It *never requires premeditation* [emphasis is mine, PWD] . . . " (Saussure 1959:14). There is no element of premeditated choice in the association of sound images with concepts in language. They cannot be willfully altered. Speaking, including its receptive and executive components, is willful in that it involves a selection from among these associations for each of its occurrences.

Third, language is passive, but speaking is active. Language is passive synchronically in that it is the sum of what has been learned (Saussure 1959: 13). Speaking, the whole of it, being an instance of individual willful choice from this sum of passively acquired knowledge, is active.

Because speaking is individual and willful, it has a fourth characteristic: heterogeneity. There is no *pattern* between social context and what is said. That is, one cannot predict when someone will speak nor what he will say. Witness malapropisms. Furthermore, given a controlled context, one cannot predict the physical character of speaking. This is in part a function of individual sloppiness in articulation, close attention to articulation, and the fact that it is physically impossible to reproduce precisely a given sound. Finally, speaking is heterogeneous in that it includes a variety of kinds of phenomena: psychological, physiological, and physical. Language is homogeneous in that sound images and concepts are correlated in a constant way. The sound images of a language are not capriciously and arbitrarily associated with random concepts from time to time and from place to place. Language is homogeneous or complete only "within a collectivity" and "is not complete in any speaker" (Saussure 1959:14). If language is acquired as a "storehouse filled by members of a given community through their active use of speaking" (Saussure 1959:13), the claim that language is complete only within a collectivity can be interpreted in two ways. First, in acquiring language, a person will never be exposed to it all. A trivial instance is the continued yet never completed acquisition of all the possible lexical items of a language. Second, such a claim may mean that if speaking is an individual function, individual idiosyncracies may be acquired by others and these idiosyncracies are not representative of the whole of the community's language. They are assigned to speaking. Thus the homogeneity of language will be the "average" of the community. "Among all the individuals that are linked together by speech, some sort of average will be set up: all will reproduce [in speaking]—not exactly of course, but approximately—the *same* signs [sound images] united with the *same* concepts [emphases mine, PWD]" (Saussure 1959:13). Finally, language is homogeneous in that it is composed of a single kind of phenomenon: the psychological.

We have now examined some of the features Saussure attributes to language and speaking.

SPEECH

Speaking	*Language*
Individual	Social
Willful	Nonwillful
Active	Passive
Heterogeneous	Homogeneous

Language is what is learned; speaking is use of that knowledge; and the speech act is the manifestation of that use. We can see from these features of language one compelling reason for making it the primary subject matter of linguistics. It is in language alone that patterning is discoverable, and it is pattern that is requisite in the subject matter of a science.

The Theory

Before discussing the theory Saussure develops to account for this subject matter, we will consider some further features attributed to language. We mentioned that language involves the association of sound and meaning, that this association is psychological and has pattern. The principal comments to be made at this point involve the term *sign*. In the last quotation we took from Saussure, the term "sign" was used in the sense of something representing or standing for meaning. "Sign" in a more important sense is used to indicate the association of sound and meaning. Since sound is a physical phenomenon and language is psychological, psychological equivalents are used in place of both sound and meaning, i. e., *sound image* and *concept*. The sound image and the concept may be associated by mutual implication, and these three (sound image, concept, and mutual implication) constitute the sign.

The sound image and the concept, when mutual implication is established, are termed the *signifier* (*significant*) and the *signified* (*signifié*), respectively.

A characteristic of the sign is its *arbitrariness*. That is, within a particular language the particular signifier and the particular signified that contract mutual implication is simply a datum. It does not follow from a particular sound image that some particular concept should be associated with it. There is no way of predicting which signified will be associated with a signifier, and vice versa. If this were the only characteristic of signs, an accounting would consist of a simple inventory in which signifieds are associated with signifiers.

Language is said, however, to be a *system* of signs; it is not a mere list. Within a system, each sign is defined relative to every other sign and not each independently of the others. The implication of this will be explored in more detail later.

A further characteristic of the system of signs is that each distinctly defined sign need not be completely unlike the others in the system. There are patterns. For example, the signs *thief*, *thievery*, and *theft* (also *thievery*, *bravery*, and *slavery*) are partially alike and thus exhibit a pattern, whereas the signs *thief*, *quickly*, and *go* exhibit none. This possible partial likeness of signs implies their complexity, for it is in terms of parts of signs that the pattern of signs is stated. Signs, then, may be minimal or they may be complex. The extent of this complexity is vaguely defined. Saussure would exclude, for example, most sentences from language data, claiming that they are the result of willful construction on the part of the speaker, hence part of speaking. The basis for this position is the claimed heterogeneity of sentences: "If we picture to ourselves in their totality the sentences that could be uttered, their most striking characteristic is that they in no way resemble one another" (Saussure 1959:106). They fail to meet the criterion of pattern and are completely arbitrary. Some sentences with fixed form, such as clichés, greetings, and the like are, however, to be considered part of language. It is not possible to say with assurance what is a sentence, thus not language, and what is a cliché or other complex sign and thus language: ". . . there is no clear-cut boundary between the language fact, which is a sign of collective usage, and the fact that belongs to speaking and depends on individual freedom" (Saussure 1959:125). From this it follows that the subject data are not clearly determined, at least not on first examination.

There are two senses in which the term "arbitrary" is used: to characterize the mutual implication of signifier and signified and to characterize pattern or partial likeness among signs. In the first sense, language is arbitrary; in the second, it is partially arbitrary.

It is these features of language that Saussure has in mind in developing a theoretical framework to account for particular languages. Although Saussure never speaks explicitly of developing a theory, he does mention "fixed principles that the linguist meets again and again in passing from one [idiom] to another" (Saussure 1959:99) and claims that "the diversity of idioms hides a profound unity" (Saussure 1959:99). He thus distinguishes between a universal framework, in terms of which accountings of individual languages are made, and the individual languages themselves.

The Attitude of Realism

The shape of Saussure's theory is in part determined by an adopted condition of realism. This condition is at least in the following weak form: assumptions and definitions of the theory must be so constructed that *each* instance of them in the *accountings* of language data has a one-to-one relationship to pieces of data. It is not clear that Saussure holds a stronger form of realism, i.e., that assumptions and definitions of *both* theory *and* the accountings must have this isomorphic realization. To adopt the stronger form of realism would be equivalent to claiming that speakers of distinct languages possess identical representation of some single object, the theory, for the elements of the theory are necessarily universal. The identical representation cannot be social in origin, since the speakers of distinct languages will have been formed by different social environments. The distinct language-identical representation conflict may be resolved by further claiming that the identical representation is innate, that every person, by virtue of being a human being, is born with knowledge that is the representation of the elements of theory. Saussure (1959: 9–11) speaks briefly of a *faculty of speech*, but it is not clear if he extends his realism to elements of the theory itself to account for this faculty. He insists clearly and frequently on the "concrete," real character of language but never on some innate ability to acquire it. We assume Saussure accepts the weaker form of realism. The acceptance of this condition has a corresponding effect on the terms posited as part of his theory; that is, they may be part of the theory if and only if they are shown to have a concrete psychological interpretation when they occur within an accounting.

Saussure distinguishes theory/accounting from language data, but it is not clear in all passages of the *Course* whether he is speaking in terms of accounting for a language or in terms of the psychological data of the particular language being accounted for. Thus when Saussure (1959:102) writes, "The signs that make up language are not abstractions but real objects . . . ; signs and their relations are what linguistics studies; they are the *concrete entities* of our science. . . ," it is not clear if he is speaking of (1) signs as theoretical terms occurring *in some accounting* of a language or (2) signs as occurring *in their psychological context* and constituting part of some language data. This ambiguity, which results from the fact that "language" labels both the data and also the accounting of that data within the theory, need not bother us in light of Saussure's assumption of a form of realism. That such statements *are* ambiguous and that Saussure does hold a form of realism will be made clearer later when we discuss how this position restricts his theory.

Operationalism Rejected

Saussure (1959:102–7) considers briefly an operational theory of language but finds it lacking. It may be instructive to examine his dismissal of such an approach. In terms of delimiting signs, the operational approach would involve general principles for identifying sound images and concepts in the data so that the signs, signifieds, and signifiers in the resulting accounting would have identifiable psychological correlates. In this approach, the first problem involves segmenting sound images and concepts, for language (as data) "does not offer itself as a set of predelimited signs that need to be studied according to their meaning and arrangement; it is a confused mass . . ." (Saussure 1959:104). This operation is performed by comparing portions of sound images, which are considered to be linear, and identifying the smallest portions that correspond to or are associated with concepts. The result of this operation is then checked, and confirmed or invalidated by comparing it with results of the same operation on other sound images. Discovering the same sound image associated with the same concept in other sound images supports the posited sign. Thus *rat* in *rattrap* and *catch the rat* are separate instances of the same sign occurring in complex signs. However, *rat* in *he ratted on me*, although the same sound image, enters a distinct sign, for it is associated with a concept that is not the same as the concept associated with *rat* in *rattrap*.

Such a theory of language based on an operational definition of the sign in terms of the operations of segmentation and association is rejected by Saussure for two reasons. First, signs characterized in this fashion fail to meet his restriction of realism. To use Saussure's example, one may segment two sound images in French, *mwa* and *mwaz*, in the complex sound images, *sɛtmwa* (*cet mois*) 'this month' and *ləmwazaprɛ* (*le mois après*) 'the month after'. One would be impelled to claim that with respect to these segments there is a single sign with the concept/signified "month" and a sound image/signifier; but actually there are two signifiers. To establish a single signifier (which is necessary because a sign is defined by the association of a signifier with a signified) it is necessary to resort to an *abstraction* that in some way contains or links both *mwa* and *mwaz*. Similar examples are numerous; thus an operational theory fails with respect to realism. Sign, as a term of the theory and accounting established by segmentation and association, fails to meet Saussure's restriction.

Second, an operational approach does not account for the signs of a language as a system. Each smallest sound image is delimited and identified without relating it to the other sound images; they are defined independently of one another. Thus the resulting set of signs constitutes an inventory, not a system. Such a theory fails to account for the systemic characteristic of the subject matter. Signs defined simply by the "union of a certain sound with a certain concept . . . would isolate the term from its system; it would mean assuming one could start from the terms and construct the system by adding them together when, on the contrary it is from the interdependent whole that one must start and through analysis obtain its elements" (Saussure 1959:113).

The last part of the quotation in the preceding paragraph indicates the kind of theory Saussure will attempt to construct. He adds:

> *Being unable to seize the concrete entities or units of language directly [i.e., by a set of operations, PWD], we shall work with words. While the word does not conform exactly to the definition of the linguistic unit [i.e., simple and complex signs including some sentences, PWD], it at least bears a rough resemblance to the unit and has the advantage of being concrete; consequently we shall use words as* specimens equivalent to real terms *[emphasis mine, PWD] in a synchronic system, and the principles that we evolve with respect to words will be valid for entities in general (Saussure 1959: 114).*

We will use the term "sign" when speaking of data and the term "word" when speaking of theories or accountings. It will be an explanatory theory of language. There will be a theoretical element, "word," which will enter into patterns that are expressed by "word" being analyzed into constituent elements; "word" will consist of constituent elements. Thus

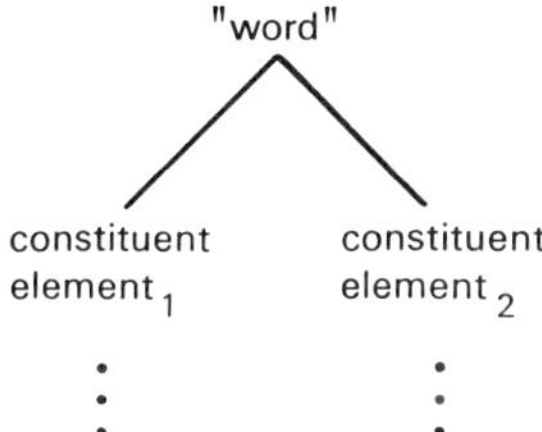

Notice that, given the kinds of signs that enter into a system (simple, e.g., *brave;* complex, e.g., *bravery;* some sentences) and that all these signs are instances of the element "word," it is possible to determine the number of analyses (the number of constituent levels) "word" will have only with respect to data. That is, the number of analyses is determined by the number needed to account correctly for the pattern present in the sign data. The examples Saussure chooses as illustrations never require more than one analysis into at most two constituents. His examples are limited to simple or complex signs to the exclusion of sentences.

Speaking now of the data this apparatus is in part to account for, the complex signs exhibit patterns of resemblance with other signs, so that parts (but not the whole) of the complex sign may be identical or similar to parts of one or more distinct complex signs or to the whole of some simple sign. For example, *bravery* exhibits a partial resemblance to *thievery* and to *brave. Bravery* is complex because it contains at least two constituent elements, *brave* and *ry*, which happen to be instances of simple signs. In other words, these constituent elements do not partially resemble other signs in terms of at least two constituent elements, *br* and *ave*. It is to account for patterns of this kind that Saussure assumes a theoretical framework including "word," which may be analyzed into constituents; for if patterns are stated in terms of parts of signs, these statements require that these parts be identified. Analysis is then a component of a complete accounting of language pattern. Thus:

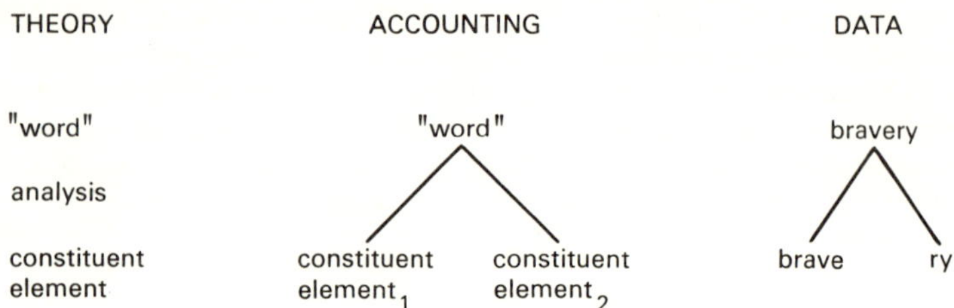

We set aside for the present mechanisms for stating the patterns between two pieces of data such as

Restriction of the Theory

At this point we return to Saussure's realism with respect to its effect on accountings and the definition of the system of signs. In speaking earlier about the theoretical apparatus that must be provided to account for patterns on the basis of analyses, we did not consider the question of how we in fact know that *bravery* is a complex sign and that in terms of its constituents it in fact is similar to some other sign. That is, up to now we have not considered how data are collected: what experimental methods are used to collect data. The method proposed by Saussure (1959:14) is introspection. "It [language] never requires premeditation, and reflection enters in only for the purpose of classification [for the purpose of collecting data, PWD] . . . " Saussure never questions the validity of this method of obtaining data (and we will accept it here without argument), although he does place certain restrictions on it as a technique. These restrictions concern the question of how much of language can be discovered by introspection. Without doubt, one can obtain data that show that *bravery* is complex. But (to use Saussure's example) can one also obtain by this method the data that show the signs *domin-ī, reg-is,* and *ros-ārum* exhibit a pattern, that they are partially the same in their second constituent sign? Or can one determine that the second simple signs in *žen-a, žen-y, žen-e, žen-u, žen-oj,* and *žen-e* in Russian are linked and pattern as a paradigm or that *domin, reg,* and *ros,* although distinct signs, have a pattern, a similarity, in that they are all substantives? Finally, can one establish that *politicians finagle, the flower fades,* and *snow melts* (assuming for the sake of example that these sentences are included in language) are similar in that they are all statements with a substantive and verb, that is, are "types of syntagms"? And to add a type that Saussure does not explicitly consider can introspection establish that different "types of syntagms" (e.g., *brave, thievery, do flowers fade, go!,* etc.) are all similar in that they are all instances of "word"? Are they related in that they are all signs of some sort? These considerations ascend in inclusiveness or "generality" in the order given and seemingly for Saussure become less certain in that order. Saussure (1959: 138) claims, however, "all these things exist in language, but as *abstract entities* [hypotheses, PWD]; their study is difficult because we never know exactly whether or not the *awareness* [emphasis mine, PWD] of the speakers goes as far as the analyses of the grammarian." Because the data are limited by the extent of the speakers' awareness and because of the realism, Saussure is prevented from positing theoretical elements to account for classes of syntagms or classes of signs such as substantives and the like. Patterns of signs in language data are those of which the speakers are aware. If the speakers are not aware of these "higher" patterns, then they do not exist as language patterns; and given the realism condition, the theory does not account for them. If it did, accountings would contain terms such as "paradigm," which would correspond to no piece of language data obtained by experiment, thus contravening the condition of realism.

All this has the following effect on the accountings within such a restricted theory. Consider *bravery* and *stupidity* and possible analyses of them:

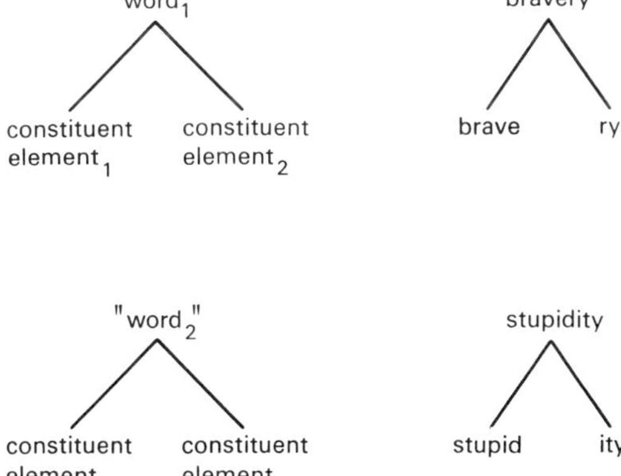

and

One detects a pattern in the data, perhaps as a grammarian and not as a speaker, in which both *bravery* and *stupidity* are complex signs, and moreover both are abstract nouns; the first constituent sign in both is an adjective and the second is a suffix deriving abstract nouns. Assuming this as data, we can express the pattern formally, which would require equating or linking "$word_1$" and "$word_2$" as "$word_a$"; constituent $elements_{1\&3}$ as constituent $element_a$ and the second constituent elements of *bravery* and *stupidity* as constituent $element_b$. Then an analysis might run as follows:

ACCOUNTING   DATA

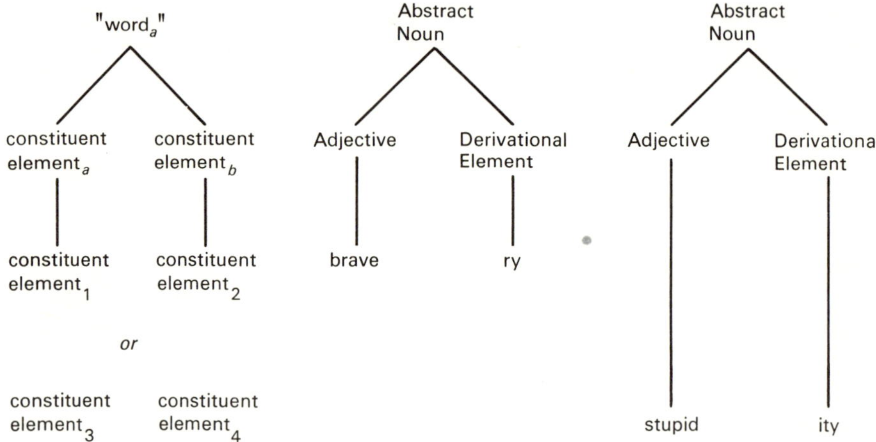

But this type of analysis and accounting for pattern requires theoretical elements of a sort that according to Saussure have no (or at best, doubtful) psychological reality and thus for him are not permissible elements of the theory.

Given Saussure's initial condition that all elements within an accounting must correspond to some part of the data, constituent $elements_{a\&b}$ would predict the existence or discovery by introspection of data-links between *brave/stupid* and *ry/ity* as well as between *bravery/stupidity:* the existence or discovery of, say, "adjective," "abstract-noun derivation," and "abstract noun." The unsubstantiality of these last terms, as a function of the uncertain depth of the speaker's introspection, is reflected directly in the tenuousness (or absence) of the theoretical apparatus to account for them as data. Saussure apparently requires that patterns and types of patterns be discovered as data *before* introducing elements into the theory to account for them. This procedure of theory construction guarantees that all elements in the accountings of data will exhibit a correspondence within the data and that the condition of realism will be met. This cautious approach prevents, however, hypothesizing theoretical elements like "constituent $elements_{a\&b}$" and prevents the accounting of the pattern existing between *bravery* and *stupidity* and their parts in the data. The theory, and thus the accounting, permits no prediction that (with or without some future sharpening of experimental techniques) such data patterns may or will be discovered.

But again the existence and discovery of that data pattern by introspection is nonexistent (or at best uncertain); thus there is no pattern (or an uncertain one) here to be missed. The possible argument that Saussure's theory to this point is open to criticism on the basis of incomplete accounting of data resolves itself into an argument of what is in fact data and what is not data. The method of introspection as used by Saussure places a condition on possible data: that the speaker be conscious ("aware") of data (data here in terms of pattern). That the speaker may be guided by the grammarian toward the discovery of some data is excluded. If the discovery of data is not automatic on the part of the speaker, it is not data but an "abstract entity." Criticism of the lack of generality of the theory in accounting for certain kinds of data then leads not to the discovery of some shortcoming in the theory Saussure proposes but to the discovery of another characteristic of the data, language; that while requiring no "premeditation" in its acquisition, patterns exist only if they are directly discoverable by introspection on the part of the speaker with no guidance by the grammarian.

There is an uncertainty at this point. It is possible to find passages in the *Course* and elsewhere that apparently contradict this interpretation. For example: "The very fact that *enseignement* is a substantive creates a relation with all other substantives in the form of an associative series" (Saussure 1969: 41). Were one to accept this alternative statement of Saussure's, then the theory would have a shape more like the one we have just outlined. The principal difference would be the addition of an either-or primitive that is missing from the theory as presented at the end of the chapter and the addition of suitable "abstract entities" to the theory such as "word$_a$" and the like. Saussure's strong insistence that language data be concrete, however, inclines one toward the interpretation given below.

Furthermore, the fact that in the *Course* sentences are clearly excluded from language by Saussure and are not part of the data of the theory supports the interpretation set forth in the remainder of this chapter. This conclusion results from the following argument. If "substantive," and the like, were concrete language data (assuming the alternative statement), then it would follow that many *sentences exhibit pattern* in that they are partially identical in terms of "substantive," "verb," and so on. But Saussure's exclusion of most sentences from language is not open to doubt; there are no conflicting statements on this point. Thus the assumption that leads to its contradiction—namely, that "substantive," and the like, are real, discoverable by observation, and are part of the data—must be excluded. To accept the assumption and its result would further indicate that Saussure consistently ignores part of the data of language.

If the theoretical elements "word$_a$", "constituent elements$_{a\&b}$", and the like, had been accepted, system could have been defined in terms of minimum words, the last elements in an analysis. The nonminimim words might then have been accounted for as some defined "combinations" of minimim words. For example, *brave, stupid, ry,* and *ity* would have been terms of the system, while *bravery,* and the like, would have been nonminimum words defined in terms of minimum words related in some appropriate way. With the rejection of "abstract entities," however, all signs, complex or not, make up part of and enter into the definition of language as a system of signs (now: some simple, some complex).

From the argument given above, there is not *one* initial "word" in the theory but a system of "words" to account for a system of signs (required, according to Saussure, because the uninstructed speaker does not feel that all signs have something in common, say, "signness," and exhibit pattern). Where signs are complex (exhibit pattern), "word" may be analyzed into constituent elements to provide an accounting for these language data. The pattern of these signs (stated in terms of their constituents) will require the addition of some elements to the theory in order to provide accountings of this pattern. Thus for each sign:

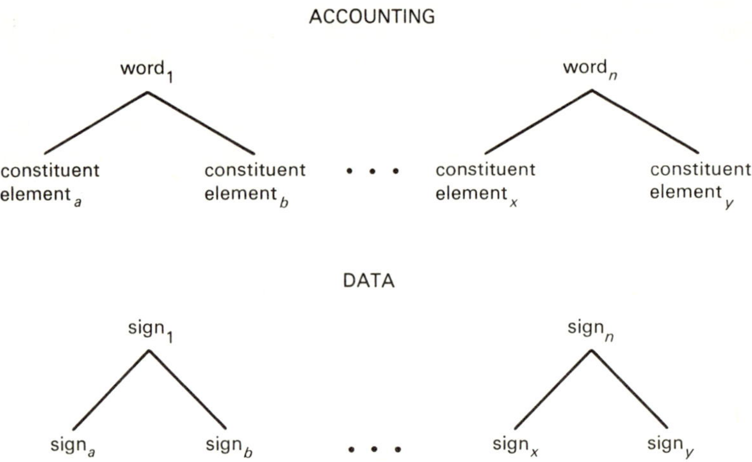

Notice that signs$_{a...y}$ will all be minimum or simple, while signs$_{1...n}$ will include both minimum and complex signs. Signs$_{1...n}$ and signs$_{a...y}$ constitute a system. Accordingly, words$_{1...n}$ and constituent elements$_{a...y}$ will be defined as a system to account for the sign data.

System and Value

At this point we examine Saussure's definition of system based on *value.* Value is a relationship characteristic of signifieds and signifiers. It is also a defining characteristic. A signifier or signified is said to have value (have a relationship of value) if it is different from the other signifiers and signifieds, respectively. Each signifier and signified is then defined systemically as the conjunction of what it is *not*. "The value of any term is accordingly determined by its environment" (Saussure 1959: 116). To give a graphic example, consider the three figures in Figure 1. Each is defined in the following way:

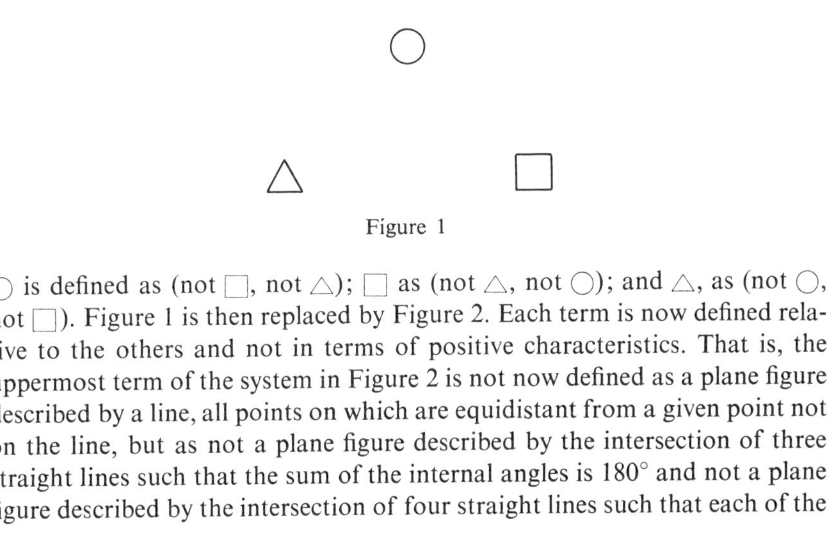

Figure 1

○ is defined as (not □, not △); □ as (not △, not ○); and △, as (not ○, not □). Figure 1 is then replaced by Figure 2. Each term is now defined relative to the others and not in terms of positive characteristics. That is, the uppermost term of the system in Figure 2 is not now defined as a plane figure described by a line, all points on which are equidistant from a given point not on the line, but as not a plane figure described by the intersection of three straight lines such that the sum of the internal angles is 180° and not a plane figure described by the intersection of four straight lines such that each of the

(not □, not △)

(not ○, not □)   (not △, not ○)

Figure 2

four internal angles equals 90°. It is obvious that any change in the number of terms in the system will affect the definitions of *all* terms within the system. Any change in the number defines a completely different system, for the definitions of all the terms have been changed.

The example Saussure uses in this respect is that of a monetary system. A dime, say, is defined as not-a-quarter and not-a-nickel. How the dime is defined positively (in terms of its silver and base-metal content or in terms of what it will buy) is irrelevant. The dime may be produced of aluminum or in ten years it may purchase what a nickel does now. These changes would have no effect on the systemic definition of the dime. If, however, a new coin, say a quickle, were introduced, the definitions of quarter, dime, and nickel would be altered correspondingly.

Each positive term of the system is now described by the intersection or conjunction of relationships relating each term to all other terms of the system and is fully defined within the system by the intersection of these relationships. Thus let (1) _____ = not-△ relationship, (2) ...... = not-○ relationship, and (3) _ _ _ _ _ = not-□ relationship. Then the intersection at

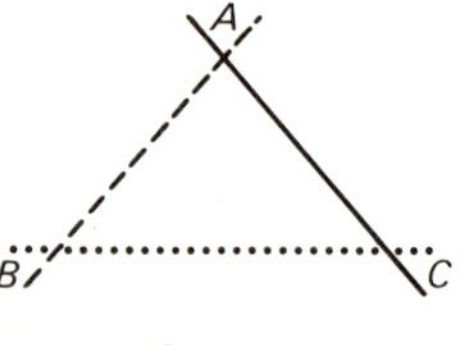

Figure 3

A yields a term defined by the intersection of the not-△ relationship and the not-□ relationship. Similarly, for the intersections at *B* and *C*. The concept of value does not involve what a term is different from, but only that it *is* different. Accordingly, the distinction between △, ○, and □, or the unbroken, dashed, and dotted lines, are to be replaced by pure difference. In Figure 4 we have defined three nonidentical terms by the intersection of three

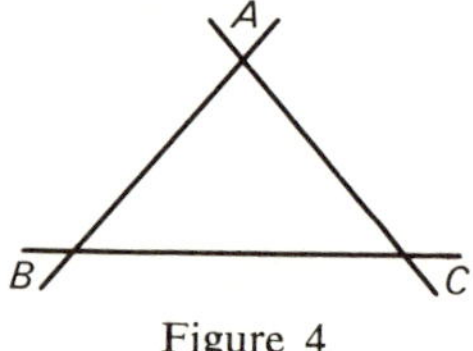

Figure 4

relationships of difference. Whether they are a circle, triangle, and a square, or doctor, lawyer, and Indian chief is irrelevant to their systemic definition. The correspondence of these three different terms to concrete things—pieces of data—is a matter of interpretation. By statements such as "Let *A* be a circle . . ." we provide some content to the terms of the system.

The definition of signifieds systemically without regard to positive content or association external to language may be illustrated in the following way. Consider the color spectrum from red to violet. English has within its system of signifieds some that correspond to the color spectrum outside of language; but within the system of signifieds they are defined solely in terms of value relationships. Some other language, such as Bella Coola, may also have within its system of signifieds some that correspond externally to the spectrum as illustrated in Figure 5. Although these two sets of signifieds are associated externally with the same range of physical phenomena, systemically (internal to the language of each) they receive definitions such that they are completely distinct. The signifieds are defined independently of one another and of any shared positive characteristic.

Signifiers are analogously defined. Each signifier is determined by what it is not; *mat* has value by virtue of its being not *bat, mad, might, mit, met,* or *rhinoceros.* Its positive definition as *m-a-t* or [mæt] is irrelevant to the definition of its place in the system of signifiers.

The system of words—corresponding one-to-one to a system of signs in the data—may be defined by associating the terms in the system of signifiers

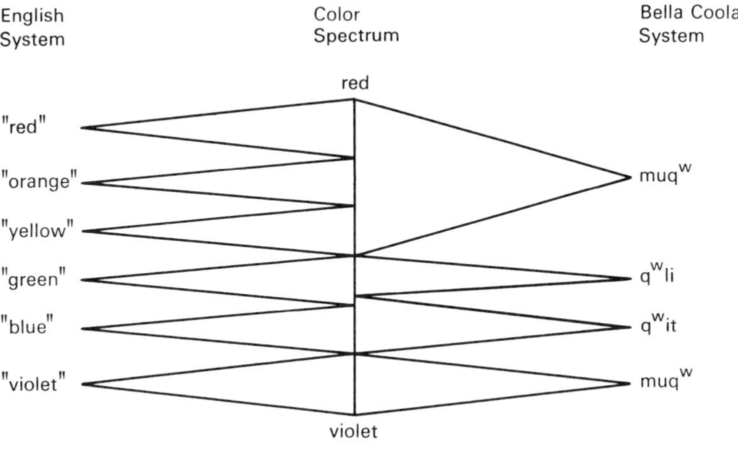

Figure 5

(defined as intersections of relationships) with terms in the system of signifieds, also defined as intersections of relationships. That association is specifically mutual implication. Thus for a three-termed system, represented in Figure 6, the number of occurrences of the solid lines representing mutual

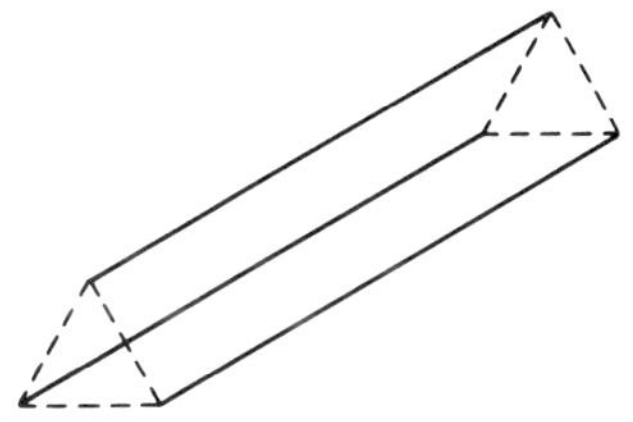

Figure 6

implication determines the number of words in the system. Notice that while the system of signifiers and signifieds is defined relationally in negative terms, the system of words is defined as the positive and arbitrary association of distinct signifiers and signifieds. Thus, Saussure (1959:121) says that signifiers and signifieds within their systems are *different* from one another, but signs are *opposed* to one another.

The theoretical apparatus to account for data with the characteristics outlined above includes: (1) value or relationships of nonidentity (not-*a* relationships, wherein *a* is equal to the number of terms in the system), (2) a way of relating the relationships in (1), called conjunction, and (3) a mutual implication relationship. These are the present assumptions of the theory. Given these primitives, one may define two systems in terms of value relationships and by stating mutual implications between points of intersection in the two systems, define a system of words. The accounting at this point consists of certain chosen systems defined according to the rules of the theory with no meaning attached to the terms. This accounting may be interpreted in the following way, thus imparting content to the definitions of the accounting. The elements of one of the systems may be interpreted or given meaning by letting $term_1$ of $system_1$ defined by the intersection of not_{a-d} correspond to $signifier_1$ in the data defined by the intersection of $not_{\alpha-\delta}$, and so on, until the members of $system_1$ of the accounting have been assigned correspondence in the data. Then the same procedure may be followed for the second system. That is, let $term_x$ of $system_2$ of the accounting defined by the intersection of not_{m-r}, which is related by mutual implication to $term_1$ of $system_1$, correspond to $signified_1$ defined by the intersection of $not_{\mu-\rho}$, which is related by mutual implication to $signifier_1$. This process continues until all the defined terms have been assigned correspondences within the data or, equivalently, until these sets of definitions consistent with the assumptions of the theory have been interpreted. Thus we arrive at an accounting of the system of signs given as data and represented graphically in Figure 7.

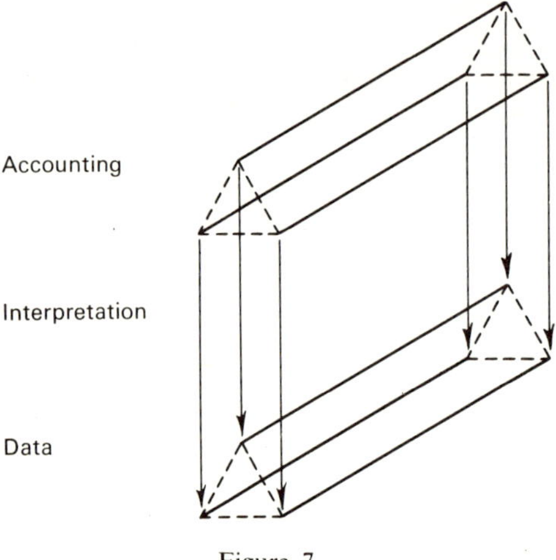

Figure 7

Notice that the assumptions of the theory and the definitions of the accountings are made without reference to content and provide a very abstract framework that potentially may account for a great many phenomena. For example, in Figure 7 the terms of $system_1$ of the accounting might be interpreted not as corresponding to a system that is positively characterized as sound images, but to a system that is positively characterized as body movements (a dance) or as modes of behavior (carrying an attaché case to work, or a book bag, or growing long hair and a beard). We see, then, that such a theory potentially could account for much more than the data of language. All "meaningful" or symbolic behavior might be the data of such a theory and the field of some science. Saussure suggests this and proposes the

name *semiology* for its study. Within the science of semiology, linguistics
would be a specialized branch of study in which the theory is interpreted as
systems that are associated positively with sound images and concepts.

Complexity may now be considered systemically. A complex sign is complex by virtue of pattern. Pattern requires complexity, for the former is
identity of parts of a whole. Both the whole and the parts are signs within the
system. For such a whole-part to exist, both are required. Signs cannot be
parts of some sign without relation to that complex whole; nor can a sign be
considered complex without parts. Hence, there is a mutual implication between whole and part, which suggests that complexity might be characterized
by relations between words in the word system. By identifying the whole-word
and its part-words, relating them by mutual implication, complex and simple
words can be defined. In Figure 8 the solid line (a mutual implication between

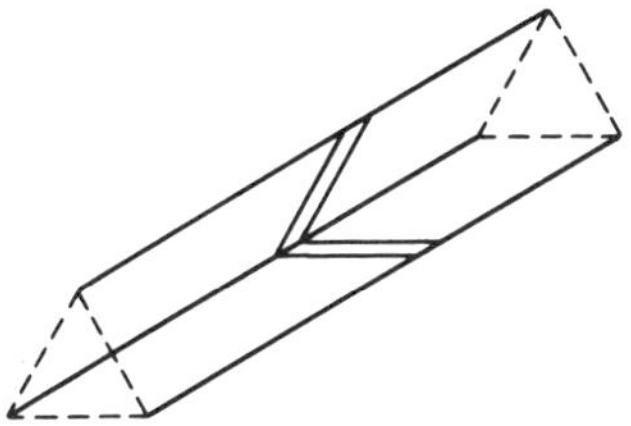

Figure 8

a signifier and a signified) intersected by *two* double lines (mutual implication
between words) defines that intersected line as complex. The two single
lines (words) related to the complex line (word) are defined as parts. Thus,
mutual implication involving three or more words, one of which is defined
as complex-whole, the others as the parts, defines complex and simple words.
Mutual implication may now hold between words as well as between signifiers and signifieds. Notice that there is no distinction drawn between
two possible types of simple signs: (1) a simple sign as a simple-whole and
as a part of a complex-whole and (2) a simple sign as part of a complex-whole
alone (*slave* and *slavery* versus *ry* and *slavery*). In terms of the theory, mutual
implication may hold between words; whole, complex, and part may be
defined of words. The relationship between complex-whole words and less
complex-part words, and correspondingly in the data between complex-whole
signs and less complex-part signs, is called *syntagmatic solidarity* (Saussure
1959: 127–28). Notice that the part elements are less complex but need not
necessarily be minimum. Recall the discussion of extent of analysis and
Saussure's choice of examples with one-step complexity. For simplicity of
exposition, we deal only with this uncomplicated type of complexity.

We have mentioned one property of language—whole-part relationships
or complexity—and pointed out how one might account for it within the
theory as developed to this point. We also mentioned that this property of

complexity was requisite for pattern within the system. Now we consider the patterns discoverable within a system of complex and minimum signs.

The Pattern of Signs

Saussure finds two types of patterns in the data: *associative* and *syntagmatic* (*not* syntagmatic solidarity) (Saussure 1959: 122–27). Associative patterns are divided into several subtypes. First, two different complex signs may be analyzed into their respective less complex signs such that they share some sign, that is, share a constituent sign and are partially identical. Thus *burglary* and *burglarize*, analyzed, respectively, into *burglar* and (*r*)*y* and *burglar* and *ize*, share a sign in common. *Burglar, burglarize,* and *burglary* exhibit a pattern that is an associative relationship by virtue of the shared sign.

The second type of associative pattern is based on "analogy" of signifieds. Saussure's example is a series of complex signs: enseignement, instruction, apprentisage, and education. The constituent signs (double underlining) are the parts of each complex sign that exhibit the analogy of signifieds. This claim of an associative pattern as characterized requires an assumption not explicitly made by Saussure, namely, that signifieds may be partially alike. This assumption contradicts the definition of system that defines the individual signifieds within the system of signifieds by intersections of nonidentity relations, for Saussure's claim of pattern based on partial identity of signifieds requires some positive characterization of signifieds. One may attempt to resolve this contradiction assuming that signifieds may be in some way complex, that signifieds may consist of signifieds. That is, signifieds of signs may be complex in the same way signs are complex, and furthermore, the two different signifieds of two opposed signs may have constituent signifieds in common. This assumption is equivalent to assuming a hierarchy within the system of signifieds. A second possible resolution of the problem might be to assume that the shared identity of the signifieds is external to language. If we assume that signifieds, viewed as part of the speech act, are connected to some external field (activity, objects, culture, etc.), then the signifieds may overlap in terms of these external fields. This assumption admits nonsystemic considerations in the form of patterns into language.

A similar associative pattern is claimed relative to signifiers. Two signs may exhibit pattern if the signifier of each is partially identical. Saussure's example is *enseigne-ment* and *juste-ment*, wherein $ment_1$ means 'ing' (*teaching*) and $ment_2$ means 'ly' (*justly*). The comments of the preceding paragraph apply here.

What these two subtypes of associative pattern hint at but do not explicitly develop (see Chapter 3 for an explicit statement) is that once a stage of analysis is reached in which the signs are minimal, the signifieds and signifiers may be analyzed independently (Saussure 1959:130–31). The signifieds would be analyzed into constituents and some may be said to be complex, exhibiting pattern by sharing constituents and being partially identical with other signifieds. Similarly for signifiers. This pattern, however, requires a multileveled theory of language.

A level within a theory of language may be thought of as follows. Assume that the function of linguistics may be roughly described as accounting for the way meanings and sounds are associated and also as providing tangible content to the terms "meaning" and "sounds." One way to accomplish that task would be to record sounds, produce a permanent record of them in some way, and associate stretches of sound, say those defined by alternations of speakers in a conversation, with the corresponding meanings, also recorded in some way, say in an ideographic script. Thus

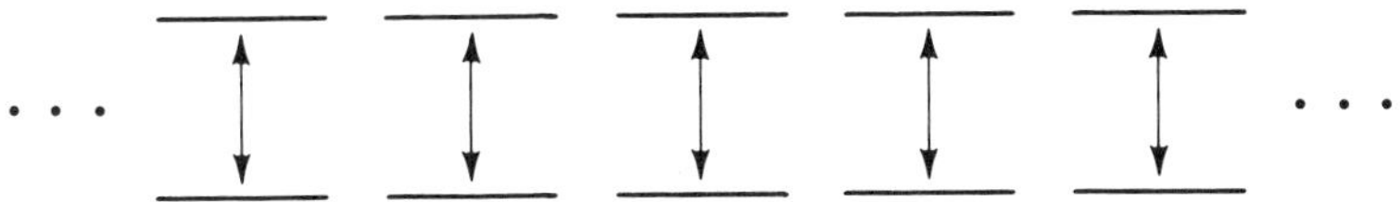

in which the top lines are meaning stretches; the bottom are sound stretches; and $\updownarrow$ means "are associated together." In this way each unit is unique; it would never recur. This is equivalent to claiming that there is no patterning, no similarities between pieces of data. If this *were* true, such phenomena would be of no scientific interest, besides being unlearnable and an impossible basis for speaking. If linguistics is a science, the data must be amenable to patterned statements. The notion of level can be roughly equated with kinds of patterning. Saussure initially assumes one kind of patterning in the data, a patterning in terms of signs. Thus

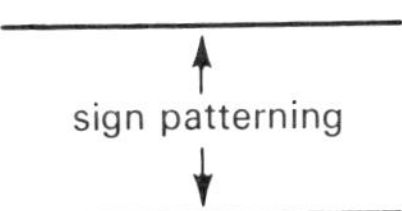

"sound" and "meaning" are connected, and these mediating connections are patterned. They are not each unique, but exhibit similarities in terms of partial identities. With some indication now that Saussure would introduce other kinds of patterning, partial identities of signifiers and signifieds, thus perhaps

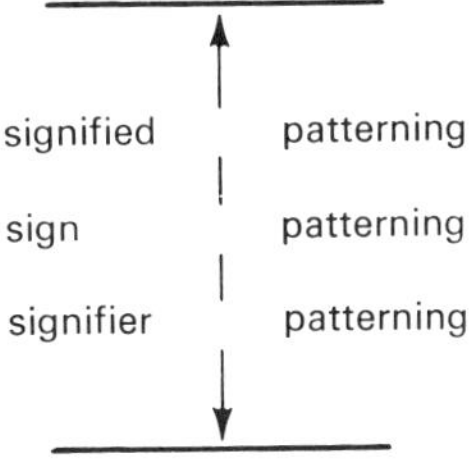

Saussure does not consider the implications of assuming associative patterns of the last two types mentioned above. It would be a definite extension of the theory to incorporate more than one level; it would not be the theory of most of the *Course*. (See again Chapter 3 for such an extension into a *two*-leveled theory.) Here we will consider Saussure's theory as one that accounts for one kind of patterning on one level, that of sign patterning.

Related to level is hierarchy internal to it. Given a level based on a kind of patterning, that pattern will be in terms of something. For Saussure that something is signs (when speaking of data). Internal hierarchy is in part defined by size. One might distinguish size-levels within a level. Within Saussure's theory/data two such size-levels are well-defined. The first is that system of words/signs defined without regard to complexity or pattern. Here a word/sign is considered and defined as neither complex nor simple but as a unit, a term in a system. The second size-level is that defined by identifying just the minimal words/signs after making a distinction between complex/ noncomplex, that is, after analysis is introduced. Here by definition all terms are minimum. Furthermore, according to an interpretation of Saussure's theory, under which elements like "substantive" are not data and therefore need no theoretical apparatus to account for them, there would be only two size-levels: that size-level of signs considered without analysis and that size-level of signs defined as minimum by virtue of analysis. Intermediate levels of the hierarchy would exist in the data in terms of "substantive," but these are nonexistent in language.

Returning to the discussion of types of patterning, besides the associative types, there is a syntagmatic type. This patterning is based on a property of linearity that we have assumed but not yet discussed. One of the properties of sign data is that the signifiers of signs are linear. "The signifier, being auditory, is unfolded solely in time from which it gets the following characteristics: (a) it represents a span and (b) the span is measurable in a single dimension; it is a line" (Saussure 1959: 70). The signifieds are not linear. Furthermore, *constituent signs are linear* with respect to their whole sign. That is, if a complex sign consists, say, of two constituent signs, then these two are in a fixed order. The signifier of constituent sign$_1$ is linear (as is that of constituent sign$_2$), and furthermore, the signifier of the complex sign of which these are parts is linear; the signifier of constituent sign has a fixed linear relationship to the signifier of constituent sign$_2$. The linear property of constituent signs follows from the linear property of the signifiers. The linear relationship of the signifiers indicates the linear relationship of their respective signs. The linear "sequence" of signifier and/or sign is a *syntagm*. Hence, "In the syntagm a term acquires its value only because it stands in opposition to everything that precedes or follows it or both" (Saussure 1959: 123).

The constituent elements of some complex sign, in addition to being related to each other by being in mutual implication with the complex sign, are related linearly (syntagmatically.) Thus the special term for mutual implication between signs: *syntagmatic solidarity.*

The two types of relationships or patterns between signs may be distinguished in several ways. First, the associative pattern is nonlinear; the syntagmatic is linear. Second, the number of elements that may enter into an associative pattern is much larger (perhaps unlimited) and the number in a syntagmatic pattern is relatively small and fixed. For example, *redo* contains the constituent signs *re* and *do* in a syntagmatic relationship. *Re* in *redo* is also a constituent in the large set of verbs *re* + verb; thus *redo* is associatively related to this number of complex signs. Saussure illustrates these differences between associative and syntagmatic patterns with the analogy of a building constructed of columns. The whole building is the complex sign. The columns connected by architraves are the minimal signs related linearly (syntagmatically). Buildings that are partially identical in that they share one or more column types (doric, ionic, etc.) establish an associative pattern between themselves. The columns of the building and the building as a whole are related by syntagmatic solidarity. Third, the associative and syntagmatic patterns differ in that the first is determined by (partial) identity of complex signs while the second is determined by opposition between signs.

One final comment on a relationship between these two types of pattern: they presuppose each other. That is, a syntagmatic pattern cannot exist unless at least *one* of the terms is shared with or is (1) the constituent element of (is part of) another opposed complex sign or is (2) the whole of some sign that happens to be simple. The associative pattern requires that the complex sign consist of parts, that it be complex. It requires analysis. Hence, "[in *painful*, for example] the suffix is non-existent when [*painful* is] . . . considered independently; what gives it a place in the language is a series of common terms like *delight-ful* . . ." (Saussure 1959:128). Notice that syntagmatic pattern and syntagmatic solidarity also mutually imply each other; neither exists without the other. Hence, each of the three mutually implies the other two. Mutual implication is a relation that is reciprocal and transitive.

Summary

The preceding discussion of pattern was in terms of its existence in the sign data. To account for such data the theory has to provide either definitions in terms of existing assumptions and definitions or definitions in terms of new assumptions. Saussure's formalism for accounting for such data is a display such as Figure 9, in which ________ indicates the (complex) word; and X and Y between ________ indicate the constituent elements related by syntagmatic solidarity with X Y and with one another in the order given: X then Y, from left to right. The elements ________ about X Y indicate the latter's associative relation with the former (which may be simple or complex, i. e., Z or W may be null). The ordering is formally defined by the

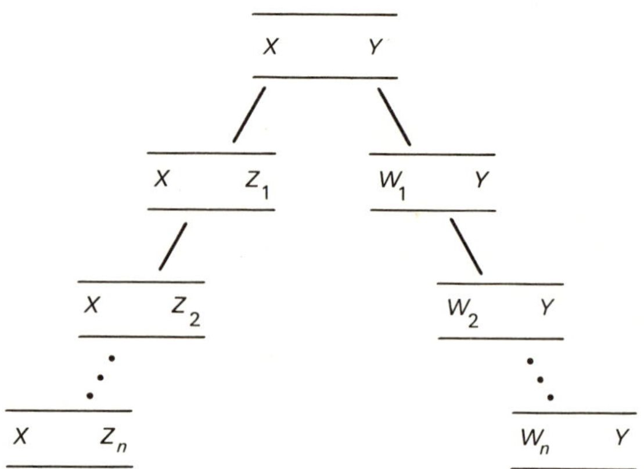

Figure 9

point of intersection of these radiating elements with $\overline{X\ Y}$; this point also identifies that shared element X or Y. $\overline{X\ Z_1} \ldots \overline{X\ Z_n}$ intersects $\overline{X\ Y}$ at X in Figure 9, thus accounting for the associative pattern of $\overline{X\ Y}$ with $\overline{X\ Z_1} \ldots \overline{X\ Z_n}$ by virtue of the shared X. It is obvious that any account of even slightly more complicated data in these terms will become completely unwieldly; one may settle for accountings in terms of prose statements based on the following primitives and definitions of the theory:

Primitives.
1. *Nonidentity, value relationships*
2. *Linearity*
3. *Conjunction*
4. *Mutual implication*

Definitions.
1. *Word system:* Defined in terms of mutual implication holding between conjunctions of two systems that are in turn defined by conjunctions of nonidentity relationships.
2. *Syntagmatic solidarity:* Defined as the relationship of mutual implication holding between n elements of the word system in which $n \geq 3$ and $n - 1$ of the terms are linearly related.
3. *Complex word:* Defined as the element of a syntagmatic solidarity with no linear relation with the other elements of the syntagmatic solidarity.
4. *Simple words:* Defined as (a) the linearly related elements of a syntagmatic solidarity or (b) elements of the word system not related by syntagmatic solidarity.
5. *Analysis:* Defined in terms of word system, syntagmatic solidarity, complex word, and simple words.
6. *Associative relationship:* Defined in terms of (a) complex words analyzed such that at least one of the simple words of each is the same (e.g., *burglary* and *burglarize*), or (b) a complex word and a simple word such that they are

related by syntagmatic solidarity (e.g., *burglar* and *burglary* or *ry* and *burglary*), or (c) the relationship between simple signs if the complexity of signifieds and signifiers is admitted.

7. *Syntagmatic relationship:*   Defined in terms of simple words related to the same complex word by syntagmatic solidarity and to one another by linearity.

This is a semiformal interpretation of the theory Saussure proposes as a definition of language. One accounting that follows from it is given in Figure 9. With proper interpretation it is possible to deduce the data *burglar*, *burglarize*, *burglary*, *thievery*, and *slavery* and the patterns holding between them. An accounting in this theory would then consist of the following:

1. A definition of a word system
2. A definition of the complex and simple words
3. A definition of an analysis holding between the complex and simple words
4. A statement of the associative relationships among words
5. A statement of the syntagmatic relationships of minimum words holding between them as elements related to complex words
6. An interpretation of statements (1)–(5) such that the elements and statements given there predict the signs and patterns, and only those, in the sign data
7. An evaluation of the extent to which (6) is met and a reworking of (1)–(5) until (6) is met and the correct data are predicted.

To meet (6) is to provide an explanation of the data.

Accountings are evaluated in the following manner. First, does some systemically defined configuration of accounting statements that is consistent with the assumptions and definitions predict the signs and patterns discovered in the data? Can the terms of the accounting be interpreted so that they predict the data? Do the relations defined in the accounting, when interpreted, predict the exact patterns found in the sign data? "Yes" to these questions indicates an acceptable accounting. Increasing numbers of "no" answers indicate less acceptable accountings. Notice that the choice of accounting is never determined by nor requires any operation on the data beyond that they be collected by introspection; that is, there are no operational definitions within the theory.

We consider now whether this theory can yield two accountings that will correctly predict the data and whether these two can differ in simplicity. The answer is "no." Pattern is part of the data, and each term of the accounting, considering the realism condition, is related by the interpretation to one part of the data. Accountings and data are isomorphic. Making a simpler description by using fewer statements (removing some part of the accounting) will directly alter the predictions the accounting makes and produce an incorrect accounting. The accounting that *correctly* predicts the data is *fixed* in simplicity. To alter the simplicity is to alter the correctness of the accounting. We see now that two accountings consistent with some theory may both predict the data *and* differ in simplicity (one having fewer statements) *only if* there is no realism condition dictating that *all* terms in the accounting must have some direct correspondence in the data. Otherwise there is a *single*, *unique* correct accounting that it is the task of the grammarian to find.

This concludes the explanation of the theory in the *Course in General Linguistics*. We can now easily understand Saussure's (1959: 122) dictum that "language is a form and not a substance." Language is relationships; positive characteristics are a secondary concern. In the following chapter we detail the theory of Hjelmslev's *Prolegomena to a Theory of Language*, which further develops the idea of language as form.

ADDITIONAL READING

BLOOMFIELD, LEONARD. 1924. Review of Saussure, *Cours de linguistique générale. Modern Language Journal* 8.317–19.

EGE, NIELS. 1949. "Le signe linguistique est arbitraire." *Travaux du Cercle Linguistique de Copenhague* 5.11–29.

GODEL, ROBERT. 1961. "L'école saussurienne de Genève," in *Trends in European and American Linguistics 1930–1960*, eds. Christine Mohrmann, Alf Sommerfelt, and Joshua Whatmough. Utrecht: Spectrum. Pp. 294–99.

————. 1966. "F. de Saussure's theory of language," in *Current Trends in Linguistics* III, ed. Thomas A. Sebeok. The Hague: Mouton & Co. Pp. 479–93.

SAUSSURE, FERDINAND DE. 1959. *Course in General Linguistics*, trans. Wade Baskin. New York: Philosophical Library.

————. 1969. "Linguistique statique: quelque principes généraux," in *A Geneva School Reader in Linguistics*, ed. Robert Godel. Bloomington: Indiana University Press. Pp. 39–52.

WELLS, RULON. 1947. "De Saussure's system of linguistics." *Word* 3.1–31. Reprinted in Joos (1958).

CHAPTER 3

Louis Hjelmslev

The comments to be made here on the theory of language suggested by Louis Hjelmslev will be based primarily on his *Prolegomena to a Theory of Language*. As with Saussure, we begin with some pre-theoretical discussion of what the relevant data are considered to be and the approach taken to provide a theory of them. The data of this theory are called the *text*, which may consist, for example, of all utterances made in English over a period of time (in which case it is a restricted text) or of all possible utterances in English (in which case it is an unrestricted text). The text is not necessarily oral. It may be written or manifested in any material whatsoever. Pattern, the discovery of which is the goal of science, is not assumed to be present and exhibited within the text. Pattern and constancy lie elsewhere, and the text is simply assumed to be amenable to systematic accounting. This assumption with respect to the nature of the data (which characterizes any science) is the only one made of the nature of the text within this approach to a theory of language. Strictly, then, the text is not a given. An analogous situation arises in any science with respect to its data. First, the data of the theory must be delimited from all other possible data and this delimitation has to be justified. Second, handling techniques or operations have to be applied to the data. These are the parameters of experimentation; say, a device for splitting atoms and a method for recording the array of segmentations. These methods may or may not be assumed by the theory (be primitives of the theory). The results of the operations, the segmentations or the terms in which they are described, may be included within the theory as primitives without the theory's being operational. A theory may, for example, assume a phonetics without being itself operational. If such primitives are adopted, the theory loses part of its abstract character, and its validity and usefulness will depend in part on the correctness of the segmentation. Here, neither terms involved in the description of the text segmented by handling techniques (a phonetics) nor the operations of segmentation are assumed by the theory, which will provide a segmentation in its own terms, a linguistic segmentation. Concerning the first delimitation, that of texts from nontexts:

> *The philosophy of science leads to the view that the description of the universe is a continuum. A description of a particular object is therefore in principle only part of the description of the whole universe and cannot be regarded as definitive . . . until all the pieces have been fitted into their places in the great picture puzzle. To be absolutely sure of the description of, say, an English text, one would have to begin with the analysis of the universe in the first operation of the procedure and descend gradually until the text, or some slightly larger unit comprising it is reached . . . . "He [the scientist] assumes that in considering a small portion of the universe he can neglect the rest. He goes on on this assumption until he finds it is wrong. If it is wrong he looks around and brings another bit of the universe into his ken, and continues altering his field of observation until his isolated structure behaves as though it were really isolated [Ritchie, A. D. 1923.* Scientific Method. London: Kegan Paul. *Pp. 6-7.]" (Uldall 1957: 30).*

The first delimitation of data is arbitrary, but each delimitation is justified by the fact that systematic statements can be made of and within each in terms of some theory.

The justification of the identification of a particular object as text requires a preliminary introduction of some of the theory. The systematic statements of this theory, which if applicable justify the delimitation, are made within a framework of a taxonomy: generally, of elements defined as classes and simultaneously as components of classes, that is, a hierarchy of classes. The taxonomy is elaborated by characteristic dependences or relationships existing between a class and its components and among the components themselves. The dependences among components order them as members of a class. These dependences are *interdependence* (Saussure's mutual implication relation wherein X implies Y and Y implies X), *determination* (wherein X implies Y but not the reverse), and *constellation* (neither X nor Y implies the other). An object chosen from among those possible as the object of a science must have interdependences and determinations predicable of it. ". . . the aim of science is always to register cohesions [interdependences and determinations, PWD], and if an object presents only the possibility of registering constellations or absences of function, exact treatment is no longer possible" (Hjelmslev 1961: 83). There is no possible science of the latter object.

The extension of text, as opposed to nontext, might be identified as the largest portion of the universe of whose parts a statement in terms of one of the dependences (here interdependence or determination, since constellation may be predicated of any division) may be made. Thus

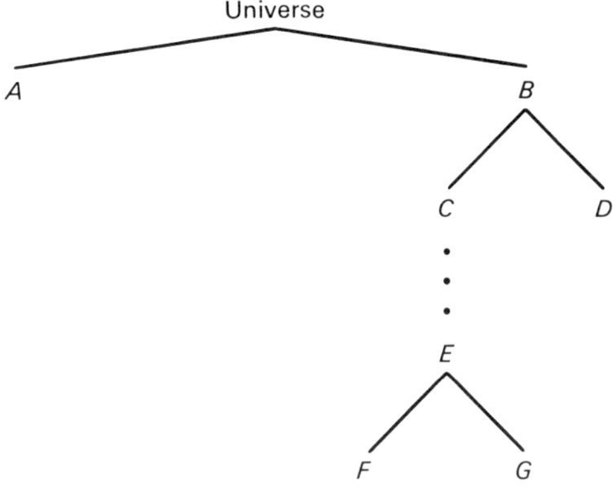

If, say, there is interdependence between *F* and *G* as components of *E*, then *E* may be coherent and amenable to patterned statements, while constellation holds between *C* and *D* of *B*, and *B* is not so amenable. If such is the case of *E*, we are justified in taking *E* as data of the theory. If no systematic statements are applicable, different divisions are tried until such statements apply. Even at this early point it is impossible to talk of data except in relation to theoretical terms. Let us suppose we find that the theory provides one set of statements as applicable to a portion of the universe and then discover a second portion for which the theory also provides applicable statements; and furthermore, we find that the two sets of statements differ, although both derive from the theory. This is roughly the basis for distinguishing between two texts as manifestations of distinct languages. This second text, along with *E* and any others, constitutes the set of texts within the universe: the manifestations of possible language. We delimit the set of texts from all else within the universe and then distinguish among individual texts.

If *E* is identified as a possible text by the theory, that is, if it is amenable to the systematic statements provided us by the theory, then it will always be first resolved into two components called *content* and *expression* related by interdependence. The data, here the content and expression portions of an individual text, may be delimited further by nonlinguistic handling techniques exterior to the theory. Bits of expression may be derived by the techniques of a phonetics or a physics, by techniques that are not part of the theory itself. The expression may be a continuum of speech sound, a series of marks on a piece of paper, or the dots and dashes of a code. In an unrestricted text, the expression is the possibility of an unlimited number of these elements. The content may be segmented in terms of a psychology, an anthropology, or a physics. It is, very roughly, that which is talked about. This segmentation of content, like the segmentation of expression, is accomplished by techniques that are not part of the theory. Since in an unrestricted text it will be possible to talk of anything, the content is potentially the universe itself. This segmentation of the text by nonlinguistic sciences is not presupposed by the theory of language. The theory of language imposes its own segmentation on the text, both expression and content, as it did on the universe. This potentially segmentable stuff of a text is called *purport*. The two segmentations of expression and content via nonlinguistic and linguistic sciences are distinct; each is a segmentation with respect to distinct theories. The association of the linguistic segmentation with purport projects an order onto the latter, which is a *substance*.

The integral, unsegmented text is the object of the linguistic accounting. We now consider some of the statements one may want to make in accounting for it. We seek a regularity. Initially, given a theory of taxonomy and dependences, we may want to account for the text through a division of it, since it is presented to us as a whole. Segmenting the text into a hierarchy of classes may serve as such an accounting, but such statements, being unique to the portion under scrutiny, may not be confirmed by the unscrutinized portion. Furthermore, such an accounting would be subject to lapses and mistakes and would miss possible identities; what may be identical items and susceptible to being accounted for with a single statement may be treated separately. In general, an accounting based directly on the nonlinguistic segmentation of the text would miss the pattern or the constancy behind the fluctuation that is requisite for a science. This property of constancy is not attributed to the text and is not to be found through a direct nonlinguistic segmentation of the text. Although the text has no internal structure, one may be imposed on it through a segmentation by a linguistic or nonlinguistic science, but neither of these *exists* within the text. We may contrast this approach with Saussure's, according to which the results of introspection (sameness or identifications, partial samenesses or identifications, and differences) were "concrete" within certain restrictions placed on the technique of introspection and were centered in the brain. Here an existence within the data, the text, is not claimed for the results of the nonlinguistic handling techniques nor for those of the linguistic theory. The reverse is most emphatically stated:

> . . . *the purport* [*unsegmented text, PWD*] *can be known only through some formation, and thus has no scientific existence apart from it . . . From a projection of the results of linguistics on the results of these other sciences will come a projection of the linguistic form on the purport in a given language* (*Hjelmslev 1961: 76–77*).

As Saussure assumed an attitude of realism with respect to the relation between theory/accounting and data, Hjelmslev adopts an instrumentalist attitude. Neither theory nor accountings will be directly derived from observation of a text. It is assumed that constancy is present in the form of the theory and the accountings themselves. These accountings are evaluated and justified in terms of how well they satisfy a set of criteria for theories and accountings.

Two properties Hjelmslev (1961: 14–15) attributes to theory in general are *arbitrariness* and *appropriateness*. The first quality is in part equivalent to our observation that theory cannot be derived inductively. Arbitrariness of theory, further exhibited by the absence of an assumption of structure inherent within the data and consequently by the assumption that pattern will be present only in the form of the theory and accountings and by the absence of primitives derived from handling techniques and the consequent explanatory character of any theory based on such an approach, is so emphasized by Hjelmslev that he gives this approach a distinct name: *glossematics*. Glossematics is not a theory of language, but a set of attitudes toward what may qualify as a theory of language. As characterized, glossematics specifies theories of language in which language is immanent within the theories and their accountings and is contrasted with a linguistics whose theories of language define language as transcendent by assuming structure and pattern inherent to data (realism) and which include elements provided by the handling techniques as primitives. The second property, appropriateness, results from the fact that the theory, although arbitrary, is based on what the theoretician might guess is necessary to define and account for some actual range of data. These two properties of theory as interpreted by Hjelmslev mark his theory as explanatory. Although he speaks of procedure, it is not to be interpreted as operational. (Cf. below.) Recall that the segmentation of the text is predicted by an accounting of the theory; an accounting segments purport. The segmentation of purport by some nonlinguistic science is a prerequisite neither for linguistic theory nor for a linguistic accounting. Recall also that the definition of the range of data, text, came out of the theoretical considerations.

With respect to the possible accountings within the theory, Hjelmslev (1961: 11) specifies a hierarchy of evaluative criteria that he calls the "empirical principle":

> *The description shall be free of contradiction (self-consistent), exhaustive, and as simple as possible. The requirement of freedom from contradiction takes precedence over the requirement of exhaustive description. The requirement of exhaustive description takes precedence over the requirement of simplicity.*

The first condition required of accountings is simply that they be accountings of the given theory; if not, they are to be immediately dismissed. The second two correspond to the evaluative criteria of accountings introduced in Chapter 1: exactness and simplicity. Exactness is here interpreted as accounting for all the data, stating all the patterns that the text affirms. Simplicity is further elaborated into a "simplicity principle":

> *If . . . linguistic theory ends by constructing several possible methods of procedure, all of which can provide a self-consistent and exhaustive description of any given text and thereby any language whatsoever, then, among those possible methods of procedure, that one shall be chosen that results in the simplest possible description. If several methods yield equally simple descriptions, that one is to be chosen that leads to the result through the simplest procedure (Hjelmslev 1961: 18).*

Simplicity of description means economy of elements in the accounting: roughly, classes and members of classes. For example, in considering a possible accounting of a text derived from nonlinguistic segmentation, we mentioned that it erred in not making possible identifications; the results of the accounting were more than they could have been, and simplicity was violated. Simplicity of procedure must await explanation until we have a better understanding of what "procedure" as a technical term means.

The criteria of simplicity of description and exhaustiveness are important in the construction of Hjelmslev's theory. The types of patterns assumed to be assertable of a text and thus to be available to possible accountings are motivated by these two evaluative criteria.

The Shape of an Accounting

We begin the discussion of the theory with the three dependences (interdependence, determination, and constellation) and an extremely restricted text: *in*. We assume that some nonlinguistic science has provided us with a segmentation of this text: [ɪn] and 'within a container' via, say, physics and anthropology. From the point of view of linguistic science, the text is as yet unanalyzed. We may provide a linguistic accounting of the data in the following way:

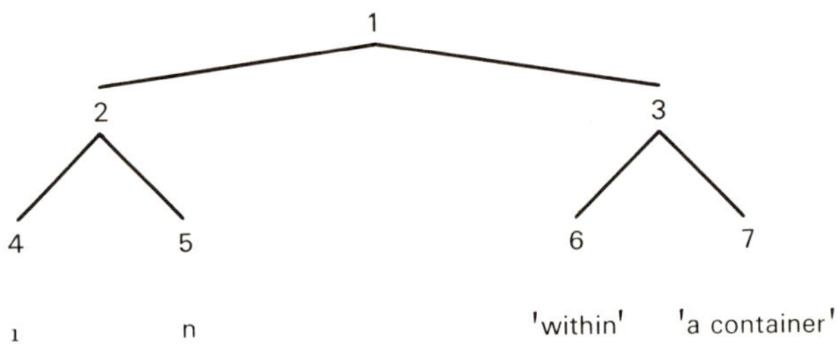

in which the four terminuses (numbered 4, 5, 6, and 7) indicate the four segments that, when related to purport, will provide a linguistic accounting of the text. We have provided a linguistic accounting of the whole by this segmentation. Within the framework of our primitives we may define 2 as the dependence between 4 and 5: an interdependence; 3 is defined as the dependence, again, interdependence, between 6 annd 7; 1 is a dependence between dependences 2 and 3 and is an interdependence; 4 and 5 may be defined as objects between which there is interdependence; and 6 and 7, as the objects between which another interdependence exists. Dependence 2 and 3 may also be defined as objects between which an interdependence exists, namely, 1. The statement of these patterns introduces a new primitive: *object*. It is justified within the theory in part by exhaustiveness. There are two ways in which 2 and 3 may be described—as dependences (between 4 and 5 and 6 and 7, respectively) and as terminuses of a dependence (i.e., 1). Exhaustiveness requires that all this be stated. Notice that 4, 5, 6, and 7 can at this stage be defined only as terminuses, objects, of a dependence, but not as dependences. Should it turn out that objects are always dependences, then every required definition in which "object" occurs may be restated with "dependence" replacing "object." The fact that all dependences are here interdependences is an accident of the text. Because of its restricted nature, no portion of the text occurs without the remainder; each portion thus presupposes the remainder.

An accounting, then, is in terms of dependences between dependences, and if an accounting is to be exhaustive, each dependence must be defined as the first and as the second "dependence" in "dependence of dependences." The similarity between the abstract, relational character of the primitives, and needed definitions involving intersections of them, and the relational character of the primitives and definitions of Saussure's theory of language should be apparent. Saussure's definition of a system of signifiers or signifieds is based on the conjunctions of one type of relationship (distinctiveness or value). The conjunctions or intersections define the terms of a Saussurean system interpreted as acoustic images or concepts. The terms of a Hjelmslevian linguistic segmentation are similarly defined. The term labeled "2" is the conjunction or intersection of the relationship between 4 and 5, which in turn has a relationship with 3. This latter relationship is labeled "1". The conjunctions of relationships are not immediately—hence, not equally—related to all others. The terms are hierarchically associated with the other members within the network of terms. This hierarchy is clearer in our second sample text (cf. below), in which 8 and 9 are more closely related than 8 and 10.

Analysis is defined as the "description of an object by the uniform dependences of other objects on it and each other" (Hjelmslev 1961: 131). Within this definition the described object and the describing objects presuppose one another; neither is logically prior (Hjelmslev 1961: 48). The dependence between the described object and its describing objects is interdependence. Each implies the other. Uniformity ensures that the describing objects together describe or define only one object: that they, with whatever kind of dependence between them, enter into an interdependence with a single described object, namely, the dependence between them. If there is a dependence of determination between X and Y, then the dependence is the described object and X and Y are the describing objects. The relationship between the two groups of described and describing objects is interdependence, and the describing objects bear that interdependence with no other described object. They, together, describe no other object than the one identified in the analysis. In an analogous fashion, a class exists by virtue of having membership, and its members are members by virtue of membership in a class. Class and member hold a relationship of interdependence in the same way that the described object of an analysis holds interdependence with its describing objects. The definition of analysis is exemplified in the definition of complex word in Saussure's theory. The complex word is analogous to the described object and the simple words are analogous to the describing objects. A complex word is complex by virtue of its relationship to simple words, and simple words are simple by virtue of their relationship to the complex word. Interdependence or mutual implication exists between the complex word and simple words; that particular relationship is syntagmatic solidarity. Uniformity within Saussurean theory is assured by the linearity of the $n - 1$ elements of the syntagmatic solidarity. *Burglar* and *ry*, linearly related, held mutual implication with *burglary*, as did *burglar* and *ize* with *burglarize*. The fact that *burglar* was linearly related with *ize* and that these two words entered into mutual implication with *burglarize* was irrelevant to the syntagmatic solidarity between the complex word *burglary* and the simple words *burglar* and *ry*, for *burglar*, *ize*, and *ry* held no relation of linearity among themselves and mutual implication with some complex word. The relationship between two objects, which may themselves be dependences, and the dependence they describe is interdependence. If that last dependence is taken as 2 above, then 2 may be described by the uniform dependence of 4 and 5 upon it (2) and each other. The latter—the relationship between 4 and 5—within this accounting was also an interdependence, although it might have been a determination or constellation with respect to some other text. The relationship (their dependence) that 4 and 5, the describing objects, hold with 2, the described object, will always be an interdependence.

A *class* is the "object that is subjected to analysis" (Hjelmslev 1961: 131) and *components* are "objects that are registered by a single analysis as uniformly dependent on the class and each other" (Hjelmslev 1961: 131). Here 1, 2, and 3 are classes; 2, 3, 4, 5, 6, and 7 are all components.

Now we can make some additional observations. Recall that the first division predicated of any text as data was a division into exactly two pieces called "expression" and "content." These two terms are also names for particular components of an analysis. The components within the analysis, when interpreted, project an exhaustive division of the text—purport—into exactly two pieces. Expression and content apply to the theoretical terms (two identifiable components within an accounting) and to two pieces within the data identified when the accounting (provided in part by the analysis) is interpreted. Without regard to interpretation, the two components are not differentiable within the accounting. Expression and content, always bearing the relationship of interdependence, are describing components of the most inclusive class of the accounting. To call one expression and the other content is arbitrary. "Their functional definition [in terms of dependences, PWD] provides no justification for calling one, and not the other, of these entities *expression*, or one, and not the other *content*" (Hjelmslev 1961: 60). Externally, the two are differentiated. The part of purport we called content, with reference to an unrestricted text, included/subsumed everything that one could talk of, potentially the universe itself. The part of purport labeled expression was more restricted and, furthermore, must be included within content. One can talk about the sounds one makes or can make, about the marks one makes or can make on paper, and so on. The component of the accounting, which, when further defined, segments or provides a segmentation for the including part of purport, the universe, is identified as content versus the component of the accounting that segments the included part of purport, expression. Thus

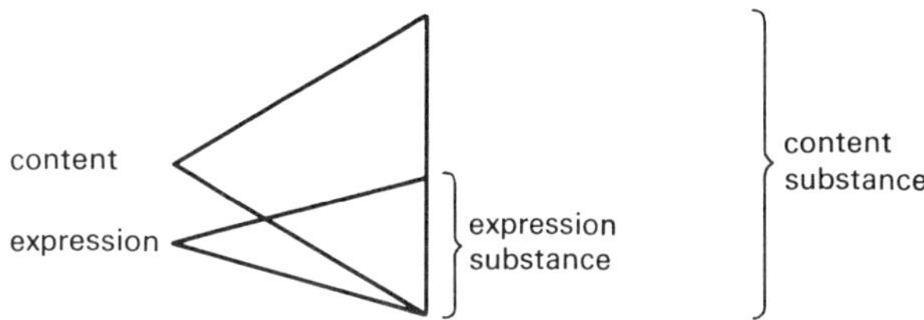

A nonarbitrary labeling of two terms of the accounting as content and expression results only from relating them to purport via an interpretation. Within the accounting we have of the restricted text, 2 and 3 are expression and content, although we don't know which is expression and which is content until an interpretation is made.

We have now added three primitives to the theory: description, object, and uniformity. Analysis has been defined with these primitives. A selection of statements in terms of analysis constitutes a partial accounting, but one which, as we mentioned, is not exhaustive. Dependences described by analysis as a class must also be described as components of (a) class(es) if the accounting is to be exhaustive. *Synthesis* is the "description of an object as a component of a class" (Hjelmslev 1961: 131). If we restate the definition of synthesis, replacing the term "class" with the words that define it, then synthesis is "the description of an object as a component of an 'object that is subjected to analysis'," and it is easily seen that synthesis presupposes analysis. Describing an object by analysis results in a single statement in terms of the describing objects, which follows from the uniformity stipulation in the definition of analysis. Describing an object by synthesis, however, may result in a set of statements that is not those of analysis in reverse order, because an object described as component may be a component of more than one class. There is no example of this in our text *in*, but it is apparent in the *burglary-burglarize* example wherein analysis would eventually make *burglar* a component of both *burglary* and *burglarize*, thus necessitating more than one description of *burglar* as a component. We ignore here the condition required to recognize the *burglar* of *burglary* as the same as *burglar* of *burglarize*.

At this point we find this array:

THEORY	ACCOUNTING

Primitives
   Description
   Dependence
   Interdependence
   Determination
   Constellation
   Object
   Uniformity
	A set of statements in terms of analysis describing the two components of the initial class

Definitions
   Analysis
   Class
   Component
   Synthesis
	A set of statements in terms of synthesis describing the two components of the initial class

A class defined by two components holding a both-and independence (= content and expression)	An interpretation of the segmentation resulting from analyses and syntheses by ordering to them the two segmentations of purport by the nonlinguistic sciences
	An evaluation of the self-consistency, exhaustiveness, and simplicity of the analysis and synthesis
	A reworking of analysis and synthesis until the highest valued set of statements in terms of analysis and synthesis is identified.

Language will be identified as the definition of the specific class defined last within the theory; we are concerned now with its elaboration.

We introduce three additional definitions: function, functive, and hierarchy. *Function* is a "dependence that fulfills [causes to be fulfilled, PWD] the conditions for an analysis" (Hjelmslev 1961: 131). Function is exemplified in the accounting by the interdependences between 2 and 3, 4 and 5, and 6 and 7. A requisite for the description in terms of analysis is the dependence among describing components. Another requisite is the dependence between class and components. This dependence, which is also a function in that it causes the necessary conditions of an analysis to be fulfilled, will always be an interdependence and universal to all analyses. A *functive* is an "object that has function to other objects" (Hjelmslev 1961: 131). In our example, 2, 3, 4, 5, 6, and 7 are functives. A functive is the describing object that contracts constellation, determination, or interdependence with some other describing object (also a functive), both of which presuppose and are presupposed by a dependence (the function) between the describing and the described objects. If a functive is in turn described as a dependence by analysis, then it is also a function. A dependence when analyzed is a class; and when its components are analyzed, they, too, are identified as classes. Thus there exists a class of components that are in turn classes, or a class of classes. A *hierarchy* is a "class of classes" (Hjelmslev 1961: 131). In our example the whole analysis is a hierarchy: 1 is a class consisting of the components 2 and 3, which are classes by virtue of analysis into 4 and 5 and 6 and 7.

Hjelmslev defines two terms, "constant" and "variable," in terms of which interdependence, determination, and constellation are removed from the list of primitives and placed in the list of definitions. *Constant* is defined as the "functive whose presence is a necessary condition for the presence of the functive to which it has function" (Hjelmslev 1961: 131), which requires the additional primitives: presence, necessary, and condition. *Variable* is defined as the "functive whose presence is not a necessary condition for the presence the functive to which it has function" (Hjelmslev 1961: 131). Now interdependence is defined as the "function between two constants" (Hjelmslev 1961: 132); determination as the "function between a constant and a variable" (Hjelmslev 1961: 132); and constellation as the "function between two variables" (Hjelmslev 1961: 132). With this information our preliminary theory is modified as follows:

THEORY

Primitives	Definitions	
Description	Analysis	A class defined by two
Dependence	Class	components holding a
Object	Component	both-and interdepen-
Uniformity	Synthesis	dence such that the
Presence	Function	components are hierar-
Necessary	Functive	chies
Condition	Hierarchy	
	Constant	
	Variable	
	Interdependence	
	Determination	
	Constellation	

In the following section we take up the nature of the hierarchies of content and expression.

The Empirical Principle, Process, and System

Let us now consider an only slightly more complex example. We assume a restricted text *in in* that by some nonlinguistic science has the following segmentation:

$$[\, ?\text{ın} \qquad\qquad \text{ın}\,]$$

'within a container'   'within a container'

Again, from the point of view of linguistic theory, the text is unanalyzed. We may assume the following linguistic accounting:

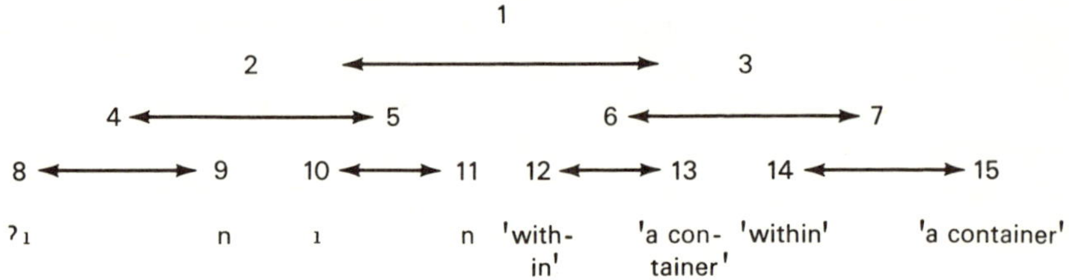

Again, 2 and 3 are identifiable as expression and content, although which content and which expression cannot be formally determined. There is interdependence between 2 and 3, 4 and 5, 8 and 9, 10 and 11, 6 and 7, 12 and 13, and 14 and 15, symbolized by $\leftrightarrow$. It is an accident of the restricted text that all the dependences are again described as interdependences (with the exception of 2 and 3, which is always an interdependence).

Assuming the self-consistency and exhaustiveness of the accounting, we consider it with respect to simplicity. Let us propose an alternative accounting:

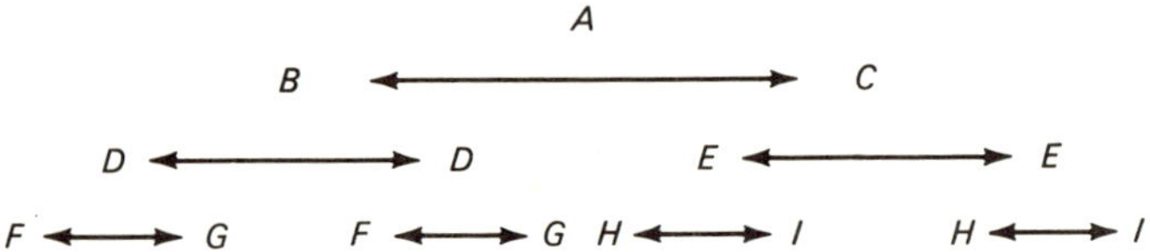

The second accounting differs from the first in that 4 and 5 and 6 and 7 have been identified as D and E, respectively. Furthermore, the components 8 and 9 of 4 and 10 and 11 of 5 have been identified (8 and 10 as F and 9 and 11 as G). Similarly, we have identified 6 and 7 and the components of 6 and 7. The dependences between components of a same class remain interdependences as before. B is a dependence described as an interdependence between D and D, and D is a dependence described as an interdependence between F and G.

This second accounting is the simpler in that it requires fewer *distinct* dependences and objects, nine versus fifteen, and is to be preferred assuming a constant degree of self-consistency and exhaustiveness. This second description requires a condition under which two terms, 4 and 5, may be identified. We assume this condition for the present and further assume that it is met by 4 and 5 and the others. Such a simpler accounting may be obtained in two ways. It may be derived independently of the first, or it may be obtained from the first by a set of heuristic techniques. For exposition we will adopt the second approach in deriving a maximally simple accounting. These techniques in no way determine what is a possible self-consistent, exhaustive, and simple accounting, but are of practical use in attaining a maximally simple one from the set of possibilities.

The derivation of the second accounting from the first may work in the following way. If two or more classes or components within some accounting meet the condition for identification, then they must be described as a single component within some class. If 8 and 10 meet the condition for identification, the number of describing objects is reduced, while exhaustiveness is not affected by the change. This heuristic technique is useful here only with respect to increasing the simplicity of accountings, then, not the exhaustiveness of accountings. The latter enters into consideration only if the condition of identity is violated, for example, by describing as same in the second, derived accounting dependences that are in fact distinct. Should this be the case, the second accounting, although simpler, is less exhaustive. Since exhaustiveness is the more important criterion, the first accounting, more exhaustive although less simple, is the preferred one. As 8 and 10 above, 4 and 5 also meet the condition for identification and are described by synthesis as components of D. When such a set of identifications are made, the simpler description results. This technique is summarized as the *principle of reduction* (Hjelmslev 1961: 61).

From our example we may observe relationships between terms of the two accountings. The two terms 8 and 10 are components of the class F. Because of the class-component relationship, 8 and 10 together as components maintain interdependence with their class F. This relationship between accountings holds whenever identifications are made. The terms of the first accounting are *variants* of the class within the second accounting, which are *invariants* (Hjelmslev 1961: 62); 8 and 10 are variants of the invariant F. The heuristic technique involves examining the accounting to make certain that only invariants are present. Where two terms are found to be variants, a derived accounting is made in which they are identified (treated as invariants).

At this point we have introduced an additional relationship. For each occurrence of an invariant within the second accounting, we find within the first accounting only *one* variant at that point within the linguistic segmentation of the text. Thus F at either of its occurrences within the second accounting will have the variant [ʔɪ] *or* [ɪ] but not both. This is an either-or relationship that contrasts with the relationship of the invariants to each other within the second accounting. There we have two D's occurring simultaneously. This latter relationship is a both-and relationship. The either-or and both-and relationships enter the theory as primitives; they are additional dependences.

It should be pointed out that both-and and either-or are not dependences distinguished with respect to linearity versus absence of linearity. Synonyms for a both-and function used temporarily by Hjelmslev (1961: 37–38) are "conjunction" and "coexistence"; for either-or "disjunction" and "alternation" are used. These synonyms are replaced by *relation*—a both-and function—and *correlation*—an either-or function. None of these terms implies linearity. The nonlinear nature of these two new dependences is further indicated by the fact that the two classes in an accounting that may be identified as content and expression (*B* and *C* in our second accounting) are related by a both-and dependence (Hjelmslev 1961: 48) that is an interdependence. There is no implication in this that the both-and relationship between content and expression is linear. The fact that, internal to the accounting, it is not possible to determine which of the two classes is content and which is expression further indicates the nonlinear character of the both-and and either-or dependences. Thus with respect to these new dependences, functives related by both-and or either-or are commutative, that is, $XY = YX$.

Let us now consider a slightly more complex example to see what is required for a maximally exhaustive and simple description. The text may be *on the bar under the bar on a barstool under a barstool a bar the bar the barstool.* Here we will consider accountings of this text concentrating on that hierarchy that can be labeled expression. What is relevant to this hierarchy will apply equally to the hierarchy of content. A possible first description is on page 53. Dependence 1, which will be identified as expression, is described by seven components holding the dependence of interdependence. Within this text each of the components 2 through 8 occurs with the other six, each apparently presupposing the others. The division of expression purport into just seven segments (and the boundaries between these segments) is at this point arbitrary and will have to be justified. The descriptions of 2 through 8 by analysis is also based on the dependence of interdependence. All describing components, in addition to holding an interdependence among themselves, hold a both-and dependence. Analogous statements apply to the remaining classes of the description. Given this restricted text, each object (e.g., 9) presupposes some other object, here 10, because 9 never occurs without it. In fact, 9 occurs only once. It is unique until a simpler description based on the assumption of identities is made, after which, when 9 is identified with 13, an interdependence no longer exists between 9 and 10, for 10 being identified with 7 occurs without 9, thus no longer presupposing it. When the identifications are made, we can give a different, simpler accounting of the text as on page 54. The single-headed arrow indicates the relationship of determination. Here the descriptive statements involve sixteen distinct elements versus the thirty-six of the first accounting.

Considering the second accounting, several patterns remain to be stated and are absent from this accounting. First, classes *B* through *H* exhibit very similar patterns. In *B* through *E* there is some term, either *I* or *J*, that presupposes some term, either *G* or *K*. Also, classes *F*, *G*, *H*, and *K* exhibit

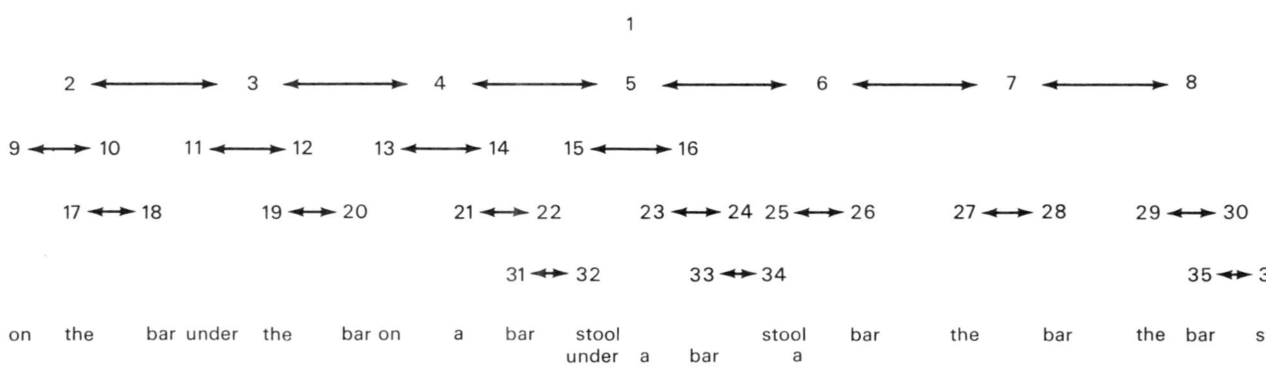

1
2 3 4 5 6 7 8
9 10 11 12 13 14 15 16
17 18 19 20 21 22 23 24 25 26 27 28 29 30
31 32 33 34 35 36
on the bar under the bar on a bar stool stool bar the bar the bar stool
under a bar a

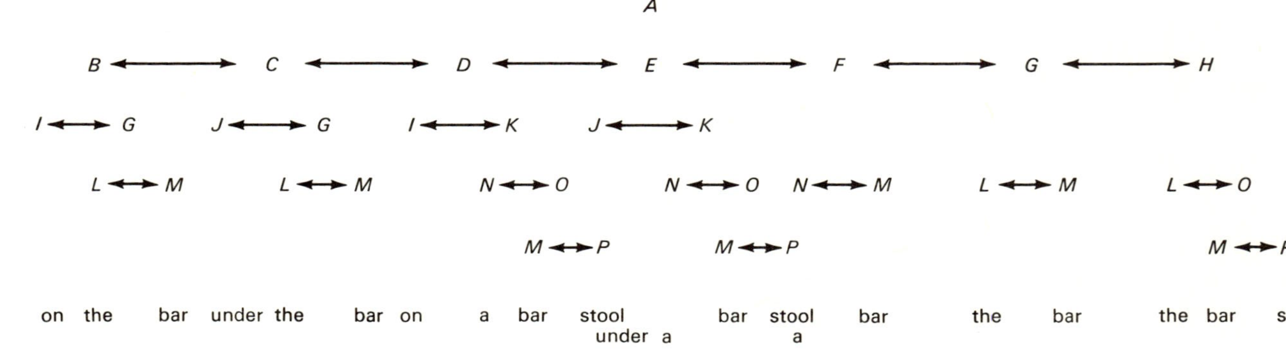
A
B C D E F G H
I G J G I K J K
L M L M N O N O N M L M L O
M P M P M P
on the bar under the bar on a bar stool bar stool bar the bar the bar stool
under a a

similar patterns; either *L* or *N* maintains interdependence with either *M* or *O*. This *L*-to-*N* relationship is shared by *B* through *H*. Suppose that *F*, *G*, *H*, and *K* are components of a class labeled NP and that they are related by either-or, and let us also suppose that *I* and *J* are similarly either-or related components of a class that we label Prep. Now the class Prep presupposes the class NP, but NP does not presuppose Prep. Either Prep *and* NP occurs or NP occurs. Let us relate these two terms as either-or components of a class and label it Phrase. What we have done to this point may be represented as follows:

(1)   Phrase

(2)   Prep *and* NP   *or*   NP

By asserting that terms *L* and *N* are either-or components of a class labeled Det and that terms *M* and *O* are either-or components of a class labeled Noun, we may further describe NP:

(2)   Prep *and* NP   *or*   NP

(3)   Det *and* Noun   Det *and* Noun

Since *M* and *O* exhibit similar patterns (share a same *M*), we may claim that a determination exists between *M* and *P*; the latter presupposes the former. Labeling *M* Bar and *O* Stool, either Bar or Bar *and* Stool describe Noun. We again expand what we have:

(3)   Det *and* Noun   Det *and* Noun

(4)   Bar *or* Bar *and* Stool   Bar *or* Bar *and* Stool

In stages (2) and (4), a describing component, NP in (2) and Bar in (4), occurs twice in the description of a single class. We may reduce this complexity—the recurrence of sames—by claiming that at stage (2) we have two (not three) describing components of Phrase (Prep and NP) and that the dependence between them is an either-or determination. Prep presupposes (determines) NP. In analogous fashion there are two describing components of the class Noun: Stool holding an either-or determination with Bar. Stool presupposes (determines) Bar. If we rewrite the description of Phrase and Noun as

(1)   Phrase

(2)   Prep *either-or determination* NP

and

(3)   . . . Noun

(4)   Bar *either-or determination* Stool such that NP and Bar occur once in each description, we claim that the either-or description of Phrase, for example, is an abbreviation—that is, a simplification—of two descriptions. The two descriptions are implied as instances of the two either-or components of Phrase. Either NP instances Phrase, or Prep instances Phrase; but the determination of Prep for NP also implies the occurrence of NP if Prep instances Phrase. This either-or description of Phrase then implies

(1)   Phrase

(2)   NP

and

(1)   Phrase

(2)   Prep *both-and determination* NP

Similarly, the either-or description of Noun implies

(3)   Noun

(4)   Bar

and

(3)   Noun

(4)   Bar *both-and determination* Stool

Stool, analogous to Prep describing Phrase, implies the co-occurrence of a term, Bar. Carrying this further, we may describe NP entirely on the basis of either-or.

(2)   NP

(3)   Det *either-or interdependence* Noun

Here the choice of either component to instance NP yields

(2)   NP

(3)   Det *both-and interdependence* Noun

Finally, within the second accounting *I* and *J* are either-or components of class Prep; *I* and *J* are labeled Under and On, respectively, within the derived accounting. Prep is instanced as either Under or On; neither implies the other, and Prep is described

(2)   Prep ...

Under *either-or constellation* On

L and *N* are either-or describing components of class Det; we label them, respectively, The and A. The description of Det, like Prep, is an either-or constellation between The and A.

We have had occasion to use such constructions as "either-or determination" (of Prep and NP as describing components of Phrase) and "either-or constellation" (of On and Under as describing components of Prep). Furthermore, the relationship of Prep and NP as describing components of Phrase implied by the either-or description is a "both-and determination"; and the relationship of Det and Noun describing NP is a "both-and interdependence," implied by the either-or interdependence of Det and Noun describing NP. Before proceeding, let us give such complex relationships names in the following way (Hjelmslev 1961: 41):

	Both-and	*Either-or*
Interdependence	Solidarity	Complementarity
Determination	Selection	Specification
Constellation	Combination	Autonomy

Now we may say that specification holds between Prep and NP as describing components of Phrase, and that selection holds between Prep and NP as describing components of Phrase implied by the specification. The presupposing term determines the presupposed one, to select it if the relationship is also a both-and function and to specify it if the relationship is an either-or function.

In working toward a third accounting of our data, we have used the words "claim" and "suppose" for the validity of pattern. We cannot always see the pattern within the given text; our assumed predictions—the pattern—remain to be tested. Our present description of Noun (as Bar specified by Stool) is an example of the kind of mistake we may make, for we will also find as additional text *barrail, footstool, footrail,* and *foot.* The class of autonomous Bar and Foot, which we label $Noun_1$, is specified by the class described by autonomous Stool and Rail, which we label $Noun_2$. We alter the description of Noun as follows:

(3)		...		Noun	
(4)		$Noun_1$	*specified by*		$Noun_2$
(5)	Bar *autonomy* Foot			Stool *autonomy* Rail	

We can now summarize as the third accounting the patterns assumed to be exemplified in the description by the second accounting:

(1)			Phrase		
(2)	Prep	*specifies*	NP		
(3)			Det	*complementarity*	Noun
(4)				$Noun_1$ *specified by*	$Noun_2$
(5)	Under *autonomy* On The *autonomy* A Bar *autonomy* Foot Stool *autonomy* Rail				

This third accounting implies a set of possibilities or choices. An instance of one of the possible set of choices is

Phrase

Prep	*determines*	NP	
		Det *solidarity* Noun	
			Noun$_1$
Under		The	Bar

interpreted as

under	*the*	*bar*

We postpone for the moment the possibility of some relationship between Under, The, and Bar, and any implication that may have for the either-or description. The remaining Phrases into which the text is linguistically segmented are described similarly as alternate choices of the either-or related terms of the third accounting. As an additional example, *a barstool* has the following description:

Phrase

NP

Det	*solidarity*	Noun	
		Noun$_1$ *selected by* Noun$_2$	
A		Bar	Stool

interpreted as

a	*bar*	*stool*

It should be reemphasized that both-and does not imply linearity. The placing of Bar to the left of Stool is a concession to the actual sequence within the data. Specification and selection are nonreciprocal relationships; the choice of linear writing we happen to make in representing the terms on paper dictates whether we say "specifies" or "specified by," "selects" or "selected by." Again the choice is our own, and not suggested by the theory. At some point in our accounting we must include the observation that Bar is interpreted as a portion of data that is linearly related to the interpretation of Stool. No way of performing this interpretation is indicated in the *Prolegomena*.

In accounting for certain classes, such as Prep and Det at stage (2) within the either-or and both-and description, we have postponed their description to some succeeding, nonimmediate stage. Prep at stage (2) is not described as an autonomy of Under and On at stage (3): it is so described at stage (5).

We require some way of recognizing when to make such a postponement. The basis is a "rule of transference" (Hjelmslev 1961 : 41) according to which a class is transferred unanalyzed past a stage when "given conditions," not elaborated in the *Prolegomena*, are met and that seem to apply here. If one of two components of a class is analyzed on the basis of some dependence between components, while the other component has a single describing component, the latter is stuctureless at that point and is transferred unanalyzed to some stage at which the basis chosen (constellation in our example) permits analysis.

The complete text is now predicted as embodying a number of choices of Phrase (seven) related by combination (both-and constellation). This situation implies that none of the instances of Phrase in the text presupposes any of the remaining instances of Phrase. Within the text, it is claimed that classes *B, C, D, E, F, G,* and *H* in fact hold a combination (both-and constellation) in place of the interdependence that was previously claimed for them. The third accounting of the expression hierarchy of our text is a hierarchy based *entirely* on either-or, and it is here that the description attains maximum exhaustiveness and simplicity. In the first accounting no identifications were made. In the second, identifications were assumed. The second accounting was a simpler description in that the number of distinct terms was reduced, but the number of occurrences of the terms and the number of descriptions were more than necessary. By identifying lack of simplicity in describing Phrase by "Prep *and* NP *or* NP," and by recognizing that we were describing the same thing (NP) twice, while ideally we would want to describe it but once, we take another step toward a description that more adequately satisfies the empirical principle. In reducing the number of descriptions (as well as the number of described objects), we had to distinguish two hierarchies—two descriptions—one based entirely on both-and and one entirely on either-or. It was only within the third description that we find a maximally exhaustive and maximally simple accounting. The increased exhaustiveness of the description based on either-or results from the following observations. One of the possible text-portions implied by the third description based on either-or is *on the bar* occurring in the text. Another of the possible interpretations will be *on a bar*, a sequence that is nowhere recorded in our data. The third accounting, then, is more exhaustive in that it registers dependences between functives that are not registered in the second accounting based on both-and; and in so doing, it predicts a possible, but not yet extant, addition to the text. The third accounting defines "possible text," and in its prediction it is more exhaustive. The description provided by the second accounting is of a restricted text; the third accounting describes an unrestricted text. The correctness of the predictions justifies the third accounting and the linguistic segmentation implied by it. The accounting based on either-or generates possible texts of "the same premised nature" (Hjelmslev 1961 : 16) as the given one, which is a desired result.

A *system* is a "correlational [either-or] hierarchy," and a *process* is a "relational [both-and] hierarchy" (Hjelmslev 1961: 132). We have seen that a maximally exhaustive and simple accounting of a text requires that analysis and synthesis statements be expanded beyond the basis of interdependences, determinations, and constellations in terms of both-and to a basis of analysis and synthesis in terms of either-or. Our second accounting takes the shape of a process; the third, of a system. In terms of the heuristic technique for determining increasingly satisfactory accountings, the either-or hierarchy will follow and presuppose the description in terms of the process:

> *... linguistic theory prescribes a* textual analysis *which leads us to recognize a linguistic form behind the "substance" immediately accessible to observation by the senses* [and the nonlinguistic sciences, PWD], *and behind the text a language (system) . . . (Hjelmslev 1961: 96).*

In terms of the statements in the accounting, however, the direction of the presupposition is reversed. The process presupposes the system:

> *A closer investigation of this function* [between system and process, PWD] *soon shows us that it is a determination in which the system is the constant:* the process determines [presupposes, PWD] the system. *The decisive point is not the superficial relationship consisting in the fact that the process is the more immediately accessible for observation, while the system must be "ordered to" the process—"discovered" behind it by means of a procedure—and so is only mediately knowable insofar as it is not presented to us on the basis of a previously performed procedure. This superficial relationship might make it seem that the process can exist without a system but not* vice versa. *But the decisive point is that the existence of a system is a necessary premiss for the existence of a process: the process comes into existence by virtue of a system's being present behind it, a system which governs and determines it in its possible development. A process is unimaginable—because it would be in an absolute and irrevocable sense inexplicable—without a system lying behind it. On the other hand, a system is not unimaginable without a process; the existence of a system does not presuppose the existence of a process. The system does not come into existence by virtue of a process's being found (Hjelmslev 1961: 39).*

Recall here our discussion of the various possible interpretations of "explanation." Here it is clear that explanation is used in the deductive sense. What we have done for our third text is to contrive—by whatever means available—a system. That system implies (we may deduce from it) the process that is our text when interpreted. Conversely, we have no means of logically inducing a system from a description of the process. Our theory informs us of a set of possible systems, and the empirical principle tells us which of these is the correct one for the text.

The Empirical Principle and Procedure

The accounting that satisfies the empirical principle to the highest degree is termed an *operation:* "a description that is in agreement with the empirical principle" (Hjelmslev 1961: 131). This definition and the terms it presupposes, "agreement" plus those occurring within the elaborated empirical principle (self-consistency, exhaustiveness, and simplicity), are not presupposed by nor required for any definition of the theory in shaping the set of possible accountings and thus possible language. We exclude them from the set of necessary primitives of the theory.

From our example, the description of A by analysis and synthesis is an operation *if* it is self-consistent, exhaustive, and maximally simple. The description of A in the second accounting is not maximally simple; therefore it is not in agreement with the empirical principle, and hence is not an operation. Our accounting will contain a number of descriptions (it will contain one for each term within it), and to the degree that these descriptions attain the stipulations of the empirical principle, the accounting will contain a number of operations (one for each term). Notice that for a description of an object to be an operation it is necessarily presupposed that the terms that are used to describe it are in turn described by operations. Had we written a description of the system for some text such as

```
                                 A
            B                                       C
      D         E        F                          .
   G      H  I     J  K      L                      .
                                                    .
```

in which components D, E, and F of some class B are the fewest possible consistent with exhaustiveness, but these components are *not* described as classes by the *simplest* set of describing components (D by G and H; E by I and J; and F by K and L), assuming that H and J meet the condition of identity but have been treated as distinct, then the description of D and E by G, H, I, and J is not an operation. They are partially alike (sharing the identity of H and J) but they have been treated as completely unlike. Their description is not consistent with the empirical principle. The simpler description of D and E results in an altered, simpler description of B

```
                  B
          X               F
      Y       Z       K       L
   G    I
```

in which *G* and *I* describe a class in relationship with the identity of *H* and *J*. This description reduces the describing components of *B* by one. If the description of one of the components of a class is not an operation, the description of that class itself will not be an operation. A description of an object or class that is an operation presupposes that the describing objects are in turn described in such a way that their descriptions are operations. In short, operations mutually presuppose one another. A correct accounting, then, is one that is a complex of operations (Hjelmslev 1961: 30–31): a hierarchy such that the descriptions of its classes and components by analysis and synthesis are operations. Such an accounting, which is an operation, complex to the degree that it satisfies the empirical principle, is termed a *procedure:* "a class of operations with mutual determination" (Hjelmslev 1961: 132).

It should be emphasized that the notion of procedure is external to the notion of possible description (or possible language). The theory specifies a set of accountings of the shape we have in part already outlined. The evaluative criterion—the empirical principle—identifies one of these sets as the correct accounting with respect to a given text. It identifies one of the accountings implied by the theory as a procedure with respect to a text. If this is so, then "theory" and "*possible* accounting," or "description," in Hjelmslev's terms, must not be determined by "procedure." That is, considerations involved in determining procedure must not be involved in determining the set of *possible* accountings. Hjelmslev (1961: 18) points out that procedure "can provide" or "result in" a description and that "*The description is made through a procedure*" (Hjelmslev 1961: 61). Possible description and procedure are not equated. In addition to this interpretation of procedure as an element outside the theory itself, consider these comments:

> *By virtue of its appropriateness the work of linguistic theory is empirical [it is here procedure functions within the empirical principle, PWD], and by virtue of its arbitrariness [in terms of primitives and definitions, PWD] it is calculative (Hjelmslev 1961: 17).*

The "general calculus, in which all conceivable cases are foreseen" (Hjelmslev 1961: 18) provides the "tools" for some accounting. The particular subtlety, via the simplicity principle, involved in recognizing correct accountings requires that "the aim of linguistic theory. . . [be] to provide a procedural method by means of which a given text can be comprehended through a self-consistent and exhaustive description" (Hjelmslev 1961: 16). Notice again that procedure and possible description are distinguished. Procedure is identified by the empirical principle as a particular description of a text from among those possible, but this does not affect the definition of possible accounting. This is again clear from Hjelmslev's (1961:17) statement:

> *... it is of the greatest importance not to confuse the theory with its applications or with the practical method (procedure) of application. The theory will lead to a procedure, but no (practical) "discovery procedure" will be set forth ....*

Procedure does, as indicated, have a status within glossematics although it is not part of the theory itself based on this approach. It is the simplicity principle that provides this status. Recall that in determining the maximally appropriate accounting for a text, Hjelmslev proposed a hierarchy of evaluative criteria: self-consistency, exhaustiveness, simplicity of description, and simplicity of procedure, which he expanded further as the simplicity principle (Hjelmslev 1961: 18) and the principles of economy and reduction (Hjelmslev 1961: 61). It is here that a knowledge of procedure is required. The simplicity principle in which procedure functions, like arbitrariness and appropriateness of theory, is an extra-theoretical consideration. All these principles are outside the theory itself but co-exist with the theory as elements of glossematics and may function in distinguishing glossematics from other approaches to language, such as transcendent linguistics. Self-consistency specifies that the result of our work *be* an accounting; exhaustiveness specifies that this accounting identify all the relationships of invariants; and the imposition of simplicity on the set of these statements identifies one as a procedure—the simplest both in distinct terms *and* descriptions, hence the correct set of self-consistent, maximally exhaustive statements accounting for the data, one of the possible systems. We can now understand how simplicity of procedure functions and why it is a concern in glossematics.

Returning to our text, we now admit that our original segmentation of it was not exhaustive. A more complete segmentation by nonlinguistic means is the following (in a broad phonetic transcription):

[own ðə bar əndər ðə bar own ə bar stuwl əndər

ə bar stuwl ə bar ðə bar ðə bar stuwl]

In providing an accounting for this additional nonlinguistic segmentation, we again assume the condition of identity. In the restricted text we notice that [ə] does not presuppose additional terms. We will assume that in the unrestricted text the terms [ow], [a], and [uw] also do not presuppose additional terms. We see further in this restricted text that the terms [n], [b], [r], [st], and [l] presuppose some term, that is, one of [ə], [ow], [a], or [uw]. Let us label the class of the presupposing terms C and the class of presupposed terms V. We label the class that is described by them Syll(able). We also see that to account for a piece of data like [bar] we must allow for two C's to select V; to do this let us assume two classes, C_1 and C_2. In this restricted text the components of the two classes C_1 and C_2 have the same components and have the appearance of not being distinct. We separate them here and take up the problem of their nonidentity in the next section; there, we will find the problem is not whether C_1 and C_2 are identical but whether their components may be identified. The pattern behind this text is in part the system

Syll

C_1 *specifies* V *specified by* C_2

Again we emphasize that the co-occurrence within the process implied by this system is not linear. With this fact in mind, the processes implied by this partial description are C_1 selecting V, V selected by C_2, C_1 selecting V selected by C_2, and V. The components labeled *ə*, *ow*, *a*, *u*, and *uw* (interpreted as [ə], [ow], [a], [u], and [uw], respectively) describing class V are related by autonomy (either-or constellation). The components labeled *n, b, r, d, st, t, f*, and *l* (interpreted as [n], [b], [r], [d], [st], [t], [f], and [l], respectively) are describing components of C_1; *n, b, r, d, st, t, f*, and *l* (interpreted as before) are the describing components of C_2 related autonomously.

The correctness of this initial description receives justification when we find as additional data [ow] *owe*, [aj] *eye*, [ej] *A*, [bow] *bow*, [baj] *by*, [bej] *bay*, [paj] *pie*, [gaj] *guy*, and [raj] *rye*. We find two additional terms, [aj] and [ej], which presuppose no term. The description of class V is revised to include them as describing components related to the others by autonomy. The terms [p] and [g] are in the new text, and like the describing components of C_1 and C_2, they presuppose some term. The descriptions of classes C_1 and C_2 are revised to admit describing components *p* and *g* (interpreted as [p] and [g]). The description of the class Syll by the two component classes C_1 and C_2 in specification with class V is otherwise unchanged. A text expanded to include data such as [ówvər] *over*, [bĭníjθ] *beneath*, and [bárbĭkjŭw] *barbecue* alter this description. We observe that [ów], [níjθ], and [bár] will presuppose no other terms co-occurring with them in a text, while the terms [vər], [bĭ], and [kjŭw] do presuppose some co-occurring term; unstressed syllables presuppose some stressed syllable. We account for this in the following manner:

Word

$Syll_1$ *specifies* $Syll_2$ *specified by* $Syll_2$

Again noticing that the linearity is not indicated by the description, this implies the following possible co-occurrences within the process: $Syll_1$ selecting $Syll_2$; $Syll_2$ selected by $Syll_3$; $Syll_1$ selecting $Syll_2$ selected by $Syll_3$; and $Syll_2$.

If this pattern is intergrated with the patterns previously accounted for, the more complete description of our text takes this shape:

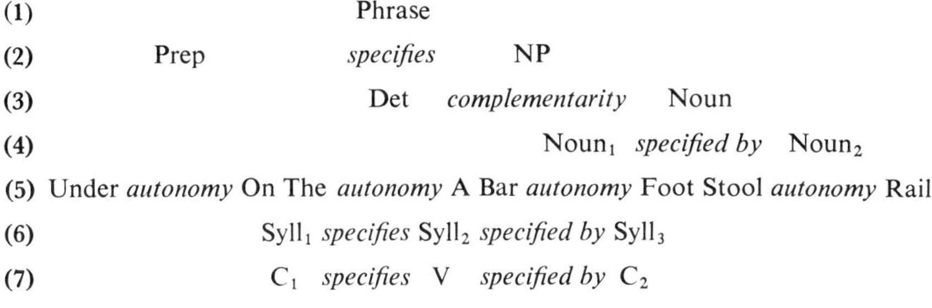

(1)   Phrase

(2)   Prep   *specifies*   NP

(3)   Det *complementarity* Noun

(4)   Noun₁ *specified by* Noun₂

(5) Under *autonomy* On The *autonomy* A Bar *autonomy* Foot Stool *autonomy* Rail

(6)   Syll₁ *specifies* Syll₂ *specified by* Syll₃

(7)   C₁ *specifies* V   *specified by* C₂

wherein at stage (8), C_1 is further described by *n, b, r, d, st, l, p, g, t,* and *f* holding autonomy among themselves; V is further described by *ə, ow, a, uw, aj, ej,* and *u* holding autonomy; and C_2 is described by *n, b, r, d, st, l, p, g, t,* and *f* related by autonomy. Each class at stage (5) is described by a particular choice of the terms at stage (6) forward. The process description of Under is

(5)   Under

(6)   Syll₂   *selected by* Syll₃

(7)   V *selected by* C₂   C₁ *selects*   V *selected by* C₂

(8)   ə   n   d   ə   r

interpreted as

         [ə   n   d   ə   r]

Following is the process description of the text *on the bay*:

(1)   Phrase

(2)   Prep   *selects*   NP

(3)   Det *solidarity* Noun

(4)   Noun₁

(5)   On   The   Bay

(6)   Syll₂   Syll₂   Syll₂

(7)   V *selected by* C₂   C₁ *selects* V   C₁ *selects* V

(8)   ow   n   ð   ə   b   ej

interpreted as

         [ow   n   ð   ə   b   ej]

At each stage (1) through (8), one of the choices implied by the system is manifest. At stage (1) one instance of Phrase occurs; at stage (2) Prep is chosen, which selects NP, and so on.

Extending the accounting of our text beyond our initial nonlinguistic segmentation is motivated by exhaustiveness. Given a nonlinguistic segmentation of the text by a phonetics, a linguistic segmentation—our system—may evoke predictions that are borne out. Pattern is predicable of this further kind of segmentation, and any empirically adequate theory must provide for its inclusion. But where do we stop in our analysis? Is there any motivated way of determining the boundaries of pattern in our hierarchies of expression and content? The boundary between language and nonlanguage was identified as that point where we could identify an object among all other objects to which the definitions of our theory were applicable. That point identified the (set) of object(s) that could be described by a particular configuration of dependences. At that point constellation disappeared, and we began to find determinations and interdependences—cohesions—and statements in terms of them had predictive power. We have now extended those statements to apply to two solidary hierarchies—content and expression. As elaboration of the hierarchies by analytic (and synthetic) description continues, the point at which we stop—like the point at which we began—is indicated by the disappearance of cohesions. In the description of the process, "a stage will be reached in which selection is used for the last time as the basis of analysis" (Hjelmslev 1961: 99). At further stages in the description of the process, either two or more terms of the description occur freely with one another (constellation), or they always occur together (interdependence). The presence of constellation and interdependence to the exclusion of determination implies no pattern, an all-or-none. At this point we have reached the "bottom" of the process hierarchy. The terms of this stage are *taxemes*. The terms of the system that generate the taxemes are *glossemes*, "minimal forms which the theory leads us to establish as bases of explanation, the irreducible invariants" (Hjelmslev 1961: 135).

Let us take an example from the expression hierarchy. We assume a number of terms within expression that select a particular term. To simplify, let us say the selected term is *ow* (interpreted as above). We assume that we find the terms selecting *ow* to be *p, t, k, b, d, g, f, s,* and *x* (interpreted as [p t k b d g f s x], respectively). Within the system, we may describe a class C by these terms related by autonomy (as we did above), but this violates the empirical principle, for we find a pattern of complementarity justifiably asserted within the system at this point. Let us alternatively describe C within the system by two classes labeled Position and Manner related by interdependence. Let Position be described by components labeled Bilabial, Dental, and Velar, related by constellation. Let Manner be described by components labeled Voice and Obstruction, related by interdependence; Voice is further described by components labeled Voiced and Voiceless; and Obstruction is described by the components labeled Stop and Fricative. Then

                                    C

                Position   *complementarity*   Manner
                                        Voice   *complementarity* Obstruction
    Bilabial *autonomy* Dental *autonomy* Velar   Voiced *autonomy* Voiceless   Stop *autonomy* Fricative

(1)   C

        Position   *solidarity*   Manner
                                    Voice   *solidarity*   Obstruction
        Bilabial   Voiceless   Stop

(2)   C

        Position   *solidarity*   Manner
                                    Voice   *solidarity*   Obstruction
        Bilabial   Voiced   Stop

and so on; that is, what we have labeled *p*, *b*, etc. Interpreting Bilabial as a phonetic property of bilabial articulation, Voiceless as the phonetic property of open glottis, and Stop as the phonetic property of blocked egressive air stream at the point of articulation, we have interpreted the both-and related

Bilabial, Voiceless, and Stop as $\begin{bmatrix} \text{Bilabial} \\ \text{Voiceless} \\ \text{Stop} \end{bmatrix}$ or [p]. A taxeme corresponds

roughly to what may be called a phoneme; a glosseme corresponds roughly to a feature of a phoneme. Such descriptions are the last within the linguistic segmentations.

Saussure would end his description with terms such as *under*, *on*, *the*, and so on; in other words, with signs. Hjelmslev's theory extends beyond this stage. The possible theoretical formulation of Hjelmslev's theory may extend "upwards" beyond this point, discovering what we call paragraphs, chapters, works, literary productions, and the like (Hjelmslev 1954: 180); but the upper boundary of pattern within the two hierarchies of expression and content, like the lower, is found where selection is used for the first time (Hjelmslev 1954: 180–81). Garvin (1954: 85) points out that constellation most likely exists among terms at the stage traditionally called "sentence." The upper boundary of pattern in Hjelmslevian language, then, is the traditional sentence. Again, our labels, Phrase, and the like, are only labels, and their intuitive content is not intended to correlate with the interpretation of the classes of expression that they label. No distinction is made within the expression (or content) hierarchy between what is traditionally called morphology or syntax (Hjelmslev 1961: 26). The only break within each of the hierarchies of expression and content occurs between signs and *figurae* (see page 75).

The theory has now been elaborated by adding definitions of two types of hierarchies—process and system—and elaborating the characterization of the initial class by stipulating that the two hierarchies that are its components (content and expression) be systems. The distinction between process and system is motivated by the empirical principle. A correct accounting of a text, a procedure, is the continued description by analysis and synthesis of the two universal classes, which are the hierarchies of expression and content, on the basis of either-or (that is, as systems). The systems of expression and content imply an expression and a content process, a both-and hierarchy, which in turn is associated with the nonlinguistic segmentation. ACCOUNTING thus is modified in its first two statements. It now consists of the description of the system of expression and content in terms of analysis and synthesis and the description of a process in terms of analysis and synthesis. The last three statements in regard to evaluating and reworking the accounting remain unaltered.

The Condition of Identity and Mutation

We take up now the discussion of the condition of identity, postponed earlier. First, let us introduce another definition. *Derivates* are "components and components-of-components of a class within one and the same 'continued analysis or analysis complex with determination between the analyses that enter therein'" (Hjelmslev 1961: 132). (The words within single quotation marks define *deduction*. A continued analysis results from the description of a class by analysis and the description of the resulting components by analysis, and so forth, for an arbitrary number of times ≥ 2. Within the continued analysis each analysis presupposes the preceding one.) From our example, $Noun_1$ and $Noun_2$ are either-or derivates of Noun; Bar and Stool are also derivates of Noun, but indirectly with an intermediate stage. Thus, $Noun_1$ and $Noun_2$ are first-degree derivates of Noun while Bar and Stool are second-degree derivates of Noun and also first-degree derivates of $Noun_1$ and $Noun_2$, respectively. Within the process portion of the accounting, Det and Noun are first-degree derivates of NP, while $Noun_1$ and $Noun_2$ are second-degree derivates of NP. Expression and content are first-degree derivates of the class that will include the whole text: the initial class. Within expression (system or process) or within content (system or process), first-degree derivates exhibit interdependence, determination, or constellation. Second- (and greater-) degree derivates of a single class usually are related by a constellation. (The phenomena of government and agreement would be instances in which determination and interdependence, respectively, exist between second- or greater-degree derivates of a single class.) Within the system, the *particular* describing components of Det (The and A), for example, do not presuppose nor are they presupposed by *particular* describing components of NP (that is, Bar and Stool). Det and Noun as first-degree, either-or components of NP are related by specification, but The and Bar describing NP are related by autonomy as greater than first-degree derivates of NP. Now consider $Noun_1$ and $Noun_2$ as first-degree derivates of Noun described on the basis of both-and. $Noun_2$ presupposes $Noun_1$, and the relationship is a selection; but the second-degree derivate of Noun (Stool, one of the either-or related components describing $Noun_2$) does not presuppose Bar nor any *particular* greater than first-degree derivate of Noun. Among these derivates of a class (here, Noun) a combination (both-and constellation) exists.

For an accounting to be exhaustive, such relationships must be described. To this end we introduce the definition of *sum*: "class that has function to one or more classes within the same rank" (Hjelmslev 1961: 134). (Rank is constituted by the derivates of a single class, all of which are of the same degree.) Derivates, if they are classes and are described by analysis, may be described by synthesis with respect to the other derivate(s) of the same rank and the function relating them. Thus, in *on the bar*, *on* will be described as a sum with respect to other derivates of the same degree, *the* and *bar*, and the function relating them. This is an instance of a sum within the hierarchy of both-and; such a sum is a *unit*. For an example of a sum within the either-or hierarchy, consider The and Bar as third-degree derivates of NP. The term "The" would be described by the other third-degree derivates of NP (Bar, and the function between them, a constellation). Again, the description is by synthesis. A sum within a system is a *category*.

The descriptions to be made by synthesis are now expanded. Initially, synthesis was restricted to components that were *first*-degree derivates of the same class. Now the description by synthesis is extended to account for components as second- , third-, and greater-degree derivates. This addition requires no new definitions or primitives within the theory but only an extension of the descriptive statements in terms of synthesis beyond the limitations of the rank of first-degree derivates.

Beyond the description of sums as elements of the same rank such that the described and describing sums *all* lie within *either* content *or* expression, a sum within expression (or content) may be described in terms of the function that relates it to a sum within content (or expression). Again, this is simply an extension of the description of an object by synthesis. The function between two such sums is a solidarity. We can take as an example the process portion of the accounting of the text we used earlier, with content now brought into the sample:

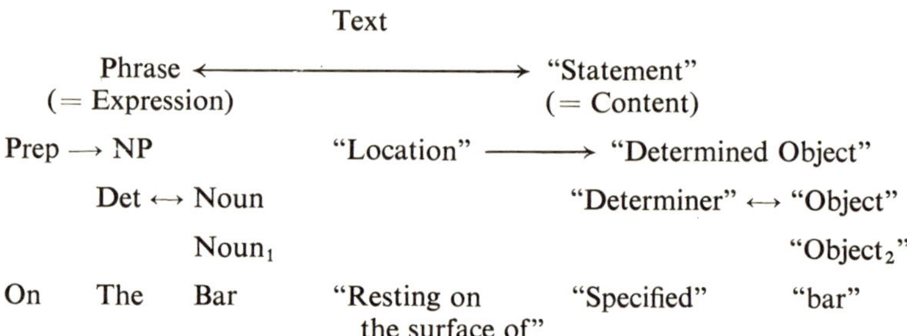

Again, dependences are arbitrarily labeled for convenience, and again we emphasize that these are only labels. On may be described by its relation to same degree derivates within expression (= Phrase, here) and also by its relation to terms of the same rank within content (= "Statement," here). This second description is satisfied by stating that a solidarity holds between On and "Resting on the surface of." Thus, within an unrestricted text predicted by the accounting, wherein any portion that interprets On occurs, we will also find another element in the same portion that interprets "Resting on the surface

	Phrase			Text		
	solidarity			"Statement"		
Prep *specifies* NP			"Location" *specifies* "Determined Object"		
Det *complementarity* Noun			"Determiner" *complementarity* "Object"		
Noun$_1$ *specified by* Noun$_2$			"Object$_1$" *specified by* "Object$_2$"		

The	Bar	Stool	"Particular"	"Bar"	"Stool"
autonomy	*autonomy*	*autonomy*	*autonomy*	*autonomy*	*autonomy*
A	Foot	Rail	"A"	"Foot"	"Rail"

of," and vice versa. A sum so related by the function of solidarity is a *sign:* "the name for the unit consisting of content-form and expression-form and established by the solidarity that we have called the sign function" (Hjelmslev 1961: 58).

Similar to the relationship between second- and greater-degree derivates lying solely within either expression or content, it is possible to find relationships among functions at second- and greater-degree ranks of the initial class, the sign function, one of which lies within expression and the other within content. And again, within an accounting that is exhaustive, these relationships must be stated. This relationship of elements of expression and elements of content is a *mutation*, defined as the "function existing between first-degree derivates of one and the same class and belonging to one and the same rank" (Hjelmslev 1961: 133–34). Let us return to our example. Identifying and describing functions as mutations involves the following steps. First, first-degree derivates of some class within expression, say, Prep and NP of the class Phrase described on the basis of both-and (within the process), and first-degree derivates of the class "Statement" within content described on the basis of both-and, "Location" and "Determined Object," must be identified. Second, the analytic description of Phrase and "Statement" must be completed by stating the function relating Prep and NP and "Location" and "Determined Object," which is a selection in both cases. Third, each derivate of this rank, such as Prep, must be described as a sum with respect to (a) derivate(s) in the opposing hierarchy ("Location"). Here, this description is accomplished by stating that Prep holds a solidarity with "Location," and that NP holds a solidarity with "Determined Object." Fourth, each selection (the selection between Prep and NP and the selection between "Location" and "Determined Object") must be described by synthesis in terms of the relationship each holds with the other. If such a fourth statement can be made of the function between Prep and NP and between "Location" and "Determined Object," then these functions are mutations. Any of the six possible functions may be described by synthesis as mutations. The relationship between first-degree derivates may be, in addition to the six possible complex ones, a mutation if the conditions are met. The selections between Prep and NP and "Location" and "Determined Object" are mutations, as are the solidarities between Det and Noun and between "Determiner" and "Object." The constellation between On and The and Bar in the process description of *on the bar* are not mutations because the constellation does not hold between *first*-degree derivates of the same class, Phrase.

Functions as mutations can also be described, and must be where appropriate, within the system. Consider the chart on page 71. The specification between Prep and NP as first-degree derivates of the single class Phrase is described by the relation between Phrase and the specification between

"Location" and "Determined Object" as first-degree derivates of "Statement."

We can now add some definitions based on the relationships we have just defined. A semiotic is a "hierarchy, any of whose components admits of a further analysis into classes defined by mutual relation, so that any of these classes admits of an analysis into derivates defined by mutual mutation" (Hjelmslev 1961: 134). Here, in the preceding example, the hierarchy Text has components Phrase and "Statement" and is described by analysis by these components related by solidarity. The describing components of Phrase and "Statement" are mutually related such that the functions of components describing them are also mutations. For example, NP, a describing component of Phrase, is in part defined by mutual relation to "Determined Object" in "Statement," as is Prep of Phrase by mutual relation to "Location." The function between Prep and NP meets the definition of mutation. Prep and NP are further defined by mutation. Thus the hierarchy of Text is a semiotic. *Commutation* is "mutation between the members of a 'class within a semiotic system'," and *permutation* is "mutation between the parts of a 'class within a semiotic process'" (Hjelmslev 1961: 135). (The expressions within single quotation marks are definitions of *paradigm* and *chain*, respectively.) The mutation between Prep and NP within the system is an example of a commutation, and the mutation between Prep and NP within the process is an example of permutation.

We now designate the condition of identity as *substitution*, the "absence of mutation between members of a paradigm" (Hjelmslev 1961: 135). (For restricting substitution to a paradigm, recall that identifying or equating elements has involved identifying or equating them as components related by either-or within some class.) Suppose that within some text we found not only [ownəbar] *on a bar* and other examples of [own] but also [anəbar] *on a bar* and that we had equated An [an], On [own], and Under [əndər] as describing components of the class Prep within the system but had not identified them. Then considering them as first-degree derivates of Prep, in an exhaustive accounting, we would have discovered a mutation between On and Under; their constellation within the expression hierarchy bears a relation to the constellation between "Resting on the surface of" and "Beneath the surface of" as first-degree derivates of "Location" within the content hierarchy; furthermore, Prep and "Location" belong to one and the same rank. Thus a mutation (specifically, a commutation) exists between On and Under. An and Under likewise are related by a constellation, Under bearing a relation to the constellation between "Resting on the surface of" and "Beneath the surface of." Thus there is a mutation between An and Under. On and An, in this modification, bear a constellation as first-degree derivates of Prep, but the constellation has no relation to some function in content because [own] and [an] as sums are described by synthesis as being in solidarity with a *single* same derivate within content, "Resting on the surface of." Hence the constellation between On and An is not a mutation, but a substitution. Here the accounting of the modified text is less than maximally simple. The condition for identity being met, the two terms should be reduced to a single one. In the maximally simple accounting there will be no substitution. Substitution occurs only within less simple accountings and functions in order to locate where identifications are to be made. It functions only within the heuristic technique of deriving the most highly valued accounting from a less highly valued one. Searching accountings, assuring the existence of mutations between first-degree derivates of a single class and simplifying the accounting when such mutations are absent, is summarized as the *commutation test*. A clear distinction must be made between mutation (also commutation and permutation), a necessary relationship within the theory and accountings, and the commutation test, a technique for writing satisfactory accountings (cf. Fischer-Jørgensen 1956: 141).

Let us consider a second modification of the text, this time adding to the either-or description of "Location" the component "Resting on the bottom side of." Here the mutation within content will hold between "Resting on the surface of" and "Resting on the bottom side of" and between "Resting on the surface of" and "Beneath the surface of." But "Resting on the bottom side of" and "Beneath the surface of" will not be in commutation, for their constellation is not related to any function among derivates of the same degree within expression, because they, described as sums, both are related by solidarity to a single sum within expression—Under. Commutation exists, then, within both expression and content, as may substitution in less desirable accountings; and the commutation test may be applied within both hierarchies to assure maximally simple accountings.

The commutation test (but not commutation itself) will not apply to such possible pieces of data as *on the bank*, wherein *bank* is a single additional describing component of Noun. Within content "Object" may have two components "Financial institution" and "Land adjoining a lake or stream." Describing these components as sums of content will involve describing them by synthesis as related to the single term Bank in expression. The autonomy between the two elements of content, as in the example in the preceding paragraph, will not meet the definition of commutation. The resulting reduction within content is counter-intuitive. Ignoring the commutation test, two describing components of Noun, $Bank_1$ and $Bank_2$, may be postulated, such that commutation is met. This requires some formal way of identifying instances in which the test may be ignored, in which the heuristic technique is to be abandoned, and accountings are to be written arbitrarily but more appropriately. Neither the problem nor the solution is considered in the *Prolegomena* (cf. Hjelmslev 1954: 184–85).

Notice in the example expanded to include content that the description of content was such that each functive and function corresponded to exactly one functive and function with expression. Expression and content were isomorphic. While that was so in this particular case, it does not always hold, nor did we make an assumption of isomorphism between the two. The theory must describe the relationship of sums to some appropriate sum(s) in the opposite hierarchy of expression or content. Notice that we have described each dependence, such as Noun, by analysis without regard for the description by analysis of any other class, such as Det. In the description of the two hierarchies of expression and content, each is similarly described by analysis independently of the other. But notice also that less satisfactory accountings did not exhibit isomorphism. For example, in the modifications of the example, "Resting on the surface of" corresponded to two elements, On and An in expression. Only in the more satisfactory, simpler accounting in which there was no substitution were expression and content isomorphic. The class of objects we are characterizing exhibit functions that are mutations. Functions that are substitutions mark an object that is not a possible member of this class. The apparent isomorphism is the product of the evaluative criterion of simplicity and an accidental result of the requirement for a maximally simple accounting.

While it is assumed that for all texts there will be statements describing sums synthetically, holding a function to some sum in the opposing hierarchy (expression or content), it is also assumed that a point will be reached in the hierarchies of content and expression when this is no longer true. This stage is exemplified in our example at the stage where the classes labeled Syll are reached. Neither Syllables nor their derivates are related to an element within content. Analogous to expression, a point will be reached in the analysis of content such that neither the elements of content at this stage nor their derivates will be related as sums to expression. The elements of both expression and content of any rank of which this is true are called *figurae* (Hjelmslev 1961: 41–47). With this assumption, we will find that expression and content cannot be isomorphic as it seemed previously. The justification for extending the accounting beyond the rank of words or signs to include figurae in both hierarchies is exhaustivenesss. We may make predictions of cohesion for figurae as well as for nonfigurae. If such predictions are appropriate, then the theory must provide for their inclusion, as we did within expression. Within content, as within expression, it is necessary to analyze into figure the minimum sums holding a relation to a sum of expression. Here we may use Hjelmslev's (1961: 70) example:

"ram"	"man"	"boy"	"stallion"	"he"
"ewe"	"woman"	"girl"	"mare"	"she"
"sheep"	"human"	"child"	"horse"	

These terms, Hjelmslev argues, may be described by analysis on the basis of both-and and the components "SHEEP," HUMAN," "CHILD," "HORSE," "HE," and "SHE." Thus "ram" would be described by a relation between "HE" and "SHEEP"; "ewe," by a relation between "SHE" and "SHEEP"; and so on. The *Prolegomena* does not indicate whether additional stages are required within content; that is, whether "HE," "SHE," and so on, are to be described by analysis. It has been argued (Martinet 1946: 39 and Spang-Hanssen 1961: 143–44) that the describing elements "HE," "SHE," and so on, are in fact not figurae because they correspond to elements in expression, such as [hij] *he*, [šij] *she*. The apparent content figurae are sums bearing a relation to a sum in expression, which, however, would contradict the general assumption that sums are described by other sums of the *same* rank. If "HE" belongs to n rank, then He, the sum within expression to which it might conceivably be related by solidarity, belongs to $n-1$ rank, and "HE" cannot be described as a sum with respect to He. Likewise, within expression, one of the describing components of C_2 may be a term interpreted as [s]. That one of the sums in solidarity with the derivate "Plural" within content may also be interpreted as [s] does not imply that the describing component of C_2 ($=$ [s]) is not one of the expression figurae.

We have established the necessity of extending the accounting beyond the sums related to a derivate in the opposite hierarchy of expression or content. Figurae, as well as nonfigurae, are described within a framework of analysis and synthesis statements. We may describe Syllables and their derivates as sums, but here we find that the description by synthesis is restricted to sums within the same hierarchy of expression. Expression figurae (or content figurae) bear relationships to other figurae of the same rank only if those describing figurae lie within expression (or content). Thus p, b, r, and so on, bear no relationship to one of the content figurae. The absence of the sign function among figurae (the formal distinction between them and nonfigurae) makes it impossible, for example, to define mutation between p, b, and r as first-degree derivates of C_1. This impossibility in turn raises the problem within the heuristic technique with respect to the condition of identity defined as the absence of mutation.

The problem of identity arising from the lack of requisites for the definition of mutation may be resolved in two ways. First, we may modify the commutation test in such a way that it will apply to figurae, or second, we may simply consider all possible identities of the component figurae describing a class and judge the resulting accountings relative to the evaluative criteria. Hjelmslev chooses the altered technique; the commutation test is modified to apply to figurae. For example, consider p and t as components of C_1 wherein the co-occurring elements of both p and t are the same choices of V ($= aj$) and C_2 ($= p$). Thus:

$$C_1 \quad V \quad C_2$$

$$p$$

$$or \quad aj \quad p$$

$$t \quad \cdot \quad \cdot$$
$$\cdot \quad \cdot$$
$$\cdot \quad \cdot$$

The commutation test will work here in the following way. Are p and aj and p descriptive of some word and t and aj and p descriptive of some second word such that the function between the two identified words is a commutation? A "yes" answer indicates the nonidentity of p and t. They are distinct describing elements of C_1. A "no" answer indicates that the two are to be identified as a single describing component of C_1. The choice of co-occurring elements, here aj and p, is free. Thus we might have picked simply aj. The words involved would have differed, but the relationship between p and t would have been the same. Thus Hjelmslev (1961: 66) may write:

> *The difference between signs and figurae in this respect [the commutation test, PWD], is only that, in the case of signs, it will always be the same difference of content that is entailed by one and the same difference of expression, but in the case of figurae, one and the same difference of expression may, in each instance, entail different changes between entities of the content (e.g., pet-pat, led-lad, ten-tan).*

If the commutation test applied to figurae yields a "yes" answer and thus a nonidentity between p and t, we still may not assert that the autonomy between the figurae p and t is a commutation without also implying an altered definition of mutation, hence also of commutation and permutation. We may say that there is a relationship of contrast between p and t rather than commutation (cf. Fischer-Jørgensen 1956: 147).

In this reformulation of the commutation test an additional difficulty may be encountered. In selecting V and C_2, we have assumed that the aj and p co-occurring with p of C_1 are identical with the aj and p co-occurring with t of C_1. But their identity also presupposes the commutation test. Within the heuristic technique, a co-occurring identity is assumed as a frame for objects being tested, but this identity presupposes a previous application of the test to the frame. The problem is neither raised nor solved in the *Prolegomena* (cf. Spang-Hanssen 1961: 157–58).

A second possible problem of identification involves the identity or nonidentity of the describing elements of C_1 with those of C_2. Although p describing C_1 will be of the same rank as p describing C_2, they will not be first-degree derivates of one and the same class. An additional requisite for the presence of mutation or its absence is not met. Nothing can be said of their identity in terms of the commutation test. Hjelmslev (1961: 63–64) points out that "phonemes [e.g., the describing components of C_1, V, etc., PWD] can differ simply by belonging to different categories." Such identification is, however, implied by the following:

> . . . *the commutation between* p *and* b *in Danish (which applies, e.g., in initial position:* pære *'pear'—* bære *'carry') is suspended when, for example,* p *and/or* b *contract(s) relation with a preceding central part of a syllable (Hjelmslev 1961: 88).*

The statement of suspension of commutation between *p* and *b* as describing elements of one class implies their identification with distinct *p* and *b* describing another class. Such a reduction would result in a simpler accounting and is to be desired.

This kind of problem exists throughout any accounting and must be resolved by the theory. We may take as an example the following from the nonfigurae stage of an accounting of the expression hierarchy (again the class names are intended only as convenient labels):

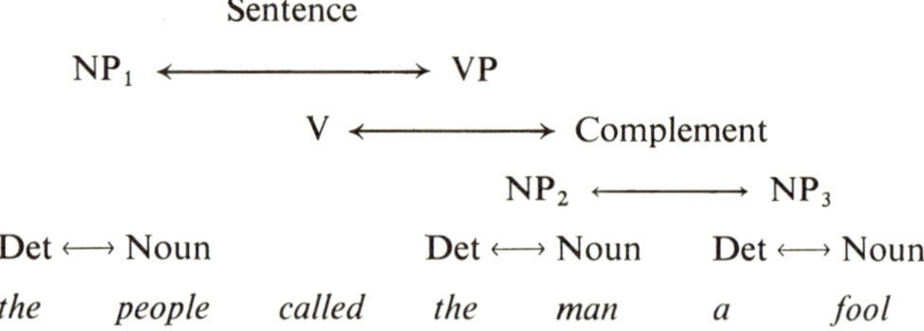

We would intuitively claim that the *the* of NP_1 is identified with the *the* of NP_2, and indeed, the NP's describing Complement (which do meet requisite conditions for a definition of mutation) are identical with the NP component of Sentence. But NP_1 and NP_2/NP_3 are not first-degree derivates of a single same class. In terms of mutation, we have no way of comparing them, thus no way of identifying them. The same problem would arise in describing the system.

Although the condition of identity in these cases is not broached in the *Prolegomena*, it is considered by Fischer-Jørgensen (1949: 219–34), who concludes that simplicity of interpretation suffices as a criterion. If *p* of C_1 were identified with the *p* of C_2, they could be interpreted by a single statement as [p]. Or if some nonlinguistic science registers *p* of C_1 as [p'] and the *p* of C_2 as [p⌐], the two statements would not be identical, but they would remain similar to each other. The similarity, or partial likeness, of these statements is greater than the similarity between the two required statements if we identify *p* of C_1 with *t* of C_2 (or make no identification at all). This greater similarity results in more statements of interpretation being present only once. That is, interpret p as [p] and add ['] if p is of C_1 and [⌐] if of C_2. Nonidentity requires two statements of two distinct objects described by [p], one for p of C_1 and again for p of C_2. Identification may result in a simpler inventory and a simpler interpretation. Wrong identifications will be recognized by no decrease in simplicity of interpretations, as in the wrong identification of p of C_1 and t of C_2. Generalizing, we may extend this argument of simplicity of interpretation to nonfigurae. Any two classes within an accounting whose interpretations cover the same range of purport are considered identical. We may be tempted to see here a solution to the problem of ambiguity with respect to the commutation test. We may choose to abandon the test as a technique if the resulting identity yields an interpretation that is not simpler—for example, if a class of content is interpreted as two widely disparate portions of the nonlinguistic segmentation of purport as "Financial institution" and "Land adjoining a lake or stream." The hierarchy of simplicity and simplicity of procedure have been reversed. The problem of conflicting hierarchies of criteria within the figurae stage is raised by Fischer-Jørgensen (1949: 228–34).

Another problem with the revised commutation test should be mentioned. Assume that we are considering possible describing components of V, say a and ow co-occurring with n as a component of C_2. Furthermore, assume that a and n describe some word which is not in commutation with the word described by ow and n: the on of the example. The test would identify the two as a single describing component of V. However, had we chosen as co-occurring elements the l of C_1 and n of C_2, the two sequences would have described two words in commutation: *loan* and *lawn*. Here the test would indicate two describing components of V. Let us look at another example. Suppose we have a text with some class Syll in its accounting, described by analysis by C_1, C_2, and V, with specification between C_1 and V and between C_2 and V. Suppose also that t and d are distinct describing elements of C_1, but considering them possible describing elements of C_2, we find that the two descriptions correspond to no two words related by commutation, regardless of the possible variety of same co-occurring elements from C_1 and V. An *overlapping* exists between t and d as describing elements of C_2. A *syncretism* is a "category that is established by a 'suspended mutation between two functives'" (Hjelmslev 1961: 136). (The phrase within single quotation marks is the definition of overlapping.) The syncretism (and not t and d) is the first-degree describing component of C_2. A principle of generalization (Hjelmslev 1961: 69–70) indicates that syncretism should be removed from the description if possible and C_2 described by one of the describing components already in the accounting at this stage. (This principle also applies to the description of clusters such as st. If there exists as describing components of some C, st, s, and t, then st is to be removed from the accounting as a describing component and accounted for by a conjunction of the already occurring s and t.) If this can be done, the syncretism is *resolved*. This heuristic technique is as follows. Determine the co-occurring elements that are presupposed by the syncretism: the conditioning environment. Let us assume here that the condition is the absence of a component of V to the right of C_2; that is, if a describing component of V occurs to the right, there is no syncretism. Thus

$$\text{Word}_x \qquad \text{Word}_y \qquad \text{Word}_x \qquad \text{Word}_y$$

$$C_1 \quad V \quad C_2 \; : \; C_1 \quad V \quad C_2 \; :: \; C_1 \quad V \quad C_2 \quad V \; : \; C_1 \quad V \quad C_2 \quad V$$

$$t \quad o \quad t/d \quad t \quad o \quad t/d \quad t \quad o \quad t \quad\quad t \quad o \quad d$$

$$(1) \qquad\qquad (2) \qquad\qquad (3) \qquad\qquad (4)$$

Here t/d is used to mark the syncretism of t and d. The syncretism is resolved by introducing the analogous element, d of (4), in place of the element involved in the syncretism t/d in (2), furnishing a description of Word$_y$ under (2) as *tod*. The syncretism in the description of Word$_x$ is resolved by introducing the t describing C_2 in (3) as the describing component of C_2 in (1), now described as *tot*. The result of such a resolution is an *ideal* "notation," which under given conditions is manifested by or interpreted as the syncretism, an *actualized* notation. An ideal notation is a simpler accounting, for the describing components of C_1 and C_2 are reduced by one (the syncretism t/d), and C_2, instead of being described by the syncretism as component, is described by elements already present at that stage as describing components, t and d. Furthermore, Word$_x$ and Word$_y$ receive a single description each: *tot* and *tod*, respectively. Notice again that the technique of resolution presupposes identifying the components describing C_1 with those describing C_2. If an analogy cannot be stated, the syncretism cannot be resolved. For example, if in C_1VC_2 the i and e of V commute before all components of C_2 except m, n, and η, as in the description of *tin* and *ten* in some varieties of English, there is no description of either *tin* or *ten* such that the components of V, i and e, do not occur before n, and the syncretism cannot be resolved because no analogy can be offered as basis of generalization. Another such example involves [own] *on* and [an] *on* There is no way of describing *on* that would resolve the syncretism ow/a; there is no analogy to serve as basis for its resolution.

If the interpretation of the elements describing a syncretism is the same as the description of some but as not all of the elements outside the syncretism (that is, those elements into which the syncretism is resoluble), the syncretism is also an *implication*. Thus t and d above, co-occurring with the syncretism, are interpreted as [t] alone, while the elements into which the syncretism was resolved were interpreted as [t, d] when not co-occurring with the syncretism. That syncretism was an implication. If the syncretism is such that its interpretation is the same as all or none of the commuting elements whose suspension forms the syncretism, the syncretism is also a *fusion*. The Danish example cited by Hjelmslev of the syncretism of p and b when they describe C_2 in C_1VC_2 is an instance of a syncretism that is a fusion. The interpretation is [p] or [b], the same as for both elements whose suspended commutation forms the syncretism when they exist outside the syncretism and describe C_1. Here the interpretation is the same as for all the components of the syncretism when they are outside its conditions. If in the *tin/ten* example the interpretation of the syncretism *i/e* is [ɪˇ] distinct from the interpretation of either *i* [ɪ] or *e* [ɛ] outside the environment of the syncretism, then this is an example of a fusion of the second type.

One problem involved in the phenomenon of syncretism and not resolved in the *Prolegomena* is linearity. In the syncretism of *t/d*, the conditions involved a statement "to the right of." Hjelmslev, in stating the condition for the syncretism of *p* and *b* in Danish, uses the term "preceding," but the theory has no way of identifying linear relationships. Such difficulties may be resolved by introducing linearity into the theory, or we may try to state the conditions in terms of both-and and distinct classes. Thus the commutation between *t* and *d* is suspended when they describe C_2. If a Syll presupposing the Syll of which C_2 is a component co-occurs and is described by V or VC_2, then the commutation of *t* and *d* when describing C_2 of the presupposing Syll is not suspended. Such a statement of the condition of suspension presupposes that C_1 is not identified with C_2. If it were, linearity would be required at this point in the accounting; but we have already implicitly assumed the presupposing Syll to be "to the right of" the presupposed Syll, and linearity is again introduced. The relationship of the conditioning of a syncretism and linearity remains unsolved.

We consider one last example of syncretism. Let us add the words *field* and *feel* from a variety of English in which they are both registered as [fijl] such that the C_2 of their accounting is *l*. The items may occur under conditions wherein the describing component of C_2 occurs before a component of $V_{\cdot,}$ thus $C_1 VC_2V$, in which case C_2 is also described by *ld*. We find that *d* does not commute with the absence of *d* outside this condition. There is a suspension between *d* and an element that is interpreted as no segment of the nonlinguistic segmentation, ⊘ (Hjelmslev 1961 : 93). The condition for the syncretism of *d/⊘* is the absence of a co-occurring component of V to the right of C_2. (We ignore the linearity problem.) The syncretism may be resolved by the following analogy:

Word$_x$	Word$_y$	Word$_x$	Word$_y$
C_1 V C_2 :	C_1 V C_2 ::	C_1 V C_2 V :	C_1 V C_2 V
f ij l	*f ij l*	*f ij l*	*f ij ld*
(1)	(2)	(3)	(4)

We introduce *d* into the description of (2), thus *fijld*. Consistency would require that we introduce zero, $\varnothing$, into the description of (1), *fijl*$\varnothing$, and that it also be a describing component of C_2 of (3), also *fijl*$\varnothing$; but this is not clear from the *Prolegomena*. The syncretism of *d*/$\varnothing$ would be an implication.

Another problem revolves around the zero component. Suppose we had written an accounting that had predicted that Phrase would be described on the basis of both-and by Prep and NP, but in some addition to the text we found [ın] without accompanying material. We might have two recourses. First, we may assume that [ın] by itself is possible and should be predicted by the accounting, which is accordingly altered by changing the selection between Prep and NP to a combination within the process and by changing the specification to an autonomy within the system. Second, we might assume the solitary [ın] to be atypical of the text. An accumulation of such accidents, if they are not atypical but are of the same premised nature as the given text, will reduce the accounting to a statement without cohesions. Such a text would not be amenable to scientific treatment. The number of such "accidents" necessary to convince us that the aberrant sequence is in fact a valid part of the data is undetermined. Assuming that we do consider [ın] to be aberrant, we may account for it by *catalysis*. Catalysis, like the resolution of the syncretism *d*/$\varnothing$, involves introducing an element that has zero interpretation; but unlike the syncretism example, no analogy is required. The occurrence of [ın] without accompanying matter in the text is unique or numerically very small, while [ın] with accompanying matter occurs throughout the remainder of the text, which serves as a basis for the encatalysis of some element within the accounting. The elements required to account for the aberrant case must not be more than can be inferred on the basis of [ın] alone. In, as a component of Prep presupposes NP, and NP may be described by Det and Noun mutually determining each other within process and system. Here the encatalysis of elements stops. Constellation is reached at this point. In presupposes no particular choice of Det, A or The, nor any particular choice of Noun. Hjelmslev (1961: 95) points out that we might here consider the describing components of Det and Noun to be irresoluble syncretisms of their describing components; Det is then described by the syncretism A/The, and so forth. Notice that catalysis functions within the technique of deriving exhaustive accountings. Not accounting for such accidents produces less than an exhaustive description. Syncretism, on the other hand, is a relationship that occurs in the interpretation of the accounting if it is resoluble; or it may occur within the accounting if it is irresoluble. The resolution of the syncretism is a technique like encatalysis, functioning in the derivation of more highly valued accountings.

Summary

We have now reached the point where we may summarize the theory developed in the *Prolegomena*. The theory as interpreted here will consist of the following primitives and definitions:

THEORY

Primitives

1. Description
2. Dependence
3. Object
4. Uniformity
5. Presence
6. Necessary
7. Condition
8. Both-and
9. Either-or
10. Identity and nonidentity

Definitions

1. Analysis
2. Synthesis
3. Interdependence
4. Determination
5. Constellation
6. Dependence described by two solidary components ($=$ expression and content)
7. The components of (6) being in turn described
   a. By analysis on the basis of either-or and interdependence, determination, and constellation, and
   b. By analysis of the classes of (a) on the basis of both-and and interdependence, determination, and constellation such that
   c. Description by synthesis of each component of (a) and (b) with respect to
      i. First-degree derivates of the same class as the described component, and
      ii. Greater-degree derivates of the same rank of one and the same class as the described component such that both sums lie within expression or content—both within one of the solidary classes of (6), and
      iii. First-degree derivates of some class in the opposing hierarchy (in expression if the described sum is within content or in content if the described sum is within expression), which class is of the same rank as the class of the described sum, such that (iii) does not hold beyond some rank n within (a) and (b), while (i) and (ii) hold for components at a rank greater than n.
   d. Yields a mutation holding between first-degree derivates of each class to rank n.

Nonprimitives such as "solidary" should be defined before they are used in definitions. We assume that they were defined as (1) through (5) were and omit them here to simplify the overall definition of language.

The theory summarized here is expanded beyond the preliminary profile outlined on pages 48–9. There the object characterized was a simple dependence described by analysis and synthesis. Now the dependence is elaborated internally to consist of two solidary components, which are themselves hierarchies. They, labeled content and expression, constitute what may be interpreted as levels within the theory. Thus

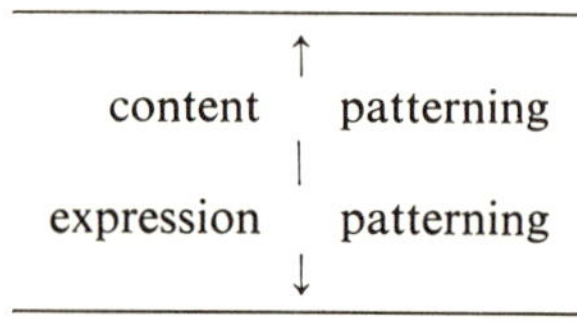

Internally, each level is characterized by two hierarchies (7 and 6), one on the basis of either-or, the other on the basis of both-and. Each of these hierarchies is delimited by analysis and synthesis on the basis of interdependence, determination, and constellation. The relationships between levels as wholes is a solidarity, as are the relationships between elements of one level and the second. The definitions (7ci and ii) provide for the description of each term within both expression and content and also within the process and system in terms of synthesis. (7ciii) extends that statement of synthetic description to include relationships to a term in the opposing hierarchy—content or expression. This is the basis of (7d): that relationships between sums that are first-degree derivates of a class within process or system of expression and content are mutations to rank n; n defines the distinction between signs and figurae. Terms at and above n are signs; those below are figurae. All this—(6) and (7) of THEORY—characterizes the dependence of (6) as a hierarchy satisfying the definition of a semiotic, but a particular kind of semiotic because of the stipulation that a distinction be made between signs and figurae. This stipulation assures that the levels of content and expression not be isomorphic, and it is this nonconformity of expression and content that requires their separation (as their conformity required their merger in Saussure's theory). If they were found to be conformal, simplicity would dictate that they not be distinguished.

The implementation of the theory with respect to some text will entail the following:

ACCOUNTING

1. Definition of a system by analysis of the two solidary components of a dependence defined by (6) of the theory
2. Definition of a process by analysis of the classes of the system
3. Description of the resulting components in both (1) and (2) by synthesis as
   a. First-degree derivates with respect to other first-degree derivates of the same class
   b. Greater-degree derivates with respect to derivates of the same rank of one and the same class such that both are within either of the two solidary components of (1)
   c. Greater-degree derivates with respect to derivates of the same degree of

> one and the same class such that the describing derivates lie in the oppos-
> ing level

4. Description of the functions among first-degree derivates as mutations where appropriate
5. Interpretation by establishing determination between the classes/components of the process described in (1)–(4) and the nonlinguistic segmentation of purport
6. Evaluation of
   a. The self-consistency of (1)–(4)
   b. The exhaustiveness of (1)–(4)
   c. The simplicity of (1)–(4)
   d. The simplicity of (5)
7. Reworking (1)–(5) until (6) is maximally satisfied (in part by eliminating all substitution, resolving syncretisms, and encatalysis).

With relationship to the data projection, the accounting constitutes a *form*, the constant or presupposed in a selection among the hierarchies of the accounting (Hjelmslev 1961: 134) and their projection upon the formless purport. Purport organized by the projection of the hierarchies of the accounting on it is *substance*, the variable or presupposing element in the selection (Hjelmslev 1961: 134). The same selection holds of the set of all possible accountings (the theory) with regard to the set of all possible purports.

The use of the term "language" is restricted to a portion of the theory: the system. We may understand this restriction if we relate language to constancy. The data have no inherent pattern. The theory and accountings are patterned, but constancy is equated with absence of instantiation, which may be predicated of system but not process. Recall that a partial accounting of the data exclusively on the basis of both-and involved a choice of elements from the system. The accounting by both-and was particular to a segment of the data. Description on the basis of either-or does not involve such a choice and is not particular. Language as a technical term is defined as a system within a semiotic whose classes are manifested by all purports (Hjelmslev 1961: 137). Saussure, unlike Hjelmslev, used "language" within the data and the theory based on the assumption that both were patterned; and although he noted that syntagmatic relationships involved choices (Saussure 1959: 130), "language" was not restricted to the system of associative patterns. Choice or instantiation was eliminated by the exclusion of sentences as possible data.

We now find that the term "text" is ambiguous. It has been used as a synonym for data (Hjelmslev 1961: 12 et passim), but it has application as a technical term (Hjelmslev 1961: 137) designating a process within a semiotic whose classes, if expanded indefinitely, is manifested by all purports.

The notion of grammar is associated with the level of content (cf. Hjelmslev 1961: 25–26 and 84), and no distinction is supposed between the traditional studies of morphology and syntax (Hjelmslev 1961: 27 and 73). Insofar as the two levels of content and expression are isomorphic and the distinction between the two is undeterminable within the theory, labeling a particular portion of the theory as grammar is arbitrary. Notice again the arbitrariness of our labels in the descriptions of pieces of data throughout the discussion. Given Hjelmslev's application of "grammar" to the level of content, our use of Phrase, NP, and so forth, within the level of expression is incorrect; there, however, they served only as convenient names for classes and components, with no further implication.

We will conclude the discussion of Hjelmslev with a remark about the appropriateness of the theory with regard to a characteristic we may intuitively attribute to language, however delimited by a theory. First, data may be imagined such that its accounting in terms of the formalism of the theory projected onto purport encompasses only a portion of the universe. The system of that semiotic would not be manifested by all purports, nor could its text be extended indefinitely. If the theory as presented is to be a definition of possible natural language, this stipulation that the system be manifested by all purports must be added to delimit natural (unrestricted) languages from unnatural (restricted) languages. It is a characteristic of natural language that all semiotics (restricted and unrestricted) may be translated into it (Hjelmslev 1961: 109), but a characterization of natural language in such a way involves terms outside the formalism. That is, an object is or is not a language with respect to the unrestricted or restricted nature of the predicted purport. Given the defining stricture of glossematics to strictly formal primitives and definitions, there can be no formal distinction between a natural language in which one can talk about everything and an unnatural language, which is restricted. Like Saussure's theory, Hjelmslev's ends by characterizing objects we would want to call languages but also some we would not.

ADDITIONAL READING

FISCHER-JØRGENSEN, ELI. 1949. "Remarques sur les principes de l'analyse phonémique." *Travaux du Cercle Linguistique de Copenhague* 5. 214–34.

GARVIN, PAUL. 1954. Review of Hjelmslev, *Prolegomena to a Theory of Language*. *Language* 30. 69–96.

HJELMSLEV, LOUIS. 1959. *Essais linguistiques* (= *Travaux du Cercle Linguistique de Copenhague* 12). Copenhagen: Nordisk Sprog- og Kulturforlag.

———. 1961. *Prolegomena to a Theory of Language* (revised English edition), trans. Francis J. Whitfield. Madison: The University of Wisconsin Press.

LAMB, SYDNEY. 1966. "Epilogomena to a theory of language." *Romance Philology* 19. 531–73.

MARTINET, ANDRÉ. 1946. "Au sujet des Fondements de la théorie linguistique de Louis Hjelmslev." *Bulletin de la Société Linguistique de Paris* 42. 19–42.

SPANG-HANSSEN, HENNING. 1961. "Glossematics," in *Trends in European and American Linguistics 1930–1960*, eds. Christine Mohrmann, Alf Sommerfelt, and Joshua Whatmough. Utrecht: Spectrum.

CHAPTER 4

Leonard Bloomfield

Historically, the theory of language developed by Leonard Bloomfield has formed the basis for a great deal of work on the nature of language. As expected in a developing science, not all of this activity has been theoretically conformal. Some of it has been done within Bloomfield's framework but some involves alterations of Bloomfieldian theory. Here we take up a theory of language developed primarily in Bloomfield 1926 and 1933. We will see that these two sources imply different theories of language; what we finally acknowledge as Bloomfieldian theory involves aspects of both and forms the basis for a later modification into a theory that may be termed post-Bloomfieldian (cf. Chapter 5).

The kind of data that is the subject of this theory is in part determined by what is considered to be acceptable scientific statement. Let us begin with some general considerations. In constructing a theory, we decide informally and without constraint the kinds of things we want to account for; then with a set of primitives and definitions we delimit formally that set of objects. We are relatively free in choosing the primitives. Our choice is justified to the extent that the resulting definitions (theory) permit correct statements within the areas of prediction, generality, exactness, and simplicity. One restriction placed on empirical theories (i.e., theories of some range of data) and, therefore, on the constituents of these theories, is that they be liable to testing or invalidation. We must be able to recognize when, where, and how theories are mistaken. The primitives may be chosen subject to these constraints.

Now, the primitives may be relatively abstract (e.g., implication), or they may be less abstract (e.g., sound segment). Primitives of the sound segment type are directly associated with some part of the data; they are the result of some operation on that material. And if taken as primitives of the theory, the theory presupposes the operation(s) on the data that derive(s) those primitives. Hjelmslev's glossematics is an example of explicit rejection of such primitives. Rejection of nonlinguistic (or prelinguistic) operations places more emphasis on the interpretation of accountings based on such a theory. Since terms of the accounting are abstract (not derived from some previous segmentation of or operation on possible data), none of the terms of the accounting is guaranteed constant association with any part of the data. Each term of an accounting which has interpretation requires the *explicit* assertion of its correspondance to data for each of its occurrences. Without such interpretation, the accounting tells nothing about the data; it is devoid of empirical content. The interpretation of the accounting (and thus the possibility of invalidation) depends on the possibility of this association between accounting and data. A test of the correctness of an accounting (and eventually of the theory) presupposes interpretation; we can say nothing about the value of accountings (and theories) with respect to some data if they have no relationship to those data. A theory that contains primitives such as sound segment [i], [e], and the like has a built-in interpretation. Within accountings of such theories, these terms will always be associated with some portion of the data without explicitly stating the association by virtue of their natural content. As such terms increase, explicit interpretations within individual accountings decrease. To the degree that we adopt such primitives for use within a theory, we build in a guarantee of interpretation and therefore of testability. A concern with the testability of statements is expressed by Bloomfield (1939a: 46): "Science deals with phases of response that are alike for all normal persons. Its observations and predictions can be tested by anyone" (cf. also Bloomfield 1933: 38 et passim and 1936).

A concern with testability by itself does not in any way restrict possible data—what we conceive as a manifest, possible language. We satisfy this concern by choosing, when possible, primitives that result from nonlinguistic operations, guaranteeing to that extent the interpretation of the accountings and their possible invalidation. This approach to theory construction is taken by Bloomfield.

Let us again emphasize that restricting ourselves to particular kinds of primitives does not by itself restrict what is possible data. If, however, we choose to designate certain nonlinguistic operations as unacceptable, then we have limited what may qualify as possible data. If we find that some possible primitives are the result of operations (or the result of theories of some nonlinguistic science) that are of questionable validity or of doubtful interpretation, or are uninterpretable, then we gain nothing toward our goal of constructing a testable theory by accepting the results of these operations and theories as primitives. In accepting such primitives, we would actually move away from our goal of testability. One technique that Bloomfield finds particularly unacceptable as an operational source for primitives in constructing an acceptable theory is introspection:

> *The working of the nervous system is not accessible to observation from without, and the person himself has no sense-organs . . . with which he himself could observe what goes on in his nerves . . . . It is a mistake, for instance, to suppose that language enables a person to observe things for which he has no sense-organs, such as the workings of his own nervous system (Bloomfield 1933: 34).*

Results from this technique, such as "idea" and "concept," are judged an unsuitable basis for a theory (Bloomfield 1933: 142). This restriction on possible theory has the following effect on the range of possible data. If there is no valid technique for observing data, it is impossible to provide a testable theory or accounting of those data. If the workings of the nervous system can be observed only by introspection, which has been judged unacceptable, then there can be no theory of those data such that testable predictions or accountings may be made of them. Because of the constraint on theories which requires the highest possible degree of testability, no acceptable theory can be constructed on primitives to account for data with respect to which the primitives have no interpretation; accountings (and theories) based on them may not be invalidated. Data of the nervous system recorded by introspection are so characterized, and a theory of introspectively acquired data is disqualified.

The kinds of data we may consider are those that are amenable to a valid, applicable handling technique from which we may derive our primitives. The sounds a person may make; his physical environment while making these sounds; his relationship to other persons present or absent; his physical behavior before, during, or after he makes the sounds; physical behavior of others before, during, or after he makes the sounds are all amenable to the techniques of one or another science (physics, biology, anthropology), which are acceptable sources of primitives. Such observations by these techniques may be and are taken as the data of linguistics. These techiques are illustrated by Bloomfield (1933: 22) with an anecdote. Suppose that Jack and Jill are walking along a road. Jill sees an apple on a tree beside the road and says to Jack that she is hungry and wants the apple. Jack in turn walks to the tree, climbs it, picks the apple, and brings it to Jill. Schematically, this scene can be represented as follows (Bloomfield 1933: 26):

$$S \longrightarrow r \ldots s \longrightarrow R$$

It is the result of an initial segmentation of a sequential continuum of activity by our assumed techniques or theories. The label S corresponds to that part of the sequence bounded by the beginning of the anecdote and Jill's first observing the apple; the first $\longrightarrow$ represents Jill's internal workings from the point when she sees the apple to when she begins to speak; the r labels her activity (articulation) in speaking; the . . . represents the physical sound itself; s represents Jack's perception of that sound; the second ⟶ labels Jack's internal workings subsequent to his perceiving . . . and prior to his acting on Jill's request; and, finally, R represents Jack's act in getting the apple. Were it possible to apply an operation, say that of a physiology, to the ⟶ portions, the result would be linguistically uninteresting, for such portions differ from time to time and from person to person (Bloomfield 1933: 142). It would not be possible to attribute patterns to such data. The r . . . s portion, called the *act of speech*, *speech-signal*, or *speech utterance* (Bloomfield 1933: 23, 29, 144), is said to recur; and here we may find some subject for scientific treatment. The r . . . s portion may be subjected to a physiological operation (on r and s) or to a physical operation (on . . .). If we assume an equivalence between the three, that is, if we assume that regardless of whether we take the production of sound, the sound itself, or the perception of sound, we will obtain equivalent patterns, then it makes no difference which we deal with. The S and R portions are collectively termed the *meaning* of the speech-signal (Bloomfield 1933: 32 and 1939a: 18). Further statements are based on an assumption of patterned relationship between the speech-signal and meaning.

With respect to the dichotomy between introspection and other techniques, we may introduce the distinction of language-as-knowledge, as a property of the nervous system, and language-as-behavior, as activity of human beings in an environment. It is possible that language exists as one or the other datatypes. Given this dichotomy and the concerns we have just discussed, we may make an assumption; namely, that were it possible to develop a theory of language-as-knowledge, as a property of the nervous system, we would not find any patterns that we could not also find and express in a theory that considered language as behavior. Simply, the assumption claims that a theory of language-as-knowledge reduces to a special case of a theory of human behavior. Such a view holds that no primitives other than those within a theory of behavior are necessary to account for language. A contrary view would hold that there are indeed features of language-as-knowledge exhibited in patterns not present nor predicable of language-as-behavior. Not all the relevant patterns of language can be found in behavior. This argument may be formulated by claiming as necessary primitives that are not present within a theory of language-as-behavior. "Concept" may be one such primitive. The additional, required primitives of this view share the unreliable nature of Bloomfield's rejected introspection. They have no statable correspondence to data other than that collected by introspection. The argument claims that the designated primitives are not present in a theory of language-as-behavior, and no theory without them can account for the relevant patterns. The two points of view are called *mechanism* and *mentalism* (or vitalism), respectively (cf. Hempel 1966: 101–10). There are two criteria for the mechanistic attitude: (1) that language-as-knowledge reveals no patterns not also manifest in language-as-behavior and (2) that no primitives beyond those neccessary to define language-as-behavior are required should we account for language-as-knowledge. Mentalism is the negation of (1) and (2).

Vis-à-vis this dichotomy, we place the theory of language developed by Bloomfield on the side of mechanism. We have already indicated the kind of data we will be interested in, and it is all data independent of mental phenomena. Mental phenomena, although not of interest here, can also be characterized as physical and chemical activity, as "obscure and highly variable muscular contractions and glandular secretions . . . not represented by conventional speech forms . . . the speaker reports these as *images, feelings*, and so on and they differ not only from speaker to speaker, but for every occasion of speech . . . " (Bloomfield 1933: 142–43). Here it is assumed that all so-called mental data are in fact physico-chemical in nature. The theories of Saussure and Hjelmslev do not neatly reflect one or the other of these attitudes. Saussure distinguishes between *langue* and *parole* (the former mental, the latter mental, physiological, and physical), further assuming that pattern exists within *langue* alone. One may not reduce patterns of *langue* to patterns of *parole* nor patterns of language-as-knowledge to patterns of language-as-behavior. But the primitives assumed to account for the pattern of language are such that they may also be found within a theory of behavior. They are abstract: nonidentity, conjunction, linearity, and mutual implication. They are neither characteristically mental nor physical; they are not derived from operations on either mental or nonmental phenomena. Terms such as "concept" and "sound-image" are associated with introspection, but introspection plays no role within the theory itself. This theory does not meet the second criterion of the mechanist-mentalist distinction; it accounts for mental data but is not mentalistic. Hjelmslev's theory meets neither criterion of the dichotomy. The data on which pattern may be based are either mental or nonmental or both, indifferently. The primitives used in developing a statement of possible pattern, like Saussure's, are drawn from results of no set operations on any data. Hjelmslevian theory, then, is not classifiable with respect to this dichotomy of mechanism and mentalism; this reflects the glossematic view of the immanent nature of language.

The Theory

We now turn to developing a theory of the data that we have found interesting, the speech-signal (r . . . s) and its relationship to meaning (S and R). The relationship between these terms is clearly instable from one point of view. For example, in the anecdote Jack might have turned his back on Jill and walked off instead of behaving as he did. Bloomfield (1933: 37) observes that "Some actions are highly variable in each person. . . . " To obviate this lack of pattern when individual pieces of data are considered, we may restrict ourselves to "the study of conventional actions. . . . Here the linguist is in a fortunate position: in no other respect are the activities of a group as rigidly standardized [patterned, PWD] as in the forms of a language" (Bloomfield 1933: 37). The behavioral data after individual variation is subtracted are termed *habits* (Bloomfield 1933: 30–31, 37 et passim). This assumption of conventional actions parallels the "average" characterization of language within Saussure's theory and catalysis within Hjelmslev's theory. All are designed to free the accountings from a basis of accidence within data and to identify phenomena as exceptional if statements of them are to be made within the accounting.

The S/R portion of the data raises a problem with respect to handling technique. Certain situations are difficult or perhaps impossible to characterize correctly by nonlinguistic means:

> *Linguistic forms . . . result, for the most part in far more accurate, specific, and delicate co-ordination than could be reached by non-linguistic means; to see this one need only listen to a few chance speeches:* Four feet three and a half inches.—If you don't hear from me by eight o'clock go without me.—Where's the small bottle of ammonia? (*Bloomfield 1933: 144*)

The lack of technique for characterizing all meanings makes it impossible to demonstrate pattern holding between r . . . s and S/R and leads to what Bloomfield (1933: 144) terms the fundamental assumption of linguistics. "*In certain communities (speech communities) some speech-utterances are alike as to form and meaning*"; or in an earlier formulation (Bloomfield 1926: 154), "Within certain communities successive utterances are alike or partly alike."

This assumption—in the second formulation—presupposes the terms *community, utterance,* and *alike.* Utterance is a defined term based on an additional presupposed term, *act of speech:* "An act of speech is an utterance" (Bloomfield 1926: 154). The primitive "act of speech" is a complex consisting of the elements identified in the Jack-and-Jill anecdote: speech signal, here consisting of vocal features or sounds implying in turn the segmentation of speech signal, and the stimulus-response features, the plural again implying their segmentation.

In terms of utterance, community, and the fundamental assumption, a particular type of community, a speech community, is defined. It is any community in which the fundamental assumption holds. Language is then identified as the set of possible utterances within a speech community. Bloomfield uses the term "language" to label the set of possible data, unlike Hjelmslev, who used the term to identify part of his theory but none of the data, and Saussure, who used the term for both data and the theory.

Bloomfield (1926) gives an account of his theory in terms of assumptions and definitions. The distinction is important. We cannot have been exposed to all languages (all sets of possible utterances for all possible speech communities); therefore, we cannot have demonstrated that whatever patterns we may have encountered in some languages (and for which we want to provide a theory) will hold for all languages. We have to assume this. Nor can we demonstrate that speech-signals are associated with meanings, because we cannot identify each meaning within the data. (But notice that such a handling technique is assumed within act of speech.) Therefore, we assume such an association exists and that such associations recur. The assumptions state the patterned properties inhere in any set of data, in any language. The assumption of the predicability of patterns in data is present in any empirical theory. The definitions provide the framework for the statement of these patterns.

The patterns predicated of sets of data inhere in that data. Bloomfield's (1926) assumptions concern the set of vocal features, claiming that certain patterns exist within the r . . . s portion of the act of speech. Bloomfieldian theory is not constrained, as Saussurean theory, to introduce only definitions that correspond to assumed patterns in the data. Nor does Bloomfieldian theory, unlike Hjelsmlevian theory, claim that patterns exist immanently, only within the theory. The framework—theory—established to express those patterns will include some terms that correspond to elements within the data, but also some that do not. The data are linear pieces of behavior existing through time. Some definitions of the theory are set forth in terms holding nonlinear relationships, e.g., form class. These do not occur in the data. Recall that Saussure believed that certain pieces of data (e.g., substantive) were of uncertain validity. These data would have required a theoretical apparatus analogous to form classes; but Saussure declined to include them, and thus their necessary apparatus, in the theory because of the condition that required all terms of an accounting to correspond to some patterned portion of the data. Bloomfield, not assuming form classes to occur within the data, nevertheless includes them as definitions of the theory. Bloomfieldian theory is not constrained by realism to the same extent as is Saussurean theory. Definitions involving linear, conjunctive relationships (morphemes consisting of phonemes or phonemes themselves) do correspond to elements assumed to occur in the data. The theory also differs from Hjelmslevian theory, which claims that its definitions do not correspond to inherent patterns in the data; Bloomfield seems to hold a position between the two extremes of Saussurean and Hjelmslevian theory. The attitude Bloomfield adopts on the relationship of definitions occurring in accountings and patterns inherent in the data appears to be a descriptivist one, but it is not a goal here to revise or restrict the theory so that all or none of its terms occurring in accountings correspond to elements in the data. The theory is constructed to express patterns assumed to exist in sets of data, but not all of its terms occurring in accountings of specific data will be amenable to interpretation (cf. Hockett 1968: 151).

Grammatical Patterning

The use of "alike" in the fundamental assumption as cited from Bloom-field 1933 further specifies coincidence of sound features and stimulus-response features. In comparing utterances *cap* and *capsule* and *ripe* and *gripe*, we may note a likeness in terms of sound features but not stimulus-response features. In *cap* and *capsule* [kæp] is not associated with some same meaning; similarly for [rajp] in *ripe* and *gripe*. The two pairs of utterances are not partially alike with respect to the first assumption. Each of the two pairs, *cap* and *caps*, and *ripe* and *riper*, however, shares an identity of vocal features that corresponds to a same meaning. The members of each pair are thus partially alike. Such sames of vocal features, that is, "vocal features common to same [alike] or partially same utterances" (Bloomfield 1926: 155) are *forms*. Thus *cap* and *capsule* (but not the *cap* of *capsule*), *ripe*, *gripe* (but not the *ripe* of *gripe*), *er*, and *s* are all forms, as are *caps* and *riper*. All utterances are forms, but not all forms are utterances. Neither *er* nor *s* are utterance forms. They do not occur by themselves as speech acts. We distinguish between these two by identifying some forms as *free* and some as *bound* (Bloomfield 1926: 155 and 1933: 159–60). A form that occurs as an utterance is free; one that does not is bound. An utterance is, then, equivalent to a free form; all free forms are utterances.

A minimal pattern emerges from our observation that different utterances may be partially alike, which implies that utterances are "made up of" segments of vocal features that are forms. An utterance, to be partially like another, must consist of at least two parts: one part shared by the second utterance and one part not so shared. After we have identified forms in examining some set of data, we exhaust the segmentation of the data without leaving a residue of vocal features that are not forms. Every vocal feature is within some form. These two observations (that utterances, themselves forms, are related to forms by the relation "made up of" and that utterances are exhaustively made up of forms) are generalized to all languages by Bloomfield's (1926: 155) second assumption: "Every utterance is made up wholly of forms." All this is a kind of pattern assumed to be inherent in language. To account for this we use the primitives speech act (complex as indicated), community, alike, and made-up-of, to construct an initial theoretical framework to account for these observations. The definitions we require are form, free, and bound. Data such as the half-dozen or so speech acts cited above may be accounted for by designating some of them as free forms and indicating the forms (free or bound) of which they consist. Patterns of partial identity are indicated by a shared form. Such an accounting might take the following shape:

| Free Forms | *cap* | *caps* | *capsule* | *ripe* | *riper* | *gripe* |

consist of

| Forms | *cap* | *s* | *capsule* | *ripe* | *er* | *gripe* |

The pattern is essentially one of identifying forms, free and bound, and showing how they may be arranged into exclusively free forms. Bound forms are identified by their restriction to co-occurrence with some form in making up a free form within the set of free forms. All other forms are free. An interpretation would involve associating each form with a set of vocal features, *cap* with [kæp], and so on. The preliminary pattern identified here is of one kind: forms.

There is a similarity among certain of the utterances of our data. Some consist of a single form, others consist of two. This difference is recognized by distinguishing between *minimum* and *nonminimum*. "A *minimum* X is an X which does not consist entirely [wholly, PWD] of lesser X's" (Bloomfield 1926: 155). Thus, some forms are minimum (= *morphemes*); they consist of a single form. Others are nonminimum and free, consisting of two or more forms each of which is free; such nonminimim forms are *phrases*. And some forms are free and minimum such that they consist of only one free form, plus perhaps some forms that are not free. Such minimum forms are *words*. Within our data *cap*, *caps*, *capsule*, *ripe*, *riper*, and *gripe* are words; *s* and *er* are morphemes. Additionally, *cap*, *capsule*, *ripe*, and *gripe* are morphemes; they satisfy the conditions of the definitions of both word and morpheme. The possible number of forms within an utterance is not, of course, restricted to two. *The bartender served me a glass of beer* is an utterance consisting of eleven forms: *the, bar, tend, er, serve, d, me, a, glass, of,* and *beer*. The number of forms within an utterance is not a defining property of what is a possible utterance. In an accounting we know one point at which our statements cease: the point at which forms making up utterances are minimum. The made-up-of relationship ceases at that point. What constitutes the upper boundary (loosely, a sentence, paragraph, chapter, or whatever) is similarly determined by the relationship made-up-of. An utterance that does not in part make up (is not included within) another utterance is the upper boundary of the pattern of inclusion: a maximum utterance. The set of utterances that fulfill that condition are called *sentences* (Bloomfield 1926: 158 and 1933: 170). Thus the following:

(1)   The bartender sat on my cap

(2)   Max sat on my cap

(3)   The bartender griped a lot

(4)   Max griped a lot

These are all sentences, and like our previous data they are partially alike in certain ways. They differ from the earlier examples in that they share not a minimum form, but a nonminimum form. (1) and (3) share the forms *the bartender;* (2) and (4) share the form *Max;* (1) and (2) share the forms *sat on my cap;* and (3) and (4) share *gripes a lot.* Furthermore, all of these shared forms may themselves be sentence-utterances. *The bartender* may occur independently of some longer utterance, as may *sat on my cap* and *griped a lot,* the first in answer to "Who sat on my cap?" and the last two in answer to "What did the bartender do?" If we decide to consider this type of pattern (shared nonminimum forms) one we in fact wish to account for, we need no additional theoretical apparatus. In the accounting we simply add an intermediate stage of inclusion. Thus, refer to the accounting on page 97. (We ignore the possibility of additional intermediate stages.) The inclusion of intermediate stages here depends on the decision that these additional patterns occur in language. That such patterns are necessary is indicated by examples such as the following:

(5)　　　　　　　old bartenders and patrons

(6)　　　　　　　the coat and the gloves which fell on the floor

Each of these utterances correspond to at least two different meanings. (5) may have the meanings 'bartenders and patrons, both groups of which are old' or 'bartenders and patrons, of which only the former are old'; (6) may have the meanings 'the coat and the gloves, all of which fell on the floor' or 'the coat and the gloves, of which only the latter fell onto the floor'. We may distinguish between the forms having two meanings by differentiating among the hierarchical groupings of the minimum forms within the nonminimum ones, as follows:

Free Forms	*old-bartenders-and-patrons*	*old-bartenders-and-patrons*
consist of		
Free Forms	*old bartenders-and-patrons*	*old-bartenders and patrons*
consist of		
Forms	*old bar tend er s and patron*	

(Again we ignore possible additional intermediate stages.) Here, we require the intermediate stage to account for the fact that the two instances of (5) and (6) may correspond to different meanings. If (5) were accounted for by claiming that it consisted directly of eight forms, there would be no way to account for its association with distinct meanings. With the acceptance of this pattern as one we want to include in possible languages, we have to elaborate the taxonomic organization of forms by the relationship made-up-of into a hierarchy. If a nonminimum form is directly related to its composing forms, the latter

Free Forms   *The-bartender-sat-on-my-cap*   *Max-sat-on-my-cap*   *The-bartender-griped-a-lot*   *Max-griped-a-lot*

consist of

Free Forms   *The-bartender*   *Max*   *griped-a-lot*   *sat-on-my-cap*

consist of

Forms   *the bar tend er*   *Max*   *gripe d a lot*   *sat on my cap* are designated the *immediate constituents* of the former (Bloomfield 1933: 161). A form that contains immediate constituents is a *complex form;* the minimum forms in the hierarchy are the *ultimate constituents* (cf. Bloomfield 1933: 160–61).

We now see that the accountings of the utterances that require intermediate stages have a certain lack of simplicity. The forms appear several times within an accounting. For example, in accounting for (5), *old* appears five times, *bar* appears five times, and so on. We would like to increase the simplicity of the accountings implied by our theory. Such improvement is connected to the recognition of an additional kind of pattern. Beyond the patterns of utterances in terms of shared forms (minimum and nonminimum), we find another. Comparing the utterances

(7)   Max grabbed the beer

(8)   The bartender closes the door

we observe that they share an identity in terms of meaning that may be roughly represented as 'Actor performing an action on an object'. If we wish to ascribe the partial identity to the two speech signals, we may not do so in terms of shared forms. The only shared form is *the*; it is assuredly wrong to ascribe the partial likeness to this shared constituent. The pattern of the two may be reflected in another kind of partial sameness—order of elements. Thus:

$$\left\{\begin{matrix} \text{Max} \\ \text{The bartender} \end{matrix}\right\}_1 \quad \left\{\begin{matrix} \text{grabbed} \\ \text{closes} \end{matrix}\right\}_2 \quad \left\{\begin{matrix} \text{the beer} \\ \text{the door} \end{matrix}\right\}_3$$

These sames of order may recur in many utterances, just as forms may recur. Words, as well as the phrases (7) and (8), may be partially alike in terms of order; *boats*, *children*, and *phenomena* manifest a same order:

$$\left\{\begin{matrix} \text{boat} \\ \text{child} \\ \text{phenomen} \end{matrix}\right\}_1 \quad \left\{\begin{matrix} \text{s} \\ \text{ren} \\ \text{a} \end{matrix}\right\}_2$$

associated with the meaning we represent as 'Plural object'. This kind of pattern is generalized to all languages in the assumption (Bloomfield 1926: 157) that "Different non-minimum forms may be alike or partly alike as to the order of the constituent forms and as to stimulus-reaction features corresponding to this order." To account for this pattern we add *construction* to the definitions of the theory; "Such [corresponding to sames of stimulus-response features, PWD] recurrent sames of order are constructions" (Bloomfield 1926: 158). The ordered units of a construction are *positions*. This requires we add to our theory the primitive linear conjunction or order. Orders of the same number of positions may be distinct in the same way homophonous morphemes may be distinct, by virtue of distinct meanings.

The complexity of accountings is reduced with this modification. Let us examine the description of (5) in terms of construction and positions.

$$\textbf{(5')}\quad \text{(a)}\quad \{\quad\}_1 \qquad and \qquad \{\quad\}_2$$

$$\text{(b)}\qquad \{\quad\}_1\ and\ \{\quad\}_2\ and\ \{\quad\}_3$$

$$\text{(c)}\qquad \{\quad\}_1\ and\ \{\quad\}_2 \qquad \{\quad\}_1\ and\ \{\quad\}_2$$

$$\text{(d)}\quad old\quad bartender\quad s\quad and\quad patron\quad s$$

$$\textbf{(5'')}\quad \text{(a)}\qquad \{\quad\}_1\ and\ \{\quad\}_2\ and\ \{\quad\}_3$$

$$\text{(b)}\quad \{\quad\}_1\ and\ \{\quad\}_2$$

$$\text{(c)}\qquad \{\quad\}_1\ and\ \{\quad\}_2 \qquad \{\quad\}_1\ and\ \{\quad\}_2$$

$$\text{(d)}\quad old\quad bartender\quad s\quad and\quad patron\quad s$$

The hierarchy of (5') is associated with the meaning 'bartenders and patrons, both groups of which are old', and (5'') is associated with 'bartenders and patrons of which only the former are old'. As before, possible additional stages within the hierarchy have been ignored. The constructional accounting of (5') claims that there is a construction consisting of two positions at (5'a). Position two at (5'a) may be occupied by forms that exhibit the construction at (5'b), consisting of three positions. The first and third positions may be occupied by forms exhibiting a pattern accounted for by two constructions at (5'c). By identifying the constructions at (5'c) on the basis of sames of positions associated with sames of meaning, we claim that there are two instances of the same construction at (5'c). Allowing positions to consist of positions, we define constructional hierarchies analogous to hierarchies of form. Finally, the positions of these constructions are filled by the actual forms at (5'd). Hierarchy (5'') is a construction that consists of three positions. Again, on the basis of sameness of positional order and meaning, we identify construction (5''a) with construction (5'b). Position one consists of two positions identified as the same construction as that of (5'a). Position two of (5''b) and position three of (5''a) are described as two instances of the same construction and identical to the constructions at (5'c). Finally, the positions defined in (5''a-c) are filled by the forms in (5''d). The principal constructional difference between (5') and (5'') is that in (5') *old* fills a position in construction with a single position filled by *bartender*, while in (5'') *old* fills a position in construction with a single position filled by *bartenders and patrons*. The constructional hierarchies of (5′) and (5″), wherein the nodes are positions, are

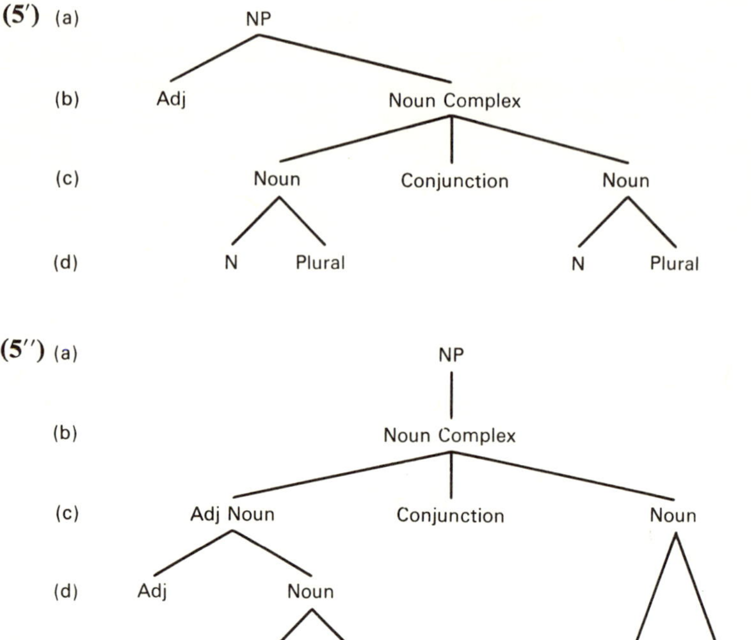

The positions at (5′a), (5′b), and so forth, are constructions within the constructional hierarchy. The constructional hierarchies of (5′) and (5″) being different—absence of sames of ordered positions associated with different meanings—marks (5′) and (5″) as constructionally distinct. The data they predict may have the same actual order while differing in their *structural order* (Bloomfield 1933: 210).

With the addition of construction to the theory, we may point out a redundancy. Previously we required the definitions form, free, bound, minimum, and nonminimum to account for patterns; but now we observe that all utterances are instances of constructions (allowing utterances such as *Run!* to manifest constructions of one position), as are any nonminimum free forms (phrases) of which utterances consist. If we assert that a set of data (utterances) may be described by a number of constructions 1 . . . *n*, such that some of them may occur not as the constituent of a construction, while others always occur as the constituent of some construction, then we have, by this hierarchy, described the notion free and bound. Forms predicted by the first construction type are free; those predicted by the second construction type are bound. If we allow constructions to consist of one or more than one position, then we have captured the notion of minimum and nonmininum forms. Minimum forms are those predicted by one-place and one-stage constructions. Nonminimum forms are predicted by multiplace constructions. The terms "utterance," "free," "bound," "minimum," and "nonminimum" are then redundant within the theory. The definitions of position, construction, and form, plus the hierarchy defined from language to language on the basis of these definitions and the primitive made-up-of, allow us to capture the notions utterance, free, bound, minimum, and nonminimum. The terms in this group apply to the data; they label patterns described by position, construction, form, and hierarchy. We accordingly modify the preliminary theory presented above to conform with these observations. For the place of "word" and "phrase" within this framework, see the discussion of morphology and syntax.

An accounting of patterning of form breaks into two portions: (1) statements of constructions and (2) lists of forms in positions. Notice that the actual forms are now entered fewer times within the accounting, at stage (d) in (5′) and (5″).

Having introduced the definition of construction into the theory, we have eliminated a complexity, namely the repetition of forms in the accountings of the first descriptions of (5) and (6), and have accounted for additional patterns. We now discover that the complex repetition of forms within the accounting has not been completely remedied. Observe for example, that in the description of (5) by (5′) and (5″) the form *old* occurs twice; the form *bartender* occurs twice, and so on. Accountings will attain maximum simplicity in this respect if we revise the theory further so that each form is listed only once within an accounting. This revision will involve a sharp distinction between statement types (1) and (2) of the preceding paragraph as *grammar* and *lexicon* (Bloomfield 1933: 138). In describing this revision we also note that we have missed a pattern based on the following observations. We have now claimed that utterances may exhibit a pattern by sharing a common term; they may be partially alike. We accounted for this condition by adding the definition of form to the theory such that utterances were forms consisting of forms. We also discovered that utterances may exhibit a pattern that is not attributable to a shared form; this pattern is not accounted for by the assumption that forms include forms. The sameness in this instance was attributed to a same, shared order of forms. Within the theory the definitions of construction and hierarchy were sufficient to state this pattern. We now take up a third type of pattern or sameness among forms. Consider

(7)   The bartender wipes the bar

(8)   Marvin wants a drink

(9)   Fred hates violence

First of all, these three utterances are instances of a single construction, which we may call "Subject-Predicate" with two positions. There is a sameness among *the bartender*, *Marvin*, and *Fred* that is not attributable to a shared form nor to a recurrent same of order. They are, in these examples, all 'Actors'. In addition to their individual meanings, they all share the meaning of 'Actors'. The formal sameness, the pattern they exhibit, is the fact that they may occur in the same position in a construction. The patterns utterances may exhibit must now be accounted for in terms of the forms of which they consist, the orders the forms manifest, and the positions the forms fill in a construction. As sameness of order required an additional definition within the theory, so sameness of occurrence in some position(s) requires one: "All forms having the same functions [occupying the same positions, PWD] constitute a *form-class*" (Bloomfield 1926: 159).

We now separate forms completely from the statements of constructions and list them in a lexicon that is a nonlinear conjunction of the minimum forms of a language. With each form is listed the form classes of which the form is a member. The lexicon is additionally structured by the fact that form classes may have internal organization. Let us examine the following:

(10)	The mayor trips
(11)	*The letter trips
(12)	The mayors trip
(13)	*The mayors trips
(14)	The letter falls
(15)	The mayor falls
(16)	The letters fall

All these examples are representative of a same "Subject-Predicate" construction with two ordered positions, which we may label "Subject" and "Predicate." The "Subject" position is in turn a construction of two positions, which we label "Determiner" and "Noun." Thus

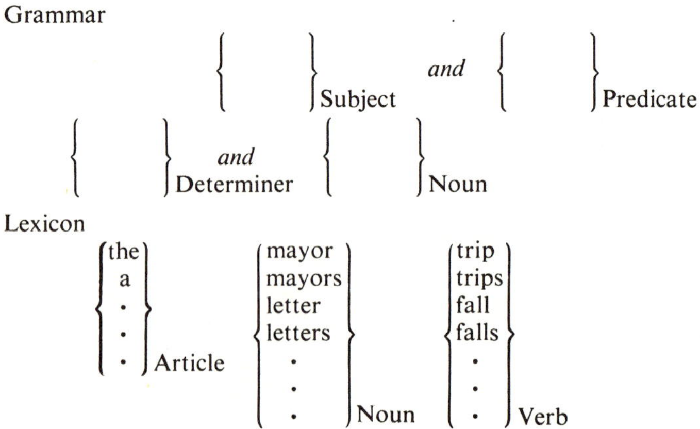

The form class Noun may be subclassified into a Noun Singular subclass (*mayor* and *letter*); a Noun Plural subclass (*mayors* and *letters*); a Noun Animate subclass (*mayor* and *mayors*); and a Noun Inanimate subclass (*letter* and *letters*). The Verb form class contains the subclasses Verb Singular (*trips* and *falls*); Verb Plural (*trip* and *fall*); and Verb Animate-subject (*trip* and *trips*). The members of subclasses are again nonlinearly related. The reason for this additional organization of the lexicon stems from observations of the following kind. Relationships may hold between members of distinct form classes. Some members of the form class Verb (*trips*) require (presuppose) a member of the Noun form class such as *mayor*. It may not occur with *letter* [see (11)]. The reverse does not hold. *Mayor* occurs with *trips* as well as with *falls*. *Mayor* does not presuppose either *trips* or *falls*. The presupposition of *trips* for *mayor* is nonreciprocal, but between some members of form classes there is reciprocal presupposition. Some members of the Noun form class (*mayors*) require a particular kind of Verb (*fall* or *trip*); and here the reverse holds. *Fall* requires a particular kind of Noun, either *letters* or *mayors*. The unidirectional relationship may be called *government* (Bloomfield 1933: 192): it is comparable to a synthetic description of a sum holding determination with a sum both of which are of the same rank two or higher in Hjelmslevian terms. The bi-directional relationship of mutual presupposition is *congruence* or *concord* (Bloomfield 1933: 191) and is comparable to the same Hjelmslevian sum described by interdependence. These restrictions are generalized beyond statements of specific pairs (or triads, and so forth) of lexical items to apply to groups of lexical items. The ordering subclassification of form classes is required for this generalization and to predict correctly only sequences of forms that in fact are possible utterances, that have some meaning. The relationship among subclasses is called *selection* (Bloomfield 1933: 165) and is required as a primitive within the theory. Selection, like act of speech, is a complex primitive. It covers the relationship of presupposition or implication, mutual (reciprocal), and nonmutual (nonreciprocal). Patterns of free and bound forms can be cast in terms of selection. The constructions designed to account for such data can be in part defined by one of the varieties of selection existing between positions.

In passing we point out that we have treated the data of plural nouns as a two-position construction, that is as data described by grammar. Bloomfield (1933: 165) treats them as we have just done, as data to be described within the lexicon by subclasses and selection relations. Specific criteria for attributing patterns to grammar or to lexicon are not supplied. Roughly, we may distinguish between treatments in the following way. If plurality is recognized as a morpheme, it has its own entry in the lexicon, its own form class membership. The morphemic treatment of *s* implies the grammatical description. If plurality is not recognized as a morpheme and is treated as a property of Noun distribution, then like other distributional properties, it is described within the lexicon via subclasses. But notice that we find *mayor* and *mayors*—Noun

Singular and Noun Plural—but we do not find *mayor*₁ and *mayor*₂—Noun Animate and Noun Inanimate. The morpheme *mayor* is invariably animate but variably singular and plural. This lexical treatment of plurality raises questions about the morphemic identity of *mayor* and *mayors*, possibly (if they are not identified) doubling the number of Noun entries in the lexicon. This may be taken as cause to treat plurality as a grammatical pattern.

The pattern imposed on morphemes in the lexicon is not a hierarchical taxonomy like grammar. Morphemes belong simultaneously to many form and subclasses; and two morphemes separated with respect to one subclass, such as *mayor* and *letter* with respect to Noun Inanimate, may both be members of another subclass, Noun Singular. The form *letter* may belong to two (or more) form classes; for example, Noun and Verb. Such *class cleavage* (Bloomfield 1933: 205–6) is characteristic of the lexicon. The largest form classes may be called *parts of speech* (Bloomfield 1926: 160 and 1933: 268). Each member has its form class and subclass membership as part of its entry in the lexicon. They are idiosyncratic, nonpatterned properties (Bloomfield 1933: 274) of morphemes as the meaning and phonological shape are (cf. below).

The distinction between grammar and lexicon is not a distinction between levels. The morphemes grouped in the lexicon constitute terms whose patterning is expressed by the grammar (Bloomfield 1933: 162–63). They are not two kinds of patterns but two integral parts of a single pattern.

We have so far discussed patterning of forms without reference to a distinction between morphology and syntax. The distinction is made (Bloomfield 1933, Chapters 12 and 13) by the terms "word" and "phrase" as already defined. The patterning of forms within the domain of words is the subject of *morphology;* and the constructions that express this are morphological constructions. The patterning of words within the domain of the phrase is the subject of *syntax*. The constructions accounting for these data are syntactical constructions. The question arises whether the distinction conforms to the notion of level in our sense of the term. Recall that we require different *kinds* of patterning for identifying levels. The distinction between morphology and syntax is motivated by arguments such as these; the patterns of words are "more elaborate," "irregular," or more "rigidly fixed" (Bloomfield 1933: 207) than patterns of syntax. No claim is made that different *kinds* of patterns exist but that *less* nondistinctive variation, or *more* statements of selection, are required. The difference is one of degree. No new definitions are required by the patterns of morphology and syntax beyond those definitions required to make the distinction. Above a certain point in the constructional hierarchies of grammar, specifically word, fewer or more, but not new, statements of a different kind are required. Given our notion of level, differentiating grammar into morphology and syntax does not correspond to two levels. Grammar and lexicon constitute a single level.

Finally, on the subject of grammar, there is an interesting difference between Hjelmslevian and Bloomfieldian theory. Let us reconsider (5′) and (5″). We have pointed out samenesses within the two grammatical hierarchies of (5′) and (5″) and eliminated redundancy to the extent that we have identified those samenesses, calling them instances of the same construction. At this point, eliminating redundancy and recognizing patterns seem to stop in Bloomfieldian grammar. Hjelmslevian theory would claim we have accounted only for the process, and to attain maximum simplicity, we must generalize further. By recognizing partial samenesses of construction (in addition to identity and nonidentity), we establish partial sameness between grammatical hierarchies. For example, we may claim that (5′) and (5″) are partially alike in that a three-place construction occurs in both, the difference being that in (5′) it occupies a position in construction with a position filled by *old*. In (5″) it does not. In Hjelmslevian terms Adj specifies what we here call Noun complex. (We ignore the fact that Adj may occur alone; that is, *old* is a free form.) By continuing to locate partial identity of constructions in terms of shared positions, we can construct the following Hjelmslevian-like system:

Adj   *specifies*   Noun complex

Adj *specifies* Noun

N *specified by* Pl

This implies the processes (of constructional hierarchies)

(a)   Noun complex

Noun

N *selected by* Pl

bartender   *s*

(b)   Noun complex

Noun   *combination*   Noun

N *selected by* Pl   N *selected by* Pl

bartender   *s*   *and*   *patron*   *s*

by choosing Noun twice, as we could choose Phrase several times in the preceding chapter (*And* is a "connective." We ignored them in the discussion of the Hjelmslevian theory and continue to do so here, cf. Hjelmslev 1961: 72).

(c)   Noun complex *combination* Noun complex

Noun   Noun

N *specified by* Pl

bartender   *and*   *patron*   *s*

(d = 5′)

Adj *specifies* Noun complex *combination* Noun complex

    Noun   Noun

   N *specified by* Pl   N *specified by* Pl

old   bartender   s and patron   s

(e = 5″)   Noun complex

Adj *specifies* Noun *combination* Noun

   N *specified by* Pl   N *specified by* Pl

old   bartender   s and patron   s

and so on. In Bloomfieldian terms all these constructional hierarchies (Hjelmslevian process instantiations of a system) are distinct. They manifest an order of positions with different meanings. They are also distinct in Hjelmslevian theory, but their partial identity is recognized and that pattern is stated. The only generalization made of constructional hierarchies in Bloomfieldian theory is to recognize *sentence-types* (Bloomfield 1933, Chapter 11). Here the pattern is expressed by classifying sentences into *full* and *minor* sentences (Bloomfield 1933: 171). In English, the full sentence-type consists of actor-action phrases and commands (Bloomfield 1933: 172). These both consist of subtypes (Bloomfield 1933: 174): explicit-action and a second sub-type, such as *I did hear him* versus *I heard him* and **Run** home versus *Run home*. Within the explicit-action, actor-action subtype, there is a further subtype: inverted versus noninverted questions, such as *Did John run away?* versus *John ran away?* The minor sentences have similar subtypes. The classification here is obviously not directed toward the recognition of sames within constructional hierarchies and the reduction of redundancy in accountings.

A second generalization is made by comparison of constructions indirectly by the properties of the forms they predict. If a construction yields a form that may occur in the same positions as one of its constituents, the construction is *endocentric* (Bloomfield 1933: 194–97). The Adj-Noun construction predicts a resultant form *acceptable merchandise*. This phrase has the same privilege of occurrence as its constituent merchandise. Both forms occur in *Max refused the . . .* , and the Adj-Noun construction is endocentric. A constituent of a phrase defines a form class to which the phrase itself belongs. This endocentric property may be recursive. In the construction Adj-Adj-Noun resulting in *expensive, acceptable merchandise*, the whole phrase has the same privilege of occurrence as *acceptable merchandise*, which in turn shares the privilege of occurrence of *merchandise*. When the maximum construction is reached such that the recursive expansion is ended, the construction is *closed* (Bloomfield 1933: 197). The construction resulting in *all the expensive, acceptable merchandise* is closed because no construction yields a longer phrase with *all the expensive, acceptable merchandise* as constituent such that both the containing phrase and constituent phrase have the same privilege of occurrence. The observation of endocentricity relates the Adj-Noun, Adj-Adj-Noun, Det-Adj-Adj-Noun, and Quantifier-Det-Adj-Adj-Noun constructions by comparing their resultant phrases; but such comparisons do not specify any partial identities in terms of shared positions. It leads to no simplification within the set of possible grammatical descriptions. If no constituent of the resultant phrase of a construction has the same privilege of occurrence as the whole phrase, the construction is *exocentric* (Bloomfied 1933: 194–95). The Subject-Predicate construction has *Max refused the merchandise* as one of its predicted forms. None of the constituents shares the privilege of occurrence of the whole phrase, and the Subject-Predicate construction is exocentric. Compare occurrence in *I said that* . . . . The classification of constructions as endocentric and exocentric, like the classification according to sentence-types, is not directed toward recognizing sames within constructional hierarchies and reducing redundancy in accountings. The emphasis of Bloomfieldian theory is on the linear, syntagmatic property of data and not the nonlinear, paradigmatic, as in Hjelmslevian theory. Bloomfieldian description of grammatical pattern requires a *set* of grammatical hierarchies: a list of syntagmatic hierarchies as opposed to a single paradigmatic hierarchy.

Sound Patterning and Identity

The ultimate terms in the hierarchy of an accounting have been assumed to be minimum forms, and the patterns we have so far discussed have been patterns of forms. Morphemes have been treated as if they had no internal structure, no partial similarity. We now see that they do exhibit patterning and that they are internally complex. Given the morphemes

strew	*stray*	*stay*	*say*	*sigh*	*sue*
true	*tray*		*ray*	*rye*	*rue*

we may identify partial samenesses. *Strew* shares the vocal features recorded as [str] with *stray*. Comparing *strew* with *stay* produces a shared [st], while comparing *strew* with *say* identifies a shared [s]. Pairwise comparison will eventually identify ultimate units [s], [t], [r], [e], [a], [j], and [uw] such that none of them consists of units shared with another unit. That is, comparison will lead to the observation that [st] consists of [s] and [t] and eventually to minimum units. These observations presuppose a phonetics capable of segmenting the speech signal, thus providing the basis for the comparison. The pattern in *strew*, and so forth, is generalized as characteristic of language by the assumption (Bloomfield 1926: 157) that "Different morphemes may be alike or partly alike as to vocal features." In these terms, the partial likeness of *cap* and *capsule* and *ripe* and *gripe* is finally established. Just as utterances patterned by shared vocal features and stimulus-response features required the definition of "form," so the partial identity of morphemes with respect to vocal features alone requires a new definition in the theory. Bloomfield (1926: 157) worded this definition as "minimum same of vocal feature"—a *phoneme*. Given this definition, if our given segmentation of the speech signal were very delicate and precise, none of the vocal features would recur. That is, there would be no sames of vocal features among the morphemes listed. Different instances of what we had thought to be the same morpheme shared no same of vocal feature, that is, *strew* on one occasion might have been [str̥ów] and on another, [s·tɹúy̥]. This is a difficulty only if "same" is taken as a phonetic (nonlanguage) term belonging to the laboratory technique. Bloomfield (1933: 79) subsequently defines phoneme as "a minimum unit of distinctive sound feature," and it is clearer that "same" or "alike" and "distinctive" are terms of the theory and not of the laboratory procedure for recording data.

The introduction of "distinctive" (along with its synonyms and antonyms into the theory) brings us to a discussion of the place of identity in Bloomfieldian theory, and thus to its operational or explanatory character. A theory that assumes identity as a primitive—implicitly or explicitly—will be explanatory. One that defines identity such that we may determine identity within a set of data by applying a set of handling techniques is operational. A theory that defines identity such that determination is not possible by these techniques may still be called an operational theory, but a poor or incomplete one. Whether Bloomfieldian theory is explanatory—as it seems by the assumption of an identity relationship—can be resolved by examining the way accountings are written or intended to be written in principle.

First, the accounting may be made arbitrarily and evaluated against some criteria. In this case nonidentity ("distinct," "same," etc.) enters the theory as a primitive and the theory is explanatory. Second, "distinctive" may enter the theory not as a primitive, but as a definition such that it is constrained to correspond to some operation that can be performed on the data. In phonology we would examine in some fashion two given segments, determine whether certain defining conditions of identity or nonidentity were met, and thus derive an accounting. The procedure may be ambiguous and point to a plurality of accountings for one set of data. In this circumstance we would require an evaluation of the resulting accountings to select the preferred one nonarbitrarily.

A characterization of "distinctive" as applicable to the definition of phoneme is given by Bloomfield (1933: 77) in the following way:

> *Part of the gross acoustic features are indifferent* (non-distinctive) *and only part are connected with meanings and essential to communication* (distinctive).

Distinctive and nondistinctive are determined by the following kind of activity (Bloomfield 1933: 78–79). Examine pairs of sounds, such as [t] and [d] in [tawt] *tout*, and [dawt] *doubt*, respectively, and determine whether they, being phonetically distinct, occur in forms (or utterances) that correspond to different meanings. If so, they are language distinct; if not, they are nondistinctive. This operation assumes several things: first, that the two segments are comparable in that they occur initially in the same positions with respect to the remainder of the vocal features. Second, it is assumed that the remainder in both cases is identical such that difference in meaning can be attributed without ambiguity to the single difference of vocal feature occurring in comparable positions. Third, behind such techniques lies the assumption of a record of the stimulus-response analogous to the record of vocal data. Without this assumption we have no meanings to attribute to comparable phonetic differences. "It is important to remember that practical phonetics and phonology presuppose a knowledge of meanings: without this knowledge we could not ascertain the phonemic features" (Bloomfield 1933: 137–38). Fourth, it is assumed that we know the identity between terms of this stimulus-response record. Had we recorded two phonetic utterances [sṭɹʊ́w] and [stɹʊ́w] such that our data show the first to correspond to a stimulus-response recording labeled "scatter about with one hand," while the second phonetic record corresponds to "scatter about with both hands," we would conclude that the two *t*'s are distinct, following the technique outlined. That is, we would so conclude unless we also knew that the two records of the stimulus-response are not distinctive and that "scattering about with one or both hands" corresponds to either [sṭɹʊ́w] or [stɹʊ́w] indifferently.

In cases where two vocal features are incomparable (occur in complementary environments, as the two *t*'s in [tawt]), "a little practice will enable the observer to recognize a phoneme even when it appears in different parts of words" (Bloomfield 1933: 79).

The techniques that are intended to yield information of identity in grammar are even less formalized. "In the case of a strange language we have to learn such things [whether two instances of forms are the same, PWD] by trial and error, or to obtain the meanings from some one that knows the language" (Bloomfield 1933: 78).

It is not clear whether these activities, which are called experiments (Bloomfield 1933: 78), are intended to correspond to a definition of "distinctive" or "nonidentical" or whether they are intended only as helpful hints to initiate the investigator into the writing of accountings. Identity and nonidentity are nowhere defined; we are given imprecise directions on how to recognize them in specific data. In Bloomfield 1926 and 1933 we find two different attitudes toward integrating the relation into the theory. In Bloomfield 1926, identity is premised by the first assumption: "Within certain communities successive utterances are *alike* or partly *alike* [emphases mine, PWD]"

(Bloomfield 1926: 154). "Alike" occurs in later definitions and assumptions, but no definition of the term is alluded to nor are any techniques indicated that would tell us how to recognize the relationship of alikeness with respect to any data. The relationship of identity in Bloomfield 1926 is clearly an assumed one, and the outline of a theory presented there is an explanatory one. In Bloomfield 1933, the same first assumption of Bloomfield 1926 occurs, and again the identity relationship appears assumed by it (cf. Hockett 1952: 117). Here, however, it is clear that the assumption of identity is an admission of a lack/shortcoming in the techniques available to the linguist. That is, the assumption is made only because we have no way of recording the data of stimulus-response. Were such a laboratory technique available, we would then be able to define a relationship of distinctiveness or identity and eliminate the assumed identity from the theory. "Since we have no way of defining most meanings and of demonstrating their constancy [identity as recurrent instead of infinite variation, PWD], we have to take the specific and stable character of language as a presupposition of linguistic study . . ." (Bloomfield 1933: 144). The ideal would be to attain the requisites and to eliminate the assumption of identity from the theory. The experiments or quasi-operations outlined above are inadequate to determine identity or nonidentity: "So long as the analysis of meaning remains outside the powers of science, the analysis and recording of languages will remain an art or a practical skill" (Bloomfield 1933: 93). The point is that a theory should ideally be an operational one, but the required techniques—a recording of meaning—are not available. We have two choices of interpretation here: the theory as it is or the theory as it should ideally be. Subsequent development of the theory (cf. Chapter 5) is characterized to a great extent by attempts to introduce identity versus nonidentity as definitions (complementary distribution and free variation versus contrast, respectively), thus sharpening the operational property of the theory. Our choice is to treat Bloomfieldian theory as operational while simultaneously recognizing its incompleteness. That is, the technique analogous to phonetics for recording stimulus-response features of speech act and a definition of distinctiveness (nonidentity) will be entered in the theory as primitive and definition, respectively, but no further elaboration of them will be made. Attempts at such elaboration will be covered in the following chapter.

As indicated, in an operational theory the relationship of identity-nonidentity may yield, with respect to some data, more than one possible description. Similarly, an explanatory theory may be such that it provides a plurality of descriptions for some data. In each case, operational and explanatory, it is desirable that theory be modified such that a single accounting is possible for each distinct set of data (and conversely for each distinct accounting of the theory there be a single possible set of data). This would be the most exact, precise definition possible of the object of the theory—language.

In the absence of such a definition, there must be in each case some means of nonarbitrarily selecting one of these accountings as the preferred one.

Bloomfieldian theory admits multiple accountings for a single set of data. Possible evaluative criteria are uniformity of statement (Bloomfield 1933: 164); generality of statement (Bloomfield 1933: 213); convenience of statement (Bloomfield 1933: 179); compactness of statement (Bloomfield 1933: 237); and simplicity of statement (Bloomfield 1933: 131, 135, 164, 212, 218, and 239). There is no general discussion of criteria, and we may assume that the listed criteria differentiate accountings that are equally exact. If one or more accountings predict all the patterns, then they may differ in generality reflected formally by the compactness (Bloomfield 1933: 237–38):

> *... our traditional grammars fall short of scientific compactness by dealing with an identical feature over and over again ... when, of course, it should be noted only once ...*

As applied to our data, the criteria would prevent identification of the first segment of *strew, stray, stay, say, sigh,* and *sue* with the first segment of *ray* and the notation *Xej* for both *say* and *ray.* To correctly predict that the first segment of *ray* is [ɹ] would require a very nongeneral statement identifying the *X* as occurring specifically in the morpheme *ray* when interpreted as [ɹ]. Incorrect identification of distinctive sound features is paralleled by necessary, but nongeneral statements to predict correctly the actual, occurring sound feature. Should we distinguish the second element of *strew, stray,* and *stay* from the first element of *true* and *tray,* then we would find that two sets of interpretive statements for the two units largely repeat each other. Again, lack of generality or compactness—reflected in the repetition—indicates an incorrect statement. Considering the [h] and [ŋ] of *hang,* their identification would result in no simpler description, for the separate descriptions do not overlap such that a repetition is eliminated by their identification. The sum of criteria, compactness, and so forth, are in essence those of simplicity of description and procedure developed with Hjelmslev's theory of language.

In a fashion parallel to patterning of forms, there arises the question of determining whether forms consist directly of their constituent phonemes and whether there are intervening stages of patterning. Not all possible combinations of phonemes occur (Bloomfield 1926: 157); and forms may share a nonminimum phoneme sequence just as utterances may share a nonminimum sequence of forms. The patterns of forms were systematized within the theory by defining construction and hierarchy and specifying for each form the positions it might occupy. As the maximum domain of such pattern was termed the sentence, the maximum domain of shared phoneme sequences is the word (Bloomfield 1926: 157 and 1933: 130–36). Just as there were no recurrent relationships (sames of order) between sequences of sentences, and hence no pattern, there are no recurrent relationships assumed to exist in the orders of phonemes beyond the boundary of word. Within the domain of phonological patterning, the mediating construction between word and phoneme is the syllable. The word is described phonologically as a construction consisting of one or more positions that themselves consist of positions. This second mediating construction size-level is the syllable.

Using a scale of sonority (Bloomfield 1933: 120) given by the set of operations that segment the speech act and provide information about sameness among the phonetic segments, a scale is established within an utterance such that variations of sonority or loudness may be identified, and the segments higher on this scale than surrounding segments are called peaks or crests of sonority. These peaks of sonority are termed *syllabics* and the non-peaks, *nonsyllabics* (Bloomfield 1933: 120–24). A syllable will always contain a syllabic; thus the number of syllables within an utterance is equal to the number of syllabics. The syllable may, in addition, contain nonsyllabic segments to the left and/or right of the syllabic. These observations are made in terms of data and lead to operations on those data, namely assigning a value of the scale of sonority to each segment; determining the peaks (higher environmental values) of sonority. These operations constrain a definition of syllable as a term within theory. There is no operation, however, that delimits the boundaries of syllables in all cases. "In a word like *dimity* ['dimitij] or *patroness* ['pejtrones], the stress merely drops off after its high point on the first syllable. Evidently there are three syllables, because there are three crests of natural sonority, but it should be impossible to say where one syllable ends and the next begins" (Bloomfield 1933: 126). The operational definition of syllable is incompletely specified (as were previous ones associated with definitions of the theory) and possible alternative accountings must be differentiated presumably by reference to the evaluative criteria. We would select the one that led to the simplest, most compact prediction of data.

Words, then, may be described as consisting of one or more positions called syllables that are themselves constructions of positions. The positions of the syllables may be labeled syllabic and nonsyllabic. These in turn may consist of one or more positions, and so forth, until minimum positions are reached within the hierarchy. If we consider a possible description of patterning of phonemes in English, we may find something like the chart on page 113. If we restrict ourselves to discussion of the initial nonsyllabic of three positions, C_1, C_2, and C_3, which occur in the initial syllable of a monosyllabic word, we may distinguish the following classes of phonemes identified, as membership of form classes was, by their occurrence in certain positions, the three C positions detailed above. The C_1 position may be occupied by a class of one member: *s*. The C_2 position may be filled by a class *p*, *t*, and *k*. The position C_3 is filled by a class made up of *w*, *r*, *l*, and *j*. C_3 members are ordered into the subclasses 3A ($= j, r$, and *l*); 3B ($= r$); and 3C ($= w, j$, and *r*). Just as selection imposed restrictions on co-occurrence of morphemes

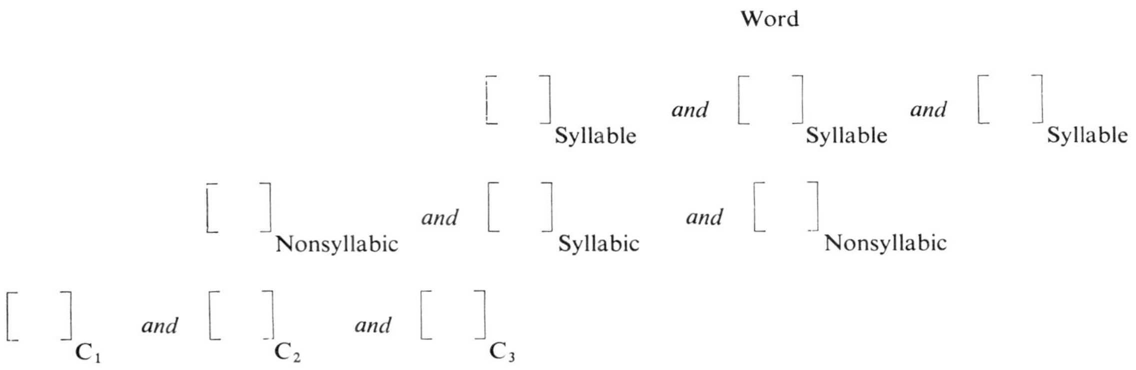

Word

$$[\ ]\ \textit{Syllable} \quad \textit{and} \quad [\ ]\ \textit{Syllable} \quad \textit{and} \quad [\ ]\ \textit{Syllable}$$

$$[\ ]\ \textit{Nonsyllabic} \quad \textit{and} \quad [\ ]\ \textit{Syllabic} \quad \textit{and} \quad [\ ]\ \textit{Nonsyllabic}$$

$$[\ ]\ C_1 \quad \textit{and} \quad [\ ]\ C_2 \quad \textit{and} \quad [\ ]\ C_3$$

as members of classes, so a similar government-like relationship occurs in the description of co-occurrences of phonemes. For example, given our word-initial, nonsyllabic construction of three positions, only subclass s may occur here. The occurrence of this class s presupposes p, t, or k in position C_2. (Class s may precede other members belonging to class 2, but only when position C_3 does not follow; that is, in a nonsyllabic construction [ ]$_{C_1}$ *and* [ ]$_{C_2}$, position C_2 may be occupied by a subclass of C_2 consisting of p, t, k, f, m, and n.). Subclass p, t, k breaks down into three further subclasses: one consisting of p, one of t, and the last of k. The p subclass selects subclass 3A ($= j$, r, and l) as in *spew*, *spray*, and *splat*. The t subclass selects the subclass 3B ($= r$) as in *straight*. The k subclass selects 3C ($= w$, j, and r) as in *square*, *skew*, and *scrape*.

In a nonsyllabic construction consisting of the positions C_2 and C_3, we find other relationships among the subclasses of the total classes that may occupy those positions. If we discover that j in C_3 occurs in this three-position construction only if the segment occupying the syllabic position of the syllable construction is [ʊ́w], then we might claim that it is not the subclass of p or k that selects j in C_3 but the fourth position, which is outside the nonsyllabic construction. Subclass 3A consists of l; and 3C consists of w and r. Eventually, complete assignment of all the phonological segments to classes and subclasses will identify each by a particular configuration of occurrences. The statement of the phonological constructions and the class and subclass organization of the inventory of phonemes, plus the selection relationships that exist among them, account for the *sound-pattern* (Bloomfield 1926: 157) or *phonetic structure* (Bloomfield 1933: 127–29) of language.

The notation of the class and subclass membership of phonemes apparently follows the model of the notation of morphemic form classes and subclasses. "For convenience, I [Bloomfield] shall place a number before each phoneme or group of phonemes that shows any peculiarity in its structural behavior" (Bloomfield 1933: 131). The number denotes membership in a class or subclass. An alternative way to indicate this property of phonemes is by a taxonomic hierarchy analogous to grammatical constructional hierarchies but based on disjunction instead of linear conjunction. The alternatives have an implication for the theory. With a simplified example, the alternatives look as follows (the numbers indicate membership in the distribution classes):

```
(a)  p  1  2  4   6     (b)
     b  1  2  4   7                        1
     t  1  2  5   8                 2             3
     d  1  2  5   9              4        5
     k  1  3      10          6  7  8  9  10  11
     g  1  3      11          p  b  t  d  k  g
```

wherein 2 and 3, 4 and 5, 6 and 7, 8 and 9, and 10 and 11 are either-or related. The construction of (b) assumes no cross-classification. With an inventory cross-classified as (c)

$$
\begin{array}{cccccc}
(c) & p & 1 & 2 & 4 & 6 \\
    & b & 1 & 2 & 4 & 7 \\
    & t & 1 & 2 & 5 & 6 \\
    & d & 1 & 2 & 5 & 7 \\
    & k & 1 & 3 &   & 6 \\
    & g & 1 & 3 &   & 7 \\
\end{array}
$$

we cannot construct a systemic hierarchy on the model of (b). Only if we consider phonemes themselves to be constructs (nonlinear conjunctions of distinct properties), can we fashion such a taxonomic ordering of the inventory:

$$
\begin{array}{c}
(c') \\[1ex]
1 \\
2 \qquad 3 \\
4 \qquad 5 \\
6 \quad 7 \quad 6 \quad 7 \quad 6 \quad 7 \\
p \quad b \quad t \quad d \quad k \quad g \\
\end{array}
$$

Here 6 is the distributional class of "voice"; 7, that of "voiceless"; 4, that of "bilabial"; 5, that of "dental"; 2, that of "nonvelar"; 3, that of "velar"; and 1, that of "obstruent." This contrasts with (b) where 6 is the distribution class of p, not of properties of p. As in (b), 6 and 7, 4 and 5, and 2 and 3 in (c′) are either-or related. The minimum unit of phonology is not, however, the segment features of (c′) but the segments themselves (cf. the description of Chicago English in Bloomfield 1933: 129–35 and 1935); and the ordering of these segments involves cross-classification as the morpheme classes and subclasses do. The ordering here must be by the unique notation of class membership for each phoneme in the inventory. The phoneme inventory of a language is then a nonlinear conjunction of the phonemes. This is consistent with our observation on grammatical pattern that the emphasis of the theory is on the linear, syntagmatic aspect of pattern. With this conclusion we eliminate completely any disjunctive, systemic relationship within the theory.

Grammar and Phonology

Unlike the distinction between morphology and syntax, which was one of degree, the patternings of grammar and phonology differ in kind. Words and morphemes and their patterns were identified as patterns of the same kind of things—forms. The patterns of phonology and grammar are patterns of different kinds of terms: phonemes and forms. These are not, like word and morpheme, terms that differ only as to minimum-nonminimum, free-bound, and the like. They differ by their distinct definitions as well as their patterns. There is no definition of the theory such that phoneme and form are simply different aspects of it in the way that phrase and word are different aspects of form. If we retain the notion of level as kinds of patterning, then the patterning of phonemes—phonology—and the patterning of forms—grammar and lexicon—constitute two levels within the theory.

While phoneme and form are not reducible to some single term or definition, both are defined as certain configurations of sound or vocal features. By observing phonetic transcription, say, certain portions of the data may be identified as phonemes, other portions as forms. Comparing these forms and phonemes reveals patterning we have just discussed. Our identification of forms and phonemes as made up of vocal features (they *are* particular vocal features) satisfies one of our concerns with testability—the proposed interpretation. A phoneme is identified as one or more sound features to the exclusion of other features. English *p* is identified phonologically as the sound features bilabiality, voicelessness, and stopness; the co-occurring features of aspiration, release, tense, or whatever, are not distinctive or phonemic. They do not constitute phonemes in English. Statements of interpretation supply features that are predictable from the environment in which the phoneme occurs. Without such interpretive statements of nondistinctive features we would still have a minimal interpretation—a definite connection between the terms of the theory (phonemes) and the data as recorded by our phonetics. This interpretation is ensured by the definition of phonemes as certain selected portions of that record based on universal phonetic properties. Likewise, as selected properties of that same record, forms are ensured an interpretation. The interpretation of forms or their relationship to data is not, however, direct but is mediated by the phonology. "Every form is made up wholly of phonemes" (Bloomfield 1926: 157). We now have to make precise the relationship of morphemes to phonemes.

Each morpheme must be identified as to meaning, form class and subclass membership, and phonological shape. The list of morphemes with this information is the lexicon. If a morpheme may occur in a number of shapes, such as the morpheme of plurality, which is phonologically *iz*, *z*, and *s*, we can list the individual shapes themselves or list a single shape and predict somehow the variety of its phonological appearance. The latter has the virtue, with respect to the evaluative criteria, of simplifying the entries in the lexicon and is the choice taken by Bloomfield. Morphemes are entered in the lexicon in terms of a single *basic alternant* (Bloomfield 1933: 164). This basic alternant may be an actually occurring form; we may pick one of the varieties as basic. If the morpheme occurs as a word, a free form, then the choice of the form entered in the lexicon is its shape in such an occurrence. This is termed an *absolute form* (Bloomfield 1933: 186). This choice is not made if some other basic alternant will lead to a simpler statement of actually occurring shapes (Bloomfield 1933: 218–19). For example, in some language in which, among the obstruent sounds, only voiceless obstruents occur finally in a word, we may find morphemes (which are also free forms) occurring with a voiceless obstruent in its absolute form as well as a voiced obstruent in nonabsolute (or included) form and morphemes with voiceless obstruents in both forms. If we choose the absolute forms as basic, then from the basic form alone we cannot predict which morpheme will have a voiced alternant in included position and which will not, unless we provide this information separately for each form. If, however, we choose the nonabsolute form as basic, we can predict the correct alternant simply by stating that voiced obstruents are replaced by voiceless ones in absolute position. An included alternant chosen in place of an absolute alternant is when the form is also free, termed an *artificial* or *theoretical* basic form (Bloomfield 1933: 218–19). The entry of the basic alternant of bound forms occurring exclusively in included positions is determined by this criterion of simplicity alone. There is no operation that will lead directly to the determination of basic forms; we must simply evaluate the alternatives with respect to the criteria we have (Bloomfield 1933: 211–12).

Taking as an example the English plural morpheme in its three variants *iz*, *z*, and *s*, Bloomfield chooses the *iz* variant as basic, for the same statements will apply to it as apply to the "is" form of "be," which in its absolute—and also basic—form is the same as the plural variant *iz* and also has the same variant shapes. To predict the occurring variants, we require two statements:

> (a)   *i* is lost except after sibilants (*s, z, č, ž, š, ž*)

> (b)   *z* is replaced by *s* after voiceless obstruents (*p, t, k, f, θ*)

Thus the basic forms

	churches	*homes*	*desks*
	čurčiz	*howmiz*	*deskiz*
by (a) become		*howmz*	*deskz*
and by (b)			*desks*

These statements have the added virtue with respect to simplicity of also applying to the third singular morpheme co-occurring with verbs, as in *teaches, roams,* and *rants* as well as the possessive morpheme in *Ross's, Wyn's,* and *Matt's.*

In addition to the types of statements such as (a) and (b), we require some that are slightly different when we consider such singular-plural pairs as *wife:*

wives. Here the morpheme *wife* occurs in two variants [wajf]: [wajv]. If we take the absolute form (*wife* is a free form) as basic, then we require a way of predicting the alternant [wajv]. We may not, as in (a) and (b), predict alternants in terms of the shape of co-occurring phonemes, for the possessive of *wife* is [wajfs] and not *[wajvz]. We are forced to predict the variant in terms of the plural morpheme itself. Thus

> (c) *f* is replaced by *v* before the plural morpheme.

Furthermore, (c) does not apply to all nouns as (a) and (b) do. The plural of *cliff* is *cliffs*, not **clivs;* (c) must be altered.

> (c′) *f* is replaced by *v* before the plural morpheme
> in the following morphemes: wife, . . .

As membership in form classes and subclasses was included in the information about each lexical entry, so must we include information about each morpheme that is exceptional with respect to these statements predicting actually occurring alternants.

Another complication arises with respect to statements (a), (b), and (c). They must be made such that (a) and (c′) precede (b). For (b) to apply to *deskiz*, (a) must be made first, deleting the *i;* otherwise, the sequence voiceless obstruent plus *z* to which (b) applies is not present. Similarly, (c′) must precede (b), producing the intermediate form *wajvs*, or an incorrect form will be predicted. The sequence *wajfiz* by (a) yields *wajfz;* by (b), *wajfs;* and by (c′), *wajvs*. We might not order our statements and still predict the correct variants by letting (b) apply twice to *deskiz*. Thus, *deskiz* becomes by nonapplication of (b) *deskiz*, by the application of (a) *deskz*, and *desks* by the second application of (b). In the case of *wajfiz*, application of (a) may yield *wajfz;* application of (b) may yield *wajfs;* application of (c′) yields *wajvs;* and application of (b), in a revised reverse form (another complication), finally yields *wajvz*. In each case repetition and/or additional complication of statement is required. All this is avoided and the maximally simple accounting is obtained by providing for the ordered application of these statements. As certain other portions of accountings have no correspondent within the data, so these statements predicting occurring forms from underlying forms are theoretical devices only and have no interpretation (Bloomfield 1933: 213).

The elements making up basic forms are not sharply distinguished from those making up the variants. The statements of patterns of phonemes may or may not be identical for both underlying forms and variants. The description of phonetic patterns, the restrictions in co-occurrence of phonemes, seems to be made not for the distribution of elements making up basic forms but for the phonemes occurring in variants. In later work the shape of basic forms are distinguished and termed morphophonemes, and those of the variants, phonemes. (See Bloomfield 1939b for a further discussion of the principle of ordering within the theory.)

Having decided to enter morphemes in the lexicon in a single basic form and to predict variants by statements such as above, we have introduced relationships encountered here for the first time. These are addition (Bloomfield 1933: 188, 213, and 217), loss (Bloomfield 1933: 188 and 212), and replacement (Bloomfield 1933: 212, 213, and 215 and Bloomfield 1939b: 106 et passim). The patterns we have so far asserted of language data have been based on a taxonomic relationship expressed as made-up-of (Bloomfield), describe (Hjelmslev), or syntagmatic solidarity (Saussure). Additional patterning has been expressed by elaborating this taxonomic relationship to define a taxonomic hierarchy (in Bloomfieldian and Hjelmslevian, but not Saussurean, theory). Finally, patterning has been expressed by relationships between members of a class: selection (Bloomfield), dependence (Hjelmslev), or a linear, syntagmatic relationship (Saussure). These three types of relationships (class-member plus ordering of members by hierarchy or some second means) characterize a taxonomic theory. The add-loss-replacement relationships differ from these in the following way. They express relationships that hold not *within* a taxonomy (or taxonomic hierarchy) but *between* two taxonomies (or taxonomic hierarchies). One taxonomy is defined by the terms that represent the basic forms and a second by those representing the actual, occurring shapes of forms. The add-loss-replacement relations state the correlation between the two; they are extra-taxonomic (and therefore non-taxonomic) in the sense that they exist, not within a taxonomy or taxonomic hierarchy, but between two taxonomies. These relationships can be made taxonomic by considering the terms of the basic forms to be made up of those manifesting the actual forms (cf., for example, Harris 1951: 232 fn. 30). The treatment of the relationship of basic forms to actual forms (and of substitution, cf. page 124) is consistently in terms of add-loss-replace and not in terms of made-up-of. For this reason we adopt the interpretation given here and assume a nontaxonomic relationship. The relationship of grammar-lexicon to phonology is still one of made-up-of. Bloomfield places the add-loss-replace relationships within the phonological pattern, and the description of the sound-pattern and patterns between basic alternants and occurring alternants, termed *alternation* (Bloomfield 1926: 160) or *phonetic modification* (Bloomfield 1933: 163–64 et passim), together constitute the *phonetic pattern* (Bloomfield 1926: 161).

We also find here for the first time the explicit requirement that statements within an accounting may (and must in some optimal accountings) be ordered. This ordering, unlike the ordering of forms in the data and of positions in a construction, is nonlinear. It holds between statements within an accounting, not between pieces of data or terms of a theory and its accountings. Unlike the linear sequences of pieces of data, which reflect the ordering of positions in constructions, there is nothing in the data reflecting the ordering of these statements. The latter is called *descriptive order* (Bloomfield 1933: 213) and is another instance of the absence of realism between accountings and data.

With the distinction between these two levels, we can see that their relationship differs in principle from the relationship between content and expression in Hjelmslev's theory. The relationship between levels may be reciprocal or nonreciprocal. In the first instance the levels are not hierarchically related; in the second, they are. The relationship between content and expression is solidarity—a reciprocal both-and implication—and the levels within Hjelmslevian theory are nonhierarchically related. The relationship of grammar-lexicon and phonology is based on made-up-of. This relationship is not reciprocal. If two levels are distinct and one is made up of terms of the other, the reverse cannot also hold without the loss of distinction. The Bloomfieldian levels of grammar-lexicon and phonology are nonreciprocally, and therefore hierarchically, related.

Grammar and Meaning

The kinds of patterns assumed so far for language have been expressed as two kinds of configurations of vocal features: phonemes and forms. Stimulus-response features have been mentioned only in the definitions of form and phoneme. No patterned configurations of stimulus-response features analogous to those of vocal features has been proposed. The term "language"—the data of this theory—has been identified with the possible configurations of vocal features: language is the possible set of patterns of phonemes and forms. Unlike Hjelmslev's theory, meaning patterns (stimulus-response patterns) are not assumed to require a theoretical device separate from any already outlined. Meanings are assumed to be recorded by an operation analogous to phonetics (but recall the observation that such a technique is imperfect) and to "correspond" in a one-to-one fashion with certain terms of the theory.

A meaning associated with a morpheme is a *sememe;* meaning corresponding to a construction is a *constructional meaning;* meaning corresponding to a position within a construction is a *functional meaning;* and meaning corresponding to a form class is a *class meaning* (Bloomfield 1926: 155, 158, and 159). A class meaning is simply the conjunction of all the functional meanings of the positions that may be occupied by the members of a form class. In addition to the Subject position, the three forms *the bartender, Marvin,* and *Fred* may occur in other same positions. For example,

(17)   The customer shouted to the bartender

(18)   The girl whistled to Marvin

(19)   We waved to Fred

The form class constituted by *the bartender*, *Marvin*, and *Fred* has a class meaning that is the meaning of the Subject position and this second one. This renders the class meaning different from the functional meaning; class meaning can no longer be identified with the functional meaning of a single position but is the conjunction of all the functional meanings of the positions in which the members of the form class Noun may occur. If the terms of formal patterning have meaning, we may construct a taxonomy of meaning parallel to the taxonomic hierarchy of constructions of positions with each element of one hierarchy mutually presupposing an element in the other. But because such a meaning hierarchy would be isomorphic with that of grammar and the sememes isomorphic with the entries in the lexicon, the two must be made into a single one. Grammar and lexicon account for patterns of meaning. Hence, the two are together called *semantics* (Bloomfield 1933: 138). As phonology is interpreted by relating it to a phonetic record of the r . . . s data, semantics would be interpreted by relating it to the record of stimulus-response data. As the nonconformity of content and expression forced their separation in Hjelmslevian theory, the assumed conformity of grammar-lexicon hierarchy with meaning requires that the two be made into one in Bloomfieldian theory.

Each of these theories distinguishes two levels. Loosely, the distinctions may be compared in the following way. Hjelmslevian theory assumes one patterning for expression purport (Bloomfieldian r . . . s) and another for content purport (Bloomfieldian S/R). Within each kind of patterning a distinction is possible between figurae and nonfigurae. Hjelmslevian levels are those of expression and content form. Bloomfieldian theory finds a patterning for vocal features and a distinction analogous to Hjelmslevian figurae and nonfigurae, namely, phonemes and forms. The patterning of stimulus-response features, is isomorphic with the patterning of form and conflated with it. Bloomfield's levels would "correspond" to Hjelmslev's expression figurae and expression and content nonfigurae. Levels within the respective theories are distinguished "perpendicularly":

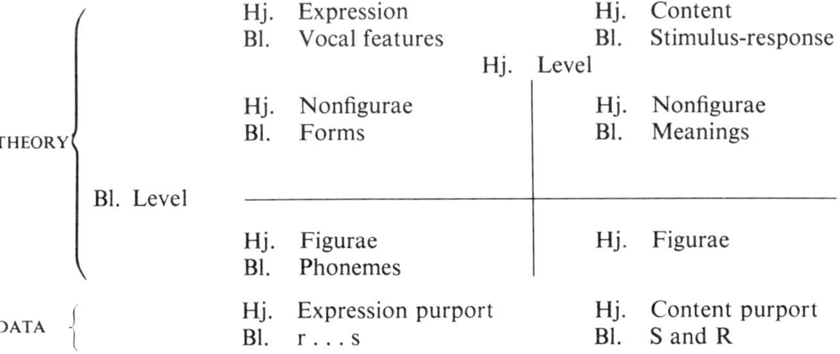

		Hj. Expression		Hj. Content	
		Bl. Vocal features		Bl. Stimulus-response	
			Hj. Level		
		Hj. Nonfigurae		Hj. Nonfigurae	
THEORY		Bl. Forms		Bl. Meanings	
	Bl. Level				
		Hj. Figurae		Hj. Figurae	
		Bl. Phonemes			
DATA		Hj. Expression purport		Hj. Content purport	
		Bl. r . . . s		Bl. S and R	

Unlike the formal hierarchy in which morphemes exhibit partial samenesses in terms of morphemes alone, the hierarchy of meaning ends with sememes. Sememes do not exhibit partial samenesses analogous to the phonological shapes of morphemes. In Hjelmslevian terms, the claim is that there are no content figurae, and there are no synonyms (Bloomfield 1933: 145).

Having made this comparison we should emphasize that strictly the terms of different theories are not comparable. (Cf. Scheffler 1967, Chapter 4, esp. pp. 82–84., where this constitutes incommensurability on the first-order level.) Terms within each theory defined in terms of the primitives of each theory present no basis for direct comparison. Strictly, we cannot equate patterning of figurae directly with patterning of phonemes any more than we can compare a pencil with love. We can compare and contrast theories on the basis of things they have in common: in terms of the operational explanatory dichotomy, the taxonomic-nontaxonomic dichotomy, the realism-descriptivism-instrumentalism distinction, that is, externally with respect to scientific methodology. This is Scheffler's (1967: 83) comparison as the second-order level. Among the kinds of comparisons we may make this way is comparison of data; we assume we have some theory-free way of talking about those data. This comparison of Hjelmslev's and Bloomfield's theories is based on the observation of comparable data; that is, there is an overlap in the data recorded by Hjelmslev's nonlinguistic science (and accounted for by expression) and the data recorded by Bloomfield's phonetics (and accounted for by phonology). Given such overlaps, what we have compared above are the differing places each theoretician asserts patterning; the allotment of the common data to portions of the theories is such that the lines of allotment cross one another.

Summary

We have identified the data of Bloomfieldian theory, observed certain patterns within those data, and provided a theoretical framework to account for those patterns. The primitives of the theory are:

1. *Speech-act:*   This is actually a complex of primitives. It includes a technique for segmenting the r . . . s continuum into vocal features and an analogous technique applicable to the S and R context yielding features of stimulus-response.
2. *Made-up-of*
3. *Linearity*
4. *Nonlinearity*
5. *Conjunction*
6. *Selection:*   This is another complex of primitives, including reciprocal, nonreciprocal, and implication.
7. *Replace*

8. *Add*
9. *Delete*

In the following set of definitions based on these primitives we omit "speech community" and "language" as expressing the assumption common to all science: that the data are patterned. The term "language" can still be applied to data, namely, those sets of data to which the definitions are applicable. The definitions required to delimit the set of possible languages are the following:

1. *Identity* (= distinctive) *and nonidentity* (= nondistinctive): Unspecified. Cf. the discussion on pages 108–10.
2. *Phoneme:* Defined as a distinctive vocal feature (segment) that is not made up of two or more distinctive vocal features (segments).
3. *Form:* Defined as an identity of phonemes corresponding to identities of stimulus-response features within a speech act.
4. *Position:* Defined as the relation of linear conjunction a form or phoneme holds with other forms or phonemes, respectively. For example, two forms that hold linear conjunction to the same forms (the latter in the same linear order) occupy an identical position.
5. *Construction:* Defined as identities of linear conjunction of positions. In the absence of partial identities of constructions and paradigmatic description, the relationship among the positions of a construction is reciprocal implication.
6. *Constructional hierarchy:* Defined by two or more constructions such that one or more positions of one construction are made up of positions that constitute a second construction. A constructional hierarchy may have two or more "stages" or "size-levels."
7. *Phonological construction:* Defined as a construction whose positions are filled by phonemes.
8. *Phonological constructional hierarchy:* Defined as constructional hierarchy whose constructions are phonological constructions.
9. *Phonological class:* Defined as the nonlinear conjunction of phonemes that occupy identical positions within one or more phonological constructions.
10. *Phonological subclass:* Defined as the members of a phonological class that are nonidentical with the remainder of that class because of the nonidentical selection they hold with one or more members of a nonidentical phonological class.
11. *Grammatical construction:* Defined as a construction whose positions are filled by forms.
12. *Grammatical constructional hierarchy:* Defined as a constructional hierarchy whose constructions are grammatical constructions.
13. *Morpheme:* Defined as a form that is not made up of two or more forms.
14. *Form class:* Defined as the set of morphemes that occupy identical positions within one or more grammatical constructions.
15. *Grammatical subclass:* Defined as the members of a form class that are nonidentical with the remainder of that class because of the nonidentical selection they hold with one or more members of a nonidentical form class.

16. *Grammar:*   Defined as the nonlinear conjunction of the grammatical constructions and constructional hierarchies.
17. *Lexicon:*   Defined as the nonlinear conjunction of the morphemes identified by its stimulus-response features (= sememe), form class and grammatical subclass membership, and a single linear conjunction of phonemes (= basic form).
18. *Phonetic modification:*   The relation of replace, add, and/or delete holding between the basic forms of the morphemes and their phonological shape in positions of a construction and linearly related to other morphemes.
19. *Phonology:*   Defined as including statements of phonetic modification; phonological constructions and constructional hierarchies of the patterns of the actual phonological shapes of morphemes; and the phonemes ordered by their membership in phonological classes and subclasses.

We have so far ignored one kind of pattern—substitution—and have not included it in the summary of Bloomfieldian theory. It appears in Bloomfield 1933 (Chapter 15) but not Bloomfield 1926. Substitution involves relationships among subclasses of form classes. As example, some subclass of Nouns, human-masculine-singular, may hold a relationship to a single morpheme *he*, which carries the meaning of the human-masculine-singular subclass such that under "certain conventional conditions" (Bloomfield 1933: 247) the term *he* "replaces" (Bloomfield 1933: 249) any member of the first subclass. In such sentences as *Ask that policeman and he will tell you* or *Stop that man who saw the accident*, *he* replaces a second occurrence of *that policeman* in the first sentence and *who* replaces *that man* in the second. The "conventional conditions" would determine whether the replacing morpheme is *he* or *who*. This substitution relationship seems to imply the occurrence at some point in the accounting of the sequences **Ask that policeman and that policeman will tell you* and **Stop that man that man saw the accident*, in which one term (subclass member) is obligatorily replaced by another. Notice, however, that what is replaced is not a single morpheme but a complex form that exemplifies a two-or-more-positioned construction. Such relationships are pointed out but not elaborated. We have not included such possible patterns within the theory above. If it were included, it would expand the nontaxonomic portion of the theory, giving it an outline as follows:

Grammar and lexicon yield the

Basic syntactic forms which yield via

    replace

Variant syntactic forms consisting of basic phonological forms which yield via

    replace, *add*, and *delete*

Variant phonological forms

The relationship among the basic syntactic forms established by filling the positions of a construction and the variant syntactic forms is analogous to the relationship among basic forms and the variant, occurring forms. If included, it would modify the selection statements existing between subclasses in the lexicon. The work of these statements would in part be converted to statements of substitution. Such substitution forms as *he*, *who*, and so on, occur outside the substitution conditions illustrated, as in the sentences *He drank my beer* and *Who did it?* These examples show that the substitution forms are not entirely predictable in their occurrence and require their own entry in the lexicon. In the substitution position they occur with antecedents, and in their unpredictable positions they occur without antecedents. In the former position they are termed *dependent* and in the latter, *independent* (Bloomfield 1933: 249). Within the framework we have outlined, we can account for this type of pattern by selection. In certain constructions in which the position class Noun occurs twice, certain subclasses within the first occurrence, such as *that policeman* or *the man*, select a particular subclass with the second Noun position, *he* or *who*. The exact conditions again remain unspecified.

An accounting within the theory would consist of the following:

1. A definition of the phonemes
2. A definition of the forms
3. A definition of the phonological constructions
4. A definition of the phonological constructional hierarchies
5. A definition of the phonological classes and subclasses
6. A definition of the grammatical constructions
7. A definition of the grammatical constructional hierarchies
8. A definition of the morphemes
9. A definition of the form classes and the grammatical subclasses
10. A definition of a lexicon
11. A definition of the relationships of phonetic modification
12. An interpretation of the phonemes and the constructions, positions, form classes, grammatical subclasses, and morphemes associating them with the phonetic or stimulus-response record
13. An evaluation of (1)–(12) with respect to exactness, simplicity, compactness, etc.
14. A reworking of (1)–(12) such that (13) is maximally satisfied

The above two-level interpretation of Bloomfieldian theory is primarily that of Bloomfield 1926. In Bloomfield 1933 the framework is modified with respect to the levels. The following observations are the basis of that modification. In discussing patterns of forms and phonemes, we have pointed out certain similarities between the two levels in that construction-like, form class-like, and subclass-like things were required to express form and phoneme patterns. Bloomfield notes an additional similarity. First, morphemes, which correspond to some meaning, consist of phonemes, which do not correspond to some meaning. Meaningful things consist of meaningless things. In analogous fashion, meaningful things occur in grammar: the constructions and positions. We may adopt the view that

> (a)   morpheme is to phoneme as
>
> (b)   grammar is to X.

To fill out the proportion we need to find meaningless things of which constructions consist. These meaningless things are order, selection (expanded to include the notion of form class, subclass, as well as selection in our narrower sense), phonetic modification, and modulation (Bloomfield 1933: 163–69). We have already discussed the first three. Modulation consists of the sets of secondary phonemes (pitch and stress contours) that may accompany an utterance. These meaningless elements are assumed to combine in different ways to define the meaningful constructions. The meaningless items are *taxemes* and their meaningful combinations are *tagmemes* (Bloomfield 1933: 166–67). Thus

> (a)   morpheme is to phoneme as
>
> (b)   tagmeme is to taxeme.

This reorganizes the patterns of the theory such that grammar (b) consists of statements of taxemes and tagmemes, and the lexicon (a) consists of the preceding lexicon (modified by the substraction of form class, subclass, and selection statements) and phonology.

The relation between the two levels is not mediated by made-up-of (as in our interpretation), since taxemes, the minimum terms of grammar, do not consist of morphemes. In this formulation of levels, the relation between grammar and lexicon is made by morphemes filling positions (Bloomfield 1933: 266). The interlevel relationship is not further specified.

Of the two following theories we will take up, the post-Bloomfieldian is essentially an elaboration of Bloomfieldian theory as we have interpreted it, namely, Bloomfield 1926 with the operational emphasis of Bloomfield 1933. The second, tagmemic theory, developed primarily by K. L. Pike, elaborates the Bloomfield 1933 grammar-lexicon distinction into a grammar-lexicon-phonology theory of language.

ADDITIONAL READING

BLOOMFIELD, LEONARD. 1926. "A set of postulates for the science of language." *Language* 2. 153–64.

———. 1933. *Language*. New York: Henry Holt and Company.

————. 1939a. *Linguistic Aspects of Science (= International Encyclopedia of Unified Science, Vol. 1, No. 4)*. Chicago: The University of Chicago Press.

————. 1939b. "Menomini morphophonemics." *Travaux du Cercle Linguistique de Prague* 8. 105–15.

HOCKETT, CHARLES F., ed. 1970. *A Leonard Bloomfield Anthology*. Bloomington: Indiana University Press.

CHAPTER 5

Post-Bloomfieldian Theory

Post-Bloomfieldian theory is in fact not a single theory but a cluster of distinct, closely related theories that are based on the work of Leonard Bloomfield. Their development is the work of many people since the mid-1930's. As we proceed, we will see points of divergence and will indicate, where possible, the assumptions that underly the differences. Finally, for the sake of exposition, we will arbitrarily select a particular variant and consider it to be post-Bloomfieldian theory, while emphasizing that there are several.

In Bloomfieldian theory the association of definitions with operations is an ideal not realized in any detail. In the development of an operational constraint on theory it is important that the order of definitions within the theory conform to the sequence of performable operations. If one operation or experiment presupposes a second, the definition associated with the presupposed operation must precede the definition associated with the presupposing operation. The nonoperational character of the theoretical framework of Bloomfield 1926 is indicated not only by the assumption of the identity relation, but also by the sequence of the definitions. The definition of form presupposes identities of vocal features (phonemes), but precedes the definition (and operation, if such is intended) that yields them. If the sequence of operations is indicated by the order of chapters (phonology, then grammar) in Bloomfield 1933, then the definition of form preceding phoneme is not consistent with an operationally constrained theory. Post-Bloomfieldian theory differs from Bloomfieldian primarily in the elaboration of these operations, and it is important that the sequence of definitions conform to the sequence of possible operations. The content of these techniques for handling assumed language data is important, for Bloomfieldian theory is modified at several points, and these modifications are often the result of the patterns implied by the operations. Pattern in language must be such that applicable operations are associated with it. If the operations adopted yield a pattern different from that within Bloomfieldian theory, a corresponding alteration is made in the theory. The data of both Bloomfieldian and post-Bloomfieldian theory remain the same (cf. Hockett 1942: 3–4; 1948a; and 1958: 322).

It should perhaps be reemphasized here that the operational constraint on possible theory is intended to preserve objectivity or testability of the theory and individual accountings. What we actually do in constructing an accounting need not follow the prescribed operations step by step (Hockett 1949: 49–50). We may use whatever means we want in attaining an accounting, but it should always be *possible* to reach that accounting via the operations. Simply, each accounting must be one permitted by the theory; how we find it, by whatever "shortcuts" (Bloch 1948: 5), is our own business. A necessary concern with the physical activity involved in constructing an accounting and the consistency of this activity with the theory arises only when the theory has an operational constraint. In an explanatory theory, the activity of writing has no potential effect on the theory itself.

Operations and Phonemics

The operations of post-Bloomfieldian theory are such that grammatical operations and grammatical pattern presuppose phonemic operations and phonemic pattern. The reverse sequence is entirely possible and consistent with the notion of an operational theory, but it is contingent on the development of the necessary operations. Given the nature of the proposed techniques, we take up first the discussion of the sound pattern of language.

The framework for the statement of this pattern and an instance of it in a description of some language is termed *phonemics* (Trager 1949: 5). The level of phonemics in a language plus its interpretation as a set of phonetic data is *phonology* (Trager 1949: 5). The interpretative statements are sometimes called the *phonetic system* (Hockett 1958: 138). We will use the term "phonetics" for the technique intended for recording the speech continuum.

Bloomfieldian and post-Bloomfieldian theory (Hockett 1958: 142) assume that the data are structured or that structure may be predicated of the data and expressed as a set of elements holding a fixed set of relationships. In terms of these relationships, the operations must first provide us with information about the identity and nonidentity of units of sound patterns and at the same time provide a basis for defining those units. We begin the construction of our operations by examining the results of our phonetics, sets of *phones* (Hockett

1942: 8–9), and determining the relationships that may exist among them. Let us take as an example the following utterances:

[tuwí·t']   [tuwé·t']   [tuwέ·t']

Let us consider the phones [í·] [é·] and [έ·]. We first see that they occur in an identical phonetic environment and relate them in pairs holding this relationship. If we sharpen our technique by listening carefully, we will increase the number of phones in this environment to an extent limited only by our powers of observation. Thus, we may find in this same phonetic environment [í·], [í·ˇ], [é·ˆ], [é·], [é·ˇ], [έ·ˆ], [έ·], and [έ·ˇ]. Clearly, in defining a structure (here, language), we must be capable of characterizing the terms entering into it, or it will not be well-defined. The potentially infinite variation must have limits placed on it, which is accomplished in the following way. Let us associate some meaning (supplied to us as data by our assumed record of stimulus-response) with each of the utterances:

[tuwí·t']	'great hunter'
[tuwí·ˇt']	'great hunter'
[tuwé·ˆt']	'great hunter'
[tuwé·t']	'great hunter'
[tuwé·ˇt']	'great hunter'
[tuwέ·ˆt']	'who?'
[tuwέ·t']	'who?'
[tuwέ·ˇt']	'who?'

Next, we revise our notion of possible relationship existing among phones and distinguish two ways of relating them. The first is based on the coincidence of two observations: (1) the two phones occur in the same phonetic environment, and (2) the meanings of the utterances in which they occur (each phone plus its environment) are distinct. The second relationship is based on determining that (1) the two phones occur in the same phonetic environment, and (2) the meanings of the utterances in which they occur have the same meaning. In these terms, [í·], [í·ˇ], [é·ˆ], [é·], and [é·ˇ] as pairs, exhibit the second relationship, as do [έ·ˆ], [έ·] and [έ·ˇ]. If we take pairs made up of a member of the first set and a member of the second set, we find that they exhibit the first relationship.

The assumptions of these relationships require no grammatical operation. We presuppose speech acts recorded phonetically plus information of associated stimulus-responses. This association of meaning is to an utterance and not to any subpart of that utterance. We do not require information about forms, morphemes, or any other term derived from grammatical operations.

In practice, an utterance may turn out to be a minimum form or morpheme if grammatical operations are applied, but this result is fortuitous and irrelevant for our observations here.

The two relationships we have identified may be made criteria for identity such that phones related by the first relationship are nonidentical and phones related by the second relationship are identical. They are named respectively, *contrast* (Trager and Bloch 1941: 223; Bloch and Trager 1942: 38; and Hockett 1942: 9) and *free variation* (Bloch and Trager 1942: 42 and Hockett 1942: 7). In terms of these relations we may first define phoneme as a class of phones in free variation. The phones so related are called *allophones* (Bloch 1941: 278 and Trager and Bloch 1941: 223) with respect to the single phoneme to which they are related. A phoneme is a *class* of phonetic data (Trager and Bloch 1941: 223; Bloch and Trager 1942: 40; Hockett 1942: 9; and Bloch 1948: 36). The definition of a phoneme as a class differs from its definition within Bloomfieldian theory. In Bloomfieldian theory, a phoneme is a composite of phonetic properties—a minimum unit of a distinctive *sound* feature—which, when interpreted, implies a set of phonetically distinct elements. A Bloomfieldian phoneme is a phonetic object in the same way that the vocal features from which it is abstracted are phonetic. A phoneme in Bloomfieldian theory is selected portions of that phonetic record, and it has a minimal interpretation implicit within the properties it contains, even if no additional statements of interpretation are added. The phoneme in post-Bloomfieldian theory differs in that it is *not* a phonetic thing. The phonetic data are records of events or occurrences, and we may say that phones occur. But a phoneme as a class of events (Bloch 1948: 36) does not occur as data occur. The symbols used to label the phonemes of a set of data, unlike phonetic symbols, do not have empirical content; they are "symbols for enclosure between solidi" (Hockett 1947b: 258). A phoneme determines a set of data occurrences only when interpreted. Without that interpretation—and ignoring the operations that yielded it—a phoneme implies no data; not being a phonetic object, it has of itself no interpretation. Empirical content is provided by a separate set of statements associating phonemes with data. The operations associated with the definition of phoneme function here to ensure that such statements are available, for in the history of an accounting, it is through such statements that the set of phonemes is derived.

Let us consider what such a preliminary definition presupposes. In choosing to perform our operations on phones, we have assumed a technique that divides a sequence of continuous sound into segments such that we may identify some as physical recurrences; we assume phonetic identity. We have, for example, assumed that the phonetic environments of our phones under consideration were identical. Assuming a phonetics alone is not sufficient to determine contrast and free variation. We require information of samenesses and differences of utterances, information provided by what we may call a technique of stimulus-response. This technique may consist either of observing the stimulus-response or bio-social environment of sound and the identification of some portions as recurrent sames and others as different; or our technique may consist, in abbreviated form, of simply inquiring of the speaker(s) of the language whether a pair of successive sound sequences "mean" the same or do not. With these two techniques and their product taken as primitives and our operations that yield observations about pairs of phones, we may tentatively define contrast, free variation, and phoneme as above.

Returning to a consideration of possible relationships between phones, we find a third. Given the following data from a Salish language,

[kɛ́·lʌc]	'many'	[ɬqǽ·t']	'wide, to widen'
[tɛ́·ʔ]	'grandmother'	[qǽ·pɛt']	'to tie something'
[lɛ́·lʌm]	'house'	[θqǽ·t']	'tree'

let us determine the relationship of the pair [ɛ·] and [ǽ·]. Here we find two phones that do not occur in identical phonetic environments, and neither of our two relationships are applicable. If we were to expand the number of utterances, it would turn out that [ǽ·] always occurs after [q] or a phone articulated in postvelar position in the vocal tract, while [ɛ·] always occurs in other phonetic environments. Our operations are as yet incapable of handling these data. On the basis of such observations, we establish a third possible relationship defined by occurrence in complementary phonetic environments and term it *complementary distribution* (Trager and Bloch 1941: 223 and Hockett 1942: 9). The definition of this relationship in terms of complementary phonetic environments is sufficient to distinguish it from our first two relationships, and we need to make no mention of meaning associated with utterances in its characterization.

At this point, we must decide how complementary distribution is to be integrated with our definition of phoneme, that is, whether it is a criterion for identity or nonidentity of phones. In this respect let us consider two pairs of phones from an English example: [ǽ:] and [ǽ] and [h] and [ŋ]. We take the following utterances as typical of their occurrence

[hǽt]	'hat'	[ɹǽːŋ]	'rang'
[hǽč]	'hatch'	[bǽːŋ]	'bang'
[hǽk]	'hack'	[sǽːŋ]	'sang'
[hǽːd]	'had'	[hǽːŋ]	'hang'
[hǽːg]	'hag'	[gǽːŋ]	'gang'

and observe that [h] occurs initially and [ŋ], finally. Although these two phones are in complementary distribution, they are not classed together as allophones (e.g., Trager and Bloch 1941: 229). The phone [ǽ] occurs before phonetically voiceless stop consonants; [æ:] occurs before voiced consonants. This pair, like the preceding, are in complementary distribution, but they *are* classed as allophones of the same phoneme (e.g., Trager and Bloch 1941: 229–30). The contradictory treatment of the two pairs is resolved with respect to a fourth relationship that may hold between phones: their *phonetic similarity*.

We have assumed that our phonetics provides us with a segmentation of data and information of the samenesses or differences of those segments. Now we require that our phonetics give us information in addition to identity or nonidentity. We assume that phones may be partially alike, sharing some properties and differing in others, which implies that phonetic segments are a complex of simultaneous or overlapping properties. If we do not accept this characterization of our phonetics, we can determine only the phonetic identity or nonidentity of atomic units. Our phonetics is accordingly modified to provide segments that are complexes of phonetic properties. The properties are identified via parameters of articulation as opposed to those of physical sound or aural impression (Bloch 1948: 9). One of these parameters is obstruction of a movement of air in the vocal tract, from complete obstruction to its absence. Intersecting this, there is a second parameter of position of obstruction, from bilabial to glottal. At each position, we may break the continuum of the parameter of obstruction into a discrete set ranging from complete obstruction (stops) to a movement toward or away from complete obstruction (glides). Each of these may co-occur with glottal vibration (voice) or without it, or with the velum lowered or closed. The group of possible sounds articulated without obstruction (vowels) may be further divided by the intersecting parameter of tongue position from close to open and from front to back and the rounding or spreading of the lips. Certain of the possible choices from these sets of articulation possibilities is designated by one of a set of symbols constituting a phonetic alphabet (Pike 1947c: 246). Additional secondary articulations are possible. Consonants may be rounded, aspirated, palatalized, pharyngalized, glottalized, implosive, and so on. Vowels may be nasalized, pharyngalized, long, accented, voiceless, and the like. Each of these secondary articulations is denoted by the appropriate alphabetic symbol plus a diacritic indicating an additional element in the articulation. Diacritics may also be used with alphabetic symbols to indicate a value along one of the primary parameters that is intermediate between two points provided with a letter from the phonetic alphabet. Thus, if [t] indicated an alvealar stop, [ṭ] might indicate a retracted, calcuminal articulation falling in position between [t] and [č] (an alveo-palatal affricate). In this way it is possible in principle to provide every distinguishable articulation with a distinct symbol. Now, phones may be distinct phonetically without being completely different if they share one or more same values along the same parameters. Increasing numbers of shared same values of parameters indicate increasing phonetic similarity between two phones.

Returning to the contradictory treatment of two pairs of complementarily distributed phones, we now find that the phones [h] and [ŋ] share a phonetic property of obstruction, but differ in the degree of obstruction as well as in values for position, voice, and nasality. We term them dissimilar; [æ̆] and [æ̆ː] are similar, differing only in degree of length while sharing the same values for obstruction (both are vowels), tongue height (open), tongue position (front), lip configuration (spread), and stress. In like fashion, the two phones [é·] and [æ̆·] from the preceding example differ only in the degree of tongue height. They are phonetically similar.

The relationship we find operationally useful is not complementary distribution, but complementary distribution plus phonetic similarity or phonetic dissimilarity. We may alter the conditions of identity to make it equivalent to the relationship of free variation or complementary distribution plus phonetic similarity. Nonidentity is equivalent to contrast or complementary distribution plus phonetic dissimilarity. The definition of phoneme is elaborated as a class of phones that are in free variation or in complementary distribution and are phonetically similar.

Operations and Economy

In considering the third relationship of complementary distribution to be associated with a valid operation, we have assumed two things. First, we have assumed that the phones in different environments are comparable in principle. Recall that Hjelmslevian theory did not permit the comparison or identity of terms not first-degree components of the same class; the commutation test presupposed this condition and did not extend to cases analogous to complementary distribution. That we do want to compare such data in post-Bloomfieldian theory is expressed in the criterion of *economy* (Hockett 1942: 9). Hjelmslevian theory was constructed such that analogous classes or components in complementary distribution were in principle not comparable; post-Bloomfieldian theory is constructed on operations that permit that comparison. The second assumption underlying their comparison is the grid of phonetic similarity that serves as a basis for that comparison.

The criterion of economy is not peculiar to the definition of identity and nonidentity; it is the underlying scientific criterion of simplicity of accounting that motivates our search for such definitions. These definitions of identity and nonidentity function as constraints on economy; the performance of the operations associated with them inform us where economy is lacking and where identifications are to be made or where such identification cannot be made.

We now examine economy (or simplicity or generality) of description in terms of the ease of statement of phonemic membership, taking as an example the hypothetical data of Swadesh (1935). We assume a language with the following vowel phones:

Environment   ...*CV*   ...*C*#

[i   ɪ

   e   ɛ

   ɛ   æ]

in which ≠ indicates a second consonant or the end of an utterance. The phones [i e ɛ] contrast in the phonetic environment ...CV (in open syllables), and [ɪ ɛ æ] contrast in ...C# (in closed syllables). Each of the phones in the first set is in complementary distribution with each of the second set. The relationship of phonetic similarity holds in its strongest form (phonetic identity) between [ɛ] in ...CV and [ɛ] in ...C#. If we assume that our phonetics also indicates a greater degree of closeness between [ɪ] and [i] than between [ɪ] and [e], then we might have the following phonemic inventory:

/i/   [i ɪ]

/e/   [e æ]

/ɛ/   [ɛ]

(We assume for the sake of argument that [e] and [æ] may be classed together. If not, the point of the example is not only still valid but reinforced.) In stating the complementarily distributed memberships of /i e ɛ/, we must make five distinct statements:

1. /i/ has a close front vowel allophone in open syllables *and* a slightly lower front vowel allophone in closed syllables;

2. /e/ has a half-close, front vowel allophone in open syllables *and* an open, front vowel allophone in closed syllables;

3. /ɛ/ has a half-open vowel allophone in all positions.

Statements (1) and (2) differ in that the degrees of increased openness in the closed syllables are not the same for both /i/ and /e/: say, one degree for /i/ and two for /e/. If, however, we classify phones as follows:

/i/   [i ɪ]

/e/   [e ɛ]

/ɛ/   [ɛ æ]

then a modified set of four statements predicting the membership can be made.

1. /i/ is a close, front vowel in open syllables;

2. /e/ is a half-close vowel in open syllables;

3. /ɛ/ is a half-open vowel in open syllables;

4. /i e ɛ/ are one degree more open in closed syllables than in open, respectively, [ɪ ɛ æ].

The reduced number of statements reflects a more economical description of the data with respect to the statement of members of phonemes, but we have violated phonetic similarity. The greatest degree of phonetic similarity (identity between [ɛ] in ...CV and [ɛ] in ...C#) has been ignored. To obtain this alternative solution we must modify what we mean by phonetically similar.

If we consider *relative* values for each position, namely, that in ...CV [i] is close relative to [e] and [ɛ]; that [e] is mid relative to [i] and [ɛ]; and that [ɛ] is open relative to [i] and [e], then we may also find in ...C# that [ɪ] is close with respect to [ɛ] and [æ]; that [ɛ] is mid with respect to [ɪ] and [æ]; and that [æ] is open with respect to [ɪ] and [ɛ]. In terms of these relative values, [i] and [ɪ] are both close, [e] and [ɛ] (in ...C#) are both mid, and [ɛ] (in ...CV) and [æ] are both open. On the basis of these relative (as opposed to absolute) similarities, we may class complementarily distributed phones as in the second description. The increase in economy of statement is reflected in the proportion i :ɪ :: e:ɛ :: ɛ:æ, in which the first members of the ratio occur in some same environment as do the second members, and the difference within each ratio is one degree of height. This proportion between the memberships of phonemes, maximized where possible (requiring an interpretation of phonetic similarity as relative and not absolute), is termed "parallelism of allophones" (Harris 1944: 200) or "phonetic symmetry" (Harris 1951: 68–71), or included under the term "pattern congruity" (Hockett 1955: 158).

This alternative interpretation of phonetic similarity provides a point of disagreement in post-Bloomfieldian theory. One of the implications of its acceptance is the permission of *partial overlapping* or *intersection,* and it is on this point that the disagreement is voiced. Trager and Bloch (1941: 223) and Bloch (1941: 281) permit it; Hockett (1942: 9) and Wells (1945: 27) do not permit it. Partial intersection exists when a phone [x] occurs in complementary environments (1) [a...b] and (2) [c...d] and is a member of class /P/ in (1), but a member of class /Q/ in (2). The phonemes partially overlap or intersect in their shared phone. The rejection of relative phonetic similarity leads to a rejection of partial intersection and the requirement of nonintersection of phoneme classes in their allophonic membership.

Furthermore, if two phones contrast in some position, say [e] and [ɛ] when they are not followed in the next syllable by a vowel, as in a variety of French: [metʁ] *maître* and [mɛtʁ] *mettre*. It follows from absolute phonetic similarity that all occurrences of [e] and [ɛ] are assigned to /e/ and /ɛ/, respectively, even if they are in complementary distribution in all phonetic positions except one. This additional result of absolute phonetic similarity is summarized in the maxim "Once a phoneme, always a phoneme." The choice of alternatives, absolute or relative phonetic similarity, has corollaries:

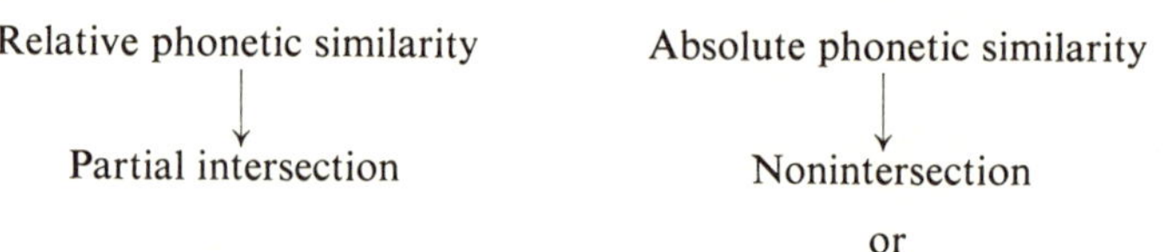

Relative phonetic similarity	Absolute phonetic similarity
↓	↓
Partial intersection	Nonintersection
	or
	"Once a phoneme, always a phoneme"

We have examined the criterion of economy as it affects (1) inventory and (2) the statement of membership of phonemes. Economy also interplays with the statement of distribution which allows the establishment of complementary distribution. Suppose that two phones [x] and [y] are in complementary distribution and are phonetically similar, but the statement of their complementarity requires a moderately long list of disparate phonetic environments, and further, that their statement applies only to the distribution of phones [x] and [y]. This condition contrasts with the relative simplicity of the statement of complementarity in our previous examples. Further along this scale, suppose that two phones occur in similar environments, but never in identical environments. Here contrast as defined does not hold; but if we chose to list the shape of each utterance, we might establish complementary distribution. At the extreme along this scale, suppose that the two phones are in contrast, as defined. Complementation of a kind could be established if we list the utterance meaning as a conditioning factor; that is, [x] (manifesting phoneme /P/) occurs in some utterance meaning one thing, while [y] (manifesting phoneme /P/) occurs in an utterance having some second distinct meaning. Here we find a scale of complementarity determined by economy. Economy of identity of units conflicts with the decreasing economy of the statement of complementary distribution permitting that identity.

<table>
<tr><td>

I

[x] in env. [p];

[y] elsewhere and several other pairs of phones are in complementary distribution described by the same statement [p] vs. non-[p], e.g., [p'] : [p], [t'] : [t], and [k'] : [k] in English.

</td><td>

II

[x] in env.'s [p], [q], [r], and [s];

[y] elsewhere and the statement of complementary distribution describes only the relationship of [x] and [y], e.g., the allophones of /a/ in Swahili (Harris 1951: 123).

</td></tr>
<tr><td>

III

[x] in env. [P];

[y] elsewhere, where [P] is a list of one hundred plus disparate phonetic environments, e.g., [ž] and [ǯ] in English (cf. Hockett 1958: 17–22).

</td><td>

IV

[x] in env. P;

[y] elsewhere, where P is a list of meanings distinguishing a phonetic environment that is otherwise identical with the phonetic environments in which [y] occurs.

</td></tr>
</table>

In I through IV, the general criterion of economy of phonemes is served by the identification of [x] and [y] in each case; but as we progress from I to IV, the price of that economy is increasing lack of economy elsewhere in the accounting, namely, in the statement of complementarity permitting economy of units.

Situation IV differs in kind from the first three. It permits the least amount of economy in the statement of complementarity and furthermore, unlike the first three cases, the conditioning factor is meaning. The stimulus-response record associated with [x] and its phonetic environments differs from those associated with [y] and its phonetic environments. This property of IV, if allowed, would be equivalent to denying a sound pattern in language. All phonetic segments of each utterance would be predictable in terms of meanings; the phonetic properties of utterances and the level of phonemics would be redundant. There would exist no level within the theory in terms of which the partial phonetic sameness of utterances might be expressed. The assumption of a pattern of utterances expressed as partial identities of sound (that is, a level of phonemics) is rationale for the exclusion of statements exemplified in IV from the set of acceptable statements of complementary distribution. The statement of complementarity *must* be in terms of phonetic environment. If statements of complementarity exist only in terms of IV, they are rejected. In phonetic terms, IV is in fact contrast.

Situations I-III are opposed to IV in that the statements of complementarity are made wholly in phonetic terms. There is, however, a distinction to be made among them. Situations I and II are opposed to III; III, like IV, is rejected as an acceptable statement of complementary distribution. The rejection of III is not based on the same objections voiced against IV, but follows from the application of the criterion of economy. The economy effected by the identity of [x] and [y] permitted by the statement of complementary distribution in III is outweighed by the complexity of that statement. Although distinct from IV in principle, III is also called contrast (Bloch 1950: 90), and the definition of contrast is now altered to include the occurrence of two phones in identical (IV) or similar (III) phonetic environments.

With this, we face the problem of determining the point at which dissimilarity of phonetic environment (defining complementary distribution) fades into similarity (defining contrast). Put differently, we must determine a scale of economy in such a way that we can recognize instances in which economy of identity is outweighed by the complexity of the statement of complementarity permitting that identity. Within our operations we require a measure of economy; without this, our operations permit two or more possible descriptions for a single set of data. We return to this general problem in the discussion of operations and evaluative criteria.

Acceptance of the principle of contrast as a relationship of nonidentity is reflected by the universal rejection of what is called *complete overlapping* or *complete intersection* (Bloch 1941). The problem of the preceding paragraphs concerned instances in which identity could not hold between two phones. Complete intersection involves a situation in which identity must be made; it exists when a single phone [x] occurs in an environment [a...b] and in some instances is considered to be a member allophone of /P/ and in others an allophone of /Q/. If we compare our possible relationships in their distributional aspects,

	Complementary Distribution		Contrast		Ignoring Contrast		Complete Intersection	
Phoneme Class	/P/		/P/	/Q/	/P/		/P/	/Q/
Phones in	[x]	[y]	[x]	[y]	[x]	[y]	[x]	[x]
Environment	[a...b]	[c...d]	[a...b]	[a...b]	[a...b]	[a...b]	[a...b]	[a...b]

we can see that complete intersection is the converse of ignoring contrast. In the latter, two phones have been (incorrectly) identified as allophones of a single phoneme; in the former, two occurrences of a single phone have been (incorrectly) not identified and assigned to two different phonemes. Contrast is rejected as a relationship of identity because such an interpretation of it denies the possibility of a level of sound patterning within the theory. The rejection of complete intersection can be based on the same argument. Given the Russian utterances and phonemic description:

Phonetic Data	Stimulus-response Data	Phonemic Description
[nʌgá]	'naked (fem. sg.)'	/nagá/
[nák]	'naked (masc. sg.)'	/nák/
[nʌgá]	'foot'	/nogá/
[nók]	'feet (gen. pl.)'	/nók/

the phonemic class /a/ and /o/ completely overlap in [ʌ] in the environment [n...gá]. To determine the phoneme of which [ʌ] is an allophone in this environment, we require the meaning associated with each utterance. The phone [ʌ] is assigned to the phonemic class /a/ when it occurs in the environment [n...gá] if the utterance is associated with the meaning 'naked (fem. sg.)'; if the associated meaning is 'foot', then [ʌ] is assigned to /o/. This is a perfectly performable operation with the data we have assumed: a phonetic record and a stimulus-response record associated with the phonetic record of speech acts. But as in the case in which contrast was ignored, the prediction is in terms of stimulus-response, not in terms of the phonetic environment. The existence of sound pattern is again denied. When contrast is ignored, the phonetic record is predicted in terms of meaning associated with the utterance; and when complete overlap is permitted, the attribution of phones to phonemes is in terms of specific meanings associated with the phonetic record of the utterance. If these two relationships are rejected, the prediction of the phonetic record is in terms of phonemes in an environment of phonemes; and the attribution of phones to phonemes is in terms of phones in a phonetic environment. These last statements are the level of sound pattern ignored by the admission of complete overlap and ignoring contrast.

Another argument against complete intersection is the claim that it assumes an operation that has not yet been performed. A phonemic operation assumes a grammatical operation. This argument is applicable in instances such as the following. Let us assume our same four Russian utterances, and additionally, that each of them is a part of larger utterances and that the added portions differ in each of the four cases. Now we can no longer say [ʌ] is assigned to the phonemic class /a/ when the utterance is associated with the meaning 'naked (fem. sg.)', because the complete utterance has in addition, some remaining meaning associated with it. Identifying that *portion* of the utterance that is associated with the meaning 'naked (fem. sg.)' is a grammatical operation, and the result of this operation is what is required to make the assignment correctly. Here the statement is that [ʌ] is assigned to the phonemic class /a/ if it occurs in a particular position of a *portion* of a larger utterance and has the given meaning. This is also true of the phone when the associated meaning is 'foot' and the whole is a part of a larger utterance. Some grammatical operation is required to identify that portion that is associated with that meaning. Here the operation of assignment is circular in that a phonemic operation presupposes a grammatical one; this contradicts the supposed sequence of applicable operations, and such are rejected. The argument against complete intersection is usually based on these observations of possible circularity (Hockett 1949 and 1951).

The rejection of complete intersection as a possible accounting consistent with the theory is expressed by the requirement that accountings be *bi-unique* (Hockett 1951: 340. Cf. also Harris 1951: 72). The bi-uniqueness of accountings is attained by constraining our operations to the use of nonidentities and identities of meaning and excluding use of the actual specification of the associated stimulus-response record (Hockett 1949: 46). Having done so, we can determine that the utterance environment of [ʌ] is the same in two instances, but we cannot assign the phone to /o/ or /a/ without using the specific meaning, either 'foot' or 'naked (fem. sg.)'. Bi-uniqueness is not a condition that has to be stated separately within the theory. It follows directly from our operations (using only identities or nonidentities of meaning) and the definitions of the theory, constrained such that they are associated with the operations plus the general requirement that accountings be logically consistent with the theory from which they are derived. Nonbi-unique descriptions are such that they cannot in principle be attained by the operations associated with the theory, and therefore are not a possible description within the theory. They are logically inconsistent with post-Bloomfieldian theory.

Notice that a theory that allows partial overlapping, as well as a theory that disallows it, meets the criterion of bi-uniqueness. The operational criterion of noncircular bi-uniqueness is met by both variants. The distinction between them turns on whether one requires phonetic symmetry or not, all other things being equal. There are no general distinctions to which we may relate this disagreement. Both variants of post-Bloomfieldian theory (admission and exclusion of partial intersection) meet the requirements of a possible operational theory. They simply differ at this point.

Operations and Evaluative Criteria

In the preceding sections we have given an outline of operations regarded as sufficient to a definition of phoneme. The operations are not such that a definition presupposing them admits only a single description for each set of data. Recall the discussion of the conflict of economy of inventory and economy of statement of complementary distribution and the resulting vagueness in the operations underlying the distinction between contrast and complementary distribution. This imprecision permits two or more ways of describing data. There are two ways of obviating an arbitrary choice between the alternatives. First, we may make the operations underlying contrast and complementary distribution more precise, further narrowing the definition of possible phoneme based on them such that for each set of data there is a single description. Second, we may add some way of evaluating the plurality of descriptions such that the preferred one is distinguished from all possible ones. The first solution requires that we specify what "phonetically similar" and "phonetically dissimilar" mean in the definitions of contrast and complementary distribution. We may look to a further refinement of our phonetics for this specification. The second solution requires that we establish an evaluative criterion of economy such that we can measure the relative worth of varying economy of inventory versus varying economy of statement of complementary distribution.

The same problem turns up at another point in the theory. Let us assume that our phonetics provides us with information of degrees of phonetic likeness and consider what happens should we find in our data a phone distributed complementarily with two or more phones that contrast, the phone being phonetically similar to all. We take as an example a problem in English (Trager and Bloch 1941). We observe in the following set of utterances

[pít]	'pit'	[pʊ́t]	'put'
[pét]	'pet'	[pʌ́t]	'put'
[pǽt]	'pat'	[kɔ́t]	'caught'
	[pát]	'pot'	

that the stressed vowels contrast and English must be described with at least seven vowel phonemes. As in the case of [æ]: [æː] from the previous English example, each phoneme will have allophones that differ in length according to the following consonant. In a second set of utterances, [bí^i̯t]   'beat'   [bʊ́^u̯t]   'boot'

[bé̜^ɪt]   'bait'   [bɔ́^o̯t]   'boat'

[bǽ̜t]   'bite'/[bǽo̯t]   'bout'

we observe stressed [ɪ^ ɛ^ a ʊ^ ɔ^] in complementary distribution with the previous set of seven stressed vowels. The phones of the second set of data occur
before nonsyllabic elements denoted by [˯]; the phones of the first set occur
before consonants with a greater degree of obstruction. Assuming phonetic
similarity, we may class them /i/ [ɪ ɪ^], /e/ [ɛ ɛ^], /a/ [a], /u/ [ʊ ʊ^], and /o/
[ɔ ɔ^]. Consideration of a third set yields

[bí^i̯]   'bee'   [bʊ́^u̯]   'boo'

[bé̜^ɪ̯]   'bay'   [bɔ́^o̯]   'bow (of a ribbon)'

[bǽ̜]   'buy'/[bǽo̯]   'bow (of a boat)'

and the stressed vowels are again grouped similarly to those of the second set.
The problem concerns the nonsyllabic [i̯ ɪ̯ e̯ u̯ o̯ o̯].

To further set the framework for a decision, we must consider a property
of phonemes and the level of phonemics. Bloomfield's assumption (1926:
157) that not all possible combinations of phonemes will occur in a language
has been taken over into post-Bloomfieldian theory. With respect to given
phonemic environments, phonemes will have varying degrees of similarity in
their privilege of occurrence. The co-occurrences are patterned, not random.
A complete description of the level of phonemics will consist of (1) the inventory of phonemes, (2) the statement of the members—allophones, and (3)
their distribution relative to one another. In expressing this third pattern, it
is going to be more economical and simpler if statements of distributions are
valid for the largest possible number of phonemes. In that distribution statements are valid for smaller numbers, an increasing number of separate statements will be required, and the description will be less economical in this
respect.

Let us now return to the example and consider some possible groupings
of the nonsyllabic phones. We might first class them with vowel phonemes in
the following way:

/i/   [ɪ ɪ^ i̯ e̯]   /u/   [ʊ ʊ^ u̯ o̯]

/e/   [ɛ ɛ^ ɪ̯]   /o/   [ɔ ɔ^ o̯]

/a/   [a]

Phones [ɪ ɪ^] are in complementary distribution with [i̯ e̯]; the former occur
stressed, the latter unstressed following a vowel. Phones [i̯] and [e̯] are also in
complementary distribution; [i̯] occurs after [ɪ^] and [e̯], after [a]. All four are
phonetically similar in terms of tongue fronting and lip spreading and tongue

height, mid-close or higher. With this description (cf., for example, Swadesh 1947), *bee, bay, buy, bow, boo,* and *bow* would be represented as /bíi/, /bée/, /bái/, /báu/, /búu/, and /bóo/, respectively.

An alternative description might group the phones as follows:

/i/	[ɪ ɪˆ ẹ]	/u/	[ʋ ʋˆ ǫ]
/e/	[ɛ ɛˆ]	/o/	[ɔ ɔˆ]
	/a/	[a]	
	/ː/	[ị ɪ ụ ʋ̣]	

The phoneme of length contains four phones distributed complementarily. The unrounded phones occur after unrounded stressed vowels; round phones occur after rounded stressed vowels. The close phones occur after close vowels; the more open phones occur after raised half-open vowels. All four share the phonetic properties of being nonsyllabic and of relatively close tongue height. The phones [ẹ] and [ǫ] contrast after [a] and must be allotted to separate classes; here, as before, to /i/ and /u/, respectively. Our six utterances in this description (cf., for example, Pike 1947b) would be represented as /bíː/ *bee,* /béː/ *bay,* /bái/ *buy,* /báu/ *bow,* /búː/ *boo,* and /bóː/ *bow.*

A third alternative involves the observation that the glides [j] and [w] as in [jés] *yes* and [wét] *wet* occur initially, but not finally before consonants or after vowels, and they are in complementary distribution with the nonsyllabic phones. Furthermore, [j] and [w] are nonsyllabic and share tongue position with the front and back nonsyllabic vowels, respectively. Glide [j] involves movement away from a close, front tongue position and [ị ɪ ẹ] share a non-open tongue position; they also share the property of lip spreading. Analogous statements hold for [w] and [ụ ʋ ǫ], and we may group our phones

/i/	[ɪ ɪˆ]	/u/	[ʋ ʋˆ]
/e/	[ɛ ɛˆ]	/o/	[ɔ ɔˆ]
	/a/	[a]	
/j/	[j ị ɪ ẹ]	/w/	[w ụ ʋ̣ ǫ]

and represent out utterances /bíj/ *bee,* /béj/ *bay,* /báj/ *buy,* /báw/ *bow,* /búw/ *boo,* and /bów/ *bow* (cf. Trager and Bloch 1941).

If it is assumed, as we have, that phonetic similarity indicates none of the three descriptions as preferable, then any of the three descriptions of English is permitted by our theory. The potential arbitrariness here may yield to either of the two alternatives we indicated at the beginning of this section. We can refine our phonetics such that the three descriptions differ with respect to phonetic similarity and one satisfies that relationship to a higher degree than the other two; or we may introduce the evaluative criterion of economy. Economy in this instance affects the statements of the distribution of phonemes; this is the fourth place in the theory in which economy has been employed. It may be formulated as requiring us to allot the phones to classes in such a way that the simplest statements of distribution of phonemes results. The application of the criterion would give a higher value to the third solution. If chosen, the description of stressed vowels is stated as occurrence before consonants, and the statement that obstruents occur initially and finally is extended to /j/ and /w/. The second description yields an additional phoneme /:/, which occurs only after vowels. The first yields small sets of phonemes in terms of occurrence; /i/ occurs after /i/ and /a/; /u/ occurs after /u/ and /a/; /e/ occurs after /e/; and /o/ occurs after /o/. All occur before consonants. The third description gains still higher value when utterances like [ló:] *law* and [pá:] *pa* are considered. After [a], [:] contrasts with /j/ [ę] and /w/ [ǫ], that is, [páę] *pie* and [páǫ] *pow*. One consonant with which [:] is in complementary distribution is [h]. If classed with /h/ [h:], representations such as /lóh/ *law* and /páh/ *pa* extend the statement that consonants occur initially and finally even further; /ŋ/ [ŋ], in its restricted occurrence, is the only exception. This criterion of economy in its application at this particular point within descriptions is termed *pattern congruity* (Swadesh 1934: 124; Twaddell 1935: 66; Trager and Bloch 1941: 229; Hockett 1942: 9; and Hockett 1955: 159).

There are different attitudes toward the use of pattern congruity in the theory. Haugen and Twaddell (1942: 235) disagree with the analysis of English proposed by Trager and Bloch (1941); "The additional concept of 'phonetic interrelationship' or 'pattern analysis' . . . seems to be little more than a covert appeal to the system that *is to be* established and therefore a circular argument." Similar disagreement may be found in Saporta 1956. The choice of admitting pattern congruity (and economy in general) or refusing it any status turns on whether we admit as possible theory one that exhibits evaluative criteria in addition to the operations, primitives, and definitions. The rejection of pattern congruity implies that we either accept the arbitrariness or we revise our techniques such that a single description results from their application to a set of data. The insistence is here that the operations be mechanical. Under this version of operationalism, evaluative criteria would have no status because they would not be required; the operations alone would be sufficient. If pattern congruity is introduced into a mechanically operational theory, it must be part of the operation on which phoneme is based, for there are no evaluative criteria. Inclusion of pattern congruity as defined (presupposing statements of distribution) as part of the operation yielding those distributed elements does produce a circularity. Pattern congruity is included in the operational basis of phoneme here, because the notion of possible theory provides for no other place for it; but it is part of that basis only because we have adopted an extreme notion of a mechanically operational theory. If we do not require the theory to be mechanically operational, we may include pattern congruity without contradiction; within this weaker version of the operational constraint the evaluative criterion need not be part of the operational basis of phoneme. Our operations yield a set of possible descriptions, and we evaluate and choose the most highly valued one in the manner of an explanatory theory. In this less constrained theory, the evaluative criterion plays no part in the operations nor in the definition of phoneme.

The previous indications of arbitrariness in the theory are subject to this same divergent opinion. They all turn on the refinement of the notion of phonetic similarity or the introduction of the evaluative criterion of economy. If we assume that a possible theory can be only one that is mechanically operational, then our only recourse is to increase the delicacy of our phonetics. This, in general, has not been done (cf., however, Austin 1957).

In instances in which a phone is in complementary distribution with two contrasting phones and is as phonetically similar to one as the other, it has been suggested (Hockett 1942: 10, fn.11 and Bloch 1950: 107) that a classification be made with neither. The phone is placed in a third class. Another suggestion is made by Harris (1944 and 1951), who develops an operation of "rephonemicization" involving segmentations of phones into simultaneous features and reallotting them such that the phonemic classes of "long components" result. The benefit of this operation is phonemes of freer distribution. The operation can, however, be arbitrary (Postal 1968: 93–94) within a mechanically operational assumption because it permits at least two descriptions of a set of data.

Evaluative Criteria and Juncture

We have seen that economy, simplicity, generality, or whatever we choose to call the evaluative criterion can apply at several points in a description: (1) the phoneme inventory, (2) the statements of the patterns of occurrence of the phonemes, (3) the statements interpreting the phonemes as allophones, and (4) the statements that express the complementary distribution of these allophones. The evaluative criterion applied at (1) is termed, simply, economy; applied at (2), it is called pattern congruity; at (3), it is allophonic parallelism; at (4), it has no name unless it be complementary distribution. The application of the evaluative criterion at one point in a description can yield less than maximal satisfaction of that same criterion at another point. We have seen that economy of inventory can conflict with economy of the statement of complementary distribution and with economy of the statement of the patterns of occurrence of phonemes. We take up now one last instance of economy.

Consider the following two pairs of utterances;

[ná·et‘ɹɛ̀^ɪ̩t]   'nitrate'   [ʔʌnɛ́^ɪ̩m]   'a name'

[náet·ɹɛ̀^ɪ̩t]   'night rate'   [ʔʌn·ɛ́^ɪ̩m]   'an aim'

The two pairs of phones [t'] and [t·] and [n] and [n·] are apparently in contrast. The phonetic environments of each are similar, and the utterances are associated with distinct meanings. Unlike Bloomfieldian theory, post-Bloomfieldian theory may not take advantage of the fact that word boundaries are present; we cannot claim that the pairs of phones are in complementary distribution with respect to a preceding or following morpheme boundary without assuming an unperformed grammatical operation. Our operational constraint apparently forces us to accept a phonemic class for each of the four phones. Numerous parallel examples may be adduced that quickly add to the number of contrasting phones and the number of phonemes (with restricted privilege of occurrence) necessary for the description of English.

In an attempt to avoid this conclusion, which is unsatisfactory from the point of view of both economy of inventory and pattern congruity, let us consider [t·] as simultaneous features of articulation. Recall that the alphabet symbols and diacritics are abbreviations for such. Let us take the unaspirated articulation and length of [t·] and assign it to a phonemic class, denote it /+/ ("plus") and write it to the right of the phonemic class to which the remainder of [t·] has been assigned. We treat the length of [n·] in the same way. Phonemically, our items are

/nájtrèjt/	'nitrate'	/ənéjm/	'a name'
/nájt + rèjt/	'night rate'	/ən + éjm/	'an aim'

Now, the stressed [a·] and [a], which we have so far ignored, are in complementary distribution. The latter occurs short before [t·]; the former occurs elsewhere. We may predict the phonetic length of /a/ in terms of the absence of /+/ following the consonant to the right and the absence of length by a following sequence of consonant and /+/ in the phonemic transcription.

The types of phonemic classes resulting from this segmentation and classification are called *junctures* (cf. Trager 1962 and the references cited there). We can describe English and other languages with equal exactness either with or without junctures (Hockett 1949: 38). If, however, we accept the kind of operation based on segmenting phones into simultaneous bundles of phonetic properties and assigning them to different phonemic classes, we are faced with arbitrariness. We have at least two possible descriptions for the data we have considered. The decision to describe them as we have, accepting junctures, is based on the decision to accept the evaluative criteria of economy of inventory and pattern congruity. Within a mechanically operational theory, we must limit our operations such that only one operation is applicable here, or we must accept the arbitrariness. If we eliminate the plurality of possible operations by rejecting the kind of segmentation we have performed, then we must accept the description of English that acknowledges several kinds of *t*-phonemes and *n*-phonemes. Juncture results from the acceptance of evaluative criteria and is not possible in a theory constrained by a mechanical operationalism.

Implicit in the acceptance of junctures is the classification of simultaneously occurring features of a single phonetic segment to different phonemes. This is also done when the articulatory features of stress, length, nasality, intonation, and so on, are separated from vowels and assigned to one phoneme while the remaining features are assigned (along with complementarily distributed and phonetically similar vowels) to a second phoneme. We performed this operation without commenting on it in the discussion of the English nonsyllabics and pattern congruity. Similarly, a description of English that contains the utterances [kæ̃t] 'can't', [kæ̃nd] 'canned', and [kæt] 'cat' (where there is no [kæ̃nt]) represented as /kænt/, /kænd/, and /kæt/, is based on the same type of assignment. Here, the /n/ has [~] as one of its allophones occurring simultaneously with a preceding vowel allophone when /n/ occurs before a phoneme manifested as a voiceless consonant. Were we to reject the above as a possible description, we would be assuming that a linear sequence of phonetic segments must correspond one-to-one with a linear sequence of phonemic classes. The acceptance of juncture, stress, and so forth, as possible phonemes indicates that no such assumption is made.

There are two ways of treating junctures, each of which satisfies the evaluative criteria. One version of the operation is to insert into the phonemic notation a symbol /+/, but assign no phonetic value or membership to it (Moulton 1947: 223 and Harris 1951: 82–83). Hockett (1949) would require the simultaneous segmentation of phones and assignment of some features to /+/ such as manifestation. With regard to the overall character of the theory, this difference is minor. The approach that permits zero manifestation of juncture does not violate the condition of bi-uniqueness. We know that every medial [t·] is to be phonetically /t+/, and so forth, without recourse to grammatical operations. We do not have some [t·]'s in a single phonetic environment allotted to /t/ and others to /t+/. The permission of zero phonetic manifestation of junctures would reduce the number of instances in which simultaneous phonetic features are assigned to linearly related phonemic classes, but it would not eliminate them entirely.

The observation that junctures often occur where grammatical boundaries are identified (Wells 1947b: 98) has led some (Leopold 1948) to criticize juncture as contradicting the prescribed sequence of operations and being circular; and it has led others (Hill 1958) to base grammatical operations on the occurrence of juncture. The introduction of juncture follows from the acceptance of evaluative criteria, and it is circular in principle only within a theory that does not permit such criteria, i.e., a mechanically operational one. As all varieties of post-Bloomfieldian theory agree on bi-uniqueness, all agree on the necessity of juncture, for none would describe English with more than one *t*-phoneme. The inconsistency of juncture in a mechanically operational theory is overlooked.

The data we have discussed here as basis for admitting juncture exclude pitch and/or pause as a member allophone. Junctures so restricted are termed plus or *internal open juncture* (Bloch and Trager 1942: 47 and Trager and Smith 1951: 38). An utterance containing an internal pause may contrast with the same sequence without that pause, as utterances may contrast solely by differences in pitch. The contrasting features of pause and *in part* those of pitch may be segmented from the co-occurring articulatory features and assigned their own phonemic class. (Some differences in pitch remain and are assigned to pitch phonemes, phonemes whose allophones are exclusively various pitch levels.) Phonemes whose membership is pitch and pause are termed *external junctures* (Trager and Smith 1951: 45–49, who find three of these in the description of English).

Meaning and Alternative Operations

An additional divergence in post-Bloomfieldian theory turns on the acceptance or rejection of one of the primitive techniques: the recording of stimulus-response. The negative position argues that the technique of stimulus-response, unlike phonetics, is incapable of producing a segmentation of data coincident with phonetic utterance segments and is even more incapable of providing information about identity or nonidentity of pairs of these stimulus-response segments (Harris 1951: 188–89). Recall that the same admission was made by Bloomfield. This attitude requires that we modify the operations that are the basis of the definitions of contrast and free variation, for each definition required information about the sameness or difference of meaning of the whole phonetic sequences in which the phones under investigation occurred. Without such information, we are unable to distinguish between the two relationships and have no way of precluding the assignment of all phonetically similar phones to a single class. The relationship of complementary distribution is unaffected; no presupposition of meaning is required for its identification.

One who holds this alternative position may develop other operations that reduce any reference to meaning to the status of "shortcuts." One may, however, continue to use information about meaning while acknowledging its deficiencies (Hockett 1947c: 330–31). This procedure is similar to continued recourse to phonetic similarity while recognizing its limitations. In either instance, the theory is less complete than one with precise techniques of phonetics and stimulus-response.

With the rejection of an assumed stimulus-response record, the operational basis of contrast and free variation is developed in at least two different ways. Bloch (1948) relies on distributional information of the phones; Harris (1951) relies on judgments of the native speakers of the language. Bloch proceeds in the following way. If for *every* token of an utterance-environment in which we find [x] we find a corresponding phonetic sequence differing only in that [x] is replaced by [y], then the relationship between [x] and [y] is free variation. Second, if in some environment E we find [x] and [y] in free variation, while in other occurrences outside E they are in complementary distribution (share no same environment), then [x] and [y] are in noncontrastive distribution. Third, if [x] and [y] "have some but not all their environments in common, and are not in free variation with each other" (Bloch 1948: 26), then [x] and [y] are in contrast. The definitions of free variation and noncontrastive distribution defined on these operational observations are taken as the basis for the definition of identity; contrast is the basis for nonidentity. Pike (1952a: 112–15) points out that if the term "free variation" in the definition of contrast is replaced by the words that define it, we find the following tautology: [x] and [y] "have some but not all their environments in common, and . . . [do] not 'have all their environments in common'." That is, in the environment E, [x] and [y] do not have all their environments in common. This statement of contrast simply further divides E into two portions:

$$
\begin{array}{lll}
E_1 & E_2 & E \\
[\text{x}] & [\text{y}] & [\text{x}] \\
 & & [\text{y}]
\end{array}
\quad\Longrightarrow\quad
\begin{array}{lllll}
E_1 & E_2 & & E & \\
 & & \overbrace{E_a \;\; E_b \;\; E_c} & & \\
[\text{x}] & [\text{y}] & [\text{x}] \;\; [\text{y}] \;\; [\text{x}] & & \\
 & & \qquad\qquad\;\; [\text{y}] & &
\end{array}
$$

The situation to the left of the arrow illustrates noncontrastive distribution and the first portion of the definition of contrast. To distinguish the two, the situation is modified on the right of the arrow by altering the distribution in E such that [x] and [y] do not have all their environments in common. This alteration repeats within E the initial situation to the left of the arrow. We now must alter E_c such that [x] and [y] do not share all their environments in common. This alteration, however, results in resolving E_c as we resolved E and leads to an infinite regress: an unperformable operation. If the term "free variation" in the definition of contrast means noncontrastive distribution, then the tautology and infinite regress are avoided, but there is no operational (distributional) distinction between the two. Either we have an operation that involves infinite regress and is not performable or we have one that does not provide a basis for defining identity distinct from nonidentity. (See Bloch 1953.)

The second method of avoiding an assumption of a stimulus-response record presupposes an operation yielding judgments of a native speaker (Harris 1951: 31–33). Given two phones [x] and [y] in a single utterance environment, we record one occurrence of each, then construct a tape with random occurrences of the two. Playing the tape, we ask the native speaker to sort out the occurrences as instances of the first utterance or the second.

High scores in the discrimination (abstracting loss of attention, and so forth) is the basis for defining contrast; low or random scores indicates free variation. This procedure assumes that the speaker of the language will hear no difference among phones in free variation but will hear the utterances as different if they are in contrast. Such definitions of contrast and free variation introduce the possibility of a third type of primitive technique in addition to phonetics and stimulus-response. An analogous technique may be used to obtain a stimulus-response record if the sameness/difference judgments of the native speaker are in terms of the meanings of the utterances; this technique is opposed to the technique of observing the occurrence of utterances in same/different stimulus-response environments (Hockett 1942: 6 and 1949: 45 and Fries 1954: 65. Cf. Hoijer 1958 for discussion).

Having examined a variety of attitudes in post-Bloomfieldian theory, we arbitrarily select for the purpose of exposition the one that (1) presupposes a technique of phonetics and stimulus-response, and (2) is not mechanically operational. The second condition implies that we accept the evaluative criterion of economy (economy per se, pattern congruity, allophonic parallelism, and economy of ease of statement of complementarity), permit relative phonetic similarity and partial intersection, and the use of juncture phonemes. On the basis of our primitives we may define free variation (identity), contrast (nonidentity), and complementary distribution (identity) as we already have, such that possible operations are associated with them. We then define phoneme as a class of phones holding free variation or complementary distribution and phonetic similarity. The ambiguities of description are resolved with respect to the evaluative criteria. The theory to this point is taxonomic; patterns involve the inclusion of phones into classes.

Phonemic Constructions

We have indicated that patterns of occurrence of phonemes must be expressed but have as yet said nothing of the framework for that expression. We assume again, as Bloomfield assumed, that not all possible distributions or combinations will be possible. The assumption of such patterning holds true to a certain point. Within some domain, some bounded stretch, such restrictions will be found, but beyond that domain we may find any sequence and no pattern. Bloomfield took the relevant domain to be the word or morpheme. In the attempt to render the theory consistently operational, we must exclude these essentially grammatical boundaries from this phonemic statement.

One sequence in which we may find patterns of distribution is the syllable (Bloch 1950: 118 and Haugen 1956). The syllable may in turn pattern within or be coterminous with a sequence of phonemes bounded by two internal open junctures or an internal open juncture and an external open juncture (Trager and Bloch 1941: 226), which we may call a *phonemic word*. We can define a post-Bloomfieldian phonemic constructional hierarchy somewhat as follows:

phonemic word *and* . . .

syllable *and* syllable *and* . . .

onset *and* peak *and* coda

wherein a phonemic word consists of one or more syllables, and a syllable consists of a peak and perhaps an onset and/or coda. As in Bloomfieldian theory, a syllable is partially identified by peaks of sonority. Syllable boundaries, except initially and finally in an utterance, may be undetermined. Those phonemes occurring as peaks constitute one distribution class of phonemes. Those nonsyllabics occurring to the left of a peak constitute the class of onsets; those to the right are the codas (Hockett 1955: 52). One procedure for identifying internal syllable boundaries is the following. Consider, first, utterances describable by any one syllable, one containing a single peak. Observe the pattern of nonsyllabics as onsets and codas. Where these patterns differ, we can match utterance internal sequences of nonpeaks as identical to the identified onsets but not codas or as identical to codas but not onsets. In the first case, the syllable boundary is made to the left of the internal sequence of nonsyllabics, and in the second, the boundary is placed to the right. If the internal sequence cannot be identified with either utterance initial onset or utterance final coda, determine if some boundary internal to the sequence will produce resultant sequences that can be so matched. If so, we can identify syllable boundaries. If not, no motivated choice can be made, and the nonsyllabics are here called *interludes* (Hockett 1955: 52). The motivation is a variety of economy. We wish to describe our occurrence patterns by a hierarchy that requires the fewest distinctions. The initial and final structures of nonsyllabics are undoubtedly boundaries of syllables. To the extent that we can generalize internal sequences to ones already required, we increase the economy of the phonemic constructional hierarchy. The inclusion of this evaluation criterion indicated that the operation constraining possible phonemic constructional hierarchy is not mechanical. It yields possible descriptions that are then evaluated.

The complete phonemic hierarchy will consist of higher constructs. Phonemic words, for example, will be constituted of *phonemic phrases* (Trager and Bloch 1941: 226): a "unit . . . contain[ing] any number of subordinate stresses in addition to the one loud stress, and any number of internal open junctures." Hockett (1955) replaces the phonemic word with *microsegment* defined as a sequence of phonemes bounded by at least one plus juncture (Hockett 1955: 61) and the phonemic phrase with the *phonological word* or *macrosegment* defined as bounded by pause (external open) junctures (Hockett 1949: 36 and 1955: 51). Any speech act, then, instances at least one phonemic phrase (or macrosegment). To define this hierarchy operationally we need only information about the phonetic property of sonority plus information about the occurrence of juncture. We assume that our phonetics provides information of sonority as one of the articulatory properties.

The statement of the patterns now requires a definition of possible hierarchy based on the above operations. Here, there is a difference between Bloomfieldian and post-Bloomfieldian theory. Recall that Bloomfieldian constructions were based on a definition of position. A position is not a class in that it may consist of phonemes, but in that it consists (possibly) of other positions. The phonemic inventory in Bloomfieldian theory was ordered to those positions; for each entry in the phonemic inventory there was a notation of its privileges of occurrence with respect to positions in the phonological constructional hierarchies. Each phoneme in the inventory was listed *once;* the position classes were listed *multiply*. If, however, we take the constructional hierarchy not to be a hierarchy of positions but of disjunctive classes, then the members of each disjunctive class must be given. Here, the position classes are listed once, and the phonemes are listed multiply: once for each class membership. This conception is the one chosen by Bloch (1950: 118), Martin (1951: 525–26), and Haugen (1956: 220–21). Position in this approach functions *only* within the operation. We identify positions, determine the phonemes that may occur in the position, and then describe those occurrences within a framework of disjunctive classes. It is the linear sequence of these classes that enter the theory as defining (in part) phonetic pattern.

A phonemic constructional hierarchy consists of linear conjunctions of disjunctive classes (= Bloomfield's linear conjunction of positions). The hierarchy is based on a disjunctive class consisting of phonemes, such as

onset	*and*	peak	*and*	coda
p		*i*		p
or		*or*		*or*
t		u		t
or		*or*		*or*
k		e		k
or		*or*		*or*
sp		o		sp
.		.		.
.		.		.
.		.		.

The phonemic structural hierarchy describes co-occurrence pattern by identifying large substitution classes, say, all sequences that are syllables. Within this, further substitution patterns are observable; thus the sequences of phonemes that are syllables are ordered.

Syllable
consists of

$$\left\{ \left\{ \begin{matrix} \text{Onset} \\ 0 \end{matrix} \right\} \quad \text{Peak} \quad \left\{ \begin{matrix} \text{Coda} \\ 0 \end{matrix} \right\} \right\}$$

and so forth, until the smallest classes that contain only disjunctively related phonemes, but no phoneme sequences, are reached.

An alternative is the retention of a phonological constructional hierarchy built on position (cf. Harris 1951: 150–55) with ordering of the phoneme inventory in the manner of Bloomfield. The pattern of grammar repeats this shift in theory: the introduction of disjunctive classes absent from Bloomfieldian theory. Both here and below we adopt the variant of post-Bloomfieldian theory which employs disjunction as possible pattern.

Operations and Grammar

The theoretical framework required to account for patterns that were accounted for by Bloomfield's grammar are based in part on operations analogous to those developed for phonemics, and similar problems arise. Just as the assumption that language was a structure and the establishment of possible operation together required items—phonetic segments, initially—so here the assumption requires a segmentation. The segments—*morphs* (Hockett 1947c: 322)—are derived by the following technique. Compare utterances in phonemic notation. Where partial sames of meaning are found, determine whether the utterances are partially same in some sequence of one or more phonemes. If so, segment the shared sequence of phonemes from the remainder in each utterance. The sequences of phonemes resulting from this operation may be related as pairs in ways analogous to phones. If two morphs stand in an identical morph environment and differ in meaning, they are in contrast. If the first condition holds, but not the second, they are in free variation. The relationship of free variation in grammar is termed *free alternation* (Hockett 1947c: 328). If the morphs occur in mutually exclusive morph environments, the relationship between them is complementary distribution. As before, contrast is a criterion for nonidentity and assigning morphs to different classes (the morphemes), and free variation is a criterion for identity and assigning morphs to the same morpheme class. Morphs that are members of the same morpheme are *allomorphs* (Nida 1948: 420) or *morpheme alternants* (Harris 1942: 170).

If the operations and the relationships derived from them were completely analogous to those of phonology, we would expect complementary distribution to be constrained by a scale of similarity. For example, /əgén/ *again* and /ówvər/ *over* occur as utterances and hold the relationship of contrast. In /rìjdúw/ *redo*, *re* is in complementary distribution with both *over* and *again*. Should *re* be classed with *again*, *over*, or with neither? One might suggest that the answer be predicated on a criterion of stimulus-response similarity. In the absence of such a scale, we would require identity of meaning. The latter is the course adopted (Harris 1942: 171 and Hockett 1947c: 342), and we assume that synonyms do not exist (Hockett 1947c: 330). The rejection of stimulus-response similarity preserves the Bloomfieldian notion that the meanings associated with morphemes are atomic; the assumption of a partial likeness in terms of meaning assumes that such are complexes of properties, some of which are shared by different morphemes. As before, the operation of grammar assumes that we have information of stimulus-response identity and nonidentity at our disposal.

If we allow the morphs /gud/ and /bet/ in *good* and *better* to be grouped as allomorphs in the way we allow two instances of /big/ in *big* and *bigger*, to be grouped, then phonemic similarity between morphs cannot be relevant to identity or nonidentity of morphs.

We find the same divergent view of the use of stimulus-response in grammatical operations that we found in phonemics. Harris (1951) suggests an operation in which segmentation is performed without using sames of meaning. Two sequences of phonemes that are partially identical may be segmented for possible grammatical classification if they occur independently of each other in some environment. In the environment *I hired a . . . , worker* is segmented into *work* and *er* because *er* occurs in that environment with *labor*. This will produce a great many potential morpheme members, and not all of them will be acceptable. The alternative possible solutions are restricted by the grammatical equivalent of pattern congruity. We require a morphemic inventory such that the pattern of the morphemes can be expressed in terms of classes of morphemes that have the largest possible membership. Conversely, we want no morpheme whose distribution is unique. This procedure is then not mechanical, but requires that we evaluate many possible descriptions against a criterion of economy. Identity is predicated in part on free variation, which is operationally distinguished from contrast in the same manner proposed by Bloch for phonemic operations (Harris 1951: 198); that is, two morphs that are identical in *all* their occurrences are considered to be in free variation. Here, the difficulty in distinguishing between noncontrastive distribution and contrast must be repeated. Not having at our disposal information of identities of meaning, we have to consider more possible descriptions than if identities of meaning were available for use. The possible descriptions that would be excluded by its use must now be considered. The criterion for accepting certain identities permitted by complementary distribution while rejecting others is solely that of economy in stating the distribution patterns of the inventory.

Consistent with our previous selection, we will arbitrarily choose that variant of post-Bloomfieldian theory that accepts a record of stimulus-response as data. This variant also contains the grammatical variant of the criterion of pattern congruity. It is expressed in the requirement that a grouping of morphs should not be chosen that produces a morphemic class of unique distribution (Hockett 1947c: 331). In attempting to satisfy this criterion, we are led to consider the relationship of the level of grammar to that of phonemics.

Morphemes and Phonemes

The relationship of morphemes to phonemic sequences is varied. Let us consider an example from French (taken from Hockett 1947c):

(a)	/ala/	'to the [fem.]'
(b)	/ale/	'to the [pl.]'
(c)	/o/	'to the [masc.]'

Having identified two morphs in (a) and (b), /a/ 'to' and /l/ 'the', we might expect to find a similar sequence in (c); but we find instead a single phonemic segment. To attain some degree of congruity of pattern, we have to describe (c) as having two morphemes {*to*} and {*the*} in spite of our inability to identify two morphs in the phonemic representation. We assume the sequence of morphemes in 'to the [masc.]' to be parallel to that in (a) and (b). Eventually we may find /alɔm/ 'to the man' to support this. Where we have two or more morphemes assumed to be manifested by a single sequence of phonemes, that sequence of phonemes is termed a *portmanteau morph* (Hockett 1947c: 333).

Partially intersecting morphemes may occur in the phonemic sequences representing them. Consider the following data:

(a)	/ðejgow/	'they go'
(b)	/juwgow/	'you go'
(c)	/didðejgow/	'did they go'
(d)	/dižuwgow/	'did you go'

The morph in (d) that would be assigned to {*did*} is present as /diž/; the final alveolar stop is present as an affricate. The /j/ of /juw/ is present perhaps in the same affricate. Here, unlike the portmanteau example, we can identify part of the sequence with other occurrences. The morphemes overlap in their phonemic sequences, but are not completely fused in an unsegmentable sequence.

A final difficulty may be found in these data:

(a)	/hawziz/	'house-pl.'
(b)	/dogz/	'dog-pl.'
(c)	/raks/	'rock-pl.'
(d)	/šijp/	'sheep-pl.'
(e)	/fiš/	'fish-pl.'
(f)	/kad/	'cod-pl.'

On the basis of (a)—(c) we establish three morphs with a same plural meaning in complementary distribution. Given (d)—(f), we assume on the basis of meaning the occurrence of the morpheme {Pl.}, but have no phonemic manifestation to assign to it.

In accounting for phonemic pattern, we had to deal with similar instances of lack of fit between phonemes and phones. The sequences of phonemes did not always correspond to a sequence of phones in our data, but there we had less problem with our operations, for the phones consisted of simultaneous features as well as occurring in linear sequence. In the treatment of [kæ̃t] as /kænt/ 'can't', we had no problem in finding phonetic stuff to assign to phonemes. In the treatment of /dižuw/ 'did you' we face a difficulty in that a phoneme is a unit and not a complex of properties; we cannot divide /ž̌/ into parts and attribute these to morphemic classes. The relationship of phonemics to phonetics and of grammar to phonemics involves relating a unity to a variety. The former relationship was included under the rubric of phonology or termed the phonetic system. The latter is called *morphophonemics* (Hockett 1942: 20 and 1958: 137 and 271–76). Because of this lack of fit between grammar and phonemics it is important that we specify exactly the relationship between the two.

There are two distinct problems bound up in resolving the grammar-phonemics relationship: (1) whether the relationship of a grammatical term to a phonemic term is made-up-of or some other, and (2) the points within grammar and phonology we choose as the relateds of the grammar-phonemics relationship. The points may be chosen from any size-level within the hierarchy. Normally we would want to take the minimum unit of grammatical pattern and state its relation to phonemics. This minimum unit varies as our notion of grammatical pattern varies. Whatever position we take, we want to minimize the number of relateds.

One way to resolve the unity-variety relationship between the two levels is to eliminate the variety within the phonology. In post-Bloomfieldian theory, where this can be done without sacrificing the bi-uniqueness of the notation, this procedure is called "normalization" (Hockett 1947c: 341). In English, our phonemic constructions predict no sibilant-sibilant sequence within their domains. The phonemic variety of the plural morpheme /iz z s/ can be reduced if we take advantage of this situation. We may write /čurčz/ *churches*, /howmz/ *homes*, and /deskz/ *desks*. Our statements of the manifestation of /z/ are unambiguous. After the obstruents /s z č ž̌ š ž/, the /z/ is represented by [ɪz]; after the set of phonemes that are phonetically voiceless obstruents, /z/ is represented as [s]; elsewhere /z/ is represented by [z]. To retain bi-uniqueness, every phonetic voiceless obstruent plus [s] must be phonemic /z/. *Max* ([mæks]) as well as *desks* ([dɛsks]) is written /kz/ in its last two segments. Not all variation can be reduced to phonemic unity while retaining bi-uniqueness. Let us take an example from Russian.

	Phonetic Record	Phonemic Representation	Normalization
[nʌgá]	'naked (fem. sg.)'	/nagá/	nagá
[nák]	'naked (masc. sg.)'	/nák/	nág
[gərʌdá]	'cities'	/garadá/	gorodá
[górət]	'city'	/górat/	górod
[gʌródņik]	'mayor'	/garódņik/	goródņik
[ḷitá]	'summers'	/ḷitá/	ḷetá
[ḷétə]	'summer'	/ḷéta/	ḷéta

The phoneme class /a/ contains allophones [ə ʌ a]. The [a] occurs stressed, [ʌ] before a stressed vowel and following a nonpalatalized consonant, and [ə] elsewhere following a nonpalatalized consonant. The phonetic similarity they share is nonclose, nonfront, and unrounded vowel articulation. (Of the five vowel phonemes of Russian /i u e o a/ only /i u a/ occur unstressed after a nonpalatalized consonant. Unstressed after a palatalized consonant, only /i u/ occur.) To obtain a unique notation we remark that the vowels of 'city', when stressed, are phonemically /o/, while the vowel of 'naked' is /a/ when stressed; and the vowel of 'summer' is /e/ when stressed. Furthermore, it is only in stressed position that all five vowels contrast. We establish one normalized notation for each phoneme in the position where we find the maximum number of contrasts. Hence, there are five vowels in the normalized representation. Comparing the variants of an item, we determine for each position the phonetic representation of our normalized vowels. The statements required for our data are that normalized *a* is represented phonetically by [a] when stressed, by [ʌ] when it immediately precedes a stressed vowel and follows a nonpalatalized consonant, and by [ə] elsewhere, unstressed and following a nonpalatalized consonant. Normalized *o* is phonetically [o] when stressed, phonetically [ʌ] when it immediately precedes a stressed vowel and follows a nonpalatalized consonant, and phonetically [ə] elsewhere, unstressed and following a nonpalatalized consonant. Normalized *e* is phonetically [e] when stressed; unstressed it is phonetically [i]. If we take the vowels of 'city' to be *o*, then we may correctly predict the phonetic representation. Had we chosen to derive the normalized representation from the unstressed vowels, then from *garad* we would not have been able to predict the phonetic value when stressed, for the vowel in *nag* is represented by [a] while the vowel of *garad* is [o]. The distinction in the normalized representation of *nag* and *garad* is not sufficient to predict the phonetic values. We would have had to say something like "*a* in 'city' (and list other items working the same way) is represented by [o]" when stressed. The difference in the simplicity of the two statements indicates the preferred normalization. Similar arguments justify the *g* in 'naked' and the *d* in 'city' as opposed to the *t* in 'summer'.

The normalization in the second example does not satisfy the constraint of bi-uniqueness. We do not, for example, know whether [ʌ] is to be assigned to *a* or *o* until we have performed some grammatical operations and identified the same morpheme occurring in 'city', 'cities', and 'mayor'. If we decide to treat all normalizations the same way, it follows that the normalized representations belong within grammar, because of the presupposition of grammatical operations. This leads us to say morphemes are not the minimum grammatical terms with respect to made-up-of; the terms of the normalized representation are the minimum grammatical units. These are called *morphophonemes* (Bloomfield 1939b and Harris 1945: 285) to distinguish them from phonemes; the former lie within grammar, the latter within phonemics. Unlike Bloomfieldian theory, we cannot claim that morphemes consist of phonemes and mean by that that the phonemes make up the *single* representation—the basic form—of morphemes without giving up bi-uniqueness. The difference is that Bloomfieldian theory, lacking a well-developed operational constraint, permits nonbi-unique descriptions. Post-Bloomfieldian theory does not permit them. The unity of representation within grammar (by a single morphophonemic representation) is again to be related to variety within phonemics. Our proposed normalization within phonemics, when carried through consistently, turns out to yield a representation that does not qualify as a possible phonemic description, but as a possible grammatical one. We are again left with a unity within grammar related to a variety within phonemics.

An alternative approach to the description of the lack of one-to-one fit between the terms of grammar and their manifestations in phonemics is to forego the operation of morphophonemics just described. We now assume the minimum units of grammar to be morphemes. Taking the same example from Russian, we would see that /garad/, /górat/, and /garód/ are in complementary distribution (the first before /á/, to be assigned to the plural morpheme; the second in isolation; and the third before /ŋik/, to be assigned to an agent {*er*} morpheme). Then we order the three phoneme sequences to the same morphemic class, assuming that the criteria of identity of meaning, and so forth, are met. The three phonemic sequences are the allomorphs of the morphemic class {*city*}.

The two approaches are distinct in terms of the points within grammar and phonemics we take as the related of the grammar-phonemics relationship. The first, using morphophonemes, assumes that there are two levels in language such that the minimum unit of phonemics is the phoneme and the minimum unit of grammar is the morphophoneme. The relationship between the two levels holds between morphophonemes and phonemes. As a phoneme was a class of sounds and not itself a sound, so a morphophoneme is a class of phonemes and not a phoneme. In this type of morphophonemic statement, we do not use the Bloomfieldian add, delete, and replace. That is, *d* does not "become" /t/ finally and /d/ before vowels, but is "represented by" (Hockett

1961 : 33) /t/ or /d/ in these positions. In our sense of nontaxonomic, "represented by" is as equally nontaxonomic as add, delete, and replace. They are different relationships, but they are both outside a taxonomy and express the relation between them. Thus

<table>
<tr><td>Grammar</td><td>Phonemics</td></tr>
<tr><td>.</td><td>.</td></tr>
<tr><td>.</td><td>.</td></tr>
<tr><td>.</td><td>.</td></tr>
<tr><td>morphemes</td><td>onsets, peaks, codas</td></tr>
<tr><td>consist of</td><td>consist of</td></tr>
<tr><td>morphophonemes   ⟶</td><td>phonemes</td></tr>
</table>

where the arrow represents "represented by."

If we adopt the second approach, foregoing morphophonemics, then the minimum unit of grammar is the morpheme that bears the relationship represented-by to sequences of one or more phonemes that we termed morphs. Thus

<table>
<tr><td>Grammar</td><td>Phonemics</td></tr>
<tr><td>.</td><td>.</td></tr>
<tr><td>.</td><td>.</td></tr>
<tr><td>.</td><td>.</td></tr>
<tr><td>morphemes   ⟶</td><td>morphs</td></tr>
<tr><td></td><td>consist of</td></tr>
<tr><td></td><td>phonemes</td></tr>
</table>

The lack of neat fit in the relationship between the levels is more understandable when we recognize that no single term within phonemic pattern (phoneme, onset, peak, coda, syllable, and so on) correlates with the notion of morph. The terms of the phonemic level are established prior to the grammatical level with the intention of expressing phonemic and not grammatical pattern. Any single portion of phonemic pattern can be delimited by the grammar-to-phonemics relationship.

Both these views of the relationship between the levels are consistent with some operation and are equally possible within an operational theory. We have indicated the particular relationship to be represented-by in both views. Others have been proposed. Within the view which relates morphophonemes to phonemes both the Bloomfieldian replace-add-delete relationship (Harris 1945: 285) and made-up-of (Harris 1951: 232) have been used. Within the view which relates morphemes to morphs, the relationship has been assumed to be made-up-of (Trager 1949: 5) or represented-by

(Hockett 1961: 33). We indicated that a single representation of morphemes as a combination of terms was incompatible with the notion that morphemes are made-up-of bi-unique phonemes. The morpheme-is-made-up-of-phonemes assumption implies (1) a multiple representation of morphemes within grammar or (2) that phonemically distinct morphs are morphemically distinct (cf. Hockett 1961). The rejection of both (1) and (2) as undesirable from the point of view of economy forces us to accept a relation other than made-up-of holding between grammar and phonemics in the morpheme-to-morph view. Of the attitudes outlined, we adopt the version of post-Bloomfieldian theory in which morphemes are the minimum units of grammar related to phonemics via represented-by. This relationship between the levels is nontaxonomic and nonreciprocal. Grammar and phonemics are hierarchically related.

Grammatical Pattern

Bloomfieldian theory was maximally weak with respect to constraint of grammatical patterning by operations. The provision of operations for grammatical pattern in post-Bloomfieldian theory is analogous to that for phonemic constructional hierarchy. In phonemics, however, the problem of determining the extension of patterning (distribution) was relatively easily solved by adopting certain of the phonemes within sequences as indicators of boundaries of a particular size-level. Given the use of syllabics, nonsyllabics, juncture, and pause in identifying domains of patterning within phonemics, we might expect certain morphemes to function analogously in indicating boundaries of grammatical patterning. This is not the case, and other means of segmentation must be found to determine stretches of morphemes that exhibit patterns. Two principal operations are proposed (Harris 1946 and 1951 and Wells 1947b). Both end by modifying certain properties of Bloomfieldian grammar; for example, the theoretical term on which patterning is based is no longer the position but the morpheme class—a disjunction of morphemes identified by their same linear occurrence relationships relative to some same sequence of forms. It is here we will begin the discussion of grammatical operations.

Harris (1946: 163 and 1951: 243–52) defines a morpheme class as a disjunctive set of morphemes with respect to their substitutability in a set of environments or positions. The set of morphemes that occur in *the . . .* constitutes a morpheme class. Let us call it Noun. The set of morphemes that occur in *the . . . bartender* make up a second morpheme class. Let us call it Adj. The notion of a disjunctive class can be expanded to include morpheme sequences as well as single morphemes. For example, the morpheme sequences that occur in *the . . .* also constitute a disjunctive class; *good beer, long night,* and the like, are members of this class. Let us call it AdjNoun, representing it by the sequence of morpheme classes to which its constituent morphemes belong. We observe now that some morpheme classes and morpheme class sequences can have the same privilege of occurrence. In the environment *the* . . . , both *beer* (= Noun) and *good beer* (= AdjNoun) occur. This situation is expressed formally by AdjNoun = Noun wherein the sign of equality means "substitutable for." Morpheme classes and class sequences so related form a third disjunctive class. The term to the left of the sign of equality implies a set of morpheme sequences; the term to the right, a set of morphemes. The two occurrences of Noun in the equation are taken as two occurrences of an identical class. Since Noun in AdjNoun is identical to Noun to the right of the equality sign, it follows that every occurrence of Noun can have AdjNoun substituted for it. Thus, we can substitute AdjNoun for Noun in AdjNoun, yielding AdjAdjNoun, which predicts a set of longer morpheme sequences, such as *good German beer*, which is substitutable for Noun and AdjNoun. This procedure represents a formalization of the recursive, endo-centric constructions in Bloomfieldian theory. Like those endocentric con-structions, the expansion of AdjNoun and similar morpheme class sequences exhibit closure. The morpheme class sequence NounPl is substitutable for Noun; *packages* is substitutable for *door* in *the* . . . . Its expression as NounPl = Noun will yield **packageses*, an incorrect prediction. The Noun of NounPl cannot have NounPl substituted for it. Here the two occurrences of Noun are not identical in terms of substitution. To mark this, the equation is modified by the use of superscript numbers; $\text{Noun}^1\text{Pl} = \text{Noun}^2$ indicates that the Noun^1Pl morpheme class sequence is closed. We cannot substitute a morpheme class with a higher superscript number for one with a lower number. We write all the patterns observed as

$$\text{Noun}^1\text{Pl} = \text{Noun}^2 \qquad \text{AdjNoun}^2 = \text{Noun}^2 \qquad \text{DetNoun}^2 = \text{Noun}^3$$

The morpheme class placed to the right of the equality sign functions for the whole class in that where AdjNoun^2 and Noun^2 occur in some position, say Det . . . , that substitutability is marked by using the morpheme class Noun^2 (not the morpheme sequence class AdjNoun^2) to label the membership of the more inclusive class. The substitution formulas ensure that DetNoun^2 implies DetAdjNoun^2, $\text{DetAdjNoun}^1\text{Pl}$, and so on.

The notation $\text{DetNoun}^2 = \text{Noun}^3$ (where Noun^3 is the morpheme class of proper nouns, and the substitutability is defined by . . . *rejected the mer-chandise*) predicts that the manifestations of the morpheme class sequence DetAdjNoun^2 (*a good friend*) and DetAdjAdjNoun^2 (*a good Canadian friend*) also occur in . . . *rejected the merchandise*. All these form a single substitution class:

(a)		Noun³		
(b)	Det		Noun²	
(c)	Det	Adj		Noun²
(d)	Det	Adj	Noun¹	Pl

All are disjunctively related. Furthermore, the members of the class are hier-archically ordered, because, internal to the substitution class constituted by (a)-(d), members are additionally related in that a morpheme class within one member sequence, (a), (b), (c), or (d), is substitutable for a morpheme class within another member sequence, but not vice versa. Taking (c) and (d), Noun¹ in (d) is substitutable for Noun² in (c), but not the reverse. There is "unidirectional substitutability" (Harris 1946: 170); "each higher numbered symbol represents all lower numbered identical symbols but not vice versa" (Harris 1951: 268). The hierarchy derives from this nonreciprocal, unidirec-tional substitution between morpheme classes shared by morpheme class sequences. Here, it is the shared noun that is the basis of the hierarchy and expressed by their superscript numbers. The morpheme class sequences in which Noun¹ occurs are then "lower" in the hierarchy than those in which Noun² occurs.

In the substitution class constituted by (a)-(d), the repetition of Det and Adj at each stage of the hierarchy indicates a redundancy analogous to the one between Bloomfieldian constructions. To reduce this redundancy, we can say that (b), (c), and (d), and (c) and (d) are partially identical by virtue of a shared morpheme class, Det and Adj, respectively. In Bloomfieldian theory, the analogous observation would be that two constructions shared a position. To express this partial identity between morpheme class sequences, we relate the classes differentiating the two whole sequences within a disjunctive class. In (c) and (d), the differentiating class sequences are Noun² in (c) and Noun¹Pl in (d). We relate them disjunctively and let that class—which, notice, is hierarchically ordered by Noun² and Noun¹—occur with the classes shared by (c) and (d). Thus,

$$\text{(c)} \quad \text{Det} \quad \text{Adj} \quad \left\{ \begin{array}{c} \text{Noun}^2 \\ or \\ \text{Noun}^1\text{Pl} \end{array} \right\}$$

Such conflations are *constructions* (Harris 1951: 325-34), although *not* com-parable to Bloomfield's construction. By repeating the same operation at (b) and (c) we have

$$\text{(b)} \quad \text{Det} \quad \left\{ \begin{array}{c} \text{Noun}^2 \\ or \\ \text{Adj} \quad \left\{ \begin{array}{c} \text{Noun}^2 \\ or \\ \text{Noun}^1\text{Pl} \end{array} \right\} \end{array} \right\}$$

The same superscript numbers (2) on Noun mark a nonhierarchical, recursive relation between the two members making up the disjunctive class co-occurring with Det. Finally, comparing (a) and (b), we form a disjunctive class with respect to some shared environment such as . . . *rejected the merchandise:*

$$
\text{(a)} \quad \left\{ \text{Det} \left\{ \begin{array}{l} \text{Noun}^3 \\ \textit{or} \\ \left\{ \text{Adj} \left\{ \begin{array}{l} \text{Noun}^2 \\ \textit{or} \\ \left\{ \begin{array}{l} \text{Noun}^2 \\ \textit{or} \\ \text{Noun}^1\,\text{Pl} \end{array} \right\} \end{array} \right\} \right. \end{array} \right\} \right.
$$

The distinct superscript numbers (2 and 3) indicate another hierarchical relationship.

Harris's formulas express two things: (1) the partial identity of morpheme class sequences and (2) the hierarchical relationships among them. Our final structure here is equivalent to the three formulas already presented. It is the admission of partial identity of morpheme class sequences that allows all the sequences of forms predicted here to be accounted for within a single hierarchy. Within Bloomfieldian theory these data would require a set of constructional hierarchies, not a single one. The pattern exemplified characterizes possible grammatical patterning within a language.

Harris's hierarchy differs from Bloomfieldian constructional hierarchy in these ways: (1) the hierarchy here is of morpheme class sequences and morpheme classes and not of positions; (2) the basis of the hierarchy is nonreciprocal substitution and not made-up-of; and (3) the members of the substitution classes are disjunctively related, while Bloomfieldian constructions within a hierarchy are conjunctively related. The operation identifies a number of morphemes and morpheme sequences with the same privilege of occurrence. This is an observation within the *technique;* the *pattern* is expressed by use of disjunctive classes. The operation further indicates that the members of this large disjunctive class can be ordered on the basis of nonreciprocal substitution, which is formally expressed by hierarchy. Finally, patterns in terms of shared morpheme classes or class sequences are expressed by a second use of disjunctive classes in constructions. In Hjelmslevian terms, it is a hierarchy of processes; the disjunctive members themselves are (linearly) conjunctive things—sequences of morpheme classes. The separate listing of such hierarchically ordered, disjunctive classes in the grammar indicates that the morpheme sequences they predict are acts of speech or utterances. Listing the class labeled Noun^3 in the grammar indicates that any combination of choices of the disjunctive possibilities yields a morpheme class sequence that, when each is manifested by a morpheme, is a possible utterance.

Grammar in this view requires primitives of disjunction and linear conjunction plus the previous definition of morpheme. With these elements we define morpheme class, morpheme class sequence, a disjunctive class of morpheme classes and class sequences, and construction; then we order the members of this class hierarchically, as already indicated. Each separate listing of such classes in the grammatical description of a language predicts the grammatical patterns of data.

This operation ignores meaning and the relation of grammar to stimulus-response records. Morphemes themselves have meaning (Harris 1951: 347), but our grammatical patterns—classes of various kinds and relations—have been established without reference to any association with meaning. Some of the terms of grammatical patterning can be associated with meaning. Morpheme class sequences or constructions that have a constant association with the stimulus-response record independently of the morphemes may have that meaning attributed to them. This condition is analogous to Bloomfield's constructional meaning of a linear order of positions. There is nothing comparable to class or functional meaning. Some, but not all, terms of grammatical patterning can be interpreted as stimulus-response.

The search for an operation capable of yielding patterns of grammar leads to this technique of substitution in positions. The observation that this technique can be used, plus the operational constraint that definitions be associated with operations, requires that we alter our previous concept of grammatical patterning from a hierarchy of positional constructions (which have no associated technique) to a disjunctive class of morpheme class sequences ordered hierarchically by unidirectional substitution. Because the operation of substitution does not require a distinction of word versus phrase, no distinction is proposed between morphology and syntax (Harris 1951: 262), as within Bloomfieldian grammar. Proposing different operations may well lead to different modifications in defining possible grammatical patterning to conform with the distinct operations. Theoretical alternatives in an operational theory are evaluated not solely in terms of the general scientific criteria of exactness, generality, and simplicity. Before these criteria can be applied, we must first determine which of the resultant views of grammar (Bloomfield's, Harris's, or some other) is preferred, basing that judgment on the validity of the operations constraining the definition of grammatical patterning. Only if both distinct operations are equally valid do we recognize both theories based on them as permissible ones (that is, as meeting the operational constraint on possible theory) and then proceed to judge the resulting concepts of possible patterning on general grounds. Like noncontradiction and universality, validity of operation becomes a constraint on *possible* theory; only when we have a possible theory, can we evaluate it. Of course, if the operational constraint is not adopted, we need not concern ourselves with this prior examination of the theory concerning its possibility and proceed directly to the evaluation of its merits.

A second proposed operation (Wells 1947b) differs from Harris's in its "direction." Harris's technique takes sequences of morphemes and "combines" them into more inclusive, fewer classes via substitution. Wells's proposal takes the same morpheme sequences and divides them into two portions, and each portion is segmented in turn until no more segmentations remain to be made. It works from the "top down," while Harris's works from the "bottom up." The basis of Wells's operation is substitution, and like Harris's operation, compares both morphemes and morpheme sequences in some position. The resulting classes defined by identity of occurrence in an environment are called *focus classes* (Wells 1947b: 86). This outcome is comparable to Harris's disjunctive substitution classes—Noun³, DetAdjNoun², Adj-Noun², and Noun¹ Pl. The operation can produce as many first segmentations of a morpheme sequence as there are internal morpheme boundaries. In *Max slammed the door*, there can be four segmentations: *Max* plus the remainder; *Max slam* plus the remainder; and so forth. For each segmentation we may establish a focus class. For . . . *slammed the door*, the occurrence of *the bartender* in this environment indicates that *Max* and *the bartender* constitute a focus class. For the second segmentation, in the environment . . . *ed the door*, we find *the bartender kick* as well as *Max slam* constituting a focus class.

Wells's (1947b: 84) observation that "an I-C analysis is never accepted or rejected on its own merits" shows that the operation is not mechanical and the theory based on it is not strictly operational in the sense we have given it. Harris's operation, like Wells's, is not mechanical. The environments we choose in establishing morpheme classes are arbitrary and may yield a plurality of descriptions. The evaluation of resulting descriptions is the same for both operational approaches. The purpose of this (and Harris's) grammatical technique is to provide a framework for morpheme (= grammatical) patterning. To do this we must state the restricted occurrences or distribution of morphemes in the simplest possible way, that is, by maximizing focus class membership. The accounting is simpler in that the larger the focus class, the greater the amount of data described by a single statement about a focus class. The membership of a focus class will fall into classes according to the segmentations valid for them, and the maximization of focus class membership also maximizes this diversity (or internal grammar) within a focus class. The correct segmentation is indicated by this formal property of large focus class (or morpheme class, in Harris's terms) membership.

As Harris's morpheme classes contain both morphemes and morpheme sequences as members, so Wells's focus class consists of sequence classes (comparable to Harris's morpheme class sequences). The members of a focus class are related by the principle of *expansion*. Each pair of sequence classes within a focus class are related by the fact that "When one of the sequences is at least as long as the other (contains as many morphemes) and is structurally diverse from it (does not belong to all the same sequence classes as the other), we call it an EXPANSION of that other sequence, and the other sequence itself we call a model" (Wells 1947b: 83).

We assume that the segmentation *Max-slammed the door* is the correct one. This, plus *we left* and *the bartender kicked the door*, yields a preliminary grammatical pattern expressed as

$$\left\{\begin{array}{l}\text{Max}\\\text{we}\\\text{the bartender}\end{array}\right\}_1 \quad \left\{\begin{array}{l}\text{slammed the door}\\\text{left}\\\text{kicked the door}\end{array}\right\}_2$$

in which the forms within the braces are disjunctively related (on the basis of substitution) and together constitute focus classes linearly related. Considering the segmentation of the members of the second focus class, we assume the correct segmentation falls before *the* in *slammed the door* and *kicked the door*. Focus class 2 is

$$\left\{\begin{array}{l}\left\{\begin{array}{l}\text{slammed}\\\text{kicked}\end{array}\right\}_3 \quad \left\{\text{the door}\right\}_4 \\ \\ \left\{\text{left}\right\}_5\end{array}\right\}_2$$

wherein *slammed* and *kicked* form another focus class, as does *the door*. *Left* is not affected by this segmentation; its internal grammar is not the same as the internal grammar of the other members of focus class 2. If we add the data *the man locked the window quickly* and *Max screamed furiously*, the first segmentation of the former is between *man* and *locked*, and between *Max* and *screamed* in the latter. The second portions of each substitute with the forms in focus class 2 and are members of it. *Locked the window quickly* is segmented into *locked the window* and *quickly*, and *screamed furiously* is segmented into *screamed* and *furiously*. We now see that *locked the window* is analogous to *slammed the door* and *kicked the door* and we treat it in the same way; *screamed* is treated as analogous to *left*. The sequence of focus classes 3 and 4 occur in position before *furiously* and *quickly*, as does focus class 5, which requires a description as follows

$$\left\{\begin{array}{l}\left\{\begin{array}{l}\text{slammed}\\\text{kicked}\\\text{locked}\end{array}\right\}_3 \quad \left\{\begin{array}{l}\text{the window}\\\text{the door}\end{array}\right\}_4 \quad \left\{\begin{array}{l}\text{furiously}\\\text{quickly}\end{array}\right\} \\ \\ \left\{\begin{array}{l}\text{left}\\\text{screamed}\end{array}\right\}_5 \qquad\qquad \left\{\begin{array}{l}\text{furiously}\\\text{quickly}\end{array}\right\}\end{array}\right\}_2$$

The repetition of a focus class leads to the redundancy present in Bloomfieldian theory and described by Harris's construction. The partial identity of sequences of focus classes is handled within Wells's operations in the same way. A more correct description would eliminate the repetition:

$$
\left\{
\left\{
\begin{array}{c}
\left\{\begin{array}{l}\text{slammed}\\\text{kicked}\\\text{locked}\end{array}\right\}_3 \quad \left\{\begin{array}{l}\text{the window}\\\text{the door}\end{array}\right\}_4 \\[2em]
\left\{\begin{array}{l}\text{left}\\\text{screamed}\end{array}\right\}_5
\end{array}
\right.
\left\{\begin{array}{l}\text{furiously}\\\text{quickly}\end{array}\right\}_7
\right\}_6
\right\}_2
$$

The term "construction" is not applied to the sequence of focus classes 6 and 7, but is applied to focus class 6. A construction (Wells 1947b: 94) is a class of occurrences (a registration of a token act of speech in morphemic terms) such that (1) they all belong to a same focus class—here, 6; (2) they have some meaning in common, say, 'Action' in focus class 6; and (3) the token occurrences recur in a range of environments as do the sequences of morphemes of focus class 6. A construction in Wells's approach is neither Bloomfield's nor Harris's, but it is closer to the latter. Harris used "construction" to label sequences such as $\text{Adj} \left\{\begin{array}{c}\text{Noun}^2\\\text{or}\\\text{Noun}^1\text{Pl}\end{array}\right\}$; Wells uses the term to identify a portion of that sequence, the disjunctive class marked by the braces.

The operations we have indicated proceed in this manner until no more morpheme boundaries remain. The last (smallest) focus classes contain only morphemes. Note that by our successive operations, focus classes first consist of morphemes and sequences of them, but by further segmentation, the morphemes are replaced by other focus classes as members. Focus class 2 first contained three sequences of morphemes. After additional segmentation, this membership was replaced by focus classes 3, 4, and 5. In the completed analysis only morpheme classes, the smallest focus classes, consist of morphemes.

Harris's operation proceeded by finding a single morpheme substituting for a morpheme sequence. Wells's operation, in working downward, seeks a morpheme sequence substituting for a single morpheme—again the reverse of Harris's. If this procedure were not performed, the focus class containing only morphemes would not be amenable to further segmentation; there would be no boundaries. It is for this reason that Wells's operation is directed toward a segmentation that recognizes expansions.

Possible grammatical patterning, when constrained by Wells's operations, is much like Harris's. There is linear conjunction between disjunctive classes (either Harris's morpheme classes or morpheme class sequences of Wells's focus classes or morpheme classes). The notion of construction in both operational approaches based on partial identity of focus classes (Wells) or morpheme classes or class sequences (Harris)—that is, on identity of substitution—yields hierarchy. In *XYZ* and *ABZ*, *XY* and *AB* are substitutionally identical and are made disjunctive members of a class *P*; then some focus class consists of *PZ* predicting *WYZ* and *ABZ*. In Wells's approach, *P* is the construction; in Harris's, *PZ* is the construction.

The grammatical patterns implicit in the two operational approaches differ in that Well's yields patterns based on linear conjunction of *two* focus classes, while Harris's does not. This binary element is *not* a constraint on possible patterning; it follows from the nature of the technique. The segmentation is such that we work with (1) an environment or position, and (2) the remainder defining the environment. If the morpheme or morphemes in the environment yield a highly valued focus class, then the remainder, plus the morphemes that are in substitution with it, constitute a focus class. The original sequence is a linear sequence of only two terms. That the binary result of descriptions is an accident of the operation follows from instances in which a segmentation into environment and remainder does not yield highly valued focus classes, as in *you and I*. In either case, binary segmentation *you and—I* or *you—and I*, *you and* or *and I* produces a low-valued focus class. The alternative is to recognize in these cases a ternary segmentation. The *theory* is not constrained to binary structures; the operation yields them. Harris's operation is such that a predominantly binary description does not result from its application.

The pattern of grammar (and phonemics) of post-Bloomfieldian theory is distinct from that of Bloomfieldian theory. Primarily, the difference is that Bloomfieldian grammar is based on the position, and post-Bloomfieldian grammar is based on the disjunctive class (see also Hockett 1958: 163–64, wherein the "form class" is the basis of grammatical pattern). This distinction is clearly reflected in the lexicon. Bloomfieldian theory contains a lexicon in which morphemes are listed once, and the indices of their privilege of occurrence are listed many times across the lexicon. Post-Bloomfieldian lexicon lists the morpheme classes once and the morphemes multiply (Harris 1951: 252–53). The change in the theory is motivated indirectly by the operational constraint and directly by the type of pattern that can be defined on operations composed to satisfy it. Grammar, which is based on the experimentally identifiable position, describes patterns built on substitution in that position. The theory then requires disjunctive relationships (and classes) to provide for the operationally determined substitution within a position. At this point, we see that the operations have directly affected the theory; the operations have required disjunctive relationships that were missing from the primarily syntagmatic Bloomfieldian theory, which also lacks the operations dictating their inclusion.

Summary

We now present the primitives and definitions that constitute post-Bloomfieldian theory. Here we are not interested in operations. Having satisfied ourselves that they exist, we have set boundaries to possible patterns and possible language. The theory now formalizes just those patterns yielded by our laboratory techniques. We assume as primitives:

1. *Phonetics:* This is a complex primitive involving segmentation of that portion of the speech act that is recordable as simultaneous occurrence of articulatory properties represented by a phonetic alphabet. A second component of phonetics is the scale of phonetic similarity by which we may rank pairs of segments as more or less alike.

2. *Stimulus-response:* This primitive involves segmenting the bio-social context of the phonetic segmentation associating the resulting segments with the phonetic segmentation. It yields stimulus-response segments that are the same or different; unlike phonetics, there is no scale of relative similarity.

3. *Linear conjunction*

4. *Disjunction*

5. *Represented-by*

6. *Made-up-of*

In terms of these primitives, we define:

1. *Contrast:* Defined as the relationship between terms occurring in identical or similar environments, the wholes of which are nonidentical in terms of the stimulus-record.

2. *Free variation:* Defined as the relationship between terms occurring in identical environments, the wholes of which are identical in terms of the associated stimulus-response record.

3. *Complementary distribution:* Defined as the relationship between two terms that do not occur in identical or similar environments.

4. *Phoneme:* Defined as the representate of phones in free variation or complementary distribution and which are phonetically similar. A phoneme is the index of that class and not itself a class in the sense that it is made up of phones; it is not defined in terms of the general taxonomic relationship of inclusion or made-up-of. A phoneme is the marker for a set of data associated/interpreted as the phonetic record via the relationship represented-by (cf. Hockett 1961: 40–41).

5. *Phonemic construction:* Defined as a linear conjunction of one or more disjunctive relationships of phonemes or phoneme sequences. Each disjunctive relationship is a disjunctive class made up of a number of phonemes and/or linear conjunctions of phonemes.

6. *Phonemic constructional hierarchy:* Defined by ordering the member disjunctive classes in a phonemic construction such that they are made up of phonemic constructions.

7. *Phoneme class:* Defined as a disjunctive class made up of phonemes and no phoneme sequences.

8. *Morpheme:* Defined as the representate of a linear conjunction of one or more phonemes (= morphs) in free variation (or the grammatical equivalent, free alternation. Cf. Hockett 1947c: 328) or complementary distribution and that are identical in terms of the associated stimulus-response. Like phoneme, a morpheme is not a class in that it is not made up of morphs; it is the atomic minimum grammatical unit associated with morphs via represented-by (cf. Hockett 1947c: 324 fn. 12 and 1961: 43).

9. *Grammatical construction:*   Defined as a linear conjunction of one or more disjunctive relationships of morphemes or morpheme sequences.
10. *Grammatical hierarchy:*   Defined by ordering the member disjunctive classes of a grammatical construction such that they are made up of grammatical constructions.
11. *Morpheme class:*   Defined as a disjunctive class made up of morphemes but no morpheme sequences.
12. *Morphophonemics:*   Defined as the relationships between morphemes and sequences of one or more phonemes via represented-by.
13. *Phonemics:*   Defined as the patterns expressed by the phonemes, phonemic constructions, and phonemic constructional hierarchies.
14. *Grammar:*   Defined as the patterns expressed by the morphemes, grammatical constructions, and grammatical constructional hierarchies.

In post-Bloomfieldian theory no mention is made of substitution or position; these are terms appropriate to the laboratory, our operations. The theoretical correlate of substitution is disjunction. Position is expressed in the theory by the linear conjunction of terms. The definitions of contrast, free variation, and complementary are elaborations of the unspecified definitions of non-identity and identity in Bloomfieldian theory.

In compiling a description of a set of data within this theory, we must include the following:

1. A definition of the phoneme inventory.
2. A definition of the phonemic constructions.
3. A definition of the phonemic constructional hierarchies.
4. A definition of the phoneme classes.
5. A definition of the morpheme inventory.
6. A definition of the grammatical constructions.
7. A definition of the grammatical constructional hierarchies.
8. A definition of the morpheme classes.
9. A definition of the morphophonemic relationships.
10. An interpretation of the phonemic inventory via a phonetic system (cf. Hockett 1958: 138) and of the appropriate portions of grammar (morphemes and perhaps some constructions) via a semantic system (cf. Hockett 1958: 138).
11. An evaluation of (1)–(10) in terms of economy (economy per se, pattern congruity, allophonic parallelism, and economy of the statement of complementary distribution).
12. A reworking of (1)–(10) until (11) is maximally satisfied.

Here again, we say nothing of operations. We assume that if our description is consistent with the theory, any statement within it can be derived by performing the appropriate operation(s). If this condition is met by the description, it will necessarily meet the condition of bi-uniqueness.

We find that each language has patterns that can be expressed in terms of two kinds of patterns or two levels. One consists of phonemes and their hierarchical pattern; the second is a similar hierarchical pattern based on morphemes. The relationships within each level are of linear conjunctions of disjunctive classes of phonemes or morphemes related by made-up-of. Each level is a hierarchically ordered taxonomy. The relationship between levels is expressed by the nontaxonomic, nonreciprocal represented-by. Schematically:

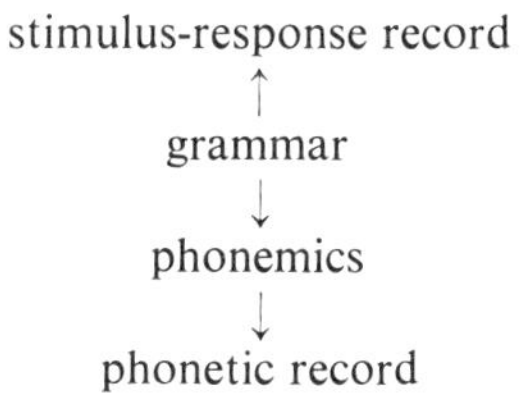

To this point we have said nothing of whether the theory is associated with an assumption of realism or not. This distinction is drawn by Householder (1952: 260–61) in terms of "God's truth," the realism assumption, and "hocus-pocus," the instrumentalist assumption. On this issue we find a final divergence of views. Some (Hockett 1948b: 270–71) assume an inherent pattern, some (Harris 1951: 18) do not. We adopt the former attitude.

Although we assume that each language has structure, it is not assumed that *each* term of our theory and accountings can be associated with some portion of language data. Some of our definitions are "artifacts" (Hockett 1961: 42) of our approach. Phonemes and morphemes are real, as are constructions. Our morphophonemics, however, do not correspond to portions of data (Hockett 1968: 151). As in Bloomfieldian theory, we find a position midway between the strict realism of Saussure and the strict instrumentalism of Hjelmslev. The partial realism of Bloomfieldian and post-Bloomfieldian theory is restricted to accountings, instances of the theory; the assumption of (partial) realism is not extended to the theory itself. The Bloomfieldian emphasis on the syntagmatic is manifest here in that only linearly conjunctive terms are "real"; disjunctive terms are not. The terms of our descriptions are interpreted by associating them with pieces of data, behavior (Hockett 1958: 322); but the patterns defined within the theory and instanced in descriptions are derived from an abstracted, refined behavior. Descriptions state patterns of habits (Hockett 1958: 137, 141–42, and 322) analogous to Bloomfield's conventional actions. Morphophonemics is part of the habits (Hockett 1958: 142) and not part of behavior; thus the interpretation of descriptions as behavior provides no real correlate for the statement of morphophonemic pattern. "Language," in the sense of specific language, is used of the habits and the description of them. The term "language" in a universal sense is attributed to the theory itself (Trager 1949: 4).

ADDITIONAL READING

BLOCH, BERNARD. 1948. "A set of postulates for phonemic analysis." *Language* 24. 3–46.

BLOCH, BERNARD, AND GEORGE L. TRAGER. 1942. *Outline of Linguistic Analysis.* Baltimore: Linguistic Society of America.

HARRIS, ZELLIG S. 1951. *Structural Linguistics.* Chicago: The University of Chicago Press.

HOCKETT, CHARLES F. 1949. "Two fundamental problems in phonemics." *Studies in Linguistics* 7. 29–51.

———. 1958. *A Course in Modern Linguistics.* New York: The Macmillan Company.

———. 1961. "Linguistic elements and their relations." *Language* 37. 29–53.

JOOS, MARTIN, ed. 1958. *Readings in Linguistics.* New York: American Council of Learned Societies.

TRAGER, GEORGE L. 1949. *The Field of Linguistics* (= *Studies in Linguistics* Occasional Papers, N° 1). Washington, D.C.: American Council of Learned Societies.

CHAPTER 6

Tagmemic Theory

The theory of language we take up now is called tagmemics, after one of the central definitions of the theory—the tagmeme. The version of tagmemics considered here is primarily that of Kenneth L. Pike's *Language in Relation to a Unified Theory of the Structure of Human Behavior*, written in the 1950's and republished in slightly revised form in 1967. On occasion we will refer to other works on tagmemics as they clarify or modify this basic point of view.

The tagmemic theory of language, like Bloomfieldian and post-Bloomfieldian theory, views language as a particular kind of human behavior. Bloomfieldian theory considered language as human vocal behavior with respect to a matrix of stimulus-response. The patterning in language was limited to verbal behavior. Language *was* patterning within that data. Although the context to which the phonetic data were related may be patterned and subject to some science (we assumed that it was at least segmentable), it was assumed to pattern isomorphically to grammar. Post-Bloomfieldian theory differs in that the minimum units of the grammatical and phonemic levels are no longer composed of phonetic material, but are more abstract markers of a set of phonemic and phonetic segments, respectively. Grammar is so defined that not all terms have a stimulus-response interpretation, but still, stimulus-response has no pattern independent of the one imposed by an interpretation of grammar. This grammatical hierarchy is now related to stimulus-response data on one side via an interpretation and to the phonemic level of the other via a hierarchy-making relationship termed "represented-by." The tagmemic view is that language data are patterned behavior within a patterned context. The patterning, however, is assumed to extend to human behavior in general (Pike 1967b: 288), and the same kinds of pattern characterize both aspects of human behavior, verbal and nonverbal. Verbal behavior now occurs within a broader context of nonverbal behavior. Pike (1967b: 26) offers support in examples of interplay between the verbal and nonverbal in a song-game in which the lyrics are progressively replaced by gestures until the complete set of lyrics is mimed. Similarly, a meeting on a street may occasion verbal behavior that may be replaced in varying degrees by gestures. Such behavior types, from the completely verbal to the completely nonverbal, are equally "meaningful." Given these instances, meaning may be manifest as either kind of behavior; both must be patterned, and the patterns must be subject to the same theory. The possible patterns of one are those of the other. The relationship between them is hierarchical. Language, as a particular portion of that patterned behavioral hierarchy, is partially defined with reference to its inclusion within a nonverbal pattern. This is somewhat like Hjelmslev's attitude toward language. Hjelmslev differentiated language from nonlanguage by determining the portions of the universe amenable to accounting by the theory. Here, it turns out that not only the relationship meaning-to-verbal behavior, but also the relationship meaning-to-nonverbal behavior is subject to the definitions of the theory. Recall Saussure's general science of semiotics.

We begin our investigation of tagmemics by considering some patterns discoverable within the verbal portion of the behavioral hierarchy. These patterns, as before, turn on the discovery of samenesses and hence of recurrences of identified sames in various ways. Consider the following utterances:

(1)   Our boss asked us to leave

(2)   We asked Max to leave

(3)   Max asked us to leave

(4)   Max was asked to leave by our boss

(5)   We elected Max boss

(6)   We elected Max to do the dirty work

(7)   We went

A kind of patterning may be descovered in that identities of sound features recur. In *boss* and *asked* we find two tokens of an identity of sound pattern; in *to* and *asked* there recurs a second identity of pattern. As before, within the representation of (1)–(7), certain stretches may be identified as same or similar in terms of sound pattern and as same in terms of meaning, e.g., *boss* in the first, fourth, and fifth sentences. To express this second type of patterning we must provide a framework for expressing this identity of items. We see that some items once identified may occur in the same positions with respect to some sequences of items. For example, *our boss* and *we* occur before *asked*, as may *Max*. This pattern may be accounted for by establishing disjunctive classes of items similar to Hjelmslevian systems and to post-Bloomfieldian form and morpheme classes. Finally, notice that in these sentences the class of *our boss, we*, and *Max* may occur initially, and in that position they are the "subject" of the sentence. The same items may occur in the frame *Someone elected . . . to do the dirty work*. Here the same items are the "object" of the sentence. (We ignore for the moment what "subject" and "object" mean and the *us* variant of *we*.) Subject is characterized by a class of items occurring initially but when we compare the occurrence of these same items in the frame *. . . was asked to leave*, we find a distinction between their occurrence there and in the frame *. . . asked someone to leave*. Here the items are Subjects-as-Objects and Subjects-as-Actors, respectively. The same items then manifest a third pattern in that they may be subjects and objects as well as members of a disjunctive class. This last functional pattern is not equivalent or reducible to class membership, for we cannot deduce that *Max* is subject or object from knowledge of its meaning or class membership. The pattern is to be formalized in some other way. These three kinds of patterns illustrate those accounted for by tagmemics: patterns of sound, patterns of meaningful items, and patterns of function. These are fully described when the inventory of sounds, items, and functions is identified, when the distribution of members of each inventory relative to one another is stated, and when the inventory of each is interpreted or manifested.

This view of language requires three levels or *modes* (Pike 1967b: 121 and 143). Language is said to be trimodally structured. The minimum units of the level accounting for patterns of sound is the *phoneme;* that of the level accounting for patterns of items is the *morpheme;* and that of the level accounting for patterns of functions is the *tagmeme.*

As in the preceding theories, the minimum or basic units within each level show patterns of distribution. Each mode contains formal apparatus to account for paradigmatic and syntagmatic patterning. Units within each level show variations when compared with the data, and a solution for the problem of identity among pieces of data with respect to units of a level must be indicated. The pattern of the relation between unity in the accounting to the observed variety within the data can be expressed in different ways. A theory may assume some arbitrary number of kinds of patterning (levels) and assume that variation within one kind of pattern is not manifested directly in the data but mediated in some way. For example, in post-Bloomfieldian theory, morphemes could be interpreted as a variety of shapes within data. This variation was not expressed by the direct relation of morphemes to the phonetically recorded data, but was mediated by the phonemic pattern (hence allomorphs and morphs). It was conversely assumed that the operations yielding the morphemic description were performed not on phonetic stuff but on phonemic units. The morphemic operations could have been assumed to apply to the phonetics. In this case, morphemes would have varied phonetically, not phonemically, and the two levels would have been independent, not hierarchically related, as they were. Thus

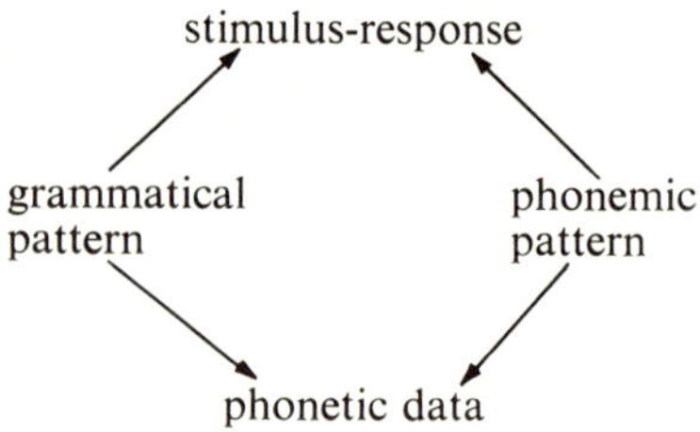

The relation of the phonemic level to stimulus-response observations would have been restricted to accounting for sameness or difference relationships. The grammatical level would have accounted for the much more complex, substantive relationships between stimulus-response and phonetics. This arrangement of the two kinds of patterning assumed for language was not considered. One reason for this lies in the observation that variations of grammatical units are patterned, and that patterning is more easily stated in phonemic terms than in phonetic. For example, in English, obstruent stops occurring finally may be unreleased, released, or occasionally released and aspirated; medially after stress an alveolar stop is lenis and voiced. In accounting for [bǽt] *bat*, a description of the phonemic pattern would require that we state the variants of /t/. A description of the morphemic or grammatical patterning of {*bat*} would require that the same statements be repeated to account for phonetic variations of the grammatical unit: [bǽt⌐], [bǽt⌐], [bǽdɪŋ] *batting*, and [bǽdɪd] *batted*, etc. This wholesale repetition of identical statements results directly from the assumption of completely independent levels. In addition, complete independence of levels would make it impossible to predict variants of phonemes with respect to grammatical patterning, although this may in part be averted by introducing terms into the phonological description (e.g., junctures) in some principled way to help predict variants. Finally, grammatical operations defined over a phonetic transcription would be much more complex than if defined over the phonemic description of data.

Tagmemics adopts a position midway between the extremes defined by post-Bloomfieldian theory and the view just presented. The three assumed levels or modes are independent in that all three may be directly interpreted as associated with some portion of meaning data. Notwithstanding this independence of levels, statements of variants with respect to verbal behavior are not expressed directly in terms of the phonetic data. The formal variants of tagmemic units are stated within the morphemic level, the formal variants of the morphemic level are stated within the phonological level; and finally, the formal variants of the phonological level are stated in terms of the phonetically recorded data. This produces a schema of relationships something like

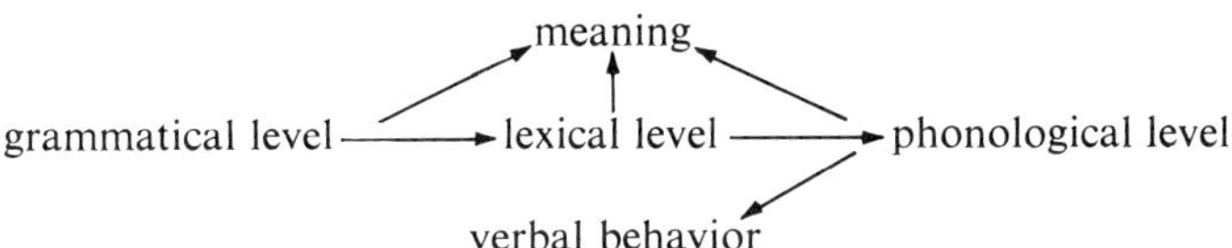

where "$X \longrightarrow Y$" means "X units have variants in terms of Y units." Not all terms within the phonological level have interpretative association with meaning. Where applicable, the association of the phonological level with meaning may be attributed to sequences of sound common to *glimmer*, *gleam*, *glow*, *glare*, and the like (cf. Pike 1967b: 606–7).

The Grammatical Level

Let us now consider the grammatical level in more detail, beginning with further observations on sentences (1) and (2). In each of these sentences, *our boss* and *we* exhibit a grammatical pattern "Subject-as-Actor." Description of this pattern consists in (1) identifying a position or slot; (2) associating a structural meaning with the slot; and (3) correlating this slot with a morpheme class within the lexical level. We might first attempt to structure this pattern with the definition of an "emic or distinctive slot," which has an interpretation as a structural meaning on one side and which is manifested as a morpheme class on the other. This preliminary attempt is, however, rejected because it is assumed that all elements of the theory will have some interpretation and correlate with some pattern inherent in the data—here verbal behavior (Pike 1967b: 38). Emic slots fail in this respect (Pike 1967b: 220–21). Slots do not occur. A distinction must be made between "manifest" and "occur." Manifestation is a unidirectional relationship between a unit and its variants. Occurrence exists under an assumption of realism when we examine data and say that a certain portion of it is some unit in the accounting. If we examine [hî^i læfs] and say that [hî^i] *is* a Subject-as-Actor tagmeme, then that tagmeme occurs in the data. All terms of an accounting have manifestations, but not all occur. The condition of realism introduced in the above paragraph is restricted. We will find it necessary to define disjunctive classes, and the condition of realism is not extended to them. They are manifested, but they do not occur (Pike 1967b: 176, 203, 209, 241, and 323). All other units, minimum and nonminimum in a level occur and are manifested. This distinction mirrors the partial realism of Bloomfieldian and post-Bloomfieldian theory.

An alternative formulation of grammatical pattern is "an emic slot correlated with a morpheme class" (Pike 1967b: 194). The unit of pattern is not a distinct position alone but one that presupposes a morpheme class. The criterion of realism is met here by assuming that the occurrence of a member of the correlated morpheme class is also an occurrence of the tagmeme (Pike 1967b: 203 and 241). Thus, *we* in *we asked our boss to leave* is the intersection of the tagmeme Subject-as-Actor and the morpheme {*we*}. Both patterns are fused in that same stretch of verbal behavior. The definition of tagmeme presupposes the terms "emic" or distinctive, "slot," "morpheme class," and "correlation." Morpheme is an undefined term at this point; "emic," "slot," and "correlation" are primitives. "Class" will be a definition presupposing the primitives made-up-of and disjunctive.

In our examples, we see that the tagmeme Subject-as-Actor may be manifest in two possible stretches of sound, e.g., *our boss* and *Max*. The unit we want to identity on the grammatical level is minimum (Pike 1967b: 194), but the tagmeme in *our boss* appears to be complex. It is present in a simple *Max*, but also in a complex, internally patterned *our boss*. This apparent inconsistency of minimum theoretical unit/complex data must be resolved without rendering the theoretical unit complex. Morphemes as minimum units of the lexical level constitute morpheme classes, as do sequences of morphemes. *Max* and *our boss* constitute a morpheme class by virtue of possible occurrences in . . . *asked us to leave*. *Max* may also occur in *our . . .*, but *our boss* may not: *our our boss* is not a pattern in English. *Boss* may occur in *our . . .*, but not in . . . *asked us to leave*. We conclude that the morpheme *Max* and the stretch of morphemes *our boss*, which manifest patterned occurrences in environments of morphemes accounted for by morpheme classes, may belong to one class defined by the environment . . . *asked us to leave*, whereas *Max* and *boss*, but not *our boss*, belong to a second class defined by occurrence in *our . . .* Thus,

Morpheme Class$_1$	Morpheme Class$_2$
Max, our boss, etc.	*Max, boss,* etc.

A morpheme class may be constituted by morphemes, morpheme stretches, or both morphemes and morpheme stretches. The apparent complexity of the tagmeme Subject-as-Actor is a function of its correlation with Morpheme Class$_1$, which contains both morphemes and morpheme stretches.

There is a distinction based on the observation that some tagmemes are correlated with morpheme classes that are constituted by morphemes alone, whereas others are correlated with morpheme classes that are constituted as well by morpheme stretches (or perhaps only by morpheme stretches). The former type of tagmeme is termed simply a tagmeme (in a constrained sense of the term), and the latter type of tagmeme is termed a *hypertagmeme* (Pike 1967b: 432 et passim). Parallel to this within the lexical level, morpheme classes that are constituted solely by morpheme stretches or morpheme stretches plus morphemes are *hypermorpheme classes,* and morpheme classes constituted by morphemes alone are simply morpheme classes. Furthermore, *boss* within the lexical level is a morpheme, whereas *our boss* is a *hypermorpheme*. Subject-as-Actor is then a hypertagmeme. The morpheme class that is manifest in the sentences as *ed* manifests a tagmeme proper of Tense. The apparent complexity within the tagmemic level is in fact a complexity within the lexical level.

A Partial Accounting

Utterances such as the tagmemically complex *We elected Max to do the dirty work* provide the basis for expanding the patterning within the tagmemic level. We may identify a hypertagmeme Sentence correlated with the morpheme class constituted by the morpheme stretch *we-elected-Max-to-do-the-dirty-work* as well as *We-elected-Max-boss, Go-home*, etc. Some morphemes and morpheme stretches may occur in English without additional co-occurring morphemes. The hypertagmeme Sentence may then be defined as a particular hypertagmeme having a slot with meaning something like 'statement' and correlated with some morpheme class of which *we elected Max to do the dirty work* is a member (See Longacre 1967).

The same stretch of items in (6) has other tagmemic descriptions than that of Sentence. We may describe it in terms of clauses. Notice as before that *we* is a member of a morpheme class correlated with the hypertagmeme Subject-as-Actor. The sequence *elected Max to the do dirty work* exhibits tagmemic patterning. Comparing this morpheme sequence with *elected Max boss*, both of which occur in the environment *we . . .* , we identify a hypermorpheme class composed of *elected, asked*, and *went*. The slot correlated with this hypermorpheme class is located relatively to the right of the Suject-as-Actor slot. The functional meaning associated with the slot may be given roughly as 'Active-Predicate'.

At this point we observe that tagmemes may be related to one another in a linear, left-to-right fashion. Such sequences of (hyper) tagmemes are called *syntagmemes* (Pike 1967b: 451). Linear patterning is generally referred to as *structural* (Pike 1967b: 506), whereas nonlinear, disjunctive patterning of the type found in (hyper) morpheme classes is *systemic* (Pike 1967b: 176 and 209). Occasionally "structure" may be used synonymously with "pattern" (cf. Pike 1967b:55–59).

The remainder of our utterances—*Max to do the dirty work*—appears to occupy a slot that is also filled by *Max boss*. The slot must be filled; **we elected* is not an acceptable pattern in English. The third slot is again identified by its relative position to the right of the Active-Predicate tagmeme slot and has a structural meaning something like 'Goal-of-Predicate'. Comparison of *we went* with *we elected Max to do the dirty work* indicates that this Object-of-Predicate tagmeme is not obligatory. The Subject-as-Actor and Active-Predicate tagmemes are. In addition to relating tagmemes linearly, we may relate them to the tagmemic sequence as either obligatory or optional. The alternative is to distinguish between two Predicate tagmemes: Transitive and Intransitive. The two syntagmemes, Subject-as-Actor and Transitive-Predicate and Goal-of-Predicate versus Subject-as-Predicate and Intransitive-Predicate, are then not only distinct by the presence or absence of a tagmeme but by the presence of two distinct tagmemes. The obligatory-optional relation is one formulation of the solidarity-selection relations in Hjelmslevian theory. This relation, plus identity of syntagmemes by virtue of shared tagmemes, permits their identification as a single syntagmeme.

This identification raises the question of predicting sentences such as those above, but not also *we went Max* and *we elected*. The tagmemic description of our utterances is now something like the following:

$$+ \text{ Subject-as-Actor} + \text{Active Predicate} \pm \text{Goal-of-Predicate}$$

in which a plus indicates obligatoriness and a plus-minus, optionality. The left-to-right order manifests the linear relationship of the tagmemes. From this description alone we cannot exclude *we went Max* from our predictions. If we add additional information of the hypermorpheme classes correlated with each hypertagmeme in the following manner,

Subject-	Hypermorpheme	Active-	Hypermorpheme	Goal-	Hypermorpheme
$\pm$ as-	: Class$_1$	+ Predicate	: Class$_2$	$\pm$ of-	: Class$_3$
Actor				Predicate	

in which the addition after each hypertagmeme identifies the hypermorpheme class correlated with each hypertagmeme, we may make further observations about the morpheme classes correlated with the Active-Predicate hypertagmeme. The presence or absence of the Goal-of-Predicate tagmeme correlates with a given hypermorpheme subclass manifesting the Active-Predicate hypertagmeme. If the Goal-of-Predicate is present, the hypermorpheme subclass correlated with Active-Predicate is constituted by *elected, designated, wanted*, etc. If the Goal-of-Predicate hypertagmeme is absent from the tagmemic sequence, the hypermorpheme class correlated with Active-Predicate is constituted by *went, walked, laugh*, etc. The two subclasses are complementary in that the first occurs only with a following Goal-of-Predicate hypertagmeme; the second occurs only when it is absent. They are both correlated with the Active-Predicate slot. The Active-Predicate hypertagmeme then has two variants or *allotagmas* (Pike 1967b: 228) predicted by presence or absence of another (hyper) tagmeme, here Goal-of-Predicate. With this much stated, we may avoid predicting nonoccurring utterances by correlating Active-Predicate with two hypermorpheme subclasses, Transitive Verb and Intransitive Verb, and stating that the class permitted within a particular syntagmeme is predicted by the presence or absence of a particular (hyper) tagmeme within the syntagmeme. The hypertagmeme Active-Predicate: Verb has two allotagmas—Active-Predicate: Transitive Verb and Active-Predicate: Intransitive Verb.

Continuing with the statement of tagmemic patterns of the phrase, we now consider *Max to do the dirty work*. *Our boss to do the dirty work* and *a boss to do the dirty work*, *Max*, and *the boss* show that certain positions or (hyper) tagmemes of the phrase syntagmeme are optional. The obligatory slot is correlated with the hypermorpheme class of *Max* and *boss* and identified relative to optional preceding and following slots. The functional meaning of the slot is vague, and we simply label it as "Nominal Head." The preceding slot correlated with the class constituted by *our* and *a* we label as "Prenominal-Modifier"; the following slot correlated with the hypermorpheme class constituted by *to do the dirty work boss*, etc., is labeled "Postnominal-Modifier." The structure (syntagmemic pattern) illustrated by *Max to do the dirty work* is then

$$\pm \text{ Prenominal-Modifier } + \text{ Nominal-Head } \pm \text{ Postnominal-Modifier.}$$

Again we face a problem in that these hypertagmemes with their associated hypermorpheme classes predict incorrect utterances as the accounting now stands; e.g., **the Max* and **a Max*. (We will assume here that *our Max* is acceptable and that the possible different meanings of *Max* in *our Max*, i.e., one of several people named "Max," and *Max*, i.e., a given individual named "Max," is to be accounted for elsewhere.) We avoid such incorrect predictions by stating that the Nominal-Head hypertagmeme has two allotagmas. To do this, we identify two hypermorpheme subclasses: one composed of *Max, Matt, Ross, Wyn*, etc., which we label "Proper Noun," and one composed of *boss, chairman*, etc., labeled "Common Noun." The Nominal-Head: Noun hypertagmeme has two variants—Nominal-Head: Proper Noun and Nominal-Head: Common Noun. The absence of the Prenominal-Modifier hypertagmeme conditions the Nominal-Head: Proper Noun variant; otherwise, either variant of Nominal-Head occurs. In terms of these manifesting hypermorpheme classes, we may predict two variants of the Prenominal-Modifier: Determiner hypertagmeme. The hypermorpheme subclass of Determiners, which we call "Possessive Determiners," manifests the hypertagmeme Prenominal-Modifier if the hypermorpheme subclass manifesting the hypertagmeme Nominal-Head is Proper Noun. Otherwise, the hypermorpheme class manifesting the Prenominal Modifier may be either the hypermorpheme subclass of Possessive or Nonpossessive Determiners.

The prediction of a variant of the hypertagmeme Prenominal-Modifier differs from that of the variants of Active-Predicate. The variants of the latter were determined in terms of presence or absence of a particular hypertagmeme. Here, the presence or absence of a hypertagmeme in a sequence is not sufficient. From the co-occurrence of Prenominal-Modifier and Nominal-Head hypertagmemes alone, we cannot predict which variant co-occurs. The prediction of one variant (the Prenominal-Modifier) is in terms of the *variants* of the second (the Nominal Head). We might consider reversing the order of prediction–that is, predicting the variants of the Nominal Head in terms of the variants of the Prenominal-Modifier. The variants of the Prenominal-Modifier would be freely occurring, and the Nominal-Head: Proper Noun variant would be predicted if the Prenominal-Modifier: Possessive Determiner variant occurred. This, however, leaves us with the problem of determining the variant of the Nominal-Head hypertagmeme when the Prenominal-Modifier tagmeme is absent. Recall that it is optional. On the basis of simplicity, we prefer our first statement of prediction. Notice that the direction of prediction, Nominal-Head variant to Prenominal-Modifier variant, was one way. In such instances as *our boss asks* and *we ask*, the hypermorpheme class of Subject-as-Actor is divided into two subclasses, Singular Noun Phrase and Plural Noun Phrase, and the Active-Predicate correlated hypermorpheme class is divided into a Singular Verb Phrase and Plural Verb Phrase. The conditioning here is mutual or reciprocal. In the schema for representing syntagmemes, the conditioning is indicated by a tie bar connecting the relevant (hyper) tagmemes:

+Subject-as-Actor   +Active-Predicate

Nonreciprocal conditioning from variant to variant covers the traditional notion of government; reciprocal conditioning covers that of congruence or agreement. In Bloomfieldian and post-Bloomfieldian theory, this type of co-occurrence restriction was accounted for by identifying subclasses within form classes and stating relations between them. In Hjelmslevian theory, such restrictions may be accounted for by stating that within a class (system), certain, describing components bear a relation of mutual implication with some but not with all of the members of another class of the same rank. In Saussure's theory such a problem would not arise. The concreteness requirement of the assumed realism would prevent the establishment of the equivalent of hypermorpheme classes, form classes, or systemic classes in the Hjelmslevian sense; and the problem of co-occurrence only arises when we define something analogous to these classes.

We now have three ways of predicting the allotagmas of syntagmemes: (1) by tagmemic environment, (2) by allotagma environment, and (3) by free variants (unconditioned). Notice that the tagmemic variants to this point have all been variants with respect to the manifesting (hyper) morpheme class indicated by choice among (hyper) morpheme subclasses. Tagmemes may have variants with respect to other properties. Order is one such property. In *yesterday we elected Max* and *we elected Max yesterday*, the optional tagmeme "Time-Adverb" correlated with a hypermorpheme class represented by *yesterday* may vary in terms of its slot from leftmost to rightmost. Here the variation is free.

If we examine the accounting we have compiled so far for the utterance *we elected Max to do the dirty work*, we find something like

(8)   +Sentence: Hypermorpheme Class$_1$

within the grammatical level correlated to

(9)   Hypermorpheme Class$_1$:
                                 we elected Max to do the dirty work
                                 we left
                                 .
                                 .
                                 .

within the lexical level. Our sentence also has this tagmemic description:

(10)

Subject-as-Actor	Hypermorpheme : Class$_2$	+ Active-Predicate	Hypermorpheme : Class$_3$	± Goal-of-Predicate	Hypermorpheme : Class$_4$

in which the hypertagmemes are correlated to the following hypermorpheme classes within the lexical level:

(11)

Hypermorpheme Class$_2$:	Hypermorpheme Class$_3$:	Hypermorpheme Class$_4$:
we	Transitive Verb:	*Max*
our boss	*elect*	*our boss*
.	*designate*	*Max to do the dirty work*
.	.	.
.	.	.
	.	.
	Intransitive Verb:	
	went	
	laugh	
	.	
	.	
	.	

Following is the grammatical description of *Max to do the dirty work*:

(12)

Prenominal Modifier	Hypermorpheme Class$_5$	+ Nominal Head	Hypermorpheme Class$_6$	± Postnominal Modifier	Hypermorpheme Class$_7$

correlated with these hypermorpheme classes within the lexical level:

(13)

Hypermorpheme Class$_5$:	Hypermorpheme Class$_6$:	Hypermorpheme Class$_7$:
Possessive Determiner:	Proper Noun:	*boss*
our	*Max*	*to do the dirty work*
my	*Matt*	
.	.	.
.	.	.
.	.	.
Nonpossessive Determiner:	Common Noun:	
the	*boss*	
a	*chairman*	
.	.	
.	.	
.	.	

In (8), (10), and (12) we have produced three accountings for a single piece of data. We must now consider their relationship to one another.

Tagmemic Hierarchy

In relating the hypertagmeme (or one-slot syntagmeme) of (8) to the syntagmemes of (10) and (12), we may say that the hypertagmeme Sentence is made up of the positions occupied by the three hypertagmemes of the syntagmeme (10); and likewise, the Goal-of-Predicate hypertagmeme in (10) is made up of three positions occupied by the hypertagmemes of (12). Such a relationship would be indicated as follows:

(14)

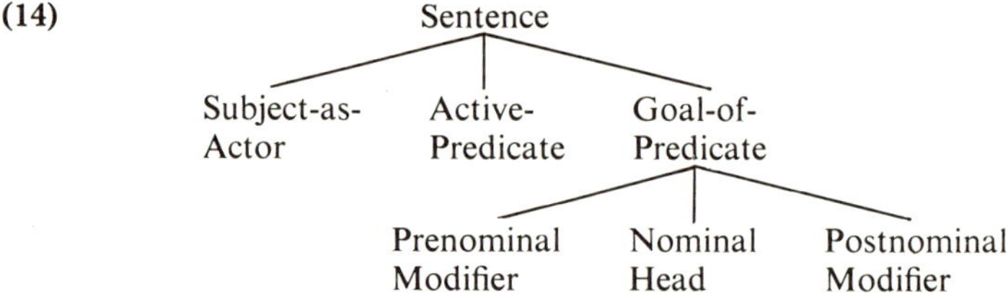

This would produce a picture of grammatical hierarchy not unlike that of Bloomfieldian theory in which constructions were defined as linearly related positions or slots that in turn consisted of positions all of which could be occupied by classes of morphemes. Within tagmemics, the argument against such a relationship is that it renders the hypertagmeme Goal-of-Predicate, for example, a grammatically complex unit in that it consists of a complex of tagmemes. The definition of (hyper) tagmeme is intended, like morpheme and phoneme, to identify a minimum unit within the grammatical level. (Recall that the distinction between hypertagmeme and tagmeme proper is in terms of morphemic, not tagmemic, complexity.) The choice to relate tagmemes to tagmemes by the relation of made-up-of would force us to modify the notion of tagmeme as the minimum element within the tagmemic level, for some tagmemes, such as the hypertagmemes, would be complex and consist of slots. The hypertagmeme would then be indistinguishable from the syntagmeme. We must seek another way of stating tagmeme-to-tagmeme relationships.

Having relinquished made-up-of as holding between tagmemes of different syntagmemes, we decide to mediate that relationship by some third term and turn to the relationship of syntagmemes to tagmeme. By definition, the former may be complex—a sequence of (hyper) tagmemes. The syntagmeme can be said to be made up of tagmemes without violating the simple nature of the tagmeme; and like the tagmeme, the syntagmeme will have a correlation with the lexical level. Consider the portrayal

$$+\text{Subject-as-Actor} \ : \ \frac{\text{Noun}}{\text{Phrase}} \ + \ \text{Active-Predicate} \ : \ \text{Intransitive Verb}$$

correlated with its hypermorpheme (sub) classes

$$
\begin{array}{ll}
\text{we} & \text{went} \\
\text{our boss} & \text{laughed} \\
\cdot & \cdot \\
\cdot & \cdot \\
\cdot & \cdot
\end{array}
$$

The syntagmeme may be considered to correlate with the sum of the morpheme sequences produced by the manifesting classes of its (the syntagmeme's) constituent (hyper) tagmemes. Thus, the syntagmeme is here correlated with, among others, the morpheme sequences *we went*, *we laughed*, etc. These sequences form a hypermorpheme class. They are in fact a subclass of the hypermorpheme class correlated with the Sentence hypertagmeme. We may now depict the relationship of the Sentence hypertagmeme to the clause syntagmeme (10) consisting of Subject-as-Actor and Active-Predicate in the following way:

(15)   Sentence : Hypermorpheme Class$_1$ $\longrightarrow$ Hypermorpheme Class$_1$

                                                        Passive Sentence

                                                        Imperative Sentence

Active Clause Syntagmeme : $\dfrac{\text{Active Clause}}{\text{Morpheme Class}}$ $\longrightarrow$ Active Sentence

Subject-as-Actor : $\dfrac{\text{Noun}}{\text{Phrase}}$ Active Predicate : $\dfrac{\text{Intransitive}}{\text{Verb}}$

in which $\longrightarrow$ means "is correlated with," and the Active Clause syntagmeme is made up of the two hypertagmemes Subject-as-Actor and Active-Predicate. The Sentence hypertagmeme is related to the Active Clause syntagmeme in that the hypermorpheme class correlated with Sentence contains subclasses, one of which is correlated with Active Clause syntagmeme. The Sentence hypertagmeme to Active Clause syntagmeme relationship is mediated by a shared, correlated hypermorpheme class. The Subject-as-Actor hypertagmeme has then only a very indirect relationship to the Sentence hypertagmeme, mediated by a syntagmeme and a hypermorpheme class.

We now find added reason for distinguishing subclasses within hypermorpheme classes, that of relating hypertagmemes to syntagmemes. Notice that the plurality of subclasses within the hypertagmeme Sentence (indicating allotagmas or variants of the Sentence) implies as many clause syntagmemes, one for each hypermorpheme subclass. It is claimed in (15) that there will be in English an Imperative Clause syntagmeme and a Passive Clause syntagmeme in addition to the Active Clause syntagmeme. Each of these three will consist of constituent hypertagmemes. The utterances *go home*, *hit the nail with the hammer*, and *shut up* are described morphemically by their membership in the hypermorpheme class of Imperative Sentence and grammatically by the clause syntagmeme

$$+ \text{Imperative-Predicate} \pm \text{Goal-of-Predicate} \pm \text{Adverb} \pm \text{Instrument}$$

The Imperative-Predicate hypertagmeme correlates with a hypermorpheme class with two subclasses, that is, it has two variants—one manifested by the Intransitive Verb hypermorpheme class (*go*, *shut up*, etc.) and the second manifested by the Transitive Verb hypermorpheme class (*hit*, *elect*, etc.). The set of utterances containing *Max was elected by us* belong to the hypermorpheme class of Passive Sentences. Tagmemically, the accounting requires a clause syntagmeme

$$+ \text{Subject-as-Goal} + \text{Passive-Predicate} \pm \text{Agent-as-Actor}$$

The Subject-as-Goal hypertagmeme is correlated with the same hypermorpheme class as the Actor-as-Subject hypertagmeme. *Max* may be equally Subject-as-Actor or Subject-as-Goal. The Passive-Predicate is correlated with the hypermorpheme class containing the hypermorpheme *was elected*, *is elected*, *was hit*, and so on. The Agent-as-Actor is correlated with the hypermorpheme class *by us*, *by our boss*, and the like.

Each of these clause syntagmemes may be related to the Sentence as the Active-Clause syntagmeme was. The presence of additional clause syntagmemes requires that we establish the relationship among them. As the relationship between the hypermorpheme class correlated with the Sentence hypertagmeme consists of disjunctively related subclasses correlated with clause syntagmemes, so the syntagmemes themselves form a system of disjunctively related terms. Our scheme of tagmemic units and relationships is now expanded:

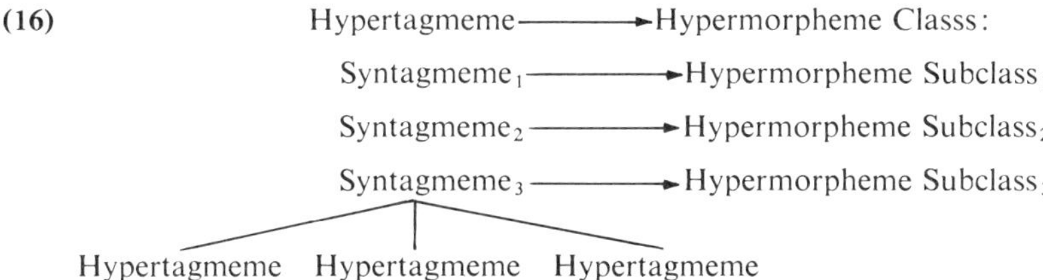

Neither the maximum and the minimum number of syntagmemes within a syntagmemic system nor the maximum and minimum number of tagmemes within a syntagmemic structure is fixed by the theory (Pike 1967b:446), and it is predicted that a language may thus have any number.

The grammatical level outlined shows patterning that falls into clusters: a system of syntagmemes and the constituent (hyper) tagmemes of each syntagmeme. These clusters of pattern are termed *levels* (Pike 1967b:436–46 and Longacre 1964a: 16–17). Because we have been using the term "level" as Pike (in one sense) uses the term "mode," we will use the compound term "size-level" to avoid confusion when we speak of Pike's levels within some mode.

Below the Sentence size-level we find names for the remaining ones: the clause size-level, the phrase size-level, and the word size-level. There is no firm distinction between morphology and syntax in terms of these size-levels (Pike: 1949 and 1967b: 481). As the number of syntagmemes within a system and the number of (hyper) tagmemes were not fixed by the theory, so the number of size-levels is not fixed (Pike 1967b: 437 and 446). This indicates that the use of a term such as "clause" in the accounting of various data has no meaning beyond its use there, for it has no universal, theoretical definition, neither relationally nor substantively. It is a label. The names of size-levels are used across different languages to designate what intuitively seems to be the same kind of patterns, but until they receive some theoretical definition their use is primarily mnemonic.

Tagmemic patterning is also assumed to be present above the Sentence size-level (Pike 1964a and 1967b: 442, 443, and 517) moving from Sentence to Utterance-Response to Monologue to Conversation. The patterning of human behavior would extend beyond this point, and the structures and systems we have introduced would be distributed in these higher patterns. These patterns also begin to involve manifestations of behavior that are not verbal. For example, a Conversation hypertagmeme might be distributed in a syntagmemic structure we may call Breakfast (Pike 1967b: 195), but not all the (hyper) tagmemes of the Breakfast syntagmeme are manifested by verbal behavior. This possible pattern beyond what we may intuitively call the Sentence was indicated by Hjelmslev. The upper boundary was indicated there by the point at which the definition of language ceased to be effective in predicting data. The definition was applicable only to language data. Bloomfieldian and post-Bloomfieldian theory assumed that patterning occur only within the Sentence. In tagmemics, the patterns determined for language are also assumed to apply to certain nonlanguage data, and the distinction between language and nonlanguage cannot be made internally with respect to same or different kinds (presence or absence of) pattern, but must be made externally with respect to whether the pattern (or accounting) is interpreted as verbal or nonverbal behavior.

Patterns in Syntagmemic Systems

The syntagmemes and their constituent (hyper) tagmemes at a size-level may show similarities. This systemic pattern is described via a *matrix* (Pike 1962, 1963a, 1963b, and 1964b). Let us now consider the system of Active and Passive clause syntagmemes in English. We repeat for convenience their tagmemic structure:

Active Clause Syntagmeme

$+$ Subject-as-Actor $+$ Active-Predicate $\pm$ Goal-of-Predicate $\pm$ Adverb $\pm$ Instrument

and

Passive Clause Syntagmeme

$+$ Subject-as-Object $+$ Passive-Predicate $\pm$ Agent-as-Actor $\pm$ Adverb $\pm$ Instrument

(We have modified the Active Clause and Passive Clause syntagmemes by including optional Adverb and Instrument tagmemes. Compare *We elected Max president yesterday by secret ballot* and *Our boss was elected by us yesterday by secret ballot.*)

One possible type of pattern between syntagmemes is that of a shared (hyper) tagmeme. We may represent this similarity by listing the shared tagmemes along one dimension of a matrix and the syntagmemes along the second:

	Adverb	Instrument
Active-Clause	$+$	$+$
Passive-Clause	$+$	$+$

In this fashion, the similarities of the syntagmemes are made explicit. The occurrence of optional Negative and Question tagmemes within these syntagmemes can also be accounted for in the same way:

	Negative	Question	Adverb	Instrument
Active-Clause	+	+	+	+
Passive-Clause	+	+	+	+

The justification for using matrices is that systemically related structures do exhibit patterning, and unless that patterning is made explicit, redundancies occur in the subscription (Pike 1962: 221 and 1963a: 216). For example, we would have to state for both of our clause syntagmemes the optional occurrence of Negative, Question, Adverb, and Instrument tagmemes as opposed to the single statement within a matrix. The matrix expresses the same kind of pattern as Harris's construction. Linear sequences of items (syntagmemes or morpheme classes) are partially alike in one or more shared items (hyper-tagmemes or morpheme classes), and that partial identity is the single entry of the shared item. Harris's constructions can be formally represented as matrices and vice versa.

The columns in the above matrices are identified with (hyper) tagmemes shared by the syntagmemes of a system at some size-level. The dimension of the rows are the propria of the syntagmeme; these are labeled the *kernel matrix* (Pike 1962: 226–29 and Pike 1967b: 473). The kernel matrix, to be a matrix, requires at least one column, i.e., at least one shared tagmeme. At first glance, such a communis is absent between Active and Passive Clauses. The criterion for establishing a dimension, column or row, of a matrix is now modified beyond identification of a shared tagmeme and extended to shared "formal contrasts of structure paralleling . . . semantic elements" (Pike 1967b: 222). Thus, the Active Clause and the Passive Clause may share a "Declarative" semantic element formally indicated by the sequence Subject-as-Actor/Goal and Active/Passive-Predicate. This contrasts with, say, the order in interrogative clauses. The only formal properties of a syntagmeme are (hyper) tagmemes and order. (See, however, Longacre 1960 for possible hierarchical groupings within a syntagmeme.) The kernel matrix is

	Declarative
Active-Clause	+
Passive-Clause	+

This kernel matrix then enters the larger matrix as a dimension and is *multiplied* (Pike 1962: 226) by the second dimension of the matrix, yielding a *derived matrix* (Pike 1962: 226). In this fashion, the system at any size-level may be characterized by a hierarchy of matrices.

The dimensions of a matrix describe patterns of shared (hyper) tagmemes or shared orders. Apparently unresolved difficulties may arise in identifying dimensions of matrices not overtly characterizable by tagmemes. For example, in establishing a formal correlate to Declarative contrasting with Interrogative, we had recourse to order of items. In identifying this sameness of order we somehow equated the Subject-as-Actor with the Subject-as-Goal saying, once they were equated, that in each syntagmeme they preceded an equated Active-Predicate and Passive-Predicate. However, no formal limitations are explicitly placed on items to be so equated. That is, what prevents us from equating Subject-as-Actor with Agent-as-Actor or even Active-Predicate and claiming that no sameness of order occurs in the clauses? The presence of the term Subject in the label is no criterion for equation unless some definition for Subject exists in the theory or at least in the accounting of each language. To use Subject as a basis for equating the two tagmemes here we must at least define Subject for English. This can be done in terms of agreement. The class of fillers (hypermorphemes) associated with the two "Subject" tagmemes may be singular or plural, and when singular, there occurs a particular suffix within the "Predicate" (Active and Passive) (hyper) tagmemes. This affix may serve as the formal basis for equating the Active and Passive-Predicate (hyper) tagmemes. On an *ad hoc* basis, we have resolved the problem for English (cf. Pike 1967b: 246). Notice that the formal contrast of order occurs on the clause size-level, whereas the formal prerequisite for identifying this order lies on a lower (word) size-level.

We have indicated that (hyper) tagmemes may have variants in terms of associated hypermorpheme subclasses and order. Syntagmemes also have variants: *allosyntagmas*. The formal properties of syntagmemes consist of order and (hyper) tagmemes, and we might expect syntagmemic variation to involve these. Variations of order have been considered variants of (hyper) tagmemic slots and not syntagmemic variants. We may say, however, that syntagmemes vary according to the presence or absence of an optional (hyper) tagmeme (Pike 1967b: 463). By doing this we in effect ascribe to the derived structures the characteristic of variants of nuclear or kernel structures. In that syntagmemes consist of orders of (hyper) tagmemes, any parameter of variation of (hyper) tagmemes will yield automatically a syntagmemic variant or allosyntagma. In describing the ways (hyper) tagmemes have variants, we also described how syntagmemes have variants.

In discussing Saussure's and Hjelmslev's comments on language we found that isomorphy or the lack of isomorphy between systems formed the basis for distinguishing two or more levels. Isomorphy between signifiers and signifieds resulted in a single-level theory of language for Saussure. The introduction of figurae and the resulting nonisomorphy of expression and content yielded the latter as two levels in Hjelmslevian theory. Here within the tagmemic theory, it is the same absence of isomorphy that yields distinct grammatical and lexical levels. The nonisomorphy follows from the observation that a (hyper) morpheme class may be correlated with more than one (hyper) tagmemic slot: thus the Subject-as-Actor, Subject-as-Goal, and Goal-of-Predicate hypertagmemes correlated with the same (hyper) morpheme class. This yields a potential many-to-one relationship between (hyper) tagmemic slots and (hyper) morphemic classes. Similarly, the set of morphemes constituting the morpheme class correlate of a tagmemic slot may, when considered as organized into subclasses, correspond to several syntagmemes. (It is here we find an analogue to Hjelmslev's rule of transference. Hjelmslev's Latin example *ī* 'go' would have a simple, one tagmeme, syntagmemic description within a succession of size-levels. Hjelmslev's failure to distinguish size-levels within nonfigurae forced the transference of the accounting of *ī* down through the hierarchy to some point where it was not simple.) The reverse one-to-many relationship does not hold between the grammatical and lexical levels, for *a* (hyper) tagmeme slot is by definition correlated with *a* (hyper) morpheme class.

The Lexical Level

The minimum unit of the lexical level is the morpheme. As the tagmeme was considered to be a "correlation" of slot with morpheme class, the morpheme is the "composite" (Pike 1967b: 163) of meaning with form. The form is the sound patterning property of language described by the phonological level. (We assume for the discussion here that we have such a description available to us.) Variants of morphemes, or allomorphs, occur as different forms (sequences of phonemes) with the same meaning. The conditioning of variants may be in terms of (1) morphemic environment (the *en*, *a*, and *s/z/es* variants of the plural morpheme in English); (2) tagmemic slot (the *we/us* variants predicted in terms of occurrence within the Subject-as-Actor tagmemic slot or the Goal-of-Predicate tagmemic slot, respectively); or (3) phonemic environment (the variants *s/z/es* within the plural morpheme as a function of the preceding segment). The conditioning factors are in part analogous to those conditioning allotagmas (or allosyntagmas); that is, the conditioning may be within the same level (morphemes conditioning morpheme variants and tagmemes conditioning tagmeme variants) or within the level "below" (phonemic shape of one morpheme variant conditioning a morpheme variant and a morpheme subclass correlated with some tagmeme, that is, an allotagma, conditioning a tagmeme variant, the choice of morpheme class that may occur in that environment). Morphemes, as composites of form and meaning, also have variants in terms of meaning. Recall the example of *Max* versus *our Max*, in which the meaning may be said to vary between 'a given individual' to 'the class of people with a given name'. Considering *Max* as morphemically same in both its occurrences produces variants in terms of meaning. Here the conditioning of that variation is the tagmemic environment. The variants of morphemes in terms of meaning are directly stated by interpretation with respect to the representation of the meaning portion of data.

Morphemes have patterns of occurrence relative to one another. These patterns—expressed with disjunctive classes—have been introduced in discussing their correlation to tagmemic slots. The distribution patterns, although correlated with the grammatical mode, exist independently in the lexical. A set of morphemes may be observed to occur in some same morphemic environment. This pattern is accounted for by grouping these morphemes into morpheme classes. Analogous observations may be made of nonminimum morpheme sequences and the description made in the same way. Morpheme classes may differ in that (1) their membership consists of morphemes alone (the class that occurs with *walk* . . . : *s, ed, ing*); (2) their membership consists only of morpheme sequences or hypermorphemes (*he* . . . : *walks, walked, is walking*); or (3) their membership consists of morphemes and hypermorphemes (*the . . . man: able, abler* and so on). Class (1) is simply a morpheme class; (2) and (3) are hypermorpheme classes. A morpheme that happens to belong to a hypermorpheme class is also a hypermorpheme, although morphemically simple (Pike 1967b: 424 fn. 2). *Able*, in the example, is a hypermorpheme with respect to that particular distribution class. The classes and their members also bear a relationship to those morpheme classes and their members with which they co-occur in a linearly conjunctive relationship.

Hypermorpheme classes, like syntagmemic systems, can be described by matrices. The hypermorpheme class of Adjective may be accounted for as follows:

	Comparative	Superlative
Stem		

wherein the dimensions are the morpheme classes shared by individual morphemes, such as {*able*}, {*abler*}, {*ablest*}, {*bigger*}, and so on. As within the grammatical level, we might identify a kernel matrix (composed of "Root" and "Derivational Affix") and construct a hierarchy of matrices. The Adjective matrix may in turn be one dimension of the matrix describing hypermorphemes like *the able man, the abler man,* and the like:

	Determiner	Adjective
Noun		

The hypermorpheme as just described would occur in a morphemic environment . . . *succeeded.* Also in this environment *he* may occur; but *he* has no matrix description as *the ablest man* does. *He* does not occur with Adjectives and Determiners. Different members of the hypermorpheme class Noun Phrase have different internal structures and thus different (or no) matrix descriptions. To account for this, we let hypermorpheme classes consist of disjunct subclasses as, for example, Noun Phrase consists of disjunctively related Pronoun and Noun Structure. Each class, Pronoun, Noun Structure, and so on, may have a matrix description of its internal structure where the dimensions are additional (hyper) morpheme classes.

This attributes a pattern to the distribution of morphemes that is exactly analogous to the pattern conceived by Harris and Wells for grammar in post-Bloomfieldian theory. Large, inclusive hypermorpheme classes (or focus classes) include disjunctively related classes of (hyper) morphemes, which according to their internal structure fall into subclasses. The structure of the items within subclasses produce linear sequences of items that again are disjunctive classes, and the hierarchy continues until morpheme classes proper (not hypermorpheme classes nor morpheme class sequences) are reached. The pattern in both is generally

$$
\left\{
\begin{array}{l}
\left\{\left\{\ \right\}_4 \left\{\ \right\}_5 \left\{\ \right\}_6\right\}_2 \\
\left\{\ \left\{\ \right\}_7 \left\{\ \right\}_8\ \right\}_3
\end{array}
\right\}_1
$$

in which 1 is the large, inclusive disjunctive class; 2 and 3 are the members— which are subclasses; 4, 5, and 6 express the internal structure of 2; and 7 and 8 express the internal structure of 3. Then 4 through 8 are treated as 1 and consist of subclasses, and the cycle repeats to the minimum classes. The pattern within a disjunctive class (for example, partial identities in internal structure between 2 and 3) are described in tagmemic theory by matrices; in post-Bloomfieldian theory, by Harris's notion of construction.

A hypermorpheme class can be alternatively viewed as a disjunctive class of matrices (= the subclasses) that consist of dimensions (= the hypermorpheme classes). The number of distinct hypermorpheme subclasses within a given class is determined by the number of (internally) structurally distinct hypermorphemes. For example, *going home, winning the game* would add another hypermorpheme subclass to Noun Phrase hypermorpheme class.

Matrices have been used in a distinct way within the morphological mode (See Pike 1963b and 1965b). Within the grammatical level, (hyper) tagmemes as minimum units were related to the lexical level simply by stating the (hyper) morpheme classes to which they were correlated. Within the lexical level, the relationship of morphemes to the phonological level are stated by establishing the forms to which morphemes are correlated. There is, however, a problem. We have noticed an arbitrariness in the relationships between levels, manifest in that the units defined of one level were not easily correlated to distinct units of a second. Recall the observations on portmanteau morphs in post-Bloomfieldian theory. Consider in this respect a present tense verb paradigm in Spanish:

	Singular	Plural
1	o	mos
2	s	is
3	∅	n

In none of these forms of the person-number is there any clear segment or sequence of segments that could correlate with any of the persons or numbers. To force a segmentation and assignment to some morpheme by correlating a meaning to these segments would be arbitrary. Unlike the example of a portmanteau morph from French, there is here no model that we may extend to account for the unclear cases. In place of segmentation, it is argued that indeterminacies exist in language patterning, not that the theory is unable to express patterning. To force a pattern of the kind we have assumed to this point on such data is to account for them incorrectly (Pike 1967b: 159 and 185). Instead of correlating meanings with discrete segments, we allow for this correlation without requiring well-defined phonological forms. It is here that the matrix enters as a device for describing morphological patterns. In the matrix just above, the form correlated with the lexical meaning of '1st person' is either /o/ or /mos/ when the person co-occurs with 'Singular' and 'Plural', respectively. Similarly, the form correlated with 'Singular' is /o/ when 'Singular' co-occurs with '1st person'. The entry of a form in a matrix indicates its correlation with the meaning of both the column and the row in which it occurs, and the multiple correlation of a form reflects the indeterminacy within the language. This same formalism may also account for instances in which the form correlated with meaning is clearly delineated. For example, in literary Turkish wherein number and case are not fused, the morpheme {*hand*} has the following paradigm:

	Singular	Plural
Nom.	el	eller
Acc.	eli	elleri
Gen.	elin	ellerin
Dat.	ele	ellere
Loc.	elde	ellerde
Abl.	elden	ellerden

where /ler/ is clearly associated with 'Plural' and no form is associated with 'Singular'. A form occurs throughout a column or row. In such a language we may still account for form-meaning composites such as morphemes in terms of a matrix. In this instance a morpheme is "isomorphic with a formative [sequences of phonemes delimited with respect to meaning, PWD] which fill every cell of one row of a matrix, or of one column of a matrix (but not both)" (Pike 1963b:16). With this formalism the entire lexical level, morphemes and their distribution, is described as matrices. The morpheme itself is identified as a portion of a matrix.

We conclude the discussion of the lexical level by pointing out one property of matrices that we have so far ignored. Matrices have been used to account for systems, but the items within the systems have been linear, either sequences of tagmemes or sequences of morphemes. This linearity can be described in two ways. First, we may list in columns the items that occur first or leftmost in the sequence and list in rows the items that co-occur, placing the leftmost item in the actual sequence in the leftmost column, and so forth. This places the linearity property of the accounting in the dimensions in the matrix. Second, we may claim the ordering of the dimensions in columns and rows is insignificant vis-à-vis sequence, and that linearity is a property of the entry where a dimension of a row intersects a dimension in a column. The linear relationship of the co-occurring dimensions is noted at the point of their intersection. The second manner of accounting for linear sequences requires, however, that sames or order be repeated at each intersection. For example, in such a description of Turkish, the intersection of the 'Abl.' row with the 'Plural' column reveals nothing about the sequence of the forms, whether /lerden/ or /denler/. Only an entry /lerden/ specifies the order. The pattern of Number preceding Case is missed in that it must be stated for each intersection. If we try to eliminate the redundancy, other problems arise. We may easily solve ordering in Turkish by stating that rows precede columns in linear order and arranging our matrix accordingly. But in matrices describing the system of clause syntagmemes in English, problems arise when we try to account for the ordering within the dimensions themselves. As an example consider the following two distinct syntagmemes: ± Question + Subject-as-Actor + Active-Predicate ± Goal-of-Predicate ± Instrument and ± Question + Subject-as-Goal + Passive-Predicate ± Agent-as-Actor ± Instrument. The former might be the description of the tagmemic clause structure of *Did we elect Max by secret ballot?* and the latter the description of *Was Max elected by us by secret ballot?* The matrix description of the partial likenesses of these two syntagmemes would be

	±Question	±Instrument
Active Syntagmeme	+	+
Passive Syntagmeme	+	+

in which the two rows are labeled by the propria of the two syntagmemes and the columns are the shared (hyper) tagmemes. The matrix fails to indicate that the Question tagmeme precedes the propria of the syntagmemes, whereas the Instrument hypertagmeme follows. Here, order might best be accounted for by the arrangement of (sequences of) tagmemes at the intersection of the dimensions, leaving the dimensions unordered. A similar problem would occur in describing discontinuous morphemes or infixes. The description of portmanteau morphs fits easily into this formalism in that they may be described by absence of linearity or absence of two units at the intersection of two dimensions. The problem is not explicitly discussed by Pike, although in practice (cf. for example, Pike 1962, 1963a, and 1965b) it would seem that the description of ordering is placed at the intersection of dimensions rather than in the ordering of the dimensions themselves.

The Phonological Level

The third level of patterning, the phonological, accounts for the sound patterns in language. The minimum unit of this level is the phoneme, which is roughly characterized as composed of distinctive, emic portions of the verbal behavior phonetically represented. The phoneme is not a class of sounds, a nonphonetic entity as in post-Bloomfieldian theory, but a phonetic unit with particular characteristics. It shares this property with Bloomfield's phoneme. It also shares the nonclass characteristic with the minimum units of the other levels. Recall that a tagmeme is not a class but a correlation of two types of things and that a morpheme is a composite of meaning with phonological forms.

Let us take as an example the restricted set of voiced and voiceless stops and voiceless spirants in English. In certain cases, say, initially before a stressed vowel and finally, we find aspiration and nonrelease, respectively, for voiceless stops; finally, voiced stops are also unreleased. Each of the eight phones [p t k b d g f s] "contrast" in each of the positions and constitute a system, a disjunctive class, in each. If we seek the phonetic properties that distinguish [b d g] from [p t k] finally, we settle on voice; all are unreleased. The set [p t k b d g] differs from [f s] by stopness. If we compare [b d], [b g], [d g] and similarly voiceless stops and spirants, we settle on the phonetic properties of bilabiality, alveolarity, and velarity as the distinguishing characteristics. Ignoring properties that do not distinguish segments in this position, we delimit /p/ as the simultaneous conjunction of bilabiality, voicelessness, and stopness; /t/ is the conjunction of alveolarity, voicelessness, and stopness. The remaining segments are similarly described. (We should emphasize that, although the slant lines / /, used to identify phonemes here, are the same as in post-Bloomfieldian notation, their meaning differs from theory to theory as the definitions of phoneme vary.) Our phonemes are certain phonetic properties of segments that occur in a given environment to the exclusion of others. The variants in this environment include the specification of nonrelease for each stop, that is, of *all* phonetic properties of a phoneme associated with the distinctive properties registered in the data. The phonemes are constituted of the properties that are not predictable in this position. Recall from the comments on contrast in post-Bloomfieldian theory that it was possible to identify a continuum of instances from complementary distribution to contrast. The intermediate range between identical and non-identical phonetic situations was called "similar or dissimilar environments." The point at which complementarity ceased and contrast began was determined by and large by the simplicity of the statement of complementarity; the measure of that simplicity was not formalized. In tagmemics there are several parameters for stating complementarity: in terms of the grammatical, lexical, or phonological levels. But, again, within any parameter the place where contrast ceases and complementarity begins is not precisely indicated.

In initial position we define /p t k b d g f s/ as we did finally, taking note that all six stops have variants here that are phonetically released, and /p t k/ are, in addition, aspirated. Implicit in the notation just used is the identification of each of the initial eight with one of the final eight. As in post-Bloomfieldian theory, this identification is based on a scale of phonetic similarity, but this criterion is not always sufficiently delicate. We cannot always identify sufficient proximity of phonetic properties to claim phonological identity (Pike 1947c: 70 and 246). Here we assume the criterion is clear in its application and identify initial [p' t' k' b˺ d˺ g˺ f s] with [p˺ t˺ k˺ b˺ d˺ g˺ f s], respectively. Again, in identifying the two sets of stops we do not establish a nonphonetic class labeling it "phoneme." The identification involves only the statement that [p'] initially is the same phoneme as the [p˺] finally. In that we may associate each member of one system with one distinct member of the second, the two systems are said to be topologically the same (Pike 1967b: 312) and hence *congruent* (Pike 1967b: 323). Should we find in some system a phoneme that is phonetically intermediate between two phonemes of a second system and no phonemes in the first that may be identified with the two of the second, then that intermediate phoneme is identified with neither and is termed an *archiphoneme* (Pike 1967b: 300–301). Should we find a phoneme in one system that is identified with no phoneme of a second because (1) it is phonetically dissimilar to all phonemes of the second, or (2) all phonemes of the second are identified with phonetically more closely related phonemes of the first, the unidentified phoneme is still termed a phoneme. Only in ambiguous cases vis-à-vis the criterion of phonetic similarity is the term "archiphoneme" invoked. Recall here Hockett's treatment of similar cases and Hjelmslev's irresoluble syncretism. These instances produce systems of phonemes that are not topologically related in a one-to-one fashion and are termed with respect to each other partially congruent (Pike 1967b: 323).

In predicting variants of phonemes, we may have recourse to properties of the grammatical or lexical level. In post-Bloomfieldian theory, phoneme variants were predictable only with respect to other phonemes. Here, that is not the case. In examples such as *nitrate/night rate*, we may predict the medial unaspirated, long [t·] of *night rate*, as opposed to the aspirated, short [t‘] of *nitrate*, in terms of its final occurrence in a morpheme without using juncture phonemes. Similar statements of the prediction of phonemic variants may be made using tagmemic environments. The conditioning of variants from level to level is now

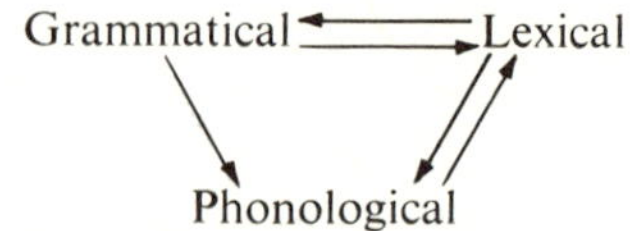

wherein "$X \longrightarrow Y$" means "X conditions variants in Y." The only absent conditioned-conditioning pattern is that of tagmeme variants with respect to phonological environment. It is assumed, however, that a phoneme sequence manifesting a (hyper) morpheme in turn manifesting a tagmeme is a variant of that tagmeme. That is, a morpheme with two variants manifests, in each of its variant shapes, a tagmeme variant. Under this assumption, a phonologically conditioned morpheme variant is also a phonologically conditioned tagmeme variant. The missing phonologically conditioned tagmeme variant is then filled in. With respect to conditioning of variants the levels are not hierarchically arranged as they were when related via manifestation. The relationship of manifestation is a nonreciprocal one establishing a hierarchy of Grammatical Level-Lexical Level-Phonological Level.

As tagmemes and morphemes were distributed into disjunctive classes and patterns of those classes into hyperclasses, so phonemes are distributed. The distribution classes of the grammatical and lexical levels were manifested as the minimum units were. Syntagmemes were manifested as sequences of morphemes. Hypermorphemes were manifested as sequences of phonemes. The sequence framework into which phonemes are distributed, syllables and the like, also have manifestations. The manifestation is not, however, merely as a sequence of sound. The syllable is said to be marked off phonetically by a chest pulse (Pike 1967b: 365–70). Syllables are distributed within a domain called the "stress group" marked phonetically by an abdominal pulse. Stress groups may occur linearly and pattern within still higher frameworks, e.g., the pause group marked by initiating movement and concluding silence; breath groups marked by intake of air; and rhetorical periods marked by change of pace. Other more inclusive distribution frameworks may exist in language, but like the number of size-levels in the grammatical and lexical levels, the number is undetermined. Unlike the size-levels in the grammatical level, the size-levels in the phonological level have a substantive occurrence marked by phonetic properties. We may speak of syllables in language X and language Y comparing them as to various characteristics; but such comparisons of clauses and the like across languages are not possible, there being no language independent or universal definition of clauses. The pattern of distribution of phonemes follows the patterning within the lexical level (Pike 1967b: 340–41) and is again analogous to the hierarchy proposed in post-Bloomfieldian phonemics.

Summary

We have now examined the kinds of patterning that are attributed to language in this theory and examined briefly some of the formal ways of accounting for this patterning. Pattern in language is claimed to be of three kinds: patterning of *particle*, of *wave*, and of *field* (Pike 1959). The particle is a discretely defined unit having properties of distribution (= field) and of manifestation (= wave). This three-way distinction is *in part* identified with the levels of the theory. The lexical level is intended to account for the particle patterning: the grammatical level formalizes the field patterning; and the phonological level accounts for the wave patterning. The assumption that language is meaningful verbal behavior is implemented by locating the unit or particle of purposive meaningful behavior in the morpheme, which in turn is described by identifying the set of morphemes of language, their distribution (field) and manifestation (wave). Manifestation is a matter of locating variants on some second level. Given the arbitrary fit between levels, manifestation must deal with units, variants, which often have ill-defined boundaries—hence, the term wave. The units within each level—tagmeme, morpheme, and phoneme—are said to be "well-defined" or "well-described" (Pike 1967b: 121) when they are accounted for as particles distributed into a field and manifested as waves.

Procedure and Explanatoriness

We have deferred the issue of identity. Up to this point in previous discussion, we have assumed the identity or nonidentity of tagmemes, morphemes, and phonemes without comment. The resolution of the problem of identity is closely tied to the explanatory or operational character of a theory. In general, it is the manner in which identity is dealt with that determines whether a theory is explanatory or operational. A theory that assumes identity-nonidentity and then provides some means for justifying or evaluating decisions of distinctiveness with respect to some data will be explanatory. A theory that does not assume identity-nonidentity, but attempts to define the relationship, will be operational.

There are several arguments to support the claim that tagmemics is an explanatory theory. (1) Much of the writing within the tagmemic framework deals with procedure (Pike 1947c and Longacre 1964a), but procedure occupies a place in tagmemics akin to procedure in glossematics in that it offers a heuristic way of arriving at accountings but does not determine possible accounting nor possible language. In a glossematic theory of language procedure and theory were separate, the former not determining the latter, which was taken as an indication of the nonoperational quality of Hjelmslevian theory. Similarly, theory and procedure are separate in tagmemics, and it is the former that provides the basis for the latter, not vice versa. Pike (1967b: 224) writes of "linguistic theory and the procedures based on it." Comments such as "The definition is useful, however, only when it is convertible into a series of operations which allows the analyst to discover these units" (Pike 1967b: 194) and "Any useful procedures must be based on an adequate theory of the nature of language" (Longacre 1964a: 12–13) indicate that the direction of determination is from theory to procedure and support the claim that tagmemics is not operational. (2) One of the principal differences between Bloomfieldian and post-Bloomfieldian theories was that the operational basis of post-Bloomfieldian definitions was more explicit. Part of this explicitness was the ordered definition of theoretical terms corresponding to the ordered operations that were their basis. The definition of phoneme preceded morpheme, and the phonemic and grammatical levels were thus ordered. We have noticed that the levels in tagmemics are not ordered but co-ordinate with respect to conditioning relations (cf. Pike 1967b:586). This, coupled with the definitions of units in the levels implying units within some second or third level, forces any operational definition of these units to presuppose operations within another level, that is, to be circular. Operational definitions of tagmeme, morpheme, and phoneme would be untenable. ". . . there is no 'starting' set of units at the 'lowest level of analysis' which can first be defined and which then serve as defined terms within definition of units of 'higher levels' of the system. Specifically, the phoneme cannot first be defined and then used to define the morpheme" (Pike 1958b: 368; see also Pike 1967b: 271 and 293 and Longacre 1964a:11–12). Related to the observation that procedure begins at no fixed point of the data is the one that units within any level may condition variants on any other level. This position contrasts with post-Bloomfieldian theory, in which only phonemic units (and not grammatical units) condition phonemic variants or allophones. We have noticed that this property follows from the logical sequence of operations. When the operations yielding a phonological description are performed, the grammatical units are not yet described, and in principle they are not available to condition phonological variants. (The disagreement between Pike (1947a and 1952a) and Hockett (1949) on the possible conditioning of phonemic variants was at cross purposes. The claims of each are equally consistent but within different theoretical frameworks—explanatory or operational.) (3) Unlike the operational post-Bloomfieldian theory, in tagmemic theory there is no consistent inference of an accounting beginning with observed data following the procedures. "We have insisted for a decade that intuitive components must enter [the analysis]. It is the necessity of these intuitive components in analysis which makes a mechanical discovery procedure impossible" (Pike 1967b:225 fn.; cf. also

Longacre 1964a: 11). Any operational interpretation of the procedures would be based on unknown and unstatable techniques, such as intuition, and yield an operational theory with an uncertain foundation.

The preceding three arguments were based in general on observations of the relation of procedure to theory, but we must also keep in mind the distinction between what a person does in writing an accounting of language data and the logical consistency of that accounting with the theory, as we did in discussing post-Bloomfieldian theory. Procedure is generally regarded as a convenient tool helping one toward an accounting. The attitude toward accountings is that they should be consistent with the theory but not that they be obtained by a fixed sequence of manipulations of data either in fact or in principle. Tagmemic procedures do not function as operations within an operational theory but as semi-formalized, heuristic techniques for handling data, and there is nothing in tagmemic theory that functions as the operations of post-Bloomfieldian theory. We conclude that tagmemics is an explanatory theory.

Having argued for the nonequivalence of tagmemic procedures and theoretical operations, we now note that "Tagmemics preserves a closer relation between the theory and procedure in that it feels that fruitful theory must to some extent be limited by analytical techniques for processing or evaluating data. Tagmemics has oscillation between theory and method rather than a one-way priority" (Pike 1967b: 509). The theory-to-method direction of influence is normal in that any theory prescribes the type of laboratory, field, or experimental activity one engages in (cf. Kuhn 1962: 24–25 et passim). But how is the reverse direction of influence to be interpreted if not as the introduction of operations? Procedure influences theory in that it may provide hints for theoretical changes or construction. "Actual work in the field which deals simultaneously with grammar and phonology and meaning is reflected in the interweaving of these components reciprocally in the basic assumptions and definitions of the theory" (Pike 1958b: 371; cf. also Longacre 1964a: 13). If it is helpful in procedure to assume a particular relationship, say, that grammar may guide one to an accounting of phonology, then this may provide motivation to alter the theory such that grammatical constructs condition variants of phonemes. Compare Pike's (1947a: 154) statement that "There must be something wrong with present-day [post-Bloomfieldian] phonemic theory if workers agree on the practical value and validity of a procedure (and of evidence) in the field which they then rule out in theoretical discussion and in presentation." This is first an indictment of the attitude of post-Bloomfieldians toward the constraint of possible theory by operationalism, and second, of the resulting theory.

Within an operational theory, descriptions can be inferred from recorded data. It is in this sequence that operations determine identity and nonidentity. Unlike an operational theory, the terms "tagmeme," "morpheme," and "phoneme" are each assumed to be *emic* (nonidentical with other) units. (Before statements of identity are made, potential tagmemes, syntagmemes, and morphemes are *etic*. After identity is established, the etic variants become emic invariants. Cf. Pike 1967b: 150, 194, and 291.) This answers our first concern of determining whether two pieces of data are variants of the same or different units. We make educated guesses via the procedures concerning identities, but this leaves the problem all explanatory theories must face. There must be some way of evaluating our guesses and of identifying the more correct accounting from among other possible ones. As a preliminary specification of this evaluative criterion Pike (1947a: 155) writes:

> It [*the argument of the article*] *assumes that the best description of any set of data is that statement about them (1) which accounts fully and accurately for all the facts and (2) which at the same time is the most concise and simple and convenient.*

The first requirement of an accounting is equivalent to Hjelmslev's criterion of exhaustiveness. In discussing what simplicity may mean, we should first eliminate from consideration reference to it as it has applied, for example, in the justification of matrices. Their introduction as a formal device produced simpler possible descriptions. This use of simplicity is an instance of the general motivation for theories—it is simpler to discover patterns and state regular items in terms of them than to treat data as patternless. The argument from simplicity is here an extension of the more general concern of identifying as much pattern as possible within a phenomenon and providing some way of representing it in the theory. Patterning was found in syntagmemic systems, and matrices were proposed to account for it.

A second instance of this type of simplicity is the requirement that syntagmemes, to be distinct, must differ in two of their tagmemic constituents, one of which must be nuclear (Longacre 1960: 75 and 1964a: 47–48). (One criterion for tagmemic nuclearity is obligatoriness within the syntagmeme. Cf. Longacre 1964a: 48–49 and Cook 1969: 27. Here we deal with obligatory and optional tagmemes.) Without this condition of identity of syntagmemes, we would treat the following two syntagmemes as distinct but partially alike:

A

A   B

With the modified provision we have one syntagmeme: $+A \pm B$ and the concept of obligatoriness and optionality. Given the syntagmemes

A   B

A

C

C   D

but no C B nor A D, the first two are identical as are the last two. The resulting syntagmemes differ in two tagmemic components, and they are not
identified. If two tagmemes are optional, as in

$$
\begin{array}{lll}
A & B & \\
A & & C \\
A & B & C
\end{array}
$$

then again the three syntagmemes are not distinct, i.e., $+A \pm B \pm C$. Given
the four tagmemic sequences,

$$
\begin{array}{lll}
A & B & C \\
A & B & \\
D & E & C \\
D & E &
\end{array}
$$

the first two would be identified as $+A +B \pm C$; the second two would
similarly be identified as $+D +E \pm C$. These two syntagmemes cannot be
identified, for they differ in two obligatory tagmemes. They are, however,
partially alike and should be related in a matrix:

$$
\begin{array}{lll}
 & & \pm C \\
+A & +B & + \\
+D & +E & +
\end{array}
$$

The definition of syntagmeme and the determination of what may be a distinct syntagmeme and consequently the determination of the system of
syntagmemes require the introduction of obligatory/optional. An accounting
of data that now fails to identify the three syntagmemes, A, AB, and AC as
etic variants of the same syntagmeme will differ in simplicity from an accounting that does identify them. But the difference between the two accountings is
also one of exhaustiveness. The accounting that makes the identification
recognizes more pattern and is hence simpler than the accounting that does
not. The simpler accounting is also the more exhaustive; the distinction
between exhaustiveness and simplicity is lost in judging accountings.

A third instance of simplicity as recognized patterning is the introduction
of co-existent systems (Fries and Pike 1947). Mazateco has a phoneme /t/
with two allophones [t d], the second after /n/; [t] occurs elsewhere. Borrow-
ings from Spanish, such as [siento] *ciento* 'one hundred', destroy this pattern
by introducing a contrast [t] $\neq$ [d]. These Spanish items, however, are more
properly exceptions to the Mazateco phonological system. To preserve the
expression of regular patterning in the Mazateco system, Fries and Pike suggest that the phonological level be allowed to consist of two (or more) sys-

tems. Again, the motivation is the provision of a theory capable of expressing occurring pattern, i.e., for *possible* simplicity of statement.

The definition of a possible language involves specifying sames and partial sames. This specification determines what is simple with respect to an accounting of a given language. In an accounting, simplicity merges with conciseness and exhaustiveness; convenience is an extra-theoretical concern. The criterion of exhaustiveness-conciseness-simplicity with which we are left is incapable of identifying a single, best accounting from the competing ones. It is claimed that there may be non-unique solutions; " . . . descriptions will differ widely, and there are no uniquely correct descriptions, since only a multi-faceted description could present all the phases of such a structure, and since theory and procedure are currently inadequate (and may always remain so) to exhaust the description of any one system" (Pike 1958b: 368). If there are two or more competing accountings, one may be faulty in that it did not consider all the facts (cf. Pike 1947c: 76). The recourse in this instance is to "try to find a third analysis which does violence to neither of the first two, but merges both analyses in a synthesis at a higher level—possibly bringing in kinds of data of other levels or data which each of the earlier partial analyses rejected as nonrelevant to the immediate problem, but which now appear relevant" (Pike 1967b: 56). If missed data are not the differentiating factor, then the competing accountings are indeterminate as a function of indeterminacy in the language. Recall the introduction of language indeterminacy with respect to lexical matrices.

Representation of the Theory

We now give a version of tagmemic theory in terms of primitives and definitions. The following are the primitives:

1. *Phonetics:* Includes a way of representing verbal behavior, chest pulse, pause group, etc., and a scale of phonetic similarity.
2. *Semantics:* Includes a way of representing "purpose" or "meaning," both the lexical meanings of the lexical mode and the functional meaning of the grammatical level.
3. *Slot or position*
4. *Mutual implication* (= "composite of")
5. *Optional:* Analogous to Hjelmslev's determination. X implies Y, but not vice versa; X is optional.
6. *Obligatory*
7. *Conjunction*
8. *Disjunction*
9. *Linearity*
10. *Made-up-of*
11. *"Emic" or nonidentity*

The following set of definitions is one possible expression of the patterns for which tagmemics claims to provide accountings:

1. *Phoneme:* Defined as the set of nonidentical (nonpredictable) phonetic properties of the phonetic representation.

2. *Phonological Size-Level*, e.g., Syllable: Defined as made up of linear orders of phonemes delimited by the boundaries of a chest pulse. The number of size-levels differs from language to language.

3. *Phoneme Class:* Defined as made up of the disjunctive occurrence of one or more phonemes within a slot or position of a sequence of phonemes at a size-level. If the class contains one or more linear sequences of two or more phonemes, the class is a hyperphoneme class and its members are hyperphonemes.

4. *Phoneme Class Sequence:* Defined as made up of the optional and obligatory (= nonoptional) phoneme classes linearly related at a given size-level and disjunctively related to other such sequences within the same size-level.

5. *Matrix:* Defined as one or more disjunctively related items (= dimensions) that occur conjunctively (= intersect) with one or more items within a second dimension. The conjunctive occurrence may be simultaneous or linear; this is marked at the intersection of the dimensions.

6. *Phonological Matrix:* Defined as a matrix whose dimensions are (hyper) phoneme classes (as in the description of partial likenesses between phoneme classes within a phonological size-level) or a matrix whose dimensions are emic phonetic properties, as in the description of partial likenesses among phonemes proper within a phoneme class, e.g., /p t k b d g/ described by the consonant stop matrix

	Voiceless	Voiced
Bilabial	p	b
Dental	t	d
Velar	k	g

7. *Phonological Hierarchy:* Defined as made up of the phonological size-levels related by made-up-of. The larger (more extensive in sequence) size-level consists of smaller (less extensive in sequence) size-levels. The extension of a a size-level is determined by the phonetic properties delimiting them.

8. *Morpheme:* Defined as the mutual implication between a lexical meaning and a linear order of one or more phonemes. If the implied phoneme(s) is (are) not clearly delineated, two meanings may jointly enter mutual implication with a single order of one or more phonemes.

9. *Morpheme Class:* Defined as a disjunctive class of one or more morphemes or linear sequences of morphemes in linear relationship with an identical sequence of one or more morphemes. If the class contains linear sequences of morphemes, then it is a hypermorpheme class, and its members are hypermorphemes.

10. *Morphological Class Sequences:* Defined as the linear relation of optional and obligatory (hyper) morpheme classes.

11. *Lexical Size-Level:* Defined as a disjunction of morphological class sequences.

12. *Lexical Matrix:* Defined as a matrix (a) whose dimensions are (hyper) morpheme classes within a lexical size-level where the intersections of dimensions are filled by the linear conjunction of (hyper) morpheme classes of the dimensions, or (b) whose dimensions are lexical meanings. Matrix (b) is the one in which the intersections of the dimensions are occupied by phonemes and that, if extended, may replace the notion of morpheme.

13. *Lexical Hierarchy:* Defined as the lexical size-levels related such that the disjunctively related sequences of one size-level are sequences of (hyper) morpheme classes, which in turn are made up of the terms of another size-level.

14. *Tagmeme:* Defined as the implication of a slot or position for a functional meaning and a morpheme or a hypermorpheme class. In the second case, it is termed a hypertagmeme.

15. *Syntagmeme:* Defined as a linear conjunction of one or more optional or obligatory (hyper) tagmemes.

16. *Grammatical Size-Level:* Defined as a disjunction of one or more syntagmemes.

17. *Grammatical Matrix:* Defined as a matrix made up of dimensions that are (hyper) tagmemes or (hyper) tagmeme sequences within a grammatical size-level where the intersection of the dimensions are filled by the linear conjunction of the (hyper) tagmemes or (hyper) tagmeme sequences that are the dimensions.

18. *Grammatical Hierarchy:* Defined as made up of the grammatical size-levels related by the correlation of the syntagmemes of one size-level with (hyper) morpheme classes within the lexical level such that each subclass of the (hyper) morpheme classes so identified is also correlated to a syntagmeme on the next lowest (by virtue of that correlation) size-level.

This outline requires several comments. First, notice that although language is defined as a nonlinear conjunction of the levels—the three hierarchies—the levels exhibit a certain asymmetry. The disjunctively defined classes within the lexical and phonological levels include classes with members that are minimum (morphemes or phonemes) and nonminimum (hypermorphemes and hyperphonemes). The disjunctive classes within the grammatical level consist exclusively of syntagmemes, the nonminimum, linear sequences that make up the membership of a given size-level. This difference is reflected in the matrices defined for each level. The matrices within the lexical and phonological levels must indicate both linear conjunctions at the intersection of dimensions (for systems with nonminimum, hyperunits as members) and nonlinear conjunctions wherein the systems contain minimum units, and the similarity among the units are properties of the lower level (formatives in the case of morphological matrices and phonetic properties in the case of phonological matrices) occurring conjunctively and simultaneously. The matrices within the grammatical level express the pattern of a nonminimum, syntagmemic membership, and the linear relationship of the dimensions is expressed at the intersection of the dimensions. For there to be matrices of the second kind on the grammatical level, there would have to be disjunctive classes of tagmemes analogous to (hyper) morpheme and (hyper) phoneme classes. For this to result, we must permit syntagmemes to be adjudged same—admit patterning—if they differ in two or more tagmemes. For example, if we were to admit that *Marvin kissed Maeva* and *Maeva was kissed by Marvin* share a partial identity in that Subject-as-Actor and Subject-as-Goal occur in some same position, as do Active-Predicate and Passive-Predicate and Goal-of-Predicate and Actor-as-Agent and express this using braces

$$\begin{Bmatrix} \text{Subject-as-Actor} \\ \text{Subject-as-Goal} \end{Bmatrix} \quad \begin{Bmatrix} \text{Active-Predicate} \\ \text{Passive-Predicate} \end{Bmatrix} \quad \begin{Bmatrix} \text{Goal-of-Predicate} \\ \text{Agent-as-Actor} \end{Bmatrix}$$

then we have admitted linear sequences into the grammatical level whose elements are not (hyper) tagmemes but classes of (hyper) tagmemes. Instances that at first may seem to require classes of tagmemes are resolved without them. Consider the obvious tagmemic sameness of *walked* and *runs*. The tagmeme Verb-Stem is correlated with a (hyper) morpheme class that includes {*walk*} and {*run*}. There are not two tagmemes of Present-Tense and Past-Tense, the disjunctive class of which occurs with the tagmeme Verb-Stem, but one tagmeme of Tense correlated with the morpheme class constituted of {Present} and {Past}. Examples involving grammatical categories such as mode, aspect, person, number, case, and so on, are similarly handled. Grammatically, there would be a tagmeme for each category, and each tagmeme would be correlated with the (hyper) morpheme class consisting of the specific modes and aspects of the language. In a language with three persons and two numbers for verbs, first, second, and third persons and singular and plural numbers are not grammatical units but lexical ones. The tagmemes of Person and Number are the grammatical units. If we allowed tagmemes to be made up of tagmemes, we would again permit disjunctive systems of tagmemes, but this would destroy the minimum-unit property of the tagmeme. Pike (1967b: 246–51) tentatively admits distribution classes of tagmemes into the theory. Taking advantage of that tentativeness, we omit such here.

Another comment may be made of the asymmetry between the levels. The theory is essentially taxonomic, each level constituted (1) of size-levels (classes) related by a disjunctive made-up-of to (2) the components that in turn are classes related by a linear conjunctive made-up-of to (3) components that are again classes related by a disjunctive made-up-of to (4) components that constitute the next lowest size-level. The hierarchy is of class-member alternating between disjunctive membership and linear, conjunctive membership. This characterizes the lexical and phonological levels. The grammatical level differs. This follows from the assumption that tagmemes do not consist of tagmemes, either conjunctively or disjunctively. This breaks the made-up-of sequence within the hierarchy between (3) and (4). Within the grammatical level (1) corresponds to some size-level; (2) corresponds to the syntagmemes; (3) corresponds to the tagmemes that are not classes of syntagmemes of the next lowest size-level. Taxonomic hierarchy exists within a grammatical size-level. The tagmeme-to-syntagmeme-on-the-next-size-level relationship is mediated by hypermorpheme classes as indicated above, and the implication between tagmeme and syntagmeme and these lexical classes.

A further comment is in order on the definition of size-levels and the systems of hyperunits constituting them. Within phonology, each hyperunit of a particular size-level is characterized physically by a phonetic property, such as a chest pulse, and the units that belong to a given size-level are delimited by its boundaries. This is not necessarily true of hypermorphemes and syntagmemes. Their borders do not always fall at the borders of hyperphonemes, and where they do not, there is no consistent phonetic marking of these lexical and grammatical hyperunits. There is no way of consistently identifying a grammatical or lexical size-level with respect to phonetic properties. Here, we reverse the sequence of definitions, identifying the hyperunit first then defining the size-level in terms of it. The boundaries of these units are perhaps determined by the identification of patterning within some, but not all, morphemes of a morpheme sequence and within some, but not all, tagmemes of a tagmeme sequence. The patterning may be in terms of optional/obligatory or peripheral/nuclear relationships between some, but not all, of a sequence of units. The clustering of such relationships between units is assumed to indicate breaks of structure within the sequence and to identify hyperunits, either syntagmemes or hypermorpheme sequence classes (cf. Pike 1967b: 467–69). Size-levels within the grammatical and lexical levels are then defined as systems of these units.

Notice also that as the grammatical and lexical size-levels are defined there is no assurance that there will be the same number within each level, even though *a* morpheme boundary is always *a* tagmeme boundary, and vice versa. Nor should we, apparently, assume there would be the same number (cf. Pike 1967b: 578–80 and Longacre 1967: 24); this emphasizes the distinctiveness of the three levels.

A final observation should be made with respect to a concern that the definitions of the theory may be circular (cf. Pike 1967b: 270 and Hockett 1949: 40). Some of the definitions in tagmemics may in fact be circular. Compare Longacre's definition of "clause" as "ranking above such syntagmemes as the phrase and word and below such syntagmemes as sentence and discourse" (Longacre 1964a: 35) and his definition of "phrase" as "ranking above such syntagmemes as the word and/or stem and below such syntagmemes as the clause and sentence" (Longacre 1964a: 74). Such definitions will be circular insofar as no other specification of "sentence" is given than "ranking above clause," and so forth. The definitions we have outlined, however, presuppose only the primitives and preceding definitions. Characterizing such terms as "tagmeme" as correlated with a morpheme class and in turn defining a "morpheme class" as distributed within a tagmemic slot as Pike does may give the impression of circularity. The circularity lies not in theory, but in the procedure on which we may base accountings. The fact that the procedures follow no precise order and require no fixed beginning point results in a possible circularity in arriving at the definitions of tagmeme, morpheme, phoneme, and the like, for a *given* language, but the definitions within the theory remain noncircularly defined. The circularity enters again when we evaluate an accounting for exhaustiveness. For example, a maximally exhaustive accounting of a language will be one in which all phonetic properties of a phoneme that are predictable are not described as emic. This implies examination of grammatical and lexical constructs for possible conditioning factors. Similarly, an exhaustive accounting will be one in which all variants of morphemes are predicted, and this involves the reverse procedure of examining phonology for possible conditioning of lexical variants. All this occurs in the construction of a description of a language and is circular. Its purpose is to maximize the integration (Pike 1967b: 587) of the levels, and in so doing each level presupposes the others in their own definitions. There is no reason why procedure should not be circular, for our theory has *no* formal relationship to it.

We now outline a possible accounting within this theory:

1. A definition of the phonemes
2. A definition of the phonological size-levels
3. A definition of the (hyper) phoneme classes within each size-level
4. A definition of the phoneme class sequences within each size-level and their patterning by phonological matrices
5. A definition of the phonological hierarchy
6. A definition of the morphemes
7. A definition of the (hyper) morpheme classes
8. A definition of the morpheme class sequences and their disjunctive relationships at lexical size-levels
9. A definition of the patterning of morpheme class sequences within a size-level by lexical matrices
10. A definition of the lexical hierarchy
11. A definition of the (hyper) tagmemes
12. A definition of the syntagmemes and their disjunctive relationships at grammatical size-levels
13. A definition of the patterning of syntagmemes within a size-level by grammatical matrices
14. A definition of the grammatical hierarchy
15. An interpretation of (1)–(14)
16. An evaluation of the exhaustiveness and simplicity of (1)–(15)
17. A reworking of (1)–(15) until the evaluation is maximally satisfied.

In such an accounting, a partial interpretation or association of the definitions with the data is ensured. The definition of tagmemes as a mutual implication of slot with a morpheme class; the definition of the morphemes of the morpheme classes as a mutual implication of meaning with phonological forms; and the definition of phonemes as distinctive phonetic properties assure us that all these definitions imply directly or indirectly some phonetic data. Similarly, the definition of tagmemic slots as associated with functional meaning and the definition of morphemes as meanings associated with phonological forms ensures that our definitions are also associated with semantic data.

Variation in Pattern

There is an observable interplay of variation and uniformity of patterning within language whether we take it to be behavior or knowledge; and in constructing a theory of language we must choose some point and say all data to one side are subject to the theory and everything else is not. The issue here is how much variation we allow in the data we take as manifesting language. At one extreme we find individual mistakes; false starts, and the like, are completely without pattern. This extreme would be potentially bothersome only if we regard language as behavior of some sort; presumably it will be absent in language-as-knowledge. Next to this extreme, we may identify a pattern for one individual that differs "slightly" from that of the remainder of individuals; and continuing, we may find patterns for a group of individuals differing "slightly" from the remaining individuals. Finally, we may find patterns that hold for the entire group. Eventually, we will find as many slightly varying patterns as there are speakers. For convenience we will term this variation across individuals *dialects*. Within the behavior/knowledge of an individual, group of individuals, or the entire group (that is, within a dialect), we may find at times one pattern and at other times another. This second kind of variation within a dialect we will call *style*. We make the distinction between dialect and style by determining whether the variation is across individuals or within an individual or individuals. The distinction tends to fade when we observe that patterns for an individual—styles—may be elsewhere distributed across individuals and hence be dialects. Although the distinction is perhaps fleeting, we retain it for the purpose of discussion. The relationship of dialect to style may be represented as follows:

	Individual Pattern	*Group Pattern*	...	*Pattern Shared by all*
Style$_1$				
Style$_2$				
.				
.				
.				

The intersections are a particular style within a particular dialect. Either the columns or the rows may be increased, for dialectal and stylistic variation is a gradation with an unspecified number of points. Intersecting the schema of variation and uniformity in patterning is a third parameter, that of exception versus regularity. Placing boundaries within this outline and determining what if any variation is allowed within the data of theories differs from theory to theory.

In Saussurean theory, uniformity of pattern across individuals was ensured by taking the "average," that which was common to all as language and attributing any variation across individuals to speaking. Style is not explicitly discussed in the *Course;* we might expect that insofar as style did not characterize all, that is, insofar as we did not have two averages, style was also speaking. (See the entry "stylistique" in Engler 1968: 48.) There would be no exceptions in Saussurean theory for the theory provides no predictions beyond observed data. Only if we were permitted to abstract an associative or syntagmatic pattern and claim that complex words patterned in accordance with the predictions would there be a basis for exceptions. For there to be exceptions, there have to be regularities, but all observations of patterning are made without distinction as to exception or regularity.

Hjelmslev admitted variation or nonpatterning in the data in the form of mistakes, and accounted for it by catalysis. A framework for integrating stylistic and dialectal variations in patterning is also provided in the *Prolegomena.* Dialectal variation, or a semiotic pattern that is limited in extent, may have associated with it a kind of meaning such as of a particular locale (a "southern accent"), or if unique to an individual, the meaning may be the identification or "linguistic physiognomy" (Hjelmslev 1961: 118–19) of that individual. These semiotics, then, are the expressions of contents such as locale, individual person, and the like. The pattern variation among them is provided for by defining a *connotative semiotic:* "a semiotic one plane of which (namely the expression plane) is a semiotic" (Hjelmsev 1961: 119). The dialectal variations, the semiotics proper, are then resolved at a higher point in the hierarchy. The semiotics enter this hierarchy as commutative either-or members of a class holding a sign function with commutative members of an either-or class that are the content of the semiotics. For example:

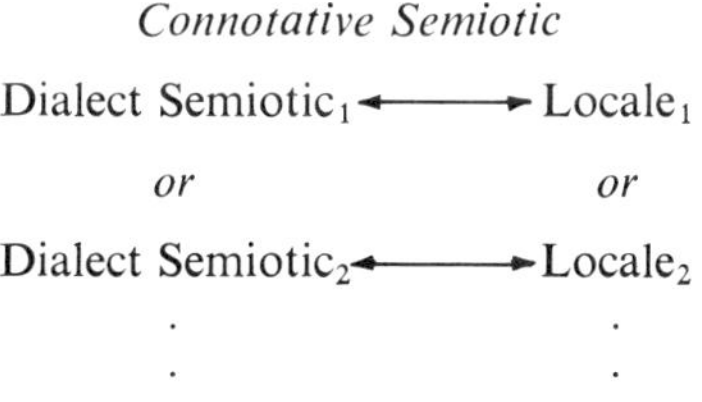

If we assume that the patterns of language are different from person to person, it would follow that semiotic as defined is limited to a text produced by individuals. Stylistic variation is not distinguished from dialectal variation and would be described similarly. If styles exist in dialectal semiotics, the hierarchy might be modified such that dialectal semiotics were also connotative semiotics consisting of an expression plane of style semiotics holding a sign function with a content plane consisting of objects such as "high style," "low style," and so on. This is not suggested in the *Prolegomena*. Exceptions, insofar as they are not attributable to style (as in the use of [ʁezɔ̃dɛtʁ] *raison d'être* in an "educated style" of English that would introduce an exceptional nasal vowel and uvular, voiced trill if the text is not attributed to some style other than "normal"), are not distinguishable from regularities.

Bloomfield broaches the problem first by avoiding it. "These differences [dialectal] play a very important part in the history of languages; the linguist is forced to consider them very carefully, even though in some of his work he is forced provisionally to ignore them. When he does this, he is merely employing the method of abstraction, a method essential to scientific investigation, but the results so obtained have to be corrected before they can be used in most kinds of further work" (Bloomfield 1933: 45). It is not clear that the synthesis of dialectal variations is not simply a requisite for the historical study of language and that synchronically nothing is said of such variation. Recall that in Bloomfieldian theory the data are characterized as "conventional." This implies that we ignore everything that is not conventional or is idiosyncratic to an individual or subgroup, thus guaranteeing us uniformity of patterning much like Saussure's "average" did. Stylistic variations manifested in choice of forms may be accounted for by attributing a distinctive component ("connotation") to their associated meanings (Bloomfield 1933: 151–57). That two forms have the same connotation is not easily reconcilable with the assertion that sememes are atomic and that there are no synonyms. Connotation fails to account for variant style patterns not attributable to connotational meaning, e.g., variant constructions or phonetic modifications. These are discussed in Bloomfield 1933 only as they co-exist in forms that are also semantically identified as members of a different style. Since constructions have constructional meanings, stylistic variants of these may also be associated with connotations. Favorite and minor sentence types do not coincide with the exception/regularity distinction. Irregularities of morphemes or complex forms with respect to their form class, phonetic modification, or selection are noted in the lexicon in the entry of that form (Bloomfield 1933: 269). Irregularities in constructs are not indicated unless they are complex forms entered in the lexicon. Irregularities in phonology are not discussed except indirectly to exclude them; "the terms *regular* and *irregular* are used only of features that appear in the grammar" (Bloomfield 1933: 275).

In post-Bloomfieldian linguistics, it is possible to find a variety of positions. Bloch adopts an extreme stance that limits data to one speaker (= idiolect) in one style (Bloch 1948: 7) and makes no provision for exceptions (Bloch 1950: 87). Unlike Bloomfield, who chooses first to ignore variation across individuals to obtain uniformity, Bloch would describe the data of an individual speaker, ensuring uniformity in this alternative manner. The problem is then how (and whether) to integrate the descriptions of different speakers. Hockett (1958: 321), following Bloomfield more directly, distinguishes between *descriptive linguistics*, the study of a speech community with dialectal variations ignored, and *synchronic dialectology*, which is the study of these variations. The two studies make up *synchronic linguistics*. The later reintegration mentioned by Bloomfield is the province of synchronic linguistics. The relationship between dialects or idiolects may be expressed in terms of intelligibility, common core, or overall pattern. The first relationship requires a method of determining intelligibility. Assuming this, dialects may be grouped in two ways; those dialects that are mutually intelligible and those that are one-way intelligible, i.e., the speakers of one dialect understand those of another dialect but not vice versa. This is expressed by identifying some idiolects as forming L-simplexes and others related as L-complexes, respectively. The variation of data we eliminated from descriptive linguistics will, when reintroduced, at least show our data to be an L-complex: there will be no relationship among the descriptions of the speech of individuals that is not at least one-way intelligible. The alternative methods of relating dialectal variation deal more directly with formal statements of patterning. A common core (Hockett 1955: 18–22 and 1958: 331–37) is that pattern that is shared by two or more dialects distinguished by indicating those points in their descriptions at which they differ. Overall or total patterning is the reverse of this. Here, the pattern of all dialects is attributed to a single description. The variations are then identified by the choices from the total pattern exhibited by them. This last attitude is that of Trager and Smith 1951. The three approaches to dialectal variation are (1) ensured uniformity by restricting data to an idiolect, (2) uniformity by ignoring dialectal variations, and (3) treating all patterning as data for the theory regardless of variation.

We have already pointed out one approach to stylistic variation (Bloch 1948). An earlier one (Bloch 1947) is based on the nonabstraction of stylistic variants from the data in a fashion analogous to the total pattern approach to dialectal variation. In this way the description yields higher numbers of contrasts. For example, English *will* is described as three morphemes: (1) {*will*} with allomorph /wəl/, (2) {*will*} with allomorph /əl/, and (3) {*will*} with allomorph /1/. Nonseparation of the data into distinct sets as in Bloch 1948 and nonadmission of conditioning factors forces this multiplication. A third attitude toward style (as we have defined it) is that of Stockwell, Bowen, and Silva-Fuenzalida 1956. Here, the data admit variation, but style itself is admitted as a conditioning factor. "Vocalizations" (Stockwell, Bowen, and Silva-Fuenzalida 1956: 465) are introduced into the description as nonidentical, and the variations in patterning are noncontrastive in terms of them. It is not indicated whether these same vocalizations may co-occur on the grammatical level, or whether some other device may be used in place of them.

The attitude toward exceptions in post-Bloomfieldian theory generally follows Bloch (1948) and Hockett (1948b: 269). No distinction is made between them and regularities.

The attitude toward variation in tagmemics is similar to that of Stockwell, Bowen, and Silva-Fuenzalida's toward style. Dialect, style, and exception variations are not ignored, and theory is constructed via co-existent systems to extend to their description. The mechanism for this was indicated above: co-existent systems. Differences in language patterns across individuals and groups may be accounted for by integrating them as members of a higher *hypersystem* (Pike 1967b: 583). To the extent that the components of each dialect are related to components of other dialects in a one-to-one fashion, the co-existent systems are topologically same or congruent. This degree of congruency determines what Pike (1967b: 583), like Hockett, terms the "common core" of these dialects and their degree of relatedness. It may be that two dialects are completely congruent and still differ. In this case the difference lies in the variants, the interpretation, of the patterns. For example, one dialect may have contrastive vowels [i e u o a], whereas the second differs only in that it has [ɪ ɛ ʊ ɔ ɑ]. Topologically, the two do not differ. The distinction within each is with respect to the manifestation of the variants of the pattern. In such instances the phonemic systems are the same within the hypersystem, which is indicated by using the same symbols for phonetic pairs [i] and [ɪ], and so forth. The variation is predicted by the occurrence of the phonemes within separate, but co-existent, systems of the hypersystem, here the dialects. With this, we introduce an additional kind of conditioning factor into tagmemics, the system or disjunctive class within which a unit occurs. The discussion of dialectal variation so far has assumed that the members of the hypersystem are trimodally patterned objects as defined by the theory; that is, the hypersystem consists of two or more disjunctive languages as defined above. But it may be that the dialect variation is a factor not of differences in the whole language system (all three modes), but of differences between one (or two) levels, whereas the other(s) are identical across dialects; or the difference may be further restricted and localized at a size-level within a level, whereas the remainder of the level and the remaining levels are congruent across dialects. Style and exceptions are treated in the same way as dialect variation. The nonuniformity of exceptions, unlike that of style and dialects, will be limited to a size-level within a level; there may be exceptions to size-level systems, but not to an entire level nor to the three levels taken together. These latter variations are either stylistic or dialectal. The distinction among dialect, style, and exception is not clearly delineated formally. All are accounted for by co-existent systems. A sharper distinction is made between exceptions versus dialect/style than between dialect and style. Compare Pike's

(1967b: 582) statement that "When speakers of a language come from different social strata of a culture [speaking variant social dialects, PWD] their language subsystems may differ somewhat as styles differ."

With the exception of Saussurean theory, all theories we have examined provide some way of expressing variation in patterning. They differ in whether the variation is integrated within the definition of language, thus making that variation an intralanguage phenomenon, of whether the variation is expressed by relating languages, thus making that variation an interlanguage phenomenon. Dialectal variation of pattern is not expressed in post-Bloomfieldian theory as we have presented it. The methods of intelligibility or common core state whether languages (as defined) may be related, but they do not constrain what is language. Tagmemics, with the introduction of co-existent systems and the definition of a language as (perhaps) a hypersystem wherein such variation is present, integrates that variation as an intralanguage datum. Post-Bloomfieldian theory and tagmemics differ at this point in what they take as data, and tagmemic theory is more general in that it includes more kinds of data in its definitions. If we accept natural language as a semiotic in Hjelmslevian theory, then the patterns accounted by connotative semiotics are outside the concept of language. Style and dialect variations are interlanguage relationships. Exceptions are not distinguished from regularities; both are intralanguage data. In Bloomfieldian theory, variations of style and exceptions, to the extent that they are acknowledged, are intralanguage variations. Dialectal variations in pattern, disregarded in the description of a set of data, are to be reintroduced as interlanguage relationships. In post-Bloomfieldian theory we find differences as to what are intralanguage or interlanguage variations. In one formulation, Bloch would exclude, as Hjelmslev does, dialectal and stylistic variations as intralanguage, while failing to distinguish formally between exceptions and regularities. Hockett, like Bloomfield, in initially ignoring dialect variations excludes them from the concept of language. Such variations are reintroduced as interlanguage phenomena. In Trager and Smith 1951, dialect variations are an intralanguage datum, for such are not excluded from the data subjected to the operations of theory. Like Bloomfield, Stockwell, Bowen, and Silva-Fuenzalida interpret style as an intralanguage variation. Tagmemics recognizes all three types of pattern variation. As we have defined language, a conjunction of three levels, any co-existent systems that consisted of two or more of such level complexes would be an interlanguage relationship; co-existent systems within individual levels would be an intralanguage relationship. Style and dialect are then potentially intralanguage or interlanguage relationships depending on the extent of the variation in what enters the co-existent systems. How much of this hierarchy of hypersystems is to be termed language is undetermined: " . . . there is doubt as to how large a unit is conveniently considered as part of the language system or hypersystem . . . " (Pike 1967b: 584). Until this is resolved there is uncertainty as to what are intralanguage data or more generally what language is.

Regardless of whether a theoretician of language assumes language to be manifest as behavior or knowledge, he must face the problem of deciding the amount of variation he allows in the object he is trying to define. He must set the boundaries on language; and in doing this, boundaries must be determined along the three parameters of dialect, style, and exception. The placement of these boundaries determines whether the resultant definition of language coincides with what we intuitively call a language, or whether it is restricted to what we intuitively call a dialect, or, finally, whether it is restricted to a single individual. The question "Do these two people speak the same language?" will receive different answers as the amount of variation allowed within a language is altered. The problem of variation and uniformity of pattern is one of the central concerns of the next theory we take up, that of the Prague School.

ADDITIONAL READING

FRIES, CHARLES C., AND KENNETH L. PIKE. 1949. "Coexistent phonemic systems." *Language* 25. 29–50.

LONGACRE, ROBERT E. 1960. "String constituent analysis." *Language* 36. 63–88.

———. 1964. *Grammar Discovery Procedures*. The Hague: Mouton & Co.

PIKE, KENNETH L. 1947. "Grammatical prerequisites to phonemic analysis." *Word* 3. 155–72.

———. 1959. "Language as particle, wave, and field." *The Texas Quarterly* 2. 2. 37–54.

———. 1962. "Dimensions of grammatical constructions." *Language* 38. 221–44.

———. 1963. "A syntactic paradigm." *Language* 39. 216–30.

———. 1967. *Language in Relation to a Unified Theory of the Structure of Human Behavior*. The Hague: Mouton & Co.

CHAPTER 7

Prague School Theory

The Prague School Theory of language presents a practical difficulty in that the material we take as source of the theory is the work of many people, none of whom individually presents a comprehensive view of language. Their work covers an extended period; their opinions necessarily change and develop. Our interpretation of Prague School theory must be arbitrary and false to the extent that it will not be attributable to any one person at a given point of time. We will take the work represented in *Travaux du Cercle Linguistique du Prague* and Vachek 1964 as basic and concentrate on the decade of activity 1929–1939, marking the years of publication of the *Travaux*, the period termed the "golden age" of the Prague School (Austerlitz 1964: 459).

We begin our investigation with an examination of the Prague School conception of the speech act. This consists of a speaker and a listener, as Saussure's conception did, but includes a third term, the things spoken of. In this scheme the speaker produces sound perceived by the listener, and the sound is said to have three different kinds of meaning or function. It may contain information of the items external to both speaker and listener, or the meaning associated with the sound may be of the speaker himself. In the second function, the sound may broadly identify the speaker somewhat like Hjelmslev's connotative semiotic, the content of which was in part the linguistic physiognomy of the speaker. Under this particular function we may include sounds emitted by the speaker which serve to identify his emotional state or internal condition. A third kind of possible meaningful sound function serves to elicit a response from the listener. Questions, commands, exhortations, appeals, and the like, are examples of this function. The three functions—broad classes of meanings with which speech sound may be associated—are called *representation*, *expression*, and *appeal*, respectively (Bühler 1934: 28–29). The third function is also sometimes called the *conative* (Trubetzkoy 1969: 20 and Isačenko 1964). The speaker has these functions at his disposal and may "choose" a particular one consistent with his communicative needs or goals. The functions form a system, a disjunctive class, from which a choice is made.

A distinction should be made between the choice as manifest in a particular sound complex with its associated meaning and the range of possible choices. Following Saussure, the former is termed *parole* and the latter, *langue* or language. The act of choice is individual and linguistically unpatterned but directed toward communication, whereas the fund of possible choices is nonindividual or social and available to all who speak/know the language; this fund of choices, lacking the unpredictable element of choice, is patterned. (This recalls Hjelmslev's restriction of the term "language" to the system of the semiotic while excluding the process or text as involving a choice—a particular, unpatterned thing—not partaking of the immanent property of language.) A distinction may be made, then, between (1) the fund of choices, (2) the choosing, and (3) the manifestation of the choice. The choice manifest in an act of speech is assumed to be not completely unpatterned, but to reflect in part the pattern of the language. ". . . in each concrete manifestation [*Äusserung*] through which a part of language, even though small, is realized, there is to be found the whole structure of language, because what is realized in speech exists as linguistic fact through its structural relations to all the rest which remains unrealized in the given instance somewhat in the way each of innumerable pieces of a broken mirror reflects the picture of its surroundings as a whole" (Kořinek 1936: 24).

The pattern of language is for the Prague School, as it was for Saussure, a psychological reality that underlies and is manifest as acts of speech and judgments of the speaker about what he conceives as "language." This assumption of the psychological reality of language is evident from continued references to linguistic consciousness (German *Sprachbewusstein* or French *conscience linguistique*) and to "psychological reality" itself (Trubetzkoy 1969: 88). (Cf. Trubetzkoy 1929b: 42, 1931a: 98–99, 1934: 22–23, 28 et passim, 1969: 64 and 85; Karcevskij 1931: 197; Mathesius 1931: 151; Martinet 1936: 50; Jakobson 1929: 6 and 12; and Artymovič 1964: 78–79.) This attitude of realism is further evident in the concern shown for patterns of linguistic judgments made by the speaker of a language (Trubetzkoy 1936a: 30–31; 1936b: 12–13; and 1969: 78). Realism must here be kept clearly distinct from the early approach in the Prague School that defines theoretical terms with psychological primitives. For example, an early definition of a unit of sound patterning—the phoneme—was phrased as an "acoustico-motor image" (Thèses 1929: 10) assuming the primitive of psychological "images."

Such definitions are later rejected. "Reference to psychology must be avoided in defining the phoneme since the latter is a linguistic and not a psychological concept" (Trubetzkoy 1969: 38). Although psychological primitives are rejected, the assumption of psychological reality of language remains characteristic of Prague School theory. It should be continuously emphasized that an assumption of realism (psychological or otherwise) is distinct from the problem of choosing primitives for a theory.

An act of speech then is a choice from the resources available to—and located in—the brain of the speaker. Language here, as for Saussure, is conceived as knowledge, not as behavior. One difference between the Saussurean and Praguean concepts of language should be immediately noted. Whereas Saussure grouped all sentence-like things together as a portion of *parole*, treating them as patternless things, the Prague School treats them both within speech and language (Mathesius 1936: 105–6 and Artymovič 1964: 77). The utterance of a sentence-like thing is an act of speech, a person's choice, but the choice is made from a patterned system of choices in language. Sentences have pattern and are to be accounted for within any complete treatment of language data.

Speech consists of the manifest choices of sound complexes associated with a function or meaning. Language consists of the range of choices constituted by the language equivalent of sound complexes associated with the language equivalent of meanings. The items that make up the three functional systems of language are the units composed of the mutual implication of the language-equivalents-of-sounds and the language-equivalents-of-meanings, or signs. We now have a picture of language something like the following:

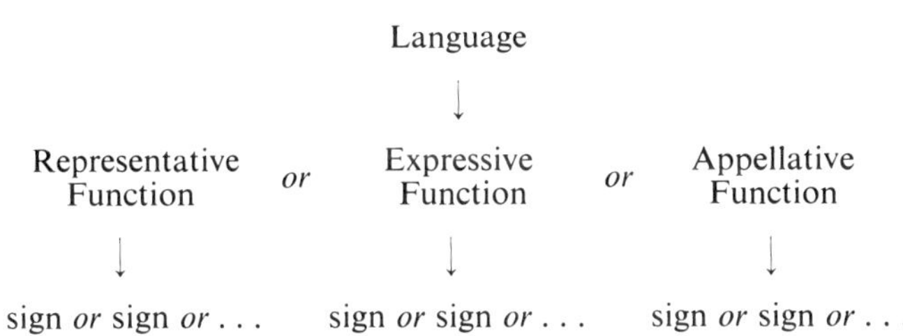

Language is a system of functions, each of which is a system of signs.

Levels of Pattern

We now take up the question of the patterning of these signs. Are they each unique and is there no pattern within each function? Or are the signs partially similar and are they patterned? If so, what kinds of patterns may we expect to find? In providing a preliminary answer to these questions, recall that Saussure's theory was interpreted as having a single level. Language was considered a system of signs, and patterning existed only in terms of signs. In modifying this scheme, we may first take note of the effect that possible homonymy and synonymy have for a theory of language. In terms of signs, homonymy exists when a sound complex, as expression or signifier of a sign, is in mutual implication with more than one meaning. Synonymy is the reverse; a single meaning, content or signified, is in mutual implication with two or more sound complexes. Hjelmslevian theory exhibits one effect such patterning has on a theory. There, simplicity had to be modified to prevent the identification of two or more meanings in the case of homonymy and the intuitively incorrect reduction of the system by one member. Without modification, the theory would not correctly account for instances of homonymy. The refusal to identify two meanings as variants of an invariant in the case of homonymy, or two sound complexes in the case of synonymy, and their acceptance as facts of language imply a lack of isomorphism between meaning and sound. Thus:

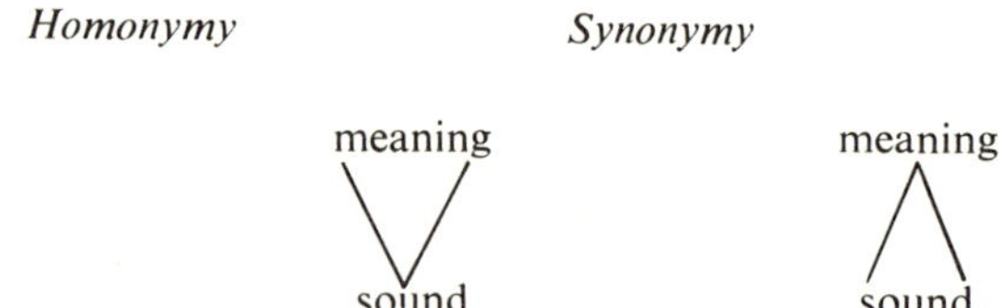

This, in part, is the point of Karcevskij 1929 (cf. also Mathesius 1964b: 21–22). Recall now that the lack of isomorphism between two patterns requires that they be distinct kinds of patterning. With the inclusion of homonymy and synonymy, we have the basis for two levels of language patterning within the sign, and hence within language.

Language now consists in part of a semantic patterning and a sound patterning and mutual implication between points in each kind of pattern. This picture is further modified by a property of language we have mentioned several times: the arbitrary fit between levels. The unit boundaries of one level do not correspond to those of another level. If the association of meanings with sound segmented the latter (or vice versa) such that the resulting units were the same as the unit patterning of sound independent of such a projection, no problem would exist. In post-Bloomfieldian theory this would eliminate the problem of integrating morphs into the hierarchy of phonemic segments. Similarly, tagmemic theory would not have to deal with a wave-like property of language. In Prague School theory that arbitrariness is manifest in the postulation of a level mediating the level of semantic patterning and the level of sound patterning. This intermediate level—grammar—has units and patterning that are neither those of the semantic level nor those of sound patterning. The pattern of meaning in language is termed the *lexical* (Karcevskij 1931: 188–89 and Havránek 1964b: 415) or the *semasiological* (Trnka 1964: 329) level; the intermediate level is called the *grammatical*

(Havránek 1964b: 415) or *morphological* (Thèses 1929: 13; Mathesius 1936: 98; and Trnka 1964: 329); and the level of sound pattern is termed the *phonological* (Trubetzkoy 1969). This three-level structure of language is that hinted at by Saussure but not fully developed in the *Course*. It should be pointed out that the term "level" (German *Ebene* or French *plan*) is used ambiguously to indicate patterns within a level (Trubetzkoy 1931a: 112 and Skalička 1936: 133) or to indicate the members of the primary functional system of language (Isačenko 1964: 92) as well as the three levels here.

The supposition of three distinct levels depends as before on the lack of isomorphism among them. Let us look more closely at the lexical and grammatical levels by returning to consideration of the speech act. In addition to the speaker's action in choosing one of the three functions, he must make an additional choice in the form of a reaction to the third term of the speech act outside the speaker and hearer. This reaction may take two forms; that is, the speaker has two "choices." In the representative function, for example, he may react to an item or items in the third portion of the speech act. In Bühler's (1934: 28) terminology, he reacts to "objects" (*Gegenstände*). This reaction, termed the *naming* (*dénominatrice*) *activity* (Thèses 1929: 11), is expressed linguistically by the utterance of sound complexes whose meanings are those objects. The second reaction is to an item or items in the same third term of the speech act and also to their relationships. In Bühler's terminology again, the speaker reacts to the "arrangement" (*Sachverhalte*) of the objects. This is termed *syntagmatic activity* (Thèses 1929: 13). Linguistically, this action takes the form of sound complexes whose meanings are the named objects and their relationships. This latter activity accounted for within the lexical level requires a *theme* and an *enunciation* (Thèses 1929: 13 and Mathesius 1964a: 61) or *rheme* (Vachek 1966b: 18). The theme within the lexical level corresponds to that portion of the meaning of which something is predicated, e.g., a quality or relationship to some object is stated of some given object. The enunciation corresponds to that portion that is the quality, relationship, and so on. Something is named (theme); then something is placed in relation to it (enunciation). The grammatical level accounts for the formal properties of this theme-enunciation and is the formal exponent of the lexical level (Trnka 1964: 329). The grammatical accounting of syntagmatic activity is in terms of systems or disjunctive classes (Trubetzkoy 1934: 5) or "parts of speech (noun, verb, adjective, adverb)" (Karcevskij 1931: 221). In the grammatical level, the unit of syntagmatic activity is assumed to consist of two constituents. The grammatical description of an utterance may consist of two large disjunctive classes, say, subject and predicate.

With this short outline of a portion of the lexical and grammatical levels, we can now turn to the issue of nonisomorphism between the two. Let us consider the following two acts of speech from this point of view:

(1)   Jiny wrote the poem
(2)   The poem was written by Jiny

Assuming that (1) and (2) are synonymous (that they are both answers to "Who wrote the poem?"), *Jiny* is the enunciation or rheme in both, the added information. The "written poem" is the theme. The grammatical subject then corresponds to a rheme in (1) and to a theme in (2). A single lexical pattern of theme-rheme is associated with two grammatical patterns. Karcevskij (1931: 205) observes that "The division of the phrase [unit of syntagmatic activity on the lexical level, PWD] . . . has nothing to do with the distinction subject and predicate nor, in general, with the opposition of any grammatical units." Isomorphism fails to hold between the two levels, and they must be distinguished.

We may also find a lack of isomorphism between the lexical and grammatical levels in terms of disjunctive classes accounting for the choices available to the naming activity. We mentioned that disjunctive classes exist within the grammatical level. Within the lexical level they will also form disjunctive classes, but the membership there is not derived from their formal affinities, but from semantic ones. From this it follows that two lexical units within a single lexical class may be associated with their respective grammatical exponents such that the latter belong to distinct classes. In this case, the disjunctive classes within each level will fail to be isomorphic. For example, two lexical units within the same disjunctive class by virtue of their shared sex, e.g., Russian *mal'čik* 'boy' and *vojevoda* 'general', are both male but correspond to exponents of two distinct disjunctive grammatical classes defined on the basis of declensional form. Simply, sex is not gender.

Nonisomorphism between grammar and phonology may be found in instances of homonymy. The sound sequence [p'aǫnd] *pound* as a naming activity corresponds to at least two distinct objects of the third term of the speech act. Accordingly, there are two distinct lexical accountings of that utterance; the two lexical units 'unit of weight measurement' and 'to strike forcefully' enter distinct lexical classes. Grammatically, there are also two distinct descriptions. In one case it is a member of a disjunctive class containing *ounce, ton,* etc.; in another it is a member of a disjunctive class containing *touch, throw,* etc. Within the phonological level there is but a single accounting. Two distinct grammatical units correspond to a single phonological one. A similar lack of isomorphism characterizes syntagmatic activity. A sequence such as *old men and women* pertains to two distinct arrangements of objects and has two distinct lexical descriptions. Grammatically, one sequence consists of constituent classes exponed first by *old* and then *men and women,* while the other consists of *old men* then *and* and *women.* The grammatically distinct accountings are associated with a single phonological one. Again, isomorphism fails to obtain. On the basis of these observations, three distinct levels must be included in the theory to account for the three kinds of patterning.

We now examine the act of speech for additional theoretical implications. Naming and syntagmatic activity result in two large classes of speech acts.

The units of the former are *words* (Thèses 1929: 11); those of the latter are *word groups* (Thèses 1929: 13). The result of either type of activity—the class of speech acts in general—are sentences. "The sentence is an elementary speech utterance, through which the speaker (or writer) reacts to some reality, concrete or abstract, and which in its formal character appears to realize grammatical possibilities of the respective language and to be subjectively, that is, from the point of view of the speaker (or writer) complete" (Mathesius 1936: 105–6 fn.). The sentence may be either a word or word group; "one single word . . . may function as a sentence without combining with other words" (Mathesius 1936: 97). The word and word group are not simply related as alternate, either-or choices, as the functions were. In the speech act the word group consists of words, but no one function consisted of another. The use of the term "word group" itself implies this, but also such phrases as the following imply such a word group-word relationship: "the word in relation to the word group [*Wortverbindung*], that is, the word as member of the sentence" (Jakobson 1931: 154) and "the word thought of as member of a sentence [*Satzteil*]" (Trubetzkoy 1934: 5).

In speech acts, words and word groups do not together form a system. A speech act as an element of naming or syntagmatic activity is a datum. Within a series of such acts, we may identify at least two kinds of pattern. Naming activity implies patterning in one word, whereas syntagmatic activity implies patterning between two (or more) words. In the theory—the construct designed to account for speech act data—the dichotomy of word and word-group patterning cuts across the three-way distinct lexical-grammatical-phonological levels producing lexical, grammatical, and phonological word and word-group patterns. Within the grammatical level, for example, "These systems are studied by morphology [grammar, PWD] understood of course in the more general sense of the word which is not placed beside the theories of naming and syntagmatics as a parallel discipline . . . but which intersects them both" (Thèses 1929: 13). (Cf. also Mathesius 1936: 98.) In phonology this intersection is manifest in the distinction between word phonology and sentence phonology (Projet 1931: 321). Schematically,

	Lexical	*Grammatical*	*Phonological*
Functional Syntax	system of word-group patterns ↓ system of minimum units	system of word-group patterns ↓ system of minimum units	system of word-group patterns ↓ system of minimum units
Functional Onomatology	system of words ↓ system of minimum units	system of words ↓ system of minimum units	system of words ↓ system of minimum units

In grammar, the intersection produces a distinction between syntax and morphology in a narrow sense of the word (cf. Karcevskij 1931: 188 et passim, where, however, the two are treated as distinct levels). No consistent term is provided for the distinction within the lexical level; the portion of the lexical level intended to account for the pattern of words is sometimes termed *vocabulary* (Thèses 1929: 26–27). The patterning of words and word groups cutting across the three levels has been called *functional onomatology* (the "lower") and *functional syntax* (the "higher") (Mathesius 1936: 98).

All of this may tempt us to draw the conclusion that accounting for word and word-group patterns within a given level involves two aspects of a single level; specifically, that morphology and syntax, for example, are two size-levels within the level of grammar. Prague School usage generally contradicts this stance. The two are regarded not as size-levels but as distinct levels in themselves (cf. Karcevskij 1929). For the two to be related as size-levels, we would have to assume syntax to be simply a further accounting of word patterns, say, patterns of distribution of the word within some context chosen for the purpose, as in post-Bloomfieldian theory. Bloomfieldian theory made the distinction between morphology and syntax as a matter of degree, and on that basis we have interpreted them as a single level. In Praguean theory, the distinction is one of kind, not degree. Syntax deals with terms of "subject" and "predicate," not word classes (Mathesius 1964a: 66 et passim). Another indication that word-group patterning in the theory is not a mere extension of word patterning is found in the relationship of sentence to word phonology. If a size-level relationship exists between the two, we might expect sentences to be distinguished by the presence of phonetically distinct sounds. That is, the word groups *It turned out funny* and *It turned out sunny* would be considered distinct by virtue of distinct meanings coinciding with a phonetic distinction—[f] in the first and [s] in the second. If word and sentence phonology bore a "consists of" relationship characteristic of size-level relationships, we would expect the two sentences to be distinct at whatever size-level within phonology we spoke of them. This is not the case. Such differences are patterns attributed solely to word phonology. In terms of sentence phonological pattern, the two sentences are identical. Even greater distinctions between word groups do not necessarily indicate different sentence phonological distinctions. The patterns of word phonology cannot be extended such that they become sentence phonology. The patterns of sentence phonology consist of statements about pause, tone or intonation, and accent as they distinguish word groups (Trubetzkoy 1969: 202–8). The two treat differently patterning phenomena and hence must be treated as distinct levels. There is a relationship between them expressed in statements of boundary markers (*Grenzsignale*) and of culminative markers, but these relationships are not disjunctive, nor do they tie word phonology to sentence phonology such that the latter is a body of expanded statements about units of the former. It would be incorrect then, to treat the two studies of functional onomatology and functional syntax within each level as a "consists of" size-level relationship.

On the basis of these observations, we interpret the theory as having three levels and two sublevels (not size-levels) within each. The data of speech acts are such that they manifest patterns of both functional onomatology and functional syntax, but never patterns of functional syntax alone nor patterns of functional onomatology alone. The utterance of a single word in fact exhibits pattern of functional syntax (Mathesius 1936: 97), but these utterances are "extreme" (Mathesius 1936: 97) or "pathological" (Mathesius 1936: 105). Whether excluded or retained as language patterns, a speech act manifests a pattern of functional onomatology and syntax simultaneously in the same choice, in the same way that it manifests a lexical, grammatical, and phonological pattern simultaneously. Functional onomatology and functional syntax do not form a system, a disjunctive class, as the three primary functions do. The choice is not between a pattern of one or the other. They are theoretical distinctions—as the three levels were theoretical distinctions—to account for patterns present simultaneously in a speech act. Although the distinction of three levels and two sublevels within each level has been derived from a discussion of speech activity exemplifying a single function—the representative—the general scheme may be assumed also to characterize those acts of speech exemplifying the expressive and appellative functions.

It remains to establish the relationship between the levels themselves, whether it is a mutual implication as in Hjelmslevian theory, a relationship "consists of" as in one version of post-Bloomfieldian theory, or some third alternative. Trnka (1964: 329) speaks of the grammatical terms related to the lexical ones as "morphological [grammatical, PWD] exponents." Trubetzkoy (1969: 249) characterizes a term of the grammatical, the morpheme, writing that "it is a complex of phonemes present in several words and always associated with the same (material or formal) meaning." (Cf. also Jakobson 1962: 296.) From this we might infer a relationship

Lexical	Grammatical	Phonological
← mutual implication →	— consists of →	
Level	Level	Level

This asymmetry of relationship requires either explanation or resolution. We may think of this three-level theory in the following way. The lexical and phonological levels exhibit patterns that are related, but not directly. The grammatical pattern serves as a mediating one and may be viewed as the intersection of the two. Retaining the Saussurean concept of sign as a mutual implication between two things (signifier and signified or expression and content), we have one term (here, one level) too many. Jakobson (1962: 295–97) places a Saussurean sign relationship between the lexical level or content (*Inhalt*) and grammar, the latter termed the "sign." Recall Saussure's ambiguous use of "sign" as both the signifier and the mutual implication between signifier and signified. The concept of sign is then extended, so that although grammar functions as signifier to the lexical level, phonology in turn functions as signifier to the grammatical. The grammatical level is now ambiguous in that it is now both sign (as signifier) to the lexical level and signified to the phonological level. The relationship of the grammatical level to the phonological level is then one of mutual implication. The notion of morphemes consisting of phonemes is also retained, producing a dual relationship between the two. This duality is not only characteristic of the relationship of grammar and phonology. Grammatical patterns are not only patterns of arbitrary conjunctions of phonemes, but are also patterns of meaning. Jakobson's treatment of the Russian verb system and case system are considered contributions to the study of the grammatical, not the semantic, level of language (Jakobson 1936: 240 and 1964: 347). The grammatical system contains as members terms that are nonlinear conjunctions of meanings and forms (cf. also Skalička 1964: 323, wherein the minimum meaningful unit in grammar is the sema and the minimum formal unit (sequence of phonemes) is the morpheme). The dual relationship between grammar and phonology is repeated between the lexical and grammatical levels. The latter bears a consist-of relationship when the meaning properties of grammatical forms (sema) are related to the lexical level, but a mutual implication when the phonological forms (morphemes) are considered in relation to the lexical level. Similarly, when the meaning of grammatical forms are considered with respect to phonology, the relationship is a mutual implication, but when the phonological form is related to phonology, the relationship is again "consists of."

Variation in Pattern

We concluded the preceding chapter with a discussion of variation of pattern and the degree to which such variation is an internal property of language. Of the three general parameters of pattern variation—dialect, style, and exception—the last is already in part integrated into language as it now stands defined by the Prague School. Among the possible exceptions in a language are those utterances that contain sound patterns exceptional by inventory or distribution. For example, *tsk tsk*, expressing the speaker's commiseration in English, contains two voiceless, implosive, alveolar stops and no vowel. The particular stop (implosive) and the lack of vowel indicate its exceptional status in English. The functional framework allows such speech acts to be characterized as expressive and thus to be separated from the regularities of the representative function. Similarly, repeated released, voiceless, implosive, bilabial stops with no vowel used in English to call some animals are as exceptional as *tsk tsk* and are separated from the regularities by recognizing their appellative function. Not all exceptions are subject to this solution, since exceptions to pattern occur within a single function. The distinction between regularities and exceptions within a function is made by the opposition *native* versus *foreign*. Exceptions to the phonological patterns have been noted in words, that, historically, have been borrowed from a distinct language. Mathesius (1929: 68) poses the matter for phonology as follows: "More difficult is the problem of knowing if sounds originally unused in the phonological system of a given language, but having to a certain degree taken root there under the influence of foreign borrowed words, must enter the phonological system." This diachronic observation may be converted into a synchronic one about language, namely, exceptions exist and may be accounted for by providing for a distinction among types of words within a given function. Just as sentences were classified as belonging to one of three functions in terms of semantic properties, so words within a function may be further distributed among systems on a formal, synchronic basis (not a diachronic one). That formal basis is their exhibiting a regular or deviant pattern on some level. The system of words in a level may be complex or structured in that it is a system of subsystems. The regular subsystem of words is called "native," and the deviant subsystems, "foreign"—a terminology consistent with the diachronic observation of the strong correspondence between regular-native and exceptional-foreign. That the distinction is *not* a diachronic one follows from observations of "assimilation." That is, not all diachronically borrowed words are synchronically exceptional (Mathesius 1929: 68 and 1964c: 406), and not all exceptional words are diachronically borrowed (Mathesius 1964c: 408). The mechanism for integrating exceptional variations of pattern into language is the recognition of subsystems on the level at which the exception exists (Mathesius 1964c: 400 and Trubetzkoy 1969: 252).

The possibility that a word might be exceptional on one level but regular on another receives no explicit solution. For example, a word in English such as *prospectus*, phonologically exceptional in its stress placement on the second and not the first vowel (Mathesius 1964c: 408), is not exceptional grammatically (Mathesius 1964c: 403). Its plural form is *prospectuses*. Compare *alumnus: alumni*, phonologically and morphologically irregular. The solution to the problem turns on the decision to group the word *prospectus* with the grammatically regular/native words while assigning it phonologically to a subsystem of foreign words. Put differently, does the concept of native: foreign cut horizontally (according to the schema above) across all three levels, or does it cut vertically through each level separately? There is no explicit answer to this question, but the independence of pattern from level to level indicates that the exceptional or regular status of a word on one level determines nothing of its status on another.

The opposition of living/productive versus dead/unproductive (Trubetzkoy 1934: 27, 37, et passim) does not correspond to the regularity versus

exception distinction because a regular pattern does not necessarily correspond to productivity (Trubetzkoy 1934: 44).

In discussing pattern variation along the parameter of style, let us return
to consider the speech act. In principle, a speaker has choices available to him
that are not accounted for by the trifunctional distinction nor by the distinction between naming and syntagmatic activity. The speaker may choose to be
very precise about his subject. He may choose a manner of speaking in which
the words have very precise, narrow correlates within the objects of the speech
act. He may also have available to him syntagmatic choices that also are more
precise, perhaps correlating with fewer possible relationships among objects,
thus again lessening potential ambiguity. On the other hand, he may choose
partially like items from the various levels and sublevels producing various
kinds of rhymes, and while conveying meaningful content, the choices call
attention to themselves. The medium, the choices themselves, may be part of
the message. To the extent that such choices are patterned and nonidiosyn-
cratic, they represent an aspect of language and must be accounted for. This
last observation should be emphasized. The choices a speaker makes from
language systems may be random. There is no rule that prevents his choosing, say, within a single syntagmatic act, words or word groups from each of
the functions. The functions may overlap or be mixed in speech, but they
turn on a patterned basis. The choices themselves, although idiosyncratic,
may be patterned. Still, they are characteristic of that speaker alone; they are
things chosen—acts of speech and not language. In that such a pattern of
choice is (or becomes) characteristic of a group, it reflects (or comes to reflect)
the resources available to a community, and hence, language. Pattern of
language unique to an individual—the idiolect of post-Bloomfieldian
theory—has no equivalent in Prague School theory. The linguistic uniqueness
of an individual is a property of his choices (speech) and not language. Here,
there is no language unique to an individual person. This patterned-choice
property of the speech act, not reflecting language, is not the subject of linguistics itself but of *stylistics* (Kořinek 1936: 27 and Mathesius 1964b: 22–
23). One these same grounds, mistakes are excluded from consideration.
Language, for the Prague School as it was for Saussure, is necessarily social
as opposed to speech, which is individual (Mathesius 1964b: 22; Karcevskij
1929: 88; and Kořinek 1936: 27–28). The division between individual speech
(as a chosen act) and social language (as a range of possible choices) is
gradual, and the distinction is "always relative" (Kořinek 1936: 28), for the
patterning in the choice may characterize any number of people. The division between speech and language in this respect is not well-defined; it
is a continuum.

Since choices of preciseness or *intellectualization* (Havránek 1964a: 6–9)
or emphasis on the choice itself, *foregrounding* (Havránek 1964a: 9–12), are
available to a community, they indicate choices that are not attributable to

the three basic functions of language nor to those of functional syntax and onomatology. Such observations lead to the conclusion that there are more functions (Vachek 1966b: 36) than the basic three suggested by Bühler. If we assume that *within* each of the choices (normal/conversational, precise, and aesthetic) we have the choices of representation, expression, and appeal, then the functions may exhibit a structure of system and subsystems, as word classes were organized into subsystems to account for exceptions:

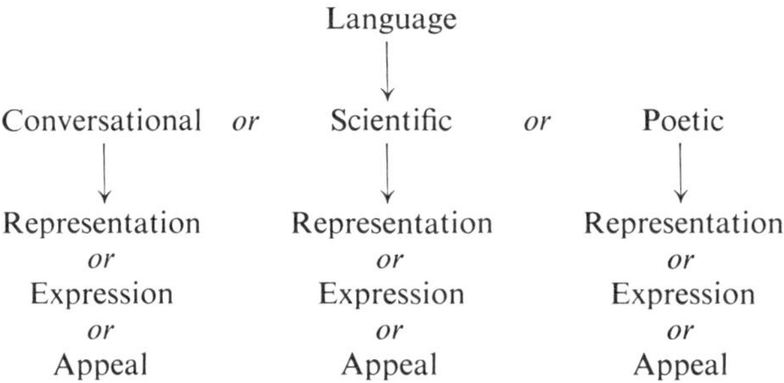

The members of the systems—conversational, scientific, and poetic—are termed *functional dialects* (Havránek 1964a: 15–16) and correspond to the parameter of pattern variation we have called style.

In a group of speakers we may find some who have available to them a different or restricted set of choices. One group may know a language with only one conversational functional dialect, while the others may know a language with two, three, or more functional dialects. Languages as systems of functional dialects may differ in the complexity of their articulation. Or the differences among different communities may lie not in the number of functional dialects but in the patterns of comparable functional dialects. The variation is across groups, not within a group. First, the term "language" is used ambiguously to designate one of the functional dialects; that is, one speaks a "poetic language" (Thèses 1929: 18) or a "language of commerce" (Vančura 1936: 162). Second, one may equally well use "language" to denote a system of functional dialects. The term "literary language" designates a system with a certain degree of development of a scientific functional dialect or a certain degree of intellectualization and, as well, a developed poetic functional dialect (Havránek 1929: 13 and 1964b: 415 and 417). Opposed to the literary language is the popular language, which lacks this development (Havránek 1929: 13 and 1964b:415). Third, the term "language" is used to identify a system that consists of terms such as the literary and popular languages (Havránek 1929: 106). One may speak of a "Czech poetic language," a "Czech literary or popular language," and a "Czech language," each indicating a different, successively higher point in a hierarchy of systems. The systemic relationship of literary and popular languages corresponds to our dialectal parameter of pattern variation, and we must face the problem of determining the degree of difference that may exist between them, such that they are still members of a language system in the third most inclusive sense of the term "language." The criterion used is not a formal one such as the degree of isomorphism between systems, but rests on the speakers' attitude toward variant patterns (Thèses 1929: 10). Horálek (1964) makes the criterion explicit. The speakers' judgment that a pattern/system is "ours" suffices as an indication of the unity of the systems within an overall language system. This relationship, like the measurement of "intelligibility" in post-Bloomfieldian theory, is not necessarily reciprocal, and the structure of such an overall system would require more than a simple disjunctive relationship among dialects. This measurement of dialectal unity, like intelligibility, may produce values intermediate between "ours" and "not ours"; and similarly across the speakers of a community with a single pattern, not all judgments will necessarily be the same. The variation in pattern along the parameter of dialects, as for the previous theories, fades at one end into stylistics or individual variation and at the other into distinct languages. No sharp boundaries exist. The Prague School theory does, however, provide formal means to account for exceptions, stylistic, and dialectal variations in patterning based in general on the introduction of subsystems at various points in a hierarchy of systems.

Phonology

Let us now consider in more detail the structure of the levels and sublevels as outlined above. Our discussion will be concerned mainly with the phonological level, and much less will be said of the remaining two because of the disparate development of the phonological versus the grammatical and lexical levels in the writings of the Prague School.

As we have observed several times, comparison of speech acts reveal differences in phonetic shape and semantic content. If a portion of some phonetic shape in a particular environment is predictable only from semantic content, the phonetic unit in that environment is considered distinctive and corresponds to a unit of phonological patterning—the phoneme. (This rough outline will be modified and further specified below.) The phonetic units in any context are accounted for by a system of phonemes. It is the structure and properties of the system that are the primary concern of the Prague School and that are most fully developed. Let us reconsider first some of the preceding theories. All of them contained some taxonomic element—classes and members—and some ordering of the members. Ordering of a membership occurs when the members are related to one another in some way in addition to being simply members of the same class. Disjunctiveness and conjunctive-ness produce no ordering of members, since any pair within either kind of class bears the same relationship as every other pair within the class.

Saussure's theory of language contained only a restricted taxonomy; the relationship of complex word to minimum words was the only class-member relationship. The members of a complex word were conjunctively related and ordered linearly. This was the only type of ordering of members of a class. Disjunctive classes were absent. The associative relationship, potentially a basis of disjunctive classes, was not a taxonomic one, for the realism constraint evident in the construction of the theory was thought to be violated by hypostatizing associative relationships as a system of distinct classes. The Hjelmslevian taxonomy defined two kinds of classes, those whose members were conjunctively related and those disjunctively related. The membership of each kind could be ordered by dependence. Since class members were themselves classes, a further order of membership was possible in the form of a hierarchy. Second-degree members of a class were ordered with respect to the class containing them all by virtue of differential membership in intervening classes of the first degree. A hierarchy results whenever the minimum units are not directly members of the largest class, but members of that class mediated by membership in some intermediate class or classes that in turn are members of the largest class. Bloomfieldian theory developed taxonomic elements based on conjunctive classes alone. One type of conjunctive class is exemplified by the lexicon. Here we find a number of taxonomies, one for each form class. Within these form classes hierarchical ordering exists in the subclasses established for the statement of selection relationships. The inventory of the phonological units is similarly organized. The second type of conjunctive class is the constructional hierarchies that account for the distribution of the units of the lexicon and phonological inventory. Here the units of the hierarchy are positions. In addition to hierarchical ordering, positions within a "higher" position are ordered linearly. In post-Bloomfieldian theory the morphemic and phonemic inventories are disjunctively related and ordered by membership in one or more distribution classes. The ordering is here not hierarchical because the membership of a class is characterized by cross classification. The constructional hierarchies involve both disjunctive and conjunctive classes. Members of the first type, such as a morpheme or focus class, are unordered; those of the second, such as a construction, are ordered linearly. If we take the morpheme class and phoneme class, as the basis of the constructional hierarchies, then these are hierarchically related. Tagmemic theory contains both conjunctive classes, e.g., a syntagmeme, and disjunctive classes, e.g., a size-level of disjunctively related syntagmemes. Hierarchical ordering is present in the disjunctive system of syntagmemes in the distinction between basic or kernel and derived syntagmemes. Hierarchy in conjunctive classes is by and large absent on the grammatical level; syntagmemes consist directly of minimum units, the (hyper) tagmemes. Within the phonological level, conjunctive classes exhibit hierarchy. That is, the class-member relationship between breath group-pause group-syllable group sequences organizes conjunctive sequences of syllables hierarchically. Within the lexical level, a similar organization of morphemes into sequences of hypermorpheme classes produced a hierarchically ordered relation among them as members of the largest hypermorpheme class. The absence of conjunctive hierarchy in grammar is another indication of the asymmetry between the levels. The distinction between optional and obligatory paralleling Hjelmslevian dependences introduced a nonhierarchical principle of ordered members of conjunctive classes. Disjunctive classes were unordered. In all theories, with the exception of Hjelmslevian theory, members of conjunctive classes are ordered linearly. In general we may summarize the taxonomies as follows as a kind of taxonomy of taxonomies:

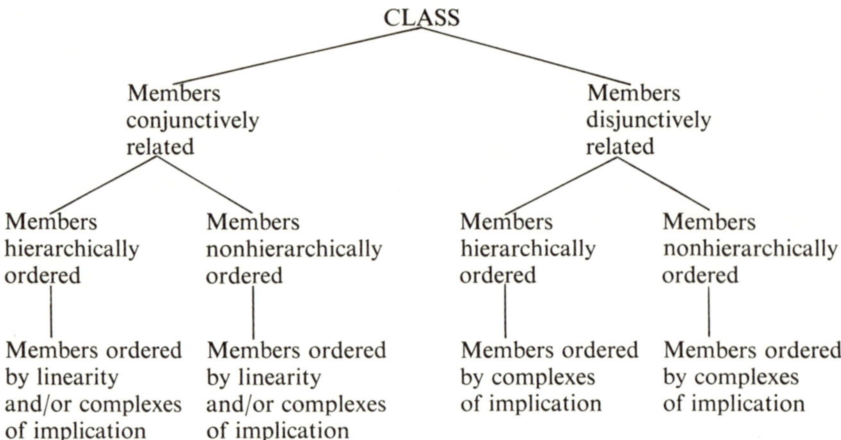

The taxonomies of all theories to this point are choices from this general scheme. Of the five so far considered, only Hjelmslev's centers on the disjunctive classes providing structure beyond simple hierarchical ordering. The Prague School, approaching the concept of language via a conceptualization of the speech act as a sequence of choices from a range (system) of possible choices, similarly emphasizes the notion of system and further elaborates the types of ordering the members of a taxonomic system may exhibit. This ordering of members of disjunct classes is the core of phonological patterning, to which we now turn.

Phonology of the Word

The level in post-Bloomfieldian theory that accounted for the sound patterning of language assumed the existence of utterances that were then compared for samenesses and differences in phonetic and meaning properties.

The tagmemic theory assumed grammatical elements, morphemes. Prague School theory assumes word and word group—the two terms of speech activity. We begin by considering the word sublevel within phonology.

Let us examine the consonant system of some language that is present in initial position of the word:

(3)

p	t	k
b	d	g
ϕ	s	x
β	z	
m	n	
	l	
	r	

In searching for possible order within this system, we begin by comparing pairs of units as *oppositions* (Trubetzkoy 1969: 31–33). Taking *p* and *b*, we see that they share properties of stopness, bilabiality, and nonnasality; no other pair of consonants within the system is so related. Similarly, *t* and *d* share dentality, stopness, and nonnasality; no other consonant within the system is so characterized. The exclusive property of liquids *l* and *r* is the escape of air around a partial obstruction without producing a sound of friction. Comparing *p* and *m* we find that they share bilabiality. The closure of *m* is not considered stopness because air escapes through the nasal cavity. In this comparison the shared property of *p* and *m* is also shared by *b*, ϕ, and β. Similarly, we find the shared properties of *p* and *t*, stopness and voicelessness, shared by *k*. We distinguish two types of relationships on the basis of these patterns: *bilateral* (or *one-dimensional*), wherein the shared properties are unique to the pair, and *multilateral* (or *multidimensional*), wherein the properties shared by the pair are also found in at least one other unit (Trubetzkoy 1936b: 7–9 and 1969: 68–69). Thus *p* and *b*, *t* and *d*, and *l* and *r* are related bilaterally; *p* and *m*, and *p* and *t* are related multilaterally.

Considering the bilateral *p* and *b* again, we see that *t* and *d* and *k* and *g* are similarly bilateral, based on share stopness plus dentality or velarity, respectively. In addition, the distinction among the three pairs is constant—either the absence or presence of voice. Taking the pair ϕ and β, we find a shared property of fricativeness, shared also by *s* and *z*. The relation of ϕ and β and *s* and *z* is bilateral, based on fricativeness and either bilabiality or dentality, respectively. Again, a constant distinguishing property is present. Taking the bilaterally related pair *l* and *r*, we find no other pair of liquids that differ by the same property of lateral versus nonlateral. The relationship between *p* and *b*, as well as between *t* and *d* and *k* and *g*, is *proportional:* ϕ and β and *s* and *z* are likewise proportionally related. The relationship between *l* and *r* is *isolated,* for there is no other pair distinguished by laterality versus nonlaterality (Trubetzkoy 1936b: 11–12 and 1969: 70–72). Considering the multilateral relationship of p and t, we find that the distinction between them—labiality versus dentality—is present in the pairs b and d and m and n. The relationship between p and t is then proportional in addition to being multilateral. Taking k and β, we find they share, along with pair g and ϕ, the property of obstruency; k and β are multilaterally related. There is no single property whose alternative values distinguishes them. The pair k and β are then multilateral and isolated.

We now have these four possible relationships:

$p\text{-}b$	$p\text{-}t$	$l\text{-}r$	$k\text{-}\beta$
bilateral	multilateral	bilateral	multilateral
proportional	proportional	isolated	isolated

A third kind of relationship can be predicated of pairs. The pair p and b differ in terms of the property of voice, by its presence or absence. There is no third member of the system differing from p and b by a third value for voice. The pair p and t differ in another way. Here the distinction is not in terms of values—presence or absence, affirmation or negation—of a single property, but the presence or absence of *two* distinct properties (bilabiality and dentality) that are mutually exclusive. The pair k and β in part differ in this manner: velar versus bilabial. The pair p and ϕ, which are related in a bilateral, proportional fashion, differ in terms of occlusion or degree of obstacle. The distinction is in terms of a single property, and within this system it is *privative*. There are only two values of occlusion. Had the system contained $p\text{-}p\widehat{\phi}\text{-}\phi$, giving the property of occlusion at least three values, p and ϕ would have been a *gradual* opposition. A vowel system with three or more degrees of openness exemplifies a gradual opposition. In terms of the kind of distinction between oppositions, they may be *privative* (e.g., voice), *equipollent* (e.g., bilabial versus dental), or *gradual* (e.g., stop versus affricate versus fricative). The pair $p\text{-}b$ now has three relationships within this system: bilateral, proportional, and privative. The pair $p\text{-}t$ is multilateral, proportional, and equipollent; $l\text{-}r$ is bilateral, isolated, and privative; and $k\text{-}\beta$ is multilateral, isolated, and equipollent with respect to bilabiality or velarity. The relation between members of a pair defined by coincidence of bilateral, proportional, and privative is given a special name: *correlation* (Trubetzkoy 1969: 84).

The fact that certain pairs are singled out and especially labeled has a basis in another kind of patterning. The pairs introduced above are not only related in that they exhibit the named relations holding or not holding between them but are also related in terms of closeness of relationship. The members of the pair $p\text{-}b$ are more closely related than those of the pair $p\text{-}t$. "The terms of bilateral oppositions are mutually related in a much more intimate way than the terms of unilateral oppositions" (Trubetzkoy 1936b:

9). Similarly, a relationship between a pair which is proportional indicates a greater degree of "intimateness" than one that is isolated (Trubetzkoy 1931a: 111). In general, on this kind of patterning, Trubetzkoy (1931a: 100) writes that *"The ability of linguistic consciousness to project different phonological oppositions onto the same or different levels according to their degree of relationship* has special importance for the construction of phonological systems. There follows from this *a natural division of phonological oppositions* according to their means of relationship. Each opposition, which is projected by linguistic consciousness onto the same level must be united into special *groups by means of relationship* [emphases, Trubetzkoy's]." The assertion of such loose-close patterning is found again in Trubetzkoy's (1969: 85 and 88) *Principles of Phonology*. Observations of loose-close are based on judgments of speakers of a language; observations of relationship type are drawn from the phonetic manifestation of language. The question arises whether these two kinds of observations are different aspects of a single pattern, one aspect manifest in judgments of intuitive feelings and the second manifest in speech acts, or whether they are manifestations of distinct properties of language. In what follows we will argue that the two kinds of patterning are in fact different manifestations of a single property of language and consider what this implies for the theory. The problem now is to provide within the theory and its accountings some single formal way of accommodating these patterns such that we may infer from the accounting both the speaker's judgments and the patterns in speech acts. In so doing, we will equate both these aspects of patterning with the formal property of ordering the members of the phonological system. The principle of this ordering will be hierarchy. This hierarchical ordering within accountings will correspond to two possible patterns—as the phonetic pattern of speech acts and judgments of loose-close.

Let us consider a different accounting of the system under examination:

(4)

		Consonant				
Obstruent		*or*		Sonorant		
			Liquid	*or*	Nasal	
Bilabial *or* Dental *or* Velar				Bilabial *or* Dental		
p-b-ɸ-β t-d-s-z k-g-x			l-r	m		n

interpreting the hierarchical arrangement in the following manner. The system (class) of consonants consists of two classes related disjunctively: obstruents and sonorants. The class of obstruents consists of three disjunctive classes: bilabials, dentals, and velars. The class of bilabials consists of four disjunctively related members: voiceless stop, voiced stop, voiceless fricative, and voiced fricative. The class of dentals consists of four analogous members. The class of velars consists of three disjunctive members: voiceless stop, voiced stop, and voiceless fricative. The class of sonorants consists of two disjunctive classes: liquids and nasals. The former, in turn, consists of disjunctively related lateral and nonlateral; the latter consists of a disjunctively related bilabial and dental. The lowest terms in the hierarchy consist of a single member. Considering the bilabial class in more detail, we observe that the four members it contains *are* bilabials; the bilabials, in turn, *are* obstruents that *are* consonants. The phonetic properties characterizing a class are related conjunctively so that the sum of class memberships in the hierarchy characterizes conjunctive occurrence of properties. For example, because lateral and nonlateral are here related to liquid by dominance, they co-occur with, and therefore are, liquids. Nondominance characterizes a disjunctive relationship. Voiceless stop and voice stop are both dominated by bilabial, but neither is a member of the other. They are both bilabials disjunctively related. The units are now completely characterized by each of the possible conjunctively related properties defined by a path from the most inclusive class to a least inclusive one, and the properties of a unit are hierarchically ordered.

Notice, however, that bilabial voiced-voiceless and stop-fricative are not hierarchically related. They could have been, for example,

(5)

	Stop	*or*	Fricative	
Voiced	*or* Voiceless		Voiced	*or* Voiceless
b	p		β	ɸ

or

(6)

	Voiced	*or*	Voiceless	
Stop	*or* Fricative		Stop	*or* Fricative
b	β		p	ɸ

The nonhierarchical arrangement of the four may be indicated by a matrix:

(7)

	Voice	*or*	Voiceless
Stop	b		p
or			
Fricative	β		ɸ

The justification of the presence or absence of hierarchical arrangements will be discussed below.

To repeat, there are three issues involved: (1) formal representation of a relationship between pairs, (2) the closeness of a relationship between pairs, and (3) showing that (1) and (2) are implicit within a hierarchy such as the one presented above. The identification of a relationship involves a "basis of comparison" (Trubetzkoy 1969: 68)—the properties of class membership a pair of units has in common. We will assume that the higher in the hierarchy two units are distinguished (the higher their basis of comparison is broken by their membership in distinct classes), the looser is their relationship; the lower in the hierarchy, the closer their relationship. The pair p-b, which are bilabial stops—the basis of comparison—are more closely related to each other than either is to l, wherein the basis of comparison is consonant. If two units are the only such members of a class, they are bilaterally related. Thus, p-b are the only stops of the bilabial class and their relationship is bilateral; p and t, however, are not the only voiceless stops of the obstruent class (because of k) and are multilaterally related. The pair p and β have in common only their membership as bilabials; their basis of comparison is a class higher in the hierarchy than stop. They share their bilabial, obstruent, consonant basis of comparison with b and ϕ; hence, they are multilaterally related. The relationship bilateral-multilateral requires for each pair that there be a basis of comparison (some class membership in common). If there are additional members of that class—the basis of comparison—that pair is multilaterally related; if not, they are bilaterally related. The basis of comparison of such bilateral relationships between units will necessarily come low in the given hierarchical arrangement and will be closely related, given our assumption of the correspondence of high-low in the hierarchy to loose-close in the relationship of units. Multilateral relationships will necessarily have their basis of comparison higher in the hierarchy and be more loosely related.

Consider now the question "Is p-b a closer bilateral relation than p-ϕ? Or is the reverse true? Or neither?" Since the basis of comparison of p-b and p-ϕ are located at the same point in the hierarchy of (4), it is claimed that the pairs are equally closely related. This is the motivation for excluding either possible hierarchical arrangement of stop-fricative and voice-voiceless. Either such arrangement would have claimed that one or the other pair was more closely related. Had we assumed the hierarchy of (5), the p-ϕ would have been bilateral by virtue of being the only voiceless members of the bilabial class, but this also claims that the pair is differentiated as bilabials and their relationship is looser than the relationship of the pair p-b, which are differentiated as stops. This imposes loose-close on the notion bilateral, claiming not all bilateral relationships are equally close. There is no indication that the notion of loose-close is extended to hold between different bilateral pairs. As such, they are equally closely related, hence the absence of hierarchy in (4) and (7). If such extension were made, the patterns could be easily accounted for by ranking stop-fricative and voiced-voiceless hierarchically. Note that our hierarchy *does* claim a difference in loose-close between multilateral pairs. The multilateral p-β differentiated as bilabials are more closely related than multilateral p-t, which are differentiated as obstruents; and both are more closely related as pairs than p-l, differentiated as consonants.

Proportionality requires the introduction of the notion of "recurrence" in the hierarchy. Recurrence and basis of comparison together indicate presence or absence of proportionality. Let us consider the pair p-b. Its basis of comparison is the class of bilabial stops. We note, however, that the class of stops co-occurring with voice-voiceless recurs, dominated by dental and velar. The thing that recurs is a portion of the whole hierarchy. To identify *p-b* as proportional, the following portion of the hierarchy must recur:

(8)   Voice   *or*   Voiceless

     Stop

Where this happens, the units included in the basis of comparison (here, stops) are proportionally related. The pairs *p-b*, *t-d*, and *k-g* then hold a proportional relationship. The recurrence of a property, like basis of comparison, is derivable from a hierarchy like that given in (4) and (7). We have observed that there did not exist an additional relationship loose-close between bilateral pairs; that is, some (by virtue of different kinds of bilaterality) were more closely related than others. With respect to further hierarchy within proportional relations, we refer to Trubetzkoy (1969: 85):

> *Depending on the correlation mark* [*the property differentiating two or more proportionally related terms in the hierarchy, PWD*], *different types of correlations are distinguished: for example, the correlation of voice* (*French* d-t, b-p, g-k, z-s, *etc.*) *or the correlation of quantity* ā-a, ī-i, *etc.*). *These various correlation types are related to each in* varying degrees [*emphasis mine, PWD*] *and can be classified in related groups. The relation of the correlation mark to other properties of the respective phonemes serves as the basis of comparison. For example, the correlation of voice* (*French* d-t, b-p) *and the correlation of aspiration* (*Sanskrit* t-th, p-ph) *belong to the same related class because their correlation marks represent different types of work performed by the larynx and different types of tensing in the oral cavity, independent of the place of articulation in the oral cavity.*

Since Sanskrit also possesses a *d-dh* and *b-bh*, the proportional relationship between *t-d*, *th-dh*, etc., would be as close a relationship as *t-th* and *p-ph*. But what would be a less closely related proportion? Let us consider the pair *p-t* from our original example. The basis of comparison is the class of voiceless, obstruent stops. The point of their differentiation is the class of obstruents. The portion of the hierarchy they manifest recurs for voiced stops, voiceless fricatives, and voiced fricatives:

(9)

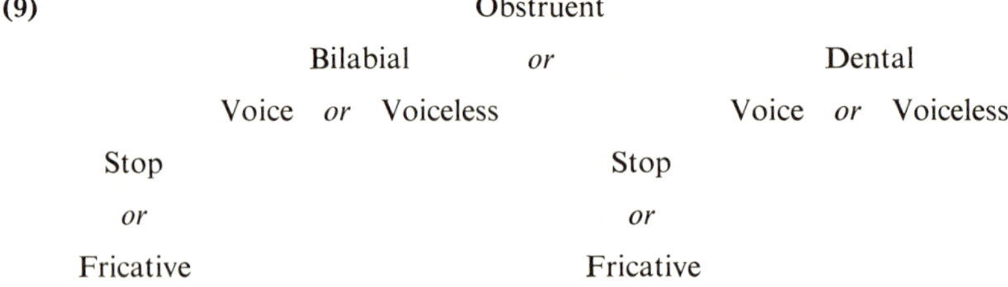

Notice that the point of differentiation (obstruent) for the proportional p-t is higher in the hierarchy than that (bilabial stop) for the proportional p-b. From this we may draw the conclusion that the proportion between p-t indicates a less close relationship than the proportion between p-b, because the former pair is differentiated higher in the hierarchy (which indicates a less close relationship) than the latter pair (which indicates a closer relationship). Although such a hierarchy of proportions is not further explicitly developed by Trubetzkoy, we may point to a later description of French (Jakobson and Lotz 1949: 157) in which a geometric representation of the consonants of French p-b (also p-f, f-v, b-v) are directly connected by a line whereas p-t (as well as p-k and t-k) are indirectly related by a line passing through a node labeled "Diluted." The relationship is mediated and less direct or close.

The loose-close distinction between proportional and isolated pairs cannot be derived from observations of where points of differentiation fall within the hierarchy. This is because we may find an isolated pair differentiated at the same point in the hierarchy as the proportional pair. Consider a system such as (3) but without z, ϕ, β, and x. The pair t-s is isolated; the pair t-d is proportional. Both pairs are differentiated as dentals, one by stop-fricative, the other by voice-voiceless. The distinction in loose-close must lie elsewhere. It can be made in terms of recurrence. One or more recurrences of a portion of a hierarchy increases the closeness of the pair characterized by the recurrent portion. Since the recurrence is explicit, we have only to state it as such a measure of loose-close. No additional theoretical apparatus is required. Observe that this implies that proportional relationships may differ in loose-close in a *second* way. In addition to distinguishing proportional pairs by the point of differentiation (e.g., p-b versus p-t), we must distinguish them as to loose-close according to the number of times the portion of the hierarchy characterizing their proportion recurs. That is, in our original example b-β would be a less close proportional relation than p-b because the first recurs only in the dentals (d-z), whereas the second recurs in the dentals (t-d) and the velars (k-g): one recurrence versus two.

The bilateral and multilateral relationships may be accounted for by a hierarchical ordering; the relative closeness of units they indicate is also derivable from such ordering. The proportional and isolated relationships are also implicit in the hierarchy. We ignore for the moment relationships based on privative-gradual-equipollent.

The multilateral relationships may be further evidenced in various types. The multilateral pair p-β, in addition to being multilateral, is *homogeneous* (Trubetzkoy 1969: 69–70) because we can interpose between p-β one or more bilateral pairs. That is, p-ϕ-β where p-ϕ and ϕ-β are bilateral. If this cannot be done, e.g., p-d, the multilateral relationship is *heterogeneous*. That is, in p-b-d, p-b is bilateral, but b-d is multilateral; we cannot relate p-d by interposing only bilateral pairs. A bilateral pair is homogeneous by definition. Homogeneous relationships are also *linear* or *nonlinear* (Trubetzkoy 1969: 70). A pair is multilateral, homogeneous, and linear if the interposed pair(s) is(are) the only possible way of relating the pair. Thus *g-x* is linear because *g-k-x* is the only such way in which they are homogeneous; but the pair *p-β* is nonlinear because both *p-b-β* and *p-ϕ-β* are possible. In terms of closeness of relationship, homogeneity implies the greater, and heterogeneity the lesser, degree of association (Trubetzkoy 1969: 88). Presumably, nonlinear and linear would be analogously related; the former indicating greater, the latter, lesser closeness. Both the definition of each of the four new relationships and their associated degrees of loose-closeness are implied in the hierarchical ordering of our system. Homogeneity, linearity, and nonlinearity are properties of a particular portion of a hierarchy, namely, the class that has units not further ordered by hierarchy or in terms of intervening subclasses. For example, in (7) *p-β* and *ϕ-b* are multilateral and homogeneous. Multilateral pairs of such a portion of the hierarchy will always be homogeneous. The multilateral pair *p-t* is not ordered by such a subhierarchy and is therefore multilateral and heterogeneous. If such a subhierarchy contains only three units, e.g.,

(10)   Velar

                                   Voice   *or*   Voiceless
                    Stop   g   k

                    or

                    Fricative   x

the multilateral pair will be linear. If it contains more units, e.g., the bilabial class, the multilateral pairs will be nonlinear.

To account for two general patterns between units in the data—closeness of relation and distinct relationship types—a single theoretical construct has been proposed: hierarchy. (The pattern of loose-close could conceivably have been attached to formal constructs other than hierarchy; we leave this type of alternative undiscussed.) It is further claimed that both patterns may be accounted for by this same hierarchy, which is defined by properties of sounds arranged hierarchically. Each distinct conjunction of these properties defines a unit and its class membership. A second way of accounting for such patterns, while retaining the concept of hierarchy, would have been to consider the units of (3) indissoluble. The hierarchy would have then been implemented not by the arrangement of properties of the units (for they would have no inherent properties beyond distinctiveness), but by their grouping into a hierarchy of classes. In the first approach a unit *p* would be defined by the conjunction of hierarchically arranged properties of consonant, obstruent, bilabial, stop, and voiceless. That *p-t-k* form a class opposed to *f-s-x* would be implied by their shared properties not also shared by *f-s-x*. In the second approach, *p* would be distinct from other units and further characterized by class memberships. Hierarchy in the second is indicated by hierarchy of class membership of a unit, whereas in the first it is given by the hierarchy of properties. If p-t-k form a class opposed to f-s-x, it has to be stated separately, for at no point in their hierarchy do p-t-k belong to some class to which f-s-x do not also belong. Both approaches implement the notion of hierarchy, but only in the choice of implementation taken by the Prague School is the notion of relation type already implicit in the hierarchy; the alternative approach would require additional theoretical apparatus in the form of added primitives and be less simple. To see that this is so, let us examine in some detail two assumptions underlying what we have done to this point.

Our argument (that patterning of a system by loose-close and the various types of relationships do not require two kinds of independent ordering within the theory, but that a hierarchy of the type adopted implies both) is based on the following assumptions: (1) that the units of sound patterning— the phonemes of the theory—are nonlinear conjunctions of primitives and (2) that the primitives (obstruent, dental, voiced, etc.) available to theory are hierarchically ordered.

The first assumption is motivated in part by simplicity. Had the units of our system been envisaged as simple, minimum units, they could still have been arranged in a hierarchy. Patterns of cross classification would have then resulted in increased complexity. For example, the accounting that considered the units p, b, ϕ, β, t, d, s, and z atomic units arranged in a hierarchy of classes

$$\left[\left[[\text{p}]_{\text{vl}}[\text{b}]_{\text{vd}}\right]_{\text{stop}}\left[[\phi]_{\text{vl}}[\beta]_{\text{vd}}\right]_{\text{fri}}\right]_{\text{bil}}\left[\left[[\text{t}]_{\text{vl}}[\text{d}]_{\text{vd}}\right]_{\text{stop}}\left[[\text{s}]_{\text{vl}}[\text{z}]_{\text{vd}}\right]_{\text{fri}}\right]_{\text{dental}}$$

(where [ ] indicates a class including all units within it and is labeled by the term at its lower right), requires the listing of voiced, voiceless twice within the bilabial and dental classes as opposed to once when the units are considered as complexes of properties. Second, treatment of the units as indissoluble requires that we impose a hierarchy either

$$\left[[\ ]_{\text{vl}}[\ ]_{\text{vd}}\right]_{\text{stop}}\left[[\ ]_{\text{vl}}[\ ]_{\text{vd}}\right]_{\text{fri}}$$

or the reverse

$$\left[[\ ]_{\text{stop}}[\ ]_{\text{fri}}\right]_{\text{vl}}\left[[\ ]_{\text{stop}}[\ ]_{\text{fri}}\right]_{\text{vd}}$$

where we do not want it. A third and more important reason for considering our units complex concerns the labels given the classes. They *are* labels and not properties of the class membership. If such labels are meant to form the basis of comparison of classes across the hierarchy by their recurrence, there is no principle constraining the notion of possible hierarchy. Given the fifteen consonants of (3), it is claimed that any of the mathematically possible hierarchies in the alternative approach may be the accounting of a consonant system within some language. In short, no constraint is placed on the notion of possible language with respect to this aspect of its pattern. Recall from the introductory chapter that although we require a theory general enough to provide accountings for all languages, we will rank them as increasingly preferable to the degree that they restrict and make the definition of possible language more precise. The application of labels fails to identify classes across the hierarchy and contains no restriction on their use. All possibilities of hierarchicalization are then predicted as possible languages. It is the first assumption coupled with the second—that the primitives are nonabstract and hierarchically related—that provides a constraint on possible ordering of a system and predicts some patterns as nonlanguage by not providing accountings for them.

Two things are important in the second assumption: the content of the primitives and their inherent hierarchical relationship. That the primitives predicting possible sound within possible language are inherently and universally arranged may be inferred from statements such as the following (Trubetzkoy 1969: 118):

> *While the properties of localization [front-back and round-unround, PWD] and the properties based on degree of apertures of the vowels are so closely linked with each other as to form a kind of 'bundle' [i.e., not hierarchical, PWD], the resonance properties [nasality and muffling, PWD] belong on quite a different plane [i.e., hierarchical level, PWD].*

(cf. also Trubetzkoy 1969: 88). The phonetic primitives accounting for vowels are then arranged hierarchically,

(a)   Vowel

(b)   Height and Localization

(c)   Nasalization and Muffling

Similar orderings are found for the properties of consonants.

It is the "natural" content of the primitives of the theory that permits the two patterns loose-close and relationship types to be combined into a single principle of ordering. To see that this is so, we may compare Prague School theory with Hjelmslev's, in which two ordering principles were distinct. In Hjelmslevian theory no primitives were derived from the data. Handling techniques, such as a phonetic alphabet, were not part of the theory of language. (Of the theories we have examined, only Saussure's shares this property with Hjelmslev's. Bloomfieldian, post-Bloomfieldian, and tagmemic theory all have assumed primitives derived from observations of possible language sound and meaning.) A theory such as Hjelmslev's with abstract primitives and the accountings based on them will have no direct connection with data unless explicitly stated in the form of an interpretation. Theories and accountings based on primitives such as some phonetic alphabet may contain a minimal interpretation in that the occurrence of such primitives in accountings by their very nature bear an inherent relation to the data. If the invariants of the theory are defined as aspects of the phonetic primitives, the minimal interpretation will hold. Bloomfieldian, tagmemic, and Praguean theories are examples of this. But if the theory assumes such primitives while defining its invariants as abstract classes (one position in post-Bloomfieldian theory), such minimal interpretation is not present in accountings. A Hjelmslevian class or component has no inherent relation to a piece of language data manifested in sound, but a Prague School primitive such as voice does. Theories based on contentive primitives we may call *empiric;* and those based on abstract primitives, we call *nonempiric.* The terms (suggested by Professor E. W. Roberts) labeling this distinction are not to be confused with the empirical-nonempirical dichotomy. The empiric basis of the hierarchy in Prague School theory makes it possible to locate identities and nonidentities. We know that two classes at different points in the hierarchy are comparable because of their empiric content. Had we labeled the classes arbitrarily with numbers or some other way, such sames and differences would not have been directly determinable. It is the possibility of determining such sames and differences that make it possible to identify bilateral, isolated, and proportional relationships, for these were derived from comparison and recurrence, which are in turn based on sames and differences. The incorporation of a hierarchy without such empiric content in Hjelmslevian theory makes it impossible to identify two components or classes as same from observation of the hierarchy alone. No further ordering beyond hierarchy is implied by the hierarchy itself. It is not possible to derive relationships of dependence from observation of hierarchy as we may derive observations of bilaterality and the like from observation of a Praguean hierarchy. The two Hjelmslevian principles of hierarchy and dependence are then independent, and the theory requires that both be stated independently in accountings. The single Praguean concept of hierarchy of features implies the relationship types by certain arrangements of these properties within the hierarchy. Hierarchy and relationship types are not independent kinds of ordering. We are not arguing that Hjelmslevian dependences and Prague School relationship types are in themselves comparable. It is only their relation—independence or dependence—to hierarchy as principles of ordering members of a system that is at issue. Although Prague School relationship types will be definable in terms of conjunction, disjunction, class-member, and hierarchically ordered phonetic alphabet, other relations will not; and like Hjelmslev's dependences, these other relations will require additional primitives.

Before leaving the discussion of phonetic primitives, several additional points should be made about them. First, the phonetic parameters used in the theory and accountings of languages are not intended to exhaust the sound-producing capabilities of humans, but only to provide those distinctions required to account for the phonological systems of any possible language. Second, there is a variant approach to the specification of phonetic primitives. Jakobson (Jakobson and Lotz 1949; Jakobson, Fant, and Halle 1951; and Jakobson and Halle 1956) proposes a set derived from a broader base, not exclusively articulatory, and maximizes the privative properties reinterpreting gradual and equipollent distinctions as two (or more) privative ones. Trubetzkoy's (1969) phonetic parameters are derived from articulatory properties, but he observes (Trubetzkoy 1969: 92) that the choice between acoustic and articulatory (or auditory) is unimportant in that the primitives, however based, are equivalent within the theory. Jakobson's proposal is based on the observation that the act of speech involves all three aspects of sound (Jakobson and Halle 1956: 34) and the role of nonarticulatory specifications of speech sound aid in capturing the properties of sound, which in turn forms the basis for describing the relations in language. That is, articulatory properties do not consistently relate those things that are related in language; additional parameters from a nonarticulatory base provide a more adequate set of primitives. The increase in privative or binary properties, those with only two values, is motivated by theoretical simplicity. The distinction bilabial-dental-palatal-velar, requiring four distinct features, is replaced by two features, grave and compact, with two values: presence and absence. Absence of grave in a segment is termed acute; absence of compactness is termed diffuse. Bilabial is then grave and diffuse; dental is acute and diffuse; palatal is compact and acute; and velar is compact and grave. Simplicity is increased in the primitives of the theory in that (1) the number of features is reduced, and (2) the values they may have are restricted to two. A second motivation is found in that the notion of possible language is further restricted. Since such a set of primitives claims there will be no language with more than four positions of consonant articulation, there should be no language which requires three or more values for a feature to account adequately for its distinctive inventory.

Complementary Systems in Word Phonology

What we have done so far is to consider one system in one environment, point out the patterns attributed to it, and attempt to provide a theory to account for it. The definition of variety of relationship types derived from the definition of a hierarchy based on the empiric primitives mentioned above is the apparatus so far introduced into phonology. We now turn to the problem to which every theory must provide an answer: identity.

We may find in the data more phonetically distinct units than the fifteen distinctions provided by the word initial consonants of (3). This is the familiar pattern of free variation; certain of the terms distinct within the speech act are not distinct within the language. Let us now add to the data of our assumed language the consonant system occurring finally:

(11)

$$
\begin{array}{ccc}
p & t & k \\
\phi & s & x \\
m & n & \\
 & l & \\
 & r &
\end{array}
$$

This system differs from the previous one. The unit p now enters only one bilateral relationship, which is with ϕ. The number of its multilateral relationships is reduced by four. Its remaining proportional, isolated, homogeneous, heterogeneous, linear, and nonlinear relationships also differ in this position. If we assume these units to be conjunctions of properties and further assert (Trubetzkoy 1969: 66–68) that they receive their definition in each system by the relationships—the hierarchy—their properties enter into, then the definition of p initially differs from p finally. Final p has no value for the property of voice; initial p does. The relationships final p enters are different from those of initial p. How then is identity to be asserted of the two p's? Or is it?

We approach the problem from another direction. Across languages or dialects, we may record phonetically in some environment a system of consonants that are objectively, phonetically the same, but the patterns of identity may differ from language to language or dialect to dialect. The difference lies in where the line of identity is drawn. If we assume the distinct *phonetic* segments arranged in a hierarchy as the one above and additionally assume that it becomes a hierarchy of distinct *phonological* segments by imposing the relationship of identity (or nonidentity) upon it, the relationship of identity may vary up and down within the hierarchy embracing more or fewer segments. In one language it may include two phonetically distinguishable segments; in another it may be broader and include three, or be narrower and contain but one. In the same way that a same phonetic system varies in its identity relationships from language to language, so a same phonetic system within a language may vary in its identity relationships from environment to environment. Furthermore, the phonetic systems themselves may vary, implying different identity relationships.

Returning to our two consonant systems of (3) and (11), in the first the relationship of identity falls below the distinction of voice-voiceless so that p-b are not considered the same. In the second, word final system, the relationship of identity is made higher so that voice-voiceless is irrelevant. Identity exists between these systems-in-environments in the same way identity held between phonemes-in-environments. A phonological system may have variants in the same way that a phoneme in some position may have variants (Trubetzkoy 1969: 228). The variants are the distinct systems as they occur initially and finally. The overall, constant system of which the others are variants is outside such environments. The conditioning factors that allow prediction of the variants of the system are the environments in which it may occur. The variant system, or system in an environment, is called a *partial system*, and the phonological system considered outside an environment is the *total system* (Trubetzkoy 1969: 106, 110, et passim). The data of partial systems may differ in that (1) the phonetic segments of one position are a subset of those that occur in another, as in the example under consideration, i.e., the data of the two differ according to the number of segments in each, or (2) the phonetic segments of one position are different from those occurring in another. More likely, both (1) and (2) will form the difference between systems. In the first case, the partial systems differ in the place the relationship of identity is located in the hierarchy. In the second, the place of identity is unchanged—and thus the two partial systems are the same—but the variants of units within the two systems differ (cf., however, the discussion of explanatoriness and evaluative criteria on pages 253–55, where the second case may be interpreted differently). Here the distinction lies not in the structure of the system but in the necessary statements of interpretation.

Let us take up what implications are to be drawn from the different placement of the identity relationship from partial system to partial system. Looking at the same data in another way, observe that in place of p and b bilaterally related in the initial system, only p occurs finally; similarly for the pairs t-d, k-g, ϕ-β, and s-z. The opposition in each instance is said to be *neutralized* (Trubetzkoy 1936a: 30; 1936b: 12; and 1969: 78). That is, the relationship of identity shifts upward in the hierarchy of the partial system—here, the final partial system—so that voice-voiceless no longer distinguishes two units; the opposition is then neutralized. The basis of comparison of the neutralized pair (e.g., in p-b it is consonant, obstruent, bilabial, and stop) is then termed an *archiphoneme* (Trubetzkoy 1936a: 31–32; 1936b: 13; and 1969: 74). The term "archiphoneme" applies to the bases of comparison of any bilateral pairs that may be neutralized. In a system wherein a given pair is nowhere neutralized, the opposition is termed *constant* (Trubetzkoy 1936a: 30; 1936b: 12; and 1969: 77).

The phenomenon of neutralization results in additional patterning or structure within the overall, total phonological system. The problem is now (1) to identify that pattern in its loose-close and relationship aspects, and (2) to determine whether our initial description of word initial consonants can be reworked so that it accounts for the total system and not a partial one. Taking up the first task, we see that in the *total* system the pair p-b is additionally related by *markedness*, pattern via relationship type. The member of the pair occurring in the position where both do not, i.e., *p*, is *unmarked* in the total system; the member that occurs in the restricted position is *marked* (Trubetzkoy 1936a: 34 and 1969: 81). We caution here that the terms "marked" and "unmarked" have a second distinct use within the partial system. Among the privative oppositions, those units that are characterized by the presence of that property are also termed marked; those characterized by the absence of the privative property are unmarked (Projet 1931: 314 and Trubetzkoy 1969: 75). Phonetically, outside a phonological system, two segments are always gradual and equipollent and never privative (Trubetzkoy 1969: 75). The two uses of "marked" and "unmarked" are differently defined: one in terms of characteristics of the total phonological system and one in terms of the partial phonological system. The pair *p-b* may be unmarked and marked, respectively, in terms of voice, and marked and unmarked, respectively, in terms of tenseness. The presence of a privative phonetic property indicates a segment farther from a neutral articulation, the act of breathing (Trubetzkoy 1969: 146). The member of a privative pair that deviates in these terms is the marked member of the opposition. Although the terms "marked" and "unmarked" have two definitions, their use is apparently parallel. In our example, *p* is phonologically unmarked in the total system, and *p* is phonetically unvoiced and therefore phonetically unmarked. If *b* occurred in some environment in the absence of *p*, then *b* would be phonologically unmarked and *p* marked. Phonetically, *b* is marked if voice is the property distinguishing them in the hierarchy; but if that is the case, phonological markedness is not equivalent to phonetic markedness. In such cases the distinguishing property is reinterpreted to be not voice, but tenseness; and in these terms the phonologically unmarked *b* is also the phonetically unmarked, whereas the phonologically *p* is also the phonetically marked. Again, phonological and phonetic markedness coincide, as do phonological and phonetic unmarkedness (cf. Trubetzkoy 1969: 76–77). We may take advantage of the empiric nature of our primitives and identify the distinction between a bilateral, privative pair in the hierarchy by a choice of feature such that phonological and phonetic markedness coincide. If voice is used to distinguish *p-b*, then we know that *p* is phonetically unmarked; if tenseness is used, we know that *b* is the unmarked member.

There is a problem in this suggestion. The bilabial portion of the total system identical with (7) identifies *p* as unmarked and *b* as marked. If neutralization does not occur, there is a single partial system in all environments. The relationship between *p-b* is not the same as in the total system, where *p-b* is neutralized in some partial system, yet the representation would be that of (7). We know from the portion of the hierarchy that *p* is phonetically unmarked, but this representation says nothing of its phonological markedness. We have a way of incorporating phonetic markedness, but we require some way of indicating neutralization. We may seek a solution in the second aspect of the pattern of neutralization. The relationship *p-b* in a total system wherein they are never distinct (where they are variants of a phoneme) exhibits the maximum degree of closeness in loose-close patterning; their relationship in a total system wherein the opposition is constant in all positions exhibits a lesser degree of closeness in the cline of loose-close. Trubetzkoy (1936a: 30) observes that "The extraphonological [phonologically nondistinctive, PWD] opposition of sound is usually completely overlooked [*gar nicht bemerkt*] by the phonetically untrained speaker of a given language. But the constant phonological oppositions are clearly perceived even by a phonetically untrained member of the language community, and the members of such an opposition are considered two different 'sounds'. With respect to neutralizable oppositions perception varies . . . . Even in the position where they are opposed [*Relevanzstellung*] the members of a neutralizable opposition are felt only as two meaning differentiating nuances, as two different but nevertheless closely related sound units . . . . " We may try to integrate this pattern into our accounting in the following way:

(12)

(a) Bilabial	(b) Bilabial	(c) Bilabial
Stop	Stop *or* Fricative	Voice *or* Voiceless
or Voice *or* Voiceless	Voice *or* Voiceless Stop	Stop
Fricative		*or*
		Fricative

In (12a), *p-b* are variants, and voice is not represented in the phonological hierarchy. In (12b), *p-b* are opposed in some position, but neutralized in some other. In (12c), the opposition *p-b* is constant. The difference in the pattern of loose-close in the data is correlated in the accounting with the notion of hierarchy. The place of voice from absence to lowest position to co-occurrence with stop-fricative (its placement from lower to higher) correlates with the increasing "looseness" or distance between *p* and *b*. We may claim that the hierarchical arrangement of voice-voiceless and stop-fricative indicates that voice is neutralized in some position, and that *p* is phonologically unmarked. The absence of such hierarchy (as in 12c) indicates absence of neutralization and no phonological markedness of the pair *p-b*.

This proposal raises a second problem. Compare a language with the constant opposition *p-b*, but without other bilabial obstruents, with a second language identical to the first except that *p-b* is neutralized in some partial system. The hierarchical representation of both their orderings is:

(13)   Bilabial

Voice   *or*   Voiceless

Stop and fricative are absent from the phonological hierarchy because the hierarchy distinguishes no pairs. Now there is no class within Bilabial to which Voice may be hierarchically ordered to indicate the distinction of neutralized versus constant. Pertinent to this is Trubetzkoy's (1969: 77) statement that "if from the standpoint of the functioning of the phonemic system neither d nor t can be considered unmarked, the opposition t-d must be regarded as equipollent." That is, if the opposition is constant, yielding no phonological relationship of unmarked-marked, what seems to be a privative relationship is in fact equipollent. This implies two distinct uses of the terms "privative," "gradual," and "equipollent." The term "privative" was introduced to designate both the property distinguishing a pair of units and the relationship between the units if no third unit was distinguished from the first two by a third value of degree or the same distinguishing property. The pair p-b are privatively related if no third unit of the system differs from p-b by a third degree of voice. If there exists such a third unit within the system, the property and the relationship are gradual. The pair i-e in a vowel system of i, e, $æ$, a, o, and u is gradual because i-e, distinguished by values for height, co-exists with $æ$ differing from i-e by a third degree of the same property. If two units are not distinguished solely by two different values of a single property, they are equipollent. The second use of these terms does not turn on relationships internal *within a single system*, but on those arising externally from the occurrence of the *total system within an environment*. Within partial systems, the internal definitions of these relationships hold; within the total system, the external definition holds. In a language in which p-b is a constant opposition and does not differ from a third phoneme by a third degree of voice, p-b are privative in partial systems but equipollent in the total system. Had the language neutralized p-b, the opposition would still have been privative in the partial systems retaining the opposition, and p-b would be privative in the total system also, unlike the preceding case. The distinction between the two uses of these terms is made terminologically by *logical* and *actual*. A relationship (privative, gradual, or equipollent) is logically privative, gradual, or equipollent in the partial system. In the total system relationships are actually privative, gradual, or equipollent or not. As we have seen, the two do not necessarily coincide.

Within the phonological system an actually privative opposition means the opposition is neutralized in some partial system; actually, equipollent means the opposition is not so neutralized. This distinction between actually privative and actually equipollent is not equivalent to marked and unmarked. That p-b is actually privative does not in itself indicate which value of voice is phonologically marked or unmarked but only that phonological markedness is present, that a logically privative opposition is neutralized in some environment.

Our proposals (1) of subhierarchy or no subhierarchy and (2) the indication of some feature within the total hierarchy as actually privative or actually equipollent are alternative ways of integrating the distinction between constant and neutralized into the theory. Once that integration is solved, the marked-unmarked relationship is implied by the empiric nature of the primitives; voiceless *p* will necessarily be unmarked once we determine how to indicate within the theory the fact that *p-b* is neutralized in some position.

There are then two issues here: (1) how to account formally for neutralization, which is a pattern of loose-closeness and relationship type (actually privative-equipollent) within an opposition, and (2) how to account for phonologically marked-unmarked members of an opposition, which is a pattern of relationship type. Neither of the alternatives (subhierarchy or actually privative-equipollent) is explicitly developed by Trubetzkoy as the formal means of accounting for neutralization. A third seems to be adopted. Instead of indicating the neutralization directly within the total system, we may adopt some adequate statement of the total system. By stating its variants, partial systems, the whole (total system plus variant systems) will identify those oppositions that are neutralized. Neutralization, then, is not internal to the system but is derived externally from, and is implicit in, the system in some environment, from its functioning (Trubetzkoy 1969: 76).

Our example or word initial and word final consonant systems would be accounted for by setting forth a hierarchy that is identical to that of word initial and then stating the variants of that system; one variant occurs finally, another (which happens to be identical in shape to the total system) occurs initially. That *p-b* is neutralized in a partial system indicates within the total system that voice-voiceless is actually privative. The nature of the primitives alone then indicates *p* (or voicelessness) as unmarked. The word initial and word final bilabial portions of the partial systems are (12 c) and (12a), respectively. The fact that voice is used to distinguish *p-b* predicts that [p] will occur finally as bilabial stop because *p* is unmarked with respect to voice and the unmarked member occurs where the property of voice is absent from (neutralized in) a partial system. Had tenseness been used in the hierarchy to distinguish *p-b*, this would have predicted *b* as the bilabial stop in the partial system where tense-nontense was absent.

The discussion of neutralization-constant and marked-unmarked has been based on *p-b*, a logically privative relationship. We have derived a way of accounting for both phenomena. When logically equipollent and logically gradual oppositions are considered, we find the suggestion sufficient to account for them; but neutralization of logically equipollent and gradual oppositions do not exhibit patterns of markedness within the total system. We take up logically equipollent oppositions first. Here we must make two observations, one general to neutralization, and one particular to neutralization of logical equipollence. In discussing neutralization, we have considered partial systems and their environment only as co-occurring. A distinction must now be made within this relationship by determining whether the manifestation of the archiphoneme is similar or dissimilar to the environment or whether the manifestation is incomparable to the environment. In the first instance, the environment conditions not only the neutralization but also the manifestation of the archiphoneme. In the second instance only the neutralization is conditioned by the environment. A distinction is accordingly made between *externally* conditioned manifestations of the archiphoneme in the case of the former, and an *internally* conditioned one in the latter case (Trubetzkoy 1969: 80–81). In the former, neutralization occurs but implies nothing about the markedness of the neutralized pair in the total system. Only when the manifestation is internally conditioned is such implication present. For example, if pairs of obstruents opposed by voice are neutralized before voiceless obstruents so that voiceless members occur before voiceless obstruents, the manifestation is externally conditioned. The presence of voiceless members in this partial system does not indicate voiceless members in the total system as unmarked, nor the voiced members as marked. The phenomenon of neutralization can occur independently of phonological markedness, but not vice versa. This is relevant to logically equipollent relationships because when neutralized, the manifestation of their archiphoneme is never internally conditioned, but always externally conditioned. It follows that equipollent oppositions never enter markedness relationships.

Unlike an equipollent opposition, a gradual one when neutralized may exhibit its archiphoneme both internally and externally conditioned. When neutralized, the gradual opposition in the total system is actually gradual; when not, the gradual opposition, like the privative, is actually equipollent within the total system. When neutralized and internally conditioned, a gradual opposition does not imply a markedness relationship within the total system, as the privative opposition does. This is based on the nature of the distinction between the opposed pairs, made not by the presence or absence of a property but by a degree of that property. Let us assume a vowel system *i*, *e*, *ɛ*, *a*, *u*, *o*, and *ɔ*. The triads *i-e-ɛ* and *u-o-ɔ* are, as pairs (e.g., *i-e*, *e-ɛ*, and *i-ɛ*), gradual oppositions. Let us suppose in one language that the pairs *i-e* and *u-o* are neutralized in some partial system and that the internally conditioned manifestation is *i* and *u*. In a second language, the pairs *e-ɛ* and *o-ɔ* are neutralized and the internally conditioned manifestation is *e* and *o*. Markedness was defined phonetically in terms of presence of a property deviating from a neutral position. Here we must speak of a degree of a property. If we assume that the internally conditioned manifestation of the archiphomene is always by a sound with the minimum degree of a property (Trubetzkoy 1969: 81), then the distinction in each case here is by the property of openness. Of the pair *i-e*, the former meets the condition of lesser degree of differentiating property only if openness is chosen to distinguish between them; of the pair *e-ɛ*, *e* is the less open. In each case, *i-e* and *e-ɛ*, the first and second members represent the *extreme* member and *mid* member, respectively, of the opposition (Trubetzkoy 1969: 75 and 81–82). Phonologically extreme corresponds to phonologically unmarked within a neutralized privative

opposition, and phonologically mid, to phonologically marked. Of the pair
i-e, *i* exhibits the lesser degree of openness and is the extreme member. If
the neutralization had been manifested by *e* and *o* for the pairs *i-e* and *u-o*,
the notion of the extreme member occurring as manifestation is met by
reinterpreting the opposition not as openness, but closeness. Then, of the pair
i-e, *e* manifesting the archiphoneme is the extreme member only if the distinction between the two is made by closeness; *e* is less close than *i*. We claim then
that the neutralization of a gradual opposition is manifested by the extreme
member and choose the property distinguishing them in each instance so
that this is so. We may define a phonological extreme within the total system
as that member of a neutralized opposition identical to the manifestation of
its archiphoneme in a position of neutralization. Phonetically, extreme is the
lesser degree of a gradual property.

We make one last comment on the integration of neutralized gradual
oppositions into the theory. A gradual property differentiating not three but
four phonemes may exist such that two mid values are neutralized. In a vowel
system with four degrees of closeness or openness (e.g., *i*, *e*, *ε*, *æ*), the opposition *e-ε* may be neutralized. Because the neutralization does not involve a
mid and an extreme, the two mid vowels, Trubetzkoy (1969: 108–9) chooses
to interpret the opposition not as actually gradual, but actually privative;
and the two members enter a marked-unmarked relationship analogous to
actually privative oppositions.

In accounting for the phenomenon of neutralization or its absence, we in
effect account for the fact that certain sequences of phonemes do not occur.
The phenomenon that was accounted for by defective distribution in post-
Bloomfieldian theory is accounted for here by a partial system from which
certain phonemes are absent. With respect to the example of (3) and (11),
post-Bloomfieldian theory would state that voiced obstruents do not occur
finally. Prague School theory states that voiced obstruents are absent from
the partial system occurring finally. Not all of the pattern of distribution of
phonemes is referred to this theoretical mechanism. We may examine an
example given by Trubetzkoy (1936a: 32 and 1969: 79). In German not all
consonants occur initially before *l*. The pair *p-b* does, but the pair *t-d* does not.
If we try to account for this by claiming that it is another instance of neutralization involving the distinction between *p-t* and *t-d*, then we claim that what
in fact occurs in this partial system is the archiphoneme of *p-t* and *b-d*. In the
case of the latter, that archiphoneme is consonant, obstruent, voiced, and
stop—the properties common to *b-d*. The manifestation of this archiphoneme is the bilabial. We observe, however, that there is another phoneme
within the language that shares the properties *b* and *d* share: *g*. Furthermore,
g occurs initially before *l*. The properties distinguishing among obstruent,
voiced stops is not neutralized because a distinction is still made between
such phonemes, viz., *b* and *g*. The distinction of location between *b* and *d* is
not neutralized, and the absence of *d* (and *t*) from this environment is to be

stated separately. If restrictions in the phonemic sequence are not statable as subhierarchies, the phenomenon is not neutralization—a property of the hierarchy—but a property of individual phonemes and is stated as distributional characteristics of them relative to one another. Such statements make up *syntagmatic phonology* (Trubetzkoy 1969: 248–52). The phonemes defined by the hierarchy are grouped into disjunctive classes according to their function or privilege of occurrence. Statements are then made of the possible linear conjunctions of these classes. This type of statement produces additional ordering within the system of phonemes termed a *functional classification* (Trubetzkoy 1969: 242). It requires no new primitives in the theory to account for it.

In making this classification, we consider the distribution in a domain no longer than a word. It may in fact be shorter; the morpheme may be chosen in its place, The motivation is generality. The distribution statements should be predicated of the largest possible disjunctive classes of elements within the hierarchy of phonemes. To achieve this goal we pick the domain accordingly.

Identity

The problem of identity that initiated the discussion of neutralization now has half its answer. Variance in data is reduced to identity in two ways: (1) within some environment, and (2) independently of environment. The first corresponds to the substitution of Hjelmslev and free variation of post-Bloomfieldian theory. The second corresponds to the phenomenon of complementary distribution in post-Bloomfieldian theory; there, identity in the second case is treated as a relationship between sound segment-sized entities. In Prague School theory the identity is not among units but the partial systems themselves, which are identified as variants of a total system. Two partial systems in different environments are the same if their hierarchies are identical. If not, they are distinct partial systems, but still variants of the total system.

Once the problem of identity is stated we must determine how it is answered and in doing this we determine the operational or explanatory nature of the theory. In Trubetzkoy 1968 and 1969: 46–51, a set of "rules" is given for determining the phonemes of a given language. Rule II (Trubetzkoy 1969: 48) defines nonidentity: "If two sounds occur in exactly the same position and cannot be interchanged without a change in the meaning of the words or without rendering the word unrecognizable, the two sounds are phonetic realizations of two different phonemes." At first inspection, this may be assumed to be an operational definition of nonidentity, but if we accept that a phoneme is defined not only as distinct from all others, but also by its conjunction of features and relationships with other members of the system, then Rule II (and those accompanying it) are insufficient. A phoneme is defined by its place in the phonological system. The rules for determining phonemes are intended only as "practical rules" (Trubetzkoy 1969: 46). The definition of phoneme is given rather by the notion of possible phonological hierarchy, and there is no sequence of operations for determining a phonological hierarchy. The theory is explanatory.

Although these procedural rules do not define the phoneme as a term within the theory, they do indicate properties of the phonological system and have implicit within them a measure for indicating preferable accountings. The impression given by Rule II that the nonidentity relationships of phonemes depend completely on their relationship to the meaning of the words in which they occur—in the manner of the Hjelmslevian commutation test or post-Bloomfieldian contrast—is modified by Rule IV (Trubetzkoy 1969: 50): "Two sounds that otherwise meet the condition of Rule III [stating conditions for identity of two sounds in different environments, PWD] cannot still be regarded as variants of the same phoneme, if, in a given language, they can occur next to each other, that is, if they are part of a sound sequence in those positions where one of the sounds also occurs in isolation." Rule I states the equivalent of free variation; Rules II and IV, that of contrast; and Rule III, that of complementary distribution. Rule IV in its supplemental, *ad hoc* nature (as compared to the preceding three) seems curiously out of place. Through Rule IV we can see the actual condition for nonidentity. Trubetzkoy's example is [r] and [ə] in [pərfekšn] 'perfection' and [prəfešn] 'profession'. If [r] and [ə] occur in complementary environments and are similar, Rule III states that they are to be identified. The first portion of each word then has an identical sequence of phonemes pXX where X is the symbol for the [r]/[ə] phoneme; but from this transcription it cannot be predicted when X is [ə] or when [r], unless we know the word in which it occurs—a very patternless kind of conditioning. The solution is to keep [r] and [ə] phonologically distinct. The motivation is one of generality in predicting variants. The prescription of Rule II can be related to the same motivation. In [rat] 'rot' and [rɔt] 'wrought', the identification of [a] and [ɔ] yields a single transcription rXt. Again with no knowledge of the particular word involved, it is impossible to predict the phonetic quality of the vowel. The consideration involved is the same as the post-Bloomfieldian concern with generality in stating the conditioning of complementary distribution. These examples are analogous to the extreme case IV in Chapter 5. With this modification Rules II and IV say the same; and Rule IV is not so unrelated to the others as it seemed. Pattern of predictability of phonetic variants is the condition of identity, and nonpatterned predictability is the condition of nonidentity. This, then, is in fact a measure of good or bad accountings. Accountings that violate Rule II/IV are very ungeneral; each statement of phonetic variants must be made separately for each word in which the phoneme occurs. Rule III is another manifestation of the generality evaluation in that identity of sounds in complementary environments is predicated on phonetic relatedness. In predicting variants, two pieces of information must be known: (1) the environment, and (2) the manifestation. Rules I and II/IV are concerned with generality of (1); Rule III is concerned with (2).

Additional rules are introduced to prescribe whether a sound is to be one phoneme or two (Trubetzkoy 1969: 55–62). Rules I–III of this set state conditions under which the choice of interpretation as one or two phonemes is not obvious; Rules IV–VII provide for the decisions. Rule IV is the same as the post-Bloomfieldian criterion of pattern congruity. Rule V states "symmetry" in the hierarchy is preferable; that is, a possible biphonemic interpretation is to be rejected if the monophonemic interpretation adds to the proportional or bilateral relationships. Rule VI states the equivalent of Hjelmslevian economy; the smallest number of units is preferable to a larger number. Rule VII restates the criteria of the preceding rule in a different context. All the rules favor the most general accounting, differing only in that they apply to different parts of the phonology: statement of phonetic variants or interpretation, statement of distribution, statement of the phonological hierarchy, and statement of the number of units within that hierarchy. Generality may be manifest or absent at all these points in an accounting, and the more general one is preferable. Possible conflicts among such criteria may exist, e.g., between post-Bloomfieldian pattern congruity and phonetic similarity (here in the form of generality in statement of distribution and simplicity of interpretation). Such problems are not considered, but the criterion for evaluating accountings is clear: generality.

Although we have interpreted the definition of phoneme to be nonoperational and independent definitionally from the meanings of grammatical words (or identities of words), phonemes do bear a relationship to them. We have indicated that grammatical elements "consist of" or are linear conjunctions of phonemes. In this lies their function or their relation to grammar. They are the diacritica of grammatical elements (Skalička 1936: 130 and Jakobson 1962: 304). Their function in distinguishing between grammatical words and morphemes is termed the *distinctive function* (Trubetzkoy 1969: 27–28). We have argued that this relationship or function is not their defining property, which is also revealed by the statement that "Oppositions of sound capable of differentiating the lexical meaning of words in a particular language are *phonological* or *phonologically distinctive* or *distinctive oppositions*" (Trubetzkoy 1969: 30). This is not conversely true. Not all phonological oppositions are capable of differentiating the lexical meanings of two words in a particular language, yet they are phonologically distinct. Such oppositions are called *indirectly distinctive* (Trubetzkoy 1969: 33); an example is [h] and [ŋ] in English. The distinctive function then is not a necessary criterion for the nonidentity of phonemes. If it is not necessary to determine nonidentity (distinctive opposition) between [h] and [ŋ], it is not necessary to distinguish [h] and [k], [ŋ] and [k], and so forth. The definition of phonological elements is independent of distinctive function. The latter is present in the theory only as the relationship of phonology to grammar and is implied by the statement that morphemes consist of phonemes.

The indication that the theory is explanatory provides the answer to the second part of the problem of identity within data. Identity is assumed, not defined, and is justified in individual languages by the degree of generality the identification adds to the accounting, and rejected when such identification detracts from the generality.

The outline of word phonology to this point consists of a set of phonetic primitives hierarchically related and the primitives of word (as possible speech act), disjunction, conjunction, linearity, and nonlinearity plus the definition of phonological hierarchy. Certain portions of the hierarchy are identified as phonemes, i.e., as nonlinear conjunctions of phonetic primitives. Through the hierarchy of conjunctive phonetic primitives defining phonemes, the latter are further defined as entering relationships in pairs with each of the others. The phonological hierarchy recurs linearly. We may view linear sequences of the phonological hierarchy in the following way. Grammatical words and morphemes consist of phonemes. As such, we may interpret them as series of "choices" from the hierarchy in a sequence of linear positions. That is, *Al'osha* in Russian, phonologically *aḷóša*, consists of five choices from those possible within the phonological hierarchy of Russian, which recurs five times in sequence. But, given certain choices in some position, other choices are not possible. Having chosen stressed *o* in third position, no stressed vowel may recur in the word. These restrictions are patterned. A group of choices in some position may preclude choices in another. If these choices (made and precluded) are identifiable subhierarchies within the total hierarchy, we find subhierarchies—but not the total hierarchy—possible in some positions. The subhierarchies are the partial systems and the restriction in choice is neutralization. The relation of subhierarchies to one another is a property of the total system. From these definitions inferences can be drawn not only in predicting possible sound and sound sequence within a language, but also concerning the speakers' judgments of relatedness between pairs of phonemes.

Sentence Phonology

There remains within phonology the second sublevel—word groups—to be accounted for, plus specifying the relation of word phonology to sentence phonology. The phonology of word groups is worked out in much less detail than word phonology. A subset of the phonetic primitives assumed for word phonology form the basis of the systems of sentence phonology. These are intonation, tone, stress, and pause (Trubetzkoy 1969:201–7): the subset of prosodic features. Given a set of word groups we may find they are distinct with respect to intonation, stress, and pause. We may find *Virginia wrote* with level intonation and falling intonation and no way of predicting when one or the other will occur. We attribute rising intonation of questions to the appeal function (cf. Jakobson 1962: 289). We may discover differences of stress (*Virgínia wróte* and *Virginia wrôte*) and differences in pause (*the Russian, the Armenian, and the Georgian* versus *the Russian Armenian, and the Georgian*, where the commas indicate pause). To account for these unpredictable differences we posit a system:

Prosodic

Level versus		First versus second		Pause versus
falling intonation	*or*	versus third stress	*or*	nonpause

wherein intonation, stress, and pause are equipollent. Rising and falling intonation are privative and isolated. Stress is gradual and isolated. Pause is privative and isolated. Possible patterns of neutralization are not treated, but in general we might expect sentence phonology to exhibit the same patterns as word phonology.

The relation of word phonology to sentence phonology is not based on "consists of" although phonological sentences consist of phonological words. Certain properties of the phonology of words may indicate the number of words or the boundaries of words as they occur in groups. Statements of neutralization, of phoneme sequences, or of interpretation may occur only at word boundaries or not at word boundaries to indicate presence or absence of word boundaries. Certain phonological properties, e.g., stress or pitch, may occur once in each phonological word and indicate the number of words within a word group. Those properties of word phonology that indicate boundaries have a *delimitative function* (Trubetzkoy 1969: 27) with respect to sentence phonology, whereas those that indicate the number of words have a *culminative function* (Trubetzkoy 1969: 27–28). As word phonology bore a distinctive function to the word sublevel of grammar, so it bears the additional relationships to its co-level within phonology. Also, as the distinctive function had no bearing on the definition of phoneme, so the delimitative and culminative functions do not restrict the definition of phoneme. Note that both distinctive and nondistinctive portions of word phonology may bear delimitative function to sentence phonology.

The Grammatical Level

In discussing the relationship between levels, we have observed that grammar, as the intersection of patterns of the two extreme levels, produced a third distinct pattern. The terms of that pattern were different from either lexical or phonological patterns in that they were conjunctions of meaning patterns and sound patterns. (This in general recalls post-Bloomfieldian theory, wherein morphemes were meaningful, formal terms, as opposed to

Bloomfieldian theory, wherein morphemes were purely formal and separate from a distinct, but isomorphic, patterning of meaning, the minimum term of which was the sememe corresponding to the morpheme. Post-Bloomfieldian theory took advantage of that assumed isomorphy to combine the two.) Prague School theory differs from Bloomfieldian and post-Bloomfieldian theory in assuming that the lexical pattern itself is nonisomorphic with its intersection with phonological pattern; hence, although grammar involves sound-meaning patterns, both sound and meaning patterns remain distinct as the phonological and lexical levels. Although the terms of grammar are seemingly more complex in some way than either lexical or phonological terms, they exhibit patterns analogous to the phonological level. It is on this basis that Jakobson (1964) develops a study of the Russian verb. In a study of Russian case, Jakobson (1936), continuing the parallel, presents the following hierarchy of eight cases in Russian:

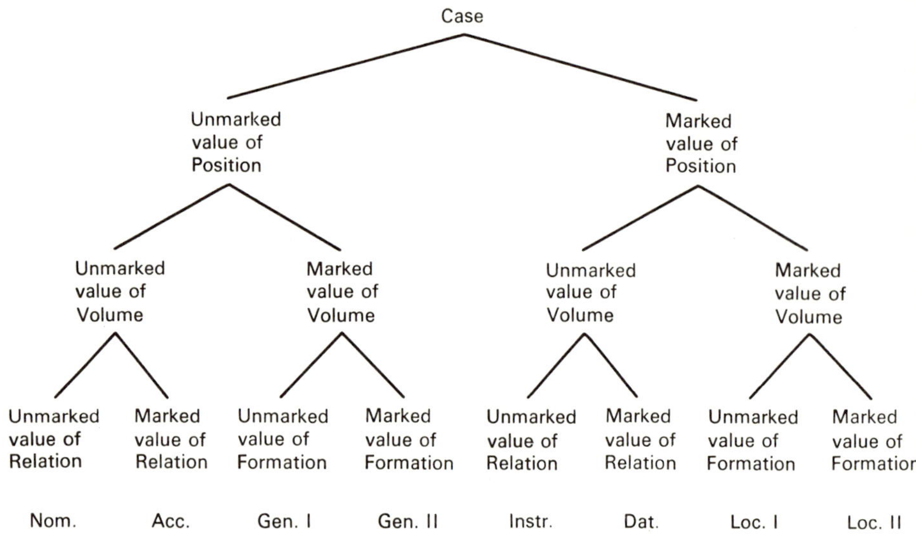

The hierarchy here is characteristic of the meaning portion of Russian grammar. Like phonological ordering systems, we may define bilateral, proportional, and neutralization relationships in pairs among the cases. The description assumes a set of empiric primitives analogous to those within phonology, i.e., position, volume, relation, and formation plus the notion of semantic markedness.

The description of case represents only a portion of the grammatical hierarchy within the word sublevel. A complete hierarchy would account for the entirety of grammatical words, ordering them by including them in subsystems. The first layer in the hierarchy would produce classes of inflectional or paradigmatic formation (Trubetzkoy 1934: 5); additional lower layers would be classes of stem or derivational formation. The class of words may then be ordered into classes of Verbs and Nonverbs; and the Nonverbs into Adjective, Pronoun, Noun, and Number (Trubetzkoy 1934: 5–10). These categories are defined, as phonemes were defined, as a nonlinear conjunction of properties. Thus, Pronouns are defined by the conjunction of a property of NonTense (Nonverb), Case, Number, and Gender without entering a characterization by value for Sentence Position. These properties of Tense, Case, Number, Gender, and Sentence Position, like those above for Case, are the primitives that, when hierarchically arranged, define the ordering of words within the grammatical system of words. Such an ordering is made or defined over a set of primitives with empiric semantic content and do not necessarily yield the same distribution of grammatical words into the hierarchy as when another—nonsemantic—basis is used. "The . . . classification of Russian verb forms [into approximately a dozen classes, PWD] refers to the inner, conceptual side of these forms. According to the external, sound side the Russian verb forms fall into two groups or partial systems . . . " (Trubetzkoy 1934: 8). The two classifications do not correspond, and although their relationship remains an intragrammatical one, its nature is not made clear. The nonsemantic basis is supplied by a subclassification or ordering by phonemic shape under the rubric of *morphonology* (Trubetzkoy 1929a, 1931b, and 1934).

An ordering of grammatical words by formal—phonological—properties involves (1) the patterns of the form, e.g., consonant-vowel-consonant as opposed to consonant-vowel; (2) the observation that not all morphemes considered the same have the same phonological shape and the statement of the patterns of those various shapes; and (3) the patterns of sounds that occur disjunctively at some point in the shape of a morpheme. The conditioning of these various shapes is statable by the morpheme environment of the affected morpheme. We may conceive of morphemes, and hence grammatical words, as consisting of a sequence of phonemes that are choices from a phonological system. In some morpheme environments, not all choices are possible, and a choice in one morphemic environment is replaced in a second. Before the diminutive morpheme *ka* in Russian, *k* is replaced by *č*; thus *reka* 'river' and *rečka* 'little river'. The exponent of 'river' has shapes *rek* and *reč*. Statements of these patterns satisfy (2); the ordering of phonemes by their relationships formed in these patterns constitutes (3). Thus, we may view morphonology as a hierarchy of statements classifying phonological shapes of morphemes in this way. The shapes are classified according to consonant and vowel sequences and by the hierarchical ordering of phonemes within a consonant or vowel class. Thus, in a CVC class, the last C may consist of among others: *k/č*, *č*, *x/š*, and *š*. Each entry represents a possible choice permitted by the pattern of (2). The morpheme "river" has *k/č* from the second C. The particular consonant, *k* or *č*, is conditioned by morpheme environment. Such an ordering resembles the phonological hierarchy but differs in crucial ways. The ordering itself within the morphonological and phonological hierarchies differs. Second, the conditioning of the morphonological subhierarchy—*k* or *č*—is the morphemic environment, whereas the conditioning of phonological subsystems was a co-occurring term within an adjacent phonological hierarchy. The presence of *k* or *č* is not only conditioned by *ka* 'dimunitive' but also by *on'ka* 'pejorative', *rečon'ka*. The shapes *ka* and *on'ka* do not form a subsystem within the phonological hierarchy. The conditioning factor is their identity as particular morphemes. The exclusion of *k* in certain environments resembles the phenomenon of neutralization within phonology; but it is different, and this is emphasized by the terminology. The basis of comparison within a neutralized opposition was called an archiphoneme. Although the terms involved in a morphonological neutralization do not necessarily have bases of comparison (something may be replaced by nothing), their conjunction shown by grammatical neutralization is called a *morphoneme* (Trubetzkoy 1934: 30). Archiphoneme and morphoneme are not to be confused. The latter is used only for phonemes related by neutralization within *grammar*. A phoneme at some position within a morpheme that is not grammatically neutralized in some morphemic environment is not a morphoneme; only either-or conjunctions are.

The pattern of syntax might be expected to parallel that of sentence phonology with a system of sentences ordered on some principle capable of distinguishing among lexical sentences. Possible devices such as word order or linearity and hierarchy may form such a basis. Two new relationships appear within syntax: *determiner* and *determined* (Karcevskij 1936 and Trubetzkoy 1966). Here the relationship is based on a syntagmatic—linear, conjunctive—pair of terms unlike the nonlinear disjunctive ones in morphology and word and sentence phonology. Such a pair is a *determinative syntagm*. Trubetzkoy (1966: 134) adds to this a *predicative* and an *associative syntagm*. The former consists of a subject and predicate, the latter of two determiners both in relation to a determined. It is tempting to see in this the selection (= determinative syntagm), solidarity (= predicative syntagm) and combination (= associative syntagm) relationships of Hjelmslev. The structure of a syntagm is binary (Karcevskij 1931: 189), like the grammatical constructions of one version of post-Bloomfieldian grammar. Possible examples are:

falling rocks	(Determining Determined)	
	Determinative	
money talks	(Subject Predicate)	
	Predicative	
a curious thing	((Determining Determining)	Determined)
	Associative	Determinative
ten thousand loves	((Determining Determined)	Determined)
	Determinative	Determinative

Summary

The lexical level—both word and word group—receives even less development, and we omit commenting on it except for our earlier discussion. In the summary of Prague School theory we present only definitions pertinent to the phonological level, since it is the only well-developed one; we may expect the remaining ones to parallel it in outline. The primitives are:

1. A set of hierarchically related phonetic primitives, including specification of phonetic markedness, privativeness, gradualness, and equipollence.
2. A set of hierarchically related semantic primitives, including representation, appeal, expression, markedness, etc.
3. Disjunction
4. Conjunction
5. Linearity
6. Nonlinearity
7. Word
8. Word group
9. Identity and nonidentity.

Definitions based on these are:

1. *Phonological hierarchy:*   Defined as a subset of the phonetic primitives. They are distinctive, phonological, or nonidentical by virtue of their occurrence in the hierarchy.
2. *Phoneme:*   Defined as any of the possible nonlinear conjunctions of hierarchically arranged, distinctive elements of the phonological hierarchy, nonidentical to every such conjunction in the phonological hierarchy.
3. *Opposition:*   Defined by two nonidentical phonemes.
4. *Basis of comparison:*   Defined as the distinctive features common to an opposition.
5. *Bilateral:*   Defined as the relation between the phonemes of an opposition whose basis of comparison does not recur in a third distinct phoneme.
6. *Multilateral:*   Defined as the relationship between the phonemes of an opposition whose basis of comparison does recur in a third distinct phoneme.
7. *Proportional:*   Defined as the relationship between the phonemes of an opposition whose distinguishing features also distinguish the phonemes of at least one additional opposition.
8. *Isolated:*   Defined as the relationship between the phonemes of an opposition whose distinguishing features do not also distinguish the phonemes of a second opposition.
9. *Homogeneous:*   Defined as a multilateral opposition whose distinguishing features are not hierarchically related to the feature(s) distinguishing the additional member(s) sharing that basis of comparison.
10. *Heterogeneous:*   Defined as a multilateral opposition whose distinguishing

features are hierarchically related to the feature(s) distinguishing the additional member(s) sharing that basis of comparison.

11. *Linear:*   Defined as a homogeneous opposition whose basis of comparison is shared by only one additional phoneme.

12. *Nonlinear:*   Defined as a homogeneous opposition whose basis of comparison is shared by at least two additional phonemes.

13. *Partial phonological system:*   Defined as a phonological hierarchy that occurs in linear conjunction with a phonological hierarchy, i.e., in a context.

14. *Total phonological system:*   Defined as a phonological hierarchy that includes all the oppositions of the partial phonological systems and does not occur in linear conjunction with a phonological system.

15. *Neutralization:*   Defined as a bilateral opposition occurring in one partial system of a total phonological system but not occurring in at least one partial system of the same total system. Neutralization is the absence of that opposition within the partial system(s).

16. *Archiphoneme:*   Defined as the basis of comparison of a neutralized opposition within the partial and total phonological systems.

17. *Assimilated:*   Defined as an archiphoneme within a partial phonological system whose nondistinctive properties occur distinctively with the same value within a second partial system co-occurring linearly with the first.

18. *Dissimilated:*   Defined as an archiphoneme within a partial phonological system whose nondistinctive properties occur distinctively with the opposite value within a second partial phonological system co-occurring linearly with the first.

19. *Contextually determined:*   Defined as the property of assimilation or dissimilation.

20. *Structurally determined:*   Defined as the absence of the property of assimilation or dissimilation.

21. *Logically privative:*   Defined as an opposition within a partial phonological system distinguished by a feature that has only two values within that system.

22. *Logically gradual:*   Defined as an opposition within a partial phonological system distinguished by a feature that has three or more values within that system.

23. *Logically equipollent:*   Defined as an opposition within a partial system distinguished by distinct features.

24. *Phonologically unmarked:*   Defined as (a) the phonetically unmarked member of a neutralized, logically privative opposition within the total phonological system when the archiphoneme of the opposition neutralized in some partial phonological system is structurally determined, and (b) the phonetically mid member opposed to a phonetically mid member within a neutralized, logically gradual opposition (such that the first member is phonetically less extreme than the second) within the total phonological system when the archiphoneme of the neutralized opposition is structurally determined.

25. *Phonologically marked:*   Defined as (a) the phonetically marked member of a neutralized, logically privative opposition within the total system when the archiphoneme of the neutralized opposition is structurally determined in some partial phonological system, and (b) the phonetically mid member opposed to a mid member within a neutralized, logically gradual opposition

(such that the second member is phonetically less extreme than the second) within the total phonological system when the archiphoneme of the neutralized opposition is structurally determined.

26. *Phonologically extreme:* Defined as the phonetically extreme member of a neutralized, logically gradual opposition within the total phonological system when the archiphoneme of the neutralized opposition is structurally determined.

27. *Phonologically mid:* Defined as the phonetically mid member opposed to a phonetically extreme member within a neutralized, logically gradual opposition within the total phonological system when the archiphoneme of the neutralized opposition is structurally determined.

28. *Actually privative:* Defined as an opposition within the total phonological system whose members are phonologically marked and unmarked.

29. *Actually gradual:* Defined as an opposition within the total phonological system whose members are phonologically extreme and mid.

30. *Actually equipollent:* Defined as an opposition within the total phonological system whose members are opposed neither as phonologically marked and unmarked nor phonologically extreme and mid.

31. *Phoneme distribution:* Defined by the membership of phonemes in nonlinear conjunctions and the statement of the linear occurrence of these relative to one another.

32. *Word phonology:* Defined by definitions (1)–(31) over the subsets of words within the disjunctive representative, appellative, and expressive functions.

33. *Sentence phonology:* Defined by the definition of (1)–(31) over the subsets of word groups within the representative, appellative, and expressive functions.

34. *Culminative function:* Defined by the distinctive and nondistinctive properties of word phonology that occur in a word group such that the word phonology of the three principal functions is related to the sentence phonology of the respective functions.

35. *Delimitative function:* Defined by the distinctive properties of word phonology that occur only at word boundaries or only within words, thus marking presence or absence of word boundaries within word groups such that the word phonology of the three principal functions is related to the sentence phonology of the respective functions.

36. *Phonological level:* Defined by sentence phonology, word phonology, and the relationships between them.

37. *Grammatical level:* Definition omitted.

38. *Lexical level:* Definition omitted.

Up to this point we have not commented on statements such as the following: "Every language has thus a vowel system with oppositions based on degrees of aperture" (Trubetzkoy 1969: 106) and "There is no language in which the properties of localization of the consonantal phonemes would be phonologically irrelevant" (Trubetzkoy 1969: 122) and "We can establish two groups of *universally inadmissible* phoneme combinations . . . Only the combination 'consonantal phoneme + vowel phoneme' can probably be considered a *universally admissible* phoneme combination . . . " (Trubetzkoy 1969:

246–47). These statements have no place in the definition of language just outlined. One type of universal can be integrated into the theory. The claim that "in any single [vowel] system only four classes of timbre can exist at the most" (Trubetzkoy 1969: 98) can be accounted for by restricting the phonetic primitives in such a way that they are incapable of making more distinctions than the four. This in effect restricts the definition of possible language. Such suggestions were made by Jakobson (cf. page 244). The converse property of language—not maximum presence, but minimum—cannot be solved by modifying the set of primitives. Neither the primitives nor the definitions are modified to include these properties of language. If such statements as the four quoted above are to be made in defining properties of language, they are present within the theory in the form of axioms appended to the primitives and definitions of theory.

A second area of comment has been omitted—patterns of frequency within language. Here, a distinction among kinds of frequencies must be made. One passing comment on the topic was made with respect to the recurrence of the distinctive oppositions within a series of proportional oppositions. The reference there was by way of deriving or accounting for the intuitive judgments of closeness of a relationship on the part of the native speaker. The greater the recurrence within the system, the greater the closeness. We now take up briefly additional patterns of frequency (cf. Mathesius 1929; 1931; and Trubetzkoy 1969: 256–69). The first deals with frequency of items, say, length of words in phonemes, within a speech act. Apparent patterns may be attributed to individuals, in which case they are not language patterns, but speech patterns studied by stylistics, or attributed to groups of individuals in which the pattern is social and a property of language. Frequency differences across styles are characteristic of those individual styles. That is, two styles may differ in that the more frequent words of one are phonologically longer than those within the second. This difference may result from patterns of derivation in grammar or be simply a result of phonologically longer "spellings" of morphemes. Whatever the cause, the differences in frequency of length of words is accounted for by the descriptions of the styles themselves. A second type of frequency compares the possible (archi) phonemic occurrences in a variety of environments. The morphonemic description of grammatical words then classifies and subclassifies morphemes according to general phonological shape; and within each shape the phonological system defines possibilities. In a CVC shape occurring initially, wherein the C system has twenty (archi) phonemes, each C has a probability of 0.05. Given a thousand morphemes or words of this shape, fifty of them would begin with any given C. This is one probability. The actual occurrence of a given C within this framework may differ from the expected. Similarly, given CVC, CV, and VC shapes for morphemes, we would expect the morphemes to be equally distributed among the shapes; but this does not necessarily happen. One possible cause is that a small (semantico-) grammatical class has a second morphonemic shape. The ratio of expected-to-actual may also be used in observing speech acts. No universal claims are made of such ratios (cf. Trubetzkoy 1969: 268). Until such claims are made, observations of frequency within data have no place in the definition of language; and the only way frequency impinges on the definition of language is in the characterization of loose-close relationships and exceptions. These observations about frequency in individual languages compare to the definition of language as idiolects to individual language. As idiolectal properties are not properties of the language they manifest, so accidental frequencies within individual languages are not properties of language.

A possible accounting of a language based on the theory given above would contain the following:

1. A definition of a phonological level by
    a. A definition of a phonological hierarchy for the word and word group, including
        i. A definition of the oppositions and their relationships as bilateral, multilateral, proportional, isolated, homogeneous, linear, and nonlinear.
        ii. A definition of the partial and total phonological systems.
        iii. A definition of the archiphonemes as contextually or structurally determined.
        iv. A definition of the oppositions in the partial systems as logically privative, gradual, and equipollent.
        v. A definition of the members of the archiphonemes as marked or unmarked and extreme or mid.
        vi. A definition of the oppositions of the total system as actually privative, gradual, and equipollent.
        vii. A definition of the phonemes and the disjunctive classes they form in their linear occurrences.
    b. A definition of the delimitative and culminative functions of the word phonology.
2. A definition of a grammatical level.
3. A definition of a lexical level.
4. An evaluation of (1)–(3) with respect to the generality of the statements involved.
5. A reworking of (1)–(3) until (4) is maximally satisfied.

Prague School theory is unique among those we have examined in the structuring of pattern within a level. Previous theories have in general defined some unit, grouped similarly patterning units within disjunctive classes, and made statements about these classes as they occurred linearly or conjunctively. The general outline may be repeated a sufficient number of times to exhaust patterning. The statements made in this way are claims made of the minimum units. The introduction of classes and the associated apparatus has been motivated by generalizing statements as much as possible, and the pattern involved in such a level was a single pattern in some portion of the data. Prague School theory has altered this by seeing two distinct patterns in the same data level. Previous theories have seen distinct patterning as distinct levels based on the pattern between sound and meaning and language as pattern in some form between them. The next theory we take up—Firthian or London School theory—combines the two. The Prague School conception of two (or more) kinds of pattern within a single set of data, which yielded sublevels, and the Firthian view that meaning and sound are not to be separated, yields a view of language somewhat like Prague School sublevels. There, levels will be derived from observations of different patterns within data viewed monistically.

ADDITIONAL READING

JAKOBSON, ROMAN. 1936. "Beitrag zur algemeinen Kasuslehre." *Travaux du Cercle Linguistique de Prague* 6. 240–88.

TRUBETZKOY, N. S. 1931. "Die phonologischen Systeme." *Travaux du Cercle Linguistique de Prague* 4. 96–116.

———. 1936. "Essai d'une théorie des oppositions phonologiques." *Journal de Psychologie* 33. 5–18.

———. 1969. *Principles of Phonology*, trans. Christiane A. M. Baltaxe. Berkeley: University of California Press.

VACHEK, JOSEF [compiler]. 1964. *A Prague School Reader in Linguistics.* Bloomington: Indiana University Press.

———. 1966. *The Linguistic School of Prague.* Bloomington: Indiana University Press.

CHAPTER 8

Firthian Linguistics

The theory of this chapter, which we will call Firthian—sometimes the name "London School" (Langendoen 1968) is used—is based on the work of J. R. Firth, but also includes much that is the work of others. See the bibliography under Allen, Carnochan, Haas, Halliday, Henderson, Mitchell, Palmer, Robins, Scott, Simon, Sprigg, and Waterson. As usual when this happens, we find not a single theory, but a number of more or less closely related ones. The fundamental outline of the theory is drawn from Firth (1957b). The statements we find there are largely programmatic (cf. Bursill-Hall 1961: 184 and Robins 1963: 22); and for elaboration of the theory and exemplification we must turn to the sources cited above. Firthian linguistics is then not all the work of Firth; we will point out divergent developments in the theory as they appear.

The subject of this theory is behavior within a context; but the attitude toward the behavioral data is unlike that of other theories that have regarded language as human activity. Those theories that have adopted a view of language as behavior—Bloomfieldian, post-Bloomfieldian, and tagmemic—have adopted the Saussurean distinction between concept/signified versus sound image/signifier, reinterpreting it in behavioral terms, roughly as stimulus-response, context, or meaning versus sound; and the pattern in language is predicable of relationships between these two aspects of data. Hjelmslevian theory, which considers language independently of its manifestation as behavior or knowledge, reinterprets language as the formal relationships predicable of content and expression purport. The number of distinct kinds of patternings assumed in this relationship yields what we have called levels:

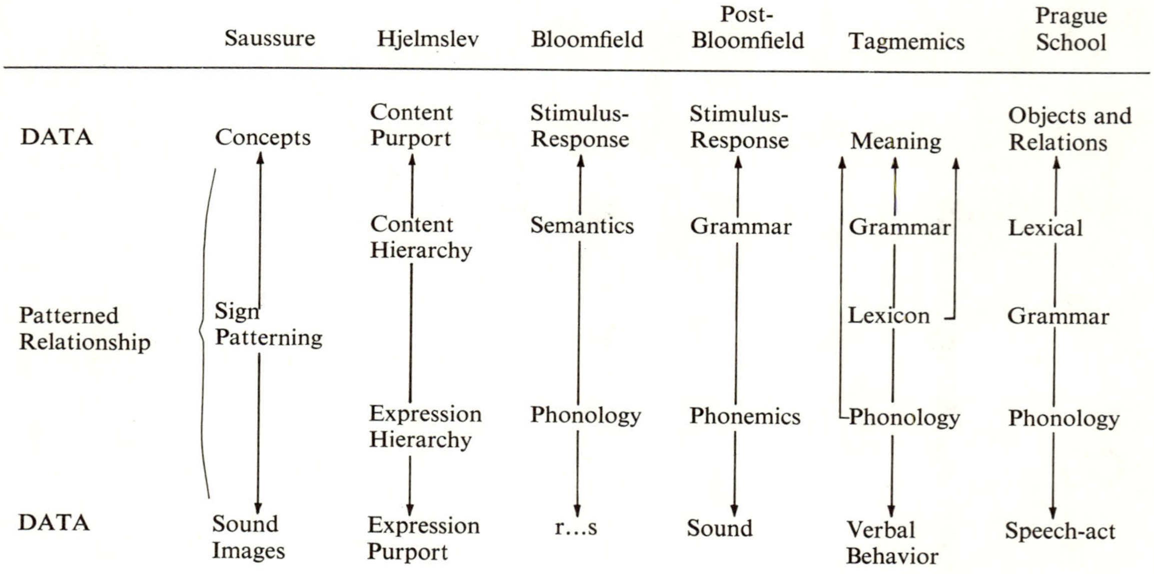

	Saussure	Hjelmslev	Bloomfield	Post-Bloomfield	Tagmemics	Prague School
DATA	Concepts	Content Purport	Stimulus-Response	Stimulus-Response	Meaning	Objects and Relations
		Content Hierarchy	Semantics	Grammar	Grammar	Lexical
Patterned Relationship	Sign Patterning				Lexicon	Grammar
		Expression Hierarchy	Phonology	Phonemics	Phonology	Phonology
DATA	Sound Images	Expression Purport	r…s	Sound	Verbal Behavior	Speech-act

If two or more levels are distinguished, the relationship between them is (1) hierarchical (e.g., Bloomfield's use of made-up-of, Pike's use of manifest, and represented-by in post-Bloomfieldian theory); (2) nonhierarchical (e.g., Hjelmslev's use of the reciprocal relationship of solidarity); and (3) a combination (e.g., Prague School use of both mutual implication and made-up-of).

Firth adopts the attitude that pattern is to be asserted of verbal, behavioral data within a context, but the relationship between behavior and context is not Saussurean. Unlike the preceding six theories, pattern is not expressed by a series of levels relating two terms. The verbal behavior we are interested in is termed *phonic data* (Firth 1957b: 226 and Allen 1954: 558) restricted by occurrence within a context. Phonic data, like Hjelmslevian purport, are the verbal continuum with no imposed segmentation. The broadest context is *culture* (Firth 1957b: 36). Subcontexts of culture are *contexts of situation* (Firth 1957b: 27, 35–36, 181–83, 192, and 226; and Firth 1957c: 7–13). With these distinctions, we can outline the shape of Firthian theory.

Unlike Saussure, Firth assumes that patterning—a segmentation—is predicable of phonic data independently of its relationship to context. To ensure that we do not attempt also to predicate pattern of gibberish—nonlanguage patterned, phonic phenomena—the phonic data are required to occur with a context if they are a manifest portion of an actual language. Context is not in fact dispensable, but still, patterning is attributed to phonic data alone. The claim is that wherever we find pattern predicable of phonic data, we will also find that the phonic data occurs within a context. This contextualization of phonic data is formally expressed by associating portions of the statement of patterning with pieces of that context. If such statements are not possible, we may assume that the phonic data we have taken as manifest language are in fact not. The context serves only as assurance that we have dealt with a valid piece of language data. The relationship of context to phonic data is not a *source* of pattern. "All linguistic statements must ultimately be founded upon phonetic observation, but not upon the observation of their meaning" (Palmer 1958a: 237). Two kinds of patterns are distinguished: grammar and phonology, which are nonhierarchically related. (Cf. the discussion of levels on pages 274–75.) This yields a schema expressing the theory-to-data relationship somewhat as follows (Allen 1956: 145):

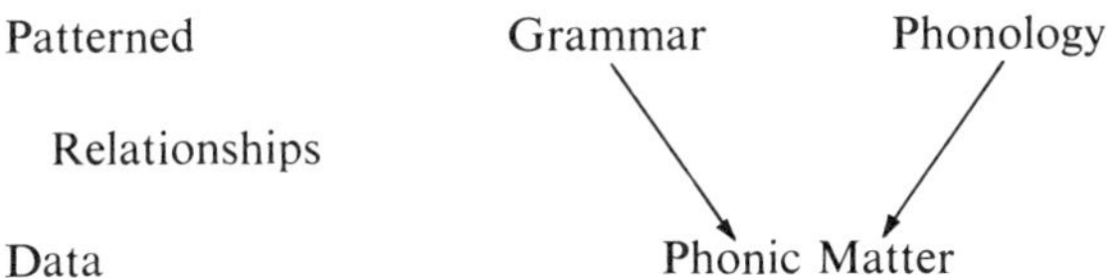

The distinction between contexts of culture and situation correlate with, and in part are motivated by, considerations of variation in patterning. The other theories we have studied admit or even require the data described to be social as opposed to individual. Saussure used the concept of "average"; in Bloomfieldian and post-Bloomfieldian theories, the same notion was called "convention." Prague School theory excluded studies of individual pattern from possible data, terming it "stylistics." The social property of language was related to the assumption that only such data were regular; only within social data were portions identifiable and recurrent. A less extreme attitude toward individual data is that they are not unpatterned, but manifest a variant pattern along with other (social or individual) data, and they all should be accounted for as intralanguage phenomena. Saussurean, Bloomfieldian, and Praguean theories take the view that data from individuals is highly variable and does not yield regularities; it is not language. Hence, the term *parole*, and so forth, to label it. A variant of post-Bloomfieldian theory, along with tagmemic theory, integrates individual (and dialectal) manifestations of language as variations of the pattern. Compare the respective terms "idiolect," "coexistent systems," and "hypersystems" used for this integration. Hjelmslevian theory similarly merges individual and dialectal variation under the term "connotative semiotic," but the boundary of language is drawn so that it includes semiotics but not connotative semiotics. Praguean theory, although rejecting individual patterning as nonlanguage, integrates dialectal patterning as language, making a three-way distinction within the parameter of variation of patterning across individuals. The remaining make a two-way distinction idiolect/dialect versus language or idiolect versus dialect/language. The Firthian position is that data taken from an individual person are valid (Firth 1957b: 143 and 187), and furthermore, such data may or may not be *typical* (Firth 1957b: 188; 1957c: 8; and Allen 1957: 68). Typical is predicated of patterns that are attributable to more than one person, but the same patterns are not necessarily attributable to all speakers linked by a shared context of situation. There is no "une langue une" (Firth 1957b: 29), but a collection of what we have called dialects.

This parameter of variation in patterning across persons requires limits. One of these limits is the identification of the single speaker. The upper limit, the boundary of one language versus another, remains to be determined. There is no proposal that the limit be made in terms of patterning, e.g., by the use of degrees of congruence of accountings such as Hockett's common core. The limit can also be determined by extralinguistic phenomena such as the Prague School's attitude toward data ("ours" versus "not ours"). Firthian theory distinguishes boundaries between one language and another by similar means. The framework used is the context of culture (Firth 1957b: 185–86), an extra-language, and nonlinguistic construct. Speakers who share no such context speak different languages. This places the problem of one versus two languages outside linguistics. Variation of patterning across individuals is an extra-language phenomenon not to be accounted for by our theory of language, for we take phonic data in a single context of situation as our language data. The variation among dialects is not integrated into the notion of possible language. The question, "Do these two people speak the same language?" is external to the definitions of the theory. An answer is provided only insofar as we refer to the results of a nonlinguistic science that segments portions of the universe into distinct cultures and situations, thus providing us with a means (external to the theory of language) of ranking our dialects in terms of close or distant.

We have now identified one variation in the statements that may be made of language data and have delimited its extremes. The middle ground—the systematic statement of patterns of one dialect versus another—is delimited by referring to contexts of situation. The context of situation delimits dialect from individual patterning. All individuals whose behavior in a context of situation is described as the same speak the same dialect. The parameter of variation in patterning that we have called style also conforms to distinctions in context of situation, and there is no formal difference among different dialects and different styles.

The data we take as subject of our statements are the behavior of individual(s) in a context of situation, not the individual abstracted from that context. The individual within that context is a *personality* (Firth 1950). Thus, we will talk henceforth not of behavior of speakers or individuals, but of persons and personalities implying the context. Any valid statement about patterns will necessarily be referrable to a context of situation. The sets of patterns that are valid for data of a particular context of situation make up a *restricted language* (Firth 1956: 138; Palmer 1958a: 237; and Robins 1963: 17). We take as data "speech sequences, verbally complete in themselves and operating in contexts of situation which are typical, recurrent, and repeatedly observable. Such contexts of situation should themselves be placed in categories of some sort, sociological and linguistic,within the wider context of culture" (Firth 1957b: 35).

Patterns based on sets of data center on the terms *meaning* and *technique*. Meaning in Firthian linguistics does not mean the same thing it did in the other theories where it involved the association of theoretical terms occurring in descriptions to portions of data. Firthian linguistics expands the notion of context, and meaning is expressed by contextualizations. Contextualization identifies the *function* (Firth 1957b: 19) of the thing contextualized. One type of contextualization we have already mentioned involved phonic data in a context of situation. Such a contextualization in a situation or culture is extralinguistic (Robins 1963: 27) and is called the *semantic function* (Firth 1957b: 27). The second kind of contextualization is intralinguistic (Robins 1963: 19); and it is here that we find a second "meaning" in formal, linguistic constructions occurring in a formal, linguistic context. With respect to this variety of meanings, Firth orders his approach to its statement by factoring contextualization into a series of statements. Here, the metaphor of light broken into the spectrum of its component colors is introduced (Firth 1957b:

170–71 and 1957c: 6). The statement of language patterning is intralinguistic contextualization; that is, the description of language data deals entirely with the statement of meanings in this sense.

Like Hjelmslev, Firth adopts an instrumentalist attitude toward the hypostatization of these formal contextual constructs. Neither the contexts of culture and situation nor the contextualized formal terms exist beyond their formation by the linguist (Firth 1957b: 181–82; Allen 1956: 164; and Robins 1963: 21). Consistent with this attitude, Firth speaks more often of a hierarchy of techniques for the statement of pattern than of theory. Recognizing that systematization of statements requires a technical language (Firth 1957b: 140), the instrumental approach indirectly constrains what goes into that technical language. Firthian theory will contain no general categories. There is no universal definition of terms such as "Noun," "Verb," "Word," "Sentence," "Subject," "Predicate," and the like. None of the theories we have so far studied has attempted to characterize all of these universally, but several have used the terms "Word," "Phoneme," and "Sentence," necessarily giving them a different meaning from theory to theory. The distinction between what has been defined theoretically and what has not correlates roughly to the position of things at different size-levels in a hierarchy, e.g., "Word" versus "Sentence," against terms that may occur at the same size-level, e.g., "Noun" versus "Verb." The former terms, if they can be identified with properties of the hierarchy defined by the theory, may be defined universally. The latter group of terms cannot be so defined; they are assumed to correlate with no formal, universal properties of the hierarchy and thus are defined *ad hoc* from language to language. Firthian linguistics adopts an even more conservative stance, and the terms "Word," "Sentence," and so on, are used *ad hoc* in each set of data (Firth 1957b: 144). This attitude is carried to an extreme in the assertion that "it is not the task of linguistics to say what 'language' is" (Firth 1957b: 177). The function of a theory is to provide a tool for stating what the linguist sees as patterns without rendering those patterns themselves as part of theory. Firthian linguistics is concerned with the techniques of that linguistic statement. With respect to such attitudes, we can distinguish between theories of language and linguistic theories. The latter treat language data, but are not concerned with specifying possible subject matter; the former extend to the definition of possible language. We shall extract those techniques that seem universally applicable and treat them, contrary to claim, as a theory of language analogous to those we have examined; but it should be kept in mind that although we treat Firthian linguistics as a theory of language, this claim is not made by its author(s), who assert that it is only a linguistic theory (Firth 1957c: 21 and 31–32).

The techniques are further characterized as hierarchical. This hierarchy results from two considerations: (1) contexts and (2) the instrumental attitude. Our techniques are directed toward the expression of Firthian meaning of items in a context. These contexts are assumed to form a hierarchy.

The number of contexts in the hierarchy is not definitely fixed (Robins 1963: 18). The formal patterns must be extracted from the phonic data in a context of situation, the latter in a context of culture. Within the formal patterns, additional, formally defined terms are established in a context. We thus have asserted a contextual hierarchy of the data:

1. formal item in
2. formal context in
3. situational context in
4. cultural context

Further, additional hierarchy may be asserted of (1) and (2). For example, with respect to formal patterning, we find the following schema (Firth 1957b: 26–27):

1'. phonetic term(s) in
2'. phonetic context in
3'. vocabulary context in
4'. morphological context in
5'. syntactic context in
6'. situational context in
7'. cultural context

"The technique I [Firth] have here sketched is an empirical rather than a theoretical analysis of meaning. It can be described as a serial contextualization of our facts, context within context, each one being a function, an organ of the bigger context and all contexts in finding a place in what may be called the context of culture" (Firth 1957b: 32). In this view, techniques are intended to establish the pattern for each of these stages of contextualization. Now the instrumentalist attitude toward these techniques can be manifested in a quasi-operational way. Techniques should lead to activities that form the basis of other activities, the sum providing the statement of pattern within a hierarchical context. Otherwise, they are not techniques, or they are bad ones. As in the operational post-Bloomfieldian theory, the application of these techniques may begin at the bottom (sound data) of this assumed contextual hierarchy and work upward to context of culture, or begin at the top and work downward. The techniques are usually viewed as working from the top down (Firth 1957b: 23 [up], 171 fn. 1 [down], 192 [up or down], and 220 [down]; Halliday 1957: 58 [down]; Palmer 1958a: 239 [down]; Robins 1953a: 109–10 [down] and 1953b: 138 [up]). Whichever is chosen, the hierarchy of context should be observed in applying our theoretical tools to the data. The hierarchy of techniques is then a consequence of assuming meaning as hierarchical contextualization combined with the quasi-operational assumption that our statements must follow from the sequential application of these techniques to this hierarchy. The techniques are ordered hierarchically, parallel to the contextual hierarchy, in the same way that the operations of phonetics, phonemics, and grammar follow the hierarchy of levels in post-Bloomfieldian theory.

We have twice used the term "quasi-operational." This is to distinguish the Firthian attitude toward the instrumental function of the theory from the post-Bloomfieldian attitude that techniques or operations constrain the definitions of the theory. This is not the case here. The techniques are separate and derive from what we will interpret as universal and defining properties of language, but the desire for functional techniques does not constrain the definitions of the theory in any explicit way. Firthian theory is explanatory in the sense we have described the term, and not operational. The theory with its definitions provides the basis for describing language data. This is unlike an operational theory in which the prior statement of operations is the basis of the definitions of the theory. Firthian techniques are not equivalent to post-Bloomfieldian operations (Haas 1966: 122). Furthermore, although the theory claims a hierarchy of items-in-context, it is not necessary to match that hierarchy by the sequence in which we handle data in individual languages (Halliday 1956: 179–80 and Robins 1959: 144). There is no fixed direction of the hierarchy, from item to context or from context to item, although the second seems to be preferred in practice. Within the techniques there is no constraint in principle on whether context defines items or the reverse.

If the hierarchy of techniques does not constrain the definitions of Firthian theory, it is important that we separate them from the discussion of theory. It is especially important to distinguish between technique and level in our sense of the term as a kind of patterning. Firth does not consistently make this distinction, and "technique" and "level" are occasionally used interchangeably. A technique applied to a particular item-in-context is given the name of that context; thus, the technique for dealing with items-in-syntactic context is the "technique of syntax" (Firth 1957b: 192). The name given to the complex "items-in-syntactic-context" is "level of syntax" (cf. Firth 1957c: 8) and corresponds to levels of inclusion in the hierarchy of contexts. "The use of the term *levels* in the phrase *levels of analysis* is not to be confused with other uses—for example, its use by Bloomfield in *Language*" (Firth 1957c: 7). Bloomfield's intention is closer to ours.

Having made the distinction between technique at some level and level in our sense, we do not identify phonetics, phonology, lexicology, morphology, and syntax (e.g., Firth 1957b: 26–27), i.e., the contexts, as separate levels. That a Firthian contextual level and a level of kind of pattern are not the same is indicated by the statement that levels (outside the phrase "levels of analysis") do not form a hierarchy analogous to the hierarchy of techniques and, therefore, the hierarchy of contexts (Bursill-Hall 1961: 164). We will discover that hierarchy exists in the pattern but that it is intralevel.

On the issue of the number of levels and their relationship, we find various positions. The number varies from two (Allen 1956: 145 and Firth 1957b:33) to four (Palmer 1958a: 241) to five (Firth 1957b: 26–27). Firth's (1957b: 26–27) five levels are levels of analysis. Generally, discussion of levels does not consistently recognize the distinction between level of analysis and level as kind of pattern. Similar variation is found on the relationship between the levels. Allen (1956) indicates a nonhierachical relationship, as does Firth (1957c: 8). Palmer (1958a) insists on a hierarchy. (Cf. Bursill-Hall 1961: 164–66 and Robins 1963: 22–23.) Again, the relationship between levels is not always discussed within a context in which levels of analysis are sharply distinguished from levels of pattern. We adopt here the variety of Firthian theory that distinguishes two kinds of patterning and relates them nonhierarchically. Henceforth, we will be concerned with levels of analysis only insofar as they relate to or find place within levels of patterning.

Phonology

The data of which patterning is predicated are the phonic data—verbal behavior in some context. In making this distinction between behavior and its context, we necessarily impose a segmentation on the universe and begin a definition of language. Further segmentation is made by focusing on the phonic portion. The technique of the first segmentation is one adopted from sociology or anthropology; the second is a purely linguistic one—phonetics. The technique of phonetics provides the terms with which we work in establishing pattern of phonology. As a technique, it may be applied to all sets of phonic data (Firth 1957b: 145), but the resulting segments should be such that they reflect phonological patterns. That is, it may be that a phonetic alphabet presents us with items for recording phonic data; sometimes, however, it is not these terms that manifest the pattern, but another segmentation cutting across those possible within the alphabet (Firth 1957b: 145–46 and Allen 1954: 557). Our initial segmentation independent of the language pattern may not be indicated by the pattern itself. Our technique of phonetics, then, is not based on a phonetic alphabet, but a combination of the parameters of that alphabet plus "some degree of arbitrary labelling" (Allen 1954: 557 fn. 3; see also Sprigg 1957: 108).

Having assumed a technique for recording phonic data, we now seek predicable patterning. Predicable patterning is not attributable to the whole text, but we will find that it can be asserted of portions of our phonetic record. We now assume a second segmentation, actually grouping, of stretches of the record and deal with them. At this point all our segmentations are arbitrary. Out of many possibilities, we choose to consider just one. The choice remains to be justified or replaced by another. We defer discussion of evaluation to later on.

Let us begin with an example (Old Church Slavic) and determine the nature of the patterns we assert of it:

(1)

[ḍɪṇɪ	koža
domʋ	bogʋ
ḍælo	žilɑ
dɨmʋ	șilo
duşa	țæṇɪ
duxʋ	çelo
daṇɪ	șiți
țɪma	șümʋ
poļe	piți]

In this set of data we observe sequences that can be termed phonetically "consonant" and "vowel." If we abstract this syntagmatic pattern, we can establish a *structure* (Firth 1957c: 17) that is valid for all our utterances: $C_1V_1C_2C_2$.

This is an abstraction and C is a term of phonological pattern, not a phonetic term (Firth 1957b: 145–46). It follows, then, that these phonological abstractions, C and V, have no universal content. We cannot say that V is always associated with the phonetic properties of vowels. For example, we find the following data in another language (Bella Coola):

(2)

[ƛ'ɬ]	'dry'	[q's]	'seriously ill'
[c's]	'noisy'	[t'ɬ]	'strong'
[sx̣]	'bad'	[t'x̣]	'cut'

Abstracting a structure CV, we find that the term V is not associated with the phonetic vowel properties of the phonetic system utilized. The terms C and V of the patterning are nonempiric, and their interpretation has to be stated *ad hoc* from language to language. There is no automatic, universal interpretation of them.

A second point is to be made about this statement of patterning. Since our terms C and V are not themselves universal, the theory will provide no definition of phonological consonant and vowel. These are labels for items that occur in an order defining a structure. What is universal and required to be part of the theory are the terms of syntagmatic structure, the items forming that structure—*categories* (Firth 1957c: 5)—and an order of mutual expectancy (Firth 1957c: 17) between those categories. In the same way that categories exemplified by C and V are nonempiric, so the relationship between categories is nonempiric. The distinction is made terminologically by *order* and *sequence*. The former is a phonological relationship, and the latter is a phonetic term (Palmer 1964: 123). As the categories require an explicit statement of interpretation, so does their order. The left-to-right order of categories does not imply left-to-right sequence of the record from which they are abstracted (Firth 1957b: 137).

The CVCV structure of (1), then requires an interpretation; by itself it says nothing of data. It is nonempirical as well as nonempiric until we associate it with exponents, a segmentation imposed on phonic data (Firth 1957c: 15). Such exponency may take the following form. Let C_1 be interpreted as [p], [ṗ], [t], [ṭ], [k], etc.; let V_1 be interpreted as [i], [ɨ], [ü], [u], etc.; let C_2 be interpreted as [m], [l], [ḷ], [x], etc.; and let V_2 be interpreted as [ɪ], [ʋ], [e], [o], etc. This interpretation imposes a second pattern on the data. Portions of the phonic material are abstracted and related disjunctively with respect to a category of structure. Classes established to express this are *systems* (Firth 1957c: 17), and the categories within any system are *terms* or *units* (Firth 1957c: 17). The phonological terms within our system that mediates between C and V and the phonetic exponents are *phonematic units* (Firth 1957b: 137–38; Robins 1957a: 3 and 1963: 28). The systemic abstraction, like the structural, yields categories that are nonempiric. Although abstracted from phonic data, the phonematic units are not bits of that material arranged disjunctively. "From the percepta of experience certain phonic data are selected (and phonetically described) as characterizing the various phonological units, of which they are termed 'exponents' and to which they may be said to be 'allotted'. The phonological units otherwise have value given only by their mutual relations as terms of systems and elements of structure" (Allen 1957: 69). Phonematic units are relationally defined with respect to other terms within the same system, but they have no other content. They do not consist of phonic stuff. The system requires a structural category for its establishment, for the terms are a system only with respect to their category. Without their associated category, they form no system; and a category requires a manifestation, an associated system of terms and their exponents. It is important to remember that a structural category is not made up of terms; a category is not itself a system of phonematic units.

The opposition of structure and system to phonetic exponents is somewhat like Hjelmslev's relationship between form and substance. The structural categories and phonematic units are established *ad hoc* for the data in the same way as Hjelmslevian form, e.g., a semiotic. Like Hjelmslevian form, they are nonempiric and associated with data by explicit statement. The terms with which they are associated are those given by the phonetics, analogous to Hjelmslev's nonlinguistic science. The association of the structure and system with the phonetic terms imposes an organization on the terms analogous to Hjelmslevian linguistic segmentation of the purport, a substance. The substance is expressed in Firthian theory as the phonetic statement of phonic data. A linguistic segmentation of phonic data presupposes structure and system in the same way that Hjelmslevian substance presupposes form.

The presupposition of system by structure is of a different order; it follows from the empirical requirement that categories have an interpretation or a *renewal of connection* (Firth 1957c: 17). The relationship of categories to form a structure is universal to all languages; so is the notion of system. But the particular system, like the particular categories and structure, are established *ad hoc* with respect to a set of data.

To account for the pattern of the data in (1), we require a theory that interprets category, ordered, unordered, conjunction, and disjunction as primitives. We define a structure as an ordered conjunction of categories, each category written arbitrarily by the symbols C and V. We may additionally define *place* (Firth 1957c: 5) as the relationships of order a category holds with the other categories of the structure. Associated with each of the structural categories is a system, defined as a disjunction of categories. Each category within a system is a phonematic unit. The implementation of this preliminary theoretic framework is arbitrary with respect to a particular set of data. The technique of phonetics and those at any level of analysis are not part of the definition of language. If they are used, it is as aids in constructing a description. The segmentation a description implies—the phonetic segmentation of phonic data—requires an evaluation (cf. pages 287–88). Validation requires contextualization within a situation or culture. The terms of this contextualization are external to a definition of possible language patterning.

The pattern so far identified emphasizes the syntagmatic, as Bloomfieldian theory does. All of our data in (1) are instances of a structure CVCV. The pattern formally expressed is similarly a syntagmatic one.

Prosody

We can identify additional patterning in (1). Observe that sequences manifesting any CV order exhibit the following properties. The terms manifesting a C have the phonetic value of palatalization or nonpalatalization. The terms manifesting a V have the phonetic property of frontness or backness. The linear sequence of these properties is such that nonpalatalization is followed by backness, and palatalization is followed by frontness. There is a redundancy here in the form of a sequential constraint on these four properties. The pattern based on the data in (1) fails to remove this redundancy. Pattern is left unstated. We can incorporate this by modifying the description. Let us remove the properties of palatalization, frontness, and backness from the manifestations of C and V. To account for these four abstracted features, we establish a *prosody* (Firth 1957b: 121–38; 1957c: 15–17; Allen 1957: 69; and Robins 1957a), which is related to the structure by unordered conjunction. Prosodies, like structural and systemic categories, have no inherent content, and their interpretation must be explicitly stated and related to the interpretation of the structure. This involves relating the prosody to certain portions—orders of categories—within the structure. In (1), that is each CV combination of the CVCV structure. The interpretation is expressed by stating that the prosody of tongue-involvement is associated with a *prosodic system* (Firth 1957b: 122) made up of "tongue-front articulation" and "tongue-back articulation" for each CV portion. The representation takes the following form:

$$\begin{array}{ll} \text{Prosody} & \text{T--I} \quad \text{T--I} \\ \text{Structure} & C_1 V_1 C_2 V_2 \end{array}$$

The interpretation is now:

The system at C_1 is interpreted by the phonetic segments [p t k], etc.
The system at C_2 is interpreted by the phonetic segments [m l n], etc.
The system at V_1 is interpreted by the phonetic segments of [i u ɪ], etc.
The system at V_2 is interpreted by the phonetic segments of [ɪ e a], etc.

The prosody T–I is associated with the system "tongue-front articulation" or "tongue-back articulation" for each CV order. The "tongue-front articulation" member of the prosodic system is interpreted as phonetic palatalization when it co-occurs with consonant features, and as phonetic frontness when it co-occurs with vowel features; "tongue-back articulation" is phonetically nonpalatalization with consonant features and backness with vowel features.

The data ordered to the phonological structure now differ in that consonant palatalization and frontness and backness of vowels are no longer accounted for by the structure. Here we find a place where our phonetic alphabet fails us. The phonetic symbol [i], for example, implies "tongue-front position" as part of a phonetic alphabet; in the same way, [p] implies "tongue-front lowered" or nonpalatalization. This is not what we want them to mean; they should give *no* information at all of tongue position (front or back) when they indicate exponents of the modified structure. The interpretation of the phonological structure does not now segment these properties from the phonic data; the prosody does. We may use these symbols giving them *ad hoc* meanings (as here) or use a longer prose specification.

Removing sequential redundancy reduces the phonematic units manifesting the categories of the structure; we have here effected a simplification in the systems. The previous systemic terms *i* and *ɨ*, phonetically distinct by tongue-front or tongue-back position, are no longer distinct when these features are subtracted (similarly for [ü] and [u]). The distinction between the previous systemic terms *ɪ* and *ʋ* is also removed. They differed phonetically both by tongue position and by having the lips spread or rounded. When tongue front or back properties are removed, the lips-spread or rounded properties become redundant; *i* in the second modified description abbreviates the phonetic description "tongue raised to half-close position, vowel." The interpretation of the prosody of tongue-involvement adds either "tongue-front position" or "tongue-back position." When the "tongue-front position" is added, "tongue raised to half-closed position, tongue-front position, vowel" implies the additional property of "lips spread." If the prosody is interpreted as "tongue-back position," this plus "tongue raised to half-close position, vowel" implies "lips-rounded" articulation. The same is true of *e* and *o* of the first description when modified by the introduction of the prosody: *e* within the V_1 system of the second description is exponed as "tongue half-open position, vowel." Analogous simplification cannot be made for the vowels that are "tongue close"; the characterization "tongue raised to close, tongue-front [by interpretation of the prosody], vowel" cannot imply roundedness because of the presence in the system of *two* phonematic units exponed as "tongue raised to close, tongue-front [by interpretation of the prosody], vowels," viz., [i] and [ü]. The same is true with respect to the close vowels [ɨ] and [u]. Among the open vowels, the distinction between [a] and [ɑ] in the first description is removed from the system of V_1 in the second accounting in the same way that the distinction between [i] and [ɨ] is removed.

We began our modification by observing a sequential redundancy and provided prosody to remove it in principle from descriptions. A second kind of redundancy occurs; the phonetically simultaneous "tongue half-close" plus "tongue front" or "tongue back" predicts "lips spread" or "lips rounded." This simultaneous redundancy may be stated when the phonetic record is related to the phonic data. The phonetic record does not then record all the phonic data. The phonological description, prosodies and structure plus the systems of each, determines what of the phonic data is recorded. "The phonetic statement must, therefore, to some degree, depend upon the rest of the analysis, but it depends upon it in the sense that what is determined by the analysis at other levels is the *selection* of the phonetic features from the phonic data" (Palmer 1958a: 234). What enters the phonetic record are features not redundant or predictable with respect to a category, or features that are sequentially redundant. The remaining features of phonic data are either predictably simultaneous redundancies in the phonetic transcription or are random, such that no pattern may be predicated of them. Sequential simultaneous redundancies are predicted at two separate points in the phonological description.

The pattern expressed by a prosody is syntagmatic. Partial identities of phonetic properties recur in sequences of phonetic record. It follows from this that we would find no prosody defined over a single phonematic unit (Allen 1954: 560 and Carnochan 1957: 163). A prosody may, however, have a prosodic system that is cumulative with the system of a single phonematic unit. Henderson (1949) defines a "syllable initial" prosody in a description of

Thai that derives from a constraint on phonetic sequence. Given the phonetic sequences exponing CVC, there is a constraint on what may occur initially exponing the first C. Henderson abstracts plosion, aspiration, affrication, friction, voice, lateralization, and rhotacization, such that singly or in combination they constitute a prosodic system associated with the syllable initial prosody. The remaining phonetic properties are taken as exponing the initial C. These are allotted to the phonematic units k, t, p, η, n, m, and *zeta*. The last has no phonetic property, and the phonic data initial in a sequence from which *zeta* is abstracted are attributed to the prosodies, either plosion [ʔ], aspiration [h], lateralization [l], rhotacization [r], or labialization [w]. The phonetic properties of the remaining exponents of C are not abstracted because they occur finally in the stretches under consideration and thus exhibit no sequential constraint or pattern. Clusters, for example, [pr], [pl], [phr], [phl] are treated prosodically. The [p] is an exponent of C. The rhotacization of [pr] is predicted by the prosodic exponent of rhotacization within the prosodic system co-occurring with the exponent [p] of the phonematic unit p; [phr] is predicted by the prosodic exponent of aspiration and rhotacization occurring with the C exponent [p].

We have as yet given no definition of prosody. Structure has been defined as categories related by order. Using the primitive category, we can define prosody as a category in unordered conjunction with a structure. By this, we effect a certain economy in not considering prosody as a primitive.

A single piece of our data, [ɖælo], is as follows:

Prosody	Tongue-Involvement		Tongue-Involvement	
Structure	C	V	C	V
System	[tongue-front articulation]		[tongue-back articulation]	
	[dental, voiced stop, consonant]	[tongue open vowel]	[lateral consonant]	[tongue half-open, vowel]
Phonetic Exponents in Transcription	ɖ	æ	l	o

Tongue-front articulation along with consonant articulation is phonetic palatalization; tongue-back articulation with consonant articulation is non-palatalization. Tongue-front articulation with vowel articulation is fronting; tongue-back articulation with vowel articulation is backing. Phonetic backing with half-close articulation implies lips-rounded articulation, hence [o]. The system, as given, is not complete; it illustrates only the disjunctive choices in the prediction of [ḏælo]. By taking choices from among the systems manifesting the prosody and phonematic units, we predict the particular data.

Let us now pay more attention to the manner in which prosodies are exponed. They are associated with a system as the structural categories C and V are. But unlike phonological elements, a domain must be stated over which the exponing phonetic properties of the prosody extend. This may be a continuous stretch (as Tongue-Involvement is over the phonological elements CV) or a discontinuous stretch, say, all V's, but no C's (cf. Firth 1957c: 31). This domain is the reference point (Allen 1957: 72). In terms of our CV reference point, the sequence of phonological elements may be divided into shorter orders, and given names. We may call our CVCV order a "word" and our CV order a "syllable." These are arbitrary with respect to individual data and have no status in the theory. The formal statement of the reference point may be given within the notation of the phonological structure, e.g.,

$$\frac{\text{T-I}}{\text{C} \quad \text{V}} \qquad \frac{\text{T-I}}{\text{C} \quad \text{V}} \quad or \quad \text{T-I} \quad (\text{CV}) \qquad \text{T-I} \quad (\text{CV})$$

(Cf. Allen 1951: 941 et passim and Henderson 1949: 213–15.) As a notational variant, the reference point may be given in prose statements such as we have used on page 279 (cf. Carnochan 1957: 154 and Waterson 1955: 580).

The justification for identifying such things as syllables within orders of phonological categories in a structure is entirely prosodic. "Syllable structures are prosodic as such, and further prosodies may be referred to them" (Firth 1957c: 31). The statement that syllable structures are prosodic *as such* implies the following. We have seen that prosodies express the sequential redundancies of phonetic transcription. An example was the consonant-vowel quality correlation. Now, we can also say that the sequence of phonetic properties consonant and vowel are redundant. We have incorporated a sequential redundancy in the order CVCV itself. In the data of (1), a phonetic consonant implies a following vowel. Strictly, these properties should also be removed from allotment to phonological categories of the structure and should be expressed as a second prosody. Such features, however, are not so abstracted. (See Robins 1957a for a survey of prosodic studies to that time.) The properties abstracted as prosodies involve position of consonant or vowel or manner of consonant or vowel, but not consonantality and vocalicity themselves. No explicit constraint on prosodic analysis is given to justify this limitation. In a prosodic treatment of Thai (Henderson 1949), the order of phonological categories is CVC, which retains a phonetic sequential redundancy in the phonological description of the structure. Observe that Henderson's treatment of Thai allows in part a complete allotment of some initial phonetic material to prosodies, leaving *zeta* (phonetically nothing) as a phonematic unit of C. The constraint in Thai that prohibits allotment of all phonetic nonsyllabic matter to the prosody is the recurrence of that phonetic matter finally; this is taken as indicating lack of sequential constraint, and hence no prosodic treatment is called for.

Longer pieces of phonetic data than our abstracted word may have pattern validly asserted of it. The justification of studying longer pieces lies in the discovery of additional prosodies that characterize and delimit them in the way our tongue-involvement prosody delimited syllables. In this manner we may find prosodies of the word, syllable groups, phrase, sentence parts, and sentence. These terms, like syllable, are arbitrary labels for the structural domains of prosodies. There will be as many distinct prosodies as there are distinct domains or reference points defined in terms of structural categories. Associated with each prosody is its system of exponents.

Let us now add the following data to the data of (1):

(3)

	[iziţi	iţi
	izdaţi	daţi
	iškesaţi	česaţi
	isţekaţi	ţekaţi
	isxoḍiţi	xoḍiţi
	ižegõ	žegõ]

First of all, we take the pieces [iz], [iš], [is], and [iž] and ascribe the phonological structure VC to them. The remainder of each piece of data has the phonological structure CVCV or CVCVCV. When still additional data are considered:

(4)

	[raziţi	iţi
	razdajaţi	daţi
	rašķıtõ	čıtõ
	rasxoḍiţi	xoḍiţi
	ražegõ	žegõ]

we find pieces [raz], [raš], [ras], and [raž] and allot them to the structure CVC. The remainders in (4) have structures as the remainders in (3). We now note a sequential constraint independent of the particular structural orders. In our data (3) and (4), wherever we find juxtaposition of structures such that a CC order occurs, there are constraints on phonetic properties exponing each C. If the following C is exponed as a palatal consonant, the first is exponed as a palatal consonant. If the second is exponed as a voiceless consonant, so is the first. To avoid this redundancy we extract from the phonetic record the phonetic property of palatal-nonpalatal and voiceless-voiced and allot them to prosodies. Now the phonematic unit within the system interpreting the last C in CVC and VC is "fricative consonant." The presence or absence of voice and palatal position co-occurring with exponents of C is predicted by the prosody. The exponents of the initial C in CVCV and CVCVCV are not [bdtčx] but those phonetic objects without specification for voice and/or palatal position: either presence or absence. To predict the correct phonetic sequence in (3) and (4), we must interpret both prosody and structural category. Phonologically, we may represent our description as

$$\frac{X}{...C \ \ C...}$$

The properties of voice and palatal position allotted to the X prosody are independent of each other; we may find voice and palatalization occurring together, or voice and nonpalatal position, or voiced and palatal position, or voiceless and nonpalatal position. We abbreviate this as VPal, VNp, VlPal, and VlNp, respectively. Our X prosody is then associated with a system of four members. The piece of data [iškesați] is as follows (including the T-I prosody):

(5) Prosodies

		T-I		T-I	T-I
Structure	V	C	C	V	C V	C V
System		[tongue-front]				

	[voiceless	palatal]	
[i]	[fricative	[affricate	[half-close
	consonant]	consonant]	vowel]

The cumulative "tongue-front," "voiceless palatal," and "affricate consonant" predicts [č]. However, a combination fricative plus fricative ([šš], [ss], etc.) or fricative plus affricate ([šč], [žǯ], etc.) does not occur. This is another sequential constraint. Only fricative plus nonfricative occurs. (We take up later the [sx] sequence.) The system of our prosody must be enlarged by allotting fricative and affricate as members. The X prosody is now associated with a system of twelve values; our previous four plus those four times two, the values of fricative or affricate. The domain remains unchanged. When the exponent involves affricate, it is manifested as fricative simultaneous with the exponent of the first C and nonfricative with the second. When the exponent involves fricative, the two C's are exponed as a single fricative. With this revision the same piece of data in (5) is described by

(6) Prosodies   <u>T-I</u>   <u>T-I</u>   <u>T-I</u>

            X

Structure   V   <u>C   C</u>   V   C V   C V

System   [tongue-front   ]

        [VlPal Affricate   ]

      [i]   [consonant]   [consonant   [half-close   ...
                      stop]   vowel]

This description raises two problems. First, we would like to give the phonological description of a piece of data in a single statement (Sprigg 1957: 106). In longer orders, CVCVCV may occur without VC or CVC; it can, for example, occur with a preceding CV order. In this case the phonetic characterization of our data is [počesɑṭi] (= CVCVCVCV). The phonematic units of our second C remain unchanged, interpreting C here as "stop consonant," among others. Under certain conditions, properties of phonetic terms are allotted to prosodies, leaving others to be allotted to phonological categories of the structure. If we assume that the same order of structural categories occur without that prosody, then the exponents of the categories are insufficient to predict our data correctly. Without the co-occurring X prosody, all the properties of the phonetic segment [č] are not specified in the system of phonematic units; nor can they be derived from "stop consonant" by a statement of simultaneous redundancy. The result is a failure to renew connection (Firth 1957c: 15) or to provide a complete interpretation. The disadvantage of the present phonological description can be obviated if we allow double allotment of the same phonetic property to both phonological categories of the structure and the prosodies (Firth 1957c: 15 and Allen 1957: 69). If such is allowed, we may simultaneously allot some phonetic feature to prosodies wherein sequential constraints are found and also allot those same features to structural categories. The phonetic feature of palatal articulation would now be an exponent of both the C under consideration and the X prosody. "Palatal stop consonant" as an exponent of C is sufficient to predict simultaneous redundant "voiceless and affricate." (We ignore in these data the [ž] ~ [ḍ] in [žegõ] ~ [rażḍegõ]. This would require that we allot "voice" to both structural category and prosody.) With this modification our final description of [iṣ̌ḵesaṭi] is

(7)   Prosodies

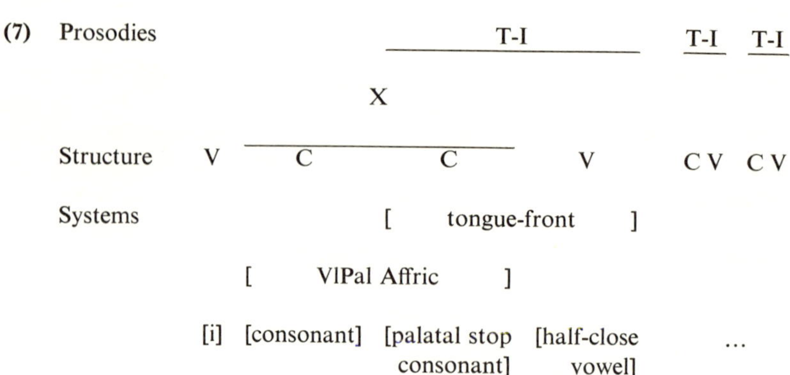

A similar problem arises with [iz] and [iž]. In the domain of the X prosody the palatal position of the exponent of C in VC is predictable; outside this domain, e.g., [iziṭi], the phonetic dental property of the exponent is unspecified. Within the system ordered to the C in VC, the exponents are all dental in position, and we predict dentality as a simultaneous redundancy.

The X prosody and our T-I syllable prosody are such that their domains are not included one within the other, nor are they coterminous. Syllable, word, and syllable group prosodies are such that their domains *are* included one within the other. The X prosody abstracted for the above data only partially overlaps the syllable prosody. If a prosodic boundary partially includes a second prosody related to a third set by complete inclusion, the first prosody may be termed a *junction* (cf. Firth 1957b: 122–23 and Sprigg 1957). In

(8)   A   ________________________

         B   __ __________   __________

         C   __ __ __ __   __ __ __

         D   __   __

          C V C C V C V C V C C V C V C V

D prosody is junctional; A, B, and C are not.

The second problem involved in the description of the data of (1) and (3) involves the correct prediction of exponents of prosodies and the structural categories in varying structures. Let us return to our data in (3) and the X prosody. The second C of its domain was associated with the system of *d, t, č, x,* and *ž*. If we expanded the data, we would find [p b v k g], among others, as exponents of this C. Now [v] and [x] are fricatives, and from our prosody we would expect [zv] and [sx] not to occur. They do, e.g., [rɑsxoḍiṭi].

The prosody as stated is cumulative with all exponents of the second C. The problem is to exclude at least [v] and [x] from its domain while including [szšžč]. This can be done in either of two ways. We may order our statement of exponents (Sprigg 1957: 127), exponing first the prosody, then saying that the second C of its domain is exponed as [dtč...] (but not [v] or [x]) if certain exponents of X prosody are part of the environment, or the second C is exponed as [dtčvx...] if they are not. Alternatively, we may say that X prosody has such-and-such a prosodic system and the second C has such-and-such a system without regard to the [zv]-[sx] problem. Then we state correlations (Carnochan 1957: 163) among certain of the phonematic units of the systems associated with the structural categories and certain of those of the system associated with the prosody. These correlations, analogous to Bloomfield's selection, order the system into subsystems, stating that one subsystem of the prosodic system occurs with one subsystem within the system associated with the C.

A similar problem in the description of Thai is handled by Henderson (1949) in a manner analogous to Carnochan. In the CVC monosyllabic word, the first C has a system k, t, p, m, $ŋ$, n, and *zeta*. The prosodic system of the syllable initial prosody contains plosion, aspiration, voice, affrication, friction, labialization, and rhotacization, but these do not occur freely with all phonematic units of the system associated with C. The system of the latter is organized into six subsystems: (1) k, t, p, and *zeta*, which occur with plosion; (2) k and p, which occur with (a) plosion and lateralization and (b) plosion, aspiration, and lateralization, or (c) plosion, aspiration, and rhotacization; (3) k, t, and p, which occur with plosion and rhotacization or with plosion and aspiration; (4) t and p, which occur with plosion and voice or with friction; (5) t, which occurs with (a) affrication, (b) affrication and aspiration, or (c) affrication and voice; and (6) *zeta*, which occurs with aspiration, lateralization, rhotacization, or labialization (Henderson 1949: 193). The subsystems of the system associated with C and those of the prosody are said to "combine" (Henderson 1949: 192), which is equivalent to Carnochan's "correlate." If we adopt this second method of expressing co-occurrence restrictions, then subsystems of different systems may be in mutual implication in the same way that categories of the phonological structure are.

We have not yet justified treating the data in the example of (1) and (3) as we have. The pieces with which we began were arbitrarily selected; certain sequences of data have been described as CVCV or CVCVCV or VC. In some cases such as [isxoḍiṭi], the sequence has been broken up and assigned to different structures, VC and CVCVCV. In others, the whole stretch was described by a single structure CVCV. We could have equally well considered longer or shorter or entirely different pieces of data. Our choice is eventually not arbitrary, for there is an evaluation to which our statements are subject: *congruence* (Firth 1957c: 8; Robins 1957a: 7 and 1963: 22). Roughly, congruence is the condition that, wherever possible, the structural orders of phonematic units and the associated prosodies have an exponency within phonetics that is coterminous with the exponents of the categories abstracted in the description of grammatical pattern. Two projections will be made on the phonic data: one implied by the phonology and one by the grammar. If we can minimize the phonetic segmentation, we have simplified our accounting. For the data of (1), it turns out that the CVCV orders we abstracted from the data coincide more closely with the grammatical structures than the CV ones (or C, V, CVC, etc.). Grammatically, the phonetic sequence [ḍælo] behaves as a whole, [ḍæ] or [lo] do not. Should phonology indicate one phonetic segmentation and grammar a second, we necessarily complicate the description; but at any point where we are presented with a choice of description, we choose the one that leads to the fewer segments projected on the data. The divisions we have proposed are then not arbitrary. The phonetic record identified by the phonological structure VC, for example, will also be identified by the projection of a portion of grammatical structure on the phonic data. The sequence [iz] will be identified as the projection of a grammatical Verbal Prefix as well as a phonological VC structure; [xoḍiṭi] will be delimited from the phonic data by the grammatical projection of Verb as well as by the projection of CVCVCV within phonology.

Polysystemicity

Associated with the evaluative criterion of congruence is the problem of identity. The attitude toward permissible identity is similar to Hjelmslev's. Before identity can be considered, the terms must belong to the same system or disjunctive class. Given [dɑvɑṭi], we cannot consider the initial [d] as identical to the [d] in [domʋ], the phonetic identity notwithstanding, because they are allotted to and described by different structures, the first one by CVCVCV congruent with the grammatical category Verb, the second by CVCV congruent with the grammatical category Noun. This does not imply that we must construct a distinct phonological structure for each grammatical category, but that we may, if it leads to an increase of congruence. The same attitude is carried over to the orders of categories within a single phonological structure. Were we to find a structure CVC with [p t k] as exponents of the first C and a phonetically identical [p t k] exponing the second C, we again cannot consider identity among the terms of the two systems, for the units are not members of a same class.

This implies that each category within a phonological structure is non-identical to every other. The repetition of C and V is not to be taken as a recurrence of identical categories (Allen 1951: 943 and Firth 1957b: 71). This attitude toward identity yields a plurality of systems of phonematic units, one for each structural category, a theoretical characteristic expressed by the term *polysystemic* (Firth 1957b: 137). Polysystemicity implies not only that the phonematic units within a system are in principle not identifiable with units within a second system associated with the same structure at a different place, but also that they are not identifiable with units of a system within a different structure.

We have considered (and rejected) identity among categories of a single structure and of units within systems associated with different categories of that structure. As yet we have not considered partial identities of hierarchies. Our prosodies have delimited structures of varying extent. If we find two sequences of phonic data delimited by the same prosodies, a question arises concerning our treatment of the nonprosodic data if they are attributed to different structures at the same prosodic size-level as in

(9)   (i)   (ii)

        (a)   C V C V C V C V   V C C V C V C V

        (b)   C V C   V C V C V   V C   C V C V C V

               [r ɑ z   u ɱ æ ʈ i]   [i z   d ɑ v ɑ ʈ i]

in which some prosody identifies both (ai) and (aii); a second prosody identifies CVC of (bi) and VC of (bii); and a third marks VCVCV of (bi) and CVCVCV of (bii). We have a choice of describing the data [uɱæʈi] and [dɑvɑʈi] with two structures VCVCV and CVCVCV or devising some description using a single structure. If we consider them to be disjunctive members of a class—a system—at a position defined by a single prosody, the identity—complete or partial—is possible in principle. This is shown by

(10)   (a)   {C V C V C V C V}
                                         {V C C V C V C V}

                                   (b)   {C V C} {V C V C V }
                                         { V C} {C V C V C V}

wherein the braces indicate disjunctive classes. It is only now that we can consider possible identity. If we allow our phonological categories to be associated with a system that includes null as a member (Robins 1957b: 88), then we may establish a single structure CVCVCV at (b) and similarly CVC for [raz] and [iz]. The initial C of CVCVCV has among its phonematic units both the *d* of [dɑvɑʈi] and the null of [uɱæʈi]. A notation employing parentheses that describes the data as (C) VCVCV (cf. for example, Robins 1957b: 94), if it abbreviates the distinct structures CVCVCV and VCVCV, implies the identity of the categories not included within parentheses and in general the identity of categories across structures, but nevertheless, structures belonging to the same disjunctive class. This is consistent with the notion of identity given on pages 288-89. If the parenthesis notation is taken to mean that the C in (C) has null as one of its exponents, it intrudes a statement of systems into the statement of structures. If we additionally observe that the optionality of initial C is expressible as implication (initial C implies VCVCV, but VCVCV does not imply C) then the relationship between these categories, C and VCVCV, is not a mutual implication. Firth (1957c: 17 and 30) points out that the relationship among categories is a "mutual expectancy" or implication. This condition implies that we recognize not partial identities among structures, using the parenthesis or "optional" notation, but that we recognize in the data differing exponents of a single structure; that is, we recognize identity of structures, expressed CVCVCV, and allow a null member to occur as phonematic unit in the system associated with a category of a structure. Within a size-level identified by a prosody, two structures are either completely alike or completely distinct. Partial identity is not possible.

The polysystemic view of phonology is opposed to the single system in Bloomfieldian and post-Bloomfieldian phonology. Accountings implied in Hjelmslevian theory, like Firthian theory, would necessarily postulate a number of systems of figurae. Tagmemic and Praguean theory allow for a plurality of co-existent systems, but do not require it. These two theories, unlike Firthian theory, require that terms be identified in different environments. Compare Pike's identification of the same phoneme in various positions of a syntagmatic structure and Praguean partial systems as positional variants of a total system. The possible plurality is exploited in the variation of patterning within data. Exceptions are not allowed to prevent the general statement of the regularities and are expressed by one or more co-existent systems. Firthian theory takes advantage of this necessary plurality of structures and systems to express exceptions as one or more additional structures or subsystems in the phonology or grammar. Henderson (1951: 132) refers to *primary systems*, which express the regularities, and to *secondary systems*, which express the exceptions. The term "system" here refers not only to the system of phonematic units, but to the opposition of regular phonology (structures and systems) to irregular phonology (structures and systems). It may be that the exceptions are not phonologically irregular with respect to their structures and that they require only a separate subclass within the systems of phonematic units of a regular structure. Or, they may require statement of a structure unlike the remainder of the data. A secondary system covers both these instances.

Within phonological patterning we recognize a hierarchy of size-levels, each identified by a prosody of the sentence, clause, word, syllable, and so on. In the data characterized by those prosodies, we reduce the data at each size-level to structures, using null members within systems if necessary. The minimum terms of this hierarchy—orders of C and V—as well as the prosodies, are associated with systems whose units, when interpreted, express the values of these categories. This statement provides empirical content for nonempiric theoretical units. We require the primitives of category, order, conjunction, disjunction, and made-up-of to express this. With these we define an ordered conjunction of categories in unordered conjunction with a category. The latter is the prosody; the former, the structure of ordered C and V units. By allowing the structures such as (10a) to be complex, i.e., to be made up of two or more substructures such as (10b), each with its prosody (unordered, conjunctively related category), we define a phonological hierarchy.

Grammar

If the pattern of grammar were parallel to phonology, we would expect a distinction between structure and system, and within the former, a distinction between ordered categories and unordered prosodies. Let us begin by examining a set of data from Spanish:

(11)   (a)   las muchachas buenas corren   'The good girls run'

(b)   los muchachos buenos corren   'The good boys run'

(c)   la muchacha buena corre   'The good girl runs'

(d)   el muchacho bueno corre   'The good boy runs'

In a larger set of data, these examples are typical. Note also that a relatively large number of terms may occur in place of *muchach*, *buen*, and *corr*. Conversely, in data exhibiting this same pattern we will find restrictions on sequential occurrences. In data analogous to (11a), we find . . . *as* . . . *as* . . . *as* . . . *en*; in (11b) we find . . . *os* . . . *os* . . . *os* . . . *en*; in (11c), . . . *a* . . . *a* . . . *a* . . . *e*; and in (11d), *e* . . . *o* . . *o* . . . *e*. Comparing (11a) and (11b) with (11c) and (11d), we find either *s* . . . *s* . . . *s* . . . *n* or its absence. Taking (11a) and (11c) versus (11b) and (11d), we find *a* . . . *a* . . . *a* or *e/o* . . . *o* . . . *o*. These two constraints have different domains. The first covers the entire sequence of data; the latter covers only the first portion. We express this pattern—using mnemonically helpful, but grammatically extraneous labels—as follows:

(12)   Number   _______________________________________

Gender   ____________________________________

Structure   Determiner   Noun   Adjective   Verb

associated with the systems

(13)

	Determiner	Noun	Adjective	Verb
Number	$\begin{bmatrix} s \\ \varnothing \end{bmatrix}$	$\begin{bmatrix} s \\ \varnothing \end{bmatrix}$	$\begin{bmatrix} s \\ \varnothing \end{bmatrix}$	$\begin{bmatrix} n \\ \varnothing \end{bmatrix}$
Gender	$\begin{bmatrix} a \\ e \quad o \end{bmatrix}$	$\begin{bmatrix} o \\ a \end{bmatrix}$	$\begin{bmatrix} o \\ a \end{bmatrix}$	
Structural Categories	[1]	[muchach]	[buen]	[corre]

In this statement, certain portions of the data have been allotted to grammatical prosodies. The remainder has been attributed to ordered grammatical categories. As in phonology, the domains of the prosodies delimit portions of the ordered structure of (12). We may call the whole structure a Sentence, delimited by Number; the portions delimited by Gender can be called Sentence Pieces. The portion co-occurring with Gender is a Phrase; that portion occurring without it is a Clause. The remaining portions delimited in the exponence by the interspersing of the manifestation of the Number prosody, we call Words. To the system associated with Determiner, we may add *un* 'one/a', *algun* 'some', etc.; to Noun we add *herman* 'brother/sister', *hij* 'son/daughter', etc.; to Adjective we add *mal* 'small', *ric* 'rich', etc.; to Verb we add *dice* 'say', *escribe* 'write', etc. This predicts among the possible data *algunas hijas malas escriben*. The exponence of Gender with the Determiner *l* requires subsystems, as within phonology. The exponent *e* correlates with the $\varnothing$ of the Number system, and *o* correlates with the *s*. Should we add to the verbal system such items as *habla* 'talk', *canta* 'sing', etc., eventually we will see that in the category Verb there is an additional constraint. Some verbs occur with *e*, some with *a*; but always with one or the other. We can establish this as a word prosody of Tense with the domain of Verb. The exponents of Verb are now *corr, dic, escrib, habl, cant*, etc. Thus the structure

(14)   Tense   ____

                          Verb

is associated with the systems

(15)

$$
\text{Tense}\begin{Bmatrix} a \\ e \end{Bmatrix}
$$

$$
\text{Verb}\left\{ \begin{matrix} \begin{Bmatrix} \text{habl} \\ \text{cant} \end{Bmatrix} \\ \begin{Bmatrix} \text{escrib} \\ \text{corr} \\ \text{dic} \end{Bmatrix} \end{matrix} \right\}
$$

such that *a* correlates with the first subsystem of Verb system, and *e* correlates with the second subsystem. The phonetic sequences identified by the grammar, e.g., [koře] *corre*, are congruent with phonetic portions identified by the exponents of the phonological word CVCV.

No distinction has been made here between morphology and syntax. In our example all the matter that might be attributed to morphology has been allotted to prosodies. The data that elsewhere would be instances of morphological government or congruence are here described as prosodies. The remaining matter, attributed to categories, corresponds to what might be attributed to syntax. The notion of hierarchy, as in Bloomfieldian and post-Bloomfieldian theory, has no exact correlate, unless we identify the successive layers marked off by our prosodies as hierarchical, saying that the

Sentence consists of Sentence Pieces that in turn consist of Words, which again may consist of smaller ordered structures if the requisite prosodies are identified.

Having presented a view of grammar analogous to phonology, we must now determine to what extent it has actually been held. As in other theories, the development of sound patterning in Firthian theory is much more explicitly developed than grammatical patterning. Answers about the exact nature of grammar must remain incomplete. We examine first the division of sequences of data on the basis of sequential constraints—the basis of prosodies. In a study of an early form of Chinese, Halliday (1959: 43–44) delimits a term he calls Sentence on the basis of the occurrence of certain fixed sequences of sound. It is assumed that these are sequentially restricted to final position. Within the Sentence smaller portions, Clauses and Words, are likewise delimited (Halliday 1959: 65–66). In a description of Abaza, Allen (1956) distinguishes grammatical pieces by sequential constraints in terms of "suffixes occupying final place in the complex" (Allen 1956: 133), and by "a P_1 [a number of phonetic sequences called Pronouns, PWD] as its initial element" (Allen 1956: 136), and so on. Robins (1953a) similarly delimits stretches for grammatical description in Sundanese. In commenting on Sundanese phonological and grammatical structure, Robins observes that phonetic prosodies delimiting phonetic stretches for phonological description as sentences, clauses, and phrases also delimit stretches (the same) that enter into the grammatical description. "Clauses, as defined in Sundanese for the purposes of this paper . . . , are established solely by reference to the actual occurrence of high tone and the final falling tone in the sentence as uttered on Tune 1 [The tunes mark phonetic stretches for phonological description, PWD]. But when so established the divisions provide a convenient and often indispensable means to the identification of grammatical structures" (Robins 1953a: 118). To the extent that this is so, phonology and grammar are congruent. The delimitation of phonetic sequences for grammatical description are here the phonetic properties of pitch and stress. Grammatical delimitation is also recognized by restricted co-occurrence of a number of phonetic stretches termed particles (major and minor, differing in stress). The group of particles are sequentially restricted; they always presuppose some co-occurrent stretch (Robins 1953a: 127), a domain. A second group of phonetic stretches termed prefixes also delimit a stretch by their co-occurrence. The particles and prefixes in Sundanese differ in their domain in the same way a word and word group prosody differ in phonology; "minor particles are in direct syntagmatic relation with the whole words or word groups immediately following them, whereas prefixial morphemes relate directly just to the root or the remainder of the word of which they form a part" (Robins 1953a: 129–30).

The delimitation of grammatical stretches is analogous to phonology. Sequential constraints of occurrence are taken in both patterns to delimit phonological and grammatical words, phrases, clauses, and sentences. The stretches delimited by the same co-occurrence restrictions are described by an order of grammatical categories analogous to phonology, but the terms delimiting them, which we might expect to be grammatical prosodies, are not described as such. For example, in Sundanese "minor particles . . . are categorized as words . . . and prefixial morphemes are written without space before the root to which they are prefixed as constituent parts of the word" (Robins 1953a: 129). Allen (1956: 152–53) similarly considers suffixes and pronouns, which by their restricted occurrence delimit structures described by ordered categories, to be of those categories. Halliday (1959: 65–66) likewise considers the particles marking size-levels in Chinese grammar to be described as a member of the structure itself at that size-level. Grammatical patterning, then, is like phonological patterning in that successive structures of varying size-levels are delimited such that smaller ones are included within the larger. In this view, relationships of agreement and congruence are described as correlations between subsystems of systems and not as prosodies (cf. Allen 1956: 154–59).

The use of grammatical prosodies is only hinted at. Robins's observation of (partial) congruence of phonological and grammatical structures delimited by phonetic tune, pitch, and stress indicates that within grammar these delimiting features may receive a prosodic description. Allen (1956: 160–61), however, distinguishes between "non-place-making" and "place-making" elements and suggests that a portion of the data be described in a manner "rather like the prosodies in a phonological statement" (Allen 1956: 161). Firth (1957c: 14) writes that "all analyses of phonic and graphic material having in view the statement of grammatical categories usually considered morphematic, and also the description of their exponents should be applied to the piece, phrase, clause, or sentence [That is, there should be a "morphematics" of piece, phrase, clause, and sentence, PWD]. 'Morphematics' at the grammatical level is thus congruent with prosodic studies at the phonological level . . . . The various structures of sentences in any given language, comprising for example at least two nominal pieces and a verbal piece must be collated and such categories as voice, mood, affirmative, negative, tense, aspect, gender, number, person and case, if found applicable and valid in descriptive statement, are abstracted from, and referred back to the sentence *as a whole* [emphasis mine, PWD]" (Firth 1957c: 20). This programmatic statement of grammatical prosodies is little realized in applications of the theory. We arbitrarily select the variant of Firthian theory that ascribes prosodies to grammatical structures and makes no distinction between morphology and syntax, except as it is implicit in the distinction between prosody and structure.

The description of grammatical patterning is complete when the prosodies, structures, systems, and their exponents are stated. The framework of grammatical structure departs from that set forth for phonology. Halliday

(1956) treats Modern Chinese within a set of possible statements that may be represented schematically as follows:

(16)

$$\text{Sentence} \qquad \left\{ \begin{array}{ccc} & \text{Category} & \\ \text{Category}_1 & and & \text{Category}_2 \end{array} \right\}$$

$$\text{Clause} \qquad \left\{ \begin{array}{c} \text{Category} \\ \text{Category} \;\; and \;\; \text{Category} \end{array} \right\}_1 \quad \left\{ \begin{array}{c} \text{Category} \\ \text{Category} \;\; and \;\; \text{Category} \end{array} \right\}_2$$

$$\text{Word} \qquad \left\{ \begin{array}{c} \text{Category} \\ \text{Category} \;\; and \;\; \text{Category} \end{array} \right\}$$

The structure of Sentence, Clause, Word, and so on, consists of orders of one or more grammatical categories. Associated with each Sentence category is a class or system of Clause categories. For example, taking the sentence structure "Category$_1$ and Category$_2$," the Clause categories within { }$_2$ "operate at" (Halliday 1956: 180) the position of Category$_2$ in the Sentence structure. The "operate at" is a nonreciprocal relationship, and the Sentence, Clause, Word, etc., structures are hierarchically related. Halliday (1957: 58 and 1959: 50) replaces the "operate at" relationship with "consists-of"; "each term [sentence, clause, word, etc., PWD] is defined as consisting of one or more complex exponents of the term next in succession" (Halliday 1959: 50). The categories of Sentence then consist of Clauses; they are systems of Clauses. This modifies our scheme to look like

(17)

$$\left\{ \left\{ \begin{array}{l} \left\{ \begin{array}{cc} & C_a \\ C_b & C_c \end{array} \right\}_{\text{Clause}_1} \\ \left\{ \begin{array}{cc} & C_d \\ C_e & C_f \end{array} \right\}_{\text{Clause}_2} \end{array} \right\}_{C_1} \left\{ \begin{array}{l} \left\{ \begin{array}{cc} & C_g \\ C_h & C_i \end{array} \right\}_{\text{Clause}_3} \\ \left\{ \begin{array}{cc} & C_j \\ C_k & C_l \end{array} \right\}_{\text{Clause}_4} \end{array} \right\}_{C_2} \right\}_{\text{Sentence}}$$

wherein a sentence structure (only one in this representation) consists of two ordered sentence categories (C_1 and C_2), which are systems of Clauses. The clauses in turn will be an order of one or more clause categories (C), which are systems of words, etc. This gives a picture of grammar much like the post-Bloomfieldian constructional hierarchy based on Harris's and Wells's operations. There is a large disjunctive class (or system) of linearly related items (structures), the sentences. The ordered items are themselves disjunctive classes of ordered items. This continues until disjunctive classes of minimum terms are reached, i.e., terms that are themselves not an ordered conjunction of two or more categories. In post-Bloomfieldian grammar, morpheme classes were the minimum disjunctive classes of the hierarchy and the morpheme inventory was distributed in them. In Firthian linguistics, the minimum categories of the hierarchy have no fixed label; they may be "word" or in Halliday's description of Chinese, the character. The minimum categories are associated with a system of units analogous to the phonematic units in phonology.

As in phonology the problem of identity arises, but receives a slightly different solution, one that is in part consistent with the polysystemicity of phonology. In the schema of (17) we would not expect, for example, to consider the identity of C [*ategory*]$_e$ with C_k because they are members of different clauses, Clause$_2$ and Clause$_4$, respectively. Likewise we would not expect to consider Clause$_2$ as identical to Clause$_4$ because they are members of different Sentence categories. This would be so within a consistent grammatical polysystemicity. Finally, systems associated with grammatical structure would be in principle nonidentifiable with one another. This is Halliday's (1956: 192) and Robins's (1963: 20–21) position. Halliday (1959: 67) alters this; "there is some degree of lexical identification between the word classes, and a complete lexicon would certainly show some forms assigned as words to both verbal and nominal classes" (cf. also Robins 1959: 100).

Related to the solution of identity of terms across systems is that of partial identity of structures, the orders of categories. If, for example, in the schema of (17), Clause$_3$ and Clause$_4$ were identical, this would make the orders Clause$_1$ plus Clause$_3$ and Clause$_2$ plus Clause$_4$ partially alike. In post-Bloomfieldian theory, this would be recognized by establishing a construction in Harris's sense (or within tagmemic theory by a matrix):

$$(18) \qquad \left\{ \begin{matrix} \left\{ \right\}\text{Clause}_1 \\[1em] \left\{ \right\}\text{Clause}_2 \end{matrix} \right\}_{\substack{\text{Sentence}\\\text{Category}}} \qquad \left\{ \left\{ \right\}\text{Clause}_{3/4} \right\}_{\substack{\text{Sentence}\\\text{Category}}}$$

This does not contravene identity in principle because Clause$_3$ and Clause$_4$ are members of the same disjunctive class, the second Sentence Catetory. Similarly, if Clause$_1$ occurs with Clause$_3$ and Clause$_1$ also occurs without it, the two sentences would be partially alike in the shared Clause$_1$. This may be expressed as

$$(19) \qquad \left\{ \left\{ \left\{ \right\}\text{Clause}_1 \right\}_{\substack{\text{Sentence}\\\text{Category}}} \left\{ \left(\left\{ \right\}\text{Clause}_3 \right) \right\}_{\substack{\text{Sentence}\\\text{Category}}} \right\}_{\text{Sentence}}$$

indicating as in phonology that there is a category that is a system including Clause$_3$ and a null member. This position is taken by Halliday (1959: 49 et passim), wherein the units, which are themselves ordered structures making up a system of clauses, are partially identified. (N)V(N) abbreviates the systemically related structures NVN, NV, and VN, and implies the identity of the V and initial and final N's across the three structures.

The polysystemicity of phonology is then not systematically carried across to the grammar; both units in differing systems and categories within differing structures may in principle be identified. Neither was permitted in phonology.

The syntagmatic, structural relationships among grammatical categories is *colligation* (Simon 1953: 327–28 and Firth 1957c: 13). Parallel to phonology, the relationship of colligated categories is a mutual expectancy (Firth 1957c: 17). (This conflicts with Halliday's (N)V(N) notation that does not yield a mutual expectancy between V and N.) Phonological patterning was also stated in terms of correlation between subsystems. In the example three paragraphs earlier, it may be that Clause$_1$ occurs with one of the prosodic terms of the sentence, whereas Clause$_2$ occurs with another. See, for example, Robins 1953a: 114, wherein different grammatical structures correlate with different prosodic units (tunes) of the prosodic structure characterizing the sentence. This matching of grammatical structures systemically related to the systemic prosodic units of the sentence prosody requires the inclusion of statements analogous to those in phonology.

Unlike phonology, grammatical patterning includes statements of the individual units of systems associated with the minimum elements of grammatical structure. These are statements of *collocation* (Firth 1957b: 194–214; 1957c: 11–12; and Robins 1963: 23–24). Within the hierarchies of grammar and phonology, the size-levels marked by the prosodies are named arbitrarily. There is no fixed number from language to language. The size-level at which collocational statements are made is the word. A statement of collocation identifies the "order of *mutual expectancy*" (Firth 1957c: 12) between the units of word systems. The "order" may vary from pair to pair. Given *kith*, the mutual expectancy of *kin* is relatively high; given *stupid*, the expectancy of *ass* is somewhat less than of *kith* for *kin*. Note also that given *kin*, the order of expectancy of *kith* is less than the reverse. Statements of collocational relationships are statistical and derived from the restricted language. With the exception of Praguean theory, the theories we have so far encountered do not consider such patterning (e.g., Saussure) or would include its statement within the variation of pattern we have termed style. The style parameter of variant pattern is the restricted language.

Firthian theory treats possible language as one style within one dialect. Variants in style and dialect are interlanguage and not part of the defining properties of language. Collocation stated in a single restricted language is a portion of language and expresses a defining property of language. To express it, we must allow for "orders" of mutual expectancies of implications of lesser probability than 1. For some restricted language we must include statements like "the mutual expectancy of *kin* for *kith* is 0.75." Such statements are not made for all words; "form" words such as *and*, which make up those data that might have been treated as grammatical prosodies, but generally were not, do not have collocational statements made of them, for they collocate with all words (Robins 1963:24) and the probability that they occur with any given word in a single instance is very low.

Collocations of words establish one aspect of their meaning or function. Another part of the meaning of words is their contextual meaning in a situation, the statement of an association of a form with some portion of the context of situation from which the text is abstracted. The set of patterns established by them are included under the rubric of *lexis* (Halliday 1959: 156–60).

Summary

The patterns identified as defining language in Firthian theory require the following primitives:

1. Category (analogous to Hjelmslev's "object")
2. Order
3. Conjunction
4. Disjunction
5. Implication
6. Made-up-of
7. Identity and nonidentity

On the basis of these, we construct the following definitions:

1. *Structure:* Defined as an ordered conjunction of categories such that each implies the other(s).
2. *Prosody:* Defined as a category in unordered conjunction with a structure.
3. *System:* Defined as the disjunction of categories that are in mutual implication with the categories of a structure or prosody.
4. *Subsystem:* Defined as (a) a member or members of a system in mutual implication with a member or members of another system and (b) the member(s) of the second system so identified.
5. *Correlation:* Defined as the implication between systems and/or subsystems.
6. *Size-level:* Defined by a prosody and its unordered conjunction with one or more structures.
7. *Phonological hierarchy:* Defined as the relationship of a size-level to another such that the structural categories of the first are structural categories of the second (higher) size-level, e.g., in (1) CV is included in CVCV.
8. *Grammatical hierarchy:* Defined by (a) structure(s) such that its (their) categories make up a disjunctive class that are the categories of a second (higher) structure. This follows from Halliday's (1957 and 1959) introduction of "consist-of" into the grammar. The hierarchy here differs from that within phonology. Compare (8) and (10) with (17).
9. *Phonology:* Defined as a phonological hierarchy and the systems in mutual implication with structural categories and prosodies plus subsystems and correlations.

10. *Grammar:*   Defined as a grammatical hierarchy and the systems in mutual implication with structural categories and grammatical prosodies plus any subsystems and correlations.

11. *Phonematic unit:*   Defined as a category of a phonological system. A corresponding unit is not defined in grammar unless it is the morpheme (cf. Robins 1959: 100).

12. *Collocation:*   Defined as the fractional implication of one word unit for another. The "word" is undefined and the statements of collocation are made arbitrarily within an accounting. The statements are then evaluated, as the remainder of the accounting is. The most highly valued collocational statements then identify the "word" units.

The categories of grammatical structure in this view are disjunctive classes of structures lower in the hierarchy following the familiar view of grammar. Only the lowest categories that do not consist of categories (post-Bloomfieldian morpheme classes) are associated with a system of categories. The categories (C and V) of phonological structure are minimum at all size-levels. In CVCV, the categories are *not* disjunctive classes of which CV is a member. The phonological word structure is not an order of two categories such that the categories are a disjunctive class of CV, V, VC, etc. Phonological hierarchy here results solely from the identification of shorter orders of categories (via a prosody) within a longer order. Each category is associated with a system of phonematic units.

An accounting requires the following statements:

1. A definition of a phonology.
2. A definition of grammar.
3. A statement of collocational relationships.
4. An interpretation of the categories within phonological systems (phonematic units and terms of prosodic systems) and an interpretation of the categories with grammatical systems (morphemes, if they are identified as such) by associating them with portions of the phonic data.
5. An evaluation of the exhaustiveness of (1)–(4) and of the simplicity (congruence) of the segmentation projected on phonic data.
6. A reworking of (1)–(4) such that (5) is maximally satisfied.

ADDITIONAL READING

ALLEN, W. S. 1954. "Retroflexion in Sanskrit: Prosodic technique and its relevance to comparative statement." *Bulletin of the School of Oriental and African Studies* 16. 556–65.

———. 1957. "Aspiration in the Hārautī nominal," in *Studies in Linguistic Analysis.* Oxford: Basil Blackwell.

FIRTH, J. R. 1957a. *Papers in Linguistics 1934–1951.* Oxford: Oxford University Press.

————. 1957b. "A synopsis of linguistic theory 1930–55," in *Studies in Linguistic Analysis*. Oxford: Basil Blackwell.

HALLIDAY, M. A. K. 1959. *The Language of the Chinese "Secret History of the Mongols"* (= *Publications of the Philological Society 17*). Oxford: Basil Blackwell.

HENDERSON, E. J. A. 1949. "Prosodies in Siamese." *Asia Major* 1. 189–215.

ROBINS, R. H. 1953. "Formal divisions in Sundanese." *Transactions of the Philological Society* 109–42.

————. 1957. "Aspects of prosodic analysis." *Proceedings of the University of Durham Philosophical Society* 1. 1–12.

CHAPTER 9

Stratificational Grammar

The theory of language called stratificational grammar is primarily the work of Sydney M. Lamb (cf. also the bibliography under Algeo, Bennet, Gleason, Lockwood, and Reich). Fleming (1969: 39–40) identifies four distinct stages in the continuous development of stratificational theory in the 1960's. The version of the theory we develop here is Fleming's Stage IV, as exemplified in Lamb 1966c, 1966d, and 1970, and Bennett 1968.

Stratificational grammar continues the Saussurean dichotomy of signified and signifier, viewing the former as "meaning" (Lamb 1965: 50; 1966c: 1; 1970: 197; and Bennett 1968: 164 fn.) or "cognitive meaning" (Bennett 1968: 159) manifest in the "outside world" (Lamb 1965: 51) as "concepts" (Lamb 1970: 170). The signifier is manifest as articulation (Lamb 1966d: 572) or speech-sounds (Lamb 1965: 50 and 1970: 170). All theories we have examined that adopt this distinction assume two or more kinds of pattern in the relationship between signifieds and signifiers. The postulation of more than one level intervening between meaning and sound is based on the discovery or assumption of pattern that is not isomorphic with existing patterning. In Prague School theory, observations on the nonisomorphy of synonymy and homonymy provided the basis for distinguishing the lexical and phonological levels. Similar arguments are used in the construction of stratificational grammar, which, in the form we discuss, assumes six levels: the hypersemological, semological, lexological, morphological, phonological, and hypophonological (Lamb 1966c: 20). Here, they are termed stratal systems, each containing a stratum and other elements; hence, stratificational grammar.

Not all theories built on the Saussurean dichotomy need assume a hierarchical relationship among levels of patterning. Hjelmslevian theory, for example, assumes the levels of content and expression to be solidary wherever they are related. This reciprocal relationship precludes hierarchy between the levels. The nonreciprocal relationships made-up-of (Bloomfield and Prague School), represented-by (post-Bloomfield), manifest-by (tagmemics) form the basis for a hierarchy within the theories using them. Stratificational grammar relates its levels hierarchically on the basis of represented-by.

The Shape of a Stratal System

Let us consider some examples by way of indicating the patterns attributed to language by stratificational theory:

(1)   light

(2)   lime

(3)   right

(4)   rhyme

In terms of sound patterning, we see here as before that the four items are partially identical. We may notice that all four are distinct in meaning, but here we also discover that *light* has at least two meanings: 'light' as opposed to 'heavy' and 'light' as opposed to 'dark'. In the theories so far discussed, this would be recognized by setting forth two grammatical entities, $\{light_1\}$ and $\{light_2\}$, on the assumption that the meanings differ. In Bloomfieldian theory, for example, the lexicon would contain two entries, and the basic forms would be repeated. Similarly, *right* meaning 'correct' and 'a particular direction' force a second repetition within the lexicon. Wherever we find this phenomenon (homonymy), repetition is forced upon us. If, however, we separate the sound-patterned shape of an item from its meaning—this is not done in Bloomfieldian theory—we may say we have a number of meaningfully distinct items represented by a number of distinct shapes. The association of $light_1$ and $light_2$ with a single *lajt* by representation relieves us of the repetition. Post-Bloomfieldian theory, in the version based on represented-by, achieves this economy by recognizing such patterning. Distinct morphemes may be represented by the same morph. This distinguishes the patterning of meaning from that of shape and identifies two levels. The boundary we have described lies between lexological and morphological patterning.

If we consider some additional data and its lexological description:

(5)   light at the end of the tunnel

we find that two meanings ('the end of one's travails' and 'a brightness in a particular location') are attributable to this single sequence of sounds. We may first attempt to treat this as a second instance of the same pattern in the preceding example, but we discover a difference. If we take (5) in its second, literal meaning, the items *light* and *tunnel* occur in

(6)   The light hurts my eyes

(7)   We dug a tunnel

and mean the same that they do in the second meaning of (5). If we take (5) in its first, idiomatic meaning, then *light* and *tunnel* do not mean the same that they do in (6) and (7) or in the literal interpretation of (5). They occur nowhere else with the meanings they have in the idiomatic interpretation of (5). The idiomatic meaning of (5) is simple; the literal meaning is complex. On this basis, we distinguish the pattern of (5) from (1)–(4) and describe it within the lexological pattern. To do this, we assume two points within the lexological level. The "lower" is made up solely of minimum terms; the "higher" is characterized by the possible presence of complex terms in that some may be associated with two or more minimum ones:

(8)

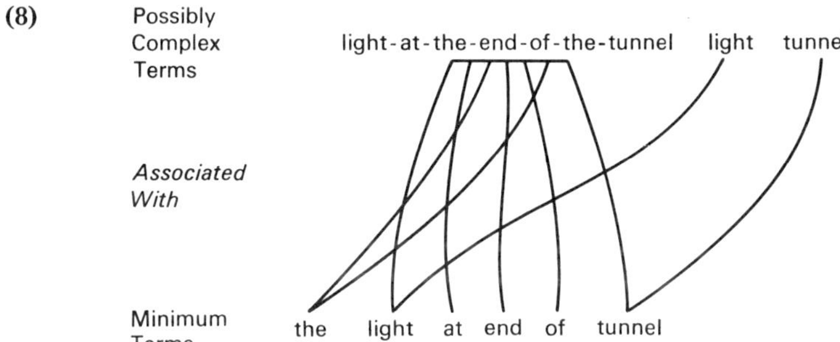

There are two observations to be made about this elaboration of the lexicological pattern. First, it provides no way of accounting for the organization of (5) in its literal meaning. Second, (5) in its idiomatic meaning patterns in the same way as *light* and *tunnel;* that is, we may say

(9)   I haven't yet seen the light at the end of the tunnel

(10)   I haven't yet seen the light

They both occur with *the* as object of a verb. To account for the first observation, we must include some way of relating terms in combinations. This is one manifestation of Bloomfield's assumption that the number of possible orders of terms within a level is a submultiple of the possible orders. We must include a *tactics* (Lamb 1966c: 12, 14–15, et passim). Having made this decision, we now have to determine the terms whose orders we describe. Generally, we would like to make our choice such that the simplest statements result. If we consider that *light-at-the-end-of-the-tunnel* functions like *light* in (9) and (10), it is perhaps best to state our tactics for the possibly complex terms of the level rather than for the minimum ones.

It turns out that we must make a third distinction before we find the terms of the tactics. Let us consider an example from Bennett (1968: 161): *on account of* and *because of*. These two terms are the same in one sense; they have identical meanings. In a second sense they are distinct; one is associated with *on, account*, and *of* (as *light-at-the-end-of-the-tunnel* is associated with *light* and so forth), whereas the other is associated with *because* and *of*. If this second aspect of their pattern is accounted for at (8), then they must be distinct at the point of "Possibly Complex Terms" within (8). If they are tactically the same as well as same with respect to meaning, then the tactics cannot hold for "Possibly Complex Terms" without making one statement for the tactics of *on account of* and repeating it for *because of*. To express the maximum amount of patterning we require a third point of pattern (where *on account of* and *because of* are identical), which provides the terms of our tactics.

We further revise the shape of our level:

(11)

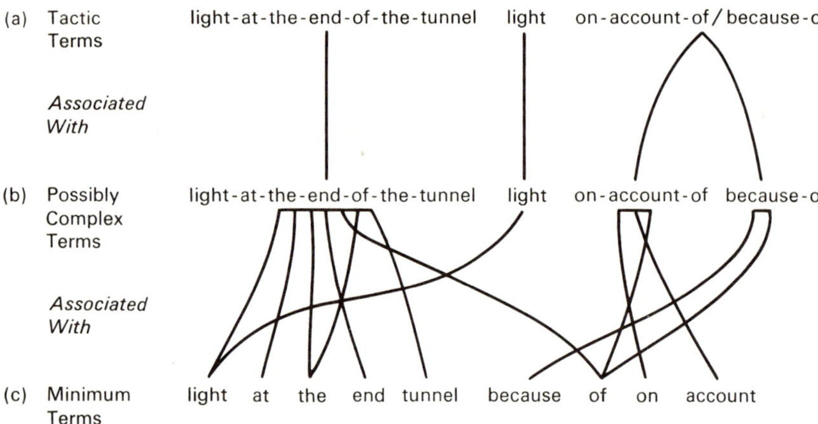

The tactics are now stated for the terms at (11a), which are *lexemes* (Lamb 1965: 45, there called *basic lexemes*). The terms at (11b) along with their associated terms at (11c) are *lexemic signs* (Lamb 1970: 198), and those at (c) are *lexons* (Lamb 1965: 45). Early stratificational terminology labeled lexemes as basic lexemes—and emes in general as basic emes—and lexemic signs as lexemes—and emic signs in general as emes. The revision is described in Lamb 1966c: 32. In Lamb 1964a, 1964b, 1965, 1966a, and 1966b, the older terms are used; in Bennett 1968, Algeo 1967, and Lamb 1966c and 1966d, the revised terms are used. Lamb (1970) occasionally reverts to the older usage. The lexemes, in addition to being the ultimate terms of the lexotactics, are also the representation of the minimum terms on the next higher level of patterning. The lexons relate the lexological patterning to the morphological via represented-by; the lexons are the *representates* or *realizates* (Lamb 1966d: 50 fn. 43) of their morphological *representations*.

We have used the neutral phrase "associated with" in specifying the relationship of terms within lexology. That relationship is also represented-by. The lexemes are represented by or realized by (Lamb 1964a: 105 fn. 2) lexemic signs. Similarly, lexemic signs are represented by lexons, and lexons are represented by terms within morphology. The expression "component" (Lamb 1966a: 571; 1966c: 31; and 1966d: 553), "composed of" (Lamb 1964b: 60; 1965: 39–40, 41, and 45–46; and 1966b: 176) and "consists of" (Lamb 1966b: 18) are often used in discussing the emic sign-to-on relationship, giving the impression of a taxonomic relationship of inclusion. This emic sign-to-on relationship is also described as one of composite realization (Lamb 1965: 41 and 1966c: 16–17). Lamb distinguishes between two kinds of hierarchies, a realizational and a tactic one, and within each level of patterning places the emic sign-to-on relationship within the former. Signs are related to ons by composite representation. We resolve the potential contradiction (made-up-of versus represented-by) in favor of a representation relationship between emic signs and ons. A lexeme and lexemic sign may be represented by one, two, or more lexemic signs and lexons, respectively; but they do not consist of them. In themselves, they are minimum.

The term "combination" (Lamb 1965: 44) is also used of one, two, or more emes as they exemplify tactic possibilities. Here the usage does indicate made-up-of. The tactic patterns offer the only source of taxonomic pattern within stratificational theory (Lamb 1966c: 31–32). Lexotactics specify the possible patterns of lexemes. The arrangements of items determined by the tactics are meaningless (Lamb 1966c: 14). In stratificational theory tactics are represented geometrically as a horizontal plane intersecting the vertical order of theoretical terms intervening between sound and meaning (cf. Algeo 1967: 272 and Bennett 1968: 163):

(12)   Meaning Data

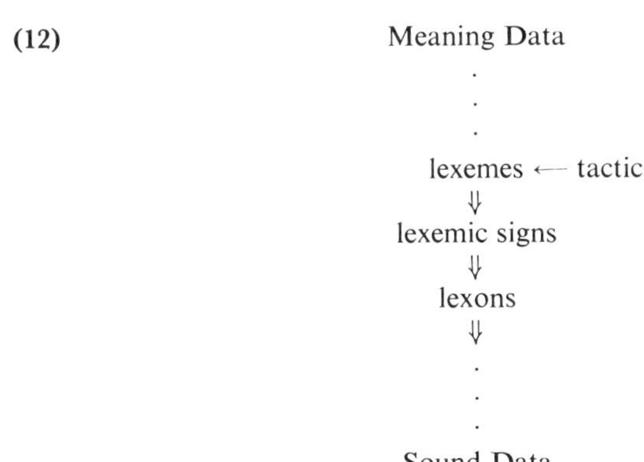

                              Sound Data

in which the double-shafted arrow is "represented-by" and the single-shafted one is "made-up-of." The tactics of lexemes specify a structure not unlike the constructional hierarchies proposed in post-Bloomfieldian theory. The distinct possible lexemic orders represent disjunctive possibilities and may share partial identity. The familiar alternation between disjunctive classes of linear conjunctions of terms, each of which term is itself a disjunctive class of terms such that each of the latter again may be linear conjunctive class, is in general that of the lexotactics. The domain within lexotactic pattern we call intuitively the sentence (Lamb 1965: 46 and 1966a: 571), and the lexotactics is sometimes equated with syntax (Lamb 1966c: 21).

To express this kind of patterning we require the primitives of represented-by, made-up-of, conjunction (or "and"), disjunction (or "or"), and order. The made-up-of relationship is the basis of the taxonomic hierarchy of the tactics. The relationships between these hierarchies is expressed by represented-by holding between emes, emic signs, and ons. Lamb (1966c: 3 and 1970: 195 and 204) emphasizes the nonempiric character of the definitions of the theory. As in Hjelmslevian theory, the definition of possible pattern or language and the description of a given pattern or language is such that there are no definitions that presuppose a phonetics, i.e., categories of possible speech sound, or a technique for representing possible meaning. Patterns are expressed in terms of relationships alone (Lamb 1970: 204). Although stratificational grammar has been presented chiefly by description and exemplification, we may formalize the taxonomy of the tactics by defining classes and members using the primitives "object" and "made-up-of" in the manner of Hjelmslev. We take the lexotactic pattern as example.

Lamb presents the general shape of patterning with a graphic notation. The classes are written as *nodes* (Lamb 1966c: 8) in two ways, depending on the conjunctive (13) and disjunctive (14) relationship of their members:

(13)

(14)

The membership is expressed by a number of lines radiating down from these nodes:

(15)

(16)

In (15) the graph indicates a conjunctive class with three members. The intersection of the membership lines with the node at three distinct points defines an ordered membership. The intersection of lines at a single point with the node in (16) indicates no ordering of the membership. As in Firthian theory, order is not linearity; this interpretation must be made by explicit statement, even though conjunctive order is always interpreted as linearity. Disjunctive order has a distinct function (cf. below). In both conjunctive and disjunctive classes the membership may be ordered or unordered. Each line radiating down from a node may lead to another node:

(17)

Within tactics, the lines themselves are not components or classes. They represent "'connective' information" (Lamb 1966c: 49). Within a taxonomic hierarchy of tactics, we may read them as "made-up-of." The primitive made-up-of and its graphic equivalent function in the manner of Hjelmslev's "description." The described object or node is connected with the describing objects or nodes by the lines. We have pointed out elsewhere that "description" is a glossematic equivalent of the taxonomic relationship of inclusion. Connective information or the graphic lines function analogously in stratificational grammar as the basis of a taxonomic hierarchy. We have labeled this basis as "made-up-of," but this might equally well be replaced by the graphic primitive "line" without altering the fact of taxonomic hierarchy. Similarly, the primitive "object" that we have assumed for the theory (taking it from Hjelmslevian theory) may be replaced by the graphic primitive "node." The statement that "describing objects or objects that make up other objects are components" and the statement that "described or made up objects are classes" may be replaced by defining "connecting nodes" as components and "connected nodes" as classes. A node may be simultaneously connecting and connected or component and class; and again we have the notion of taxonomic hierarchy.

This graphic notation is also used in the representational portion of patterning. The pattern of (11) may be graphically:

(18)

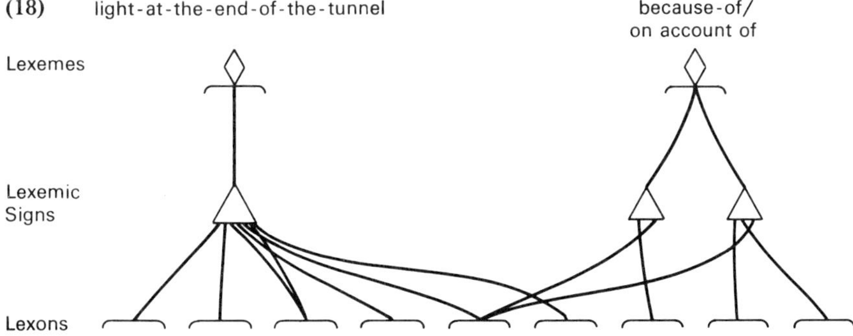

The use of lines in the representational portion of the level to mean "represented by" as in (18) renders them ambiguous when taken out of the context of their patterning.

Let us consider some possible data and its lexotactic description:

(19)

    (a)   Jiny read the poem
    (b)   Jiny is married
    (c)   Jiny wrote the poem

In post-Bloomfieldian theory these data, taken as representative, may be described as follows:

(20)

$$\left\{ \{Jiny\}_{NP} \quad \left\{ \begin{matrix} \left\{ \begin{matrix} read \\ wrote \end{matrix} \right\}_V & \{the\ poem\}_{NP} \\ \{is\}_{Cop} & \{married\}_{Adj} \end{matrix} \right\}_{VP} \right\}_S$$

wherein the final classes in a detailed description consist of morphemes. For simplicity, we will assume that the smallest classes here are morpheme classes. Within the tactic portion of a stratificational description of these data, we would find something like

(21)

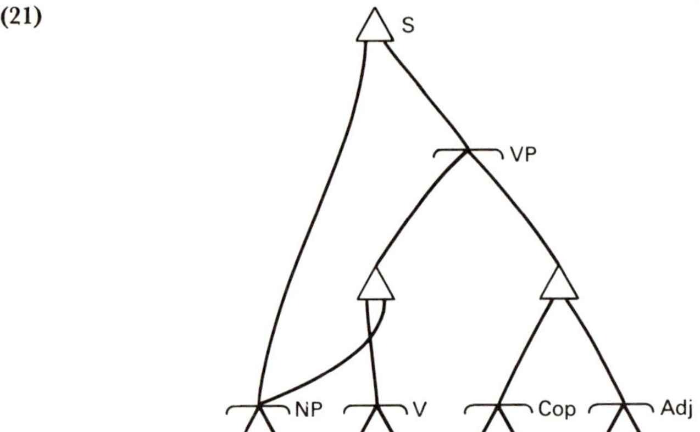

wherein the repetition of the labels in (20) and (21) show equivalence of classes. The lines leading from the bottom row of disjunctive classes connect with the constituent lexemes. One difference between (20) and (21) is immediately apparent; (20) requires that the class labeled NP be repeated, whereas (21) requires that the class appear only once in the accounting. The node NP is simultaneously a member of two classes. As in Bloomfieldian theory, each item, here lexeme, is entered once, and the places where it may occur are indicated within the tactics. Thus the lexeme ^{L}/Jiny/(represented graphically by the diamond) may be related to the tactics in somewhat the following manner

(22)

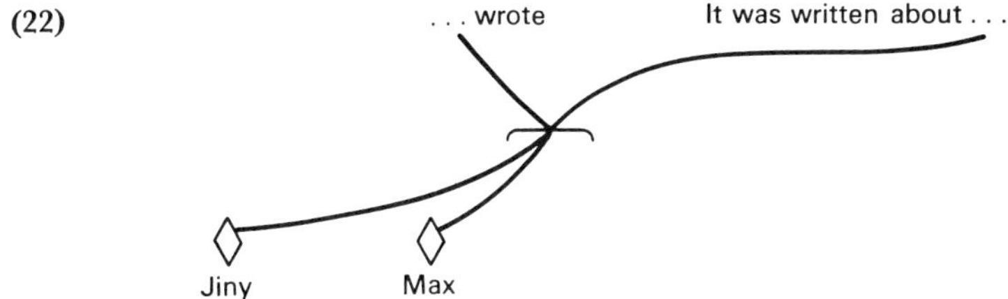

in which the lines radiating out above the *or* node specify the places within
the tactics that the lexemes, connected to that node by lines radiating out
below, may occur. The lines below the *or* node specify the disjunctive membership of the class. The disjunctive node functions analogously to the listing
of form class membership in a post-Bloomfieldian description, which is expressed by labeling these disjunctive classes as *valence classes* (Lamb 1965: 43
and 1966c: 59). The multiple connection of the valence classes to other nodes
within the tactics is an expression of cross classification of terms that we have
seen in earlier chapters. The tactics of the remaining levels do not all have the
configuration of lexotactics. (Cf. below.)

We now introduce labels for specific portions of lexological patterning.
A *stratum* is identified as the emes and their tactics (Lamb 1966c: 19). The
lexemes and lexotactics make up the lexemic stratum or lexemics. Lamb
(1964b: 60 and 1965: 39) uses the suffix "emics" to label the stratum. In Lamb
1966c: 19, the usage shifts and "emics" labels the stratal system. Here, we
retain the earlier usage. A stratum is identified by the suffix "emics"; a stratal
system, by the suffix "ology." We observe two distinctions within patterns of
representation: those wherein the representations are disjunctively related
with respect to their representate (in the on-to-eme and the eme-to-emic sign
relationships) and those in which the representations are conjunctively related
with respect to their representate (in the emic sign-to-on relationship). The
former are termed *alternation patterns* (Lamb 1966c: 15); the latter are *sign
patterns* (Lamb 1966c: 12). The two alternation patterns are distinguished as
upper (the on-to-eme alternation pattern) and *lower* (the eme-to-emic sign
alternation pattern). (Cf. Bennett 1968: 161–62 and Algeo 1967: 270–71.)
The emes themselves form the *knot pattern* (Lamb 1966c: 15–16) or in revised
terminology (Bennett 1968: 153 fn. 3 and Lamb 1970: 212–15), the *diamond
pattern.* The two alternation patterns plus the tactic, diamond, and sign
patterns make up a *stratal system* (Lamb 1966c: 18). The two alternation
patterns plus the diamond and sign patterns constitute the *realizational portion* (Lamb 1966c: 19) of the stratal system. This is the vertical portion of (12).
This general outline characterizes (with some reservations) the six levels of
patterning in stratificational theory.

Additional Stratal Systems

Having outlined the general shape of a level, the lexological stratal system, we now consider patterns that seem to force us to accept additional such systems. There are two principal concerns that motivate this elaboration: (1) patterns of partial identity and (2) patterns of distribution, neither of which are expressible on previously assumed levels or stratal systems. The first motivation operates in the following way. Let us assume that we are constructing the lexological stratal system for some language and in so doing we find an anomaly in that certain of the lexemes—the diamonds in the tactic pattern that constitute the diamond pattern—exhibit a pattern not yet stated; they are partially alike. As defined, lexemes are minimum; lexemes, and emes in general, do not consist of objects. They are realized as objects, the signs of the stratal system. Yet this anomalous pattern—partial likeness—of lexemes implies that they are complex. Because of their minimum status, the anomalous pattern they exhibit and the complexity (tactics) this implies must be stated elsewhere—presumably in another stratal system. The alternative is to recognize the first description of the lexemes as incorrect and to alter that description, making our previous lexemes complex, that is, describing them as resulting from tactic combinations of a revised set of lexemes. This alternative may affect the tactics in one of two ways. First, the alternative may fit the previous tactic statements; the statements here are simply modified to extend to the additional pattern. Or second, the altered tactics may be such that the addition is completely unlike the statements to which they are added. The additional tactic statements may, for example, require unordered conjunctions, whereas the first set was expressible wholly with ordered conjunctions. At this point a choice must be made. Either the newly observed pattern is the same in kind as the pattern of the given stratal system or it is not. If we decide that the patterns differ in kind, we project an additional stratal system to describe this pattern. This choice makes a claim about the nature of possible language. In general, patterns that do not fit the emes and the tactics of emes of a stratal system are evidence of an additional stratal system (Lamb 1965: 47). This criterion of decision-making is part of the strategy of theory construction, and like the remainder of the theory, the results of the strategy are subject to confirmation or rejection. The considerations involved here are the same we found in Bloomfield's distinction between postulates and definitions. The former expressed assumed properties of language to be either confirmed or rejected; the latter formalized those assumptions into a system for testing. Here, the conclusion that anomalous patterns on one level or stratal system indicate an additional stratal system is a postulate about language that, formalized as an additional stratal system, is subject to test.

The second—tactic—motivation for additional stratal systems is closely bound to differences in emic patterns, and we have touched upon it in the preceding paragraph. The tactic motivation, however, may come to our attention not as a result of observed partial likenesses of emes. If we construct a tactic pattern within some stratal system, the tactics, as stated, may predict incorrect as well as correct combinations of emes. The tactics of (21) predict *The poem read Jiny* as well as *Jiny read the poem*. This may be resolved in two ways. First, we may alter the tactics so that the inaccuracy is removed; or we may assume that the tactic discrepancy is in fact a pattern that is to be expressed and resolved within some other stratum. If the first alternative requires that we admit a different kind of tactic principle into the tactics of that stratum (and it turns out that the complication is required for all examined languages), we may decide that we have conflated what are in fact two distinct tactics, and hence have combined two distinct stratal systems. This problem may be illustrated in post-Bloomfieldian theory. We notice that phonemes combine in certain ways and express this within a phonemic constructional hierarchy. We then notice that certain combinations of phonemes (morphs) recur and these recurrences themselves combine in certain ways. The choice is, first, whether this second pattern is a defining pattern of language. If it is so assumed, then we must decide (1) to express this in terms of phonemes and their constructions, or (2) to posit a different unit—the morpheme, which is represented by combinations of phonemes—and to express the second combinatory pattern in terms of morphemes. The complexity of (1), which involves attempting to align morphs and their combinations with constructs of the phonemic constructional hierarchy, is motivation for the supposition of a second, grammatical level within language. Simplicity and consistency of tactics are here desiderata in the strategy of theory construction. We want to posit stratal systems such that the tactics are as simple and as consistent as possible. What seems to complicate this may be taken as evidence for the elaboration of stratal systems.

These considerations require that competing theories—unelaborated and elaborated—be evaluated. The criteria involved in the evaluation are exhaustiveness and simplicity. The unelaborated theory is simpler (by at least one stratal system) but less exhaustive in that at least one kind of pattern has remained unexpressed. The elaborated theory is less simple but more exhaustive. It is also closer to the goal of a general but not too general theory, because when we elaborate the theory, we exclude as possible languages all candidates that do not manifest that additional assumed pattern.

Semology and Hypersemology

Both motivations developed above are exemplified in the supposition of a semological stratal system adjacent to and higher than the lexological in the representational hierarchy of stratal systems. Patterns of partial likeness among lexemes may be observed in the following data (cf. Lamb 1964b: 68):

(23)			
	ram	man	stallion
	ewe	woman	mare
	sheep	human	horse

Within the lexemic stratum, these data are described via nine distinct lexemes. We observe, with Hjelmslev, that they nevertheless share partial identities. The rows share a meaning something like 'male', 'female', and 'unspecified sex'. Similarly, the columns share a meaning 'sheep', 'human', and 'horse'. With this, our nine lexemes are no longer minimum if this pattern is expressed within the lexemic stratum. *Ram*, for example, represents a combination or construction of the terms 'male' and 'sheep'. We also discover that the combination of these new minimum terms are based on unordered conjunctions that are missing from the sample lexotactics of (21). This pattern seems to exemplify our strategic motivation for the supposition of an additional stratal system.

Similar patterns are adduced (Lamb 1964b: 68–69; 1965: 45–46; and 1970: 208–10) from certain sets of adjectives:

(24)		
	big	little
	long	short
	wide	narrow
	deep	shallow

The first examination of the adjective lexemes shows that within each row the relation is one of opposites (*big* versus *little*). Second, the adjectives of the first column are "unmarked" (Lamb 1970: 208). In utterances such as *How . . . is it*?, only *big*, *long*, and so on, occur, to the exclusion of *little*, *short*, etc. The adjective lexemes of the second column are then taken to be somehow complex; they exhibit the meaning of their paired opposite in the first column, e.g., 'big', plus some additional component, 'un', the negation of that meaning. The pairs are partially alike in terms of a shared meaning, 'big', 'long', and so on. The expression of this pattern in terms of lexemes requires us to recognize *little*, *short*, etc., as no longer lexemes, but predicted by the tactics as combinations of minimum terms. As in the preceding example, such a decision again requires that we complicate the tactics by admitting classes that are unordered conjunctions, unlike the previous tactic constructs. The data of (24) point to a separate stratal system in the manner of (23).

Other evidence for an additional stratal system can be found in the tactics we have indicated for the lexemic stratum. The combinations permitted there state restrictions on sequences according to categories or valence classes. Roughly, the tactics claim that what may be called a Noun Phrase can precede what we labeled V. Nothing is said in lexotactics about restrictions between members of the valence class Noun Phrase and members of the class V. Such combinations as *The poem read Jiny* may be excluded by increasing the number of statements; that is, by establishing one pattern for *Jiny read the poem* in which *the poem* may not occur before *read* and another, e.g., *Jiny pleased everyone* in which *the poem* may also occur. This, however, requires that we ignore the tactic identity of NP plus V plus NP in both instances, thus complicating the tactics. Alternatively, we may retain the tactics as outlined and attempt to make the distinction within the diamond pattern by stating restrictions between lexemes in the manner of Bloomfield's selection relationship.

This latter alternative presents a conflict with respect to such data (Lamb 1964b: 74; 1965: 48; and 1970: 207) as:

(25)   (a) big_1 rock   (c) big_3 sister

              (b) big_2 fool   (d) big_4 man

The term *big* has at least four meanings here: 'large in size' (25a), 'extreme' (25b), 'elder' (25c), and 'important' (25d). In the meaning 'large in size', *big* has a synonym *large*. In all four meanings *big* occurs in a general tactic position preceding a valence class Noun. To prevent such incorrect predictions as *big_3 rock* by selection, we must explicitly recognize that *sister* is complex. *Big_3* occurs with a term characterized as 'sibling'. We do not say *big_3 man*, *big_3 father*, *big_3 cousin*, etc., but only *big_3 brother* and *big_3 sister*. Thus, *brother* and *sister* must be partially alike, sharing an element 'sibling', with which *big_3* co-occurs, and differing by a component 'male' and 'female'. Then *big_3* may be said to select 'sibling'. As in previous examples, such a solution assumes that what were previously considered minimum lexemes are in fact complex; and the new construct *sister*, built of the elements 'sibling' and 'female', is unlike the ordered conjunction constructions of the lexotactics. The tactic problem of co-occurrence restrictions exemplified by (25) and semantic anomalies in general are resolved on a stratum other than the lexemic.

The above examples demonstrate that certain patterns of emes (and the tactics of these patterns) may characterize language data and that they are sufficiently unlike the patterns of the lexological stratal system to warrant the assumption of an additional—semological—stratal system for their expression. The semological stratal system, like the lexological, includes a sememic stratum (semotactics plus a sememic diamond pattern), an upper and lower alternation pattern, and a sememic sign pattern of sememic signs and semons, the latter represented by lexemes within the lexemic stratum. This parallels the shape of the lexological stratal system; the semotactics, however, will differ from that of the lexotactics. (Cf. below.)

Bennett (1968) adduces additional evidence for this elaboration of theory from observations on synonymy in English. Before we consider the examples, we first examine the notion of synonymy and conditioned representation or realization. Synonymy is a pattern exhibited by two terms that (1) are distinct in the description at or above the point of the lexemic sign pattern, and (2) share at least one tactic position (Bennett 1968: 158 and 161–62). The lexemes ᴸ/big/ and ᴸ/large/ are distinct within the lexemic stratum, but identical within the sememic; and they share certain lexotactic positions. They are therefore synonyms. The lexemes ᴸ/nevertheless/ and ᴸ/in spite of/ are lexemically distinct, but sememically alike; but unlike ᴸ/big/ and ᴸ/large/, they share no lexotactic position (Bennett 1968: 158). The first belongs to the valence class of Adverb, and the second, to Preposition. They are not synonyms.

The problem of conditioning arises whenever two terms are identified at some point in an accounting. Recall, for example, the relationship of complementary distribution and the statement of complementary environments. Such disjunctive diversity occurs in two places in stratificational grammar: the upper and lower alternation patterns of a stratal system. Certain lexemes are semonically identical, and certain lexemic signs are lexemically identical. Only in these two types of alternation patterns do we find terms represented by *either* one *or* another term lower in the representational hierarchy. (Within the sign pattern the ons are related conjunctively, not disjunctively.) Alternatives of representation, where they are required, may be conditioned or unconditioned. If we identify the conditioning factor with environment of some kind, then conditioned realization must occur only within the upper alternation pattern, for only there, within the tactics, is environment expressed. Within the lower alternation pattern we find only unconditioned realization—the equivalent of post-Bloomfieldian free variation/alternation holds among signs with respect to emes. Conditioned realization occurs within the upper alternation pattern; unconditioned, free realization occurs within the lower alternation pattern (cf. Bennett 1968: 162). But see the discussion of portmanteau on page 329.

Now we consider some examples of synonymy with respect to the alternation patterns of the lexological and semological stratal systems (cf. Bennett 1968: 161):

(26)   (a)   Max stayed over on account of the rain

        (b)   Max stayed over because of the rain

The sequences *on account of* and *because of* have the same meaning 'cause'. The problem is now to determine whether their identity-diversity is placed within the sememe-to-sememic sign, semon-to-lexeme, or lexeme-to-lexemic sign relationship. The solution to this lies in their identical lexotactic distribution. We want to state this identical distribution once, and to do this we must treat them as lexemically identical. Their diversity then lies within the relationship of lexemes-to-lexemic signs, and they exhibit the equivalent of free alternation. In a variety of English in which *on account of* occurs before what we may label Clause, but *because of* does not, as in

(27)   (a)   Max stayed over on account of it started to rain

        (b)   *Max stayed over because of it started to rain

the two terms are no longer lexotactically identical. The statement of their diversity is now best stated within the semon-to-lexeme alternation pattern. As distinct lexemes, different lexotactic characteristics may be assigned to them as members of distinct valence classes. At this point the formulation of conditioning must be determined, i.e., how the tactics is imposed on the possible, alternate realizations. The on (here a semon) has alternate realizations in (28),

(28)

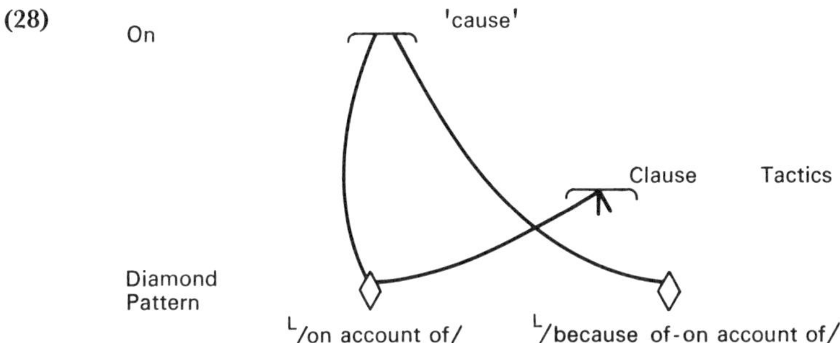

and the choice is determined by the tactics of the lower stratum (here the lexotactics). The lexemes are disjunctively related with respect to their representation of the semon, and this disjunction is ordered. The order here is motivated by simplicity of statement. In Bloomfieldian and post-Bloomfieldian theories, order is used in the statements relating morphemes to allomorphs and phonemes to allophones. This permits us to identify restricted environment(s) first by explicit statement, then to say that in all other cases ("elsewhere") the morpheme or phoneme has the alternate representation. The reverse order or no order of these statements would require that the "elsewhere" environment be explicitly stated. Often this is a quite lengthy statement. If, of two allophones, one occurs in X environment, then the environment of the second includes the remainder of the positions in which the phoneme may occur; these latter can be numerous and disparate. The order essentially allows use of a cover symbol; the first, restricted statements specify some environment(s), and the last "elsewhere" is simply the negation of all the previously specified ones: X and not-X. The degree of simplicity of the ordered realization versus the degree of the unordered statement varies according to the range of the "elsewhere." In (28), the semon ^{SN}/cause/ is realized as the lexeme ^{L}/on account of/ if the lexeme co-occurs with a following Clause; if not, it is realized as the alternate.

The utterances in (29) exhibit synonymy at a third point within the description (cf. Bennett 1968: 162–63):

(29)   (a)   Max encountered an old friend

      (b)   Max came across an old friend

Within the lexological stratal system the diversity of *encountered* and *came*

across is free or unconditioned, analogous to *on account of* and *because of* in
(26). That the diversity of (29) is not to be accounted for within the lexeme-
to-lexemic sign relationship follows from the identification of *came* and
across with the lexemes ^{L}/came/ and ^{L}/across/ in

(30)   (a)   Max came into the room

                             (b)   Max is across the street

Came of (29b) and (30a) and *across* of (29b) and (30b) are sememically alike,
whereas, *on* and *of* of (26) are not sememically identical with *on* and *of* in

(31)   (a)   Max is on the stool

                             (b)   He's a friend of mine

Generally, if the meaning of a sequence of lexemes is the "sum" of the individual meanings, the sequence is lexemically complex. If the meaning is not
such a sum, the sequence is to be considered as lexemic unit and complex
(or a sequence) at the point of the lexemic sign-to-lexon relationship (Lamb
1966b: 180). This is illustrated by (5), which in its idiomatic sense is a lexeme
and in its literal sense, a sequence of lexemes. *Came across*, like (5) in its
literal sense, is lexemically complex; *encountered* is not. The diversity of
came across and *encountered* must be stated above the lexemic description and
not in the lexeme-to-lexemic sign relationship. The alternative is a point
higher in the hierarchy of stratal systems where conditioning is not present,
i.e., within the sememe-to-sememic sign relationship. The sememic sign
^{SS}/come-across/ is then represented by the conjunction of semons ^{SN}/come/
and ^{SN}/across/.

The examples of (27) and (29), if taken as characteristic of language, indicate a stratal system higher than the lexemic, in the same way those of (23)–
(25) do. Extending this line of argument, Bennett (1968: 161) introduces an
example that seems to indicate a still higher stratal system. In the following
data,

(32)   (a)   Max is before us

                             (b)   Max is in front of us

                             (c)   Max came before long

                             (d)   *Max came in front of long

in front of is lexemically complex in the way *came across* is. The meaning of
the whole is the sum of the meanings of its parts. *Before* and *in front of* are
meaningfully the same at some point, that identity labeled 'anteriority' (Bennet 1968: 161). If they are semotactically identical, then the identity is as a
single sememe; and their diversity is specified within the sememe-to-sememic
sign or semon-to-lexeme relationship. But (32c-d) show that they differ within
semotactics; *before* occurs with sememes of ^{S}/space/ and ^{S}/time/ whereas

in front of occurs with only the sememe of ^{S}/space/. In the same way that the co-occurrence restrictions eliminating a possible **big₃ man* were stated at a higher point within the realizational chain, the co-occurrence restriction of ^{S}/in front of/ and ^{S}/long/ indicates a higher unit that is the identity of *before* and *in front of*. The diversity is then conditioned by the semotactics. Thus

(33) 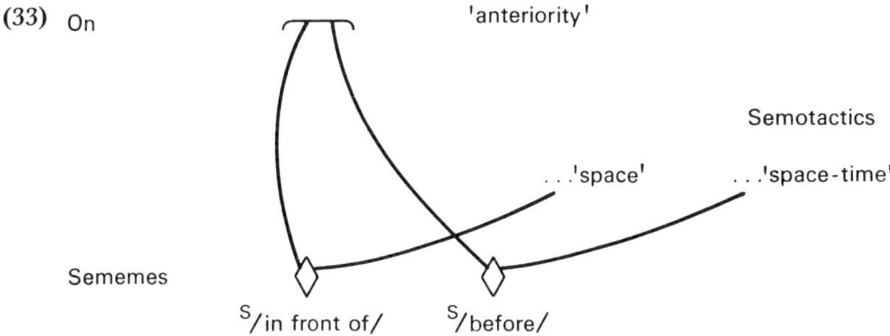

The identity of *in front of* and *before* is a *hypersemon* (Lamb 1966c: 20, 32, and 56 and Bennett 1968: 162). On the basis of this example we may expect an additional (hypersemological) stratal system complete with alternation, sign, and tactic patterns above the semological.

The theoretical units to account for the patterns assigned to any stratal system are nonempiric. Hence, we cannot distinguish between stratal systems by referring to the substance accounted for at some point within an accounting. We cannot distinguish them by saying one deals with sound pattern, whereas another deals with meaning. We may recognize stratal systems as distinct by their place within the realizational hierarchy of stratal systems and by the tactics of each stratum. The patterns of each stratum may differ in permitted shape. The lexotactics were based on a hierarchy within ordered conjunctions, much like post-Bloomfieldian grammar. The semotactics are based on a nonlinear pattern of possible co-occurrence. The tentative semotactic description of *The man caught the tiger* (Lamb 1964b: 62 and 1966b: 185. Cf. also Lamb 1965: 47)

(34) 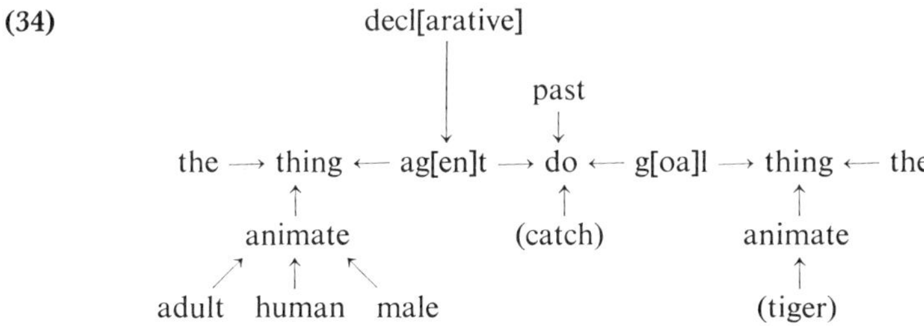

illustrates the principles involved. Generally, two things are involved in a semotactic description. First, there is a taxonomic structure that relates the sememes with one another as an expanded portion of (34):

(35)

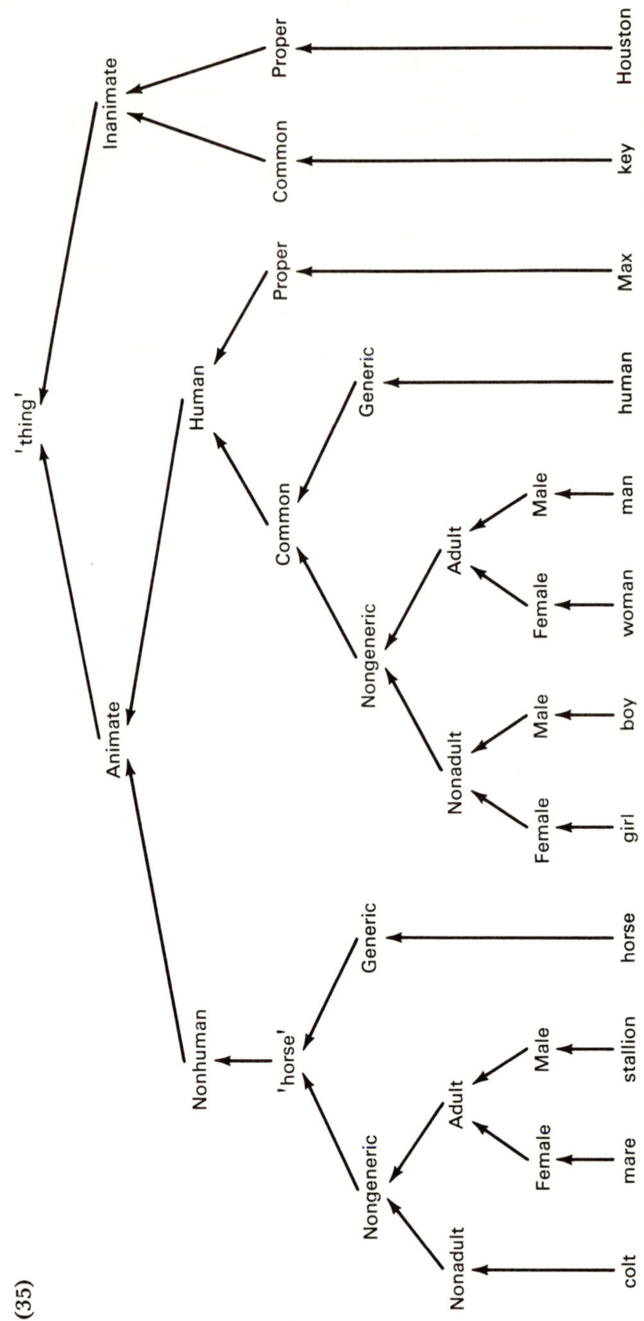

'thing'
Inanimate
Proper
Common
Houston
key
Animate
Human
Proper
Max
Common
Generic
human
Nongeneric
Adult
Male
man
Female
woman
Nonadult
Male
boy
Female
girl
Nonhuman
'horse'
Generic
horse
Nongeneric
Adult
Male
stallion
Female
mare
Nonadult
colt

Here each sememe is defined by its place in the taxonomic hierarchy. (Cf. Lamb 1970: 220 for an expanded taxonomy of "living things" and Lamb 1969: 47.) Each conjunction of sememes in the hierarchy is realized as a sememic sign that is, in turn, represented by one or more semons. Thus, 'thing-animate-horse-nongeneric-adult-male' is realized as a sememic sign, in turn, realized by a single semon, which eventually is *stallion*. The conjunction of 'thing-animate-human-generic' is realized as two sememic signs, one with a single semon (eventually *man*), the other with two semons (eventually *human being*). The scheme of (35) and those like it provide the mechanism for the expression of the patterns of (23) and (24), and (25).

The essential portion of semotactic structure is illustrated in (34) by the terms relating the taxonomies,

(36)   (a)   decl
                                              ↓
                                          ← agt →

                                   (b)   ← gl →

These express specific relationships or "connections" (Lamb 1969: 48) among portions of hierarchies such as (35). At this point we would find that not all portions of a hierarchy can be so related to a portion of the same or another hierarchy. In (35), "agt" holds between the sememe ^{S}/animate/ and the hierarchical portion representing ^{S}/catch/, but not between the ^{S}/inanimate/ portion of that hierarchy and the sememic representation of *catch*. Thus, *the key caught the tiger* is sememically anomalous, although lexemically well-formed. Its anomaly is a function of the fact that the sememe ^{S}/key/ is not related by "agt" to the sememe ^{S}/catch/ within the semotactics. It is here that semantic anomalies, noted as unaccounted for by the lexotactics (including *big$_3$ man*), are generally expressed. The domain of the semotactics is the text (Lamb 1965: 47 and 1966a: 571). Recall the assumption of patterning in stretches of data above the sentence in Hjelmslevian and tagmemic theory. A semotactic construct (text) may then imply more than one lexotactic construct (sentence).

No elaboration of the semotactics is made beyond this point. The statement (Lamb 1964b: 70) that "some features of lexemic arrangement are significant; they represent sememic units" implies that the relationship of "agt," "gl," etc., are themselves sememic units (In Lamb 1964b: 66–67, "agt" and "gl" are called sememes.) of a hierarchy like (35). The sememe "agt" may be represented as *of* in *the grumbling of the bartenders*, as *by* in *complaints by bartenders*, or by linear order *the bartender ejected Max* (versus *Max ejected the bartender*). Semons have been realized as lexemes; it is not clear how the semon ^{SN}/agt/ would be realized as order of lexemes and not a lexeme itself (Lamb 1964b: 70; but cf. Lamb 1971: 114).

Neither the nature of a possible hypersemotactics nor the domain of such patterning is indicated. Since it is through this stratal system that connection is made to data, we may (but not necessarily) expect the hypersemological stratal system to parallel the hypophonological stratal system (cf. below).

Morphology and Phonology

The realization of lexons are the morphemes of the morphological stratal system. We have already discussed some of the assumed patterns of language underlying the theoretical distinction between lexology and morphology. The Russian data of (37) illustrate the patterns underlying a distinction between the morphological and the phonological stratal systems:

(37)   (a)   [górət]   'city   (d)   [durák]   'fool'

       (b)   [górədə]   'of the city' (e)   [durʌká]   'of the fool'

       (c)   [gərʌdám]   'to cities'   (f)   [durʌkám]   'to fools'

In a previous chapter we discussed some vowel alternations of Russian, pointing out that they were predicated on the place of stress. Now we find an alternation of the position of stress itself that, unlike the vowel alternation, is not predictable in terms of co-occurring shape of a form. Compare (37b) and (37e). The place of stress in this restricted example is in terms of the co-occurring realizations of lexons, i.e., morphemes. The lexon ^{LN}/Genitive/ is realized here alternately as the morpheme ^{M}/á/ or ^{M}/a/ depending on the morpheme with which it co-occurs:

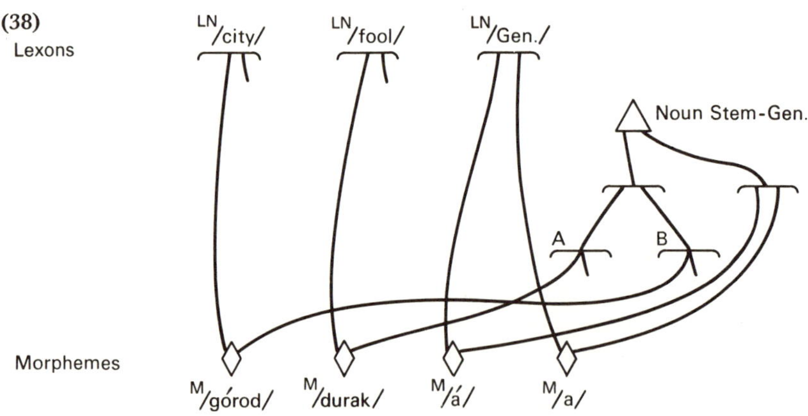

The representations of the lexon ^{LN}/Gen./ are stated in a disjunctive order. If ^{M}/Gen./ co-occurs with the valence class A of Nouns including ^{M}/durak/, then the morphemic representation of ^{LN}/Gen./ is ^{M}/á/; if not, then the representation is ᴹ/a/. (See now Lockwood 1972: 48–52 for an alternative expression of environmentally conditioned alternates.) Similar conditioning is found in complex adjectives in English. Compare *authéntic: authentícity*. Here each lexon co-occurring with the lexon realized as ᴹ/ity/ has the alternate morphemic representation in that tactic position that is eventually expressed with a stressed final vowel. We emphasize here that the morphemes, like lexemes, are atomic, and because of the minimum character of morphemes, the partial identities, or patterns in realization are not expressed. The partial likeness in the pairs *authéntic: authentícity* and *áble: abílity* is expressed only in that the second member of each is conditioned by the same morphemic *environment*. The pattern is also one of *realizations*, and this is missed being restated for each instance of an alternate representation. (Cf. Algeo 1967: 281–87 for a discussion of this unstated pattern with respect to English noun forms such as *knife: knives*.)

The variation of vowels in [górət] and [gərʌd] are not conditioned in terms of variant manifestations of lexemes, i.e., morphemes. The diversity of vowels depends on the location of stress, not the location of ᴹ/Gen./, and the like. There are perhaps three morphemes of the lexon ᴸᴺ/city/, ᴹ/górod/, ᴹ/goród/, and ᴹ/gorod/, conditioned by morphemic environment; these eventually account for the forms with stress on the first or second syllable or the absence of stress. The diversity introduced by the vowel variation is not expressed at the morphemic stratum. Only after we have stated the morphemic diversification of the lexon ᴸᴺ/city/ can we begin to consider further diversification.

Unlike the problem of *áble: abílity* and *knife: knives* in which the pattern of conditioning, but not the pattern of representation, could be stated, the vowel alternation of "city" is recognized as recurrent in other forms, e.g., [nók] 'of feet' and [nʌgá] 'foot'. To express the alternation as not specific to 'city', we must describe the morphemes as complex at some point within the accounting so that our statement of the alternation is made once and affects all those terms that are partially alike in that respect. The complexity of morphemes required for partial identity is expressed by the morphemic sign pattern (39), which shows morphemic representations of the lexons ᴸᴺ/city/ and ᴸᴺ/fool/represented by six ordered morphons:

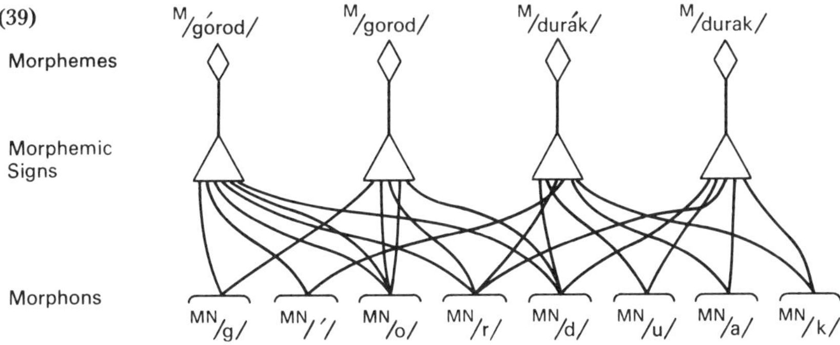

The morphonic order ^{MN}/'o/ (the particular order is apparently arbitrary) is required because morphemic signs are represented by an ordered conjunction of morphons; unordered (simultaneous) organization of morphons is not possible (Lamb 1966d: 558). The use of a morphon of stress, as opposed to morphons ^{MN}/ó/, ^{MN}/o/, etc., for all vowels is motivated by simplicity; fewer morphons are required if a morphon of stress is used.

The vowel alternation is then represented in (40) as a diversification of morphons in the morphon-to-phoneme relationship:

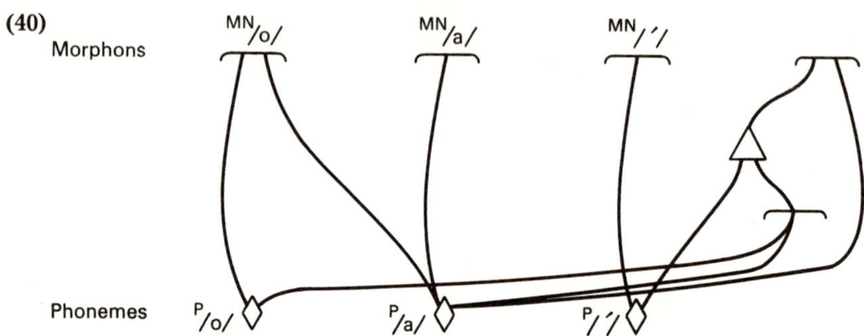

The ordered ^{P}/o/ and ^{P}/a/ as realizations of ^{MN}/o/ state that ^{P}/o/ (leftmost) is the realization of ^{MN}/o/ in a restricted environment given by the ordered disjunctive class within the phonotactics. The leftmost branch there specifies ^{P}/'/ and ^{P}/o/ as co-occurring. If that is the case, i.e., if the ^{P}/o/ is second in the phonemic order ^{P}/'o/, then the phoneme ^{P}/o/ is the representation of ^{MN}/o/. If that is not the case, the alternate representation, ^{P}/a/, of ^{MN}/o/ is predicted. The diversification of ^{P}/a/ as phonetic [ʌ] and [ə] turns out to be expressed in the eventual interpretative association of ^{P}/a/ with pieces of phonetic data.

The conditioning of divergence is an argument for two distinct stratal systems analogous to the argument based on tactics. In examining the tactics for one kind of patterning, say, the sememic, discovery of terms that did not fit the hierarchy of tactic patterning was taken as evidence of a distinct pattern. In distinguishing between morphological and phonological patterning, we find in the first case we need a conditioning environment (e.g., ^{M}/durak/ for ^{M}/á/) that, if considered as the same kind of pattern in the second case, matches neither the minimum units (e.g., the phoneme ^{P}/'/) nor constructs of these units (e.g., a syllable). The asymmetry is the same as that of the morph within the phonemic level of post-Bloomfieldian theory. Such asymmetry is taken as an indication of two kinds of patterns or stratal systems: morphological and phonological.

The argument from tactics applies as well to the distinction of morphology from phonology. In (37), for example, 'city' and 'fool', etc., are units of a tactic pattern (morphotactics) which is not the tactic pattern of the phonemic terms P/g/, P/o/, etc. The assumption of both patterns as characteristic of language and recognition of their difference supports the distinction of the two stratal systems.

Like semology and lexology, morphology and phonology are formally distinct in part by their location in the realizational hierarchy. Their tactics cover distinct domains within the data. Morphotactics expresses patterning within (and thus defines) words (Lamb 1965: 44; 1966a: 571; and 1966c: 21). Phonotactics describes the pattern of syllables (Lamb 1965: 44; 1966a: 571). Although the domains differ, the shapes of these tactics are similar and analogous to the lexotactics; they differ of course in specific statement, but they all specify possible ordered conjunctions of the emes of their respective stratal systems.

A second difference between morphology and phonology can be found in the sign patterns. Of the sign patterns of semology, lexology, morphology, and phonology, only within the last are the conjunctions of ons realizing the phonemic signs unordered (Lamb 1966c: 12). The phonemic sign PS/ó/ in Russian is realized by the four phonons PN/Vo/ (=Vocalic), PN/Lb/ (=Labial), PN/Nonhi/ (=Nonhigh), PN/Nonlo/ (=Nonlow), and PN/Str/ (= Stress):

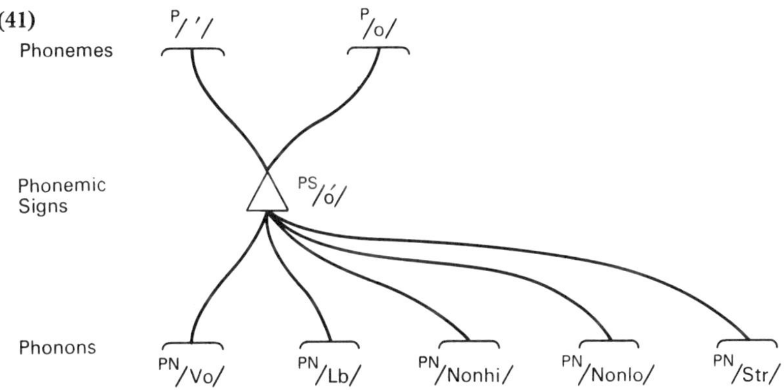

The order of P/'/ and P/o/ is converted to the unorderedness of a single phonemic sign in the lower alternation pattern of phonology.

Phonology and Hypophonology

Lamb (1966d) presents arguments for the assumption of an additional stratal system below the phonological within the realizational hierarchy. The evidence again turns on observations of possible co-occurrences that are incompatible with the tactics of phonemes. Let us reconsider the English example introduced in the discussion of Bloomfieldian constructional hierarchies. In accounting for co-occurrence of consonants initially within a monosyllabic item, we required that groups of consonants, or phonological classes and subclasses be identified:

(42)   (a) $C_1 = s$ (b) $C_2 = $ p t k   (c) $C_3 = $ j l r

                                        or   *or*

                                        p t k   r

                                        m n   *or*

                                          or   w j r

                                        p t č k

                                        b d ǯ g

                                        f   š   h

                                        v z ž

                                        m n

If the initial nonsyllabic consists of three consonants, only the subclass *p t k* of C_2 may occupy the second position. If two consonants C_1C_2 make up the initial nonsyllabic, the subclass *p t k m n* of C_2 may occupy second position. And if a single nonsyllabic occurs initially, the third subclass of C_2 occurs. Now, if the phonotactics expresses the tactics of the syllable, these co-occurrence restrictions—as the theory now stands—are to be stated within them. Within the possible sequences $C_1C_2C_3$, C_1C_2, and C_2, we find a pattern in that only voiceless stops may occur with *s* followed by C_3; only voiceless stops and nasals occur with *s* when no C_3 follows. Here we may claim that the shared phonetic properties of *p t k* are accidental and do not manifest patterns of language, or we may claim the shared properties are not accidental and do manifest language pattern. Analogous phenomena are found in Russian clusters with respect to voice. In a sequence of two or more obstruents, if the last is voiceless, the preceding are also; and if the last is voiced, so are the preceding. This requires two subclasses of obstruents which are characterized by presence or absence of voice. Now, if we decide to state these co-occurrence restrictions in terms of properties of the subclasses, i.e., voiced, voiceless, stop, and so on, we encounter a difficulty in the phonotactics. In English, for example, the phonemes ^{P}/p t k/ are atomic in the same way Russian ^{P}/a o '/ of (40) are. It is only at the point of the phonemic sign patterning that "complexity" of phonemes is expressed. The choice is (1) to alter the character of the phonotactics such that possible unordered conjunctions as well as ordered conjunctions are specified, and (2) to provide additional structure within the theory for the statement of the patterns we have observed. The parallel problem involving co-occurrence restrictions within the lexotactics was resolved by the second alternative. The solution is here the same, and an additional stratum, the hypophonemic, is recognized below the phonemic. At this point the co-occurrence restrictions stated by the hypophonotactics cover the domain of clusters (Lamb 1966d: 562).

A complete hypophonological stratal system is not assumed. There is a hypophonemic stratum plus hypophonemic signs, but no hypophonemic sign pattern (Lamb 1966d: 572). The assumption of hypophonemic signs is based on the observation that hypophonotactics predict nonsignificant elements that are not realizations of phonons. Let us consider the phonological and hypophonological descriptions of s plus p, t, and k plus glide or liquid clusters initially in English. See (43) on page 326. The partial phonotactics predict six C and V combinations: C_1VC, $C_1C_2C_3VC$, C_2VC, C_2C_3VC, C_3VC, and C_1C_3VC. No statement is made here of restrictions on consonants in clusters; the permitted consonant sequences are specified by the hypophonotactics. As the phonotactics stand, *sbl* is a possible combination, and it is the task of the hypophonotactics to filter out this incorrect co-occurrence. The single, three-member cluster predicted here by the partial hypophonotactics allows the ordered co-occurrence of the hypophoneme ^{H}/Sp/ (=Spirant) with ^{H}/Lb/ (=Labial/Bilabial), ^{H}/Ap/ (=Apical), or ^{H}/Do/ (=Dorsal/Velar). (We emphasize again that the theory is nonempiric and that the abbreviations for phonons and hypophonemes used here, and taken primarily from Lamb 1966c: 57, have no inherent phonetic content. The repetition of these in two stratal systems is not an indication that the separate occurrences are identical. They are not; the abbreviations serve merely as convenient mnemonic labels.) When ^{H}/Sp/ co-occurs with one of these three in a cluster, it predictably co-occurs with ^{H}/Vls/ (=Voiceless) and ^{H}/Ap/ in unordered conjunction. In (43) this predictability is indicated by a direct connection between the hypophonotactics and the hypophonemic sign ^{HS}/Vls/. The direct connection, bypassing the hypophoneme, expresses that the hypophoneme ^{H}/Vls/ is not distinctive in the given tactic environment. It is predictable. Also, when ^{H}/Lb/, ^{H}/Ap/, and ^{H}/Do/ co-occur with ^{H}/Sp/, the hypophonemes ^{H}/Cl/ (=Closed/Stop) and ^{H}/Vls/ are nondistinctive. This is indicated in the same way as the predictable properties of s. The class C_2 of the phonotactics is divided into subclasses within the stratal system of hypophonology by virtue of the nondistinctiveness of ^{H}/Cl/ and ^{H}/Vls/ for some representations of phonemes (i.e., those whose representations occur in the hypophonotactic environment following ^{H}/Sp/ in $C_1C_2C_3$), whereas ^{H}/Cl/ and ^{H}/Vls/ are distinctive in the representations of the remainder of the phonemes. The predictable hypophonemic sign ^{HS}/Vls/ eliminates a possible *sbl*. The observation of pattern in (42) is in fact the observation of sequentially (tactically) redundant properties characterizing subclasses of phonemes. The pattern in p, t, and k in C_2 is the redundancy of ^{H}/Cl/ and ^{H}/Vls/ in the description of these three in certain hypophonological environments. The pattern is expressed by specifying these properties in the hypophonotactics, thus identifying the number of C_2 occurring in $C_1 \ldots C_3$. The pattern in C_3 would similarly be expressed by predicting certain hypophonemes of the three subclasses as redundant, The prediction of redundancies, in turn, provides the motivation for including the hypophonemic signs. As we see in (43) a representation one step lower than hypophoneme (i.e., hypo-

(43)

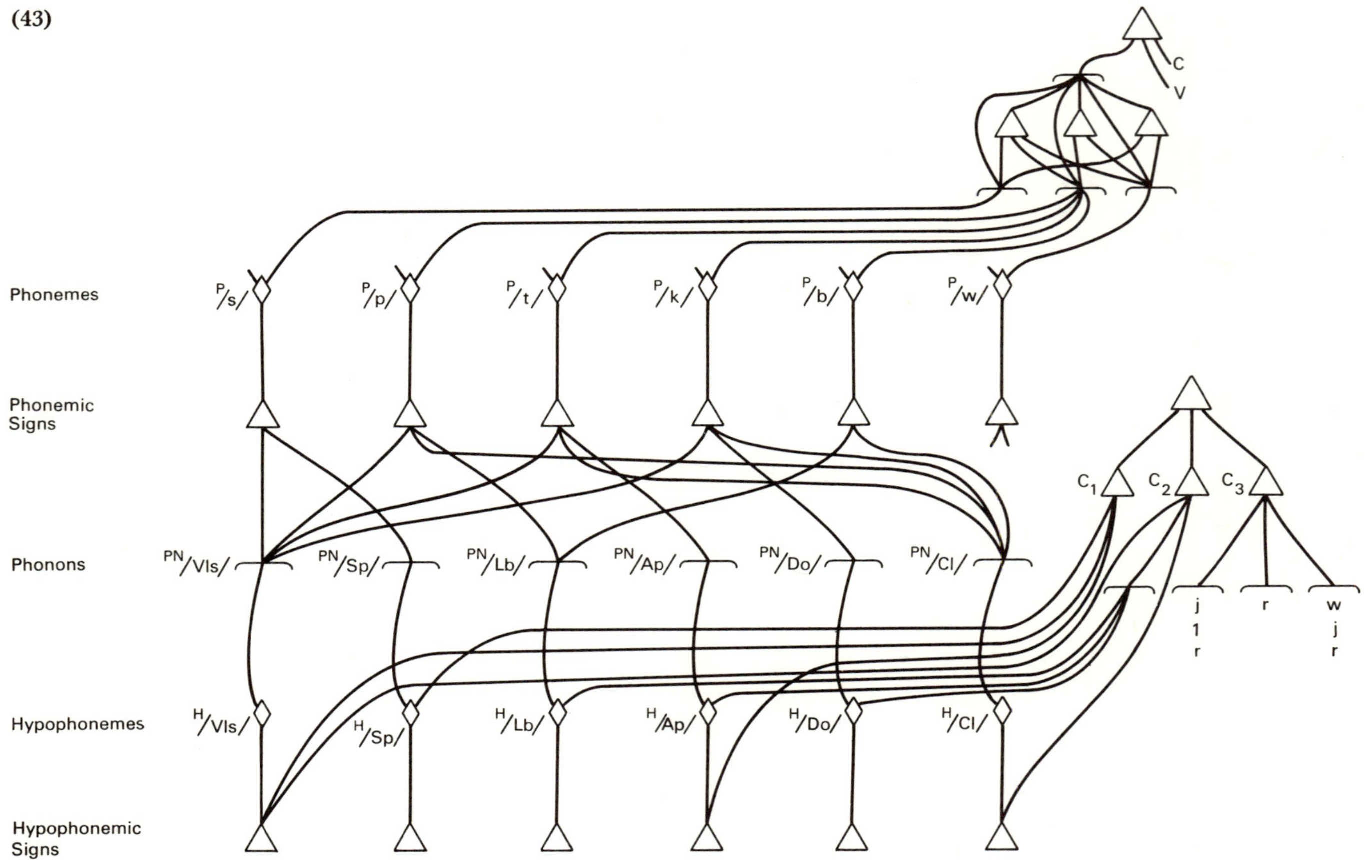

phonemic sign) is required to state the redundancy of hypophonemes. The statement of patterning such as (42) within clusters via redundancies is reason for a hypophonological stratal system developed to the point of hypophonemic signs. Like hypersememes, the hypophonemic signs are directly interpreted as pieces of the data of manifest language.

Patterns of Representation

There are five kinds of possible alternation or representational relationships between ons and emes, emes and emic signs, and emic signs and ons: one-to-one or simple, diversification, neutralization, portmanteau, and composite. Examples of simple representation are found in (43) wherein the phonemes are simply represented by phonemic signs, and the phonons are represented by hypophonemes. If the representation relationships were all simple or one-to-one, there would be a single level of patterning analogous to Saussurean signs. It is the presence of the additional realizational relationships that destroys the isomorphy between sound and meaning and motivates distinct stratal systems.

Examples of diversification are found in (28), (33), (38), and (40). All of these are instances of conditioned divergence lying in the upper alternation pattern between stratal systems. The data of (26) exemplify unconditioned diversification in the lower alternation pattern within a stratal system. Conditioned diversification presents an additional characteristic. In terms of the graphic representation, an on within some upper alternation pattern may connect to no diamond or eme. In English, the plural lexon of a small class of nouns, e.g., *sheep*, has zero morphemic representation. Graphically, this appears as (44) on page 328 wherein the first member, N_1, of the ordered disjunctive class Noun Stem in the morphotactics excludes morphemes of the class *sheep*. Thus $^{LN}/Pl/$ is realized only where *dog, cat, bartender*, and so on, co-occur with $^M/Pl/$. Elsewhere it has no realization. Here the small circle functions as indication that $^{LN}/Pl/$ has realization *only* in certain environments, the first in the ordered disjunction representation. If the ordered disjunction of the Noun Stem within the tactics can be interpreted as indicating it is the only choice that can co-occur with $^M/Pl/$ in the morphotactics, then the zero notation is not needed, for $^{LN}/Pl/$ will have realization only with the N_1 class of the morphemic stratum. Zero notation within the tactics (i.e., not within an alternation pattern) expresses optionality, presence or absence, as the plus-minus did in tagmemics. Here the zero expresses a component that is not, in turn, a class. The disjunctive or conjunctive nature is then irrelevant for this component and it is marked by zero. As the lines of the graphic notation are ambiguous—represented-by or made-up-of—so the zero occurring in realization patterns or tactic patterns is ambiguous, meaning either "no representation" or "component which is not a class."

(44)

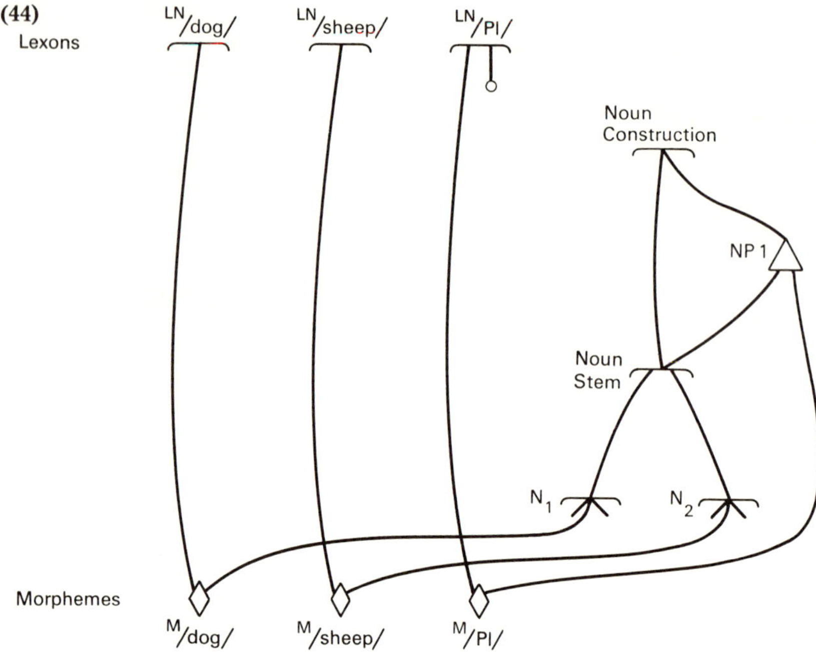

Neutralization is found in (41). Here it occurs in the lower alternation of the phonological stratal system. An example of neutralization in the lower morphemic alternation pattern is *well* as adverb and *well* as noun. They are lexemically distinct, and their morphemic realizations are also distinct, for they differ morphotactically. The noun occurs before the plural morpheme; the adverb does not. Their phonetic sameness is expressed by the unconditioned neutralization in their representation as morphemic signs:

(45)

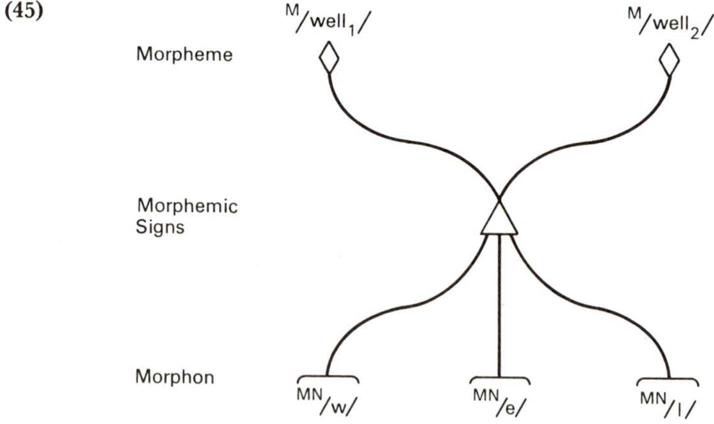

Conditioned neutralization necessarily occurs in the upper alternation patterns. In (40), the diversification of the morphon ᴹᴺ/o/ is a conditioned neutralization with the representation of the morphon ᴹᴺ/a/, conditioned by the phonotactics. Within the upper alternation pattern of the morphological system, the adverb lexon ᴸᴺ/well/ is diversely represented as the morpheme ᴹ/well/ or ᴹ/bet/. The adjective lexon ᴸᴺ/good/ is also represented as the morpheme ᴹ/good/ or ᴹ/bet/; and since the latter representation in each case is morphotactically identical, occurring before ᴹ/er/ and ᴹ/est/, the two second representations of ᴸᴺ/good/ and ᴸᴺ/well/ are a single morpheme, and the lexons are partially neutralized in the morphotactic environments of ᴹ/er/.

We have considered as yet no examples of portmanteau representation. This is an alternation type that occurs in lower alternation patterns (Lamb 1966c: 16–17). The morpheme ᴹ/bad/ and the morpheme ᴹ/er/ are represented as a single morphemic sign ᴹˢ/worse/. Elsewhere their representations are ᴹˢ/bad/ and ᴹˢ/er/. Formally, ᴹ/bad/ and ᴹ/er/ have disjunctive representations. This is expressed with an ordered disjunction for both morphemes such that the first choice of each is the same morphemic sign:

(46)

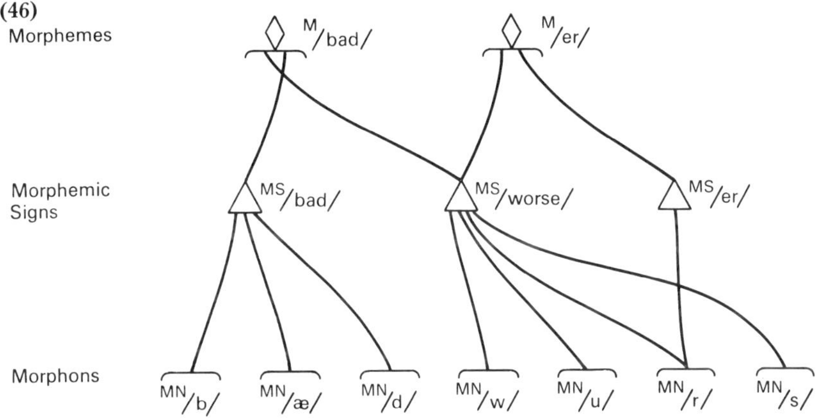

The distinction between portmanteau realization and conditioned neutralization lies in the distinct relationship of the conditioning to the conditioned. In portmanteau realization, the two terms have a single same representation, and both have a second, distinct representation. In conditioned neutralization, three terms are involved: one conditioning term and two conditioned ones. The conditioned emes have representations distinct from those of the conditioned representations, and two conditioned representations of emes are identical with respect to a single emic environment. Formally, portmanteau is more closely akin to neutralization and may be considered a partial neutralization.

A composite representation occurs if the representation of terms are conjunctively related. Given the general shape of a stratal system, this characterizes the sign pattern alone. Examples may be found in (39), (41), (43), (45), and (46). Within this general representation type, a further distinction can be made between unordered composite representation in phonology versus ordered composite representation in the higher systems.

Up and Down

A description of language data within the theory as so far developed would consist of the definitions of its patterns in terms of six tactics of emes and the relationship of the emes to emic signs, and indirectly to ons plus the interrelationship of these six by relating the ons of one to the emes of another where applicable; a description would be completed by an interpretation of the hypersememes and hypophonemic signs. This summarizes exactly half the pattern attributed to language by stratificational grammar. If we regard our theory as one of language-as-knowledge (Lamb 1966b: 173 and 1970: 195), then a further distinction is to be made. When we say "language-as-knowledge," do we mean those patterns manifest when a person speaks and understands an utterance? If not, what do we mean? We can claim that the performance of speech—*not* the utterance itself (articulation or vocal features), but the act of producing these as in Saussure's psychologically active portion of the speech act—and understanding—Saussure's psychologically passive—are patterned and are to be incorporated within the definition of language-as-knowledge. Alternatively, we can claim such activities are not patterned and that pattern of language-as-knowledge forms the basis for this performance but is not to be identified with it, although both are psychological phenomena. This alternative view parallels Saussure's position that all activity, psychological (active or passive), physiological, or physical is a property of unpatterned speaking (*parole*). Performance here is not the subject of a theory of language, which then centers on that passive, patterned aggregate of language-as-knowledge that is "used" in an unpatterned way (or conceivably used in a way patterned unlike the pattern of the used object, language) in the production and understanding of utterances. Stratificational grammar adopts the first view. Language performance (production and understanding of speech) is patterned, and furthermore, that pattern is identified with the thing used. There is no distinction; the notion of the psychologically active and passive portions of Saussurean speaking are conflated with the notion of Saussurean language.

Formally, this is expressed generally by the claim that we must construct our theory of language such that we can move from meaning data through hypersememe to hypophonemic sign and sound data, and from sound data through hypophonemic sign to hypersememe and meaning data. If we take this movement as one from representate to representation, our theory, as we have developed it, moves only in one direction, from on to eme to emic sign to on. If we further equate this direction with the data of production of an utterance, we are left with the task of completing the theory with a mechanism for describing the data of understanding utterances. We assume that if we reverse the relationships of representation in a principled way, our task will be complete. In the arbitrary graphic notation of the arrangement of stratal systems, the direction we have discussed moves downward by representation. We now have to include an upward direction. Wherever we have described terms as a representate by their representation, we must now describe that representation as a representate by the previous representate considered now as representation. For example, wherever we have described ons as represented by emes in a downward direction, we must describe emes as represented by ons in an upward direction. Because of diversity, neutralization, portmanteau, and composite representation, simple reversal of our first downward statements of representation is not an adequate statement of upward representation. Because P represents Q in a downward direction, it does not follow that Q *alone* represents P in an upward direction. The notions downward and upward just sketched recall the Hjelmslevian distinction between analysis and synthesis, respectively.

The formal apparatus for this is almost complete. We need only add the primitives "down" and "up." With this we need not multiply the notion of represented-by, conjunction, and disjunction to include primitives such as "downward-represented-by" versus "upward-represented-by."

Extending the data to include psychological performance is the basis for insisting on bi-uniqueness between the phonology and the sound data. To see that this is so, we must discuss the notion of identity and nonidentity. The nonidentical elements of phonology (We include within "phonology" here both the phonological and hypophonological stratal systems and make no distinction among terms within a stratal system.) hold a mutual relationship of *distinctiveness* (Lamb 1966d: 542–47) paraphrased as "not determined by immediate environment" (Lamb 1966d: 543). This parallels the notions of contrast and complementary distribution in post-Bloomfieldian theory distinguished by "similar" and "nonsimilar" environments. Both "nonimmediate" and "similar" are not defined, but are specified by some criterion of simplicity. We determine whether it is simpler to define the environments (making them "immediate" or "nonsimilar") rendering the relationship among terms nondistinctiveness or complementary distribution; or we determine whether it is simpler to forego that definition of environments (making them "nonimmediate" or "similar") and to render the relationship among the terms in them distinctive or contrastive. Using this notion of simplicity again, no two distinct terms occurring in the same environment will have the same phonetic representation (interpretation). This unnecessarily multiplies the number of distinct items; what is predictable from one term has been described by two. From this it follows that there exists no neutralization between phonology and phonetic data (Lamb 1964b: 72). In post-Bloomfieldian terms, there is no complete overlapping. The relationship of phonology to phonetic data is bi-unique (Lamb 1966d: 547) as a result of distinctiveness and simplicity (Lamb 1966d: 544).

Now bi-uniqueness allows the upward representations—moving from phonetic data to phonology—to be stated unambiguously in a well-defined way. Without bi-uniqueness, this is not possible. A complete overlapping (nonbi-unique relationship) presents an upward disjunction, a representate represented upward by either one or another representation. The conditioning that determines the upward describing representation in a particular instance must be made within that stratal system with reference to the tactics of that system. This parallels the conditioned downward diversity, which occurs between the ons and emes of a stratal system; the conditioning is stated within the tactics of the emes representing the higher ons, not the tactics of some lower system. There is no direct relationship of the diversity among stratal systems (downward on-to-eme) to the tactics of a lower system. The same condition applies to upward diversity; thus morphological, lexological, etc., tactics cannot determine the choice of a describing representation of a nonbi-unique, phonological upward *or*. Ambiguities within phonology cannot be resolved with reference to the higher tactics. The structure of the theory as one of the performance of understanding claims that possible ambiguities in the performance of understanding must be resolved within the stratal system where they occur. The ambiguity of an upward *or* within a nonbi-unique description has no resolution. There is none within the tactics, or there would be no nonbi-uniqueness (That is what nonbi-uniqueness means.) and there can be none within some higher tactics. The inclusion of the data of the performance of understanding, and hence upward representation, then requires a bi-unique phonology, and bi-uniqueness in general between stratal systems.

Summary

Stratificational theory is explicitly explanatory (Lamb 1964b: 71; 1966c: 6–7; and 1966d: 541). Any notion of procedure is clearly relegated to the status of a heuristic device for constructing descriptions and in no way constrains the definition of possible language. Bi-uniqueness does not result from an operational constraint as it did in post-Bloomfieldian theory but from the considerations discussed above. The explanatory character requires there be some way of determining better or worse descriptions. The evaluative criterion is that of simplicity (Lamb 1966c: 46 and 1966d: 554). This is the general criterion we have seen in previous theories. All other things—exactness or exhaustiveness—being equal, we choose the accounting that states this with the fewer statements. Lamb (1966c: 46–56) attempts to identify differences in simplicity with formal properties of the graphic notation.

Because of the tentative nature of several stratal systems (i.e., the hypersemological, hypophonological, and the semotactics), we forego a complete summary of stratificational theory to give the apparent primitives and the definition of one stratal system indicating what a complete summary would include. The primitives of the theory are:

1. Object (or node in graphic terms)
2. Represented-by (or line in graphic terms)
3. Made-up-of (or line in graphic terms)
4. Conjunction
5. Disjunction
6. Ordered
7. Unordered
8. Downward
9. Upward
10. Identity and nonidentity

With these we may construct the following definitions:

1. *Class:*   Defined as an object made up of other objects.
2. *Component:*   Defined as the objects making up an object.
3. *Taxonomic hierarchy:*   Defined as a class of classes.
4. *Eme:*   Defined as a component within a taxonomic hierarchy that is not a class, i.e., the minimum terms, downwardly represented by disjunctively related objects (or a single object) that, in turn, are downwardly represented by conjunctively related objects (or a single object). A complete definition of an eme would require further delimitation as the representation of term(s) of the higher stratal system—thus presupposing the definition of that system.
5. *Sign:*   Defined as the downward representation of an eme, the downwardly, disjunctively related objects and their conjunctive representations.
6. *On:*   Defined as the conjunctively related objects of a sign.
7. *Tactics:*   Defined as the taxonomic hierarchy and emes.
8. *Upper alternation pattern:*   Defined as the ons of the higher (presupposed) stratal system, the emes, and the relationship of representation between them.
9. *Lower alternation pattern:*   Defined as the emes and their disjunctive representations.
10. *Diamond pattern:*   Defined as the unordered conjunction of the emes.
11. *Sign pattern:*   Defined as the unordered conjunction of signs.
12. *Realizational pattern:*   Defined as the conjunction of the upper alternation pattern, diamond pattern, lower alternation pattern, and sign pattern.
13. *Stratum:*   Defined as the conjunction of the emes and their tactics.

14. *Stratal system:* Defined as the conjunction of the tactics and realizational pattern.

15. Here the downward representation patterns are to be paralleled by upward representation patterns—(a) Ons are upwardly represented by a disjunction of objects or a single object that (b) are in turn upwardly represented by (i) a conjunction of objects (emes) defining portmanteau representation or (ii) a disjunction of emes defining unconditioned neutralization, or (iii) a single eme; (c) the emes in turn are upwardly represented by a disjunction of ons on the higher stratal system or a single such on.

A schematic representation of the downward and upward realizational portion of a stratal system is as follows:

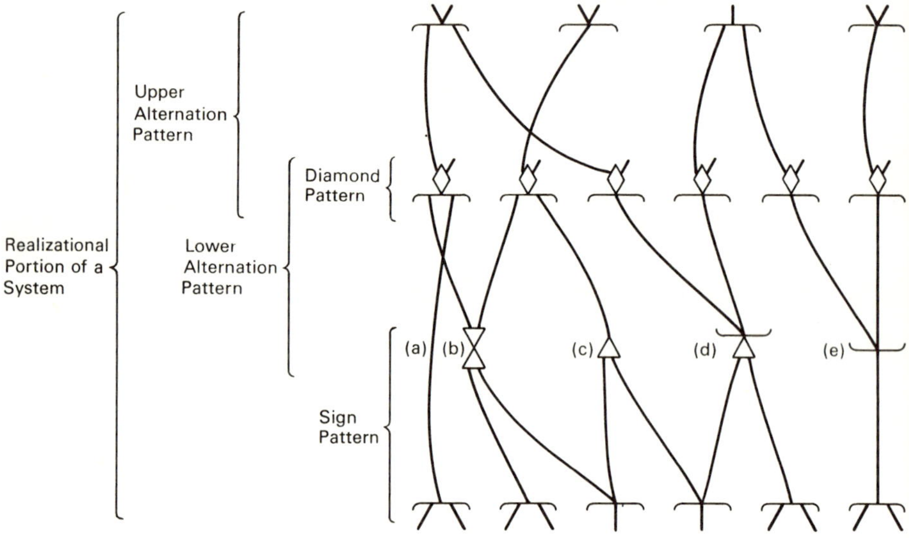

The label (b) indicates a portmanteau; (d), a neutralization. The complexes of two downward and upward nodes, e.g., (b), along with simple nodes are called *nections* (Lamb 1966c: 50). Where there is no complexity, i.e., where the representation is simple, between eme and on such as (a), there is no node. The eme is passed directly to the bottom portion of the stratal system. This recalls Hjelmslev's rule of transference according to which a class (here, representate) is passed unanalyzed (here, unrepresented) through ranks until a stage is reached at which the class is complex (here, has at least two representations). A node may be simple in both directions, that is, absent as (a); simple in the downward direction but upwardly complex as (e); simple in the upward direction but downwardly complex as (c); or complex in both directions as (b) and (d). Analogous observations hold for any pattern of nodes within the realization portion of the stratal system.

The stratal system we have outlined is not well-defined until the definitions of the remaining ones are included. Each definition is determined not only by its immediate relationships but also by indirect ones within adjacent systems. Because of the nonempiric nature of the primitives, the definition of the stratal system is not characterizable as a specific system; there is, for example, no occurrence of phonetic primitives to mark it as a (hypo) phonological system. With certain modifications, definitions (1)–(13) characterize all six stratal systems. Formal modification from system to system will include the absence of ordered conjunction within semotactics of semology; the ordered conjunction of the sign patterns except within phonology and hypophonology; the lack of a complete sign pattern in hypophonology; a more complete specification of the system of hypersemology, and so on.

A stratificational description of a language would contain the following:

1. A definition of six stratal systems including within each
   a. A definition of the tactics
   b. A definition of the realizational pattern—both upward and downward—including
      i. A definition of the upper and lower alternation patterns
      ii. A definition of the knot pattern
      iii. A definition of the sign pattern
2. An interpretation of the statements of (1)
3. An evaluation of the simplicity of (1) and (2)
4. A reworking of (1) and (2) until (3) is maximally satisfied

Stratificational grammar is unique among the theories of language that take their patterned data to be manifest as knowledge. Saussurean and Praguean theories characterize that pattern as distinct from possible pattern in its use. The former is the inert pattern of the correlation of meaning with sound; the second is the psychological manipulation of that knowledge. Transformational generative grammar, following Saussurean and Praguean theories, takes language as manifest in knowledge, distinguishing it from the patterned use of that knowledge by the terms competence and performance, respectively.

ADDITIONAL READING

ALGEO, JOHN. 1967. "On defining a stratum." *Emory University Quarterly* 23. 263–94.

BENNETT, DAVID C. 1968. "English prepositions: a stratificational approach." *Journal of Linguistics* 4. 153–72.

LAMB, SYDNEY M. 1964. "The sememic approach to structural semantics," in *Transcultural Studies in Cognition* (= *American Anthropologist* 66, No. 3, Part 2), eds. A. Kimball Romney and Roy Goodwin D'Andrade. Washington, D.C.: American Anthropological Association.

————. 1966a. *Outline of Stratificational Grammar*. Washington, D.C.: Georgetown University Press.

————. 1966b. "Prolegomena to a theory of phonology." *Language* 42. 536–73.

————. 1970. "Linguistic and cognitive networks," in *Cognition: a Multiple View*, ed. Paul L. Garvin. New York: Spartan Books.

LOCKWOOD, DAVID G. 1969. "Markedness in stratificational phonology." *Language* 45. 300–308.

————. 1972. *Introduction to Stratificational Linguistics*. New York: Harcourt Brace Jovanovich, Inc.

CHAPTER 10

Transformational
Generative Grammar

The last theory we discuss is transformational generative grammar. Since the publication of N. Chomsky's *Syntactic Structures* in 1957, the theory has passed through several stages. We arbitrarily select for discussion the version found in Chomsky's *Aspects of the Theory of Syntax*, sometimes called the "standard theory" (Chomsky 1970a: 55–56). This is not the newest elaboration of transformational generative grammar, but a summation of work done to 1965, a summation that is the base for later development of the theory into one called "generative semantics" (cf. Lakoff 1971; Jacobs and Rosenbaum 1970; and Fillmore and Langendoen 1971) and into one that is a less radically modified version of the theory we consider here (cf. Chomsky 1970a and 1970c).

Transformational generative grammar continues the Saussurean dichotomy of sound versus meaning found in all but one of our previous theories and takes language to be knowledge manifesting the patterned relationship between the two terms of that opposition. The theory differs, however, in crucial ways in its characterization of that knowledge. Saussurean and Prague School theories took language as a psychological object that formed the basis of utterances and the understanding of them; the term "language" labeled the former, and the terms "speaking" and "speech act" labeled the latter. It was assumed that the pattern (if any) of the use of that knowledge was not isomorphic with the object itself. The two, a particular knowledge and its use, were the subjects of distinct studies. Stratificational grammar assumed that isomorphy and necessarily identified the two notions. Transformational generative grammar, following Saussurean and Praguean tradition, retains the distinction of language-as-knowledge and use of language knowledge under the labels of *competence* and *performance*, respectively (Chomsky 1965: 4; 1967: 397–98; and 1968: 4).

Transformational generative grammar differs from Saussurean theory on the issue of concreteness. Recall that Saussurean theory was constrained in its construction to the supposition of only that pattern which was spontaneously attainable by introspection on the part of the speaker of a language. Any other pattern suggested by the linguist was considered quite possibly spurious. The purpose of this constraint in theory construction was the assurance of the realism of the theory. Transformational generative grammar similarly adopts a realistic attitude (Chomsky 1965: 4 and Katz 1964: 129) but does not limit itself, as Saussurean theory does, in its construction. The difference lies in their respective attitudes toward introspection as a device for collecting data. Saussure implicitly accepted it as a tool that yielded correct results. In transformational generative grammar, it is assumed that introspection is a faulty procedure (Chomsky 1965:8 and 18–24 and 1968: 22) and that the information it yields is not necessarily a direct reflection of knowledge of language. Given this assumption, there is no gain in restricting the theory to an account of introspective data. Otherwise, Saussurean theory and transformational generative grammar are quite close in their attitude toward language.

In one respect, the attitude toward introspection in Saussurean theory places it close to theories that regard language as behavior and opposes it to transformational generative grammar, viz., the assumption that the data of language are readily attainable by some experimental technique. Saussurean and post-Bloomfieldian theories, for example, assume the existence of a set of activities that yields a reliable record of manifest language. In both views, but in different senses, language is relatively concrete. Within transformational generative grammar the existence of such effective devices is not assumed. The relative intractability of language data in this view is expressed by the claim that language is abstract (Chomsky 1968: 68). Under this assumption, an operational theory is impracticable; and furthermore, within the resulting explanatory theory, heuristic procedures found in other theories are not a concern (Chomsky 1957: 56).

Syntax

Rejection of the claim that language data are concrete is not to imply that we ignore observations drawn from behavioral (say, phonetic) data or from spontaneous, unguided reactions of a speaker to his language. The claim is that there is more patterning to language than that derivable from inspection of these superficial, concrete data.

Deep and Surface Structure

We may begin our investigation of transformational generative grammar by considering some examples and the kinds of patterning they exhibit. In each of the following sentences

(1)   Sherrell was determined to teach

(2)   Will was easy to understand

we may expect to find the same pattern if our approach to the data is as before. The pattern of (1) and (2) can be expressed approximately as

(3)
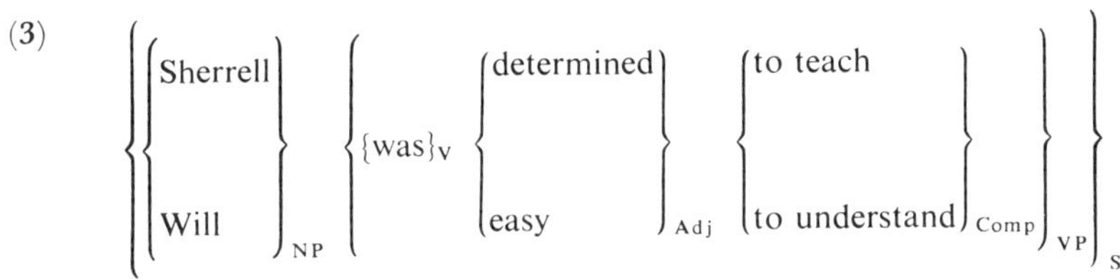

Based on observations restricted to these utterances or to untutored introspective comparison, the description of (3) may well be the extent of discoverable patterning. If, however, we free ourselves from this constraint in our search, we can ask ourselves as speakers of English "Who/what was determined?" and "Who/what was easy?" The answers for (1) and (2) are respectively "Sherrell" and "to understand Will." If we further ask "To teach whom/what?" and "To understand whom/what?" we discover additional nonparallel answers "some undetermined person(s)" and "Will." Finally, if we ask "Who did/does/will do the teaching?" and "Who understood/ understands Will?", the answers are respectively "Sherrell" and "some undetermined person(s)." This line of inquiry belies the apparent similarity of (1) and (2) and forces us to question the correctness of (3).

We add the following data to the above:

(4)   Matt was bound to telephone

(5)   Chris was fun to please

Following the same technique, we discover that (4) has a pattern like (1), and (5) parallels (2). We represent this new pattern as (6).

At this point we observe that *Sherrell, Matt, Will, Chris,* and *someone* have been variously classified as Subject or Object. Furthermore, the similar sequences *someone understand Will* and *Sherrell teach someone* have been variously classified as Subject and Object although they parallel the larger sentence structures of which they are part. We may consider replacing the functional meanings we have used to label classes with the formal ones of

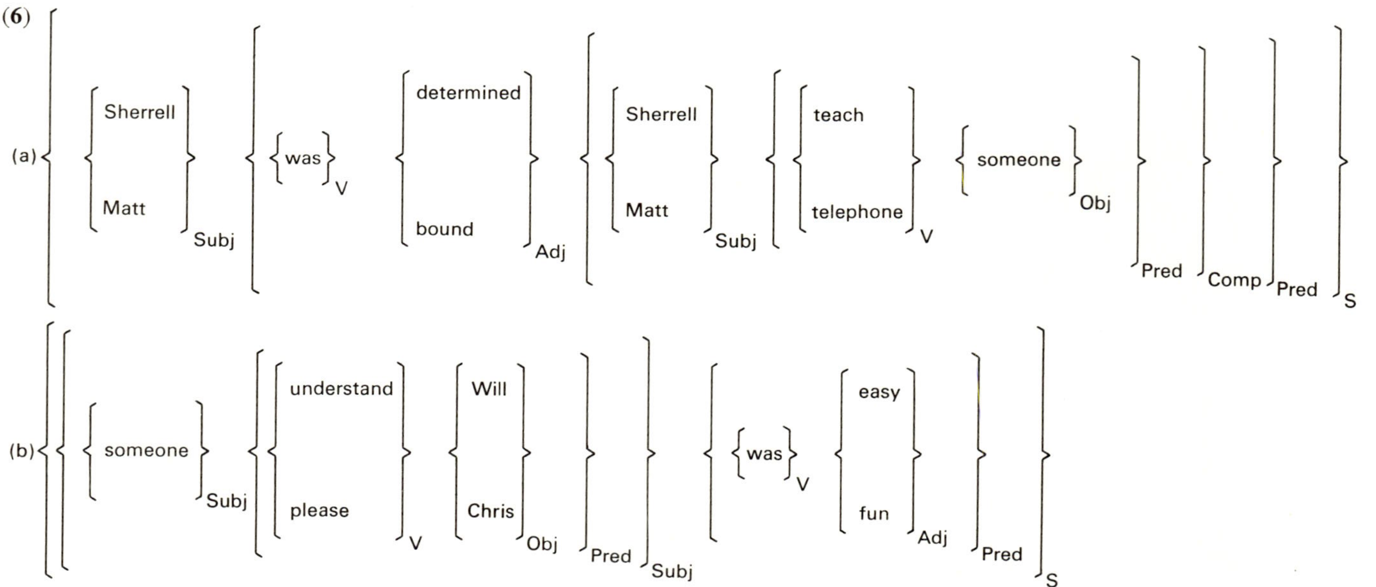

(6)
(a)
Sherrell / Matt Subj
was V
determined / bound Adj
Sherrell / Matt Subj
teach / telephone V
someone Obj
Pred
Comp
Pred
S
(b)
someone Subj
understand / please V
Will / Chris Obj
Pred Subj
was V
easy / fun Adj
Pred
S

Noun, Noun Phrase, Verb Phrase, etc., as in (3) if we can capture this formal pattern without losing the information that certain Nouns are Subjects or Objects in certain positions. Relabeling (6), replacing Object and Subject with Noun phrase (=NP) and Pred with Verb Phrase (=VP), we find that an NP that occurs to the left of a VP, such that both are constituents of a Sentence (=S), is always the Subject. The NP that occurs to the right of a Verb (=V), such that both are constituents of the class VP, is always an Object. The VP co-occurring with NP as constituent of S is always predictably the Predicate (cf. Chomsky 1965: 68–73). In making this shift, we have claimed that the varied terms that are constituents of NP and VP will pattern similarly to one another, and this sameness is expressed by placing them within a single class. This formal pattern can be expressed without loss of the information as to the location of Subject, Object, Predicate, etc., only if we take the relevant pattern to be that given in (6) and not (3). Had (3) been chosen, it would not have been possible to claim, for example, that the NP co-occurring as constituent of S is the Subject of the sentence, for in *Will was easy to understand* we would incorrectly predict *Will* as Subject, while missing that *Will* is in fact the Object of *understand* and that it is *Someone understand Will* that is the Subject. Only in the expressed pattern of (6) can information, comparable to Pike's functional meaning of the grammatical level, be directly inferred from the structure of formal classes. "In short, we must be careful not to overlook the fact that surface similarities may hide underlying distinctions of a fundamental nature and that it may be necessary to guide and draw out the speaker's intuition in fairly subtle ways before we can determine what is the actual character of his knowledge of his language or anything else" (Chomsky 1965: 24).

Having identified a portion of this underlying pattern, we must now observe that the pattern of (3) cannot be ignored. Such sequences as *Sherrell was determined Sherrell teach someone* predicted by (6) requires association with the occurring sequence *Sherrell was determined to teach* before we have an acceptable English utterance. Furthermore, in the sequence *Someone understand Will was easy* we must know as in (3) which Noun goes with the Verb *be*. Without this knowledge we cannot predict such phenomena as government and agreement. The abstract patterns do not provide this; those of (3) do. We can ignore neither the pattern of (3) nor (6); both characterize language.

With the acceptance of (3) and (6) we are faced with determining the relationship between them. It may seem that we have one pattern in terms of (6) described by a hierarchical relationship of inclusion, and a similar, but distinct pattern in (3). If we follow the outline of previous theories, we would describe them separately as distinct levels composed of terms arranged in certain ways and then state the correspondences between points of the two hierarchies. Since (3) is closer to the actual phonetic data, we may say the pattern (terms and combinatorial statements) of (6) are represented by those in (3). We have previously decided to identify such relationships between taxonomic hierarchies as nontaxonomic. In each case, such relationships have been arbitrary in one of the Saussurean senses, the lack of patterning. We can only state that correspondence; it is unique and completely unlike any other such correspondence. In post-Bloomfieldian theory the statement of the phonemic representation (allomorphs) of morphemes is without patterning. Similarly, the tagmemic manifestation of one level by another and the stratificational represented-by between stratal systems are patternless. A term within one hierarchy is simply represented by, manifested as, made up of, etc., a term within the second. All these statements apply only once within the description.

If we examine some additional data, we will discover that here the non-taxonomic relationship between our two taxonomic hierarchies is not as patternless as the previous cases. Let us add

(7)	It was easy to understand Will
(8)	To understand Will was easy
(9)	Matt was asked to telephone
(10)	Someone asked Matt to telephone

If we account for (7)–(10) on the model of (6), we find that (7) and (8) are comparable to (2). They have, in fact, the *same* description as (2), down to the same lexical items. As in (2) the first NP constituent of S in (7) and (8) is *Someone understand Will;* and the NP constituent of the VP constituent in *Someone understand Will* is *Will.* In (7), however, we find an *it* absent in (2) and (8). We modify the description of (6b) as follows:

(11)

$$\left\{ \left\{ \{\text{it}\}_{\text{N}} \left\{ \{\text{someone}\}_{\text{NP}} \left\{ \{\text{understand}\}_{\text{V}} \{\text{Will}\}_{\text{NP}} \right\}_{\text{VP}} \right\}_{\text{S}} \right\}_{\text{NP}} \left\{ \{\text{was}\}_{\text{Cop}} \{\text{easy}\}_{\text{Adj}} \right\}_{\text{VP}} \right\}_{\text{S}}$$

The alteration involves claiming that the Subject NP of the sentence is an NP with constituents N(*it*) and S (cf. Rosenbaum 1967: 12–13). The projected structure is now arbitrary but will be justified below. We find that (9) and (10) are comparable to each other, having a description in terms of (6) that is not the same as (4). In answer to "Who asked?" we have "Some unspecified person(s)." The answer to "Who was to telephone?" and "Asked whom?" is "Matt" in each case. We must modify the set of possible sentences in (6) to include

(12)

$$\left\{ \{\text{Someone}\}_{\text{NP}} \left\{ \{\text{asked}\}_{\text{V}} \{\text{Matt}\}_{\text{NP}} \left\{ \left\{ \{\text{Matt}\}_{\text{NP}} \{\text{telephone}\}_{\text{VP}} \right\}_{\text{S}} \right\}_{\text{VP}} \right\}_{\text{S}} \right\}$$

The first occurrence of *Matt* is identified as object of *ask*; the second, as Subject of *telephone*.

In relating these structures (11) and (12) to their more concrete descriptions, we may, for example, associate the sentence described in (12) directly with (9) and (10), assuming no pattern in that association. Alternatively, we may break down the association into steps, altering (12) bit by bit until it is identical to (9) and (10). In this approach one of the first things we must do in (12) is delete the second occurrence of *Matt*. To reach (10) we must also insert *to* before *telephone*. We can associate (12) with (9) if we additionally exchange positions of *someone* and *Matt*, inserting *was* to the left of *asked* and finally by deleting *someone*. We express these steps as

(13)   (a)   Matt$_1$ Matt$_2$ $\Rightarrow$ Matt$_1$

(b)   telephone $\Rightarrow$ to telephone

(c)   Someone asked Matt $\Rightarrow$ Matt was asked someone

(d)   Someone $\Rightarrow$ $\varnothing$

The steps of (13) affect only the specific structure of (12) with its lexical items. Recognizing that a great number of sentences parallel (9) and (10), we want to phrase (13) to affect all those of the same type, thus avoiding repetition of the equivalent of (13) for each additional one. We should state (13) for the structural hierarchy, not the terms occupying positions in that hierarchy, We rephrase (13) as (14):

(14)   (a) $N_1 N_2 \Rightarrow N_1$, where N_1 and N_2 are identical

(b)   [V...]$_S$ $\Rightarrow$ [to V...]$_S$

(c)   NP$_1$ V NP$_2$ $\Rightarrow$ NP$_2$ was V NP$_1$

(d)   Indefinite
$\Rightarrow$ $\varnothing$
Pronoun

Expressed in this fashion, the successive alterations effect an economy by identifying a large number of sentences as manifesting a single construct. They are not stated in terms of individual forms (cf. Chomsky 1961a: 132).

Let us now consider similar steps in associating *it someone understand Will was easy* with its variants (2), (7), and (8). First, we delete *someone*. Having the Verb *understand* with no preceding Noun, we insert *to*. Before the S category manifested by *to understand Will*, we delete the Pronoun category manifested by *it*. These steps yield *To understand Will was easy*. To associate our original structure with (7), we use the first and second steps above, but not the third. Additionally, we need to move the S category to the right of *easy* of the Adj category. This yields *It was easy to understand Will*. Finally, to associate our initial structure with *Will was easy to understand*, we require a step that removes *Will* to the initial position replacing *it*. These steps are given in (15).

(15) (a) Indefinite
$$\text{Pronoun} \Rightarrow \varnothing$$

    (b) $[\text{V}\ldots]_{\text{S}} \Rightarrow [\text{to V}\ldots]_{\text{S}}$

    (c) Definite   Definite
$$[\quad]_{\text{S}}\ \text{V Adj} \Rightarrow \quad \text{V Adj}\ [\quad]_{\text{S}}$$
      Pronoun   Pronoun

    (d) Definite
$$\text{V Adj to V NP} \Rightarrow \text{NP V Adj to V}$$
      Pronoun

Comparing (14) and (15), we find partial identity in the steps required for each: the insertion of *to* before a Verb that, as constituent of an S, has no NP to the left of it and the possible deletion of an Indefinite Pronoun category. The question arises whether this partial identity is in fact a defining pattern of language or an accident of our formulation. The observation that as we examine the patterns of English further along the lines of our present inquiry, we increase the number of partial identities among the bodies of statements associating distinct abstract structures with the more concrete structures, is motivation for assuming these partial identities as valid properties of language. We so assume.

We now notice that if we are to express this pattern, we *must* state the associations between abstract and concrete structures in steps. The nontaxonomic relationship between them must be complex in each case, so that we may identify those partial samenesses in the separate associations. Our language pattern is now expressed as the set of abstract structures, concrete structures, and the set of statements relating them. And there is a redundancy in this. As long as the nontaxonomic statements are patternless, they are necessary baggage, as were the previous relationships of represented-by and so forth. The concrete structures, being nonpredictable, were similarly necessary. But having found that the nontaxonomic statements are patterned, we discover that explicit statement of the concrete structures is unnecessary. The abstract structures plus the associative statements yield the concrete structures. The latter are redundant, and simplicity requires that we delete their explicit entry from the description. Given an abstract structure and the associative statements, we predict the concrete structure. In post-Bloomfieldian theory, the nontaxonomic relationship of represented-by between grammar and phonology told us nothing of the phonemic pattern; and both levels require explicit expression within a description. Grammar and the representation statements told us nothing of the pattern of the phonemic level, for the representation lacked patterning.

The distinctions we have discovered and labeled abstract and concrete are the *deep* and *surface structures* of syntax (Chomsky 1965: 16–18 et passim; 1967: 406–7; 1968: 25–32; and Postal 1964b). To account for these patterns we require the primitives category (cf. again the Hjelmslevian object), made-up-of or "is a" (cf. Chomsky 1965: 107 and Postal 1964a: 12), conjunction, disjunction, and linear order. Furthermore, we require either implication or the complex primitive of optionality, which includes implication, mutual, and nonmutual. We may either define optional occurrence as nonmutual implication in the manner of Hjelmslev's determination or subsume all that under the heading of optional as in tagmemic theory. These primitives are sufficient to outline the pattern of deep structure as far as we have developed it. To account for surface structure, we require a primitive relationship that permits us to add terms (e.g., 14 b and c) to delete terms (e.g., 14 a and d), to permute terms (e.g., 14c and 15c and d), and to substitute terms (e.g., 15d). These are subsumed under the complex primitive process of *transformation.*

Unlike all preceding theories we have discussed, with the exception of Bloomfieldian, pattern has been expressed within taxonomic hierarchies and ordering within those hierarchies. Nontaxonomic properties entered only insofar as distinct taxonomies (levels) were assumed to be directly related. Bloomfield proposed the relationships of addition, deletion, and substitution or replacement such that the patterned relationship of basic to actual forms was described by the application of these operations. Within grammar, a distinction was implied between a pre-substitution structure and a post-substitution structure suggesting the distinction of deep and surface structure here. Post-Bloomfieldian theory developed toward the expression of all pattern as taxonomic, retaining a nontaxonomic relationship only to express a patternless association between the hierarchies of grammar and phonemics. The distinction is made there (cf. Hockett 1954) in terms of item-and-arrangement (= taxonomic pattern) and item-and-process (= nontaxonomic pattern). The unequal development (Hockett 1954: 213–14)—item-and-arrangement more, and item-and-process less—is evidence for the post Bloomfieldian emphasis on taxonomic pattern. With the insistence here on transformational processes, this is the first of our theories to emphasize nontaxonomic pattern as central to language.

The Base: Categorial Subcomponent

Transformational generative grammar defines the pattern of language in terms of a single level of pattern—syntax—holding between sound and meaning. Syntax consists of two components: *the base component* and the *transformational* (Chomsky 1965: 141). The former provides a definition of possible deep structure and consists of two subcomponents: the *categorial* and the *lexical* (Chomsky 1965: 120 and 1968: 420). It is to the categorial subcomponent that we now turn.

We have seen that deep structure has the shape of a taxonomic hierarchy describing the possible combinations of lexical items; and furthermore, this hierarchy is such that we may derive from it the functional, semantic information of Subject, Object, etc. The categorial subcomponent describes possible combination and in transformational generative grammar functions as grammatical hierarchy does in Bloomfieldian and post-Bloomfieldian theories in determining possible combination of morphemes. We may relate categories by the primitive made-up-of or is-a in the manner familiar from Hjelmslevian theory. The relationship made-up-of holding between terms is represented by a single-shafted arrow, so that

$$(16) \qquad S \longrightarrow NP + VP$$

defines a class S as a category made up of the categories NP and VP in a specific sequence. Linearity is represented by the sequence in which the categories are written; the plus indicates conjunction. Each such statement is a *rewrite rule* (Chomsky 1964b: 916 and 1965: 66 et passim). We can construct a hierarchy by combining rewrite rules as follows:

$$(17) \qquad \text{(a)} \quad \#S\# \longrightarrow NP + VP$$

$$\text{(b)} \quad VP \longrightarrow \begin{Bmatrix} Cop + Pred \\ V \quad (NP)(\#S\#) \end{Bmatrix}$$

$$\text{(c)} \quad NP \longrightarrow N \quad (\#S\#)$$

$$\text{(d)} \quad N \longrightarrow \begin{Bmatrix} Noun \\ Pronoun \end{Bmatrix}$$

$$\text{(e)} \quad Pronoun \longrightarrow \begin{Bmatrix} Definite \\ Indefinite \end{Bmatrix}$$

$$\text{(f)} \quad Pred \longrightarrow Adj \quad (\#S\#)$$

The curly braces indicate disjunction; the parentheses, optionality. The choices offered by disjunction and optionality define a set of hierarchies, such as those of (6), (11), and (12). S is the initial category, and like the Hjelmslevian sign function, is always the first category rewritten. In deriving a specific hierarchy from (17), categories are rewritten (constituent categories specified) until all choices have yielded constituent categories that occur *only* as constituents, that is, until only those that appear on the right side of a rewrite rule are chosen. This implies that no further rules of (17) are applicable. A set of such choices is given in (18):

(18)   (a)   ≠S≠

      (b)   ≠ + NP + VP + ≠

      (c)   ≠ + NP + Cop + Pred + ≠

      (d)   ≠ + N + Cop + Pred + ≠

      (e)   ≠ + N + Cop + Adj + ≠ +   S   + ≠ + ≠

      (f)   ≠ + N + Cop + Adj + ≠ + NP + VP + ≠ + ≠

      (g)   ≠ + N + Cop + Adj + ≠ + NP + V + ≠ + ≠

      (h)   ≠ + N + Cop + Adj + ≠ + N + V + ≠ + ≠

Sequences of categories such as (18a)–(18h) are *strings*. A string produced by the application of the base rewrite rules, e.g., (18h), is a *pre-terminal string* (Chomsky 1965: 84). By inserting lexical items for the categories we form a *terminal string* (Chomsky 1965: 84) and (18a–h) is the *derivation* (Chomsky 1965: 66) of that terminal string. The structure of the terminal string of (18) is the taxonomic hierarchy

(**19**)

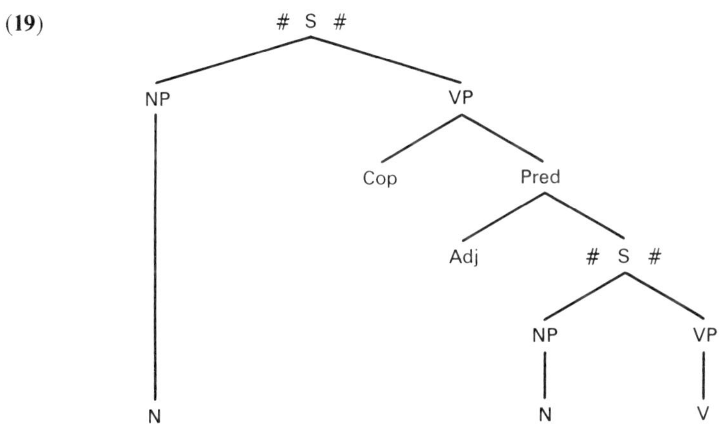

Such a hierarchy is the *phrase marker* (Chomsky 1964b: 916–17 and 1965: 65 et passim) of the terminal string.

The statements of (17) recall the Hjelmslevian system (with order added) and (19), one of the system-implied processes. Also like a Hjelmslevian system, the statements of a category definition are ordered (17a) through (17h) applying in sequence (Chomsky 1965: 67). Since the category S appears in (17a), (17c), and (17f), on different sides of the made-up-of relationship, (17a) applies first and reapplies (along with others following it) to S as long as S is chosen in (17c) or (17f). The base rewrite rules are *cyclical*

(Chomsky 1965: 134). This implies that each occurrence of S is the same class—an identity that had doubtful validity in Hjelmslevian theory—and that there is no longest string. That is, whatever string is predicted, we can always predict a longer one by choosing S in (17c) or (17f) one more time. This, in turn, predicts an unlimited number of terminal strings. We return to this later.

Observe that in (17) each relationship, rewrite rule, holds between one term (on the left) and more than one (on the right); categories are rewritten one at a time, This holds as a restriction on rewrite rules, and there is a reason for it. Notice, for example, that the transformations of (15b) and (15c) require for their operation not only categories, but the phrase marker relationship of those categories. In (15c) categories that are constituents of S in a given environment are permuted. Transformations operate not only on categories, but also on the phrase structure relationships among them. Transformations do not operate on strings, but on structures. To correctly predict the resulting surface structure, each constituent category of a structure must be unambiguously identified as a member of some category. Given, for example,

$$(20) \qquad N + S \longrightarrow Pronoun + N + V + N + V + Adj$$

in place of certain rules of (17), the transformation of (15c) cannot apply. The proper categories, those of S alone, are not identifiable. We do not know which constituent categories of (20) are constituents of S in N + S, and which are not. If we restrict base rewrite rules to rewriting one category at a time, this class-member information is preserved; and the condition of *analyzability* (Chomsky 1965: 121 and 142–43), comparable to Hjelmslevian uniformity, is met. We then know unambiguously the constituency of each single category in a phrase marker.

We have labeled the categories of the base without comment. Two attitudes can be adopted with respect to this: (1) that categories are defined from language to language, e.g., NP of (17) and (19) in a description of English is not to be identified with NP occurring in the description of any other language, and (2) that the categories are universal such that the identity eliminated in (1) is in fact possible. The attitude of (1) characterizes all theories we have previously considered. Occasionally, classes at some determinable point in a grammatical hierarchy, e.g., word, are identified and defined, but no attempt has been made to characterize universally all classes of a hierarchy. If we attempt such a universal characterization, we can proceed in two ways. Either categories are primitives of the theory, or like phrase marker, they are defined within the theory. The desirability of universal characterization is indicated in transformational generative grammar (cf. Chomsky 1965: 65–66, 73, 115–17, 120–21, and 141–42 and 1967: 418–19 and 436; Lees 1957: 392–93; and Postal 1964b: 261). The usual technique for identifiying universal categories seems to be definition (Chomsky 1965: 142, but see Chomsky 1965: 117, which suggests that they may be semantic primitives and the comments on the Q[uestion] category in Chomsky 1967:427). Such a definition would be realized if there were a universal set of base rewrite rules, i.e., a universal categorial subcomponent, such that categories occurring at specific points within the rules and phrase markers might receive a unique and universal identification. This goal is as yet unrealized, and we must take the labeling of categories here to be *ad hoc* from language to language. It follows from this that the notions of Subject, Object, etc., are also determined from language to language.

The rules of (17), and base rewrite rules in general, are *context-free* (Chomsky 1961a: 122). This means that the choice among a disjunction of constituent categories of a category being rewritten, e.g., (17b), is not conditioned by categories to the left or right in the derivation, which also characterizes the grammatical hierarchies of Bloomfieldian, tagmemic, and Firthian theories. Grammatical hierarchies in each are such that moving from size-level to size-level, any choice presented is not contingent on some adjacent choice. Bloomfieldian grammatical hierarchies offered no disjunctive choices, and the distinction between context-free and context-sensitive is not made. It is perhaps more correct to say that Bloomfieldian theory is unclassifiable with respect to this notion, rather than claim that it is context-free. In this vein, Saussurean theory, which like Bloomfieldian theory has no disjunctive classes, would also be nonclassifiable. Grammatical hierarchy in tagmemics is restricted to a size-level, e.g., clause. Within a size-level, hierarchy within syntagmemes is described via matrices, and within such a description, there are no conditioned choices from a disjunctive class (i.e., a dimension of a matrix). The propia of syntagmemes are disjunctively related as one dimension, the communis forms the second, and any members of the first dimension may occur with any of the second. Tagmemic grammar is context-free. Firthian theory contains a grammatical hierarchy such that—following Halliday—structural categories of one prosodically delimited size-level consists of a disjunction of structures of the next lowest size-level; but no constraint or condition is placed on the choice of one versus another. We may encounter constraints in the systems associated with the structural categories in the form of correlations, but none in the hierarchy of grammatical structure itself. Post-Bloomfieldian theory, in the version we examined, can be viewed as having disjunctive classes in the grammatical hierarchy such that certain choices are required (conditioned). In

(21)
$$\left\{ \begin{Bmatrix} X \\ Y \end{Bmatrix} \{ W \} \atop \{ Z \} \right\}$$

choice of W requires X or Y, but excludes Z. Such taxonomic hierarchies with constrained choices are *context-sensitive* (Chomsky 1961a: 122 and

Postal 1964a: 15). In Hjelmslevian theory, a class was analytically described by constituents independently of other descriptions of the same rank, but synthetic description of classes as constituents and the integration of the phenomena of government and agreement into the hierarchy restricts choices that can be made from the system, e.g., a sum of one rank may determine another sum of the same rank. Hjelmslevian theory is then also context-sensitive. Stratificational grammar formalizes constraints on choices within the tactics with paired, ordered disjunctive classes. In

(22)

only *A* and *C* co-occur or only *B* and *D*, but not *A* and *D* nor *B* and *C*. The choices are conditioned, and the tactics are context-sensitive. The shape of grammatical structure in Prague School theory is not so well-developed as to permit comment on its classification here.

The context-free nature of the rewrite rules of the categorial subcomponent is important because it raises a problem of co-occurrence. Were we to choose a possible phrase marker from (17),

(23)

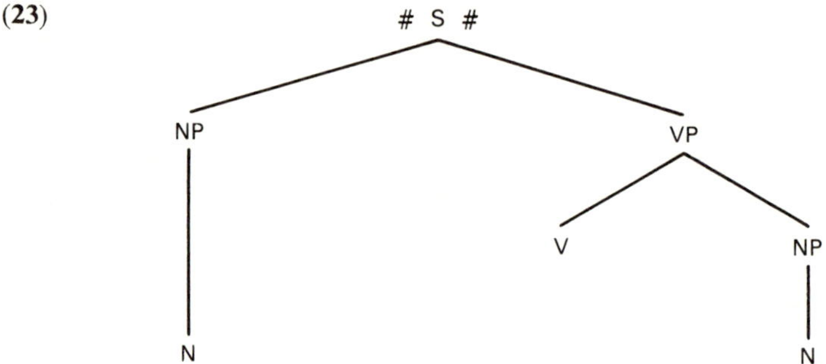

we find from what we have so far said that this is the structure of *Matt telephoned Will* as well as **Matt telephoned the merchandise*. Similarly in

(24)

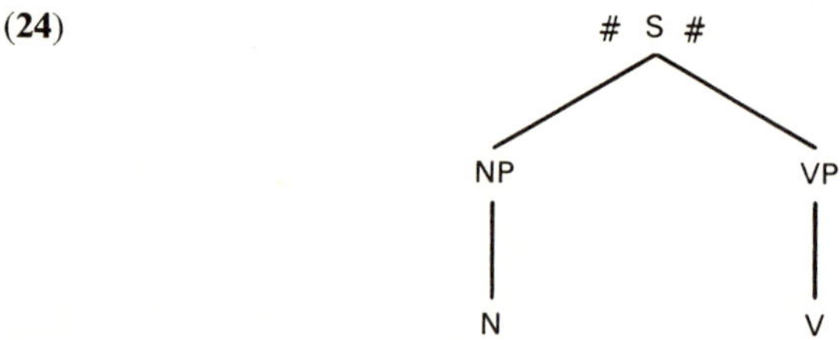

this is the structure of *Matt telephoned* as well as **Matt elected*. Nor as yet is there any thing that prevents the prediction of, say, **telephoned Matt Will* from (23). Clearly, we require some constraint on which lexical items or *formatives* (Chomsky 1964b: 915 and 1965: 3) may occur in the variety of phrase markers. The context-free rules of the categorial subcomponent say nothing of the way formatives are matched with categories. In Bloomfieldian theory this is handled within the lexicon via form class designation and selection; in tagmemic theory it is placed within the lexical mode; and in Firthian theory it is described within the systems. Similarly here, it is the lexicon, the second subcomponent of the base, that is the principal location of co-occurrence constraints.

The Base: Lexical Subcomponent

The lexicon is a conjunction of lexical entries. What interests us here is the content of an entry. Let us begin with some examples by way of determining this content:

(25)   (a)   Max was determined to please

                (b)   The bartender offed

                (c)   The dog was determined to teach

                (d)   Max stumbled the bar

                (e)   The merchandise was determined to teach

                (f)   The bartenders was determined to teach

                (g)   Max counted beer

As with our initial data, we find a pattern in (25) that is not immediately apparent. We will consider (25a) a "good" sentence and (25b) a "bad" one. Now, if asked to rank the sentences of (25) as relatively "good or bad," "funny," "deviant," etc., we find that we can in fact do that. Let us agree that the ranking from "good" to "bad" is (25a), (25c), (25e), (25f), (25g), (25d), and (25b). If it is assumed that this ranking is a manifestation of language patterning, then we have as yet no way of expressing it. Such pattern is accepted (Chomsky 1961b: 227–33), and the device that accounts for this is the same that establishes co-occurrence relationships undetermined by the context-free categorial subcomponent.

We supplement the categorial rewriting rules of the base with *subcategorizational rules* and call those of (17) *branching rules* (Chomsky 1965: 112). Each category N, V, Adj, etc., is rewritten as follows:

(26)   (a)   N ⟶ CS

                            (b)   V ⟶ CS

                            (c)   Adj ⟶ CS

The categories so rewritten are thus identified as *lexical categories* (Chomsky 1965: 74, 82, 84, and 98). Categories not so rewritten are *grammatical categories* (Chomsky 1965: 65). We have so far omitted these from our descriptions (cf. below). A category that has a lexical category among its constituents is a *major category* (Chomsky 1965: 74).

Subcategorizational rules provide content to the symbol CS (Complex Symbol) in terms of its position within the phrase marker as context-sensitive rules or independently of environment as context-free rules. A complex symbol is then a nonlinear conjunction of *syntactic features* (Chomsky 1965: 82) that also are *contextual features* (Chomsky 1965: 93 and 111) if they result from a context-sensitive subcategorizational rule.

Rule (26) requires elaboration. Let us consider the phrase markers

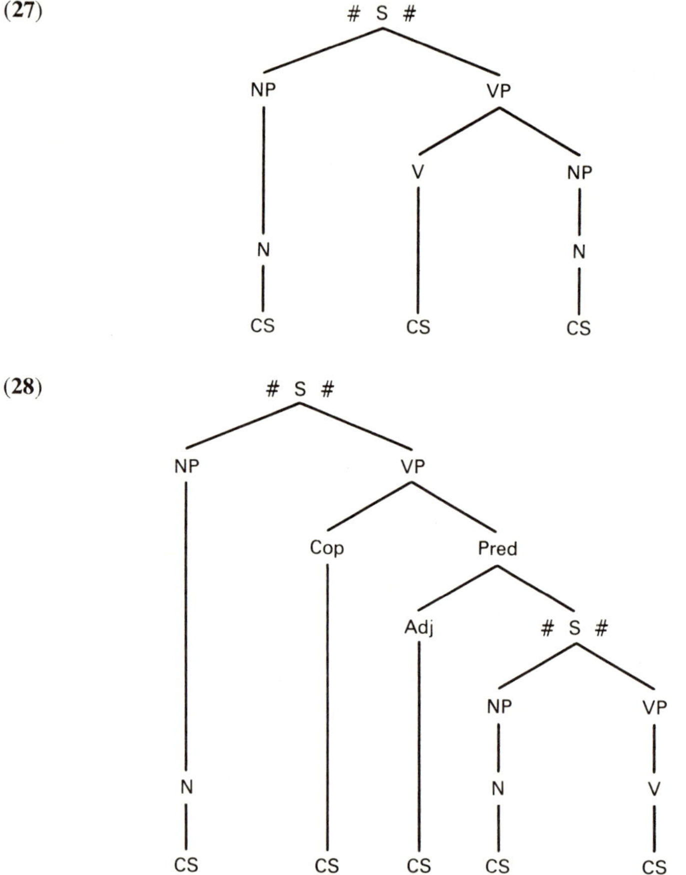

(27)

(28)

One type of subcategorization rule will specify that the complex symbol of the V category in (27) contains a set of contextual features derived from its category environment. The complex symbol here will be [+V], the plus indicating that it is a member of the category V noted by the syntactic feature [V]. It will be additionally specified as $[+\underline{\ \ } \ldots NP]$, indicating that it co-occurs with the category NP to the right. We now mark our lexical entries with the same syntactic features, associating $[+V]$ and $[+\underline{\ \ } \ldots NP]$ with every lexical item that we predict as occurring within this particular phrase marker as a member of the V category. If we mark the formatives *select*, *stumble*, and *off* as follows:

(29) (a) *select* $\begin{bmatrix} [+V] \\ [+\underline{\ \ }...NP] \end{bmatrix}$ (b) *stumble* $\begin{bmatrix} [+V] \\ [-\underline{\ \ }...NP] \end{bmatrix}$ (c) *off* $\begin{bmatrix} [-V] \end{bmatrix}$

and specify that a lexical entry may be substituted for a complex symbol where the syntactic features associated with it are not distinct (i.e., where for some syntactic feature X, the value of the complex symbol within the phrase marker and the lexical entry do not have opposite values, $+$ and $-$ or $-$ and $+$), then (25b) and (25d) are excluded. They are not predicted by any of our statements. The formative *stumble* in (25d) has been substituted for a complex symbol that contains the plus value for the syntactic feature $[\underline{\ \ } \ldots NP]$, although itself having the minus value for that feature. Specification of formatives by syntactic features based on category environment functions analogously to Bloomfield's notation of each morpheme by a form class membership. The subcategorizational rules that introduce and expand the complex symbol according to category environment are *strict subcategorizational rules* (Chomsky 1965: 95).

Since it was already pointed out that phrase markers have no upward bound of complexity, it is important to determine how much, if not all, of the category environment is relevant to strict subcategorizational rules and how that is expressed in (26). It is claimed (Chomsky 1965: 99–101) that the relevant environment for each complex symbol is just those categories of the lowest major category of a phrase marker that has the lexical category of the complex symbol in question as a constituent. Thus, the relevent environment of V in (27) is NP because the lowest major category having V as constituent is VP, which includes NP. In (28) the relevent environment for the CS of Adj is $\#S\#$; the major category defining the range of strict subcategorizational environment there is Pred. Given this assumption, we may define a universal strict subcategorizational rule once we have defined CS, lexical category (or N, V, Adj, etc.), and major category. This may take the following shape:

(30)

$$[X...Y...Z]_P \implies [X... \begin{bmatrix} \begin{bmatrix} +Y \\ +X...\underline{\ \ } \\ +\underline{\ \ }...Z \end{bmatrix}_Y \end{bmatrix} ...Z]_P$$

where (a)   Y is a lexical category,

     (b)   X, Y, and Z are categories that are immediate constituents of the major category P, and

     (c)   the terms within the square brackets labeled Y are contextual, syntactic features.

The final rewrite rule of the categorial subcomponent is now (30), which further rewrites lexical categories as a complex symbol and specifying the content in varying ways according to the relevant environment of the lexical category.

Notice that we must list within the lexicon a large number of minus values of features for each lexical entry. For example, *stumble* being [+V] is also [− __ ... NP], [−N]. [−Cop], [−Adj], [− __ ... #S#], etc. Instead of listing a large number of minus specifications, it is assumed (Chomsky 1965: 111 and 164) that we may enter only positive values, i.e., explicitly note only those environments in which a formative may occur. A *lexical redundancy rule*, a language universal convention (Chomsky 1965: 165), then specifies the complex symbol of each formative with a minus value for any feature not positively associated with it. A *lexical rule* (Chomsky 1965: 84) then states conditions for substituting lexical items for the complex symbols of a phrase marker. Like the strict subcategorizational rule and lexical redundancy rule, the lexical rule is universal to all languages:

> *If* Q *is a complex symbol of a preterminal string and* (D, C) *is a lexical entry* [*where* D *is a formative and* C, *its associated complex symbol, P W D*] *where* C *is not distinct from* Q, *then* Q *can be replaced by* D (*Chomsky 1965: 84*).

Such an extension of the theory is not sufficient to exclude all the deviant (to some degree) sentences of (25). In (25c), the problem is that *dog* is not subject NP of a sentence that has a Predicate Adj *determined;* or conversely, *determined* cannot be a Pred Adj of a sentence in which *dog* is the Subject NP. Similarly, for *merchandise* in (25e). In (25g) the problem is that a V *count* must occur with countable items, a particular type of N. In (25f), Cop must occur with N Subjects that are singular. The deviation of these sentences cannot be explained in terms of categorial environment. In *Max counted beer*, the strict subcategorizational environment of the V is not distinct from the present complex symbol of *count* in the lexicon; both are [+V] and [+__ ... NP]. The deviance lies elsewhere. Simply, *some* nouns may occur as Subject of *some* verbs, whereas others may not. Some adjectives may occur as predicate with *some* nouns as Subject; others may not.

The above observations suggest that lexical items of a particular lexical category require subclassification. Lexical items that are [+N] are either Human or nonHuman, Animate or nonAnimate, Count or nonCount, and so on. As in Bloomfieldian and Firthian theory, we further order lexical items. Using noncontextual syntactic features, we supplement the complex symbol of a lexical entry with information about its subclass membership, the membership within such a subclass being noted with a plus value for the subclass label and nonmembership by a minus. Thus, (*dog*, [+Animate]) indicates that the formative *dog* is a member of the Animate subclass of [+N]; an entry [−Human] denoting that it is not a member of the Human subclass of [+N].

Now if we have the following subclassification:

(31)

$$
\left\{
\begin{array}{l}
\{\quad\}+An \\
\{\quad\}-An \\
\{\quad\}+Hu \\
\{\quad\}-Hu
\end{array}
\right\}_{+N}
\quad
\left\{
\begin{array}{l}
\{\quad\}V_1 \\
\{\quad\}V_2 \\
\{\quad\}V_3 \\
\{\quad\}V_4
\end{array}
\right\}_{+V}
$$

such that [+An] Nouns occur with V_1 Verbs and [−An] Nouns with V_2 Verbs, but not [−An] Nouns with V_2 Verbs nor [+An] Nouns with V_1 Verbs, the question arises which determines which. Is one class, say [+N], subclassified freely such that [+V] is contextually subclassified with respect to the [+N] subclassification environment, or is the reverse true. Either choice treats the co-occurrence as analogous to government, the choice of Nouns governing the choice of Verbs. Chomsky (1965: 114–15) chooses the former, citing the greater complexity of the latter formulation and indicating that this may be true of all languages. Such an assumption may provide one step toward a universal categorial subcomponent and a universal definition of categories.

Ir his approach, a context-sensitive subcategorization rule further adds to the conjunction of contextual features of the complex symbols of all nonNoun lexical categories within a phrase marker. The relevant context for this addition is not the category environment as before, but the additional feature specification of the complex symbols provided by new context-free rewrite rules. Choosing to let the subclass of Nouns govern choice of Verb, we would require a set of rules as follows (cf. Chomsky 1965: 82–83):

(32)

    (a) $[+N] \rightarrow [\pm Common]$

    (b) $[+Common] \rightarrow [\pm Count]$

    (c) $[+Count] \rightarrow [\pm Animate]$

    (d) $[-Common] \rightarrow [\pm Animate]$

    (e) $[+Animate] \rightarrow [\pm Human]$

    (f) $[-Count] \rightarrow [\pm Abstract]$

The co-occurrence of a plus and a minus before a feature to the right of the rewrite arrow presents a disjunctive choice. The subcategorizational rules of (32) further specify the content of the complex symbol of the Noun category alone.

The complex symbol of the Verb and Adj categories are now further specified in terms of these features by a second type of context-sensitive subcategorizational rule: *selectional rules* (Chomsky 1965: 95). Following (32), the phrase marker of (28) would now be rewritten as:

(33)

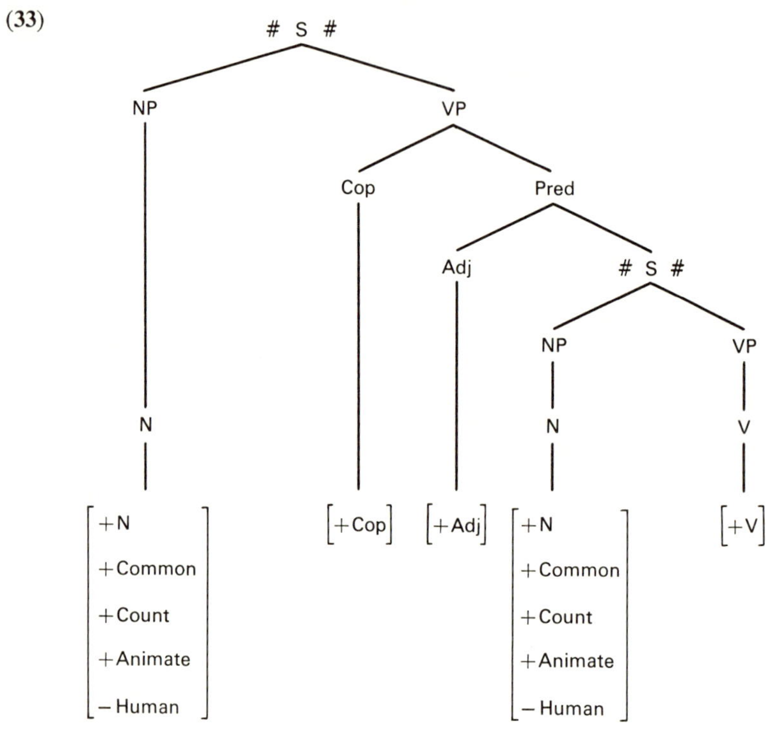

We ignore here the complete specification of the complex symbols by the strict subcategorizational rules. The complex symbol of V (indicated by the square brackets) is further specified in terms of its relevant feature environment by the selectional rule as

(34)   (a) $+V$

(b) $+[[+Common]...\_\_]$

(c) $+[[+Count]...\_\_]$

(d) $+[[+Animate]...\_\_]$

(e) $+[[-Human]...\_\_]$

Now we may substitute *dog* for the complex symbol of the N's in (33), but we may not substitute *teach* for (34), for the complex symbol of *teach* within the lexicon (ignoring irrelevant features) is

(35)

$$\begin{bmatrix} +V \\ \cdot \\ \cdot \\ \cdot \\ -[[-\text{Human}]...\_\_] \end{bmatrix}$$

Substituting (35) for (34) produces a contradiction not permitted by the lexical rule (cf. above); and *The dog was determined to teach* is correctly excluded from the predicted data. In similar fashion (25b), (25e), and (25f) are also excluded.

The selectional rule that produces the elaboration of the complex symbols as in (34) may be expressed as follows (cf. Chomsky 1965: 107):

(36)   (a) $[\alpha ... [+V] ... \beta]_S \Rightarrow [\alpha ... \begin{bmatrix} +V \\ +\alpha_1 \\ +\beta_1 \end{bmatrix} ... \beta]_S$

         (b) $[\alpha ... [+\text{Adj}] ... \beta]_S \Rightarrow [\alpha ... \begin{bmatrix} +\text{Adj} \\ +\alpha_1 \\ +\beta_1 \end{bmatrix} ... \beta]_S$

in which α and β are in each case the context-free subcategorization of the features of the N category in (32), and $+ \alpha_1$ and $+ \beta_1$ are these features copied into the complex symbols of $[+V]$ and $[+\text{Adj}]$ as contextual features. The $[\ ]_S$ indicates that the relevant Nouns are constituents of the same S category of which the modified category is a constituent, although not being a constituent of an S category excluding the affected category. This claims, for example, that the features of the leftmost N of (33) are irrelevant to the choice of Verb in the rightmost position.

We would like the selectional rules to be universal as the strict subcategorizational rule was; but in so specifying it, we need a universal definition of N, V, Adj, and so on. To claim that a $[+V]$-specified complex symbol is additionally determined in terms of the syntactic features of its N environment, we require universal identity of V and N categories. Alternatively, we may say that any complex symbol not specified by the context-free subcategorizational rules, i.e., by a rule such as (32), is further specified by the environment of those features without specifying that it is the N category affected by rule (32) and the V and Adj categories, by (36). In either case, we further require a universal characterization of the extent of that environment analogous to that of our strict subcategorizational rules. The relevant environments of the two context-sensitive subcategorizational rules are not coterminous. Notice that to exclude (25c) *teach* must be specified as $[-[\ [-\text{Human}]$ ...__]] wherein $[-\text{Human}]$ is a feature of a category outside VP, the major category determining the strict subcategorizational environment. The selectional environment is more extensive, but not outside the lowest S category of which the involved complex symbol is a constituent. In (25c), which has the phrase marker (28), the relevant syntactic feature environment is that of the N that is deleted in the surface structure by a modified version of (14a). Both the N and the V category are constituents of the S constituent of Pred; this lower S of (28), not the higher one, determines the relevant selectional environment of V. The universal specification of a selectional rule with respect to this relevant environment requires a universal identification of the S category wherever it occurs in a phrase marker (not just as the initial category), again a condition not yet satisfied. Assuming the requisite information, the universal selectional subcategorizational rule may appear as

(37)

$$[\alpha \ldots \begin{bmatrix} [\quad]_{\text{CS}} \end{bmatrix}_Y \ldots \beta]_S \Rightarrow [\alpha \ldots \begin{bmatrix} \begin{bmatrix} +\alpha_1 \\ +\beta_1 \end{bmatrix}_{\text{CS}} \end{bmatrix}_Y \ldots \beta]_S$$

where (a)   Y is a lexical category whose CS is not rewritten by (32);

     (b) α and β are the context-free subcategorization of lexical categories that, with Y, are constituents of S such that no second S is a constituent of the first S and has one of the categories as constituent; and

     (c) α_1 and β_1 are those contextual, syntactic features of α and β, respectively, copied onto the CS of Y.

We associated contextual, syntactic features introduced into the phrase marker by strict subcategorization with lexical items, such that the lexical rule determined whether those items could or could not replace a complex symbol within a phrase marker. We must now augment the complex symbols of lexical items in order to determine their behavior with respect to features introduced into the phrase marker by the selectional subcategorizational rule [cf. (36)]. As with the contextual features relevant to the strict subcategorizational rule, the minus values of the features relevant to the selectional subcategorizational rule will outnumber the plus values; and we might expect to enter only plus values in the lexicon, allowing an expanded lexical redundancy rule to specify the complex symbol of a lexical entry for minus values of any unnoted feature. The reverse may be chosen in either case subject to later evaluation. Chomsky (1965: 164) elects to specify contextual features for strict subcategorization as above and to specify those for selectional subcategorization of lexical entries as minus (i.e., to identify those subclasses to which a lexical entry does *not* belong), predicting the plus values (i.e., those subclasses to which the entry does belong). Evidence is not conclusive for either; to simplify exposition we arbitrarily choose to enter selectional subcategorization features within the lexicon as we did the strict subcategorization features.

Only the [−N] lexical categories are noted for selectional subcategorization features. The Nouns must be noted for the *inherent features* (Chomsky 1965: 165) introduced into the phrase marker by the context-free rule (32) as well as for the contextual features of the strict subcategorizational rule. In noting contextual features within the complex symbols of lexical entries, we found redundancies; and we find a redundancy also in the notation of inherent features of [+N] lexical entries, but it differs from that of the contextual features. The context-sensitive rules introduce only plus values into the complex symbol of a phrase marker, whereas (32) introduces plus and minus values. We cannot, then, use the lexical redundancy rule as formulated to predict inherent syntactical features of lexical items. The context-free rule (32) produces a hierarchy analogous to that of the branching rules (cf. Chomsky 1965: 83):

(38)

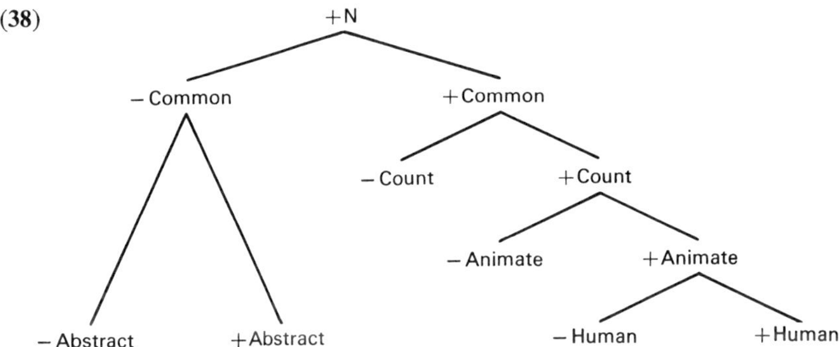

The lexical redundancy rule predicts features of the complex symbol of [+N] lexical entries in terms of the hierarchy of (38) based on observations such as the following. If we know a category is [−Human], we know it must also be [+Animate], [+Count], [+Common], and [+N] for [−Human] does not occur in the hierarchy without these features. Now, if we enter [−Human] within the complex symbol of some lexical entry, e.g., *dog*, we know from the hierarchy that *dog* must also have [+Animate], [+Count], [+Common], and [+N] within its associated complex symbol. One part of the lexical redundancy rule must then match noted inherent features within the complex symbol of lexical entries with the context-free specification—a portion of the phrase marker—and add to that complex symbol the features predictable from the hierarchy. Since only certain lexical entries will have those features (Nouns, as it turns out), only they will be affected by this portion of the redundancy rule. The lexical redundancy rule now has two parts; one predicts redundant contextual features, and one predicts redundant inherent features (cf. Chomsky 1965: 165–66).

An alternative formulation of selectional pattern is possible (Chomsky 1965: 121–23 and 1967: 423–26) in which the co-occurrence restrictions of Nouns vis-à-vis Verbs, Adj's, etc. are treated as an exclusive property of the lexicon. There is here no context-sensitive subcategorizational rules—neither strict nor selectional—within the categorial subcomponent, nor apparently is there any context-free subcategorization of the N lexical category (cf. Chomsky 1967: 424). The lexical entries are noted as before, but the lexical rule is modified such that in appropriate contexts (i.e., those of the strict subcategorizational and the selectional rules) any lexical entry whose complex symbol does not contradict the left side of the rule may be substituted for the "dummy symbol" (Chomsky 1965: 122) that rewrites all lexical categories and is replaced by lexical entries. (The dummy symbol is not a complex symbol. Unlike the latter, a dummy symbol is not a conjunction of contextual features, but a category indicating that the category it rewrites is a lexical category subject to the lexical rule.) The lexical rule is now expanded to include the statements of the strict and selectional subcategorizational rules, and the last rules of the categorial subcomponent are those specifying certain categories as dummy sumbols. It is not clear with respect to the selectional portion of the revised lexical rule whether the N category is affected first, then the remaining lexical categories, or whether the order of application to dummy symbols is free. The latter choice treats selectional co-occurrence as an agreement phenomenon and not as government; and there must be an altered condition of noncontradiction. In the former, by substituting Nouns into the phrase marker first, an environment is provided for the application of the lexical rule to Verbs, Adj's, etc. in the same way the context-free subcategorization of Nouns within the categorial subcomponent provided the feature environment for selectional rules. Chomsky (1965: 164) tentatively accepts the first expression of co-occurrence relationships using strict and selectional subcategorizational rules and context-free subcategorizational rules for Nouns within the categorial subcomponent. This is the version of the theory we accept here.

The categorial subcomponent as now modified contains two rules that are transformational processes. The context-sensitive subcategorizational rules rewrite a lexical category as a complex symbol with respect to the position of the former within the phrase marker; this is a property of transformational operations. Branching rules within the base affected only categories, e.g., (17), without regard for their structural context.

The ordering of these additional rules (first, strict subcategorizational, then context-free, then selectional) imposes a hierarchical ordering on the features within a complex symbol. It is this ordering that permits the explanation of our ranking of the sentences of (25). The ordered rules of (32) produce a hierarchy analogous to the hierarchy of the phrase marker itself [cf. (38)].

The hierarchical ordering of these features in the complex symbols of (33) is represented by their position from highest to lowest within the square brackets. A similar ordering is produced in the complex symbol of V of (33) indicated by the highest to lowest ordering in (34). The selectional rule not only copies features from an adjacent complex symbol, but also copies a portion of the hierarchy of features within that complex symbol. Now if a lexical item is substituted for (34), in (33), the complex symbol of which violates—contradicts—the value for some feature in (34), the claim is that the lower in the hierarchy of features this occurs, the less "deviant" the resultant sentence will be; the higher, the more deviant (Chomsky 1961b: 236–37). Sentence (25a) exhibits no contradictions and is not deviant. Sentence (25b) exhibits a contradiction at (34a); *off* is [−V]. Sentence (25c) exhibits a contradiction at (34e); *teach* is [− [[−Human] . . . __]]. The claim then predicts (25c) to be less deviant than (25b), and so forth. This schema recalls the Prague School hierarchy of empiric phonetic primitives and the prediction of judgments of looseness and closeness of an opposition in terms of the location within the hierarchy of the property that distinguishes its members. Notice that in the formulation of subcategorization adopted here, hierarchy is placed within the categorial subcomponent. In the rejected alternative, that hierarchy would be placed within the complex symbol associated with each lexical entry within the lexicon.

In the base component of syntax we now have the following apparatus:

Categorial Subcomponent	*Lexicon*
An ordered set of rewrite and transformational rules:	An ordered conjunction of lexical entries consisting of
Rewrite rules	A formative
Subcategorizational rules	A complex symbol—an
Strict (context-sensitive)	unordered conjunction of
Context-free	syntactic features
Selectional (context-sensitive)	Lexical redundancy rule
	Lexical rule

The formative contains necessary information for the phonological interpretation. In addition, each distinct lexical entry requires a semantic definition, provided by supplementing the components of an entry with a configuration of semantic properties drawn from an inventory of semantic primitives. The base produces terminal strings and their associated base phrase markers. These constitute the deep structure of language, and it is this that is interpreted semantically (Chomsky 1965: 135 and 1967: 427). For a discussion of the semantic interpretation and the arrangement of semantic features within the lexicon, see Katz and Fodor 1963, Katz and Postal 1964, Katz 1967, and Katz 1972.

The Transformational Component

Having developed the theoretical apparatus that defines the deep structure, we turn to the nontaxonomic portion of syntax, the transformational processes. Recall that our argument for their inclusion within language patterning turned on the discovery of partial samenesses between the associations of distinct deep and surface structures when that association was expressed as stepwise alterations of deep structures. Each of those steps consists of identifying a phrase marker or a portion thereof and its alteration in the manner indicated above. This entire step is a *transformational rule* (Chomsky 1956: 121; 1961a: 128–29; and 1967: 426). The phrase marker that is to be altered is the *structural description* (Chomsky 1962: 135) of the rule, and the result of the alteration is the *structural change*. The double-shafted arrow [cf. (14a)] indicates that the term to the right is a transform of the term to the left. Transformational rules operate on phrase markers, and the change effected by a transformational rule is likewise a phrase marker. To indicate that these new phrase markers are not those of the base, a phrase marker produced by a transformational rule is called a *derived phrase marker* (Chomsky 1961a: 131, 1964b: 944; and 1965: 128). The *final derived phrase markers* (Postal 1964b: 252) are those to which no additional, obligatory (cf. below) transformational rules can be applied; these constitute the surface structure of language. Because the semantic interpretation is determined by deep structure, no transformation may introduce nor ambiguously delete meaningful terms.

Now we observe that with the assumption of nontaxonomic, transformational pattern, we have transformations repeated in our descriptions above. Compare (14) with (15). Following the familiar notion of parsimony, we wish to reduce that repetition; and instead of having a set of transformations for *each* deep-surface association, we assume a *single* set of transformational rules applicable to the deep structures of the base in general. This has implications for the formulation of the transformational component.

In associating the single deep structure (11) with *To understand Matt was easy* and *It was easy to understand Matt*, we had to exclude a rule that applied in deriving the former from application in deriving the latter. The first required

$$(39) \qquad (a) \quad \begin{bmatrix} +\text{N} \\ +\text{Pronoun} \\ -\text{Def} \\ +\text{Human} \end{bmatrix} \implies \varnothing$$

someone

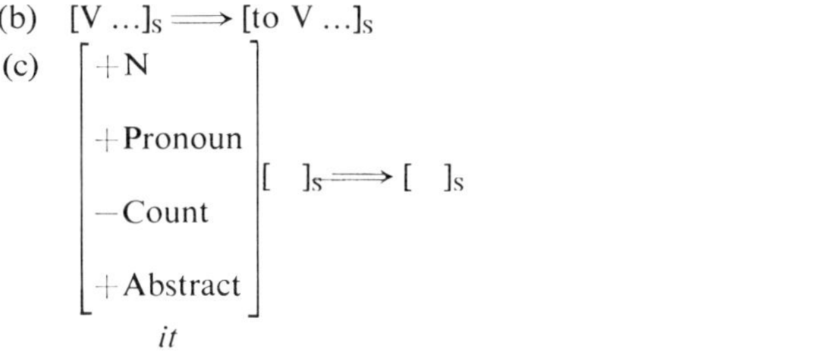

(b) $[V \ldots]_S \Longrightarrow [\text{to } V \ldots]_S$

(c) $\begin{bmatrix} +N \\ +\text{Pronoun} \\ -\text{Count} \\ +\text{Abstract} \end{bmatrix}$ $[\ \ ]_S \Longrightarrow [\ \ ]_S$

                 it

The second required

(40)   (a) $\begin{bmatrix} +N \\ +\text{Pronoun} \\ -\text{Def} \\ +\text{Human} \end{bmatrix} \Longrightarrow \varnothing$

(b) $[V \ldots]_S \Longrightarrow [\text{to } V \ldots]_S$

(c) $\begin{bmatrix} +N \\ +\text{Pronoun} \\ +\text{Def} \\ -\text{Count} \\ +\text{Abstract} \end{bmatrix} [\ \ ]_S \ V \ \text{Adj} \Longrightarrow \begin{bmatrix} +N \\ +\text{Pronoun} \\ +\text{Def} \\ -\text{Count} \\ +\text{Abstract} \end{bmatrix} V \ \text{Adj} [\ \ ]_S$

Now with the transformational processes applying in individual deep-surface structure associations combined into a single set applicable to all deep structures, we require some way of preventing the application of (39c) to the result of (39a/40a) and (39b/40b) in place of (40c). Both are equally applicable to the derived phrase marker of (39a/40a) and (39b/40b). We need to prevent that application because it yields a phrase marker to which (40c) is not applicable. Alternatively, if we accept the application of (39c) as inevitable, we must complicate (40c), providing for the reintroduction of *it*, and we must alter the structure to which (40c) applies. To avoid this we allow transformational rules to be *ordered* (Chomsky 1965: 39–40 and 134). The conflation of (39) and (40) is now the ordered sequence

(41)   (a) $\begin{bmatrix} +N \\ +\text{Pronoun} \\ -\text{Def} \\ +\text{Human} \end{bmatrix} \Longrightarrow \varnothing$

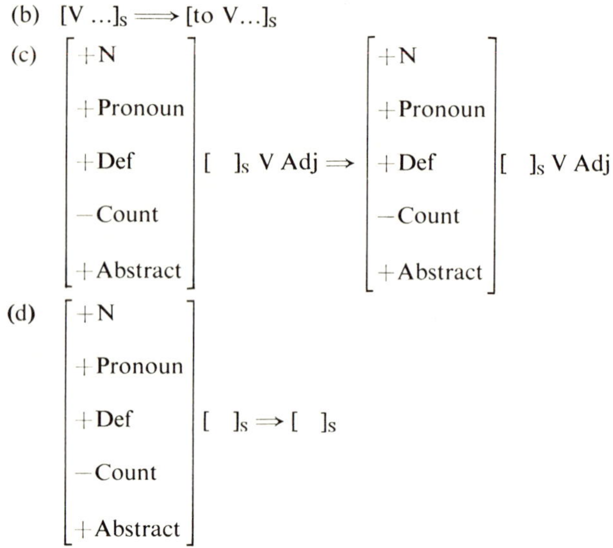

The ordered application of transformational rules as numbered in (41) allows for the simple derivation of the surface structure of *It was easy to understand Matt;* but to allow the derivation of *To understand Matt was easy,* we must make the application of (41c) *optional* (Chomsky 1957: 45). If (41c) obligatorily modifies all phrase markers to which it is applicable, (41d) can never apply and hence can never yield the surface string *To understand Matt was easy.* Not all transformational rules are optional; (14a), which deleted the second of two identical N's is *obligatory* (Chomsky 1957: 45) as are (41b) and (41d). Each pair of transformational rules may be ordered with respect to their application (but they need not always be); and each rule may be obligatory or optional. We may seek an integration of the notion of stylistic variation of pattern within the identification of optional rules; but it is indicated that stylistic variation, at least in part, may be accounted for within performance (Chomsky 1965: 126–27).

The ordering of certain of the transformational rules may be *cyclical* (Chomsky 1965: 134–35 and 143). They apply to the most deeply embedded #S# category, then reapply to the next most deeply embedded, and so forth, to the initial #S#, which is not a constituent (cf. Ross 1967 and Jacobs and Rosenbaum 1968: 235–49).

The problem of co-occurrence referred to subcategorization within the base is only partially resolved by that mechanism. If we consider a relatively simple base phrase marker there is nothing within the base subcategorization and lexicon that prohibits the choice of *Will* for the middle complex symbol dominated by N and *Chris* for the rightmost complex symbol dominated by N. Recall the context-free subcategorization of the complex symbols of the

(42)

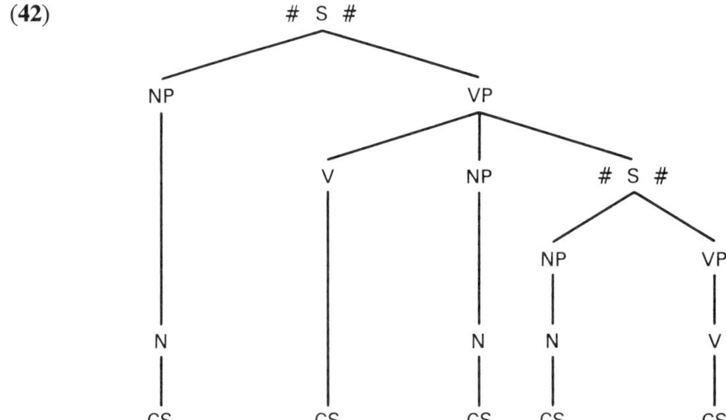

N category. The combined choices of *Will* and *Chris* should be excluded, for they predict an incorrect *Someone asked Will Chris telephone*. Furthermore, the utterance *Someone asked Will to telephone* is always interpreted such that *Will* is the Subject NP of *telephone*.

To exclude these incorrect predictions, the rule deleting identical N's is modified. Observe that the two N categories do not belong to all the same #S# categories in (42); the leftmost belongs to the highest #S# in the phrase marker hierarchy, whereas the rightmost belongs to that #S#, plus a second. Notice also that in the terminal string of which (42) is the phrase marker [cf. (18)], there is a second sentence boundary—indicated by #— within the whole string. We now modify the N deletion rule so that it deletes not only the second of two identical N's, but also the #'s to either side of the second N:

(43)
$$[+N]_1 \# ... [+N]_2 ... \# \Rightarrow [+N]_1 ......$$

where $[+N]_1 = [+N]_2$ and ... contains no $\#$

The second condition ensures the erasure of the proper boundaries. Now, if (43) does not apply or cannot apply because the two N's are not identical, the internal sentence boundaries are not erased. The transformation is said to have been *blocked* (Chomsky 1965: 138) in this instance. We define a *well-formed surface structure* as one with no occurrence of internal S boundaries and a *well-formed deep structure* as one associated with a well-formed surface structure (Chomsky 1965: 138). The transformation (43), and transformational rules in general, then acts as a *filter* (Chomsky 1965: 139) defining "well-formed" by its operation or nonoperation.

In the data we have considered, we have ignored such things as Tense of Verbs, Number of Nouns and Verbs, and Determiners of Nouns. All these things are grammatical categories introduced into deep structure along with lexical and major categories in a complete accounting of a language. Unlike the lexical categories, grammatical categories have no entry within the lexicon. Their semantic interpretation turns on the assumption that they have universal semantic content (Chomsky 1967: 427). The phonological content of grammatical categories comparable to the formative portion of lexical entries, is provided by transformational rules.

Transformational rules may have exceptions, and as in Bloomfieldian theory, that exceptionality is marked within the lexicon as a property of lexical items (cf. Lakoff 1970). Exceptions exist if a rule should apply to some phrase marker according to the structural description of that rule but cannot correctly do so; if a rule should apply to a given phrase structure but only in a small number of instances; if an obligatory rule is optional in certain instances; or if an optional rule is obligatory in certain instances, and so forth. The formal notation of exception is placed within the lexicon by use of features within the complex symbols of lexical items, indicating that the phrase marker in which the lexical item appears is an exception to the application of the transformational rule identified in the exception feature of the lexical item.

Interpretation: Phonology

The result of the transformational rules is a set of well-formed surface structures. It is these that are interpreted by associating each with a phonetic notation. This body of interpretative statements is *phonology*.

As in Bloomfieldian grammar, the lexicon contains the irregularities of a language. Among these irregularities are the arbitrary pairings of meaning and sound properties for each lexical item. Here, we consider the sound portion of an entry. Each lexical entry is in part constituted by a sequence of segments. Each segment, in turn, is an unordered conjunction of features (cf. Chomsky and Halle 1968: 293–329). As in Bloomfieldian and Praguean phonology, these ultimate terms are empiric and derive from a supposed, universal set of "phonetic properties that can in principle be controlled in speech" (Chomsky and Halle 1968: 294–95). Each phonetic property or feature is indicated as present (by a +) or as absent (by a −). The empiric nature implies that each lexical item is associated with some portion of data without additional statement.

Within a system, say, the vowels ([+ vocalic, − consonantal]) *i, u, e, o,* and *a,* the *i* and *u* are [+ high], differing in that the former is [− round, − back] and the latter is [+ round, + back]. The *e* and *o* are [− high, − low], differing in that the former is [− round, − back] and the latter, [+ round, + back]. The *a* is [+ low] and also [− round]. In a precise phonetic record, however, the *i*, for example, may be [i] in one environment and [ɪ] in a second.

To indicate this variation within the data, statements are required within phonology which permit segments not only to be characterized by the presence or absence of a feature, but also by the degree of that feature. If we indicate those degrees from 1 . . . *n* (from highest to lowest), then the [i] may be [1 high], and [ɪ] may be [2 high]; thus

(44)   *i* becomes [1 high] in some environment

                        and [2 high] in some second environment

Such statements as (44) are *detail rules* (Postal 1968: 66–69 and Chomsky and Halle 1968: 65).

This preliminary view supposes that *all i*'s (and *only i*'s) are affected by (44), and similarly for all *u*'s, *e*'s, *o*'s, and *a*'s by their respective detail rules. Let us consider the following data from Russian, again concentrating on the vowels:

(45)   (a)   γážut   'they tie'   (c)   p̡íšut   'they write'

            (b)   γizát̡   'to tie'   (d)   p̡isát̡   'to write'

If we represent the vowel of 'write' as *i* and the vowel of 'tie' as *a*, then not all *a*'s within the lexicon are treated as *a*'s by the detail rules, for the first vowels in (45 b and d) are both [ɪ] in a narrow phonetic record. This [a]∼[ɪ] alternation assumes a single entry for each lexical item. The alternative is a dual entry for 'tie', one with *a* (45a) and one with *i* (45b). But this has two undesirable effects. First, each time a lexical item shows a variation comparable (but not necessarily identical) to (45a and b), we are forced to make two (or more) entries. Second, such alternations often show patterning in that the variation recurs in many lexical items. Compare the following additional pairs:

(46)   (a)   p̡lášut   'they dance'   (c)   t̡ánut   'they pull'

            (b)   p̡lisát̡   'to dance'   (d)   t̡inút̡   'to pull'

In each case, two entries would be required, and the pattern of *a* alternating with *i* is lost; it is stated as many times as it occurs—as an exception—rather than once—as a pattern.

The statement of such patterning implies that we enter each lexical item with a single representation of its sound properties and state the alternation pattern shared by (45) and (46) only once. To express this pattern and the fact that some *a*'s emerge as [ɪ], we must include a statement such as (47) before any detail rules apply:

(47)   *a* ⟶ *i* in some environment

In a system of notation where segments are unordered conjunctions of features, we formally state (47) as (48):

(48)
$$\begin{bmatrix} +\text{vocalic} \\ -\text{consonantal} \\ +\text{low} \end{bmatrix} \longrightarrow \begin{bmatrix} +\text{high} \\ -\text{low} \end{bmatrix} \text{ in some environment}$$

Such statements as (48) differ from detail rules in that they operate on a segment (or group of segments), replacing the + or − value of some feature (s) with the opposite − or + value. Such rules are *phonological rules* (Chomsky and Halle 1968: 13–14 et passim and Postal 1968: 164). Both phonological and detail rules replace the values of one or more features with another value. Phonological rules may further add, delete, or permute segments. Both kinds are expressions of a transformational relationship between terms, and their formal statement requires no new primitives in the theory.

We now distinguish three stages of representation: (1) that within the lexicon, (2) that after the application of phonological rules, and (3) that after application of detail rules. The first is termed the *systematic phonemic representation* (Chomsky and Halle 1965: 98), and the second is the *systematic phonetic representation* (Chomsky and Halle 1965: 98). The third may be called the *narrow phonetic transcription* (Postal 1968: 6).

In our example above, we have not yet indicated why it is that we chose a particular systematic representation with the vowel *a* in 'tie' and 'dance' and 'pull' rather than *i* and include a rule

(49) $i \longrightarrow a$ in some environment

The choice turns on the general criterion of simplicity. In (48) the notation "in some environment" may be replaced by:

(50)   ç $\underline{\breve{}}$

i.e., simultaneous occurrence with [− stress] following a palatalized consonant; but in (49) "in some environment" would require a list of the lexical items affected. The environment

(51)   ç $\underline{\acute{}}$

does not suffice, for it wrongly predicts *p̦ášut 'they write'. To avoid this, we would have to append a list of lexical items affected to (49). Statement (48) is simpler and hence preferred in accordance with our general evaluative criterion. We choose our systematic phonemic representations in such a way that the phonological rules are maximally simple.

The notion of maximally simple phonological rules further implies that at least some of the rules be extrinsically ordered. Consider the following data from a South Russian dialect (the Don). Seven vowels are distinct; i, u, e, o, ϵ, $ɔ$, and a. They may be represented in the following way:

(52)

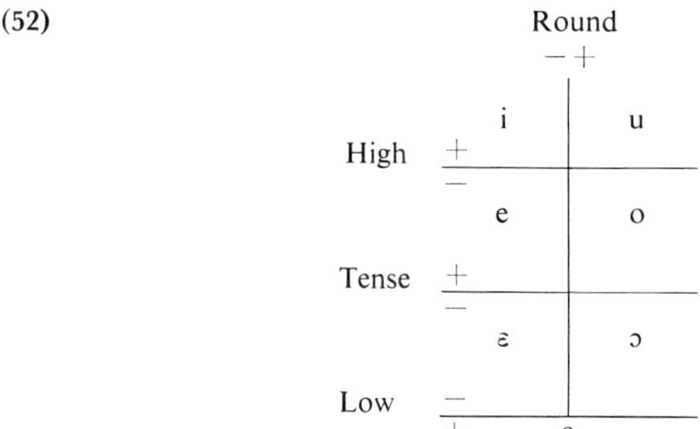

This seven-way distinction occurs only when the vowels are stressed. In a first prestressed syllable following a palatalized consonant, we find only i, u, and a. The nonhigh vowels (with the exception of systematic phonemic o and $ɔ$ which do not occur following a palatalized consonant), alternate with i and a. If the stressed vowel is high (i or u), an a manifests nonhigh vowels; if the vowel is nonhigh, an i manifests them. Thus

(53)   (a)   e ɛ a ⟶ a/Ç ___ (C) $\begin{Bmatrix} í \\ ú \end{Bmatrix}$

              (b)   e ɛ a ⟶ i/Ç ___ (C) $\begin{Bmatrix} é & ó \\ ɛ́ & ɔ́ \\ & á \end{Bmatrix}$

There is also a rule that diphthongizes the stressed, tense e and o:

(54)   (a)   é ⟶ íé

                             (b)   ó ⟶ úó

A second dialect (the Obojansk) is similar to the Don except in (53b) wherein the stressed vowels of the environment exclude systematic phonemic e and o; they condition a pretonic vowel as systematic phonemic i and u do. Rule (53) appears in the Obojansk dialect as follows:

(55)   (a)   e ɛ a ⟶ a/Ç ___ (C) $\begin{Bmatrix} í & ú \\ é & ó \end{Bmatrix}$

              (b)   e ɛ a ⟶ i/Ç ___ (C) $\begin{Bmatrix} ɛ́ & ɔ́ \\ & á \end{Bmatrix}$

If we try to state (55) in terms of systematic phonemes, then (55a) must include in the environment of the rule stressed vowels that are [+ high] (i and u) or

[— high, —low, +tense] (*e* and *o*). And (55b) must include [—high, —low, —tense] (*ɛ* and *ɔ*) or [+ low] (*a*) vowels. If we order (54) *before* (55) in the Obojansk dialect, we may state (55) more simply in terms of a distinction between [+ high] stressed vowels and [— high] stressed vowels as in the Don. Here rule (54) adds to the environment in which (55a) may apply (and simultaneously subtracts from the environments in which (55b) may apply) by replacing a nonhigh *e* and *o* with diphthongs having an initial high vowel. By ordering (54) before (55) and by allowing phonological rules to apply on some representation intermediate between the systematic phonemic and systematic phonetic representations as well as the systematic phonemic representation itself, we correctly indicate the systematic phonetic forms without complicating the environment of (55) (cf. Halle 1962: 57–58). We require no new primitives to express this, for the possible ordering of transformational rules already provides us with the necessary relationships. The two dialects differ, then, not in that their rules are different but in that their rules are alike but ordered differently. Additional arguments for the ordering of phonological rules are presented in Chomsky and Halle 1968: 340–50 and Postal 1968: 140–52.

Phonological rules are also similar to transformational rules within syntax in that some of them may apply cyclically. In English, for example, such distinctions in stress between

(56)   light housekeeper   'a person who does light housekeeping'

             lighthouse keeper   'a person who keeps lighthouses'

can be predicted from information within the surface structure: the syntactic hierarchy and the categories involved. Cf. Chomsky, Halle, and Lukoff 1956 and Chomsky and Halle 1968: 15–24 et passim. The statements that do this must first operate on the lowest elements within the hierarchy and then reapply until the largest domain—most inclusive category, here NP—is reached. The rules specifying stress levels in (56) involve *n*-ary values as the detail rules do; but cyclic application of rules switching + or — values can also be shown to be necessary. Cf. Kisseberth 1972. Again, this application requires no new primitives, for cyclic rule application is already required within syntax. The phonological rules are divided into two groups: the cyclic rules that require information of the surface structure, and postcyclic rules, which do not.

Turning again to the systematic phonemic representation, we find a pattern that is as yet unstated. There are redundancies within the sequence of segments of a lexical entry, e.g., those within consonant clusters of English discussed in Chapter 4 and Chapter 9. If we reconsider the example of *sp* initially in English, a complete specification of *s* as [— vocalic, + consonantal, + coronal, + anterior, + strident, + continuant, — voice] ([+ coronal, + anterior] identifies a dental segment) and *p* as [— vocalic, + consonantal,

— coronal, + anterior, — nasal, — strident, — continuant, — voice] ([— coronal, + anterior] identifies a labial segment) misses the pattern that *s* is the only consonant that occurs before *p* (or any other obstruent) initially within any lexical item. If we know that the second segment is [— vocalic, + consonantal], i.e., an obstruent, and if we know that the first segment is [— vocalic], i.e., not a vowel, then we know that the first segment must also—in English—contain the remaining values of the features of *s*, above. The multiple notation of these predictable features in a large number of lexical items misses a pattern. To state this regularity of English, we simply omit the predictable features of *s* in this environment and add a single statement that adds values for *s* in all lexical items wherein *s* occurs in the position indicated. The rules that do this are *morpheme structure rules* (cf. Halle 1962: 58–62 and Chomsky and Halle 1968: 380–89) or *morpheme structure conditions* (Stanley 1967). They in general account for the phenomena covered by irresoluble syncretisms in Hjelmslevian theory: subclassification and selection in Bloomfieldian theory; phoneme classes and constructions in post-Bloomfieldian and tagmemic theories; neutralization in Praguean theory; prosodies in Firthian theory; and the hypophonology of stratificational theory. The assumed domains of such patterning may differ from theory to theory. In stratificational theory, the domain was the cluster; in Bloomfieldian theory the word was the chosen domain, and in Firthian theory, the domain may possibly extend to the utterance itself if the requisite prosodies are found.

The patterns attributed to morpheme structure statements above involve sequential redundancies. Features are determined from those is adjacent segments. We now observe an additional pattern. In the Russian example (52), we know that if a segment is [+ vocalic, — consonantal, + low], it is also [— round]. This is deducible solely from features within the segment. Such simultaneous redundancies may arise only within a theory that permits unordered conjunctions of properties within phonology, for example, the glossemes of Hjelmslevian theory, the features of Praguean theory, the exponents of Firthian theory, and the phonons of stratificational theory.

Still further redundancies may be noted. In *all* languages, [+ vocalic, — consonantal] segments, i.e., vowels, are [+ continuant]. *All* [+ vocalic, — consonantal, + high] segments are [— low]; all high vowels are nonlow. Since these are universal, their specification should be stated within the theory, not within the individual grammars. Such statements are incorporated within the account of a phenomenon termed *naturalness* (Chomsky and Halle 1968: 400–402).

It is observed (1) that certain systems of systematic phonemes are "more generally found" (Chomsky and Halle 1968: 411) among the languages of the world; (2) that certain syllable types (CV) and more frequent than others (CCVC); and (3) that certain phonological rules (*k* —→ *č*) recur more frequently than others (*k* —→*k̑*). It is claimed that these phenomena are properties of language, and any theory of language should account for them. To incorporate (1) and (2) into the theory, we must construct some formal way of distinguishing between more natural and less natural systems of systematic phonemes and their sequences within the lexical items of languages. The distinction is referred to simplicity, viz., the grammar of a language with a less natural system of systematic phonemes or with less natural possible sequences of them should necessarily be less simple than that of a more natural language, all other things being equal. The formal mechanism for this is a set of *marking conventions* (Chomsky and Halle 1968: 403–14) added to the theory to specify + and − values of features (as the morpheme structure statements did) independently of individual grammars. In addition to + and − values of features, we now admit an *m* (marked) value and a *u* (unmarked) value. The *u* corresponds to a natural value of the feature, and the *m*, to an unnatural value. The simplicity of a systematic phonemic system is now calculated in terms of +'s, −'s, and *m*'s before the marking conventions convert the *u* and *m* values to + or −. The *u*, natural value, adds nothing to the complexity of individual grammars; and simplicity may be gained by maximizing the *u*'s within the lexicon, since they add nothing to complexity. All things being equal, the grammar of a language that has more *u*'s will be simpler and hence (it is claimed) more natural and more common among the languages of the world. Formally, the less simple grammar is said to be the more marked, and the simpler grammar, the less marked. Markedness is the formal correlate to naturalness (common and less common) within data.

The distinction of marked and unmarked recalls the marked: unmarked property of members of an opposition in Praguean theory; here, however, it is extended beyond markedness of segments to markedness of systems of segments and their sequences. The property of naturalness requires a set of empiric primitives for its expression, just as the ordering within phonological systems required it in Praguean theory. Had we assumed a set of nonempiric primitives, we could not have distinguished between a natural five-vowel systematic phoneme system *i, u, e, o,* and *a* and a five-vowel system *i, ü, e,* ʌ, and *a*. Because nonempiric primitives have no inherent relation to data, any system of five terms would be equivalent to any other, as would any five components of a class in Hjelmslevian theory. It is only when empiric primitives are employed that we can distinguish among terms of a system and relate them in ways (here, markedness) that are other than purely abstract.

The third expression of naturalness—by phonological rule—presupposes the formulation of marking conventions. Let us assume a system of systematic phonemic consonants as follows:

(57)   p   t   k

                                         b   d   g

                                                 s

If this language contains a rule $k/g \rightarrow \check{c}/\check{3}$ in some environment, this may be expressed as

(58)
$$
\begin{bmatrix} -\text{vocalic} \\ +\text{consonantal} \\ -\text{anterior} \end{bmatrix} \longrightarrow \begin{bmatrix} +\text{coronal} \\ +\text{delayed release} \\ +\text{strident} \\ -\text{back} \end{bmatrix} \quad \text{in some environment}
$$

Let us also assume a language which differs only in that it contains an alternative rule to (58), in which $k/g \rightarrow \underset{\wedge}{k}/\underset{\wedge}{g}$, expressed as (59):

(59)
$$
\begin{bmatrix} -\text{vocalic} \\ +\text{consonantal} \\ -\text{anterior} \end{bmatrix} \longrightarrow [-\text{back}] \quad \text{in some environment}
$$

In the first language, the resultant systematic phonetic system contains $\check{c}/\check{3}$ opposed to the $\underset{\wedge}{k}/\underset{\wedge}{g}$ of the second; but the former systematic phonetic system is more natural than the latter because the phonological rule (58) that produces it is more natural than (59). If we again refer naturalness to the formal property of simplicity, then (58) must somehow be made simpler than (59).

To implement this let us consider the following marking conventions (cf. Chomsky and Halle 1968: 421–22):

(60)

    (a) $[\text{u coronal}] \longrightarrow [+\text{coronal}] \Big/ \begin{bmatrix} \underline{} \\ -\text{anterior} \\ -\text{back} \end{bmatrix}$

    (b) $[\text{u delayed release}] \longrightarrow [+\text{delayed release}] \Big/ \begin{bmatrix} \underline{} \\ +\text{coronal} \\ -\text{anterior} \end{bmatrix}$

    (c) $[\text{u strident}] \longrightarrow [+\text{strident}] \Big/ \begin{bmatrix} \underline{} \\ +\text{delayed release} \\ +\text{coronal} \end{bmatrix}$

By linking phonological rules, specifically their output, to the environment plus output of the marking conventions, we allow the marking conventions to apply to segments produced by the structural change of phonological rules as well as to items within the lexicon. Such application is made possible by restricting linkage so that (1) the features in the structural change of the phonological rule must recur with the same values in the environment of the marking convention, (2) the segment produced by the structural change of the phonological rule must agree with the environment of the marking convention, and (3) the structural change of the phonological rule must not include the structural change of the marking convention.

We can now simplify (58) as follows:

(61)
$$
\begin{bmatrix}
-\text{vocalic} \\
+\text{consonantal} \\
-\text{anterior}
\end{bmatrix}
\rightarrow [-\text{back}] \qquad \text{in some environment}
$$

The marking convention (60a) meets all three conditions for linkage with (61) and specifies the value [+ coronal]. This in turn meets conditions for applying the marking convention (60b), which specifies [+ delayed release]; and this segment is further specified as [+ strident] by (60c). But (61) is now identical to (59), and if (59) remains unchanged, it predicts č/ǯ, as does (61). To prevent this we must add features to the structural change of (59) such that it is no longer linked to the marking conventions of (60):

(62)
$$
\begin{bmatrix}
-\text{vocalic} \\
+\text{consonantal} \\
-\text{anterior}
\end{bmatrix}
\rightarrow
\begin{bmatrix}
-\text{back} \\
-\text{coronal}
\end{bmatrix}
\qquad \text{in some enviroment}
$$

The addition of [− coronal] in (62) breaks the linkage to (60a)—specifically, the third condition for linkage—and none of the conventions of (60) applies, correctly predicting ḳ and g̑. Now, the more natural phonological rule (61) is the simpler. Marking conventions that are additionally linked to phonological rules (not all are) are termed *linking rules* (Chomsky and Halle 1968: 419–35).

In the above example, the more natural phonological rule corresponded to the more natural systematic phonetic system, and the less natural phonological rule to the less natural systematic phonetic system. It may be that a language is natural with respect to sequence of systematic phonemes, but unnatural with respect to sequence of systematic phonetic segments. The naturalness in this portion of a language is not incorporated within the above formal mechanism and finds no expression.

If the notion of the marking conventions is completely developed, it may be that they will account for all the patterns previously attributed to the morpheme structure statements. There would be a level of representation completely in terms of *u* and *m* values of features, which by the marking conventions would be converted to + or − values. No unlisted features would exist in this version and hence the expression of the morpheme structure patterns would fall completely within the province of the conventions (cf. Postal 1968: 166–67). As presented in Chomsky and Halle 1968, the representation of lexical items prior to the application of the conventions may contain + and − values as well as *u* and *m*. However this may be eventually resolved, the phonological component operates on the output of the redundancy statements, and by application of phonological and detail rules provides an interpretation of language as sound data.

Summary

In summarizing transformational generative grammar, we assume, along with Chomsky (1965: 65–66), that we do in fact have a way of identifying specific categories in a universal fashion; that is, we will assume a universal categorial subcomponent. As in our interpretation of Bloomfieldian theory, we present an idealized form of the theory.

The primitives of the theory include:

1. *A set of empiric, phonetic primitives*
2. *A set of empiric, semantic primitives*
3. *Category*
4. *Made-up-of or is-a*
5. *Conjunction*
6. *Disjunction*
7. *Linearity*
8. *Cyclical order*
9. *Contextual feature*
10. *Inherent feature*
11. *Transformation:*   a complex primitive of add, delete, replace, and permute (but cf. Chomsky 1965: 144–45)
12. *Optional*
13. *Obligatory*
14. *Identity and nonidentity*

With these primitives we may construct the following definitions:

1. *Rewrite rule:*   Defined by a category standing in a relationship of made-up-of to one or more categories. The first category is said to "dominate" (Chomsky 1961a: 123) the categories that make it up. Notice that there may occur more than one made-up-of relationship between the category and its constituent categories. As in a Hjelmslevian hierarchy, we can identify "ranks" of dominance.
2. *Categorial subcomponent:*   Defined by a sequence of rewrite rules (not further specified here), a strict subcategorizational rule on the order of (30), a context-free subcategorizational rule on the order of (32), and a selectional subcategorizational rule on the order of (37). The categorial relationships defined by the conjunction of these four portions of the categorial subcomponent identify the categories to which we have given the labels S, NP, VP, etc., as well as lexical and grammatical categories. A lexical category is one rewritten by a context-sensitive subcategorizational rule (strict or selectional). A major category is one that dominates a lexical category. Finally, syntactic features may be defined as the contextual and inherent features introduced

by the subcategorizational rules of the categorial subcomponent. Because the categorial subcomponent is universal to all languages, the syntactic features are likewise universal to all languages.

3. *Phrase marker:*   Defined as any instantiation of the rules of the categorial subcomponent selecting one possibility at each point a category is made up of disjunctively related categories or is made up of linear sequence in which one or more is optional. This may be represented as a subset of the rules of the categorial subcomponent, a branching-tree diagram, or a labeled bracketing (Chomsky 1965: 64).

4. *Formative:*   Defined by a configuration of phonetic primitives not further specified here (cf. above).

5. *Definition:*   Defined by a configuration of semantic primitives (cf. the references above).

6. *Complex symbol:*   Defined as a conjunction of contextual and inherent features.

7. *Lexical entry:*   Defined by the conjunction of a formative, definition, and complex symbol.

8. *Lexical redundancy rule:*   Defined as (a) a transformation that adds to the syntactic features of the complex symbol of a lexical entry any contextual, syntactic feature within the categorial component not present within the complex symbol of the lexical entry, marking it with a minus, and (b) a transformation that adds to the inherent, syntactic features of a complex symbol of a lexical entry that portion of the hierarchy of inherent syntactic features of the categorial subcomponent that is identified by the inherent, syntactic feature(s) noted within the complex symbol of the lexical entry. If none is entered within the complex symbol of a lexical entry, e.g., as in a [+V] entry, (b) does not apply.

9. *Lexical rule:*   Defined as a transformation that replaces a complex symbol of a phrase marker of the categorial subcomponent with a lexical entry if the complex symbol of the lexical entry is not nonidentical with the complex symbol of the phrase marker.

10. *Lexicon:*   Defined as the conjunction of lexical entries, lexical redundancy rule, and lexical rule.

11. *Transformational rule:*   Defined by the association of a transformation with a phrase marker.

12. *Derived phrase marker:*   Defined as the phrase marker that is the result of applying a transformational rule to a phrase marker. A transformational rule may affect a whole phrase marker or a portion thereof. In either case the resulting whole phrase marker is a derived phrase marker.

13. *Transformational subcomponent:*   Defined as an ordered set of optional and obligatory transformational rules; certain of them are cyclically ordered with respect to the base phrase markers, such that they apply first to the portion of a phrase marker dominated by the S category lowest in the hierarchy, then the next lowest until the highest S of the hierarchy is affected.

14. *Final derived phrase marker:*   Defined as the phrase marker to which no additional obligatory transformational rules are applicable.

15. *Surface structure:*   Defined as the conjunction of final derived phrase

markers. We may speak of the "surface structure of a sentence," meaning the individual, final derived phrase marker that predicts that piece of data.

16. *Well-formed surface structure:*   Defined as a surface structure with no occurrence of an internal sentence boundary. The latter is a term defined within the universal categorial subcomponent in the manner of other categories.

17. *Well-formed deep structure:*   Defined as a deep structure that may be transformed into a well-formed surface structure.

The summary of transformational generative grammar provides a definition of competence. As given, it admits no dialectal variation (cf. Chomsky 1965: 3). The term "language" is usually reserved for the set of phonetic interpretations of surface structures and is not applied to the patterned relationships between sound and meaning (cf., for example, Chomsky 1964b: 915). Transformational generative grammar predicts or *generates* (Chomsky 1961a: 120; 1965: 4 and 8–9; 1967: 407; and 1968: 26) a set of associations of "sound" with "meaning"; the last two terms can now be identified with the result of the interpretation of surface and deep structure, respectively.

It was indicated above that a description or *grammar* (Chomsky 1965: 25) of competence predicts an unlimited number of phrase markers and hence an unlimited number of associations of sound with meaning. This is provided for in the theory by permitting the initial category of the categorial subcomponent (S) to dominate itself as optional category at some point within the categorial subcomponent, and further by cyclically ordering these rules to reapply in sequence from the beginning for each such noninitial S. This, in turn, implies that S can be chosen again as a describing component in the second application of the rules, and so forth, without limit. Rewrite rules with such self-dominance are *recursive* (Chomsky 1961a: 123–24 and 1965: 137). This does not claim that all these predicted pairs of sound and meaning are attested nor that they ever will or can be. But transformational generative grammar is not a theory of what can or cannot be uttered; it is a theory of competence, what a speaker of a language knows. The statements that constrain the occurrence of predicted associations lie within the study of competence. The claim, then, is that a person who has competence in a specific language knows an unlimited number of objects; it is not claimed that, given world enough and time, he would or could utter all paired associations that he knows.

The set of paired associations of sound and meaning that a transformational generative grammar predicts are termed *grammatical* (Chomsky 1965: 11 and 19). As what a person knows—his competence—is not to be confused with his behavior, so the notion of grammatical is not to be confused with the experimental results cast in terms of "acceptability." Recall that experimental techniques intended to reveal portions of language are not taken as conclusively valid; competence is abstract, and intuitive judgments or introspection may not necessarily reveal competence, but reflect performance. Grammaticality and acceptability are distinct notions that do not necessarily coincide, although they did in the discussion of co-occurrence restrictions and subcategorization. There, degree of grammaticality identified as violation at varying points within a hierarchy matched judgments of the degree of deviance.

An accounting within this theory will include the following:

1. A definition of the lexical entries
2. A definition of the transformational component
3. A semantic interpretation of well-formed deep structures
4. A phonological interpretation of the well-formed surface structures
5. An evaluation of (1)–(4)
6. A reworking of (1)–(4) until (5) is maximally satisfied

In its ideal form, transformational generative grammar claims that individual languages differ among themselves only in terms of the lexical and transformational portions of syntax and in terms of the interpretations. The base—minus the lexical entries—is universal, requiring no definition from language to language.

The evaluation of accountings is generally the same as what we have seen in previous theories, a version of simplicity or generality. By virtue of being distinct, each theory defines a distinct pattern, including what may be or may not be (partially) identical. Simplicity of an accounting is a scale of the expression of pattern; "simpler" is the expression of more pattern, and "less simple" is the expression of less pattern. It is by maximization of permitted identity (equivalent to maximizing the pattern, stating all of it) that simplicity or generality is achieved. Since possible pattern, and thus identity and partial identity, varies from theory to theory, so must the implementation of simplicity vary. The constraints on theory—the evaluation of theories—are constraints on possible pattern and hence possible simplicity. In Hjelmslevian theory these were summed as "appropriateness." In transformational generative grammar this is expressed as "linguistically significant generalizations" (Chomsky 1965: 42, 93, 95, and 97). We do not know beforehand what is appropriate. We make up our theory arbitrarily. Its value emerges slowly from the application of the theory to the data; it is an empirical question of testing. Only with gradual confirmation and no invalidation do we discover that the theory or linguistic generalization is appropriate or linguistically significant and from this, what is simple.

Recalling Saussure's realism, it is claimed in transformational generative grammar that the terms of an accounting are just those that are isomorphic with the representation of a speaker's competence (Katz 1964: 129). The claim that the simplest accounting in these terms is the better translates into the claim that manifest language is, within its own locus, represented in the simplest possible way within the bounds of possible representation. Our descriptions of the bits and pieces of English in the preceding section were constructed arbitrarily. In a complete accounting of English, these may be justified as the simplest of those statements and perhaps lead to simplifications elsewhere. If so, our accounting (like the theory itself) has been arbitrarily, but appropriately constructed (cf. Chomsky 1957: 56). Being the simplest provided by the theory, it is the preferred.

This says nothing of how we recognize simplicity. In Bloomfieldian theory, it was generally recognized by the lesser number of statements, and likewise in post-Bloomfieldian theory. Recall, for example, the criterion of pattern congruity. Simplicity is here equated with brevity (cf., for example, Halle 1961: 90–91). This equation requires a formalization of the theory for its consistent application. This is the motivation for the introduction of abbreviatory devices (cf. Chomsky 1965: 42–44) that are intended to permit reduction of the length of accountings at just those points where simplicity or pattern is predicated of the data.

An accounting that predicts only the observed utterances or primary data (Chomsky 1964b: 924) is said to be *observationally adequate* (Chomsky 1964b: 923–24). One that expresses the pattern of a speaker's competence is *descriptively adequate* (Chomsky 1964b: 924 and 1965: 24). Descriptive adequacy, then, corresponds to the simplest (formally, the shortest) accounting available for the data of competence in the theory. The simplest will be closer to competence on the assumption that the representation of that competence is the simplest possible within the parameters of possible accounting/ competence. A third adequacy—*explanatory adequacy* (Chomsky 1964b: 924 and 1965: 25–27 and 30–37)—is an evaluation of theories and corresponds to our "general, but not too general" constraint on theories (cf. Chomsky 1965: 34–35). (The criteria in Chomsky 1965: 30–34 do not exclude in principle the possibility that an imagined operational theory may satisfy them. Explanatory adequacy is not then equivalent to "explanatory theory" as introduced in Chapter 1. The theory here is, however, one that is explanatory in the sense we have used the term.) The assumption that competence is represented in the simplest possible way within the framework of the theory, maximizing possible pattern, further constrains the notion of competence; it lessens the generality of the theory by excluding the less than maximally simple ones as possible accountings with respect to a given set of data. The ideal of a universal base is another point at which the variety of possible language—and hence the generality of the theory—may be constrained. Explanatory adequacy is a goal, not an achievement. Ideally, we may expect to narrow the range of possible language, such that for any set of data there would be a single possible accounting (cf. Chomsky 1965: 36–37), but this goal has not been attained by any of our theories.

ADDITIONAL READING

CHOMSKY, NOAM. 1957. *Syntactic Structures*. The Hague: Mouton & Co.

———. 1960. "Explanatory models in linguistics," in *Logic, Methodology, and Philosophy of Science*, eds. E. Nagel, P. Suppes, and A. Tarski. Stanford: Stanford University Press.

———. 1961. "Some methodological remarks on generative grammar." *Word* 17. 219–39.

———. 1965. *Aspects of the Theory of Syntax*. Cambridge, Massachusetts: The M.I.T. Press.

———. 1968. *Language and Mind*. New York: Harcourt, Brace & World, Inc.

CHOMSKY, NOAM, and MORRIS HALLE. 1965. "Some controversial questions in phonological theory." *Journal of Linguistics* 1. 97–138.

———. 1968. *The Sound Pattern of English*. New York: Harper & Row, Publishers.

HALLE, MORRIS. 1961. "On the role of simplicity in linguistic descriptions," in *Structure of Language and Its Mathematical Aspects* (= *Proceedings of the 12th Symposium in Applied Mathematics*), ed. Roman Jakobson. Providence: American Mathematical Society.

———. 1962. "Phonology in generative grammar." *Word* 18. 54–72.

KATZ, JERROLD J. 1967. "Recent issues in semantic theory." *Foundations of Language* 3. 124–94.

———. 1972. *Semantic Theory*. New York: Harper & Row, Publishers.

KATZ, JERROLD J., and PAUL M. POSTAL. 1964. *An Integrated Theory of Linguistic Descriptions*. Cambridge, Massachusetts: The M.I.T. Press.

CHAPTER **11**

Final Comment

This investigation of nine theories began with the assumption that linguistics is a science and that its purpose is to define language. One might here raise the issue of justification of these assumptions by posing the questions "Is linguistics in fact a science?" and "What then *is* language?" But the questions actually have little if any real importance.

An answer to the first is "As much as any other field of study is or can be." Science may be defined as a way of looking at an object, but it turns out that there is more than one principle of examination. "Looking" involves several components, and we may choose alternatives for each. There is no single notion of science, and we may adopt different modes of looking while remaining within its boundaries. The application of science to an object determines *a* science. Thus, the application of science or scientific methodology to objects that seem language-like to us determines the science of linguistics; but in this way, examination of *any* object can be a science. This approach to whether linguistics is a science is so broad that it means nothing.

We may ask rather "Does the application of science to language data yield an 'understanding', a definition of language?" implying that linguistics can be a science only if the answer is yes. This does not help much either. In answer, a thoughtful linguist would have to admit that he doesn't know what language is. He may claim the ability to recognize a possible one when he sees it and give perhaps some general criteria for that recognition. Still, no one knows all the properties of language nor even, really, if the ones so far postulated are the right ones. He will quite probably place different degrees of faith in the correctness of different properties. This ignorance is present in all sciences; no active science has defined its subject matter—identified it, perhaps, but defined it, no. If this were true, there would be no activity in that science and no problems to interest anyone. That we do not know what language is and cannot provide a definition of it is unimportant except as a statement of fact. It has nothing to do with linguistics as a science. All that our assumption regarding linguistics and science meant and means is (1) that we take it on faith that there is something to talk about—we assume the possibility of pattern, and (2) that we will investigate that possibility within a certain framework.

Bibliography

ALGEO, JOHN. 1967. "On defining a stratum." *Emory University Quarterly* 23. 263–94.

ALLEN W. S. 1951. "Some prosodic aspects of retroflexion and aspiration in Sanskrit." *Bulletin of the School of Oriental and African Studies* 13. 939–46.

———. 1954. "Retroflexion in Sanskrit: Prosodic technique and its relevance to comparative statement." *Bulletin of the School of Oriental and African Studies* 16. 556–65.

———. 1956. "Structure and system in the Abaza verbal complex." *Transactions of the Philological Society* 127–76.

———. 1957. "Aspiration in the Hāṛautī Nominal," in *Studies in Linguistic Analysis* (1957). Oxford: Basil Blackwell.

ARTYMOVIČ, A. 1964. "On the potentiality of language," reprinted in *A Prague School Reader in Linguistics*, ed. Josef Vachek. Bloomington: Indiana University Press.

AUSTERLITZ, ROBERT. 1964. "Review of Vachek (1964)." *Word* 20. 458–65.

AUSTIN, WILLIAM M. 1957. "Criteria for phonetic similarity." *Language* 33. 538–44.

BENNETT, DAVID C. 1968. "English prepositions: a stratificational approach." *Journal of Linguistics* 4. 153–72.

BLOCH, BERNARD. 1941. "Phonemic overlapping." *American Speech* 16. 278–84. Reprinted in Joos (1958).

———. 1946. "Studies in colloquial Japanese II: Syntax." *Language* 22. 200–248. Reprinted in Joos (1958).

———. 1947. "English verb inflection." *Language* 23. 399–418. Reprinted in Joos (1958).

———. 1948. "A set of postulates for phonemic analysis." *Language* 24. 3–46.

BLOCH, BERNARD. 1950. "Studies in colloquial Japanese IV: Phonemics." *Language* 26. 86–125. Reprinted in Joos (1958).

———. 1953. "Contrast." *Language* 29. 59–61.

BLOCH, BERNARD, and GEORGE L. TRAGER. 1942. *Outline of Linguistic Analysis.* Baltimore: Linguistic Society of America.

BLOOMFIELD, LEONARD. 1924. Review of Saussure, *Cours de linguistique générale. Modern Language Journal* 8. 317–19. Reprinted in Hockett (1970).

———. 1926. "A set of postulates for the science of language." *Language* 2. 153–64. Reprinted in *International Journal of American Linguistics* 15. 195–202 (1949), in Joos (1958), and in Hockett (1970).

———. 1927. "On recent work in general linguistics." *Modern Philology* 25. 211–30. Reprinted in Hockett (1970).

———. 1933. *Language.* New York: Henry Holt and Company.

———. 1935. "The stressed vowels of American English." *Language* 11. 97–116. Reprinted in Hockett (1970).

———. 1936. "Language or ideas." *Language* 12. 89–95. Reprinted in Hockett (1970).

———. 1939a. *Linguistic Aspects of Science* (= *International Encyclopedia of Unified Science*, Vol. 1, No. 4). Chicago: The University of Chicago Press.

———. 1939b. "Menomini morphophonemics." *Travaux du Cercle Linguistique de Prague* 8. 105–15.

———. 1942. "Outline of Ilocano syntax." *Language* 18. 193–200.

———. 1943. "Meaning." *Monatshefte für deutschen Unterricht* 35. 101–6. Reprinted in Hockett (1970).

———. 1944. "Secondary and tertiary responses to language." *Language* 20. 45–55. Reprinted in Hockett (1970).

BÜHLER, KARL. 1934. *Sprachtheorie.* Jena: Gustav Fischer.

BURSILL-HALL, G. L. 1960. "Levels analysis: J. R. Firth's theories of linguistic analysis." *Canadian Journal of Linguistics* 6. 124–35.

———. 1961. "Levels' analysis: J. R. Firth's theories of linguistic analysis (Part II)." *Canadian Journal of Linguistics* 6. 164–91.

CARNOCHAN, J. 1951. "A study of quantity in Hausa." *Bulletin of the School of Oriental and African Studies* 13. 1032–44.

———. 1952. "Glottalisation in Hausa." *Transactions of the Philological Society* 78–109.

———. 1957. "Gemination in Hausa," in *Studies in Linguistic Analysis* (1957). Oxford: Basil Blackwell.

CHOMSKY, NOAM. 1956. "Three models for the description of language." *IRE Transactions on Information Theory* IT-2. 113–24.

———. 1957. *Syntactic Structures.* The Hague: Mouton & Co.

———. 1960. "Explanatory models in linguistics," in *Logic, Methodology, and Philosophy of Science*, eds. E. Nagel, P. Suppes, and A. Tarski. Stanford: Stanford University Press.

———. 1961a. "On the notion 'rule of grammar'," in *Structure of Language and Its Mathematical Aspects* (= *Proceedings of the 12th Symposium in Applied Mathematics*), ed. Roman Jakobson. Providence: American Mathematical Society.

CHOMSKY, NOAM. 1961b. "Some methodological remarks on generative grammar." *Word* 17. 219–39.

———. 1962. "A transformational approach to syntax," in *Third Texas Conference on Problems of Linguistic Analysis in English,* ed. Archibald A. Hill. Austin: The University of Texas.

———. 1964a. *Current Issues in Linguistic Theory.* The Hague: Mouton & Co.

———. 1964b. "The logical basis of linguistic theory," in *Proceedings of the Ninth International Congress of Linguists,* ed. Horace G. Lunt. The Hague: Mouton & Co.

———. 1965. *Aspects of the Theory of Syntax.* Cambridge, Massachusetts: The M.I.T. Press.

———. 1966. *Topics in the Theory of Generative Grammar.* The Hague: Mouton & Co.

———. 1967. "The formal nature of language," in *Biological Foundations of Language,* Eric H. Lenneberg. New York: John Wiley & Sons, Inc.

———. 1968. *Language and Mind.* New York: Harcourt, Brace & World, Inc.

———. 1970a. "Deep structure, surface structure, and semantic interpretation," in *Studies in General and Oriental Linguistics,* eds. Roman Jakobson and Shigeo Kawamoto. Tokyo: TEC Company, Ltd.

———. 1970b. "Problems of explanation in linguistics," in *Explanation in the Behavioral Sciences,* ed. Robert Borger and Frank Cioffi. Cambridge: Cambridge University Press.

———. 1970c. "Remarks on nominalization," in *Readings in English Transformational Grammar,* eds. Roderick A. Jacobs and Peter S. Rosenbaum. Waltham, Massachusetts: Ginn and Company.

CHOMSKY, NOAM, and MORRIS HALLE. 1965. "Some controversial questions in phonological theory." *Journal of Linguistics* 1. 97–138.

———. 1968. *The Sound Pattern of English.* New York: Harper & Row, Publishers.

CHOMSKY, NOAM, MORRIS HALLE, and FRED LUKOFF. 1956. "On accent and juncture in English," in *For Roman Jakobson,* eds. Morris Halle *et al.* The Hague: Mouton & Co.

COOK, WALTER A., S. J. 1969. *Introduction to Tagmemic Analysis.* New York: Holt, Rinehart and Winston, Inc.

EGE, NIELS. 1949. "Le signe linguistique est arbitraire." *Travaux du Cercle Linguistique de Copenhague* 5. 11–29.

ENGLER, RUDOLF. 1968. *Lexique de la terminologie saussurienne.* Utrecht: Spectrum.

FILLMORE, CHARLES J., and D. TERENCE LANGENDOEN, eds. 1971. *Studies in Linguistic Semantics.* New York: Holt, Rinehart and Winston, Inc.

FIRTH, J. R. 1956. "Linguistic analysis and translation," in *For Roman Jakobson,* eds. Morris Halle *et al.* The Hague: Mouton & Co. Reprinted in Palmer (1968).

———. 1957a. "Applications of general linguistics." *Transactions of the Philological Society* 1–14. Reprinted in Palmer (1968).

———. 1957b. *Papers in Linguistics 1934–1951.* Oxford: Oxford University Press.

———. 1957c. "A synopsis of linguistic theory 1930–55," in *Studies in Linguistic Analysis* (1957). Oxford: Basil Blackwell.

FISCHER-JØRGENSEN, ELI. 1949. "Remarques sur les principes de l'analyse phonémique." *Travaux du Cercle Linguistique de Copenhague* 5. 214–34.

FISCHER-JØRGENSEN, ELI. 1952a. "On the definition of phoneme categories on a distributional basis." *Acta Linguistica* 7. 8–39.

———. 1952b. "The phonetic basis for identification of phonemic elements." *The Journal of the Acoustical Society of America* 24. 611–17.

———. 1956. "The commutation test and its application to phonemic analysis," in *For Roman Jakobson*, eds. Morris Halle *et al.* The Hague: Mouton & Co.

FLEMING, ILAH. 1969. "Stratificational theory: an annotated bibliography." *Journal of English Linguistics* 3. 37–65.

FRIES, CHARLES C. 1954. "Meaning and linguistic analysis." *Language* 30. 57–68.

FRIES, CHARLES C., and KENNETH L. PIKE. 1949. "Coexistent phonemic systems." *Language* 25. 29–50.

GARVIN, PAUL L. 1954. "Review of Hjelmslev, *Prolegomena to a Theory of Language.*" *Language* 30. 69–96.

GLEASON, H. A., JR. 1964. "The organization of language: a stratificational view," in *Report of the Fifteenth Annual (First International) Round Table Meeting on Linguistics and Language Studies (= Monograph Series on Languages and Linguistics 17)*, ed. C. I. J. M. Stuart. Washington, D.C.: Georgetown University Press.

GODEL, ROBERT. 1957. *Les sources manuscrites du Cours de linguistique générale de F. de Saussure.* Geneva: Librairie E. Droz.

———. 1961. "L'école saussurienne de Genève," in *Trends in European and American Linguistics 1930–1960*, eds. Christine Mohrmann, Alf Sommerfelt, and Joshua Whatmough. Utrecht: Spectrum.

———. 1966. "F. de Saussure's theory of language," in *Current Trends in Linguistics III*, ed. Thomas A. Sebeok. The Hague: Mouton & Co.

HAAS, W. 1954. "On defining linguistic units." *Transactions of the Philological Society* 54–84.

———. 1966. "Linguistic relevance," in *In Memory of J. R. Firth*, eds. C. E. Bazell, J. C. Catford, M. A. K. Halliday, and R. H. Robins. London: Longmans, Green, and Co. Ltd.

HALLE, MORRIS. 1957. "In defense of the number two," in *Studies Presented to J. Whatmough*, ed. E. Pulgram. The Hague: Mouton & Co.

———. 1961. "On the role of simplicity in linguistic descriptions," in *Structure of Language and Its Mathematical Aspects (= Proceedings of the 12th Symposium in Applied Mathematics)*, ed. Roman Jakobson. Providence: American Mathematical Society.

———. 1962. "Phonology in generative grammar." *Word* 18. 54–72.

HALLIDAY, M. A. K. 1956. "Grammatical categories in modern Chinese." *Transactions of the Philological Society* 177–224.

———. 1957. "Some aspects of systematic description and comparison in grammatical analysis," in *Studies in Linguistic Analysis* (1957). Oxford: Basil Blackwell.

———. 1959. *The Language of the Chinese "Secret History of the Mongols" (= Publications of the Philological Society 17)*. Oxford: Basil Blackwell.

HARRIS, ZELLIG S. 1942. "Morpheme alternants in linguistic analysis." *Language* 18. 169–80. Reprinted in Joos (1958).

———. 1944. "Simultaneous components in phonology." *Language* 20. 181–205. Reprinted in Joos (1958).

HARRIS, ZELLIG S. 1945. "Review of M. B. Emeneau, *Kota Texts.*" *Language* 21. 283–89.

———. 1946. "From morpheme to utterance." *Language* 22. 161–83. Reprinted in Joos (1958).

———. 1951. *Structural Linguistics.* Chicago: The University of Chicago Press.

HAUGEN, EINAR. 1956. "The syllable in linguistic description," in *For Roman Jakobson*, eds. Morris Halle *et al.* The Hague: Mouton & Co.

HAUGEN, EINAR, and W. F. TWADDELL. 1942. "Facts and phonemics." *Language* 18. 228–37.

HAVRÁNEK, BOHUSLAV. 1929. "Influence de la fonction de la langue littéraire sur la structure phonologique et grammaticale du tcheque littéraire." *Travaux du Cercle Linguistique de Prague* 1. 106–20.

———. 1931. "Zur Adaption der phonologischen Systeme in den Schriftsprachen." *Travaux du Cercle Linguistique de Prague* 4. 267–78.

———. 1964a. "The functional differentiation of the standard language," reprinted in *A Prague School Reader on Esthetics, Literary Structure, and Style*, ed. Paul L. Garvin. Washington, D.C.: Georgetown University Press.

———. 1964b. "Zum Problem der Norm in der heutigen Sprachwissenschaft und Sprachkultur," reprinted in *A Prague School Reader in Linguistics*, ed. Joseph Vachek. Bloomington: Indiana University Press.

HEMPEL, CARL G. 1966. *Philosophy of Natural Science.* Englewood Cliffs: Prentice-Hall, Inc.

HENDERSON, E. J. A. 1949. "Prosodies in Siamese." *Asia Major* 1. 189–215.

———. 1951. "The phonology of loanwords in some South-east Asian languages." *Transactions of the Philological Society* 131–58.

HILL, ARCHIBALD A. 1958. *Introduction to Linguistic Structures.* New York: Harcourt, Brace.

HJELMSLEV, LOUIS. 1954. "La stratification du langage." *Word* 10. 163–88. Reprinted in Hjelmslev (1959).

———. 1959. *Essais linguistiques* (= *Travaux du Cercle Linguistique de Copenhague XII*). Copenhagen: Nordisk Sprog-og Kulturforlag.

———. 1961. *Prolegomena to a Theory of Language* (revised English edition), trans. Francis J. Whitfield. Madison: The University of Wisconsin Press.

HOCKETT, CHARLES F. 1942. "A system of descriptive phonology." *Language* 18. 3–21. Reprinted in Joos (1958).

———. 1947a. "Componential analysis of Sierra Popoluca." *International Journal of American Linguistics* 13. 258–67.

———. 1947b. "Peiping phonology." *Journal of the American Oriental Society* 67. 253–67. Reprinted in Joos (1958).

———. 1947c. "Problems of morphemic analysis." *Language* 23. 321–43. Reprinted in Joos (1958).

———. 1948a. "Biophysics, linguistics, and the unity of science." *American Scientist* 38. 558–72.

———. 1948b. "A note on 'structure'." *International Journal of American Linguistics* 14. 269–71. Reprinted in Joos (1958).

———. 1949. "Two fundamental problems in phonemics." *Studies in Linguistics* 7. 29–51.

HOCKETT, CHARLES F. 1950. "Peiping morphophonemics." *Language* 26. 63–85. Reprinted in Joos (1958).

———. 1951. "Review of Martinet (1949)." *Language* 27. 333–42.

———. 1952. "A new study of fundamentals." *American Speech* 28. 117–21.

———. 1953. "Short and long syllable nuclei." *International Journal of American Linguistics* 19. 165–71.

———. 1954. "Two models of grammatical description." *Word* 10. 210–31. Reprinted in Joos (1958).

———. 1955. *A Manual of Phonology* (= *International Journal of American Linguistics*, Vol. 21, No. 4, Part 1). Baltimore: Indiana University.

———. 1958. *A Course in Modern Linguistics*. New York: The Macmillan Company.

———. 1961. "Linguistic elements and their relations." *Language* 37. 29–53.

———. 1968. "Review of Lamb (1966c)." *International Journal of American Linguistics* 34. 145–53.

———., ed. 1970. *A Leonard Bloomfield Anthology*. Bloomington: Indiana University Press.

HOIJER, HARRY. 1958. "Native reaction as a criterion in linguistic analysis," in *Proceedings of the Eighth International Congress of Linguists*, ed. Eva Sivertsen. Oslo: Oslo University Press.

HORÁLEK, KAREL. 1964. "La fonction de la 'structure des fonctions'," reprinted in *A Prague School Reader in Linguistics*, ed. Joseph Vachek. Bloomington: Indiana University Press.

HOUSEHOLDER, FRED W. 1952. "Review of Harris (1951)." *International Journal of American Linguistics* 18. 260–68.

ISAČENKO, A. V. 1964. "On the conative function of language," reprinted in *A Prague School Reader in Linguistics*, ed. Josef Vachek. Bloomington: Indiana University Press.

JACOBS, RODERICK A., and PETER S. ROSENBAUM. 1968. *English Transformational Grammar*. Waltham, Massachusetts: Blaisdell Publishing Company.

———, eds. 1970. *Readings in English Transformational Grammar*. Waltham, Massachusetts: Ginn and Company.

JAKOBSON, ROMAN. 1929. "Remarques sur l'evolution phonologique du russe." *Travaux du Cercle Linguistique de Prague* 2.

———. 1931. "Die Betonung und ihre Rolle in der Wort- und Syntagmaphonologie." *Travaux du Cercle Linguistique de Prague* 4. 164–82.

———. 1936. "Beitrag zur allgemeinen Kasuslehre." *Travaux du Cercle Linguistique de Prague* 6. 240–88.

———. 1962. *Selected Writings I*. The Hague: Mouton & Co.

———. 1964. "Zur Struktur des russischen Verbums," reprinted in *A Prague School Reader in Linguistics*," ed. Josef Vachek. Bloomington: Indiana University Press.

JAKOBSON, ROMAN, C. GUNNAR M. FANT, and MORRIS HALLE. 1951. *Preliminaries to Speech Analysis*. Cambridge, Massachusetts: The M.I.T. Press.

JAKOBSON, ROMAN, and MORRIS HALLE. 1956. *Fundamentals of Language*. The Hague: Mouton & Co.

JAKOBSON, ROMAN, and J. LOTZ. 1949. "Notes on the French phonemic pattern." *Word* 5. 151–58.

Joos, Martin, ed. 1958. *Readings in Linguistics*. New York: American Council of Learned Societies.

Karcevskij, S. 1929. "Du dualisme asymetrique du signe linguistique." *Travaux du Cercle Linguistique de Prague* 1. 88–93.

———. 1931. "Sur la phonologie de la phrase." *Travaux du Cercle Linguistique de Prague* 4. 188–227.

———. 1936. "Sur la nature de l'adverbe." *Travaux du Cercle Linguistique de Prague* 6. 107–11.

———. 1964. "Sur la structure du substantif russe," reprinted in *A Prague School Reader in Linguistics*," ed. Josef Vachek. Bloomington: Indiana University Press.

Katz, Jerrold J. 1964. "Mentalism in linguistics." *Language* 40. 124–37.

———. 1967. "Recent issues in semantic theory." *Foundations of Language* 3. 124–94.

———. 1972. *Semantic Theory*. New York: Harper & Row, Publishers.

Katz, Jerrold J., and Jerry Fodor. 1963. "The structure of a semantic theory." *Language* 39. 170–210.

Katz, Jerrold J., and Paul M. Postal. 1964. *An Integrated Theory of Linguistic Descriptions*. Cambridge, Massachusetts: The M.I.T. Press.

Kisseberth, Charles W. 1972. "Cyclical rules in Klamath phonology." *Linguistic Inquiry* 3. 3–39.

Koestler, Arthur. 1959. *The Sleep Walkers*. New York: The Macmillan Company.

Kořinek, J. M. 1936. "Einige Betrachtungen über Sprache und Sprechen." *Travaux du Cercle Linguistique de Prague* 6. 23–29.

———. 1939. "Laut und Wortbedeutung." *Travaux du Cercle Linguistique de Prague* 8. 58–65.

Kuhn, Thomas S. 1962. *The Structure of Scientific Revolutions* (= *International Encyclopedia of Unified Science*, Vol. II, No. 2). Chicago: The University of Chicago Press.

Lakoff, George. 1970. *Irregularity in Syntax*. New York: Holt, Rinehart and Winston, Inc.

———. 1971. "On generative semantics," in *Semantics: An Interdisciplinary Reader in Philosophy, Linguistics, and Psychology*, eds. Danny D. Steinberg and Leon A. Jakobovits. Cambridge: Cambridge University Press.

Lamb, Sydney M. 1964a. "On alternation, transformation, realization, and stratification," in *Report of the Fifteenth Annual (First International) Round Table Meeting on Linguistics and Language Studies* (= *Monograph Series on Languages and Linguistics 17*), ed. C. I. J. M. Stuart. Washington, D.C.: Georgetown University Press.

———. 1964b. "The sememic approach to structural semantics," in *Transcultural Studies in Cognition* (= *American Anthropologist 66, No. 3, Part 2*), eds. A. Kimball Romney and Roy Goodwin D'Andrade. Washington, D.C.: American Anthropological Association.

———. 1965. "Kinship terminology and linguistic structure," in *Formal Semantic Analysis* (= *American Anthropologist 67, No. 5, Part 2*), ed. E. A. Hammel. Washington, D.C.: American Anthropological Association.

———. 1966a. "Epilegomena to a theory of language." *Romance Philology* 19. 531–73.

LAMB, SYDNEY M. 1966b. "Linguistic structure and the production and decoding of discourse," in *Brain Function, Vol. III: Speech, Language, and Communication* (=*UCLA Forum in Medical Sciences, No. 4*), ed. Edward C. Carterette. Los Angeles: University of California Press.

————. 1966c. *Outline of Stratificational Grammar.* Washington, D.C.: Georgetown University Press.

————. 1966d. "Prolegomena to a theory of phonology." *Language* 42. 536–73.

————. 1966e. "The use of semantic information for the resolution of syntactic ambiguity," in *Actes du Premier Colloque International de Linguistique Appliquée.* Nancy: Faculté des Lettres et des Sciences humaines de l'Université de Nancy.

————. 1967. "Review of Chomsky (1964a and 1965)." *American Anthropologist* 69. 411–15.

————. 1968. "Lamb's reply to Teeter." *American Anthropologist* 70. 364–65.

————. 1969. "Lexicology and semantics," in *Linguistics Today*, ed. Archibald A. Hill. New York: Basic Books, Inc.

————. 1970. "Linguistic and cognitive networks," in *Cognition: a Multiple View*, ed. Paul L. Garvin. New York: Spartan Books.

————. 1971. "The crooked path of progress in cognitive linguistics," in *Report of the Twenty-Second Annual Round Table Meeting on Linguistics and Language Studies* (= *Monograph Series on Languages and Linguistics 24*), ed. Richard J. O'Brian, S. J. Washington, D.C.: Georgetown University Press.

LANGENDOEN, D. Terence. 1968. *The London School of Linguistics: A Study of the Linguistic Theories of B. Malinowski and J. R. Firth.* Cambridge, Massachusetts: The M.I.T. Press.

LEES, ROBERT B. 1957. "Review of Chomsky (1957)." *Language* 33. 375–408.

LEOPOLD, WERNER F. 1948. "German ch." *Language* 24. 179–80. Reprinted in Joos (1958).

LOCKWOOD, DAVID G. 1969. "Markedness in stratificational phonology." *Language* 45. 300–308.

————. 1972. *Introduction to Stratificational Linguistics.* New York: Harcourt Brace Jovanovich, Inc.

LONGACRE, ROBERT E. 1960. "String constituent analysis." *Language* 36. 63–88.

————. 1964a. *Grammar Discovery Procedures.* The Hague: Mouton & Co.

————. 1964b. "Prolegomena to lexical structure." *Linguistics* 5. 5–24.

————. 1965. "Some fundamental insights of tagmemics." *Language* 41. 65–76.

————. 1967. "The notion of sentence," in *Report of the Eighteenth Annual Round Table Meeting on Linguistics and Language Studies* (= *Monograph Series on Languages and Linguistics 20*), ed. E. L. Blansitt. Washington, D.C.: Georgetown University Press.

MARTIN, SAMUEL E. 1951. "Korean phonemics." *Language* 27. 519–33. Reprinted in Joos (1958).

MARTINET, ANDRÉ. 1936. "Neutralisation et archiphoneme." *Travaux du Cercle Linguistique de Prague* 6. 46–57.

————. 1946. "Au sujet des Fondements de la théorie linguistique de Louis Hjelmslev." *Bulletin de la Société Linguistique de Paris* 42. 19–42.

MARTINET, ANDRÉ. 1949. *Phonology as functional phonetics.* London: Oxford University Press.

MATHESIUS, V. 1929. "La structure phonologique du lexique du tcheque moderne." *Travaux du Cercle Linguistique de Prague* 1. 67–84.

———. 1931. "Zum Problem der Belastungs- und Kombinationsfähigkeit der Phoneme." *Travaux du Cercle Linguistique de Prague* 4. 148–52.

———. 1936. "On some problems of the systematic analysis of grammar." *Travaux du Cercle Linguistique de Prague* 6. 95–107.

———. 1964a. "On linguistic characterology with illustrations from Modern English," reprinted in *A Prague School Reader in Linguistics,* ed. Josef Vachek. Bloomington: Indiana University Press.

———. 1964b. "On the potentiality of the phenomena of language," reprinted in *A Prague School Reader in Linguistics,* ed. Josef Vachek. Bloomington: Indiana University Press.

———. 1964c. "Verstärkung und Emphase," reprinted in *A Prague School Reader in Linguistics,* ed. Josef Vachek. Bloomington: Indiana University Press.

———. 1964d. "Zur synchronischen Analyse fremden Sprachguts," reprinted in *A Prague School Reader in Linguistics,* ed. Josef Vachek. Bloomington: Indiana University Press.

MITCHELL, T. F. 1957. "Long consonants in phonology and phonetics," in *Studies in Linguistic Analysis* (1957). Oxford: Basil Blackwell.

———. 1958. "Syntagmatic relations in linguistic analysis." *Transactions of the Philological Society* 101–18.

MOULTON, WILLIAM G. 1947. "Juncture in modern standard German." *Language* 23. 212–26. Reprinted in Joos (1958).

MUKAŘOVSKY, JAN. 1929. "Rapports de la ligne phonique avec l'ordre des mots dans les vers tcheques." *Travaux du Cercle Linguistique de Prague* 1. 121–45.

———. 1931. "La phonologie et la poetique." *Travaux du Cercle Linguistique de Prague* 4. 278–88.

NAGEL, ERNEST. 1961. *The Structure of Science.* New York: Harcourt, Brace & World, Inc.

NIDA, EUGENE A. 1948. "The identification of morphemes." *Language* 24. 414–41. Reprinted in Joos (1958).

———. 1949. *Morphology: the Descriptive Analysis of Words.* Ann Arbor: University of Michigan Press.

PALMER, F. R. 1955. "The 'broken plurals' of Tigrinya." *Bulletin of the School of Oriental and African Studies* 17. 548–66.

———. 1956. "'Openness' in Tigre: a problem in prosodic statement." *Bulletin of the School of Oriental and African Studies* 18. 561–77.

———. 1957a. "Gemination in Tigrinya," in *Studies in Linguistic Analysis* (1957). Oxford: Basil Blackwell.

———. 1957b. "The verb in Bilin." *Bulletin of the School of Oriental and African Studies* 19. 131–59.

———. 1958a. "Linguistic hierarchy." *Lingua* 7. 225–41.

———. 1958b. "The noun in Bilin." *Bulletin of the School of Oriental and African Studies* 21. 376–91.

PALMER, F. R. 1964. " 'Sequence' and 'order'," in *Report of the Fifteenth Annual (First International) Round Table Meeting on Linguistics and Language Studies* (= *Monograph Series on Languages and Linguistics 17*), ed. C. I. J. M. Stuart. Washington, D.C.: Georgetown University Press.

——, ed. 1968. *Selected Papers of J. R. Firth 1952–59*. Bloomington: Indiana University Press.

PIKE, KENNETH L. 1943. "Taxemes and immediate constituents." *Language* 19. 65–82.

——. 1947a. "Grammatical prerequisites to phonemic analysis." *Word* 3. 155–72.

——. 1947b. "On the phonemic status of English diphthongs" *Language* 23. 151–59.

——. 1947c. *Phonemics: A Technique for Reducing Language to Writing* (= *University of Michigan Publications, Linguistics, 3*). Ann Arbor: University of Michigan.

——. 1949. "A problem in morphology-syntax division." *Acta Linguistica* 5. 125–38.

——. 1952a. "More on grammatical prerequisites." *Word* 8. 106–21.

——. 1952b. "Operational phonemics in reference to linguistic relativity." *Journal of the Acoustical Society of America* 24. 618–25.

——. 1953. "A note on allomorph classes and tonal technique." *International Journal of American Linguistics* 19. 101–5.

——. 1957a. "Grammemic theory in reference to restricted problems of morpheme classes." *International Journal of American Linguistics* 23. 119–28.

——. 1957b. "Grammemic theory." *General Linguistics* 2. 35–41.

——. 1958a. "On tagmemes née gramemes." *International Journal of American Linguistics* 24. 273–78.

——. 1958b. "Interpenetration of phonology, morphology, and syntax," in *Proceedings of the Eighth International Congress of Linguists*, ed. Eva Sivertsen. Oslo: Oslo University Press.

——. 1959. "Language as particle, wave, and field." *The Texas Quarterly* 2. 2. 37–54.

——. 1962. "Dimensions of grammatical constructions." *Language* 38. 221–44.

——. 1963a. "A syntactic paradigm." *Language* 39. 216–30.

——. 1963b. "Theoretical implications of matrix permutation in Fore (New Guinea)." *Anthropological Linguistics* 5. 8. 1–23.

——. 1964a. "Name fusions as high-level particles in matrix theory." *Linguistics* 6. 83–91.

——. 1964b. "On systems of grammatical structure," in *Proceedings of the Ninth International Congress of Linguists*, ed. Horace G. Lunt. The Hague: Mouton & Co.

——. 1965a. "A guide to publications related to tagmemic theory," in *Current Trends in Linguistics: American Linguistics*, ed. Thomas A. Sebeok. The Hague: Mouton & Co.

——. 1965b. "Non-linear order and antiredundancy in German morphological matrices." *Zeitschrift für Mundartforschung* 32. 193–221.

——. 1967a. "Grammar as wave," in *Report of the Eighteenth Annual Round Table Meeting on Linguistics and Language Studies* (= *Monograph Series on Languages and Linguistics 20*), ed. E. L. Blansitt, Jr. Washington, D.C.: Georgetown University Press.

————. 1967b. *Language in Relation to a Unified Theory of the Structure of Human Behavior*. The Hague: Mouton & Co.

POPPER, KARL R. 1959. *The Logic of Scientific Discovery*. New York: Basic Books, Inc.

POSTAL, PAUL M. 1964a. *Constituent Structure: A Study of Contemporary Models of Syntactic Description* (= *International Journal of American Linguistics, Vol. 30, No. 1, Part III*). Bloomington: Indiana University Press.

————. 1964b. "Underlying and superficial linguistic structure." *Harvard Educational Review* 34. 246–66.

————. 1968. *Aspects of Phonological Theory*. New York: Harper & Row, Publishers.

"Projet de terminologie phonologique standardisée." 1931. *Travaux du Cercle Linguistique de Prague* 4. 309–26.

REICH, PETER A. 1969. "The finiteness of natural language." *Language* 45. 831–43.

————. 1970. "Relational networks." *Canadian Journal of Linguistics* 15. 95–110.

ROBINS, R. H. 1952a. "Noun and verb in universal grammar." *Language* 28. 289–98.

————. 1952b. "A problem in the statement of meaning." *Lingua* 3. 121–37.

————. 1953a. "Formal divisions in Sundanese." *Transactions of the Philological Society* 109–42.

————. 1953b. "The phonology of the nasalized verbal forms in Sundanese." *Bulletin of the School of Oriental and African Studies* 15. 138–45.

————. 1957a. "Aspects of prosodic analysis." *Proceedings of the University of Durham Philosophical Society* 1. 1–12.

————. 1957b. "Vowel nasality in Sundanese: a phonological and grammatical study," in *Studies in Linguistic Analysis* (1957). Oxford: Basil Blackwell.

————. 1959. "Some considerations on the status of grammar in linguistics." *Archivum Linguisticum* 11. 91–114.

————. 1963. "General linguistics in Great Britain 1930–1960," in *Trends in Modern Linguistics*, eds. Christine Mohrmann, F. Norman, and Alf Sommerfelt. Utrecht: Spectrum.

ROSENBAUM, PETER S. 1967. *The Grammar of English Predicate Complement Constructions*. Cambridge, Massachusetts: The M.I.T. Press.

ROSS, JOHN ROBERT. 1967. "On the cyclic nature of English pronominalization," in *To Honor Roman Jakobson. Vol. III*. The Hague: Mouton & Co.

SAPORTA, SOL. 1956. "A note on Spanish semivowels." *Language* 32. 287–90. Reprinted in Joos (1958).

SAUSSURE, FERDINAND DE. 1959. *Course in General Linguistics*, trans. Wade Baskin. New York: Philosophical Library.

————. 1967. *Cours de linguistique générale*, critical edition by Rudolf Engler. Wiesbaden: Otto Harrassowitz.

————. 1969. "Linguistique statique: quelques principes généraux," in *A Geneva School Reader in Linguistics*, ed. Robert Godel. Bloomington: Indiana University Press.

SCHEFFLER, ISRAEL. 1967. *Science and Subjectivity*. New York: The Bobbs-Merrill Company, Inc.

Scott, N. C. 1956. "A phonological analysis of the Szechuanese monosyllable." *Bulletin of the School of Oriental and African Studies* 18. 556–60.

Simon, H. F. 1953. "Two substantival complexes in standard Chinese." *Bulletin of the School of Oriental and African Studies* 15. 327–55.

Skalička, V. 1936. "La fonction de l'ordre des elements linguistiques." *Travaux du Cercle Linguistique de Prague* 6. 129–33.

———. 1964. "Morphem und Sema," reprinted in *A Prague School Reader in Linguistics*, ed. Josef Vachek. Bloomington: Indiana University Press.

Slotty, F. 1929. "Wortart und Wortsinn." *Travaux du Cercle Linguistique de Prague* 1. 93–106.

———. 1936. "Zur Theorie des Nebensatzes." *Travaux du Cercle Linguistique de Prague* 6. 133–46.

Spang-Hanssen, Henning. 1961. "Glossematics," in *Trends in European and American Linguistics 1930–1960*, eds. Christine Mohrmann, Alf Sommerfelt, and Joshua Whatmough. Utrecht: Spectrum.

Stanley, Richard. 1967. "Redundancy rules in phonology." *Language* 43. 393–436.

Stockwell, Robert P., Donald Bowen, and I. Silva-Fuenzalida. 1956. "Spanish juncture and intonation." *Language* 32. 641–65. Reprinted in Joos (1958).

Swadesh, Morris. 1934. "The phonemic principle." *Language* 10. 117–29. Reprinted in Joos (1958).

———. 1935. "Twaddell on defining the phoneme." *Language* 11. 244–50.

———. 1947. "On the analysis of English syllabics." *Language* 23. 137–50.

"Thèses." 1929. *Travaux du Cercle Linguistique de Prague* 1. 5–29.

Trager, George L. 1949. *The Field of Linguisitcs* (= *Studies in Linguistics* Occasional Papers, No. 1). Washington, D.C.: American Council of Learned Societies.

———. 1958. "Paralanguage." *Studies in Linguistics.* 13. 1–12.

———. 1962. "Some thoughts on 'juncture'." *Studies in Linguistics* 16. 11–22.

Trager, George L., and Bernard Bloch. 1941. "The syllabic phonemes of English." *Language* 17. 223–46.

Trager, George L., and Henry Lee Smith, Jr. 1957. *An Outline of English Structure* (= *Studies in Linguistics* Occasional Papers, No. 3). Washington, D.C.: American Council of Learned Societies.

Trnka, B. 1929. "Methode de comparaison analytique et grammaire comparée historique." *Travaux du Cercle Linguistique de Prague* 1. 33–38.

———. 1931. "Bemerkungen zur Homonymie." *Travaux du Cercle Linguistique de Prague* 4. 152–56.

———. 1936. "General laws of phonemic combinations." *Travaux du Cercle Linguistique de Prague* 6. 57–62.

———. 1964. "Some thoughts on structural morphology," reprinted in *A Prague School Reader in Linguistics*, ed. Josef Vachek. Bloomington: Indiana University Press.

Trubetzkoy, N. 1929a. "Sur la 'Morphonologie'." *Travaux du Cercle Linguistique de Prague* 1. 85–88.

———. 1929b. "Zur allgemeinen Theorie der phonologischen Vokalsysteme." *Travaux du Cercle Linguistique de Prague* 1. 39–67.

TRUBETZKOY, N. 1931a. "Die phonologischen Systeme." *Travaux du Cercle Linguistique de Prague* 4. 96–116.

———. 1931b. "Gedanken über Morphonologie." *Travaux du Cercle Linguistique de Prague* 4. 160–63.

———. 1934. "Das morphonologische System der russischen Sprache." *Travaux du Cercle Linguistique de Prague* 5_2.

———. 1936a. "Die Aufhebung der phonologischen Gegensatze." *Travaux du Cercle Linguistique de Prague* 6. 29–45.

———. 1936b. "Essai d'une théorie des oppositions phonologiques." *Journal de Psychologie* 33. 5–18.

———. 1936c. "Die phonologische Grenzsignale," in *Proceedings of the Second International Congress of Phonetic Sciences*, eds. Daniel Jones and D. B. Fry. Cambridge: Cambridge University Press.

———. 1966. "Le rapport entre le déterminé, le déterminant, et le défini," reprinted in *Readings in Linguistics II*, eds. Eric P. Hamp, Fred W. Householder, and Robert Austerlitz. Chicago: The University of Chicago Press.

———. 1968. *Introduction to the Principles of Phonological Descriptions*, trans. L. A. Murray and ed. H. Bluhme. The Hague: Martinus Nijhoff.

———. 1969. *Principles of Phonology*, trans. Christiane A. M. Baltaxe. Berkeley: University of California Press.

TWADDELL, W. FREEMAN. 1935. *On Defining the Phoneme* (= *Language Monograph No. 16*). Baltimore: Linguistic Society of America. Reprinted in Joos (1958).

ULDALL, H. J. 1957. *Outline of Glossematics* (= *Travaux du Cercle Linguistique de Copenhague* X_1). Copenhagen: Nordisk Sprog-og Kulturforlag.

VACHEK, J. 1936. "Phonemes and phonological units." *Travaux du Cercle Linguistique de Prague* 6. 233–39.

VACHEK, JOSEF [compiler]. 1964. *A Prague School Reader in Linguistics*. Bloomington: Indiana University Press.

———. 1966a. *Dictionnaire de linguistique de l'école de Prague*. Utrecht: Spectrum.

———. 1966b. *The Linguistic School of Prague*. Bloomington: Indiana University Press.

VANČURA, Z. 1936. "The study of the language of commerce." *Travaux du Cercle Linguistique de Prague* 6. 159–64.

WATERSON, NATALIE. 1956. "Some aspects of the phonology of the nominal forms of the Turkish word." *Bulletin of the School of Oriental and African Studies* 18. 578–91.

WELLS, RULON S. 1945. "The pitch phonemes of English." *Language* 21. 27–39.

———. 1947a. "De Saussure's system of linguistics." *Word* 3. 1–31. Reprinted in Joos (1958).

———. 1947b. "Immediate constituents." *Language* 23. 81–117. Reprinted in Joos (1958).

———. 1949. "Automatic alternation." *Language* 25. 99–116.

WHITFIELD, FRANCIS J. 1956. "Linguistic usage and glossematic analysis," in *For Roman Jakobson*, eds. Morris Halle *et al.* The Hague: Mouton & Co.

Index